Praise for *Sensing Injustice*

"Many go to law school to pursue justice, but Michael Tigar has spent his career doing that, and this entertaining, insightful book tells of his many battles to use the law to make society better. He is a terrific storyteller and one learns a great deal about the United States and the progressive movement and the legal system over the last half century from this book. But most of all, one gets the strong sense of how one person can truly make a difference."—**ERWIN CHEMERINSKY**, Dean and Jesse H. Choper Distinguished Professor of Law, University of California, Berkeley School of Law

"Few lives have been as compelling and consequential as that of Michael Tigar. He is a walking encyclopedia of a half-century of law, social movements, and history, and a master storyteller. Tigar is a hero who has saved lives and is a voice for justice and peace whose life story is mesmerizing."—**ROXANNE DUNBAR-ORTIZ**, author, *An Indigenous Peoples' History of the United States*

"Michael Tigar tells the story of his lifelong struggle against injustice with wit, clarity, and astounding specificity, drawing on his profound understanding and love of history, literature, and music. I once taught a course on 'Law and Social Change.' If I were teaching today I would assign *Bleak House* by Charles Dickens and Tigar's *Sensing Injustice*."—**JERRY COHEN**, retired General Counsel at United Farm Workers (UFW)

"No one since Clarence Darrow has been in the middle of more of his generation's important legal battles than Mike Tigar. His memoir . . . is must-reading for those who wonder if law can still be exciting, heroic and moral. Tigar proves it is, with wit, high style and great stories."—**JOHN KEKER**, partner, Keker & Van Nest; formerly Irangate special prosecutor

"A must-read page turner by the Clarence Darrow of his generation. Tigar was 'in the courtroom where it happened' for blockbuster cases and describes his battles for justice with his signature wit and passion."—**PATRICIA LEE REFO**, President, American Bar Association

For Tony & Leslie compatriots, friends with warm regards [signature] 2021

Sensing Injustice

{ A LAWYER'S LIFE IN THE BATTLE FOR CHANGE }

Michael E. Tigar

MONTHLY REVIEW PRESS

New York

Library of Congress Cataloging-in-Publication Data
available from the publisher

ISBN 978-1-58367-920-3 paper
ISBN 978-1-58367-921-0 cloth

MONTHLY REVIEW PRESS, NEW YORK
monthlyreview.org

Typeset in Bulmer MT
5 4 3 2 1

Contents

*This book is dedicated to the person
who steers me into safe harbors, during a journey we have shared
these past decades. You know who you are.*

Introduction

T his is a memoir of sorts. So I had best make one thing clear. I am going to recount events differently than you may remember them. I will reach into the stream of memory and pull out this or that pebble that has been cast there by the events of my life. The pebbles when cast may have had jagged edges, but the waters wear the stones, smoothing the edges. So I tell it as memory permits, and maybe not entirely as it was. This could be called lying, but more charitably it is simply what life gives to each of us as our memories of events are shaped in ways that make us smile and help us to go on. I do not have transcripts of all the cases in the book, so I recall them as well as I can.

I have changed some names to protect privacy and to fulfill my obligation as a lawyer. Sometimes I have simply omitted the last names of those who were public figures at a certain time but who may not wish to be so now. Some people who shared these events will remember them differently. That is, to repeat, the nature of memory. It is, for lawyers in the common law tradition, the nature of what we do. We re-create events from the varying and fallible recollections of witnesses. This book contains what I remember having seen. I have argued seven Supreme Court cases, and briefed more. I have argued more than a hundred federal appeals in almost every circuit, and have been in countless federal and state trial courts, as well as before tribunals in other countries. I have written fifteen or so books, and hundreds of articles and essays.

To talk about the theme of justice requires that I choose from and arrange these experiences. Those who have known me will find details scarce about some personal relationships. In telling this story, I am not entitled to usurp the stories of others, which they may prefer to keep to themselves. Clients' stories are just that: their stories, and I can tell them only to the extent that the client has consented.

As I was working on the first edition of this memoir, in 1999, my comrade John Mage said that it was too soon to be writing a memoir, because it can lead only to embarrassment. If I went ahead and did more things than I had recounted, I would have to put out a sequel, and then I would become like one of those aging musicians who keep doing farewell tours. There is merit to that view. Somebody said: "When is your life work finished? Are you alive? Then not yet." Racehorse Haynes was questioning a prospective juror in Tyler, Texas, and asked her, "Have you lived in Tyler all your life?" She said, "Not yet." Same idea.

The years since the original book appeared in 2001 have seen important victories in the struggle against injustice, as well as challenges and setbacks. I was walking in Paris with my friend and colleague Juan Garcés and I expressed this thought. He commented, *"La bataille permanente, ni perdre ni gagne"*— The permanent battle, neither won nor lost—which expresses the dialectical nature of human history.

So this is not, and could not be, a complete work. I tell some stories for their own sake, and hope to entertain, instruct, and maybe point a direction about work yet to be done. I will in this retelling be unjust to hundreds of people with whom I have worked, for I will not mention all of their names and all they did. Brecht, writing of Cortez, asked, "Were there no cooks in his army?" More than cooks, I tell you: none of these journeys was a solo adventure. Representing people who are seeking justice, like trying to change the world by other means, is a team sport. There were comrades, partners, colleagues, clients, friends, and lovers. I salute them all, and apologize if their recollections and mine diverge. To change the image, sometimes I played only a cameo role. When I speak of victories, I don't want to be like the rooster who takes credit for the sunrise. And I don't want to forget the debt I owe to those who raised me, to my children, and to my partners.

St. Francis, it is said, prayed to understand and not to be understood. It would be entire vanity for me to suppose that this book has no element of self-justification in it. But I have tried, as with the other things I have written, to keep all that to a minimum.

I have had for a long time a sense of injustice, and have come to have a theory of history. These are the product of experience and study. I became a lawyer because I wanted to be part of the struggle for social change. I was lucky enough to have a seat from which, as participant and observer, I could do my part. In the chapters that open the book, I have sketched the people and events who figured most prominently in my younger years. The later chapters are thematic, grouping cases and other struggles that focused on particular issues. In deciding to become involved in a case, or in looking back in self-evaluation, I have tried to see how this or that story told by a justice-seeker jarred awake my sense of injustice. The thematic organization seems to make that analysis clearer. To be sure, many of these cases overlap, and the arrangement is necessarily somewhat arbitrary.

In 2018, the Rapoport Center for Human Rights, in collaboration with the Briscoe Center for American History, organized the available writings and other materials and put them online in a searchable database. The database is cited in the Notes and Sources; it owes its origin and development to Professor Karen Engle, a group of Texas law students, and Briscoe Center director Don Carleton. In this book, I often refer to arguments and witness examinations in court, to books and articles I have written, and to speeches I have made. Rather than burden the text with quotations from those items, the Notes and Sources contain hyperlinks to the text of those items, and to books and articles that report them more fully.

I am grateful to:

- All the clients—justice-seekers—who have asked me to represent them;
- Those judges and Justices who have taken the time and trouble to seek out and defy injustice;
- All the colleagues and friends who have been part of these struggles, including lawyers, law students, law clerks, legal assistants, investigators, vocal supporters;
- All the Monthly Review friends and editors who worked with me over the years, including Paul Sweezy, Leo Huberman, Martin Paddio, Susie Day, Michael Yates.
- My family, all of them.

I owe a special debt to John Mage, who was a participant in many of these events, and who brought his intellect, learning, and editorial skills to this work. Jenna Waldman, a law student at Berkeley Law, edited the manuscript and hunted down many citations and references. She read the manuscript from the reader's point of view and contributed many valuable insights.

Prologue

A ll rise!" The Supreme Court of the United States, November 20, 1969. I sat at counsel table, ready for my first Supreme Court argument. Chief Justice Warren Burger, Associate Justices William O. Douglas, Hugo Black, John M. Harlan, William J. Brennan, Jr., Potter Stewart, Byron R. White, and Thurgood Marshall. There were eight Justices, not nine. Abe Fortas has resigned in disgrace. Justice Blackmun would not be confirmed until May 1970.

The chamber is massive, with imposing columns. You can tell that President William Howard Taft, who weighed 350 pounds, had a hand in designing it. Yet the space between counsel and the Justices is relatively small, the setting more intimate than many federal courts of appeals and even some district courtrooms of the older ceremonial variety. The clerk's gavel sounded. The Justices took their seats. I thought that Justice Brennan smiled at me. I stood at a lectern, argument notes in front of me. I had not written out what I was to say; I always rely on notes. Advocacy is interactive, between the speaker and the hearer. The Justices' questions would guide the pace and structure of the argument. I had to be ready to make the basic points and respond to cues from the questioning. And so:

CHIEF JUSTICE BURGER: *Gutknecht against the United States.* [Even naming the case that way—"against"—gave one pause.] You may proceed whenever you are ready, Mr. Tigar.
MR. TIGAR: Thank you. Mr. Chief Justice, and may it please the Court. This case presents a serious question, here in *Oestereich against the Selective Service Board*, but not decided in that case, of whether the Selective Service System is being used to punish or sanction dissentient

behavior without due process, without congressional authorization and under standards so vague and broad as to offend the First Amendment. There is in addition here, two serious questions—there are here two serious questions—concerning criminal procedure in the 9.7 percent of all federal criminal prosecutions, which are represented by Selective Service prosecutions today.

JUSTICE POTTER STEWART: They are almost 10 percent of all federal prosecutions?

MR. TIGAR: Yes, Mr. Justice Stewart, 9.7 percent I believe in the last report. The petitioner, David Gutknecht, participated in an antiwar, anti-draft demonstration on the 16th of October, 1967, in the course of which he dropped his registration certificate and notice of classification, along with a mimeographed statement of his position on the Vietnam War and conscription, at the feet of a United States Marshal, in front of the Federal Building in Minneapolis. . . As soon as it could . . . under the regulations, the Petitioner's [draft] board on December 21, 1967, sent him a delin-quency notice, reprinted at page 44 of the Appendix. And a week, a day and Christmas Day after that, sent him an order to report for priority induction, taking him out of his statutorily and regulatory mandated posi-tion in the order of call. And ordering him for military service, ahead of the time, when he would otherwise have to report. [He refused to submit to induction into the armed services and was prosecuted, convicted, and sentenced to prison.]

It can't, I thought, be better than this. I am arguing a case that concerns an unpopular war in Vietnam, challenging the Selective Service System—the agency that administered the military draft. Justice Stewart's interruption, and his visible reaction to hearing that almost 10 percent of all federal crimi-nal cases involved one or another aspect of resistance to the war and the draft, signaled the perceived importance of the issue. Fifty years after that November day, I am moved to deconstruct that thought: "It can't be better than this."

"The 60s" has become a phrase laden with different meanings for dif-ferent people. February 1, 1960, saw the first sit-in demonstrations, young people of color seeking service at a lunch counter in Greensboro, North Carolina. The direct action movement spread from lunch counters to other places of public accommodation. Civil rights marches and protests took place across the country. Civil rights workers went south on segregated buses, and suffered beatings, arrests, and even death. Martin Luther King Jr. spoke on the Washington Mall on August 28, 1963. Congress passed the 1964 Civil

Rights Act. There were protests and uprisings on college campuses and in major cities, in the United States and other countries, focused on racism and on the Vietnam War.

Wielders of state power had at first accepted, to varying extents and in different ways, this upsurge of protest. But by 1969 the tone and tide had begun to turn. Richard Nixon was elected. The FBI had organized illegal surveillance and infiltration of progressive groups. Congress had given prosecutors new weapons against dissent. Winning David Gutknecht's case was by no means certain.

What was "this"? I had been a member of the bar for little more than two years. In that time, I had worked on draft cases and written a book on draft law. Mel Wulf of the American Civil Liberties Union asked me to brief and argue this case. Because at the time I had not yet been admitted to the bar, Mel had to file a motion to admit me *pro hac vice*, for this event.

"This" was an oral argument. Thirty minutes on a side, down from the hour on a side that the Court used to provide. I had been to the Supreme Court. I had helped my mentor, Edward Bennett Williams, prepare to argue, and had watched him at work. I had tried cases in trial courts, and argued in federal courts of appeal. But "this" was my argument in the highest court in the land, as much mine as it could be after weeks of working on it with co-counsel and days of intensive review of every possible question the Justices might ask.

In retrospect, it is arrogant to think of "this" as my argument. It was David Gutknecht's argument and by extension an argument on behalf of millions of young men subject to the military draft. The argument directly concerned more than 30,000 young men who had—like David Gutknecht—turned in, tossed away, or destroyed their draft cards, been ordered to report for induction, and were facing prison or were in prison for their refusal to submit. All males between 18 and 35 were required to carry these cards, showing their draft status—1-A, meaning eligible for induction, 1-O, meaning conscientious objector, and other classifications as student, clergy, and so on. There were 3,000 young men who had been prosecuted and convicted and were in prison or headed there. The war in Vietnam had already claimed tens of thousands of lives. There were protest movements across the globe. Every day in Vietnam and neighboring countries, men, women, and children were dying, cities and countrysides laid waste.

An agency known as the Selective Service System, headed by General Lewis Hershey, presided over this military draft. For General Hershey, however, the criminal penalty for not carrying your draft card was not enough, and criminal due process was too inefficient. He issued "delinquency" regulations, which provided that those who treated their draft cards with disrespect would lose their exemption or deferment and would immediately be called for service.

David Gutknecht claimed that the delinquency regulations were invalid on several grounds. In a case argued the previous day, *Breen v. Selective Service Local Board*, the petitioner contended that a young man subjected to the delinquency regulations was entitled to bring a lawsuit challenging his treatment, thus forgoing the need to refuse submission to induction in order to test the government's action. In these two cases, our goal was to deprive the Selective Service System of its power to impose hasty punishment of draft resisters, and then to take away the requirement that a draft registrant must refuse to submit to induction and incur a criminal prosecution in order to test the legality of the Selective Service System's actions.

So "this" was David Gutknecht's argument, just as one of my later cases was Gary Graham's argument, and one was Dorsie Johnson's argument. The state of Texas executed those two young African Americans, even though the jury was never told in so many words that their youthful age could mitigate against a sentence of death. "This" is a search for at least five votes out of nine, and if you get only four you lose.

"This" argument was unusual in Supreme Court history. At the government's counsel table sat William Ruckelshaus, an assistant attorney general. The Solicitor General of the United States, Erwin Griswold, sat in the spectator seats with his arms folded. Griswold, who had been dean of Harvard Law School, looked pleased to be there, and especially pleased to be sitting in the spectator section. The Solicitor General is the government's lawyer in the Supreme Court, and supervises most government appellate litigation. Supreme Court law clerks seek jobs in his office. In Gutknecht's case, Dean Griswold thought that the government's position was wrong. He told Attorney General John Mitchell that he would not sign the government's brief. This was 1969, well before Attorney General Mitchell and his Watergate cohorts were convicted of obstruction of justice and other crimes they committed along with President Nixon.

In any given year, the Solicitor General refuses to uphold the government's position in, at most, a handful of cases. That is usually the end of it. Only rarely will the Attorney General or the President overrule such a decision. The last time it had happened was 1955, when Solicitor General Simon Sobeloff refused to argue a "Red Scare" case. Then-Vice President Richard Nixon found an assistant attorney general named Warren Burger to do the job. The government lost. In 1969, Nixon nominated Warren Burger to be Chief Justice, replacing Earl Warren, who had retired.

The Solicitor General files dozens of briefs each year, either suggesting that the Court grant certiorari, or that certiorari be denied. Often, the Court "invites" the Solicitor General to express an opinion about a case in which the United States is not a party. Griswold was giving the Court permission to rule in our favor despite what the Nixon administration wanted.

Dean Griswold was a man of such evident integrity that his sitting there silently was more eloquent than I could hope to be. Griswold's legendary rectitude extended to abstinence from alcohol. Thinking of his famously bibulous predecessor, Judge Landis, people said that on average the deans of Harvard Law School drank the right amount.

In *Oestereich*, a year earlier, which I mentioned as I began my argument, Solicitor General Griswold had filed a brief expressing some doubts about the delinquency regulations, thus foreshadowing the attack we launched in Gutknecht's case.

Ruckelshaus had hardly begun his argument when Justice Douglas interrupted:

> I spent a lot of time in the *Oestereich* case reading a brief filed by the Solicitor General and it seemed to me that the attack made by the Petitioner in this case is not more massive than that made by the Solicitor General, who I see is absent from this particular brief.

Justice Douglas had written the opinion of the Court in *Oestereich*. His opinion was critical of the high-handed decision of a Wyoming draft board that revoked a draft registrant's exemption from service as a member of the clergy. The opinion did not squarely hold the delinquency procedure unlawful, but rather that Oestereich was entitled to a judicial hearing before he could be ordered to report for induction.

"This" had a quill pen. Every morning, deputy clerks put a quill pen on each counsel table, where you sit awaiting your turn to argue. If your argument is first of the day, you are supposed to take a pen as a souvenir. I hope this is right, because my children all have pens. If it is not, the Court's current clerk will, no doubt, call me up and we will work it out.

"Better" was a way of anticipating something exciting, a challenge that I was about to meet. In the Terry Lynn Nichols–Oklahoma City bombing trial, in 1997, every day just before court, my friend and co-counsel Ron Woods would say, jokingly, "Well, time to go throw up." I laughed, because I can remember throwing up every morning before court during the first major trial when I was lead counsel. Even if I can hold on to my breakfast, every time I go to court, any court, I have that same sense of anticipation. In a trial court, it may come as the jurors file in. In an appellate court, it is that time when the judges take the bench.

What was "it"? What was I looking for? What did I expect to get? Advocacy is overrated and underrated these days. It is verbally overrated by judges who hold that poor people get justice because they have access to lawyers under the Constitution. The right to counsel stops well short of the death-house door for capital defendants. Civil litigants have almost no constitutional entitlement to counsel. Some of the lawyers appointed for the poor sleep through the trial and when awake do more harm than good. Even qualified and motivated lawyers do not have equal resources. The courts that uphold such inequality do so by treating advocacy as essentially a fungible good. Any lawyer will do.

The same judges who praise an abstract idea of advocacy often show they don't really believe in it. The Supreme Court now limits argument to thirty minutes on a side. And if the Court has invited the Solicitor General to participate, it cuts some time from one or both of the lawyers for the parties. Some of the Justices don't ask questions to help clarify things, but rather to speechify. And some Justices don't ask any questions at all. In the appellate courts, oral argument is more severely rationed every year.

Some trial judges won't hear arguments on legal motions, and when trial approaches they put strict limits on the lawyers, lest a vagrant persuasive thought burst out and sway the jurors.

Even the pundits of the profession, whose official canon of ethics once firmly required the advocate to exercise "warm zeal" on behalf of the client, are backing away. In the latest versions of the American Bar Association Model Rules of Professional Responsibility—adopted by most jurisdictions to govern lawyer conduct, the words "warm zeal" have been downgraded from mandatory to advisory. The official commentary says that the rule really does permit warm zeal, but is phrased in terms of professionalism and competence and so on, because the bar leaders are afraid that if we say warm zeal, people will think that means you need to be a zealot on behalf of your client, and nobody likes zealots.

So, in the name of softening up the image of our profession, the warm zeals are a threatened species. They are clubbing the warm zeals to death to make coats for rich people. I think that's what is happening, and I don't approve. In litigation as in love, I once wrote, technical proficiency without passion is not wholly satisfying.

As advocates, we are condemned to signify. That is, we are communicators. We are trying to convince this or that decider to rule for our clients, a limited though vital meaning of signifying. We also signify in a broader sense.

The kind of work we do, the cases we take, the way in which we accept or defy injustice: the entire body of our work speaks to the world about our values. It tells the world whether and how much we believe we can get justice in the present state of things. Our advocacy to deciders is better if we continue to see the links between theory and practice, and understand the narrow and broad senses in which we signify.

Whatever "it" was, that morning, it would include warm zeal. Advocacy is an exercise in skill, craft, and daring. But would zeal be enough? When the Court decided, we would find out if it were enough for David Gutknecht. But would it be enough for me? This is really two questions. First, zeal is not enough unless I am being zealous about justice as I see it. The form of the answer may change with years and shifting perspective, but the question is always there for me. Looking back, there are some clients, causes, and actions that I took in the firm belief I was serving justice, and now I am not so sure. There are times when I declined a case, and now feel some regret. It has never been enough for me to say that the adversary system is its own justification. If advocacy is to be about more than self, it must be about the service of something.

David Gutknecht's case, and my argument that November morning, provided a textbook example of how much we can and cannot expect from the advocates, the law, the courts, and all the trappings of what is called justice. "A legal system is not what it says, but what it does," wrote Jerome Frank; and he might have added, "and what it refuses to do." The first few words of my argument affirmed that our attack on the delinquency regulations was based on the Constitution, congressional statutes, and Selective Service regulations. We did not argue that the draft system was itself unconstitutional, nor that the war in Vietnam was unlawful under United States and international law. I had made, and have made, the latter argument. By 1969, courts—including the Supreme Court—had refused even to take it seriously. Justices Douglas and Stewart had urged the Supreme Court to weigh the issue, but to no avail.

To make that broad argument in this case would not have served David Gutknecht's interest: it would have been a pointless distraction. Moreover, decisions about what arguments to present are for the client not the lawyer, to make. David's objective for this case was to head off a jail term, leaving him free to continue his valuable organizing work. The collateral effect of winning would be, and was, to free 3,000 others in similar circumstances, to forestall the impending prosecutions of more than 30,000 others, and to shore up the activities of those millions engaged in protesting the war.

Nonetheless, I was arguing in the shadow of the war. The executive branch was contending that judicial interference, in any form, with the business of raising an army was unwelcome and potentially harmful to national security.

With the backdrop of governmental hostility to free expression about the war, our brief and my argument directed the Justices to recent Supreme Court cases that rejected the government's national security claims. In most of those cases, the Court had not rested its ruling on constitutional grounds. It had chosen narrower bases of decision, presenting less challenge to executive power. I had to take account of this judicial hesitancy. I have discussed in other works, and will take up again in this book, the ways in which the Supreme Court and its members have at times ducked what seems to be, textually and historically, their constitutional responsibility.

As the argument that morning continued, the Justices' reactions gave a hint of how this case might turn out. Their questions focused almost entirely on the narrower aspects of our argument, as though they were working out a ground of decision that did not implicate the constitutional argument we were making. During Ruckelshaus's argument, JusticeDouglas interrupted to observe:

WILLIAM O. DOUGLAS: I thought something different was involved. Certainly, we don't sit to pass judgment on whether the large number of protests result in revocation of classification. We are only concerned with this man and I thought the question was whether or not as a matter of procedural due process or statutory requirement he should be entitled to a hearing on whether or not what the District Court said and the Court of Appeals said is true.

WILLIAM D. RUCKELSHAUS: Mr. Justice Douglas, that is certainly part of this case, but what I am attempting to do at the outset is define narrowly just what is involved here.

WILLIAM O. DOUGLAS: It seems to me that would be the narrowest one—as a matter of statutory, not constitutional.

Note that Ruckelshaus and I, responding to questions, address the Justice by name. I have always done that, in every court. However, one must be sure to get the name right. In 1968, the Court heard *Gregory v. City of Chicago*, involving the exercise of free speech by African-American comedian Dick Gregory and others. The city of Chicago was represented by Raymond F. Simon, Chicago's Corporation Counsel. During Simon's argument, Justice Marshall asked a question:

THURGOOD MARSHALL: Can you point to me in the record, any action at any time that the police officials took against these thousands of people? RAYMOND F. SIMON: Yes, Mr. Justice Black.

In the courtroom, there were stage whispers: "Justice *Marshall*." Simon apologized, then two minutes later made the same mistake. He lost.

Another issue was presented by the local board's "procedure" in these draft card cases. A draft board consisted of a few citizens who met more or less regularly to decide eligibility, deferment, and exemptions. In many instances, the registrant had the right to a personal appearance to present his contentions. But if the board heard—from any source it considered reliable—that a registrant had abandoned, destroyed, burned, or defaced his draft card, it would order him for induction. The regulations did not require any sort of due process hearing. Justice Marshall was concerned about that.

THURGOOD MARSHALL: Well, how can this man in this case test out the discretion of the draft board, legally and of course—
WILLIAM D. RUCKELSHAUS: He's doing it in a criminal action, which we're here before this court, Mr. Justice Marshall.

Ruckelshaus noted that the Justice Department could confess error in any case where the Department believed the registrant had been treated unjustly. Justice Marshall posed his next questions and answers in a whimsical tone, suggesting that he found the government's position less than persuasive:

THURGOOD MARSHALL: My real difficulty is that as to whether or not the Government confesses error is up to one person, the Attorney General of the United States, his uncontrolled discretion. We had the uncontrolled discretion to the board, controlled only by the uncontrolled discretion of the Attorney General of the United States. Is that your position?
WILLIAM D. RUCKELSHAUS: Mr. Justice Marshall, I don't think that we can look at a discretionary grant assuming that is going to be abused.

On January 19, 1970, the Court ruled. Justice Douglas, writing for six Justices, held that Congress had not authorized the Selective Service System to issue the delinquency regulations. His opinion traced the historical analysis we had presented in support of a narrow ground of decision. Chief Justice Burger and Justice Stewart agreed with the result. Justice Stewart wrote: "I do not reach the question whether Congress has authorized the delinquency regulations, because even under the regulations the petitioner's conviction cannot stand." He cited the local board's procedural error of ordering Gutknecht's induction while there was an administrative appeal pending. So, as the Court expressly held four years later, David Gutknecht and other resisters were free from prison or risk of prison. Chief Justice Burger and Justices

Harlan, Stewart, and White had spoken up to emphasize just how narrow a victory this was. As for the result, however, this was a unanimous victory.

In Stewart's and Burger's reluctance, and even in Justice Douglas's narrowly drawn majority opinion, one could sense this shadow of national security: an institutional indisposition to confront the executive branch, even on a matter—or so it seemed to me—of ordinary fairness and free expression. I had said in peroration:

> In conclusion, I find it quite difficult to state my sense of urgency about this case. . . . The war in Vietnam is not the issue in this case nor is conscription. The issue is whether having chosen to fight a war in Vietnam with a conscript army, we ought to tolerate, in doing so, departure from the principle that delegations of power are mistrusted when personal liberty is at stake. That no man should be condemned before he is heard. And that however outrageous a man's political conduct, it cannot be punished by invoking a system of rules which are vague and overbroad on their face. I think that if we depart from these principles, then in these very difficult times the constitutional compact is more than dishonored, it will become the cruelest of illusions.

I was, in that passage, signaling that David's case was part of a pattern of government repression and punishment of opposition to the war and the draft. For example, at every historical juncture where the state represses or punishes dissent it invokes the "national security" claim. *Salus rei publicae suprema lex.* To take one prominent example, on January 5, 1968, the Lyndon Johnson administration obtained the indictment of Dr. Benjamin Spock and four other prominent antiwar advocates for advocating draft resistance, including destruction or discarding of draft cards. By the summer before my *Gutknecht* argument, the defendants had been tried and convicted, but the court of appeals had reversed their convictions in an opinion extending First Amendment protection to their conduct, and rejecting the claim that the defendants and their movement threatened national security in any meaningful way.

Where was David? At that moment, he was on bail pending appeal. David was twenty years old, and lived in Minneapolis, the son of a working-class family. Growing up, his mother urged him to "read, read, read." He had been greatly influenced by *Liberation* magazine, founded by antiwar and civil rights leaders. He and a group of friends had organized to advocate against the war and the draft, to provide draft counseling for those seeking deferment or exemption from service, and to assist draft resisters. He abandoned his draft cards at a large demonstration in Minneapolis. That day, however, I was arguing about justice for the client named David, and not in the abstract for a cause in which he and I both believed.

I called David as I was working on this Prologue. He remains active in the antiwar movement, speaking and writing. He has had a career in the co-op movement, promoting "economic democracy." Here again is the theme of this book: our work gathers meaning only as we work with and for those whose claims for justice point toward social change. The Nigerian poet Wole Soyinka wrote: "The truth shall set you free? Maybe. But first the Truth must be set free."

I have striven for a view of justice, shaped by the needs of clients, and I want to share it with you. The great Irish advocate Daniel O'Connell was put on trial for conspiracy against English rule, and he said to his jury:

> I am ready to reassert in court all that I have said, not taking upon myself the clumsy mistakes of reporters—not abiding by the fallibility that necessarily attends the reporting of speeches, and, in particular, where those speeches are squeezed up together, as it were, for the purposes of the newspapers. I do not hesitate to say that there are many severe and harsh things of individuals, and clumsy jokes, that I would rather not have said, but the substance of what I have said I avow, and I am here respectfully to vindicate it; and as to all my actions I am ready, not only to avow them, but to justify them. I have struggled for human freedom. Others have succeeded in their endeavors, and some have failed; but succeed or fail, it is a glorious struggle.

O'Connell did his work in an Ireland under English rule, seeking open spaces in a repressive state apparatus, taking advantage of the contradictions between formal guarantees of fairness and the reality of colonial oppression. That was exciting work. That was a part of "it." O'Connell not only represented the cause of Irish independence, but also led a movement to abolish the slave trade in England and America.

Should I look back on that morning and write a book claiming that the law and the lawyers, and the courts where they are heard, hold the solution to all the injustice to which people are subject? The question answers itself. Or shall we say that "law doesn't matter," as those with state and monopoly power are at most delayed or modestly deterred from inflicting injustice by lawyer-won victory? In a play I wrote, anarchist leader Lucy Parsons mocks Clarence Darrow: "Your lawyers' victories, Clarence, are like fireflies. You catch them and put them in a jar. By morning, their light has gone out. And your bugs are dead."

Is there some middle ground? In this memoir, I reflect on that issue.

Provisional conclusion: It can make a difference, but will not always do so. To defend those seeking change, one must learn the craft and skill of advocacy, study the history of lawyers' role in social change, understand the system of social relations that the "law" is fashioned to defend, immerse oneself in the vast body of legal literature, and have the courage to venture out.

We lawyers did not really invent, and we surely do not own, the law. We act "for" and "with" our clients, seeking to identify the contradictions within the legal system that allow us to gain our—and their—victories. These are the stories in the chapters that follow.

However, invoking justice and struggle evades the second, the personal, issue of what is enough. I often say that the litigating lawyer is a massive blob of ego suspended over a chasm of insecurity. Our striving is perhaps no more compulsive or intense than that of our brothers and sisters in other parts of the profession. I don't know.

The Darrow-Parsons discussion illuminates the social responsibility issue in choosing to be a lawyer, and to represent victims of injustice. That is the question whether one is justified in taking on that work. There remains the question whether, as a personal matter, one *ought* to take it on.

As you read these accounts, you may not agree with every choice I made about whom to represent. I have debated this issue over the years with friends and with adversaries. A lawyer embarked on this profession should make self-aware choices about the use of his or her talents. We have plenty of examples of lawyers who, like Clarence Darrow, started out on one path, and changed direction.

These days, when I talk to law students, I begin by noting that, actuarily speaking, the professional path before each of them is decades long. Events and personal choices make it likely that each of them will change paths more than once. Based on my own experience, there is room for errors and corrections along the way.

I might choose to represent a client because I share his or her sense of injustice, his or her "cause," if you will. But my loyalty is to the client, who may decide to accept a result that is personally satisfying even if it does not benefit the broader cause. A worker may decide to accept a personal monetary settlement in a discrimination case, leaving others similarly situated to push their own cases.

When my decision to accept a case is challenged, I may not be able fully to defend my decision. As I wrote years ago:

We are forbidden in so many ways from telling our clients' secrets in order to justify our choices of causes and strategies. We are forbidden from expressing a personal belief in guilt or innocence. We risk crossing the lines of propriety when we say why we chose to accept a particular case, except of course to invoke the generalization that everyone is entitled to counsel and that this case raises issues that deserve to be well tried.

I hold the deepest possible conviction that the Buddhist adjuration "right livelihood" is wise counsel. But the decision itself is personal. I was *entitled* to represent David Gutknecht because he was constitutionally entitled to a capable lawyer who would do an adequate job. I *chose* to represent David, in preference to others who might want my help, because I shared many of his goals.

In this book, every time I tell of a meeting, a trial, or an appeal, I am speaking of a period of time when I was not home with my children. I am speaking of a time when I was so intensely focused on my task that I was running on adrenaline and nervous energy. For what? I remind myself of Dryden's lines:

> *A daring pilot in extremity;*
> *Pleased with the danger, when the waves went high*
> *He sought the storms; but for a calm unfit.*

In this account, you will see that in my wake were quite a few empty bottles and failed relationships. This is not a tell-all book, but some of the details will help put matters in context. I will spare you the apologies. I have tried to make all the right amends.

My father died at the age of forty-nine. I thought I would not live much longer than he did. If I were going to get anything done about justice, I would have to do it in a hurry. Indeed, if I were going to get anything done about anything, to have any experience that might be out there, I would have to do it in a hurry. A very wise therapist named Anya Rylander-Jones said to me, "You are an intensity junkie." The sheer magical sensations of trial and appellate argument, of the search for justice, fed not only my ego but also a craving so real it was almost physical.

I know, too, that I have been very lucky. Folksinger Pete Seeger tells the story of two maggots sitting on a shovel handle. A worker picked up the shovel and as he walked along the sidewalk, the maggots fell off. One fell into a crack in the sidewalk and the other bounced into the gutter and a pile of horse manure. This latter fellow ate and ate for three days, and then thought, "I better go see about my brother." So he crawled up on to the sidewalk and eventually came to the crack. His friend looked up and said, "My brother, I have been down here for three days without a drop to drink or a bite to eat.

But look at you. You look so sleek and fat. To what do you attribute your success?" "Brains and personality, brother. Brains and personality," the other replied.

There is a character in mystery stories who inquires about somebody he doesn't know by saying, "Who is he when he's at home?" It is a good question to ask of oneself. I have inveighed against the law firms that require young lawyers to bill 2,500 or 3,000 hours a year to have a chance of making partner. These firms create a culture that encourages bad lawyering while pushing young people to work such long hours and under such conditions that their personal lives suffer.

As I look back more than fifty years, and think of "It doesn't get any better than this," I am humbled. "It" was an intensity that could not be sustained. "It" was seductive. But after "it" was done, I needed to understand and even relish the quiet that inevitably overtook me. We are warriors for justice, but must also be scholars of law and society. In the afterlight of struggle, we need to look back over our work, the better to understand how to move forward.

I did not arrive at the Supreme Court that day by a magical process. There was a journey of experience and thought. In this book, I hope to analyze the times and circumstances in which I have lived and acted, to permit a critical view of how one might sense, analyze, and confront injustice. As I look back, I feel like a character in one of those eighteenth-century novels who meets and is influenced—for good or ill—by a succession of interesting characters. I tell you, though: It has been a hell of a journey. Let me share it with you.

CHAPTER 1

Growing Up among the Myths

"Were there no injustice, people would never have known the name of justice," the Greek poet and philosopher Heraclitus wrote some 2,500 years ago. Edmond Cahn captured this idea in his provocative book, *The Sense of Injustice*. I have never been able to parse all the theories of what is right—natural law, positivism, utilitarianism. Instead, I have tried to pay attention to what is going on around me, and to look at what needs correcting. This approach is necessarily based on conflict, on a sense of the dialectical way in which history moves through the struggle and resolution of opposites.

It would be more accurate to speak of a consciousness of injustice. We acquire our consciousness from observation and sensation in the social, cultural and political setting in which we grow up. Injustice is masked by rhetorical forms that conceal what is really going on—by mythologies, a topic on which I later wrote a book.

David Gutknecht's Supreme Court case provides an example. He and thousands of other young men refused to accept, as inevitable and right, the decision to send them to war. They saw that decision as unjust. They took control of their own circumstances and resisted. To turn that resistance from an act of individual courage into a process of social change, many of them banded together. They understood that in the judicial system into which their resistance thrust them, we were not going to end the Vietnam War. As it turned out, we were not even going to persuade the Supreme Court that the war was being waged by systematically deterring free expression and denying due process of law. Our victory was in that sense narrow, but when thousands of young men avoided prison, it served a purpose.

When I think today of justice and injustice, I see them as the philosopher Martha Nussbaum has described: I reject the notion "that to every argument some argument to a contradictory conclusion can be opposed; that arguments are in any case merely tools of influence, without any better sort of claim to our allegiance." Rather, again borrowing from Professor Nussbaum, my notions of justice came to "include a commitment, open-ended and revisable because grounded upon dialectical arguments that have their roots in experience, to a definite view of human flourishing and good human functioning."

Discovering injustice is not a solitary pursuit. It is a process of learning that takes place by engaging with others in the critical study of one's society and system of social relations. Jacques Derrida imagines someone coming forward and saying, "At last, I want to learn to live." One learns by stepping out of the world of ideas that one has accepted without question, being willing to be surprised, and joining with others in the common endeavor. Prince Hamlet said, "The time is out of joint. O cursèd spite, That ever I was born to set it right!" And then, conscious of his own limits, as each of us must be of our own, turned to his comrades and said, "Nay, come, let's go together."

The first edition of this memoir was titled *Fighting Injustice*. I have renamed it to more clearly illuminate my own and others' paths. My "sense of injustice" was awakened and shaped by a series of discoveries that things were not as those in charge—those in whom I was told to place confidence— had portrayed them. I was not seeking to replace one overarching ideological framework with another, to trade in the mythologies I had been given with a different set. I was seeing disjunctions between what I observed and what I was told that I was seeing.

Gore Vidal wrote to me about the first edition: "I am reading your memoir with pleasure. . . . I like your take on a subject I find it impossible to shorthand— the negative 'injustice' that arouses you to action is easier to deal with than the potentially soaring 'justice' for which we good guys fight." And he added, "I thought a somewhat overwrought sense of justice overwhelmed McVeigh."

I have also come to admire Diderot's cautionary words:

Wandering in a vast forest at night, I have only a faint light to guide me. A stranger appears and says to me: "My friend, you should blow out your candle in order to find your way more clearly." This stranger is a theologian.

I WAS BORN ON JANUARY 18, 1941, in Glendale, California, an all-white community that had an ordinance forbidding African-Americans from staying overnight in the city. The local public swimming pool was "whites only." Based on what my mother and father had told me, I saw this as unfair discrimination. Those in power said it was a recognition that the races were, well, different. By the time I was in elementary school, my parents and most of my teachers accepted without question the mentality of the Cold War and nuclear deterrence.

My sister, Sharon, was born September 29, 1943. Our mother and father were divorced when I was four. I am the product of my parents' and grandparents' influences, transmitted directly and, more amply, by what I could observe and learn of and from them. I can recall having so intense a curiosity about the world that I consumed knowledge and experience with an avidity that sometimes bewildered me.

I begin by answering a question: "What kind of a name is Tigar?" Different people ask this, sometimes to figure out which ethnic niche to put me in, and sometimes just from friendly curiosity. I sent a DNA sample to one of those "ancestry" companies, and found that my ancestors came from Britain, Ireland, Germany, and Scandinavia. They all arrived in what is now the United States and Southern Ontario by about 1725. The name "Tigar" came into being in about 1920: my father's older sister had the bright idea to change her name—from Inez Locke to Zyska Tigar.

MY FATHER AND THE UNION

My father was born Charles Henry Locke in 1906, in Ionia, Michigan, one of seven children. His father, Charles Sr., served as sheriff, constable, and chief of police. The local history, in the county library, suggests that the Lockes are descended from Benjamin Rush, who signed the Declaration of Independence. The anonymous historian gives no source for this assertion.

Charles Locke Sr. committed suicide when my father was thirteen or fourteen. The obituary read:

> After arising apparently in good spirits on Sunday morning, at 1:30 he walked through the house and upstairs to his room, passing a joking remark to his daughter on the way. A moment later the shot was heard by the family, who rushed upstairs to find Mr. Locke dying with a bullet hole in his left breast. . . . Chas. Locke . . . was fearless in the discharge of his duty when dealing with vicious characters; on the other hand [he] would deal with rare good judgment with offenders where leniency was warranted—tact which was required in the days of the open saloon, where liquor brawls were an almost hourly occurrence, and the proper place for drunkards was home rather than in jail.

My father never spoke of his father, or of the suicide. Dad's younger sister

Dorothy told us that Charles Sr. had begun to suffer from some form of arthritis, and was concerned that he would become a burden to the family. His widow, Maggie Vohlers Locke, later remarried: She died in 1934.

My father's sister, Inez, had by that time already left home to pursue a career on the vaudeville stage. She apparently considered the name Zyska Tigar more suitable for her profession. She performed a solo act in the late 1920s in and around Los Angeles: In January 1927, you could see her perform at the West Coast Walker Theatre in Santa Ana, on the same bill with other vaudeville acts and a movie starring Dolores Costello. In 1931, she copyrighted a song that perhaps recalled her Michigan origins:

> *Aunt Lou, Aunt Lou-from dear old Kalamazoo*
> *Aunt Lou-Aunt Lou, say-I'm telling you-*
> *All the men go crazy when that dame's around*
> *I wish the Lord that she'd stayed home*
> *Stayed home in our hometown-*
> *But Aunt Lou-Aunt Lou-left old Kalamazoo . . .*
> *She knocked Tom Mix right off his horse*
> *And poor Jack Dempsey got a divorce*
> *When they met Lou,-my Aunt Lou*
> *From dear old Kalamazoo...*

In 1934, Zyska won a songwriting competition at the Morosco Theater in Los Angeles. My mother took me to visit her from time to time—in the 1940s and 1950s, as I recall, when she lived alone in a Hollywood apartment. She would take out her old dancing clothes and recall the songs she had sung.

My father's older brother, Eugene, changed his last name to Tigar and became a pilot. Records show he was in the Coast Guard; perhaps that is where he learned to fly. In the 1920s, he was what was known as a "barnstormer," who entertained at county fairs with flying stunts. Gene claimed that he had gone to South America to fly in the Chaco War between Paraguay and Bolivia in the early 1930s. Other family members support this story: It is credible, based on what I later learned of Gene's character, and of the conflict itself. There was an arms embargo in place, including a prohibition on supplying aircraft to the combatants. The embargo was widely disregarded; U.S.-built airplanes were ferried into the war zone. Senator Huey Long ardently supported Paraguay's cause, and blamed Standard Oil's imperialistic designs for the conflict. I first met Gene when I was eight or nine. He seemed the very picture of adventure: boisterous and dashing. He had recently lost his pilot's license due to habitual drunkenness.

Family history is often not really "history" so much as accumulated recollection: a tapestry of imperfect observation and faded memory, colored in
by often unacknowledged bias. I grew up with, and my consciousness was
shaped by, these versions of events. William Wordsworth wrote of how he
would recall the vista of a ruined abbey, that his memory would "half-create,
and what perceive." More prosaically, *Si cela n'est vrai, il est bien trouvé.* If it
is not true it is well found. I think back on growing up to help me understand
how and why and when I decided to take up the challenges of a chosen profession and life.

My mother and father were reticent about their life experiences. Neither
of them would discuss in any detail the way they fell in love, nor the circumstances that impelled them to divorce. My mother and her mother—who was
also divorced—raised us. My father's visits were relatively infrequent, but
valuable to me nonetheless.

I know some versions of events from my father's younger sister, Dorothy.
She provided, during my youth, an oral history of the Locke-Tigar family.
Dorothy moved to Los Angeles from Michigan with her husband, Marvin
Bergstrom, in the early 1930s. Marvin had been a woodworker in Grand
Rapids, Michigan, and went to work in California at an aircraft-engine
manufacturer.

Dorothy was a regular congregant at the Catholic Church, but she scandalized the monsignor by telling fortunes, and claiming a modest ability to
foretell the future. Despite the somewhat mystical aura she created around
her accounts of family history, my research into the available archives bears
out many of her stories.

Her husband, Marvin, who went by Barney, was a surrogate dad for me
after my parents divorced. He did not attend church so regularly. At his
funeral, the priest, whose accent revealed he had not been long away from
Ireland, confined himself to a generic oration, focused on the Stations of the
Cross. "And then," he intoned, "they placed the crown of thorns on Our
Savior's head." He paused to gather inspiration, and continued, "Did you
ever have a really bad headache that wouldn't go away? That's what it was like
for Our Savior that day."

My father had left home at age fourteen, soon after his father's death, and
joined the army by lying about his age. He had only eight grades of school.
After the army found him out and discharged him, he returned to Central
Michigan. He married Grace Shreve in 1924. By the 1930 census record,
he was—by then in his mid-twenties—in charge of a private detective agency
office in Grand Rapids.

Soon thereafter, however, Dad left Michigan. He had probably divorced

Grace. He worked for a time on ranches in Wyoming, Montana, and Alberta. He moved to California, where Zyska and Gene were already living. He changed his name to Charles Tigar, for reasons he never mentioned. In Los Angeles, he found temporary labor wrangling horses at Warner Brothers.

There were good jobs in Southern California's growing aircraft industry. Douglas Aircraft was in Santa Monica, North American Aviation was in Los Angeles, Lockheed was in Burbank. In 1935, Consolidated Aircraft (later Convair) moved from Buffalo, New York, to San Diego, its CEO having decided that low wages, tax concessions, and mostly "open shop" union agreements—or none at all—made it a good move.

Employer hostility to union organization in Los Angeles was an old story. An employer group, the Merchants and Manufacturers Association, had been around since the early 1900s. Its political allies included the Los Angeles chief of police, who established a "Red Squad" and hired out police officers as strikebreakers. A local private detective agency, Glen Bodell Investigations, sent out anti-Red warnings to employers and offered to infiltrate union groups. But with the Norris-LaGuardia Act of 1932, forbidding some kinds of employer interference in organizing, and the 1932 election of FDR, things were changing. The National Labor Relations Act of 1935—the Wagner Act—recognized the right to organize and collective bargaining and created the National Labor Relations Board to supervise matters.

During the 1930s, young workers seeking employment at the aircraft plants could sign on as unskilled workers and be trained on the job. Or they could attend a local public technical school to learn the basics of metalworking.

Three main labor groups sought to organize aircraft workers:

- CIO: In 1935, the American Federation of Labor formed the Committee for Industrial Organization, which was to focus on plant-wide, as distinct from craft-by-craft, organization. Within a year, the AFL purged the CIO unions, which banded together as the Congress of Industrial Organizations and were led by radical labor voices. The CIO organizers advocated tactics such as the sit-down strike, which the union successfully employed in Detroit to win recognition at General Motors and Chrysler. In 1936, the CIO tried a sit-down strike at Douglas Aircraft, which resulted in criminal charges and other reprisals against union supporters and organizations. The CIO did win a contract with Vultee aircraft in San Diego.
- IAM: The International Association of Machinists was an old-time craft organization that had been around since the 1800s and was an integral part of the AFL. In the 1930s, its national leadership decided to admit

unskilled workers, thus allowing IAM organizers to propose essentially plant-wide bargaining units in the aircraft industry.

• Welders Union: This craft union attempted to foster bargaining units of welders in several plants, but lost out to the IAM's plant-wide efforts.

Aircraft manufacturers took varying approaches to the onrush of pro-union sentiment. War was looming in Europe, there was the prospect of military aircraft production, and a stable and reasonably contented workforce must have been a priority. Douglas and other firms decided on resistance. Lockheed took a different course; its personnel chief decided that some form of union organization was inevitable, and that if workers choose the IAM, Lockheed would not object.

The workers had their choices as well. Dad was working at Lockheed as a sheet-metal instructor. As the IAM reported:

On March 5, 1937, 440 Lockheed Aircraft Corporation employees met at Jeffries' Barn, a professional boxing club in Burbank, California, to elect union officers and to vote for a charter to the International Association of Machinists. Three days later, on March 8, 1937, Lockheed President-Treasurer Robert E. Gross and Secretary Cyril Chappellet signed a one-page document recognizing the International Association of Machinists as the sole bargaining agency for Lockheed employees. On March 30, 1937, Lockheed Aircraft Corporation and the International Association of Machinists signed a one-year labor contract, making Lockheed the first California aircraft manufacturer to enter an agreement with a union.

Lodge 727, the first IAM industrial local, was formed. Charles Tigar was its business agent and executive secretary. The IAM leaflet memorializing rec-ognition of the union includes his photo. The IAM contract, first of many, provided a wage increase and regulated hours and working conditions. Local 727 became the largest IAM local. It reached out beyond Lockheed. For exam-ple, the IAM newsletter for October 1939 reported Business Representative Charles Tigar signing a local trucking company to a contract that guaranteed a 40-hour week and time and one-half for overtime.

Rival unions chafed at the IAM having secured the contract. NLRB records reveal jurisdictional and other challenges by the CIO and the Welders in which the IAM generally prevailed. *Fortune* magazine carried a long arti-cle in March 1941, tracing aircraft labor history in the 1930s. The authors contrasted Douglas Aircraft's battle with the CIO with Lockheed's attitude toward the IAM:

But the fact remains that the C.I.O. men were arrested by the local police, while the Machinists' representatives, called in by some Lockheed workers, managed to sign up 800 or so of the then 1,000 employees and to negotiate a contract with a cordially acquiescent management, all within the space of three weeks. As soon as all hint of a C.I.O. sit-down had vanished, the Lockheed union's membership dwindled for lack of vital spark. It has been revived somewhat by its present business agent, an engaging, redheaded young ex-instructor from Lockheed's sheetmetal department, young Charlie Tigar, who has no previous union experience, no anti-company prejudices, and the background of being a police chief's son and for three years a private detective himself. As a result of his organizing activities, Burbank Lodge 727 of the I.A.M. now has 7,500 members out of Lockheed's and Vega's personnel total of 24,000 and is second in size only to the Boeing lodge.... The Lockheed-Machinists contract has been renewed, regularly, every year since its beginning, and with improvements every year.

This paragraph is problematic, even as it praises some of my father's qualities. His hair was medium brown with no hint of red. He was never "Charlie," always Chuck, and had a silver bracelet that said so. It is true that hundreds of his fellow workers met, voted to join IAM, and elected him to leadership. He was reelected to leadership. The local membership increased dramatically as war production began in earnest. He was charismatic, decisive, and principled. He did not seem to need "union experience." He had been working for a living in many jobs since he was a teenager.

In the 1941 Lockheed contract, the union won an important concession. The 1937 contract provided:

The Company has and will retain the right and power to manage the plant and direct the labor force, including the right to hire, to suspend or discharge for just cause, to demote and transfer its employees, subject to the provisions of this agreement.

The 1941 contract added this paragraph:

Any claim that the company has exercised such right and power contrary to the provisions of this Agreement may be taken up as a grievance.

This grievance procedure protected workers from discriminatory treatment, and from the institution of unsafe working conditions. The grievance procedure was not a formality: during the period 1941–45, there were 10,000 employee grievances, the overwhelming majority of which were resolved without formal arbitration.

As war production increased, the workforce changed. Aircraft manufacturers hired women and African-Americans. The figure of Rosie the Riveter became the subject of wartime propaganda. The IAM had admitted women to membership since 1911. However the union constitution limited membership to whites. On June 25, 1941, President Roosevelt issued an Executive Order declaring that "there shall be no discrimination in the employment of workers in defense industries or government because of race." Some manufacturers were slow to respect the order. Lockheed was not. Josh Sides, a historian of that period, reports:

> The Lockheed-Vega plant in Burbank proved to be, as the black press called it, "the bright spot of local aircraft employment." "We expect Negroes," a Lockheed personnel representative stated in 1941, " to work in any division for which they are able to qualify." Lockheed management was willing to employ blacks primarily because of the labor shortage, but the company also appears to have taken the FEPC seriously and worked closely with the Los Angeles Urban League.

IAM locals had varying reactions to FDR's order. Professor Sides found that:

> Local 727 of the International Association of Machinists defied the national "whites-only" policy of the IAM. The Lockheed company newspaper quoted an African-American worker: "I was struck by the courtesy of my fellow white employees and still marvel at the fact that of the thousands here, I have met with no insult, either open or veiled."

Other sources document that Local 727 repeatedly campaigned to change the national IAM whites-only policy, eventually winning in 1947. So, yes, my dad stood up against racism in the labor movement.

Lockheed did not, however, have a union shop. Management agreed, however, not to disparage the union and to offer each new employee a packet of material about the benefits of union membership.

These historical accounts of my dad's work, and the context in which he did it, are almost the only sources of my knowledge of his efforts. He seldom spoke of that period in his life, and then only in passing. Looking back at the sketchy history of Local 727, I now believe that he left his union position and went back to work at Lockheed sometime during the war. He had photographs of significant events from that time including a picture of himself riding in the confined cockpit of a Lockheed P-38, a double-fuselage fighter aircraft that was to play a significant role in he war. This experience qualified him as a member of the "P-38 Piggy-Backers," apparently a Lockheed institution that certified all those who underwent the experience as being "of unsound mind and questionable sanity."

After the war, my dad worked briefly with a company called Viking Airlines. He and my mother were divorced by that time, but he did bring me along on a Viking flight from Burbank to San Francisco when I was eight. Viking had bought a few surplus DC-3s and flew routes in the Southwest United States and across the country. It went out of business by 1950.

The man reflected in these contemporary accounts fits the image I came to have of him, as I watched him at work and spent occasional time with him until he died when I was fifteen. This is the man I wished would have spent more time with me, and in whose assurances that we would have that time "when things got straightened around" I wanted to believe. He had a prodigious memory for adventure poetry and cowboy songs. He loved to hunt. And as I saw him in various jobs in the later years, he was articulate, decisive, and capable of heroic bursts of expressive anger.

Into the late 1930s and early 1940s, my dad continued his love of horses and riding. There were—and still are—riding stables on Riverside Drive, down by the Los Angeles River in Glendale. The "river" is a concrete canyon flood control channel. He gave informal riding lessons, Western saddle only, evenings and weekends. It was there that he met Elizabeth Lang, my mother.

MY MOTHER'S FAMILY EAST TO WEST

On my mother's and her mother's side, family history traces to the East Coast and to early settlers named Gould. There were Goulds in Connecticut and Rhode Island from the 1700s. My great-great-grandmother, Margaret E. Gould, was born in Illinois on February 6, 1841. Her parents were Edmond and Jane Gould, who were married in Warwick, Rhode Island, on March 29, 1819. She married William E. Powell, who worked at the federal armory in New Orleans, on May 11, 1859. The marriage ceremony took place in St. Louis, and the couple moved to New Orleans.

Margaret kept a diary, with intermittent entries, all the remaining years of her life, until she died in about 1920. She was observant, and somewhat judgmental. Witness this entry from April 1, 1860:

> Letter from Alton from Jason Bramhall. Benjamin and Edmund Gould, my brother, have sobered up for a spell and gone to work. Thanks be.

Margaret's diary entry for January 2, 1860, begins "I believe there will be a fight between the states. Seems to be gun powder in the air. What would I do." She was right; her diary tells of the war beginning in 1861, the Confederate occupation of New Orleans, and the Union taking it back in 1862. Soldiers from whatever army was in charge at a particular time were billeted in private homes, the Bill of Rights Third Amendment notwithstanding.

In 1872, William, Margaret, and their four children headed west in a wooden wagon drawn by two mules. William died October 22, 1873, in Jefferson, Texas. Katherine Powell, my great-grandmother, married a railroad employee named McCulloch. My grandmother, Helen Margaret Lang, was born in Cleburne, Texas, November 6, 1892. Mr. McCulloch drops out of all family records; my grandmother and her mother never mentioned him. I have the feeling that there is a country-western train song lurking in there. Great-grandmother Katherine moved, with three of her children, to Seattle in about 1900.

My mother's father, Edward Merrill Lang, was born in 1890 in Fertile, Minnesota, a small farming community. He got an athletic scholarship —track and field—to the University of Washington, Seattle. There, he met and married my grandmother, Helen Margaret McCulloch.

My mother, Elizabeth, was born May 26, 1917. She had an older sister, Patricia, and a younger sister Alice. My grandmother was an accomplished violinist. Having three daughters, she gave Patricia a cello, my mother a violin, and Alice a viola. She imposed lessons on them with sufficient vigor that the resulting string quartet performed on programs with the Seattle Symphony.

In about 1930, the family moved to San Diego, where my mother's younger brothers, the twins Edward and Charles—Bud and Chuck—were born in 1933. My mother graduated from San Diego High School and San Diego State College. The Lang family moved to the Los Angeles area in the late 1930s.

SCHOOLS AND CHURCHES

My earliest real memories date from about four years of age, when I started kindergarten. My father and mother were divorced, as were my grandmother and grandfather. My mother, my sister, and I lived with my grandmother in a small three-bedroom house in Glendale, at 511 Allen Avenue, with my mother's two younger brothers. I walked five blocks to elementary school, passing the Lake Street Baptist Church where my grandmother played the violin every Sunday and my sister and I went to Sunday School.

I never saw any African-Americans in my school, in the stores, or on the streets of Glendale. Nearby, though, were the barrio and the ghetto; I saw those. My mother had learned Spanish in college and used it while working at Lockheed when foreign buyers would tour the factory. Sometimes we would go shopping in the barrio one city over from Glendale, in Burbank. For a time, my mother dated an African-American actor; my grandmother was quietly horrified. We mostly lived in that Glendale house until I was in the seventh grade. My great-grandmother lived with us there until her death when I was about five.

That Baptist Church introduced me to the literature of the Old and New Testaments, in the King James Version. Bible verses, and the stories of which they are a part, still spring to mind from the days when I won competitions for remembering more of them than other kids. In later years, I have come to a different attitude toward houses of worship. Religious belief plays a big part in the consciousness of many people, including judges, jurors, and participants in movements for social change. I have found it indispensable to understand, and be respectful of, the ways that such belief may influence decisions and actions. Whatever I may believe—or not—I want to learn as much as I can about the core beliefs of those around me. Back then, the church was the place where you learned what to believe, and you heard it and believed it. This was called faith. I was baptized in that faith, by total immersion in a big tub under a velvet painting of Jesus praying at Gethsemane.

I still visit places of worship and centers of belief, as a sort of tourist looking for insights about social structure or relations, or simply because many of them are places to sit and be quiet. I do not believe that God exists, but I have taken in moral and spiritual teachings from that time and along the way. In the places I visit, my mind always turns to consider the horrors committed in the name of faith.

No such thoughts entered my mind when, in elementary school, I went to services at the Baptist church, went to the church summer school, and even attended released-time religious services on school days. Yes, this was before the Supreme Court had begun to consider the constitutionality of this interweaving of church and state.

Even then, I had doubts. I remember one revival meeting at the church. The speaker was announced as a "missionary among the Jews of New York." I was ten or so, and I always went to the Sunday night adult services. I had no clear idea about New York, except that my mother's older sister, Patricia, lived there. I knew that Patricia was something of a family scandal, for she had gone off to Yale Music School on a scholarship in the 1930s, when most of Yale was closed to women. There she had become quite radical. My maternal grandfather had stopped speaking to her, and she to him. "My dear," she said archly, explaining this break in relations, "he told me not to go to a Paul Robeson concert, and not because Robeson is Red, but because he is Black."

Looking back, I think the revivalist-missionary was probably innocent of most of this learning as well. He described his street-corner preaching in the New York garment district, which he identified as a veritable center of Jewishness. He spoke of the crowd's indifference, and sometimes hostility, to his message. His voice rose as he intoned what must have been one of his open-air messages:

> My friends, did you ever walk past a graveyard in the middle of the night?
> And you are afraid of what is in there? And you start to hear noises? So
> you begin to whistle, to keep your courage up. My friends, the Jews are
> whistling in the dark!

This prediction of damnation for those of another faith seemed wrong. I could sing the hymns and hear the platitudes, but I could not embrace the image of a vengeful deity who welcomed believers and would destroy those who dissented or questioned. I also saw a few examples of backsliding by folks in our own congregation: being baptized was no guarantee of upright conduct. I can remember thinking that having a demeaning attitude about people whose color was different, or who professed a different faith, was strange. It seemed to represent a kind of a priorism that did not fit with the curiosity I had about the world.

I was, however, led in elementary school to view with a sort of historical curiosity the eighteenth-century Catholic missions along the California coast constructed by Franciscan friars. We were taught in general terms about the good friars' efforts to bring Christianity and agricultural knowledge to Native Americans. We were not taught that the revered Father Junipero Serra, leader of the mission-building group, began his work as Inquisitor for the territory, and in that capacity found that Native American objectors to conquest were agents of the devil, able to "fly by night" and hide out in caves. Only later did I read and understand "The missionaries go forth to Christianize the savages, as though the savages weren't dangerous enough already."

My mother and grandmother worked all day, my grandmother at the state employment bureau and my mother as a secretary. I was on my own after school from age six. There was a branch library on the way from home to elementary school, halfway along the six-block walk. I could take out ten books at a time, so some days, if I didn't want to be outside, I would get ten books, take them home, and read them. The library had a series of orange-bound biographies of historical figures. I read them all. A bus ride to the main library in downtown Glendale cost 10 cents, and I sometimes took the bus there for a better selection. Sometimes I would see a book that looked interesting, and the librarian wouldn't let me have it until my mother had called to say it was all right.

WORKING, LEARNING

By the time I was ten, I was riding my bicycle all over. From Glendale, I would ride to the Verdugo foothills and on into Burbank. I rode into Hollywood and almost to downtown Los Angeles. I rode up to Griffith Park and its observatory. I had a paper route, which took up afternoons until I switched over to delivering a morning paper. My mother had given me the bicycle I used for my paper route, but I wanted a Schwinn bike with 3-speed gears. At the Firestone store, that bike cost about $70. I figured that I could earn enough to pay that off in six months. The store manager took me seriously, and signed me up on a credit contract. Then, he came by the house one evening and got my mother to guarantee the debt. The wonderful thing about this transaction is that nobody—not the store manager, nor my mother—said that I was too young or irresponsible to choose and pay for something. I was eleven.

The morning route required me to get up at 6 a.m., but it left after-school time free. I was a member of a Boy Scout troop that met one evening a week. The adult leaders—fathers of some of the kids in the troop—took us on weekend camping trips. I took swim lessons at the YMCA downtown, going back and forth by bus.

On summer weekdays, when my mother was at work, I hung out with friends, read books, and went to movie matinees by myself. The Loma Theater in Burbank had triple features for just nine cents on weekdays, mostly older films about cowboys, pirates, and detectives. In these movies, there were messages about injustice and justice. Those messages took root. Having seen the film *Captain Blood*, I checked out the Rafael Sabatini novel on which the film was based. I watched the movie several times, but knew nothing of the social conflict in the late 1600s that led to England's "Glorious Revolution," and the installation of William of Orange as king. I had none of that lore until, on the eve of entering law school, I read a book about common law history.

I read Howard Pyle's book about Robin Hood. I listened on our huge Zenith radio to programs about Roy Rogers, Gene Autry, Bobby Benson of the B-Bar-B ranch, and Superman. In the evenings, my mother and grandmother and I listened to Jack Benny, Groucho Marx, Edgar Bergen and his chatty puppet Charlie McCarthy, and a program about doctors, *Medic*. I checked out books about the Marx Brothers and worked on learning to imitate Groucho.

I remember trying to shock my grandmother by telling that the next week on *Medic* they were going to circumcise Charlie McCarthy. Unfazed, she replied, "What are they going to use, a pencil sharpener?"

At elementary school, I enjoyed class discussion, exercises in public speaking, and school plays. My sixth-grade teacher was Wayne Sparks. The other sixth-grade class was taught by Mrs. Crane, whose stentorian admonitions to her class could be heard across the corridor. So when I was assigned to an oral report on a nature subject, and to make the report to the combined sixth-grade classes, I did my report on the "whooping crane." I got to the part about whooping cranes having five feet of windpipe curled around the breastbone before getting the giggles. I also wrote a playlet about Captain Cook, based on a book I had read that portrayed him as an intrepid explorer, supplemented with a look at our family copy of the *Encyclopedia Brittanica*.

In the books, and at the movies, I learned about the achievements of famous white men, including intrepid explorers and colonizers. I learned that there were and are bad people in the world, and that they are effectively opposed by individual men, infused with a sense of justice and duty. I sort of hoped that my mother would meet and marry a cowboy star, maybe Randolph Scott.

My images of Western heroes were burnished one December when I was about eleven. My father had moved to the Southern California desert community of Blythe, by the Colorado River. He had opened a restaurant there. My sister and I visited my dad and stepmother one Christmas in Blythe. By that time, he had closed the restaurant because it wasn't working out. I remember that visit because we were all having dinner in another restaurant in Blythe when Roy Rogers walked in with some other people. I revered Roy Rogers, along with the other heroes from the big Zenith radio and the old movies.

I had, and my son now has, autographed pictures of Roy and Gene that my dad had gotten, probably in his union days when he was moving in some pretty hot company. That night in Blythe, my dad got up from our table and went over to tell Roy Rogers that his son wanted to meet him. I shook hands with Roy, and then he and my dad got into conversation. Roy was down there to hunt duck and doves. My dad was a great hunter. I never went with him because you had to be fourteen to take the rifle training, and he died before we ever got to do it. So Roy Rogers actually asked my dad's advice on hunting, and they sat there for an hour talking. I was awestruck.

I began, however, to acquire a more realistic, today one would say holistic, image of the world. Some of this was due to my own observation. My bicycle adventures took me to some project housing down by the Los Angeles River, called Rodger Young Village, over the border from Glendale into Los Angeles itself. The project was named after a legendary World War II infantryman, about whom a song was written. The village consisted of Quonset huts left in place from the war.

The families there were black and white and brown. I had never seen a community with such diversity of people or such living conditions. Our own home was not luxurious. We did not have one of those automatic washers. My mother and grandmother drove fourteen-year-old cars to work, and so on. But we had a yard to play in, and six people in a three-bedroom house with one bathroom did not seem really crowded.

The project living conditions surprised me. I stopped off at a community center and talked to the people there. There was a sign-up sheet for volunteers to do political canvassing in the neighborhood. I thought that was a fine idea, but they said that a ten-year-old was too young for it. So I signed up my mother. When they called a few days later to set up times for her to do this work, she was at first not pleased. She worked long days, but she saw that it was important to me, and so she volunteered, and brought back more stories of that community.

Books that my mother was reading drew my attention. She had Margaret Mead's *Coming of Age in Samoa*, an anthropological study of adolescents in that island nation. I was barely twelve, and did not grasp all the lore about psychosexual development. I did see that in other societies than my own, the process of growing up, living, and making decisions was different.

My mother and I disagreed about whether I should read a book titled *My Six Convicts*, by psychologist Joseph Douglas Wilson. Wilson had spent three years working in Leavenworth Federal Penitentiary doing, as he put it, "research in drug addiction and criminality." My mother's friends, Jim and Phyllis Real, knew Dr. Wilson and had recommended the book to her. My mother insisted that the profanity, sexual discussion, and violence in the book made it unsuitable for me to read. I tried to take it out of the library but the librarian ratted me out to my mother. So I read it in the library, chapter by chapter, in the afternoons before she came home from work. This is the only book she ever discouraged me from reading. The book's epigraph, a quotation from George Bernard Shaw, continues to resonate with me:

> The first prison I ever saw had inscribed on it "Cease to Do Evil: Learn to Do Well;" but as the inscription was on the outside, the prisoners could not read it.

Wilson's book captured the narratives of the inmates, guards and staff of this maximum security prison. It awakened me to the injustices committed in the name of just punishment and rehabilitation.

When I was in the seventh grade, my aunt Patricia separated from her husband and moved from New York to California. Her daughter Leslie was about my sister Sharon's age—a couple of years younger than I. Her son John was a couple of years younger than Leslie. We moved out of my grandmother's house. My mother and Pat rented a house in Hollywood that was large enough to hold all of us.

Pat brought stories of life in New York with her husband, the French horn player John Barrows, and the musical, literary. and cultural life of this place called Greenwich Village. She shared culinary ideas. I had been doing some of the basic meal preparation, to have dinner started when my mother got home from work. Pat showed me and told me about new things to cook.

Pat's presence changed the tenor of discussion in the house. Looking back, my mother and her mother did not discuss their work lives, or much else, with us. Their lives were taken up with earning a living and caring for us. Aunt Pat was, by contrast, opinionated and loquacious. My mother had been working at Kaiser Foundation Health Plans—now known as Kaiser Permanente—for several years. When Kaiser began operation in Los Angeles, the local medical association opposed its business model, which focused on providing health care through labor-union sponsored plans that were funded by employer contributions. Retail Clerks Local 770, which represented thousands of workers, was an early adherent to Kaiser, as was the Longshore Union and the Teachers' Union. Pat got a job with Local 770, coordinating union members' health care with Kaiser.

Now the discussion in our house focused on the member unions, their disputes with employers, the right to health care, and other political and social issues. Perhaps this new current of discourse reflected Pat's and my mother's view that I was now old enough to see and understand the issues. In any event, I listened. I was getting the idea that while dynamic individuals played important roles, groups of people organized around a shared goal, and the power to change things. This was not an idea that I found in books; I was seeing and hearing about it in the lives of people close to me. I also expanded my reading list. My seventh-grade English teacher, Mr. McDonald, told us that O. Henry's short stories, and the work of Arthur Conan Doyle, were examples of good writing that he admired. I went to the library and checked out the "complete works" volumes. I found "O.Henry," whose given name was William Sidney Porter, a fascinating chronicler of people and places. Looking back, I consider such storytelling a good preparation for representing people in all social conditions of real life. As for Conan Doyle, I enjoyed the stories, but I am afraid Sherlock Holmes simply reinforced the idea that smart white men could get things done.

For eighth and ninth grades, I attended Bancroft Junior High School in Hollywood. I was student body president, and active in drama programs. I took a class in letterpress printing, learning skills I later used in an after-school job. My mother wisely suggested that I learn to type; I was one of a few boys in Ms. Cliff's typing class. I worked as a dishwasher in the cafeteria, in exchange for lunch.

At my mother's urging, I did a book report for English class on Rachel Carson's *The Sea Around Us*. I ornamented the report with an epigraph that I considered "literary": "Exploration and discovery are at the will of the sea. Man dares not challenge the abysmal depths." But at least I grasped the environmentalist values that animated Carson's work.

Mrs. Moore, our English teacher, made us memorize poetry and prose, much like the rote work of Bible study that I had done in church. In this way, bits of Emily Dickinson, William Shakespeare, and Ogden Nash came to live side-by-side in my head. Of course, with the hormonal angst of early adolescence, I was taken by such writers as William Ernest Henley and Robert Service, and would sonorously intone *Invictus* or *The Ballad of Sam McGee* at the slightest provocation.

In these years, 1954–55, Dwight Eisenhower was president, Senator Joe McCarthy had his flight of fame and then fell in disgrace, and the civil rights movement was given new energy by the Supreme Court's decision in *Brown v. Board of Education*. Amid all my comings and goings, these events shaped my perceptions.

My mother had done some volunteer work for the Adlai Stevenson presidential campaigns in 1952 and 1956. In 1954, when I was in the eighth grade, the Army-McCarthy hearings were on the radio. My mother and my aunt listened every night. The personalities and issues captivated me. I became adept at mimicking the voices of Joseph N. Welch, Senator McCarthy, and the other characters. I did not have a detailed understanding, but I saw that people were being attacked because of their political views, and that reporters my mother and aunt respected were raising objections. I read a *Harper's* magazine article about Senator McCarthy; I think it was by Richard Rovere. I took the magazine to school, and asked my social studies teacher, Mrs. Yarrow, about it. After class, Mrs. Yarrow nervously took me aside and said that while she agreed with what I was saying, would I please not bring up these issues in class because somebody might tell and she would get fired. I was startled by her fear, and then angry that she would be afraid to discuss things that we talked about at home.

From elementary school onward, we were all being taught about the evils of the USSR, and the dangers of nuclear war. We did not study these things in the sense of analyzing them. These issues were a kind of backdrop to our existence, a set of things that "went without saying." In junior high and high school we had "drop drills" as well as fire drills. The teacher would say, "Drop!" and we would crouch under our desks, assuming the position that would protect us if there were a nuclear attack. We must have known that this was nonsense, and that the only reason to crouch would be to kiss our little asses goodbye.

When I was fourteen, my mother remarried. Aunt Pat and her children moved back to New York. Our newly formed family moved to the San Fernando Valley. I enrolled at the new Reseda High School. This meant getting a new group of friends, and learning the ways of a new community.

I did not like my stepfather much. My mother wanted this relationship, and I respected that. But his presence in the house meant that I stayed away a lot. As my stepfather's business faltered, he drank more. He would come home late, having spent the evening in a bar, and by some miracle having managed to drive home. Mom and I would hold his head as he vomited into the toilet. In my high school senior year, he lost our house because he didn't make the mortgage payments; fortunately Mom's salary was enough that she could find us another house in the same school district.

Reseda High School had recruited a stellar roster of teachers. I studied Spanish with Mr. Balbuena and Ms. O'Neill. In English class, Ms. Agajanian had us read and study Christopher Fry's play *The Lady's Not for Burning*, a satirical excoriation of witch-hunting that evoked images of McCarthyism. I tried out for the football team, and didn't make it, thus illustrating the gap between lofty dreams and limited ability.

I did better at dramatics, including a portrayal of Captain Fisby in *Teahouse of the August Moon*. Our school entered a one-act play competition at the Pasadena Playhouse, and I won "Best Actor of the Day" for a portrayal of Mr. Hale in Susan Glaspell's play *Trifles*. This experience provided a signal example of education that did not get to the heart of the matter. Glaspell's play, which she later used as the basis for a short story, "A Jury of Her Peers," focuses on a farm wife who kills her abusive husband. The story and play were based on a real case, *State v. Hossack*, that was tried around 1900. The title of the story mockingly refers to the fact that all the members of Ms. Hossack's jury were white males. Our drama teacher, Mr. Farley, did a good job preparing us to perform. But despite the abundant record of Ms. Glaspell's inspiration, he did not introduce us to the deeper issues of spousal abuse and the different ways one's social circumstance determines one's perception of events. That lesson awaited me, as I headed toward becoming a lawyer. I use the play and short story when teaching criminal law.

Another student and I produced a couple of "talent shows" featuring the singing, dancing, and instrumental talents of our fellow students. One of these we called *Limerick*, based on the television series *Maverick*. That TV show featured two gamblers, Bart and Brett Maverick, who traveled from town to town in the Old West. Our character was "Brat Limerick," an itinerant Scrabble player. We set the scene in Gnatnoop Gulch, which was very daring of us because spelled backwards it was a slang word for a body part.

And, although I won a Shakespeare award as Petrucchio in *Taming of the Shrew*, the teacher did not ask me to pause and think about why Petrucchio's abuse of Kate—and her eventual acquiescence—should be considered funny.

Drama performance introduced me to the work of James Thurber. I won a prize for reading aloud Thurber's short story "The Secret Life of Walter Mitty." When the high school wanted to include my reading in a public performance of student efforts, and to charge a modest 75 cents for admission, I thought it best to ask Thurber's permission. He wrote: "You have my permission to give your presentation of Walter Mitty as outlined in your letter of December 10. Sorry I haven't been able to answer you before, but dark circumstances prevented." He signed as "Thurber." I was motivated to read everything Thurber had ever written, which perhaps enriched my writing style.

In order to have independence—to buy lunch, books, and other things I wanted, I had to get a job. I was fourteen, and under California law I could get a permit to work four hours after school and eight more hours on weekends. I took the high school print shop class. Mr. Brady, the teacher, introduced me to Milton Craw, who had a letterpress print shop on Reseda Boulevard. I ran the presses, set type, and cleaned up the shop. Home, school, and work were all within bicycling distance, although sometimes I hitchhiked.

My dad and stepmother had moved to North Hollywood, about 15 miles from Reseda. I could bicycle over and visit. My dad and I would watch television, or work on projects, or cook together. Sometimes we would go and watch professional wrestling matches. By that time, Dad worked for a small trucking company as its safety director. A couple of times we went to breakfasts at which he would have to make a speech about safety. He would betray his sense of unease. He was conscious that almost everybody in the room had a college degree, and he had only eight grades of school.

I can remember one day, during this time, telling Dad that I wanted to be a lawyer. He went into his bedroom and brought out a copy of Irving Stone's book *Clarence Darrow for the Defense*. "You need to be a lawyer like Darrow," he said. "He was for the people." I look back on that episode and wonder what my dad's study of Darrow led him to think about his time as union leader, and all the other social issues that Darrow confronted. I think my dad kept reaching for goals and then suffering because he felt he had come up short. Because he was funny, sometimes stern, and always with that edge of insecurity, it seems, looking back, that there were things he wanted to tell me and show me that somehow never came out.

I think a lot of people feel that way about their parents. Your sense of what you missed doesn't ripen until they are gone, and then it's too late. Dad's job in California came to an end. I think the trucking company wasn't doing too well. So he packed up and moved to Phoenix to take another job in June 1956, when I was fifteen. He had a mild heart attack just before he moved, but kept on going. The last time I saw him, he was smoking a cigarette and drinking a martini from a crockery cup, joking that if he could have only one drink a day it would be a good one. He spoke to me earnestly, questioning me about what I was doing and critically analyzing my answers. Maybe he was trying to fill in all the gaps in our relationship.

Two weeks later, he was working in his yard in Phoenix. He came in, sat down on the couch, and died of a heart attack. He was forty-nine. It was a Saturday. My stepmother telephoned with the news. I did not then have, nor have I developed in retrospect, a resentment of my father for leaving us. My growing up was not tragic or wounded; it was full of adventures and exploration.

The week my father died, I had begun work as a counselor and swim teacher at an upscale day camp with the posh name Egremont, five miles away in Encino. During the academic year, it was a private school. I worked there from 8 a.m. until 3 in the afternoon, then went to the print shop to put in three hours or so.

In my junior and senior years in high school, I ran for student body offices, and represented the school in community events. When I became sixteen, I got a driver's license and used my savings to buy a 1949 Plymouth for $150; it threw a piston rod within a few months and the dealer swapped me for a 1953 Ford. I kept that car until I went away to college. My campaign speech for student body president began: "I call my car Calvin Coolidge, because it does not choose to run."

There were no African-Americans at my junior high or high school, but the issue of civil rights caught our attention. I can remember the fall of 1957, when President Eisenhower sent troops to Little Rock, Arkansas, to enforce federal court desegregation orders. The papers carried those dramatic pictures, and I can remember opening a school assembly, where I was presiding as a student body officer, by saying, "Folks, we were scheduled to have a performance by a drill team from the 101st Airborne Division, but they are performing at another school this morning." This was reference to the federal troops who at that time were enforcing the school desegregation orders in Little Rock.

My friend Ken Cloke was a semester behind me at Reseda High School. We were in student government together, and he was student body president the semester after I was. Ken's father, Richard, had fought as a member of the Abraham Lincoln Brigade in the Spanish Civil War. He and Ken's mother, Shirley, were articulate, caring, and politically active. I enjoyed visiting their house, and being included in discussions. These times were a respite from the tensions at home. Ken's father introduced me to California governor Pat Brown. Ken would be a friend and colleague all through my college and law school years, and to the present day.

The summer of 1957, I returned to work at Egremont. My stepfather was still solvent enough to lease a restaurant in the resort community of Big Bear, 125 miles from Los Angeles. The place was open mainly on weekends. He mistakenly believed he could make a success of it, despite his penchant for alcohol and having assigned himself the job of bartender.

So I worked from 9 to 3 as a day camp counselor, then from 3 to 6 for Mr. Craw's print shop. At 6 or 7 in the evening on most Fridays, I would drive the 125 miles to Big Bear. Mom would have driven up after her job and would work as a waitress. I was second cook and kitchen helper. On Sunday nights, after the restaurant closed, we would all drive back home to face our Monday jobs.

In every spare moment, often at night, I would read. Mr. Lewis, at the local bookstore, helped me find more books on Clarence Darrow, including his autobiography, and I read them all.

The school had paid a lot for marching band uniforms, and I was one of the few who, being tall and slender, fit into the drum major uniform with its tall fur hat and silver buttons The band teacher asked me to be drum major, then regretted it when it turned out I had neither musical talent nor the coordination required to look good while marching. I never got the musical talent, but I could wave a baton in 4/4 time. A teacher, Richard Osborn, showed me how to do a kind of strutting walk that was odd enough to look like I was being gangly on purpose.

I read Meyer Levin's book *Compulsion*, which told of Nathan Leopold and Richard Loeb, two Chicago teenagers who murdered fourteen-year old Bobby Franks in what they conceived of as a "perfect crime." Clarence Darrow represented them. Darrow advised them to plead guilty to murder and waive a jury. I was fascinated by Darrow's argument to Judge Caverly. He wove together thoughts about the death penalty, youthful age as a mitigating factor, and psychological insight into human behavior. The judge sentenced the defendants to life in prison.

At that time, California had its gas chamber, and the fate of convicted kidnapper/murderer Caryl Chessman was being debated. Chessman's alleged crimes were robbery, sexual assault, and kidnapping. The prosecution obtained a death sentence under a California statute that would be held unconstitutional today, because the Eighth Amendment permits a death sentence only for homicide. The Chessman case dragged on until May 1960 when he was executed, still protesting his innocence and his lawyers still pointing out all the holes in the evidence and all the errors of procedure.

In 1958, my senior year in high school, I noticed a newspaper review of Arthur Koestler's book *Reflections on Hanging*. I went to Mr. Lewis's bookstore and ordered the book. Koestler's prose captured me from the opening sentence: "England is that peculiar country in Europe where people drive on the left side of the road, measure in inches and yards, and hang people by the neck until dead."

Edmond Cahn's Preface to *Reflections on Hanging* still rings true. Capital punishment is not an effective deterrent to crime. Hardly anybody seriously argues any more that it is. Cahn also noted the racial disparity in charging, convicting, and sentencing in death cases. This disparity contributed to the debate that led the Supreme Court in 1972 to declare the death penalty unconstitutional in every state that enacted it. The disparity still exists, quite dramatically, but later Supreme Court cases disparaged its significance, then put hurdles in the path of defendants who challenged their sentences on that ground.

Cahn also made the point that has come to dominate my thinking about the death penalty, after being trial and appellate counsel in a few of these cases. In capital cases, he wrote, there is a disturbing amount of police haste, sloppiness, and outright falsification of evidence. Over the past thirty years, scores of defendants have been liberated from death row because of definitive proof showing they were innocent. A crime that would lead the prosecutor to call for the death penalty is likely to have shocked the community. The media echo the public's need to have the case solved so that everybody can breathe easier. The police are encouraged to indulge their early suspicions and prejudices and make an arrest. Then the machinery goes into operation. Other leads are ignored. Exculpatory evidence is overlooked. And in a distressing number of cases, lies, false reports, and fake forensics enter the fray. I have tried those cases, seen this done, and tried to deconstruct it for juries and appellate courts. Because the system for appointing counsel in capital cases is inadequate, defense lawyers often lack the skill, commitment, and resources to challenge the falsehoods.

Cahn quoted a speech that Robespierre made in 1791. I still recall
Robespierre's warning about the finality of the death penalty:

> Hear the voice of justice and of reason; it cries that human judgments are
> never certain enough that society can put to death a person condemned by
> other persons who are subject to error. Let one imagine the most perfect
> judicial system; let one find the most honorable and enlightened judges;
> there remains the possibility of error or prejudice. Why deny yourself the
> means of redress? Why would you forbid the means of redress? Why con-
> demn yourselves to helplessness to extend a rescuing hand to oppressed
> innocence? Of what value are those sterile regrets, those illusory repara-
> tions that you accord to vain shadow and insensible ash? Those are the
> sad evidence of the barbaric recklessness of our penal laws.

Koestler's prose captured the condescending hypocrisy of English judges
who upheld death sentences, and the stories of defendants, victims, and their
families. An English Member of Parliament, Sydney Silverman, contributed
an essay on abolition of capital punishment to Koestler's book; later, I met
Silverman in London.

My dad's admonition about being a lawyer, the Darrow books and the
Koestler book opened up new questions for me. I could imagine myself
arguing against imposition of the death penalty, or emulating Darrow's summations, laden as they were with a history of struggles for justice.

In that senior year, I thought about college My grades were good. I had a
record of extracurricular activity. I did not have money. I hunted for scholarships and looked up information about colleges.

CHAPTER 2

Berkeley and Beyond

FRESHMAN YEAR: 1958–59

Looking back at the way my mind opened up in my first two years at Berkeley, I have the sense of having set foot on a path that was trod by many thousands of young men a few years later. These were the young men I counseled and represented, as the Lyndon Johnson administration dispensed billions of dollars of armaments and hundreds of thousands of human lives in the war in Vietnam. These young men came to their views about the world and their place in it by making difficult choices, like the choice David Gutknecht had made. They found that the rulers were intent on war regardless of human cost, legal rules, and rising protests. They also discovered that the rulers were willing to crush protest by any means necessary, all in the name of protecting "freedom."

At seventeen, I thought I had read and heard enough to make wise decisions, and was confident that if I did well and obeyed the rules, I would be recognized and rewarded. It was 1958. The United States had barely begun its involvement in Vietnam, having sent military advisers to bolster the Diem regime and having helped Diem stage a rigged election. The civil rights movement's dramatic escalation of direct action was not to begin until 1960.

I was relatively innocent of any detailed understanding of world events; I thought I knew more than I did. My mother's younger brothers Bud and Chuck had passed all the rigorous tests for enrollment in the regular Naval Reserve Officers' Training Corps (NROTC): the Navy paid their tuition, books, and living expenses at the college of their choice, and they became commissioned officers on graduation as Ensign USN, regular Navy not USNR, just like Annapolis graduates. They were then obliged to serve in the Navy for four years. Bud and Chuck followed an engineering curriculum at the University of Southern California; their stories of summer training cruises filled my head with wonder. Bud went off to work for Admiral Hyman Rickover in nuclear engineering, and Chuck got a good assignment on other engineering duties. My mother had known Nancy Nimitz, daughter of the famous admiral, growing up in San Diego.

The Navy offered a chance to go to sea, the best-looking uniforms, a free education at the college of my choice, and some externally imposed order in my life. It did not occur to me that there was little room, even for people studying to be officers, to debate the serious issues of war, peace, life, death, and destruction. That realization came later.

When I competed for and was awarded an NROTC scholarship, I accepted it. The Navy would pay $50 a month. I could still have my National Merit Scholarship, but I would get only $125 a year from that source. My step-mother wrote and said that my father had left $1,500 for my college expenses and I could have that at the rate of $375 every school year. I had some money saved from working during high school.

I could have gone to a private college where the tuition was expensive, but the University of California at Berkeley seemed ideal. It was away from home, but only a Greyhound bus ride away. These days, air travel has become so commonplace that college recruiters visit cities and schools; high school students tour colleges, as my own children did. I had never been east of Montana. All those eastern schools seemed foreign and far away. So I chose Berkeley. I would get a college degree, serve in the Navy for four years and then resume my intended journey and go to law school. At that time, a public university education meant just that: University of California tuition and fees came to about $150 per semester, and that included health care.

My family, my community, and most of my friends applauded my choice to accept appointment as a midshipman. Once there, I embraced the learning that was available in and out of classrooms, and ran right into contradictions that shook my worldview and forced me to make hard decisions. Even today, if I walk along the Berkeley streets, or hike along the hills of San Francisco, or stroll the waterfront, memories flood in of all the rich and varied experiences that a boy from the suburbs of Los Angeles suddenly found.

From my mother's and aunt's work with labor unions and in provid-ing health care to my father's union history, to my family's adherence to the Democratic Party, to the derision of McCarthyism, to what I learned from reading books by and about Clarence Darrow I should perhaps have seen that serving as a military officer would prove to be inconsistent with living a principled life. As things turned out, closed minds and intolerance for dissent proved to be widely shared by more people than just those in uniform.

These days, people write and ask what kind of college experience they should have to prepare for law school. I believe that college is the most luxurious opportunity one can ever have to meet and wrestle with ideas. I kept looking around and wondering if my classmates had a better high school education than I did. They seemed calmer, with less of a sense of wonder than I. They seemed not to be affected by the contradictions between what they had been taught before coming to Berkeley and what they were now seeing and hearing. Of course, we are always comparing our insides to other people's outsides, so I can't really say what they were thinking and feeling.

Ralph Waldo Emerson is said to have asked Henry David Thoreau, "What branches of learning did you find at Harvard?" Thoreau replied, "All of the branches and none of the roots." The University of California houses scholars, books, and human stories. One might not "get" an education there, but one can "find" an education. The "roots" are not always visible, and—to pursue the metaphor—there are deans and even professors who would prefer that you not dig for them.

The adventure began two weeks before classes formally began. I asked my mother and stepfather to drop me off in Berkeley, and I moved into temporary quarters at the Ridge Road Co-Operative dormitory. The co-op dorm where I was to stay, Barrington Hall, was not yet open. The co-op dorms were low-rise converted apartment buildings, where students shared double rooms. A typical suite had two double rooms, one single room and a bathroom with tub or shower that served all five residents. The Co-op required you to work five hours a week to keep the place going, but your room and three meals a day cost just $50 a month, the amount of my Navy stipend.

I chose the Co-op based not only on cost. I liked the idea that I could spend my five required hours cooking in the restaurant-style kitchen, following the menu directions issued from the Co-op central kitchen in downtown Berkeley. Those who chose the Co-op experience were a more diverse crowd than those in the dorms, fraternities, and sororities. My friend Ken Cloke arrived at Berkeley for the spring semester of 1959; we moved out of the Co-op together and shared an apartment for the next two academic years, 1959–60 and 1960–61.

I had read in *Sunset* magazine of walks one might take in San Francisco. After I unpacked my stuff, I found the Trans-Bay bus stop, paid the 75-cent fare, and went into the city. San Francisco was always referred to as "The City." Each day for a week, I repeated the ritual. I rode the bus to San Francisco's East Bay terminal, and walked or took a cable car. I covered dozens of neighborhoods, snapping pictures and visiting stores, museums, docks, and bookshops. A lot of those places have since been paved over, or "redeveloped," but every time I have a few hours in San Francisco I retrace some of those old steps. Some of the stores are still there, as are the steep stairs up Telegraph Hill, and some traces of what Fishermen's Wharf was like. I had never seen so rich and diverse a place.

TURNED ON BY THE RADIO

I walked the Berkeley campus, 1,232 acres, where more than 20,000 of us undergraduates, and another 10,000 or so graduate students, were enrolled. I noticed the metal plates embedded in the pavement at each entrance to the campus: "Property of the Regents of the University of California. Permission to enter or pass over is revocable at any time." The Regents, most of whom were appointed by the governor for twelve-year terms, and the remainder of whom were state political officials, governed the university system and its campuses. Surely, I thought somewhat whimsically, they did not "own" the campus, in the sense that they could sell it to somebody, or forbid public expression at a whim. I found out later that this was indeed a serious question.

I had a roommate at Ridge Road, a graduate student. His FM radio was usually tuned to a nonprofit radio station called KPFA-FM. He said he would sometimes volunteer as an announcer at the station, and if you wrote away for some sort of FCC license, they would even let you operate the station control board.

You mean, I could be on the radio? Radio news had been important in our house. Edward R. Murrow covered Senator McCarthy. My high school social studies teacher, Sol Kaufler, active in the Teachers' Union, asked us to listen to Edward P. Morgan's ABC radio news broadcast, which was sponsored by the AFL-CIO: "Fifteen million Americans bring you Edward P. Morgan and the news." Morgan and Murrow had the "radio voice." I looked up KPFA. A project of a nonprofit entity called Pacifica Foundation founded in the late 1940s, the station broadcast commentators with a wide range of political views, interesting literary offerings, news and interviews, and hours each day of mostly classical music, with interludes of jazz and folk. I went to KPFA's studio above the Edy's ice-cream store on Shattuck Avenue in Berkeley, and said I wanted to be a volunteer. Bill Butler, who was the station's literature and drama director, greeted me with an air of detached boredom.

"Well, we would have to see if you can speak properly," he said. He gave me a book and sat me in a studio. Those KPFA studios were soundproofed with old acoustical tiles and worn carpet. The microphone was the venerable RCA 44BX. I learned only later of the amazing qualities of this instrument.

It was ideal for interviews, for it was bi-directional—it picked up sound from two sides. But if you started by speaking into it, and then swung your head, it sounded to the listener like you were moving across the room away from him or her. We used this to great effect in drama programs.

Butler told me to read aloud Maurice Maeterlink's short story, "Massacre of the Innocents." I had never heard of it. "All of it?" I asked. "Please," he said. He adjusted the volume level from the control room, started a tape and left the engineer's booth. There were two such booths at the station, so the broadcast must have been running from the other one. I read the story, put the book down and left the studio with the tape running. Butler never reappeared. I told the receptionist that I had finished, and I left.

A few weeks later, I was walking across campus and my temporary roommate at the Co-op hailed me and said, "I heard you reading that story on the radio. Sounded great." I walked down to KFPA and saw Bill Butler. "Oh, yes," he said. "I liked the reading, so I broadcast it. I had lost your phone number. Would you like to volunteer for us?"

I wrote to the Federal Communications Commission to get a "Restricted Radio-Telephone Operator Permit," learned how to operate the control board, and became an announcer on Saturday mornings. At first, I simply announced programs and musical selections, and recorded interviews and other events. I worked my way into doing drama, news, and public affairs broadcasting. By my senior year in college, 1961–62, I was a half-time paid employee doing news and interviews.

By the late 1950s and early 1960s, KPFA was a training ground for talents who would later make their names in mainstream journalism. It was also a place where people who had mastered the craft of communication came to spend the latter part of their careers. Elsa Knight Thompson, who had worked at the BBC during World War II, knew interview techniques that we all struggled to learn. Gene Marine had made a career in print journalism. Among the younger staff members, John Leonard became cultural editor of the *New York Times*, and Chris Koch became a producer with National Public Radio. The music director was Alan Rich, who went on to write for the *New York Herald Tribune*. I worked alongside Fred Haines, who wrote the screenplay for the 1967 film *Ulysses*.

Most of the commentators who broadcast on the station would come to the studio during the evening to record their commentaries, and the volunteer on duty would set up the microphone and handle the recording process. In this way, I met an array of fascinating people. I met Paul Baran, Anthony Boucher, Alan Watts, and others.

ENROLLED

My first class that September 1958 morning was on a Monday, at ten past eight. English 1A or Speech 1A was required of all freshmen. I chose Speech 1A, and enrolled in the section that was listed as designed for those who might become lawyers. Enrollment was limited to fifty students, and I made the cut. I did not suspect from the course catalog what the Speech Department had become. It was not concerned only with oral expression, although there were courses of that nature. It had been transformed by its faculty into a department of what used to be called "Rhetoric." Courses dealt with all aspects of persuasive communication, and they even included offerings on freedom of speech. Good fortune brought me that Monday into the classroom of Jacobus tenBroek.

TenBroek held a law degree and a doctorate in law. He had been blind from an early age. His 1938 doctoral thesis dealt with constitutional interpretation. His 1951 book, *The Anti-Slavery Origins of the 14th Amendment*, was and remains a classic argument for racial justice. He was co-author of a book on the Japanese internment, and was founder and leader of a militant organization of the blind. He had been head of the California Department of Social Welfare.

That Monday morning, he strode into the classroom at 8:10, tall, with a trimmed ginger beard. He laid his white cane in the blackboard chalk tray, and called the roll from Braille cards. That way, he learned the sound of each of our voices and where we sat. He asked us to keep the same seats throughout the semester. He would thereafter recognize us when we spoke up, or call on one of us to speak.

This was Socratic instruction in the way that Socrates did it, and not the imitation variety one sees in so much law school teaching. TenBroek would take a passage from the reading and ask about it. One of us would venture an interpretation. "Oh, yes," he might say, "but have you considered what he says just one paragraph further on?" Or even, "You are forgetting how the punctuation might change the meaning." From his flawless memory of the text, he would challenge us to move deeper into what we were studying. That semester, our course book contained Plato's Dialogues on the citizen and the state, works on free expression by John Milton and John Stuart Mill, and Supreme Court cases. Almost all of it was new to me, but it opened up my eyes to the theory and value of free expression. I rejoiced at John Milton's words:

I cannot praise a fugitive and cloistered virtue, unexercised and unbreathed, that never sallies out to see her adversary. . . . That which purifies us is trial, and trial is by what is contrary.

Here was an idea not only about free expression, but also about the very dialectical process by which the world advances and great causes are disputed. We were being led, or perhaps propelled, through it by mastering both its content and its technique. TenBroek also introduced us to the work of Alexander Meiklejohn, a leading writer on the theory and practice of free expression, who was a regular commentator on KPFA.

Speech 1B turned us to equal protection of the laws, to see the tension between freedom and equality. Years later, I was asked to contribute an essay to a collection titled *Can We Be Equal and Free?* I wrote what I learned in those two magical semesters, that one is useless without the other. Free speech is valueless without equality of access to the forum.

The University required that all students take three semesters of a foreign language. I chose French, having learned basic Spanish in junior high and high school. In later years, I learned French well enough to conduct research, write about European legal history, and to teach at universities in France. I found the required university course difficult. After some introductory material on grammar and vocabulary, we were assigned to read and study Jean-Paul Sartre's 1947 novel *Les Jeux Sont Faits.* Our instructor was of French origin, and insisted firmly and repeatedly that the Algerian struggle for independence—going on at that time —was utterly wrong, because Algeria was not a colony but an overseas department of France, and must always remain so. His ability to interpret Sartre's idea of human liberation was perhaps stultified.

The Navy required us to take a general sociology course, which met three times a week in a large hall for lectures by Professor Lewis S. Feuer. We also had weekly sessions with a graduate teaching assistant in smaller sessions. Feuer had been an editor of the Marxist journal *Science and Society*, and had worked with Paul Sweezy in the 1930s to organize a union at Harvard. He had published an anthology of Marx and Engels's work. He was perhaps not well suited to discuss the work of the 1950s scholars, particularly David Riesman and C. Wright Mills, whose work addressed the post–Second World War structure of American society. Having abandoned Marxist social theory, he had become angrily intolerant of those who continued to espouse the views he had once held. He was an ardent Cold Warrior, and a good friend to Edward Teller, the physicist credited with developing the hydrogen bomb. Feuer credited Teller with "exposing" Robert Oppenheimer.

Early in the semester, he assigned us a version of Nikita Khrushchev's speech to the 20th Soviet Communist Party Congress. Khrushchev had become Party First Secretary shortly after Stalin died. In a secret speech on February 14, 1956, he attacked Stalin's policies:

> It is here that Stalin showed in a whole series of cases his intolerance, his brutality, and his abuse of power. . . . He often chose the path of repression and physical annihilation, not only against actual enemies, but also against individuals who had not committed any crimes against the party or the Soviet Government.

The speech did not remain secret for long. Within a month, extensive excerpts of it were published around the world. Along with the speech, Feuer assigned the *Communist Manifesto*, and some other work of Marx and Engels.

NAVAL SCIENCE

On the lower end of the UC Berkeley campus, toward downtown Berkeley, a modest frame building housed the Naval ROTC classrooms and storerooms. The commanding officer, Marine Corps Colonel Wilbur, had an office in the large UC gymnasium building nearby. In the gymnasium basement, Marine Sergeant Major Mills presided over an armory of old bolt-action rifles, which we were to use for target practice, and to learn how to drill with a rifle on one's shoulder.

The quartermaster who ran the storeroom issued us the books we needed for our regular classes. One day, the naval command in San Francisco sent over a tailor who fitted out the forty of us Midshipman 4th Class with uniforms—blue wool double-breasted jacket and pants with gold buttons. I had to buy straight-collar white dress shirts and a plain black tie to complete the ensemble. Our officer-instructor told us to buy one of those wire-and-springs gadgets to hold the collar straight.

Once a week, all of us NROTC midshipmen showed up in uniform, and marched around the football practice field while Sergeant Major Mills called a marching cadence. I learned to carry a a rifle in the proper "shoulder arms" position, ready at a shouted command to turn and fire on any Soviet warship that might appear in San Francisco Bay.

Our classroom course in Naval Science was taught by a young Navy lieutenant, using a textbook titled *The United States and World Sea Power*. The book was based on the work of Admiral Albert Thayer Mahan, who had taught at the Naval War College in the late nineteenth and early twentieth century. The message of this packaged history was clear. For example: "It is safe to predict that, when the opportunities for gain abroad are understood, the course of American enterprise will cleave a channel by which to reach them." And: "In unity of heart among the English-speaking races lies the best hope of humanity in the doubtful days ahead." Mahan wrote in the late nineteenth century that there would soon be a canal across the Isthmus of Panama, and United States imperial power would reach toward Asia, gobbling up the Hawaiian Islands on the way. This expansion was to be fueled by "race patriotism," and made possible by a large force of warships.

Mahan was one of several advocates for the "New Imperialism." In the United States, he stood alongside Frederick Jackson Turner, whose theory of the American "frontier" included white settlers overrunning Native American lands and civilizations, and driving out rivals such as Spain and Mexico.

This jingoistic vision of the military—and my proposed role in it—did not fit with the arguably noble mythology of a defensive force prepared to resist a possible invasion, nor with the more modest idea of policing conflicts that might threaten world order. We were being taught stories of warfare, without considering the social and historical context in which we were living.

On the other hand, I found the World War II history of naval battles in the Pacific and Atlantic, against Japan and Nazi Germany, fascinating.

Someone, probably at KPFA, recommended that I read J. A. Hobson's book *Imperialism*, written in 1902. Hobson discussed, as had Mahan, the capitalist drive for new markets, but he presented a more realistic picture of the savagery and exploitation employed in that expansion. I learned enough to be able to understand what Paul Baran was talking about in his radio commentaries.

On January 1, 1959, the forces led by Fidel Castro entered Havana. The U.S.-supported president, Fulgencio Batista, had left the country overnight in two airplanes, along with his family and other government figures. Even with the military aid that Batista had received from the United States, Batista had not held on to power. For months thereafter, KPFA and other media carried the dramatic stories: show trials of Batista collaborators, the U.S. role in putting and keeping Batista in power, and the history of U.S. financial and political dominance over Cuba in the years since 1898. I delved into the history of U.S.-Cuba relations.

I began to see Mahan's theory as a recasting of classic colonialism, driven by finance. I did not yet have tools of analysis to understand all the laws of motion of this American idea of global domination, but I was getting there. I had been immersed in this ideology, but did not understand what it was. Many years later, I read David Foster Wallace's parable: Two young fish are swimming upstream. An old fish swims by in the other direction, and calls out "Good morning, boys! How's the water?" One young fish turns to the other and says, "What's water?"

In the summer of 1959, the NROTC treated me to a learning cruise aboard the destroyer USS *Maddox*, DD 731. This warship, commissioned in 1944, had seen action in World War II. If I were ever to become a naval officer, this would be the kind of ship on which I would serve. Unlike a battleship or cruiser, it was not overwhelmingly large, about 115 meters long. Two dozen of us midshipmen were added to her crew for ten weeks.

To prepare us for this experience, we had to learn what to do if we fell in the water. I was ordered to show up at the university gymnasium swimming pool, wearing a pair of Navy-issued dungarees. A Navy petty officer directed me to climb the high-dive tower. "OK, now jump into the water." It seemed like a long way down. "Once you get in the water, take off your dungarees. Wring them out. Tie a knot at the bottom of each leg. Then hold the waistband and flip them over your head, so that the legs fill with air. Then use them as a float."

I did all of this. As a method of saving my life, I considered it on a par with hiding under my school desk during a nuclear attack. Why not give every sailor on deck a life jacket with a signaling device? Why not tether sailors to lifelines when working on deck, at least during the night? Since then, I have owned sailboats and sailed on other people's boats, logging more than 30,000 miles at sea. We wear life vests on deck, and use "jacklines"—tethers—during night watches.

During our summer training cruise, the ship's crew practiced man overboard techniques once or twice. Without notice to the crew on the bridge, someone would toss a mannequin into the sea and yell, "Man overboard" and "Starboard side" or "Port side." The officer of the deck would order "Left full rudder" or "Right full rudder," turning the ship toward the side where the mannequin went over, and then "All stop," a common order relayed to the engine room to stop engines. One crew member was assigned to keep the mannequin in sight, while a life raft was launched over the side to retrieve him. We managed not to lose the mannequin.

We midshipmen worked with all the groups and trades who were running the ship—engine room, fire room, deck officers, navigation officers. I learned elementary navigation and charting skills that I later used as a sailboat sailor. I learned that I loved the ocean, a love that led me in later years to own a sailboat and go "blue water cruising." By dint of throwing up, I learned that I would not like to be in a confined engine room or fire room inhaling fuel oil.

Our cruise began in Long Beach, California. We ventured deep into the Pacific Ocean, doing maneuvers as part of a fleet dominated by a huge aircraft carrier. We called on the ports of San Francisco, San Diego, and Seattle. Our commanding officer always looked a bit harried. The story on board was that he was a recovering alcoholic, and that this was his "make or break" command. Every morning, the ship intercom, the "1-MC," would intone: "Reveille, reveille, all hands heave out and trice up. Reveille [pronounced revel-ee]!" And then, "This is the captain speaking. Let us pray." There followed a prayer to Jesus.

Here we were, part of a military establishment that presided over weapons of mass destruction, and everybody hoped that nobody would make a fatal nuclear mistake. Yet, while docking in San Diego, the captain managed to take out 100 feet or so of the dock through a miscalculation. And, as I stood on the bridge, when we were coming in to Los Angeles Harbor, the communications officer informed the captain on the bridge what he said was our position, in latitude and longitude. The captain called back down, "Try again, Ensign. That position puts us in the middle of downtown Torrance."

Although I enjoyed being at sea, the experience of my first university year left me with a sense of unreality. We studied imperial expansion without considering its human cost. We rode around in warships, preparing for military conflict, without anyone mentioning the risks of a nuclear arms race. We read about ideological and political conflict in the USSR, and considered some works of Marx, without being encouraged to look deeply at history and context. These were indeed the branches and not the roots.

The one bright spot had been tenBroek's classes, not merely for what I learned about free expression and equality, but also for the ways that his own work and his teaching illustrated how theories about fundamental rights might be put into practice.

SOPHOMORE YEAR: 1959-60

I had signed up for four years of Naval ROTC, including the summer training cruises. However, every male United States citizen who was a student at the University of California was required to take two years of ROTC classes. A student could choose Army, Air Force, or Navy ROTC, although enrollment in the Navy program was limited. The requirement dated to the Morrill Land Grant Act of 1862, which gave land to states for building colleges, provided that each such college would offer courses in mechanics, agriculture, and military tactics. After 1918, the decision whether ROTC would be compulsory at the University of California was left to the University Regents.

On October 19, 1959, Fred Moore, a freshman student, conducted a seven-day fast on the steps of the University's administration building. Moore was conscientiously opposed to war and preparation for war, and hence to

ROTC. Conscientious objection based on religious belief had been recognized by statute as a lawful basis for refusing military service all through the twentieth century. But the Regents had decided not to honor such an objection; refusal to enroll in ROTC meant exclusion from the University. Not only that, the ROTC authorities compelled every student to take a loyalty oath as well.

Fred Moore's protest tapped into a stream of student concern that was already flowing. Early in 1957, a group of students had formed Toward An Active Student Community (TASC) to advocate against the nuclear arms race, and for human rights in the United States and internationally. TASC's overriding concern was that students be involved in debating and taking action about important social issues—from the branches to the roots. In 1958, TASC recast itself as Slate, an organization that would not only advocate but would also present a "slate" of candidates for student government offices. In the spring of 1958, Slate candidate David Armor was elected student body president for the 1959–60 academic year.

Armor's election frightened the University administration. Armor's strongest electoral support had been among graduate students. The University issued an edict removing graduate students from the student government system, barring their representatives from the Executive Committee of the Association Students of the University of California (ASUC). University president Clark Kerr followed up on this move with what became known as the "Kerr directives." These new rules forbade student government from taking positions on "off-campus issues," that is, on the matters of social concern that had been the basis for TASC's and Slate's existence.

The effort to silence student concern was not a new phenomenon. In 1956, students had organized to protest compulsory ROTC. The Dean of Students forbade students to pass out leaflets on the issue, saying that leaflets would cause litter and make more work for the janitorial staff. The dean was perhaps unaware that in 1939 the Supreme Court had rejected littering as a plausible reason to forbid handing out leaflets. Or perhaps he was overcome by his literal reading of those metal plates at the campus entrance that proclaimed the entire university to be the "property" of the Regents. The university did not object to the military handing out pro-ROTC leaflets in classes. Fred Moore's protest invigorated the fight against compulsory ROTC, but the Regents did not abolish the requirement until the fall of 1962.

The dean's interdiction had some precedent. In 1958, Berkeley citizens had gathered enough support to put an ordinance on the ballot prohibiting racial discrimination in housing. In March 1959, Slate asked the Dean of

Students' permission to hold a campus rally supporting the proposed ordinance. The dean's denial was wrapped in tortured legalistic jargon. Students would be announcing the rally as taking place at the University of California. This would amount to using the University's name in support of a political position without permission of the Board of Regents. Moreover, students were not allowed to use campus facilities to express opinions on political or social issues. The dean concluded: "Students in their individual capacities or as members of groups not recognized by the University are, of course, free to engage in political activity off the campus."

Housing discrimination was rife in Berkeley. African-Americans made up more than 20 percent of the city's population in 1958, yet were subjected to de facto segregation. In 1958, when an African-American family moved into a home they rented near campus, this triggered community turmoil and retaliation against their landlord by the Federal Housing Administration, which had guaranteed his mortgage loan. Had Berkeley's professors not noticed that they lived in all-white housing areas, many of which had racial restrictions?

From his office, the dean could see that the university campus was a public place, with streets, paths, and park-like spaces. He had apparently not heard of the Supreme Court's 1939 decision in *Hague v. CIO*:

> Wherever the title of streets and parks may rest, they have immemorially been held in trust for the use of the public and, time out of mind, have been used for purposes of assembly, communicating thoughts between citizens, and discussing public questions. Such use of the streets and public places has, from ancient times, been a part of the privileges, immunities, rights, and liberties of citizens. The privilege of a citizen of the United States to use the streets and parks for communication of views on national questions may be regulated in the interest of all; it is not absolute, but relative, and must be exercised in subordination to the general comfort and convenience, and in consonance with peace and good order; but it must not, in the guise of regulation, be abridged or denied.

The ACLU sought to persuade the dean to change his mind, to no avail. Slate members held their rally anyway, despite threats of university discipline.

By the end of the fall 1959 semester, it had become clear to me that I should change direction in my own life. I should move away from the academic field I had chosen; confront the social issues that the university was determined to ignore, and reconsider the military path on which I had embarked.

THE UNIVERSITY AS AN ISLAND

I had come to Berkeley thinking I might major in mathematics. I believed that this subject would develop my ability to analyze and reason. In high school, I had taken analytic geometry and calculus in an experimental curriculum developed by Dr. Leon M. Lessinger, a gifted teacher. I was fascinated by the idea that shapes and the movement of objects could be understood with numeric precision.

In my sophomore year at Berkeley, the sequence of math courses included the "theory of algebraic equations." The course met in a large lecture hall. One algebra book was Uspensky's *Theory of Equations*. I don't remember the other one. At first I followed the lectures. But gradually I had the sense of being ushered into a room where people were speaking in a foreign language, and I could not grasp what was being said well enough to make notes. The mathematical statements had become so complicated that I could not see the shape of a solution. I lacked the patience, and perhaps the ability, to parse them. The social and political issues that were being debated all around me seemed a more welcome field of study. I passed the math courses, and enrolled in political science and history classes. I was looking for academic experiences that would help me to interpret events.

Within a few years, I realized that I had perhaps been too quick to abandon the study of mathematics. As I began to read the work of Paul Sweezy and other economists, I saw that mathematical proof was one lens through which to view the contradictions in the present system of social and economic relations.

The university administrators had demonstrated their disregard, if not contempt, for students' right to self-expression. More than that, they saw the university as an island of acquiescence and quiet irrelevance in a sea of social conflict. Professors professed, but almost universally failed to connect their professing to the issues of war, racism, and repression that were all around us. Much less did they take action against injustice by way of example. There were a few exceptions, such as Professor tenBroek and history professor Richard Drinnon, with whom I was to study in my junior year.

Had these deans and teachers missed John Milton's message, that suppressing ideas is "vain and impossible," and that "he who were pleasantly disposed could not well avoid to liken it to the exploit of that gallant man who thought to pound up the crows by shutting his park gate"? Had they failed to notice what Justice Jackson wrote in a Supreme Court case that Professor tenBroek had assigned?

But freedom to differ is not limited to things that do not matter much. That would be the mere shadow of freedom. The test of its substance is the right to differ as to things that touch the heart of the existing order.

Some administrators were no doubt moved by the bureaucratic, though futile, desire to avoid controversy. Others, such as University of California president Clark Kerr, had a vision of the university, and the intellectuals within it, that was ahistorical as well as repressive. In 1960, Kerr published a book, *Industrialism and Industrial Man*, that set out his social theory, echoing his work as an expert on industrial relations.

Kerr foresaw a new stage in social development called "industrialism," in which society would be divided into two classes, managers and managed. The managed need to be trained to follow orders, and the managers would be agents of technological change. As for intellectuals, Kerr had both fear and contempt. "They are by nature irresponsible," he wrote. "Consequently, it is important who best attracts or captures the intellectuals and who uses them most effectively, for they may be a tool as well as a source of danger."

In industrial society, Kerr wrote, "there will not be any revolt . . . except little bureaucratic revolts that can be handled piecemeal." With that world-view, it is no wonder that the students under Kerr's care rose up in ways that he found both frightening and mystifying. His understanding of his own time proved as lamentably poor as the predictive power of his hypothesis. The domestic drive for civil rights, the antiwar protests that carried on into the 1970s, and then the worldwide upsurge of liberation movements confounded him and his theory.

With my friend Ken Cloke, I began to attend Slate meetings. We discussed ways of attacking the Kerr directives and other limits on freedom of expression. We wanted to be an effective voice for farm workers' rights, nuclear disarmament, and racial equality. Because Slate was concerned with many issues, it fostered separate organizations addressing, for example, agricultural labor, capital punishment, and civil liberties.

I was volunteering at KPFA, and I began to learn from the talented people there. At that time, radio news on commercial stations consisted mostly of five minutes at the top of the hour, where an announcer read copy torn off the Associated Press teletype. At KPFA, an AP teletype chattered away in a closet, but was only one source of our news. Gene Marine, the news director, decreed that we would do one half hour of news every weekday night at 6 p.m. Two newscasters would be on the air. Gene was usually one of them, along with Bill Plosser. The rest of the work was done by volunteers and part-timers like me.

By my sophomore year, I would come to the station in the early afternoon and pound out news stories on a manual typewriter, then be subjected to Gene's editing process. Sometimes we would use paragraphs from the Associated Press wire, but we wrote most of the stories for delivery over the radio. A radio lede is different from a print journalism lede—it has to convey more key information, and the simple declarative sentence is even more essential. A strong lede, staking out the ground on which the story will play out, that's what Gene Marine and Elsa Thompson taught me. If you look back to the Prologue of this book and the first part of my oral argument in David Gutknecht's case, you will see that I continued to heed those lessons. You would find the same technique in any of my more than a hundred oral arguments in courts of appeals, and seven Supreme Court appearances.

Because this was radio, and not an in-person or TV appearance, the timbre and tone of my speaking voice made a big difference. I had to sound like somebody who should be taken seriously and not some eighteen-year-old who had wandered in off the street. I can't remember which of the KPFA staffers took me aside and taught me: "Your voice sounds too young. Get it down into your chest." I remembered that lesson from high school drama. I worked to comply. In audio recordings of various times in my careers, you can hear what my wife calls my "radio voice." That radio voice won me an occasional spot as co-host of the evening news broadcast.

To liven up our broadcasts, we would call up people in the news and record brief interviews. On days when I was working the news, there was from about 2 p.m. to 6 p.m. the deadline pressure to produce about 3,000 words of copy. During this time, we were deciding which would be the main stories of the day. In addition to the AP, we had news from the BBC, local media, and alternative sources. We might do a news feature on political developments in a foreign country, based on sources that were several days old, but that had not been reported elsewhere. The world of internet-based instant communication did not yet exist.

At 6 p.m. the announcer would say, "And now the news, read this evening by Gene Marine and Mike Tigar." I might then say, "Good evening, this is Mike Tigar. In Havana today, Cuban President Fidel Castro. . . " That was our type of lede. Tell them where, tell them who, and then tell them what. I was "Mike" in those days.

Learning to think and write in the form of stories that would be spoken aloud was another part of my preparation to be a lawyer. Radio journalism also provided practice in asking questions, one after another, to avoid dead air and keep the discussion moving—and, most important, to listen to the answers. Elsa Thompson was one of the best interviewers I would ever meet.

She shared her experience and ideas. My techniques of courtroom examination began in those radio studios.

Around this time, with the help of Pacifica colleagues, I began to sell stories and reviews to local print publications. I wrote for a Berkeley publication, the *liberal democrat,* and for *Frontier* magazine. I wrote a few movie reviews for a San Francisco weekly newspaper, using—for a reason I cannot now recall—the nom de plume Peter Noster.

I spent as much time as I could carve out from classes, study, homework, and my NROTC duties to be at KPFA and work alongside the staff members. They willingly shared their skills and values. Because of KPFA's role as the broadcast voice of so many talented and politically active people, I could not have found a better introduction to ideas and information that began to unsettle the impressions of the world with which I had arrived at Berkeley.

NAVAL DISENGAGEMENT—PART ONE

In September 1959, Soviet First Secretary Khrushchev visited the United States for discussions with President Eisenhower. They met against the backdrop of worldwide concern with nuclear testing and the arms race. The two leaders agreed that "the question of general disarmament is the most important one facing the world today." They agreed to reopen discussions about Berlin.

As it happened, the naval science subject that second year was "naval weapons." Our NROTC instructor was Lieutenant Commander Steed. We got a new commanding officer, Captain Meyer. Steed did not present the classic image of a naval officer. His khaki uniform was usually a little rumpled, his manner diffident. A part of his job was to teach us something about foreign and military policy, from the Navy's perspective. A midshipman in our class, Pete, stood out because he was outspoken, and because we all knew he was the nephew of some high-ranking Navy officer. One day in class we were talking about the atomic bombs dropped on Hiroshima and Nagasaki. Pete raised his hand and said, "Commander, I have read that we did not need to drop those bombs, that the Japanese were ready to surrender."

Steed paused a very long time. Finally, his voice soft, he said, "Mr. X, if I believed that, I would have to turn in my uniform." I am not giving his last name because for all I know he is still a naval officer somewhere. Pete's concerns paralleled some of mine.

As part of thinking things through, I decided to clarify my views by writing them out. We were assigned a term paper, and could choose any topic related to naval weaponry in the modern age. I suppose it was expected that we would focus on the strategic importance of nuclear missiles carried by the newly launched nuclear-powered submarines. I chose to write about disarmament. We are now, I wrote, like villagers living on the slopes of Vesuvius, never knowing from one day to the next whether an unexpected calamity will wipe out our community. Why, I asked, are we living in this way? I quoted John Donne, who prayed God to deliver man from needing danger. These are the parts I remember; I am sure that I included research and analysis in addition to rhetorical flourish.

A week after I turned in the paper, Commander Steed called me. "Can you come to my house?" he asked. Somewhat fearfully, I went. We sat in his living room. At home, he looked more disheveled than on duty. I wondered where in the arc of his naval career he now was, and thought that he must be on the downward slope. He had my paper. "I have read this. It is very well done," he began. "You have a career in the Navy ahead of you, if you want it. You are bright. You present a good image. Your marks are high. You don't want something like this in your file. It would follow you. So I am going to give you a grade, and I am giving you back this paper."

I thought the concerns I raised were realistic, and that my approach to them was at least debatable. Did Steed mean that the Navy was intolerant of all but the narrowest official view of policy and history? I thought tolerance of dissent was an important American value. I thought that those destined for leadership, even in the military, should develop the habit of independent thought, and of concern for the consequences of one's acts.

During my second year at Berkeley in 1959–60, I continued attending meetings of campus political organizations. I spoke against the death penalty. I spoke in opposition to the House Committee on Un-American Activities. I became more active in Slate. I met one of the KPFA commentators who was a member of a Quaker meeting, and I attended Sunday services there a couple of times.

NO LONGER AN ISLAND

On February 1, 1960, African-American and white young people in Greensboro, North Carolina, sat-in at a lunch counter to demand service. They were arrested. Nine Chapel Hill high school students were arrested for sitting in at the Colonial Drug Store on Franklin Street. These protests signaled the beginning of a direct- action movement to end segregation. People of good will had become impatient with the glacial pace of change. Despite *Brown v. Board of Education*, and despite President Eisenhower's 1957 use of military force to enforce a school desegregation decree in

Little Rock, Arkansas, the white establishment resisted change by every possible means.

In Berkeley, we organized sympathy pickets and boycotts of the chain stores that had refused service to African-Americans in the South, principally Woolworth's and Kresge's. To the tune of "Hallelujah, I'm a Bum," the Depression ditty, we sang:

> *Hallelujah, picketing Woolworth*
> *And I like it just fine*
> *Hallelujah, I'm carryin'*
> *That big freedom sign*

During that time, the newspapers were reporting on the case of Caryl Chessman, who had been convicted and sentenced to death in 1948. I first learned of his case when I was in high school, as I recounted in chapter 1. Chessman proclaimed his innocence in dozens of appeals, some of which he pursued as his own counsel. As his February 19, 1960, execution date approached, California Governor Pat Brown issued a stay of execution and expressed the wish that Chessman's sentence be commuted to life imprisonment. However, California law at that time required that the State Supreme Court ratify commutation of sentence for a twice-convicted felon. The Court denied relief, 4 to 3. The stays of execution ran out. Chessman was executed in the gas chamber on May 2, 1960. Students from Berkeley joined a protest at San Quentin Prison, and passed out leaflets on campus opposing the death penalty.

The final significant event of that spring 1960 semester was a visit to San Francisco by the House Committee on Un-American Activities (HUAC). Politics in the San Francisco Bay Area, including Berkeley, were eclectic. The California university system had experienced its own loyalty oath crisis in the early 1950s. State senator Hugh Burns headed a "Fact-Finding Committee on Un-American Activities," which in 1951 issued a report claiming that the University of California had "aided and abetted the international communist conspiracy." Burns and his committee cooperated with the FBI and other agencies to conduct surveillance of suspected subversives. They were part of the McCarthyite machinery of the 1950s. Partly in response to attacks like Burns's, the University forbade any campus group from inviting any speaker who was a member of the Communist Party. Good thing, I thought, that Khrushchev hadn't wanted to visit.

I studied this issue. I read the history of loyalty oath fights, and of state and federal investigating committees. I read Supreme Court cases. HUAC's

San Francisco hearings were focused on alleged communist infiltration into the labor movement and education. The hearings followed a familiar pattern. The visiting subcommittee would be presided over by an ascetic midwestern or jowly southern congressman. In this case, it was Louisiana congressman Richard Willis who showed up, accompanied by Republican congressman August Johansen, from Michigan. Committee Counsel Richard Arens would by turns exude sanctimony and disgust. The hearings would begin with the public testimony of witnesses who claimed to have been members of the Communist Party, revealing insidious Communist plots, as well as giving out the names of their friends and neighbors who, so they said, had been in there with them.

This pattern was unbroken since at least the late 1940s, and indeed some of the witnesses had been recycled so often they were running out of names to name. The San Francisco hearings took their predictable course. One witness intoned the evils of Communist infiltration, and counsel Arens encouraged her by asking:

Q: Now, Mrs. Hartle, can you tell us all please whether in the ideology of communism, with its goal of world domination, is there any room for the basic ideas of God and patriotism as we are taught them at our mother's knee?

That particular question led to a spate of tasteless remarks in our group about "my mother's knee and other low joints."

Following the professional tale-bearers, the Committee had subpoenaed several prominent left-wing figures from the Bay Area as hostile witnesses, asking each under oath if they were members of the Communist Party, or had ever been, and receiving from each a Constitution-based refusal to answer. None of this "investigating" would lead to any legislation.

The Supreme Court had questioned the Committee's bona fides. Congressman James Roosevelt had begun a drive to abolish it. The May 1960 Committee hearings were different from those that had been held in other places. Thousands of students, union members, and others formed a peaceful picket line around the San Francisco City Hall, where the hearings were being held. The main theme of their signs and chants was "abolish the Committee." Slate was represented, as were Students for Civil Liberties, which was affiliated with the American Civil Liberties Union, and the Bay Area Student Committee to Abolish HUAC (BASCAHUAC).

On May 12, 1960, two California legislators addressed a large crowd in Union Square, attacking the Committee and its work. One speaker was California Assemblyman Phil Burton, who later served in Congress. I spoke briefly. The Committee, not wanting a hostile audience in the hearing room, arranged that its supporters would take up all the seats. Students lined up for places at the hearing, but were disappointed to see that their long wait in line was fruitless. Holders of Committee-issued white cards showed up and trooped in. The tension grew inside and outside the hearing room. Hostile witnesses upbraided the committee for stacking the audience. Among the witnesses was the redoubtable Archie Brown, an elected leader of the International Longshore and Warehouse Union (ILWU), who publicly proclaimed his Communist Party membership. Archie later ran for San Francisco County Board of Supervisors and got 33 percent of the vote.

On Friday, May 13, the waiting students began to show their impatience by chanting, "Mr. Willis, we're still here." San Francisco police in riot gear moved into position and turned on the powerful fire hoses. The students were on the City Hall's second-floor rotunda, just outside the hearing room door. The police washed them down the long marble stairs, and then followed them down, clubbing at them randomly as they slipped and slid to the ground floor. Police on the ground floor scooped up about a hundred demonstrators and carted them off to jail.

Upstairs, the hearings continued. The next hostile witness, William Mandel, began his first answer to a Committee question with, "Honorable beaters of children, uniformed and in plainclothes, distinguished Dixiecrat wearing the clothing of a gentleman. . . . "

Eventually the protesters were all acquitted. Pete Seeger sang at a benefit concert to raise defense money. I was the master of ceremonies, fascinated by the interplay of political action, folk music, and legal theory. As some of us met with the lawyers who volunteered to represent the arrested students, we learned more constitutional lore about direct action and the First Amendment.

HUAC, anxious to rebut the attacks on its handling of the San Francisco protest and to preserve itself if possible, sponsored a movie about the protests, *Operation Abolition*. This film was widely shown to community groups and on college campuses, and was the set piece for many debates. At some of these, Ken Cloke and I were the invited speakers, confronting Fulton Lewis III, son of the conservative columnist.

In Berkeley, we thought there should be a rebuttal to the film; Fred Haines, Ken Kitch, Jerry Gray, and I wrote and produced a 12-inch long-playing (LP) record titled *Sounds of Protest*. We used audio recordings from the demonstrations and the Committee itself. Fred and I had reported for KPFA on the hearings and demonstrations. Slate raised money for the project. We wove together a montage of sound clips from news coverage of the hearings and protests. We constructed a constitutional argument for abolishing the

Committee, stressing its chilling effect on protected expression and its lack of legitimate legislative purpose.

I was a Slate-sponsored candidate for student government office in both my junior and senior years. Slate's membership included unaffiliated folks, those who labeled themselves liberal Democrats, and socialists of various organizational tendencies. As a group, we took positions and action on issues, not ideologies. University professors, including Lewis S. Feuer and Seymour Lipset, argued that in order to be a legitimate critic of loyalty-security investigations, or an advocate of disarmament, one had to deny membership in or any affiliation with the Communist Party. They were also criticizing KPFA for airing Communist commentators as part of the station's roster of speakers expressing a wide range of views.

This academic reaction was not limited to Berkeley professors. With the advent of the Cold War, and then of McCarthyism, many professors who had been Communist Party members, Trotskyist adherents, or otherwise ardent anti-capitalists and activists in the 1930s, underwent conversions. I was reminded of Kahlil Gibran's words:

> And [what] of him who comes early to the wedding-feast, and when over-fed and tired goes his way saying that all feasts are violation and all feasters lawbreakers?

We in Slate, and those at KPFA, rejected demands for any sort of loyalty oath. Slate, like TASC before it, was an "issue-oriented" organization, open to all who shared its views on peace, disarmament, racism, labor rights, free expression, and so on. It did not matter to us whether you agreed with every single position the organization espoused, nor what ideological stance informed your ideas. We were not going to emulate McCarthyism.

By the spring of 1960, the University administration gave up most of its efforts to silence campus discussion of social issues, at least for the time being; four years later, renewal of speech curtailment led to the Free Speech movement. Slate invited Nobel Laureate and peace activist Linus Pauling to speak on campus; he accepted and the university administration did not dare stand in the way. That year, Ken Cloke and I were sharing an apartment off campus; I cooked dinner for Dr. Pauling and guests. I made spaghetti with a rather ordinary tomato sauce. My repertoire has since expanded.

INTO THE SUMMER WITH NAVY AND MARINES

My sophomore year, I managed to attend enough NROTC classes to get a B.

The 1960 Navy summer training cruise was in two parts. For the first part, I boarded a train in Los Angeles and arrived 29 hours later in San Antonio. A few hundred of us midshipmen were to spend three weeks at the naval air base, taking eight hours of flight instruction and hearing that we should choose naval aviation when we received our commissions.

As midshipmen, we were entitled to go to the Officers' Club in the evenings. I learned that Navy pilots, whose work involved being launched from and landing on aircraft carriers at sea, had prodigious thirst and capacity for alcohol. By a process I no longer recall, I was appointed commander of a company of midshipmen—seventy-five or so. This honor meant only that I was to conduct barracks inspections and march the company to meals. Maybe I got the job because I had cultivated a loud and clear outdoor speaking voice at campus rallies.

I loved flying the single-engine T-34 training aircraft, sitting in the front seat with a flight instructor in back giving instructions—and having hold of the dual controls. I resolved, however, that whatever I did in the Navy, I would not do it in South Texas in July.

On two evenings when I was free from military duties, I took a bus to San Antonio, which was an hour or so away by road. The Greensboro lunch counter sit-ins had taken place in February. What impact had the civil rights movement had in San Antonio? I was surprised to learn that most San Antonio restaurants had ended racial discrimination as of March 16, 1960. San Antonio police and the mayor had agreed with local merchants to stop enforcing segregation, on condition that African-American churches and community organizations would endorse the change and work to prevent white backlash.

The second half of the summer, our training continued in and near San Diego. Our own Captain Meyer was in charge of the midshipmen contingent, but the classroom and field instruction was done by Marine Corps officers and enlisted men. They were offering us a glimpse of what it would be like to accept a commission as a Marine Corps second lieutenant.

We learned amphibious assault tactics, including a full-scale landing on a California beach. We waded ashore from landing craft with packs and rifles, to the amazement and amusement of tourists parked along Highway 101. We penetrated into imagined enemy territory, firing blank ammunition and scaring the hell out of rabbits and chipmunks.

Another day, we were told that the next war might involve armed landings from helicopters. (Yes, in 1960, the U.S. military was already preparing to land troops in wooded terrain.) We suited up and did a mock invasion of the rolling countryside near San Diego. We leapt from helicopters and fired blank rounds at nothing in particular. We were advised that, if we smoked, we should use non-filter cigarettes, and then "field strip" the butt and scatter the bits of tobacco and paper, so as not to reveal our presence.

In San Diego, Captain Meyer made us all watch a 45-minute Technicolor film called *Communism on the Map*, produced by George S. Benson, president of Harding College, Searcy, Arkansas. Benson was an avid segregationist, devout Christian, and fervent anti-leftist. In later years, commanding officers were disciplined for showing this stuff to the troops. The story line was that the Communists were poised to take over America, as shown, for example, by the number of legislators in Hawaii who had received electoral support from the International Longshore and Warehouse Union. The film regarded every progressive political movement in America as part of a Soviet-dominated movement to destroy America.

As we marched back to our barracks from the showing, Captain Meyer fell into step beside me. "Well, Mr. Tigar, what did you think of the film?"

"I thought it was mostly half-truths, sir."

"Well, what about the rest of it?"

"The rest of it was lies, sir."

"Report to my office."

"Yes, sir."

In the office, Captain Meyer and another officer questioned me at length on my role as a film critic. I stood my ground: characterizing progressive ideas and associations as dangerous violated fundamental principles of free speech and association. What, I asked, were we supposed to be defending?

JUNIOR YEAR: 1960-61—LEAVING THE NAVY, LEARNING JOURNALISM

When the fall semester began, Captain Meyer resumed his position as commanding officer of the UC Berkeley NROTC unit. I was rooming with friends who were active in student political organizations. In October, Meyer called me into his office and handed me a report prepared by the Office of Naval Intelligence. "These are the kind of people you are associating with," he said. The office had investigated me and my roommates. Its report was full of the clichés that dominated right-wing political discourse. An example: "X [one of my roommates] is, among his other activities, chairman of the Students for Civil Liberties. This organization is affiliated with the American Civil Liberties Union, which claims to support the Constitution but which in fact is an apologist for Communist and Communist-front activity."

I was, first of all, angry at the invasion of my political privacy and that of my friends. What the hell was Naval Intelligence doing investigating students?

I was angry at the nonsense in this report, authored by a government agency and issued to guide decision-making by senior military officers. I complained to the university's Dean of Students. He was not only unconcerned, but also reported our conversation to Captain Meyer. I thought that the university would be upset about the military spying on its students, but it turned out that the administration knew about it and welcomed it.

I was also scared. I was nineteen years old. My Navy scholarship money was my main support in college. I had my part-time job at KPFA, but that didn't pay much.

It is hard to remember how many more times I sat in Captain Meyer's office, defending my views. I know it was a few. I spoke to helpful friends. I had been a good midshipman, with high ratings.

I could not talk to my family. My mother would have understood, I am sure, but my stepfather was rabid on the subject of my politics, and it was all my mother could do during his drunken rages to keep him from calling the FBI to report his disloyal stepson.

One day in October, Captain Meyer called me to his office and handed me a paper terminating my status as a midshipman; I was being "disenrolled." A couple of weeks later, I received a notice in the mail saying that because I had been a midshipman for more than two years, I was hereby enlisted as a seaman in the United States Navy, and that I would soon be told where to report for duty. I had thought that maybe they would send me a bill for the several hundred dollars the Navy had spent on my state university fees and my books. I hadn't thought they would draft me.

It was time to fight back. Captain Meyer and his cohort had swallowed whole the mentality of American empire and American military power, and of a war economy that held it together. I had been naive to suppose there was room in their world for alternative ways of seeing ideas and events. The words I had spoken in his office were as futile as trying to explain a sundial to a bat. I also reflected that much of what I needed to understand could be gathered from C. Wright Mills's book *The Power Elite*, which I had read in a sociology class.

I wrote to Francis Heisler, a lawyer in Carmel, California, whose name someone had given me. In those days before the massive Vietnam draft calls, there were not many lawyers who knew anything about military and draft law. In my letter, I told my story. Heisler called a few days later.

Heisler had immigrated from Hungary in 1918; his law practice in the United States focused on civil liberties and conscientious objection. His voice was calm and comforting. "It sounds from your letter," he began, "like you have not made up your mind. Could you participate in warfare, or not? Are your objections to particular foreign policies or to all policies that include war?" I do not remember all my words. I struggled to explain. I could see the possibility of armed forces in a true multinational force keeping the peace. I could understand how an oppressed people could take up arms. I thought that these instances were different from the use, and threat, of nuclear war as an instrument of national policy, which was what I was being asked to participate in.

Most clearly, my own experiences told a story. Whatever was noble about the World War II military resistance to Nazism, and whatever made just and necessary the armed overthrow of Batista in Cuba, I had met and heard the officers of the modern U.S. military. They were the ones under whose leadership I was to serve. They displayed utter obliquity about the dangers of nuclear war, and were uninterested in lessons of history. They encouraged suppression of opposing views and repression of those who expressed them. I was not being asked about participation in some hypothetical and indefinite conflict, but about the here and now. There was, for those in my position, only one kind of war on offer. Surely the term "war" should be understood in terms of present circumstances, and not in all the hypothetical situations one might conjure.

Was my belief "religious"? I remembered a court decision we had read in tenBroek's class: the court had held that the First Amendment required the country to grant the same tax exemption to a non-deist "Fellowship of Humanity" that was accorded to traditional churches. My decision seemed reasonable and at the same time grounded in moral principle.

This was, Heisler said, a close case. Later, when I wrote a book on selective service law during the Vietnam War, I would understand just how close. If I rejected participation in war as I understood that term, and if my objection were based on religious or ethical principles, and if my definitions were reasonable, then I would be a conscientious objector as the draft law—read in the informing light of the First Amendment—defined that term.

The trouble was that I was already in the military. The draft law conscientious objector exemption did not apply to me. In time, the military would codify conscientious objector standards almost identical to those used by the Selective Service System. This had not happened yet, nor were there regulations on processing people who claimed this status. This was 1960, before the law on conscientious objection had received the more thorough judicial consideration that it was later to receive.

Heisler urged me to write a letter describing my beliefs and send it to the Navy. "Show on the letter that you have sent a copy to me," he said. "That might do some good." I sent my letter. Months went by. John F. Kennedy was elected president. In January, shortly after the inauguration, I received an envelope from the Navy. Inside was an honorable discharge from military service, "for the convenience of the government." I don't know if I was honorably discharged as a pain in the ass or as a pacifist. Whatever the paper meant, it did not get me off the hook, because I had not served enough time to become ineligible for the draft.

In 2019, I was buying a washing machine at Lowe's. The cashier said that if I was a veteran, I would get a 10 percent discount. So I said yes. She worked at her computer terminal for about five minutes, and then said, "Oh yes, here it is. Thank you for your service."

I have recalled my conversation with Francis Heisler many times. When I became a lawyer, I tried to emulate Heisler's compassionate and gentle inquiry. I would be talking to a young man of about the age that I was at that time. He had come to reject the corrupt, morally bankrupt political-military-industrial system. Yet, to be recognized as a conscientious objector, he would have to state his views in terms that met the law's rather stringent and somewhat opaque requirements. In sum, the lawyer seeks to find in "the law" some way of recognizing and honoring a human condition.

But of all the personal decisions I faced, this had been the most difficult. Thinking through my views on warfare as policy, I came to certain tentative views about the need for transnational rules to halt slaughter while legitimately using force to protect human rights. In the sixty years since then, I have returned to these themes again and again, usually without the compulsion of personal consequences. In later years, I changed my views about violence and armed struggle. I had not considered the issue outside the context of nuclear war. I had leapt from the nonviolent struggle of the civil rights movement to the possibility of nuclear annihilation.

Later, I had to take into account such things as the South African struggle against apartheid, which included armed conflict. Such conflict was, I came to believe, necessary in the people's defense against an enemy with superior forces. One might call this defensive struggle, not war as such, thus preserving for me the label of conscientious objector. But a part of my journey has been to reject labels as being ways to falsify an underlying and changing reality. So I simply say where I was and where I am. I rejected for myself and for those whom I represented the label "coward" for not wanting to put on an American military uniform. I have been shot at by white racists in Florida, beaten up by police, and held at gunpoint by South African security forces who made us lie on the ground while they debated what to do with us. I have had my share of conflict.

LEARNING WHO I WAS AND WHAT I OUGHT TO DO

The Navy's decision, and the University's complicity, triggered my sense of injustice. I understood that this was not an injustice devised for and directed at me. Captain Meyer was acting out a role defined for him by a structure of power. What should I do about that? What career path should I choose? I could think of three alternatives.

I could be a journalist. On the radio, I had learned to do research, write the news, do interviews. I was technically proficient at editing audiotape, and had worked to develop a good "radio voice." The KPFA approach to news and public affairs reporting was principled and effective. Gene Marine and Elsa Knight Thompson had helped my writing and presentation skills.

I could get a PhD and become a university professor. I admired the work of Professor Richard Drinnon, who taught a history course I had taken. He had written *Rebel in Paradise*, a biography of anarchist leader Emma Goldman. Drinnon recommended the work of William Appleman Williams, who chronicled American imperial expansion. I admired not only Williams's scholarship but also his active engagement in social issues.

I could become a lawyer, the profession I had long thought I would pursue. My notion of lawyers had been enriched by reading about civil rights struggles, and by watching lawyers for demonstrators, union organizers, and radicals in the Bay Area.

I did not want to repeat the error that had led me into the Navy. I had taken that step based on untested assumptions and inadequate knowledge. There is a saying: It is easier to act your way into right thinking than to think yourself into right acting. I decided to study the alternatives.

These three choices seemed somehow right: related to one another, and each designed to permit me to understand and to remedy injustice.

Before I investigated my choices, however, I needed money to stay in school. KPFA offered me a part-time job, working on the news a couple of days a week, and filling in on other assignments. For a few months, I had an early morning job at the University, from 7 a.m. until 10 a.m., filing and copying records. I had to give that up, because classes in the daytime, followed by work at KPFA, followed by study and political meetings at night grew too wearing.

Ken Cloke, Charles Fleckles, and I found a lower-floor flat on the north side of campus. The landlady lived upstairs. Shortly after moving in, we had a rather noisy gathering. We heard thumping noises from upstairs. The next morning, the landlady warned us, and said that she kept an American flag in a stanchion beside her bed, which she could use to pound on the floor when the noise bothered her. Having read in the local paper what we were doing and saying on the campus, she took to calling us "Comrade Cloke" and "Comrade Tigar." We decided to find another apartment and moved to a second-floor flat on the south side of campus.

In that fall of 1960, Cloke and I were Slate candidates for the student government Executive Committee, known as ExCom. We advocated for student involvement in the issues that Slate and related organizations had been advocating. On October 14, the day before the election, the campus newspaper, *The Daily Californian*, carried an editorial endorsing my student government candidacy. UC Vice-Chancellor Alex Sherriffs was furious. He and his colleagues saw the *Daily Cal* as a kind of house organ that was to report on student activities such as sports and fraternity parties. At his behest, the majority of the Executive Committee fired the *Daily Cal* editors.

BROADCAST JOURNALIST?

By the beginning of 1961, the Pacifica Foundation had acquired two more stations: KPFK in Los Angeles and WBAI in New York. Its revenue base and potential audience correspondingly grew. I worked on the nightly news, but also on radio documentaries. I even had a brief tenure as director of children's programs. I read aloud classics such as *Treasure Island* and James Thurber's *The Thirteen Clocks*, doing the voices of all the characters and adding background music and sound effects.

The KPFA staff also produced radio documentaries on current history. Ernest Lowe had studied the lives of farmworkers, and produced *Sometimes You Work a Day*. I helped Fred Haines and Chris Koch put together a documentary on the Congo. The Republic of the Congo had become formally independent from Belgium on June 30, 1960. Patrice Lumumba was its first prime minister and Minister of Defense. Immediately, Belgium and the United States began to undermine his government, in the interest of maintaining international capital investments in Congo mining. Lumumba turned to the USSR for assistance. By the end of 1960, Lumumba had been removed as prime minister and on January 17, 1961, he was executed by firing squad. The KFPA documentary traced the history of Belgian colonialism in Africa, with attention to French, German, Dutch, and British colonial power. The title was *The Work of Civilization*. We took those words from a speech in the Belgian parliament by socialist leader Emile Vandervelde: "The work of civilization, as you call it, is an enormous and continual butchery."

The documentary connected the savage history of colonialism to what we were then seeing in the daily news reports. What were we doing, journalism or history? I saw that we were using an understanding of history as a lens through which to view the present. In recounting present events, we rely on observation and recollection by participants and observers. To evaluate those accounts, we must understand the social, cultural, and political biases of those accounts.

That spring, KPFA also produced a radio documentary on the Spanish Civil War, *Winds of the People*. The documentary told the story of the anti-fascist movement and the civil war through the words of radical poets and songwriters. The pseudonymous author of the documentary was Dolores de Viznar, literally "sorrows of Viznar." Viznar was the town where fascist soldiers shot and killed Federico Garcia Lorca in the early days of the war. My radio voice was called upon to narrate some of the evocative poetry of Lorca and others.

I saw that the present-day Franco dictatorship was the product of a disgraceful history of American and British indifference to Hitler's military support for a fascist Spain. I also committed to memory Lorca's poem "Casida del Llanto," which spoke to the failure of academics and intellectuals to hear and respond to human suffering:

It begins:

> *He cerrado mi balcón*
> *Por que no quiero oír el llanto*
> *Pero por detrás de los grises muros*
> *No se oye otra cosa que el llanto.*

> *I have shut my balcony*
> *For I do not wish to hear the weeping*
> *But from beyond the gray walls*
> *Nothing else is heard but the weeping.*

I also concluded that in the struggle for justice, the good people have the best poems and the best songs. A right-wing Scottish poet, Roy Campbell, who lived in Spain in the early 1930s, wrote a poem celebrating Franco's military prowess. He titled it "Flowering Rifle: A Poem From the Battlefield of Spain." Actually, Campbell had fled "the battlefield of Spain" when the fighting started, though he later claimed to have been a combatant. He wrote the poem in 1939, while living comfortably in Mussolini's Italy, where he was celebrated by Roman high society. It was also a bad poem.

The Scottish national poet Hugh MacDiarmid, whom I was later to meet one bibulous evening in a London pub, wrote a poem in response. The Campbell clan was notorious in history for participation in a massacre of Scottish nationalists. The surname Campbell is from the Gaelic words meaning "crooked mouth." MacDiarmid wove these themes into a poem of his own:

Franco has made no more horrible shambles
Than this poem of Campbell's
The foulest outrage his breed has to show
Since the massacre of Glencoe

And then:

Campbell they call him—"crooked mouth" that is—
But even Clan Campbell's records show no previous case
Of such extreme distortion, of a mouth like this
Slewed round from a man's bottom to his face

MacDiarmid was a pen name; his given name was Christopher Murray Grieve. I later came to appreciate his work and his insights. Christopher Brookmyre wrote that "the poet Hugh MacDiarmid once said that England destroyed nations not by conquest but by pretending they didn't exist." I took that as describing the penchant of English colonists to impose English social forms on colonized structures.

HISTORIAN?

By my junior year, I'd found that the University political science department was dominated by professors who loved to count things, to the detriment of political and social theory. I arranged to get four political science credits for a thesis project under the direction of history professor Richard Drinnon. Drinnon and I discussed the story of J. Robert Oppenheimer, the brilliant Berkeley physicist who had led the scientific team at Los Alamos in the wartime years. Oppenheimer is still known as the "Father of the Atom Bomb."

In the 1950s, Oppenheimer was subjected to a loyalty hearing by the Atomic Energy Commission, which revoked his security clearance. The hearing was largely a charade, a study in systematic character assassination of a principled and dedicated scientist. It was nominally directed at Oppenheimer, but served as a warning to the community of atomic scientists who had begun vigorously to protest nuclear armament. I read the 1,000-page hearing transcript. I studied the decision to drop the atomic bombs on Hiroshima and Nagasaki. During this study, I encountered a book by P. M. S. Blackett, *The Military and Political Consequences of Atomic Energy*, which persuasively argued that we had dropped the bombs on Japan unnecessarily. The Japanese had been ready to surrender,

Blackett concluded, and dropping the bombs was designed to keep the Soviets out of the postwar peace process in the Asian theater.

I studied the evidence that the atomic scientists at Los Alamos were told that the atomic bomb needed to be ready for possible use against the Nazis, even though by 1943 the German ability to make a nuclear weapon had been neutralized by destruction of the German heavy-water facilities.

Looking over the historical record, my research paper concluded that the military knew that Oppenheimer was a brilliant scientist and charismatic leader, and therefore overrode loyalty-security concerns and put him in charge of the bomb-building project at Los Alamos. The military supervisor of Los Alamos, General Leslie Groves, made clear after the war that he knew the bomb was being readied for a postwar confrontation with the Soviet Union. Once Oppenheimer had guided the bomb project to conclusion, plans were afoot to cast him aside. The atomic weapons program was then placed under the guidance of Dr. Edward Teller, who supervised development of the hydrogen bomb.

I studied the human consequences of dropping atomic bombs on Hiroshima and Nagasaki. Later, I visited both cities.

I drew a series of political and personal lessons from this study. The military, industrial, and political commanders of power were heedless of human consequences, and willing to incinerate two cities and trigger radioactive harm for decades in order to gain a geopolitical advantage. They did so cynically, and were later willing to destroy individual careers based on rather fanciful charges of disloyalty.

My own experience with the Navy reinforced this view. Oppenheimer was tolerated because he was necessary to a plan of which he was perhaps naive or unaware. As a *Time* magazine reviewer noted in 2005:

> As an effort to prove that he had been a party member, much less one involved in espionage, the inquest was a failure. Its real purpose was larger, however: to punish the most prominent American critic of the U.S. move from atomic weapons to the much more lethal hydrogen bomb. Oppenheimer would never again feel comfortable as a public advocate for a sane nuclear policy.

I was fascinated by the work of Oppenheimer's lawyers in the loyalty-security hearing, John W. Davis and Lloyd Garrison. Both men had records of distinguished government service. Garrison had represented civil rights figures and victims of the loyalty-security apparatus. Davis was a prominent corporate lawyer.

Reading the transcript, it seemed to me that Garrison and Davis, despite their evident concern for their client, were outflanked by their adversaries in terms of trial preparation and tactics. I wondered whether Oppenheimer had reached out to prominent lawyers with accepted political credentials, perhaps to cultivate an image of respectability. I thought of Darrow, who had abandoned doing legal work for the railroads and instead made a career of learning and telling the human stories of those threatened by injustice.

Garrison and Davis were hobbled by the atmosphere of secrecy that surrounded the hearing: The aura of "national security" skewed any rational perception of what Oppenheimer had done or not done, believed or did not believe.

If I were going to be a lawyer, I would seek to understand the mechanisms and mythologies that foster and maintain injustice, and to orient my work to oppose those mechanisms and to assist those who were victimized by them. I would challenge government efforts to conceal relevant evidence behind a shield of secrecy.

I understood that there was a "right to counsel," but that did not require any individual lawyer to represent just anybody. One of Oppenheimer's chosen lawyers, John W. Davis, was at the same time counsel to the Topeka, Kansas, Board of Education. He wrote the brief and argued in the Supreme Court for the maintenance of racially segregated schools. His brief was a farrago of discredited social theory and misstated history; his oral argument reeked of condescension toward people of color.

The hearing transcript contains much evidence that the FBI was shadowing Oppenheimer closely during the Los Alamos years. The Bureau had records of his visits to women other than his wife. It had detailed reports of dinners, parties, and other gatherings attended by alleged members of the Communist Party. The government lawyers paraded all of this evidence in an effort to paint a picture of a person who could not be trusted.

Lurking in this evidence, however, was a picture of Oppenheimer's hubris. During the war, Oppenheimer reported to security personnel that Haakon Chevalier, a professor of French literature who was a University of California colleague, had approached him in 1942 to ask about the development of an atomic bomb. Oppenheimer's version of events left a suggestion that Chevalier was a member of the Community Party and was acting on behalf of the Soviet Union. Oppenheimer's report dogged Chevalier's career for decades. There were others upon whom Oppenheimer cast suspicion as well. In 1959, Chevalier published *The Man Who Would Be God*, a novel whose central character was an atomic scientist who diverts suspicion on his friends in order to maintain his position in the face of loyalty-security inquiries. As I read Chevalier's book, and later as I interviewed him for KPFA, I saw again how this McCarthyite loyalty-security apparatus had fostered the employment of witnesses who for personal gain, temporary safety, or revenge recounted stories—often false—about the political activities of their friends and acquaintances.

My Oppenheimer paper helped me see the malign effects of Cold War ideology on freedom of expression. Here was Clark Kerr's theory of "industrialism" at work. Oppenheimer, one of the "intellectuals" in Kerr's imagined world, had to be "captured," and if not confined would be a source of social danger.

Now I had experience studying sources and putting events into context. I had done "history work." My research paper stayed in my file cabinet for decades, until the University of Texas put it into an archive. I discussed the Oppenheimer case and its lessons with historians and authors. However, I identified most closely with Oppenheimer's lawyers and the journalists who had exposed not only the injustices in his case but also the way the entire apparatus of power imposed itself on society.

My list of professional choices was getting shorter. Was it "enough" to study events and write books or articles—or radio documentaries—about them?

In trying to answer this question, I encountered teachers who were glad to provide insight. I enrolled in the two-semester basic economics course. The thrice-weekly lectures met in a cavernous lecture hall. The course was based on Paul Samuelson's book *Economics: An Introductory Analysis*. Samuelson, whose work spanned seven decades, was the archetypical pseudo-Keynesian economist, later to be adviser to Presidents Kennedy and Johnson. For two or three hours a week, we met in small sections of two dozen or so with a graduate teaching assistant, who would assign other readings, lead discussions, and grade our essay assignments. In my section, the teaching assistant was an older student named Clinton Jencks. Now, where had I heard that name?

Clinton Jencks had been leader of the International Union of Mine, Mill & Smelter Workers local in Silver City, New Mexico. A motion picture of the miners' struggle, *Salt of the Earth*, had achieved notoriety. He had been prosecuted and convicted for falsely denying that he was a member of the Communist Party. An averment on that subject was required of all labor union officers under Section 9 of the Taft-Hartley Act. The Supreme Court, in the 1957 case of *Jencks v. United States*, reversed the conviction, holding that a federal criminal defendant is entitled to receive the prior, and perhaps contradictory, prior statements of prosecution witnesses.

In Clint's case, the lead prosecution witness had been Harvey Matusow, one of the witnesses repeatedly used by the House Committee on Un-American Activities to claim that this or that person was a covert Communist. Matusow revealed in his book *False Witness* that he had been urged by Roy Cohn and Senator Joseph McCarthy to give testimony against Jencks.

Freed from prosecution, Clint was back in school to earn his PhD in economics, and would go on to write his dissertation on the life and work of miners, titled "Men Underground." As a teacher, he was anxious to share with us his insights on the way economic theory interacted with real life.

Clint's circle of friends included people I knew from KPFA and from campus political activity. It also included lawyers who had represented labor union officials who, like Clint, had been targets of government scrutiny. A group of us met with him outside class hours. He recommended that I read Paul Sweezy's book *The Theory of Capitalist Development*. I bought a copy and read it cover to cover. It was an alternative and an antidote to Samuelson. It remains a classic discussion of capitalism's history and laws of motion.

I recalled that in Professor tenBroek's class on freedom of expression, we had read a Supreme Court case, *Sweezy v. New Hampshire*. Sweezy had refused to answer questions about lectures he had given at the state university and about his political affiliations. He based his refusal on the First Amendment, and specifically on academic freedom. I read the case again, and was struck by the New Hampshire Attorney General's direct attack on the content of what a professor was teaching to students. Years later, I wrote the article on "Academic Freedom" for the *Oxford Companion to the Supreme Court*, and once again reflected on how Sweezy's courageous refusal to cooperate with the state Attorney General's investigation had helped to reinforce a basic principle about teaching and learning.

And, of course, we read and studied Clint's court case, careful to note that Cold War ideology was being used to undermine and sideline militant labor leaders who, like Clint, faced a phalanx of employer and governmental antagonists.

I also took a "survey" course in the Political Science Department, taught in lecture format by Peter Odegard. Odegard had worked in the FDR administration, had taught at several colleges and universities, and been president of Reed College in Oregon. He served on the board of directors of the Pacifica Foundation, KPFA's parent entity. He opposed the House Committee on Un-American Activities.

The graduate teaching assistant in Odegard's class was Oscar Pemantle. In class, and outside class, our discussions ranged over economics and recent history, as well as the course content on U.S. political theory. Oscar advised that I read Sweezy's collection of essays, *The Present as History*, to see beyond the structure of present society to the mechanisms by which it had come into being and could in its turn be changed. The book had a profound effect on my thinking. Sweezy opened up a view of history and society, not just a portrait of economic development. I recalled that Sweezy was a friend and colleague of Paul A. Baran, a Stanford economist who often appeared on KPFA. I bought Baran's book *The Political Economy of Growth*.

I admired the academic work of Clint Jencks, Peter Odegard, Oscar Pemantle, and Richard Drinnon, as well as that of Baran and Sweezy. I wondered whether I was patient enough to do that kind of work. Writing about history requires the discipline of careful research; the resulting publication and teaching may not have an immediate effect on events.

LAWYER?

During this time, the atmosphere of inquiry and controversy at KPFA was inspiring. I was learning to write, speak, interview, and put information together in a more or less organized way. I was listening to scholars, teachers, and activists. The Congo and Spain documentaries seemed a more immediate kind of work than historical writing.

Also, I had the opportunity to observe and report on events as they occurred, in what was later called "real time." An example: On April 17, 1961, a military force of Cuban emigrés, supported by U.S. air and naval forces, invaded Cuba at the Bay of Pigs. The emigré military force had been trained by the CIA in the United States and Guatemala. The invasion was conducted so as to make it appear that it was an uprising against the Cuban government by internal forces. Despite U.S. military support, Cuban forces defeated the invasion within a few days. U.S. ambassador to the United Nations Adlai Stevenson denied that the United States was involved in the invasion. President Kennedy falsely said, "I have emphasized before that this was a struggle of Cuban patriots against a Cuban dictator. While we could not be expected to hide our sympathies, we made it repeatedly clear that the armed forces of this country would not intervene in any way."

At KPFA, we reported the story as the successive falsehoods came unraveled. We featured a magnificent oral report by Jim Higgins, editor of the *York* (Pennsylvania) *Gazette and Daily*, who had been invited to a confidential State Department briefing on the invasion.

KPFA's free speech policy attracted opposition from those who thought that Communists or suspected Communists should not be given air time, and from those who thought that Allen Ginsberg's poetic vocabulary was obscene. In addition, KPFA was broadcasting news of loyalty-security issues and political demonstrations. Lawyers working on such matters were regular visitors to the station. In addition, Slate and other groups welcomed civil rights and civil liberties lawyers as speakers at campus events. I admired these lawyers; they seemed content with their life choices.

I met Al Bendich, an ACLU lawyer who also taught an undergraduate course in the Speech Department. Al was a good friend of Professor tenBroek, and willingly shared his ideas about civil liberties, politics, and economics. He was, indeed, voluble on topics about which he cared. At his memorial service in 2015, somebody remarked, "There was a time when I didn't speak to Al for three months, but that was because I didn't want to interrupt him."

Al had defended San Francisco poet Lawrence Ferlinghetti on obscenity charges in 1957. The charges were based on Ferlinghetti's bookstore, City Lights, having a book of Allen Ginsberg's poetry for sale on its shelves. Al also gained an acquittal for the comedian Lenny Bruce, who was charged with obscenity for having said "cocksucker" during a nightclub performance in San Francisco. The Supreme Court later held that the California statute under which Lenny was prosecuted was unconstitutional, in a case involving a young man who wore a jacket that said "Fuck the Draft." Bruce kept up a running, drug-induced patter throughout the trial. When asked whether he had said to the arresting officer, "Eat it! Eat it!" he replied, "No, I said 'Kiss it! Kiss it!'" Bendich asked, "Do you apprehend a difference?" Bruce said, "Oh yeah, man. There is a big difference between kissing your mother good-bye and eating your mother good-bye."

Years later, Al became general counsel to Fantasy Records, Fantasy Films, and Saul Zaentz Production Company, which produced the first Creedence Clearwater Revival records, and the motion pictures *Amadeus* and *One Flew Over the Cuckoo's Nest*. In the 1970s, I represented those companies and Al himself, in litigation over literary rights and tax planning,

Then, on June 5, 1961, the Supreme Court decided *Communist Party v. Subversive Activities Control Board*, by a vote of 5-4. The Court upheld a Board order requiring the Communist Party to register as a "Communist action organization," and to disclose—among other items—the names and addresses of its officers and members, the location and nature of its printing presses. The purported legislative premise of the relevant statute, the Subversive Activities Control Act, stated:

> There exists a world Communist movement which, in its origins, its development, and its present practice, is a worldwide revolutionary movement whose purpose it is, by treachery, deceit, infiltration into other

groups (governmental and otherwise), espionage, sabotage, terrorism, and any other means deemed necessary, to establish a Communist totalitarian dictatorship in the countries throughout the world through the medium of a world-wide Communist organization.

Congress had passed the Act in 1950, as the "Red Scare," McCarthyism, and the loyalty-security purges were getting underway. The Court's opinion, for five Justices, was written by Felix Frankfurter, joined by Clark, Harlan, Whittaker, and Stewart. Chief Justice Warren, and Justices Douglas, Black, and Brennan wrote separate dissents.

The case had previously been before the Court in 1956. In that decision, the Board had admitted that the record of administrative proceedings about the Party and its activities was rife with perjured testimony presented by the stable of professional witnesses who were also making the circuits of congressional committees and other public forums, as well as giving their false testimony to courts and agencies. The Supreme Court sent the case back for further hearings.

With the record (somewhat) cleansed, the case came back. The 1961 decision reflects, perhaps more than any other, how Cold War mythology and ideology overwhelmed rational and evidence-based analysis. Justice Frankfurter had written a concurring opinion in *Sweezy v. New Hampshire*, trumpeting freedom of inquiry, even when the state claimed to be protecting young people from dangerous ideas. While a professor at Harvard Law School, Frankfurter had inveighed against the unjust convictions of Sacco and Vanzetti, victims of the Red Scare that followed the First World War. In this opinion he seemed to have abandoned all the tools of discernment that had served him so well.

On that same June day, the Court also upheld, 5 to 4, the conviction under the Smith Act of Junius Scales for the crime of simply being a member of the Communist Party.

In earlier decisions, the Court had overturned statutes and ordinances in southern states that had required civil rights organizations to disclose the names of their members. It had invalidated a California law that required those handing out leaflets to put their name and address on each leaflet. These decisions had recognized and enforced a vision of free speech and association, recognizing that those publicly identified as embracing unpopular views would face public obloquy and worse.

On KPFA News, we reported on these decisions, and reached out to lawyers who could help us and our audience understand them. Al Bendich helped me see the cases in their historical context, and indeed was the first person I spoke to who pointed to the Court majority's different approaches to cases involving "Red" and "Black." In the civil rights cases from the South the Court had refused to honor the states' mythological assertion that demands for racial integration were dire threats to the social order. Yet the five-Justice majority in the Communist Party cases bought into the government's characterization of the Party and its adherents.

I was getting the idea that if different groups of judges and Justices could present shifting judicial analyses of fundamental questions, then there might be open spaces, or contradictions, within which principled lawyers could affect outcomes. Justice Frankfurter's opinion for five Justices was based on the idea of First Amendment "balancing." That is, he began by accepting the Cold War narrative about a huge social danger supposedly presented by a relatively few individuals and organizations. One should, the theory went, balance this huge danger against the free speech and association rights of the individuals and groups. By this mental process of inventing "weights" and a scale in which to "weigh" them, the First Amendment would almost always be the loser.

The dissenting opinions presented quite different ways of seeing the process of constitutional interpretation. The hope that these views might once again prevail was validated in later years, as the power of the Cold War mythology receded. Some examples: Justice Charles Evans Whittaker, who was part of the five-Justice majority, resigned from the Court in 1962; he had been, as one legal scholar opined, an "extremely weak, vacillating Justice" who was "courted by the two cliques on the Court because his vote was generally up in the air and typically went to the group that made the last, but not necessarily the best, argument."

In the years to follow, the invocation of "Communist" did not have decisive effect. In 1964, the Court held that membership in the Communist Party did not deprive someone of the right to hold a passport and to travel. In 1965, the Court struck down a provision of the 1959 Labor-Management Reporting and Disclosure Act that made it a crime for a member of the Communist Party to hold union office. The Court held, 5 to 4 in an opinion by Chief Justice Earl Warren, that the provision was a bill of attainder that punished based on status rather than on socially harmful conduct.

Then, in 1966, the Court reversed the conviction of Eugene Frank Robel, a shipyard worker from Seattle. Robel had refused to register as a member of the Communist Party, as was required by the Subversive Activities Control Board order upheld in June 1961. He was indicted for continuing to work at the shipyard without having registered. The Court, 7 to 2, invalidated the conviction on First Amendment grounds and in its opinion revived and relied upon the free association cases it had ignored in the 1961 decision.

Of course, in June 1961 I could not and did not foresee the ways in which the Supreme Court might revive the principles of free expression and association it had overridden. I did know that the Court had at times jettisoned this or that reactionary decision in the light of later argument and understanding. If I were to become a lawyer, I could perhaps be part of that change.

PERSONAL AND POLITICAL DECISIONS

As I struggled with the questions of who I wanted to be, I turned more to other students who were working on the same set of personal and political issues. Many young people my age were confronting opposition from family and friends about the choices they were making, just as I was. Our ideas and attitudes were not as widely shared as we hoped or, sometimes, thought. In the spring of 1961, I was the Slate candidate for student body president. Graduate students could not vote in the student body election. I campaigned in dormitories, fraternity and sorority houses, and in campus rallies. I lost the election, but made a respectable showing.

As I observed my mentors —lawyers, broadcasters, teachers—I looked for clues about how they lived their lives and faced challenges. My own fractured family did not give me examples I wanted to follow. Ken Cloke introduced me to Pam Jones, a freshman from Santa Monica who had begun to attend Slate meetings. Pam and I got married in September 1961. Pam's father was a UCLA English professor, her mother a physical therapist. They had been involved in progressive politics for decades, and shared their ideas with Pam and me.

SENIOR YEAR: 1961-62

No matter which path I chose, I would need to study the craft of written expression. The investigative journalists whose work informs and motivates, and then survives as something like history, are careful, skillful writers. They are not writing "history"—they are recording what they see, and the memories of what those they interview have observed. What they write is destined to be read by people who may be close enough—in time, if not also in circumstances—to do something about what is being reported.

In UC's Journalism Department was a course, "The Literature of the Press," taught by Professor Pete Steffens. Students would read the words of journalists, from Daniel Defoe, in the 1600s and 1700s, through the chroniclers of the American Revolution, to the work of John Hersey, whose book-length reportage *Hiroshima* remains a classic.

Pete Steffens was the son of Lincoln Steffens, a journalist renowned for reporting on economic injustice, labor strife, and political corruption. Pete, before turning to teaching, had worked as a journalist in the United States, Europe, and the Middle East. He had grown up in his father's circle of friends, which included in those days Clarence Darrow. The Steffens household was a kind of literary salon in Carmel-by-the-Sea, California.

Years later, I learned that Pete had been a classmate of Gore Vidal at Exeter Academy, where—as Vidal wrote to me—Pete's mother, Ella Winter, was regarded with amazement and awe when she visited the school. Ms. Winter, also a journalist, worked alongside Lincoln Steffens for decades beginning in the 1920s.

The class seemed designed to follow avenues of thought on which I was already embarked. Steffens saw journalists in the same way that Percy Shelley had, as "companions and forerunners of ... change in our social condition." We examined style and modes of expression, techniques of drawing stories from witnesses, and different visions of events and social theories. It was not rhetorical flourish nor overt advocacy that made this journalism powerful and enduring, but rather the quiet force of observed, recollected, and reported facts.

Pete and I had mutual friends, through KPFA and political activity. He introduced me to people he had known since boyhood, including long-shoremen's union leader Harry Bridges. I remember that dinner with Harry Bridges and his wife, Noriko Sawada. Bridges was part of, and had led, the militant San Francisco labor movement, and was a friend and supporter of Clinton Jencks. He had been prosecuted by the federal government in an effort to denaturalize him and deport him back to Australia, where he was born. I remember Pete Seeger's song:

> *Oh, the FBI is worried, the bosses they are scared,*
> *They can't deport six million men, they know.*
> *And we're not going to let them send Harry over the sea,*
> *We'll fight for Harry Bridges and build the C. I. O.*
> *For they can't deport six million men they know.*

I learned that evening that when Harry and Noriko went to Reno to get married in 1958, the county clerk refused to issue them a marriage license due to Nevada's law forbidding marriage between a white person and anyone of Asian or "black" or "red" race. A federal judge performed the ceremony and Nevada soon repealed its statute.

Pete shared stories of his and his father's journalistic lives. An example, which I also used in *Mythologies of State and Monopoly Power*:

During the 1930s, in California, farm labor organizers in California were prosecuted for criminal syndicalism. The Hearst newspapers supplied local district attorneys with an "expert" witness who would testify that the defendants' doctrine was based on Soviet-style Communism. Lincoln Steffens reported on the cross-examination of one such witness:

Q: You are familiar with the teachings of Karl Marx?

A: Yes.

Q: Can you define "dialectical materialism"?

A: Well, you have to take it one word at a time. "Dialect"—that's the way that foreigners talk. And "materialism," that means going after money. So "dialectical materialism" is a bunch of foreigners who are trying to take our money.

Another example: Pete was reporting from Geneva in 1954. In May 1954, the French garrison at Dien Bien Phu in Vietnam was overrun by Viet Minh forces in the decisive battle of the Vietnamese independence struggle. The news came through to the United Nations Palais des Nations on the wire service. Pete sought out the Chinese envoy, and said: "Dien Bien Phu has been captured!" The envoy looked at Pete in puzzlement, then smiled and said, "Oh! You mean 'liberated.'"

My other choice in the Journalism Department was the course "Magazine Writing," taught by Allen Temko. Temko was architecture critic for the *San Francisco Chronicle*, with a particular focus on urban architecture. He had written a book on the work of Eero Saarinen and another on the Notre Dame Cathedral. I had heard him speak on campus, and admired his gift for aphorism. He referred to UC's Dwinelle Hall, a newly constructed featureless classroom and office building, as "a symbol of man's eternal search for a lavatory." He described San Francisco's Embarcadero Freeway, which obscured views of San Francisco Bay, as something "deposited by a concrete dog with square intestines."

Then, as now, I believed that writing and speaking memorably as well as accurately was a skill worth learning. Sometimes I must be careful about this: I am tempted to let my flights of language overshadow the content of my message.

Temko was an inspiring teacher and a superb editor. We wrote short pieces on assigned subjects, and then a longer research-based article. I wrote about how Harry Bridges's International Longshore and Warehouse Union had confronted the issue of automation on the docks, seeking to preserve union jobs while accepting the inevitability of mechanization. I used what I knew about this militant union and the insights gathered from the economics learning to which Clint Jencks had led me.

Harry Bridges and the other ILWU leaders knew that under the relatively weak labor laws employers had substantial discretion to mechanize the port operations and eliminate longshore work. The ILWU therefore decided to enter a fairly long-term contract that would allow for mechanization and preserve as many jobs as possible. I saw this process through the lens that Clinton Jencks, and the works of Paul Sweezy, had given me.

I was seeing, without wholly understanding, the beginnings of globalization. Sea transport would be mechanized. Goods would be packed into containers. The loading and unloading of containers would become more and more mechanized, meaning jobs for fewer and fewer longshore workers. But anything that could be carried in a container now traveled on the sea economically. For example, it was not necessary to unload TV sets, or stoves, or automobile transmissions, from a cargo ship hold one by one. Thus, manufacturers could "outsource" manufacture to low-wage countries, where labor rights were not well enforced, if they existed at all.

I got an A in the course. Years later, the understanding I had gained helped in representing workers and labor organizations, on the docks and in industries affected by globalization. I did not find an answer to my question about career path. Would I rather report on labor struggles with automation and job loss, or would I rather have been a lawyer representing Harry Bridges and like-minded labor leaders?

That academic year, to support our married life, I added to what I earned at KPFA by typing up my class notes at night and selling them through a "note service" across the street from the UC campus. On some weekends, I worked at KABL-FM, a classical music station in San Francisco, selecting and announcing music selections. The station was owned by a purveyor of high-fidelity home sound systems, and was operated as a showcase for FM stations and their technological ability to broadcast sound through a wide range of the musical spectrum. My sonorous "radio voice" was useful. Pam free-lanced typing and editing papers.

TO FINLAND AND TO THE RADIO STATION

My friend Mike Myerson asked me to serve on a committee to organize participation by U.S. students and youth in the 8th World Festival of Youth and Students, to be held in Helsinki in the summer of 1962. I agreed, but set conditions. The Youth Festivals had been held every few years since 1947. Most of them had been held in socialist countries, and doubtless the Communist parties of the host countries had played a role in organizing them. At the 7th Festival in Vienna, there was controversy because some participants had been prevented from speaking about the Soviet incursion into Hungary and related issues. I insisted that the American group be called a "contingent" rather than a "delegation," to make clear that by attending one did not profess adherence to any ideological position. More important, the festival organizers would have to guarantee freedom of expression by all participants and set up "free speech areas," where anyone could get up and make a public address on any topic, without interference. I thought that a gathering of young people at this time in history was a good idea. "This time in history" encompassed, just to mention a few examples, the Cuban Revolution, Algeria's liberation from French colonialism, and the movements for change in Eastern Europe.

As we prepared to go to Finland, it occurred to me that I might inveigle KPFA into helping me learn more about being a journalist. I spoke with KPFA public affairs director Elsa Knight Thompson and proposed that I be assigned for six months to a year as European correspondent for KPFA and its sister Pacifica Foundation stations, KPFK and WBAI. Elsa agreed. Pacifica would pay me $300 per month and some modest expenses for travel. I would produce programs on public affairs.

I would be based in London. Elsa called on her BBC acquaintances from her time as a broadcaster in London, and on her friends Konni Zilliacus, a Labour Member of Parliament, and the historian Basil Davidson. She wrote to her former BBC colleagues. I had never been outside the United States except for a Boy Scout trip to Canada and a couple of fishing trips with my uncle Marvin in Baja California.

When classes were over, and I had my bachelor's degree, Pam and I went to London. I called Zilliacus. He had been in the Secretariat of the League of Nations between the world wars and spoke eight or ten languages. He worked with representatives of European League members, and attempted to alert the UK and other powers to the dangers of Hitler's designs for Europe. In 1945, he was elected to Parliament, having written on the foreign and military policy issues that the postwar government would face. His book, *Can the Tories Win the Peace? And How They Lost the Last One*, was influential in the 1945 parliamentary campaigns. In that period, he worked to prevent the hardening of Cold War divisions in Europe. For these efforts he was attacked as pro-Soviet in the West, while in Eastern Europe—particularly Czechoslovakia—he was branded an agent of Western espionage. Zilliacus had supported Tito's break with the USSR and had written about Khrushchev's accession to power. He was an early supporter of the movement for disarmament.

Zilliacus was also one of the most eloquent speakers in the House of Commons. Arraigning a Tory government bent on continued adherence to imperial ideas and to the arms race, he proclaimed: "The government is made up of impenitent Municheers and foiled Suez aggressors. Lord Home [the Foreign Secretary] has the melancholy distinction of being both."

Zilly, as he liked to be called, helped us find an apartment near where he lived in Maida Vale, for a weekly rental of £8. He promised to introduce me to diplomats, Members of Parliament, and other public figures, whom I could interview and on whose knowledge I could base my reporting. He also put us in touch with an obstetrician, as Pam was pregnant.

I went to introduce myself to the BBC, at the broadcasting studio in Maida Vale, rather than the imposing headquarters on Portland Place. I met Jack Aistrop, who had met Elsa Thompson. Dressed in a pinstripe suit, he was polite, helpful, and a bit formal. Also in his office was a tall slender man in khaki pants and white shirt, but without jacket or tie; he was introduced as Bill Ash. He seemed to have a southern U.S. accent.

The BBC would lend me recording equipment with which to do interviews and record events. It would provide me with audiotape to use, and would help set up the process of sending recorded tapes back to the United States. The meeting over, I went out for coffee with Bill Ash. Over time, I learned his story. He was born in Texas. He was twenty-two years old in 1939, when England declared war on Germany. Bill joined the Royal Canadian Air Force, so that he could get into the fight against Hitler. He was one of 9,000 young Americans who followed the same path; 2,000 of these were Texans, to the point where the RCAF was dubbed the Royal Canadian Texas Air Force. He trained as a fighter pilot, and began to fly combat missions. On March 24, 1942, his Spitfire aircraft was shot down over France.

He survived the crash and was taken prisoner by German forces. From that date, until he was liberated from a German prison camp in April 1945, Bill repeatedly escaped from German custody, only to be recaptured. He led several escape attempts. At least twice, he was sentenced to death as a spy; on one of those occasions, he was spared because the Luftwaffe claimed the right to hold him prisoner and got him out of the Gestapo's hands. His personal valor earned him an MBE, Member of the Order of the British Empire. In the 1963 film *The Great Escape*, Steve McQueen portrayed a character based on Bill.

This account of his life came out bit by bit, from Bill and from his friends. After the war, he became a British citizen and took a degree at Oxford's Balliol College. As a BBC broadcaster, he worked in India. While there, he met Ranjana Sidhanta; they were married in 1955. In 2005, Bill at last published his memoir, *Under the Wire*. It was, and deserves to be, a best-seller. He wrote books of politics and Marxist philosophy, and several novels.

Bill's day job was with the BBC. His passions were political action and political philosophy. Ranjana Ash had a PhD from the University of Iowa, earned as a scholarship student in 1947; she was a writer of fiction and non-fiction works.

Bill had learned a little about my political past, and knew about student radicalism at Berkeley. Over coffee, he said that he was working with community groups to oppose racism. I knew of the racial tension that had led to violence in some London neighborhoods and of the anti-immigrant sentiment openly expressed by some political figures. I later produced a news program on proposals in Parliament to ban racial incitement.

In 1962, some of the racist groups formed the National Socialist Movement, which openly embraced Hitler's legacy—or at least that part of it that did not include losing the war and seeing the Nazi leaders jailed and hanged. Colin Jordan was leader of the NSM, which planned to hold a rally in Trafalgar Square on July 2, 1962. In London, the World War II devastation had not been entirely repaired. Memories of the war were still alive.

Bill told me that he and young people with whom he was working had been attacking NSM meetings in London. What did he mean by "attacking"? Bill said that he led teams of young men with bicycle chains and other non-lethal weapons. He regarded this work as continuing his battle against Nazism.

So, he asked, would I like to attend the Trafalgar Square rally? I agreed. That day, the Nelson Monument in the Square was bedecked with Nazi flags. Colin Jordan spoke from the Monument plinth, flanked by young men in Nazi uniforms. When Jordan embarked on some of his more odious anti-Semitic stuff, members of the crowd, some of them led by Bill, rushed forward. I joined in and wrestled one of the storm troopers off the plinth. A British Bobby, in traditional uniform with the tall round hat, pulled me off and said sternly, "All right, young man. That's it. You're under arrest. Now you wait right here, and I shall return for you presently." I was impressed by his courtesy. I moved to another part of the square. The Nazi speech was being drowned out by the crowed singing, "We'll hang Colin Jordan from a sour apple tree." The police suggested that Jordan should get to a place of safety. Protected by a phalanx of supporters, and pursued by a large group that included Bill's acolytes, Jordan ran down into the Charing Cross Underground station and locked himself in a pay toilet. I took the opportunity to leave Trafalgar Square and catch the Bakerloo Line train home to Maida Vale. I suppose I am still a fugitive from British law, but nobody has made an issue of it.

After that introduction to London, Pam and I went to Helsinki for the Youth Festival, which was held from July 27 to August 8. On the whole, the Festival justified my optimism. Young people from Algeria brought stories of the struggle for Algerian independence. Young Cubans discussed their revolution, the U.S. invasion, and U.S. foreign policy. We discussed the Khrushchev-era reforms in the USSR with Soviet young people. The poet Yevgeny Yevtushenko was there; he spent hours with the U.S. group, discussing politics, poetry, and recent events. Yes, there were demonstrations against the Festival by anti-Soviet Finnish political groups, but the meeting itself supported the idea that a new generation might be able to change the world. The free speech areas were open and respected.

I went back to London to get to work. The flat we had rented in Maida Vale was sparsely furnished. We argued with the landlord to get the promised refrigerator installed; we arranged for phone service.

Pam was pregnant. Our doctor told us that hospital rooms were scarce in London, and that when Pam went into labor, we would only then learn where our child would be born. Or, the doctor said, the baby could be born at home. We were taking Lamaze Method natural childbirth classes. Pam was healthy; we decided that a home birth would be okay.

At 2 p.m. on October 8, 1962, I was at the BBC studio on Portland Place, doing a three-minute talk titled "The Americans Have a Word For It," about American English and English English. I was to receive five guineas for this witty contribution. I took the Tube home. A bicycle from the Sutherland Avenue Nurses was leaning against the rail outside the outer door of our flat.

Two nurse-midwives were in our bedroom, hanging up sterile sheets and preparing for the delivery. Jon Steven Tigar appeared shortly before midnight.

The next morning, a stout middle-aged woman appeared at our door and announced that she was the person assigned by the National Health Service to help us cope with a new baby by cooking and cleaning and showing us how to boil the diapers.

London, for a twenty-one-year-old with curiosity and concern about the world, seemed to be at the center of events, or at least a logical place from which to observe, learn, and report. I began to do radio programs. I discovered that if I telephoned or wrote to a person of prominence announcing that I was a European correspondent—never merely a "reporter"—for a chain of nonprofit American radio stations, never mind that there were only three links in the chain, I could expect agreement for me to come and do an interview.

LORD RUSSELL, CUBA, AND THE REMNANTS OF EMPIRE

A few days after Jon was born, I got a letter from Lord Bertrand Russell, replying to my request for an interview. Yes, he would give an interview, on October 23, at his home in Penrhyndeudraeth, Wales. Lord Russell, born in 1872, was a philosopher, mathematician, social critic. He had been at the center of controversy for decades. Being able to interview him was an exciting prospect. Bill Ash tried to introduce me to the main themes of Russell's philosophy, and I read accounts of his life.

Penrhyndeudraeth is 239 miles from London, six hours by train. I booked a room at a pub hotel for the evening of October 22. That night, the television in the pub carried a transatlantic broadcast from the United States, a speech by President John F. Kennedy. The United States, based on information from a spy plane, had confirmed that the Soviet Union had installed missiles and warplanes in Cuba. Cuba had requested the missiles in the aftermath of the Bay of Pigs. Kennedy announced a blockade of Cuba, a trade embargo, and a policy decision that any attack from Cuba would be considered an attack by the USSR.

I now had something topical about which to interview Lord Russell. I can still remember the old taxi pulling up in front of his stone castle. The train trip through Wales had wound among hills still green in that early fall. Sheep, the animals best adapted to the terrain, grazed. Is such an image, I wondered, a basis for the Bach Cantata 208, "Sheep May Safely Graze"?

Lord Russell was ninety years old, frail but alert. He had seen the television reports and listened to the radio. My thoughts of an interview that ranged over his philosophical thoughts went out the window. Looking back, I wish I had been more prepared for the intellectual depth and fire that I was to meet. As it was, the interview was one of my most exciting mornings. Our talk turned to the Cuban missile crisis.

"I cannot tell you," Lord Russell said in that precise acerbic tone, "how wicked I think it." He had been a prominent figure in the Campaign for Nuclear Disarmament, and had committed civil disobedience at one of its marches. Some dismissed him as a senile crank, well past any ability to think things through. Some said his private secretary, Ralph Schoenman, dominated his activities. That day, his words and actions laid all that to rest. Whether it was putting forward his views on nuclear arms or recalling his philosophical disputes of decades before, his vision and diction were clear.

The Cuban Missile Crisis, as it became known, came to a sort of resolution a month later, as the USSR withdrew the missiles from Cuba. The United States and USSR established a telephone "hot line" in an effort to ensure that nuclear war did not begin due to some misunderstanding.

I returned to London with the tape recording, and followed the ongoing dispute. The Soviets pulled back their missile-carrying ships. The risk of nuclear war seemed to recede. The conflict had, however, raised serious questions about the Western military alliance. As I continued to do interviews and to report on those issues, I formed opinions on the laws of nations that have influenced my teaching, writing, and lawyering ever since.

Throughout the fall of 1962, the French and English governments continued to discuss the missile crisis and its meaning. Harold Macmillan was prime minister, with a Conservative parliamentary majority. Hugh Gaitskell led the Labour opposition until his death in early 1963, to be succeeded by Harold Wilson. Charles de Gaulle was president of France. Macmillan was being challenged over the issue of Britain's relationship with Europe, and whether the United Kingdom should enter the Common Market.

Debates in England and France revolved around the evident fact that American military power was the principal strength of the NATO alliance and that the Americans were likely to use that power when and where they thought best. If the European members of the alliance disagreed, that was too bad. This perceived American arrogance led to different responses in England and France.

President de Gaulle insisted that France have an independent voice in nuclear decision-making, and had built a uniquely French nuclear capability, which he dubbed the "strike force," or *force de frappe*. French nuclear testing went on heedless of international agreements and at one point the French secret service destroyed a protest vessel in the South Pacific. President de Gaulle was outraged that the United States had turned a local battle with a small island nation into a potential nuclear war.

The English response was more complex. England had decided in the 1950s to develop nuclear arms. Foreign Minister Bevin's rationale was that one should not be "naked at the conference table." In the ensuing years, Britain's colonial power had eroded, and its nuclear force was inexorably tied to the Americans. The Macmillan government revealed that it had mobilized Britain's nuclear armed bombers during the missile crisis. Macmillan defended this action as an exercise of British power and sovereignty. Foreign Secretary Konni Zilliacus and other Labour MPs derided such pretensions: Zilliacus's point was that Britain had not acted independently, nor had it any realistic capacity to do so. It had used NATO nuclear might in the service of a non-NATO cause.

The Chinese Communist Party issued a statement condemning the USSR installation of missiles as "adventurism," and the decision to remove them as "capitulationism." Bill Ash supported the Chinese view. I read and reported on the statements of position of the Soviet and Chinese Communist Parties.

In deconstructing the crisis events, I had the context of having watched the Cuban Revolution as a student reporter and activist, and having watched the official lies about the Bay of Pigs invasion unravel.

I thought that any decision by any nation-state to increase the risk of nuclear war was foolish and dangerous. The way out of the Cold War confrontation had to be nuclear disarmament. Britain's Campaign for Nuclear Disarmament (CND), and comparable organizations in the United States and elsewhere, had made that point clear and millions had marched under their banners.

That said, there was—and still is—the issue of Cuban sovereignty. The major powers should not behave in the nineteenth-century fashion and dictate military policy—or economic, political, and foreign policy—to smaller states. If the United States and USSR are opposed to nuclear proliferation, they can set an example by dismantling their own stockpiles.

Taking a somewhat larger perspective, the introduction of nuclear weapons into Cuba presented an issue of collective security. The United States did not take the matter to the United Nations, where if a Soviet veto had prevented Security Council action, the General Assembly could become engaged. Looking at the eventual outcome—which was a Soviet-U.S. accord reached over the heads of the Cubans, and of every other nation—one has reason to believe that the Security Council would have been a useful forum.

Regardless of one's view of those prospects, the crisis pointed up the United States' undermining of the United Nation's intended collective security role. Because the United States refused to recognize the Chinese government, and insisted that Taiwan was China and therefore held the Chinese seat on the Security Council, that body's authority was weakened. Moreover, by 1962 the United States was taking over the French military role in Indochina, in violation of the UN Charter and other precepts of international law.

BOMBS IN PARIS

Algeria had become independent of France on March 18, 1962. Most French and Spanish colonial residents of Algeria, sometimes referred to as Pieds-Noirs, opposed independence; many of them abruptly left Algeria. Some of these exiles, who had decamped to Franco's Spain, formed a paramilitary armed force, the Secret Army Organization, Organisation Armée Secrète. In early July, Algerian troops sought to enter the city of Oran. They were fired upon by armed Pieds-Noirs. This confrontation triggered armed combat that resulted in dozens of civilian deaths.

Vowing revenge for the liberation of Algeria, and for the "Oran massacre," OAS armed cells began a series of bombings and assassinations in France. They tried to assassinate President de Gaulle, whom they viewed as responsible for freeing Algeria. The conflict in France was newsworthy. Zilliacus put me in touch with French political figures, and I took a tape recorder to Paris.

I arrived for my scheduled morning interview at the Paris apartment of Claude Bourdet, a leader of the Parti Socialiste Unifié, a socialist party founded as a left alternative to the "regular" Socialist Party. The apartment door had been blown out by a bomb that had exploded the night before. We did the interview in the rubble-strewn sitting room. I went on to interview a French Communist Party official. His office had been bombed, and we sat in the ruins to talk.

Although I had taken French as an undergraduate, and used medieval and modern French sources in my law review comment, I was not as articulate as I wished—or imagined. Through the political activity in which I was involved, I met a law student who was fluent in French, Stephen Sedley. He helped translate the Paris interviews and we became friends. I lost track of him until 2007. I was working with a team of lawyers from the UK and Mauritius, and a team of law students, on the right of the Chagossian people to return to the homeland from which they had been unlawfully expelled. There was a favorable decision from the UK court of appeals, with the principal opinion by Lord Justice Sedley. Yes, it was Stephen; we have become reacquainted and shared ideas about the role of law, lawyers, and judges.

COMMON MARKET, UNITED KINGDOM, AND THE THIRD WORLD

In the fall and winter of 1962–63, there was debate in Britain over what was then called the European Economic Community. The EEC was formed by the 1957 Treaty of Rome; its original members were West Germany, France, Italy, the Netherlands, Luxembourg. and Belgium. It was a step toward uniting the economies of Western European countries. The British left opposed Britain joining the EEC—they argued that it perpetuated the economic dependence of member states' colonies and former colonies, threatened individual member state labor rights protections, and might well limit social welfare spending by member states.

I interviewed the economist Joan Robinson, who discussed her theory that the UK could and should develop an economic policy that would benefit its former colonies and contribute to its own economic and technological development. Such an economic policy would make entering the EEC unwise and unnecessary, she argued.

I covered the 1962 Labour Party Conference in Brighton. The EEC was a major agenda item, and party leader Hugh Gaitskell made an eloquent and impassioned speech opposing Britain's entry. His theme was not the ethnocentric one that decades later dominated the Brexit debate. It was a left perspective that resisted an alliance that, he argued, would impede Britain's progress toward progressive social change.

Development economist Anila Graham, who was born in India and served as adviser to UN development agencies and to private industry, suggested I go to Geneva and report on the United Nations Conference on Trade and Development. In the UN building, Ms. Graham introduced me to economists and officials from developing countries. They provided information and insight about the ways that the post-colonial economic policies of First World countries continued to distort the economies of the former colonies. Meeting Robinson and Graham was somewhat like a graduate seminar in the political and economic theory that I had begun to study at Berkeley. I gained a deeper appreciation for Paul Baran's work on the Third World's economic dependency.

I agreed with Zilliacus and with Joan Robinson that the EEC was in the main an effort to preserve and expand the power of wealthier nations, while taking advantage of a lower-paid labor pool in the rest of Europe and the former colonies. However, its leaders phrased their ambitions in the rhetoric of bourgeois democracy.

The Council of Europe, which took shape after World War II, was, however, distinct from the EEC economic alliance, although there was an overlap of leadership and ideology. Under the Council's leadership, the European Convention on Human Rights was drafted and took effect in 1953. The Convention, and the European Court of Human Rights in Strasbourg, have been remarkably effective in policing human rights abuses in the signatory states. I did a radio program for Pacifica on the Convention and its potential future.

MUSIC AND POLITICS

The London winter of 1962–63 experienced record cold. We struggled with inadequate heat in our flat, worried that sealing up the windows against draft would create a danger from unsafe heating appliances. In the open-air market just off the Edgware Road, the only fresh vegetables were Brussels sprouts. It was years before I could eat another one.

Pam and I went on many Saturday nights to hear folk music performed by Ewan MacColl and Peggy Seeger and their friends, in pubs around London. We carried Jon, in his carry cot. Ewan and Peggy were stalwarts of the labor and peace movements. Their colleague Enoch Kent wrote a song on the current events:

> *In the land of the dollar*
> *Where everything's taller*

And everything's fine 'less you're black
They've a government leader
An old Ivy Leaguer
And his name it is President Jack.

He hands out atom missiles
Like Popish epistles
For he scatters them all 'round the globe
And Macmillan gives thanks
By Clyde's bonnie banks
For Polaris which he hopes won't explode.

This was the time in Britain of the CND, the Campaign for Nuclear Disarmament, with its symbol that has been adopted by antiwar movements around the world. The British peace movement seemed to me more self-consciously focused on nuclear alliances and imperialism than its United States counterpart. As the UK reaction to the Cuban Missile Crisis showed, the British left focused on the risk that U.S. dominance of NATO and disregard for collective security could propel the world into nuclear conflict. During a trip to Berlin, President Kennedy handed out souvenir ballpoint pens. Ewan and Peggy wrote a song:

On the banks of the Elbe
Me love and I sat down to neck
And he took out his ball pen and he wrote me out a check
And he said "My darlin' Gretchen, how'd you like to make a wreck
Of the whole bloody universe, me darlin'."

A later stanza:

There's a place they call the Congo
And it's filled with heathen Blacks
They had the nerve to try and get the Belgians off their backs
But plucky little Belgium up and gave 'em such a whack
And me Johnny smiled and gently whispered "freedom."

And the chorus:

O the banks they are rosy
And the market's doin' fine

The bulls and bears are pasturing
From Wall Street to the Rhine
The bombs are in the stockpile, only waitin' for a sign
From me Johnny, lovely Johnny, and his ball pens.

Ewan and Peggy invited Pam and me to gatherings at their home. Jon was welcome to come along; Ewan's mother, Betsy, baby-sat him. On one evening, Jon had begun teething, and was a bit cranky. But when we went to gather him up to go home, he was calmly asleep. Betsy explained that rubbing Jon's gums with a warm spoon, moistened with a drop of whisky with a little sugar, was her secret.

One evening, we were with Ewan and Peggy in a London pub, and Hugh MacDiarmid walked in, dressed in formal Scots attire. I remembered his anti-Franco poetry. He was in London to receive an award on his seventieth birthday. He had drunk a great deal, and was at the "dignified and voluble" stage of inebriation. As Pam and I got into Ewan and Peggy's car, MacDiarmid came out of the pub and made his way down the street, arm in arm with a friend. Peggy picked up the concertina from the floor of the car, and rolled down the window. She played while Ewan sang:

I'm a rover, seldom sober
I'm a rover of high degree.

We met others involved in the peace movement, including the poet Adrian Mitchell and his actor wife, Celia Mitchell. I was invited to speak at meetings where Adrian was also speaking.

At this time, Ewan and Peggy were producing radio documentaries on working people, including miners and construction workers. When they heard I was going to Geneva to report on events at the UN, they asked me to buy a Nagra tape recorder, manufactured in Switzerland. The Nagra was small and the most technologically advanced recorder then available. Since the customs duties on imports from Switzerland were very high, they gave me the funds and I brought one back.

Those months in London provided other teaching moments as well. Clint Jencks came to London to conduct research for his PhD thesis on miners' lives and work. He stayed with us, and he and Bill Ash debated Marxist economics.

Thanks to Bill Ash I met George Thomson, a Marxist scholar of ancient Greek literature and society. I read Thomson's books *Aeschylus and Athens* and *Studies in Ancient Greek Society: The Prehistoric Aegean*. Bill invited me to hear Thomson lecture and tutored me in the implications of his work. I continue to find ideas drawn from Thomson's insights into Greek culture and state power significant. We often had dinner with Jan and Konni Zilliacus—Zilly was an imaginative chef. Over dinner he shared his experience and knowledge about the origins of the Cold War.

However much I was learning from daily observation and the firsthand accounts of those I met, I did not feel that I was having an impact on the world. Pacifica Radio had lawyers who were defending its free speech rights back home; lawyers in Europe were taking cases to the European Court of Human Rights; lawyers were representing people called before investigating committees.

I wanted to be a participant and not an observer. I signed up for the LSAT, the Law School Admissions Test, and sent in my application to UC Berkeley Law School. My undergraduate record was a bit spotty, given my dispute with the Navy and the associated emotional turmoil. However my LSAT was in the 99.6 percentile, so I had a good chance of getting in.

As spring arrived, we walked in the London parks and marveled at the shades of green, of a depth and variety that I had not seen in California. We packed up and came back to the States in late spring. We moved into Pam's parents' house in Los Angeles. I went to work at KPFK, the Pacifica Radio station in Los Angeles, producing public affairs and news programs and editing the program guide. That had its own excitement, which went beyond broadcasting. KPFK's studios were near one of the movie studios' back lots, a big open space. Two devoted KPFK supporters, Ron and Phyllis Patterson, suggested that the station raise money by holding a Renaissance Pleasure Faire and May Market, re-creating a medieval market for a long weekend. This seemed a good idea, and in fact the "faires" have since become a California institution much imitated elsewhere. But I was there at the start. They needed somebody to open the faire by galloping on horseback, dressed as a knight, while brandishing a sword and giving "the call of the Faire." I was the only male staff member who knew how to sit on a horse, so I did it. Twenty-five years later I reprised the role along with my daughter Katie, who was working for the outfit that produced the Faires.

As the summer of 1963 continued, I had to make up my mind. UC Berkeley Law School had admitted me. I went to see my friend Al Bendich, the civil liberties lawyer I had met while an undergraduate and at KPFA. He convinced me that I had convinced myself—long before—that law school was in my future. But he had a warning: "It will be hard for people to take you seriously, with your history of being a dissenter, a radical. You will have to convince them. And you know how to do that? By being first in your class. And the way to be first is to study more than the next person. You see him studying twelve hours a day, you do fourteen. That's all there is to it." So I entered law school in September 1963.

CHAPTER 3

What Was Taught, and What Was Learned, in Law School

One of my mother's friends gave me books he had used in law school. Included was an early edition of T. F. T. Plucknett's *A Concise History of the Common Law*. Another was the 1952 edition of Charles Alan Wright's treatise on federal courts. Plucknett helped me to see that the law is not news from nowhere—legal rules and ideas arise in social and historical context. This may seem obvious and trivial, but since so much of the law school curriculum seems devoted to picturing law in isolation from social conditions it was a useful reminder.

Wright's book provided an introduction to how federal courts operate, and under what system of constitutional, statutory, and rule-based procedures. This was a time when civil rights and civil liberties discussions centered on what the Supreme Court and lower federal courts were doing and what they ought to do. Wright's treatise, in its successive editions, remained a basic text throughout his life, and is even now in print with the participation of new authors.

I followed Bendich's advice, and established my study routine. I typed out a brief summary of every case. I took careful notes in class, and then each night I typed up my notes and integrated them into the case briefs. This was well before the days of word processors, so my product was cut, pasted, and stapled.

FIRST-YEAR COURSES AND ISSUES

I could not drown out what was going on in the wider world. As in my undergraduate days, I would not necessarily *get* a legal education at law school.

However, I could try to *find* one. In my first year, I set out to see what I could find. I wanted to take in all that professors and casebooks were providing, get all of what was offered, and then go beyond to find out where that stuff came from, what interests it served, and what I might learn that would help to make me a useful part of the struggle against injustice.

I did not know the term "legal realism," nor any names of its exponents. Years later, I came upon a statement by Judge Jerome Frank. He was dissenting in a case involving prosecutorial misconduct: Judge Frank contended that the prosecutor's resort to ethnic slurs, and the trial judge's refusal to do something about that conduct, was—in this wartime prosecution —reversible error. As I noted in the Prologue of this book, Judge Frank arraigned the mythology of justice against the real events of trial:

> A legal system is not what it says, but what it does. Our "criminal law," then, cannot be described accurately in terms merely of substantive prohibitions; the description must also include the methods by which those prohibitions operate in practice—must include, therefore, not the substantive and procedural rules as they appear in words but as they actually work, or, as Llewellyn puts it, "The net operation of the whole official setup, taken as a whole," for it "is that net operation—it is the substantive rule only as it trickles through the screen of action—which counts in life."

Without being able to put words to the idea, that was the understanding for which I was searching. Of course I had to learn Contracts, Torts, Property, Civil Procedure, and Criminal Law. These were—and are—the basic building blocks of the present system of legal rules. But they did not justify themselves, nor did they exist as free-floating self-evident norms. We were invited by our professors and the casebooks to criticize results in cases under a fairly narrow set of criteria.

My journalistic adventures, and my undergraduate study and activism, fueled the sense that "legal education" should be more than this. The power of those events over our lives came home to us when President Kennedy was assassinated on November 22, 1963. In every one of our classes, we took time to talk about what the assassination meant.

Beyond, before, and after those events, however, the constitutional crisis in the country at large bore in upon us. The Supreme Court had begun to decide cases arising from the sit-in movement. The Court's majority reaffirmed some important principles about the right to demonstrate, and held that the state could not use its criminal justice apparatus to enforce racial segregation. These Supreme Court decisions seemed far removed from the basic first-year curriculum. Make no mistake: I thought then and think now that the first-year curriculum can be understood as giving insight into the basic structure of legal ideology. I could see how civil procedure helped lawyers to litigate civil rights cases. But the point of the private law courses, as presented to us, was sometimes hard to see.

Some of that changed when we began to study offer and acceptance in our contracts class. If a storekeeper puts up a sign, "Refrigerators $100," is that an offer, such that if I walk in and say "I'll take one" there is a binding contract? Or is it simply an invitation to make an offer? What difference does it make? In our contracts book, there was a 1901 case from the Transvaal, in South Africa, *Crawley v. Rex.* Crawley went into a tobacconist shop, but was told that he would not be served. He persisted in demanding to make a purchase and was arrested for trespass. He was convicted on the theory that the shop-keeper's sign was only an invitation to make an offer. I read the short reference to the case in the casebook note material.

Who was Crawley? What had been going on in the Transvaal? In the library, I read the entire case. Transvaal was part of South Africa. *Rex* was in the name because South Africa was under British rule. That was all I could learn. I kept digging. There had been protests in South Africa about the refusal of merchants to serve "colored" and "African" customers. Indeed, the young Mohandas Gandhi had lived and practiced law in South Africa, and had joined those protests. Gandhi had begun to preach *satyagraha*—nonviolent resistance—in 1906 in Natal Province. Was the holding in *Crawley* in some way related to racial discrimination? I never found that answer, but the case spurred me to more research.

Here, it seemed, was a theory. If Woolworth stores opened their doors to the public, why should courts not hold that they had offered to sell their merchandise and dispense the food at their lunch counters to anybody who showed up? Why not hold, in first-year, law-student terms, that the merchant had made an "offer" that was "accepted" by the customer sitting at the lunch counter? As a matter of contract law, this seemed at least arguable. I was there-fore pleased to find that Justice Douglas, concurring in the reversal of sit-in demonstrators' convictions for criminal mischief in *Lombard v. Louisiana*, had expressed a related thought.

In *Lombard*, an interracial group of young people sat-in at a lunch coun-ter. They were refused service. When they refused to leave they were arrested. The Supreme Court reversed their convictions because the local police chief had participated in the order to leave; thus, the state had been involved in the discriminatory conduct, in violation of the Fourteenth Amendment equal protection clause. Justice Douglas, concurring, wrote:

Business, such as this restaurant, is still private property. Yet there is hardly any private enterprise that does not feel the pinch of some public regulation—from price control, to health and fire inspection, to zoning, to safety measures, to minimum wages and working conditions, to unemployment insurance. When the doors of a business are open to the public, they must be open to all regardless of race if apartheid is not to become engrained in our public places. . . . There is no constitutional way, as I see it, in which a State can license and supervise a business serving the public and endow it with the authority to manage that business on the basis of apartheid, which is foreign to our Constitution.

I thought about the theoretical works I had read as an undergraduate. I was a month or so into law school, and it appeared that a major premise of first-year legal education was mythological. Contracts and Property were called "private law," to distinguish them from constitutional and criminal law, which were "public." There was "freedom of contract" and "the right of property." These were words being used to mask relationships of power. A contractual bargain did not exist unless the state was willing to enforce it.

Contract law is generally the business of state courts and legislatures. Contracts between private parties do not usually involve any constitutional command because those parties are not acting as agents of the state. The state and its agents are the only ones subject to constitutional commands. I found *Lombard* because in the searches that began with *Rex v. Crawley*, I was reading all the sit-in cases I could find. Those were the days before Westlaw and LEXIS. So I began by reading all the current sit-in cases, then followed the trail in the indices.

Justice Douglas had said that lunch counters are not unlike innkeepers and common carriers. In the old common law, those merchants had a duty to serve everyone. That is, their signage was to be regarded as an offer, which any traveler or customer would accept by demanding service. Justice Douglas's expansive view of state action and the Constitution never gained a Supreme Court majority, although it certainly reflected the reality of property and contract rights.

Having gone this far in a big hurry, I did not want the class discussion of offer and acceptance to pass by without having reached some conclusions. I tried to find other cases dealing with civil rights and based on contract principles. Even if there were not a constitutional issue here, perhaps state courts would interpret broadly the right to serve all comers. I could find only one helpful case, perhaps because I was limited to legal digests and indices. And I was, after all, less than a month into law school.

The case I found was *Johnson v. Sparrow*. The holder of a theater ticket showed up and was denied admission to the performance because he was Black. The court held that the theater was obliged to serve everyone with a ticket, as a matter of contract law. You can quibble about the case because maybe the ticket is a contract, and thus not like simply putting up a sign advertising the performance. But I was proud of my find.

At the next contracts class, I was ready. In alphabetical order, Tigar sat next to Thompson, about five rows back from the front, and in the middle. The room held a hundred or so law students. I raised my hand at the right moment and told Professor Jackson that there was authority for the view that advertising your goods or services was an offer. He demurred.

I began to read from *Johnson*. The case was from Quebec and was in French. Jackson was impatient so I blurted out, "I am sorry to be going slowly. This case is in French and I am translating as I go along." The class burst into laughter. The story has dogged me, and in some versions has the case in Latin or Greek.

This episode was relief from the dominant theme of the course. We had been required to read chapter 5 of Sir Henry Maine's 1861 work, *Ancient Law*, titled "From Status to Contract." Maine's theme was that with the abolition of the personal relationships that characterized feudal society, people were free to make their own bargains. Our course did not dwell on inequalities of bargaining power.

Our Property law professor was Stefan Riesenfeld, educated in Germany and the United States and possessing an encyclopedic knowledge of legal history and comparative law. His rigorous course began with William the Conqueror in 1066, and took us through the transition from feudal to bourgeois property norms. At least one could see, if one wished, that "property" has never truly merited the name "private." The relationship of people to things, including real estate, was always formulated in the interest of a dominant class and enforced by state power.

I had met Riesenfeld when I was an undergraduate, for he offered a Political Science Department course in international law. We met in a cavernous lecture hall, and I struggled to hear and understand him. One key concept in international, as in municipal, law is estoppel. A sovereign state may be precluded from asserting a position by its own prior conduct that is inconsistent with what it now claims. It was a week's worth of lectures, however, before I understood the word *estoppel* as pronounced by Professor Riesenfeld. What I heard was "Gestapo," and I wondered how the hell the Gestapo had such influence over modern international law.

Riesenfeld began the law school Property course by diagramming the forms of property on the blackboard. Over in the corner where intangible property rights were diagrammed, he used the classic common law term "incorporeal hereditaments." I copied the diagram faithfully. Years later, it came in handy. While arguing an appeal from a federal mail fraud conviction, I criticized the unduly vague prosecution theory of "intangible rights." In mock surprise, Judge Altimari interjected, "What? Have you never heard of incorporeal hereditaments?"

My mind flashed back to Professor Riesenfeld's chart, but instead of giving him credit, I began by saying, "Judge Altimari, in the little town in Texas where I come from, people talk of little else." Then I answered what I considered the question must have been. To be clear, at the time of that court argument, I was living in Austin, Texas—not a "little town," but close enough.

The course in Civil Procedure, taught by Professor Geoffrey Hazard, seemed more related to the use of law and lawyering in the real world. We began by studying a complaint Hazard had filed in a housing discrimination case in Berkeley. For two weeks, we worked through the lawyer's tasks in bringing, trying, and winning that lawsuit.

CIVIL LIBERTIES DOCKET: REAL WORLD LAW

That first year, we lived in the second floor of a two-story house on Roosevelt Avenue in Berkeley, within walking distance to law school. My friend from undergraduate days, Mike Myerson, lived downstairs. A week or so after the semester began, he introduced me to Dennis Roberts, who was a year ahead of me in law school. Dennis asked if I would like a part-time job with something called the *Civil Liberties Docket*. I said yes.

The *Docket* had been founded in 1955 by Ann Fagan Ginger, a progressive lawyer and legal writer. This unique publication, which Ann produced from her Berkeley home, summarized civil rights and civil liberties cases. It covered not only officially reported judicial decisions, but also unreported ones, giving readers access to material that was not otherwise generally available. We summarized briefs and pleadings, which Ann had me and Dennis collect from the lawyers involved.

Ann archived these materials in what became the Meiklejohn Civil Liberties Library. She edited a practice guide for civil rights cases that became the model of our *Selective Service Law Reporter* some years later. The *Docket* was a dream job. I sat at a typewriter and read litigation materials. If I read of a significant case in the newspapers, I would write the lawyers to get their pleadings. I felt like a medical student doing dissection, learning the anatomy of litigation. Except, of course, these were not cadavers but living cases. Voting rights, attacks on free expression by civil rights organizations, desegregation battles—all the racial justice issues that had led to the 1963 March on Washington where Martin Luther King had spoken. Ann was a superb editor and writer, and I was also learning how to state and formulate issues and legal arguments.

This job gave me a view of human rights litigation as the work of lawyers working with clients to confront injustice. This was the law as "what it does and not what it says or claims to do." I could also see the ways that people involved in movements for change became cynical, frustrated, and embittered as they discovered the limits on what law, lawyers, and courts could accomplish. I was learning how lawyers move from understanding legal rules to putting those rules to use. It was 1963, and the *Docket* was reporting on hundreds of school desegregation lawsuits. Nine years after *Brown v. Board of Education*, and southern school districts would not integrate unless some parents found a lawyer and brought a lawsuit. Lawyers for school boards used every dilatory tactic they could conjure. Little wonder that beginning in 1960 the sit-in and direct action movements began to flourish across the country.

THE OATH

In those early weeks of law school, I was deep into my books, classes, and typewriter—and my part-time job. Some law school functionary handed out a leaflet from the California bar. Every first-year law student in California was required to fill out a form stating his or her intention to practice law. (I say her, recognizing that there were just six women in our entering class of 315.) The form asked for information about one's background, and included a question something like this: "Are you now or have you ever been a member of, affiliated with, or supported any group or organization that advocates the overthrow of the government by force and violence?" A loyalty *oath*, for one had to swear to the truth of one's answers.

When I saw this question, I had a sense of foreboding. I thought back to the Supreme Court's series of decisions rejecting First Amendment claims. Among those cases were two dealing with loyalty-security inquiries as a basis for denying admittance to the bar. I knew that loyalty qualifications for bar membership were widespread, and that I would have to answer some questions about adherence to the Constitution to be eligible for the bar. In *Konigsberg v. State Bar of California*, the Supreme Court held 5 to 4 that California was justified in refusing the petitioner bar membership because he refused to answer questions concerning membership in the Communist Party. Konigsberg had said that he did not belong to any organization that to his knowledge advocated violent overthrow of the government, and did not himself believe in violent overthrow. The same 5 to 4 majority upheld denial of bar membership in an Illinois case, *In re Anastaplo*. Was there a difference between the questions that *Konigsberg* and *Anastaplo* declined to answer and the one posed by the California bar?

If not, did I want to become a test case to try to reverse the results in those cases? I quickly answered the second question "probably not." I did not want to stand alone or virtually alone in this fight, and I would surely have done so by attacking two Supreme Court decisions head-on. To the first question, I could answer "yes." The California bar question swept considerably more broadly than those upheld in *Konigsberg* and *Anastaplo*.

If I could convince some of my classmates, then we might stage a fairly effective protest against the question and actually make the bar change the form. I did some research. I began with the nature of this question. One answered it under oath. I remembered Governor Goodwin Knight of California telling an audience why he supported loyalty oaths: "You can't prosecute people for being Communists—at least the Supreme Court has made it very hard to do that. But you can ask people if they are Communists, and make them swear they are not. And if they lie, you can send 'em to jail for perjury." In thinking about that comment, I deconstructed it. I went to the library and found that despite Supreme Court decisions upholding some loyalty questions, there was a countercurrent of relevant law upon which I could argue that this particular question was improper.

One case, *Cramp v. Board of Public Instruction*, was from the same year, 1961, that had seen the Supreme Court split 5 to 4 on a number of civil liberties issues—sometimes in one direction and sometimes in another. *Cramp* from December 1961, however, was unanimous. A Florida statute required every teacher to swear under penalty of perjury that he or she had never given "aid, support, advice, counsel or influence to the Communist Party." The Court held that these terms were too vague to have any settled meaning and that the oath-taker was denied due process because he or she could not determine whether or not particular conduct fell within the oath's terms.

Later, I was to learn that in criminal law, one cannot be convicted of perjury for an allegedly false answer to an unduly vague question, nor held in contempt for violating a vague judicial order.

Armed with the *Cramp* case, I wrote a memo to all first-year students saying that I would not sign the bar form with this question on it, and invited them to join me. Before I sent the memo, I made an appointment to see

Professor Hazard, who seemed to be quite active in the California bar. I took with me volume 368 of the *U.S. Reports*, where *Cramp* was reported. I put the bar form and the case before Professor Hazard. He read both of them, looked up, and to my surprise said: "You are right. What do you want me to do?" I said, "Help me."

Hazard was witty, articulate, and given to grand gestures. He picked up the telephone and dialed the general counsel of the California bar, whose name I cannot recall. Let's call him Bill. "Bill, this is Geoff Hazard. I am sitting here with one of my students and we have been looking at this form you make all first-year law students sign." Hazard read the question aloud. "I also have a Supreme Court case right in front of me—unanimous, by the way—that holds that this question cannot be asked. Denies due process, because it's too vague. Now, Bill, the question is, are you going to delete the question, or are we going to have a dispute about it? I have to support these students, because they are right about this one." I was amazed at the alacrity and commitment of Hazard's action.

One-third of the first-year students signed on to support deleting the question, and in due course the bar relented. This vignette showed why I came to law school. If you read the cases, worked hard to understand the issues, and either had courage or found a client who had it, you might—just might—find wonder-working power in all of this doctrine.

I had worked so hard, and with such anxiety, during that first semester, that I got sick. I had fever and chest pain. I spent a few days in Cowell Hospital, on campus, and was attended by a cardiologist, all part of the University's health plan for all students. As I lay in my hospital bed, somebody delivered my first-semester grades, a series of numbers and a grade-point average computed to two places after the decimal. I was tied for third place in a class of more than 300. This was not the news I wanted to hear.

In the second semester of the first year, Criminal Law and Procedure was a required course. The professor for our section was Rex Collings. I disliked him from the first day. He appeared unkempt. His stomach peered through the stretched-out front of his dress shirt. We began the course with cases on constitutional criminal procedure. In 1961, the Supreme Court had followed the lead of the California Supreme Court and held that if the police obtained evidence by an illegal search and seizure, that evidence could not be used by the prosecution at trial. The Court thus took a long step along the road to incorporating all the criminal procedure guarantees of the Bill of Rights into the due process clause of the Fourteenth Amendment. The older idea, that state courts had to provide only those basic rights essential to "ordered liberty," was being abandoned.

This change from "ordered liberty" to "incorporation" was to continue through the 1960s. There was another aspect to it. In March 1963, the Supreme Court had decided *Fay v. Noia*. The majority opinion, by Justice Brennan, expanded the rights of state prisoners to attack their convictions by seeking habeas corpus in federal court. A longer list of federally guaranteed rights meant more possible bases on which to challenge state convictions.

Professor Collings detested these developments. In his first lectures, he did not so much analyze as deprecate. He referred to the Supreme Court's current trend as "the spreading buttocks of due process." Rising (or descending) to this level of intellectual analysis, I wrote and posted on the bulletin board (anonymously, until now), a bit of doggerel:

> *Under the spreading buttocks see*
> *The state policeman stand*
> *His blunted anti-crime implement*
> *Shriveled in his hand*
> *And see the happy criminals*
> *Frolic wild and free*
> *Secure that incorporation*
> *Has replaced ordered liberty*
> *And see the law professor*
> *He has buttocks too*
> *"O bring us back the hose and rack*
> *The sandbag and the screw!"*
> *But look out, Rex, stand back, beware!*
> *Due process' buttocks spread*
> *And with eloquent judicial groaning*
> *Shit, constitutionally, on your head.*

I got a 72 in the course, a C, but still managed to average high enough to move from third to first place in the class rankings when the end-of-year grades were computed. I remained first for the rest of law school. Given my later career in practice and teaching, it is sometimes hard to figure out why I resisted learning criminal law so strongly. I suppose it was not the subject, but Collings's approach to it.

In law practice, I have often gone back to the basic concepts of the required law school courses, to see what the old rules can yield in terms of new ideas. I learned Corporations from Professor Jennings, but after quickly moving through some historical material, he was interested in our learning about shareholders' rights. Only later did I study and write about the centuries-long history of capital-pooling devices, including the corporate form, and how those devices contributed to the rise of the bourgeoisie. Income Tax, with Professor Kragen, was a required course; I am glad I took it because the basic ideas served me well when in law practice I defended tax evasion cases.

LAW REVIEW AND THE FREE SPEECH MOVEMENT

As I began my second law school year, I was thinking about the three elements of legal education that I wanted to have in order to participate in confronting injustice. I wanted to understand the basic principles I would need to form into arguments. I wanted to study the historical and social origins and real bases of those principles, what their expression masked, and how are they being changed. And third, I wanted to acquire skills I would need to advance a view of what "the law" ought to do. My ideas about the third element were enlivened by working at the *Civil Liberties Docket*. Today, any law school worth attending has clinical legal education courses, where students can confront injustice in real life and real time. Clinical legal education was just being introduced in some law schools, though not at Berkeley, when I attended law school.

In those days, one "made law review" by being in the top 10 percent of the class. Every law school in the United States has one or more student-run journals. Being an editor of one of those is a résumé builder and an education in itself. As a second-year law review member, in addition to hours spent checking citations in submitted articles, I had to write a law review comment that could be published. I wanted to do something that stretched my consciousness, but was acceptable to the editorial board. My eye fell upon California Code of Civil Procedure section 440, which provided:

> When cross-demands have existed between persons under such circumstances that, if one had brought an action against the other, a counterclaim could have been set up, the two demands shall be deemed compensated, so far as they equal each other, and neither can be deprived of the benefit thereof by the assignment or death of the other.

Our law school casebook said simply that this section appeared to derive from the French *compensation* or Roman law *compensatio*. A California case held that this provision operated to prevent the statute of limitations from extinguishing a claim. That is, if your creditor sued you, and there had at some past time existed an offsetting claim, you could plead the offset even if your claim would otherwise be time-barred.

I am not sure why this topic interested me, but it led me on a journey that has continued to this day. The very idea of counterclaims and crossclaims, as they are now called, or "setoffs," the older word, is relatively recent in Anglo-American law. Permitting a defendant to assert claims against other or opposite parties is regarded as one of the great innovations that took root in the mid-nineteenth century with code pleading and continued with the 1937 adoption of the Federal Rules of Civil Procedure. This is, you might say, hardly the stuff of drama. It might look good on one's résumé, but was good for little else.

I was influenced by having read Plucknett's work on English legal history before starting law school. The arc of legal change was longer than I had imagined. Professor Plucknett dealt with relevant events going back to the eleventh century. Professor Riesenfeld had taken us on a similar path.

Here, however, was a legal rule that could be traced back millennia. It presented, in discrete and manageable form, an example of the ways that legal rules come into being and are enforced and changed to serve particular interests. How and why—and in whose interest—had this provision come into being? My journey began by looking at basic Roman law sources, then moving deeper into that material. Upstairs in the University law library was the Robbins Collection—books dating to the 1300s, and containing discussion of Roman, canon, and customary law. I could not bear to read only those bits having to do with bilateral agreements and offsetting claims, so my gaze wandered further. I devoured material on the origins and structure of Roman legal ideology, and glanced back at Greek procedure. I got glimpses of the nascent merchant bourgeoisie struggling to formulate rules and create forms of judicial review that were relatively simple, and relatively free from mythology.

From this study, I acquired a conviction reflected in all my later writing, teaching, and litigating. I could see the interaction of law and history, law and popular struggle. My study became broader than this single provision that simplified procedure by allowing resolution of offsetting claims in a single lawsuit. I saw how the rising merchant class had struggled to cast aside a host of arcane procedural forms.

This research carried on up to the Code Napoléon, promulgated in 1804, which contained a *compensation* provision. My curiosity was further aroused, so I struggled to read the *Conseil d'Etat* discussions of the various principles that were embodied in the Code. Those discussions focused hardly at all on legal procedures, but I gained insight into the political, economic, cultural, and regional interests at stake, and the way that the French legal profession was seeking to impose the new social order on post-revolutionary France.

This historical timeline brought events up to 1804. How did this provision become part of the California law codes of 1872? The answer lay in disputes about how law is and ought to be "made." The lawyers who wrote the Constitution and laws of the newly independent colonies, and of the United States, were trained in the English common law system. Judges in that system had great authority to devise and apply legal rules.

Jeremy Bentham and others argued that the civil law system of France and other European countries should be followed, and that law codes like the Code Napoléon would make the process making legal rules more transparent, and the rules themselves more accessible. Bentham wrote that the law is made by judges: "Do you know how they make it? Just as a man makes laws for his dog. When your dog does anything you want to break him of, you wait till he does it, and then you beat him for it."

In the 1830s and 1840s, New York lawyer David Dudley Field advocated codification and influenced the laws of New York. His brother Stephen J. Field, moved to California in 1851, was elected to the legislature, and proposed that some of his brother's codification efforts should be adopted in California.

Field's views carried weight. California's 1851 civil practice statute was drawn from David Dudley Field's work. In 1872 California adopted Civil, Civil Procedure, and Penal Codes. I went to the document repositories at UC Berkeley's Bancroft Library and at San Francisco's City Hall. I sought out original letters, documents, and newspapers. This work opened up a picture of the financial and political forces in late nineteenth-century California, beyond the debates over procedure. I saw how the views and practices that Professor tenBroek had identified as contributing to racist legislation and eventually to the Japanese internment were formed. Yes, I was looking at a simple article of the Civil Procedure Code, but in a broader sense was learning about legal ideology. The law, I found once again, is not news from nowhere.

Having managed to keep my grades up, I was elected editor-in-chief of the Law Review at the end of my second year. That position generally went to the person who was first in the class. The appointment ought, therefore, to have been unremarkable. The *San Francisco Chronicle* nonetheless reported it on June 5, 1965, under the headline, "UC Honor for Former Firebrand." I was only twenty-four, and already I was "former."

That second law school year was 1964–65. That summer and fall, the Free Speech Movement (FSM) burst upon the Berkeley scene, leading in December 1964 to a sit-in demonstration in the University's administration building. FSM began during the summer of 1964, when young Republicans supporting William Scranton for the Republican presidential nomination were prevented from handing out their materials at the entrance to the UC Berkeley campus. Their activity angered Republican Senator William Knowland, who urged the chancellor to ban the student activity. Several student groups defied the ban and maintained their literature tables at the campus entrance.

On October 1, 1964, Berkeley student Jack Weinberg was sitting at a table, handing out Congress on Racial Equality literature. He refused to show identification to Berkeley campus police. They arrested him. Students surrounded the police car that arrived to take him to jail. For 32 hours, students used the police car roof as a platform from which to speak about free speech. I was among the speakers. The University negotiated the release of Jack and of the police car, but during that time FSM was established in a series of meetings.

My law school studies kept me away from much of the FSM activity, but I kept up a lively discussion with student activists and with faculty members about the constitutional free speech issues. The FSM and its leaders have been chronicled in dozens of books, articles, and other media. My overriding sense of it all was, and remains, to marvel at the obliquity of a university administration that had learned nothing from all the preceding years of student activism.

By June 1965, the criminal cases arising from the FSM sit-in were still in the local courts. The events called for the kind of analysis that the *Law Review* could provide. What could law and lawyers tell us about campus free speech and academic freedom? We planned a *Law Review* issue devoted to those issues. We invited law professors with widely differing views to contribute. A student, David Frohnmayer, who would later be attorney general of Oregon, contributed a thoughtful comment analyzing free speech rights on the University's premises. I wrote a long introduction, trying to put the Free Speech Movement into the historical perspective of student political action at Berkeley. We were among the first to address the due process rights of university students who were subjected to school discipline. The Supreme Court's landmark decision on procedural fairness, *Goldberg v. Kelly*, was still five years away. A state university was, of course, bound to respect the Fourteenth Amendment due process clause. But that observation did not answer the question of what process would be due a student who had allegedly committed some infraction for which the university thought suspension or expulsion was appropriate.

One principal issue was factual reliability, which raised a number of specific questions. By what means could the student challenge the evidence against him or her? Cross-examination? The right to call witnesses? The right to compel attendance of witnesses subject to the university's control?

The right to testify? If the student refused to testify, might an adverse inference be drawn from the refusal?

A second issue was the relationship between the potential harm to the student from an adverse decision and the amount of due process required. That is, as the cases that came along in the 1970s explored in more detail, the process that will be due increases with the potential consequences. This tension between reliability and efficiency is key to due process analysis. These issues were, in the 1960s debates, overshadowed by the university's institutional arguments concerning its relationship with students and its autonomy from official regulation. All universities in that era claimed to act *in loco parentis*, in the place of a student's parents. They claimed an obligation not only to provide an education but also to regulate a broad range of student conduct without any outside interference.

The university was arguing, in essence, that it fulfilled a role somewhat like that of a guardian in Roman law. The students saw it differently. They argued that the university was a place where they should learn self-reliance, with the right to make their own choices and the obligation to accept corresponding consequences. They spoke of *Lehrnfreiheit*—the freedom to learn—as a basic student right. Students have a vital role to play in shaping the university's mission.

Then there was the issue of fairness in student discipline. From the student point of view, the discipline mechanism should be conducted at arm's length, rather than by the university asserting that informal procedures best suited some relationship of tutelage. The students pointed out that the disagreements between students and the administration increased the risk that charges would be brought for the wrong reasons, or on flimsy evidence, and that the informality the university craved would therefore be a cover for suspect decision-making.

As a related matter, the university stressed its institutional independence. One core meaning of academic freedom is immunity from outside interference in internal governance. Detailed due process standards for university discipline would inevitably entail judicial review of discipline decisions and hence overt state control of the discipline process. The university rejected adoption of any system that would permit that sort of control.

The students countered with their own theory of academic freedom, again using the concept of *Lehrnfreiheit*. On this theory, the Berkeley students found faculty allies, in a pattern that was to be repeated on other campuses throughout the 1960s and 1970s. In the European universities where models of academic freedom were developed, the faculty governed and the students learned, or at least that was the model. At the University of California in 1964, as with all large universities, the faculty had some power by virtue of its academic senate. But the Cold War and the loyalty-security fights of the 1950s had firmly established political control of the university's major activities and mission. Government contracts were endemic in all departments—note that the Berkeley physics department was a major resource for developing both the atomic and hydrogen bombs. Professors as well as students felt constrained by political pressures originating from the legislature and the governor's office, and were transmitted through the chancellor of the Berkeley campus and the president of the UC system.

The University had espoused a contradiction. To preserve its "independence" students should not speak on "outside" issues. Independence from what? From the political pressures that would result if students spoke out on such issues? In fact, the administration was bowing to the conservative forces that had held sway from time to time in California politics, and had become an important player in the nuclear arms race. The University's claim to independence from outside control was ironic at best. That outside control already existed in overtly political form, and the question was whether it would be mediated by the intervention of courts applying constitutional principles.

In 1965, the landscape of this debate was not so thickly planted with argument as it was to become. The other editors and I felt that we were staking out new territory.

That year also gave us a chance to work with my former professor, Jacobus tenBroek, a leader of movements to protect the dignity of welfare recipients and the disabled. He proposed that the Law Review should host a conference on "the law of the poor," and publish the conference papers. Charles Reich of Yale had published his pathbreaking 1964 essay, "The New Property," arguing that welfare benefits and other social services were not government largesse but a form of entitlement that should be protected under the due process clause just like other property. Writers had noted the similarity between shabby treatment of welfare recipients and the vagrancy laws of Elizabethan England. We had come a long way from the Supreme Court's 1837 denunciation of the "moral pestilence of paupers." Hans Linde, then a professor and later a justice of the Oregon Supreme Court, had written of "freedom in the welfare state." President Lyndon Johnson had proposed his War on Poverty.

In the end, this one Law Review issue totaled 690 pages and included more than two-dozen articles. We had raised money for the extra pages from foundations and by selling republication rights. The entire issue was then printed as a book, *The Law of the Poor,* with the Law Review getting a share of the credit. For the two conference days, and throughout the painstaking editorial process, I felt I had a front-row seat at a new and energetic debate.

We were, perhaps, helping to direct lawyers toward ideas and principles that they could use in representing the marginalized and discriminated.

STEIN, APTHEKER, JACOBS: RATIONING SPEECH

Although I had only a small role in the FSM, I was drawn into a case that sprang from it during my last year in law school. In September 1965, UC Berkeley's post-FSM chancellor, Roger Heyns, issued new rules on students' free speech rights. Law professors assisted in the drafting process; I looked at the draft rules and sent comments. The rules' basic theme was that students and faculty had the right to free expression, subject only to reasonable limitations based on "time, place and manner." The rules permitted students to speak, using microphones and amplifiers, from the steps of the University administration building, provided that a given student or group could do so only once in any calendar week, even if nobody else wanted to speak there during that week. When I saw that rule in draft form, I sent an objection to one of the law professors: As the University had decided that the administrative work would not be unduly disturbed by noontime speaking, why ration speech in that way?

In February 1966, President Johnson escalated the Vietnam War twice in one week. A student protest group wanted to hold a second rally. The administration said no, so the students set up a microphone and spoke anyway. A law professor representing the Chancellor showed up and told the students to desist. They persisted. Three students, Bettina Aptheker, Susan Stein, and Harold Jacobs, were charged with violating the rules, and with "conduct unbecoming a student." They asked me to represent them at their disciplinary hearing.

I suppose this was my first real trial. I wrote a brief arguing that the once-a-week rule was an unreasonable restriction on speech. UC was a public university, and the administration building space had historically been a public forum—indeed, the FSM had been concerned with recognizing and preserving its status as such a forum.

The hearing officer was John Hetland, a conservative law professor who taught property law. The Chancellor's choice in this respect did not augur well for our side. Facing me as prosecutors were one law professor, one political science professor, and one portly lawyer from the firm that represented the University. As part of my case, I called the law professor/prosecutor, who had argued with the students that day, to testify. I examined him about the various drafts of the proposed speech rules. He had written a note on one such draft questioning the wisdom of the very rule my clients were said to have violated.

The administration building steps were suitable for public expression, and had historically been used for that purpose. No other group wanted to speak at that time, and the speakers were orderly and not unduly amplified. In short, the once per week restriction swept broader than necessary to assure fair access to the forum, and could not therefore be justified as a valid time, place, and manner rule. Moreover, the Chancellor had issued the rules without consulting student groups, violating administrative due process. As for the "conduct unbecoming a student" charge, the rule was unduly vague. The very idea that speaking against the war was "unbecoming," on a campus where fraternity parties sometimes spilled noisily and drunkenly into the streets of peaceful neighborhoods, seemed silly.

Hetland rejected our constitutional argument, holding that he lacked authority to consider it. He found the three students guilty. The University demanded a heavy punishment. Professor Hetland said that although the students had violated a rule, he thought that having a two-day hearing with all these lawyers was a colossal waste of time and money. He sentenced the students to one semester of ineligibility for inter-collegiate sports and banishment for that period from the hamburger stand in the Student Union. Since none of the three played sports or ate hamburgers, this punishment reflected Hetland's view of the whole affair. Hetland had also barred the three students from all public speech activities on the campus for the semester; Chancellor Heyns, as a gesture toward the First Amendment, set aside this punishment.

JUSTICE BRENNAN

Constitutional law professor Robert O'Neill had clerked for Justice William J. Brennan, Jr. Professor Robert Cole had clerked for Justice Minton, during Brennan's first year on the Court. Brennan asked O'Neill for recommendations of students to be his law clerk. Being a Supreme Court law clerk is an honor. These days, most Justices choose their clerks from people already clerking on the federal courts of appeals. In 1965, this practice had not begun. Today, each Justice has four law clerks. In 1965, each Justice was allotted two clerks, although Justice William O. Douglas used one clerk position to hire an extra secretary, so he had only one clerk. During my second law school year, Cole and O'Neill asked me if I would be interested in clerking for Justice Brennan. I said yes.

In June 1965, just after the spring semester was over, Justice Brennan wrote to me. He "had just been talking with Professors Cole and O'Neill" and they had said I would like to be his clerk. Would I accept that position?

The night I received the letter, I went home and celebrated. Jon was two and a half. Pam was six months' pregnant. We had a cheap record player and had just bought an album of Clancy Brothers songs. My friend Al Katz came over, and we listened to "Brennan on the Moor," a fine Irish song about "a brave young highwayman, Willie Brennan was his name." We played it over and over, and drank cheap rum. I can remember a dreadful hangover the next day, which passed in time for Pam and me to go to San Francisco and spend more money for dinner at the Mark Hopkins Hotel, with a view of the Bay, than we would normally spend on food in two weeks.

The summer of 1965 had a magical quality. I was editor-in-chief of the Law Review; I worked at the American Civil Liberties Union in San Francisco. I attended a summer symposium on law and economics. In September, our daughter Kate was born. In the fall, when word of the clerkship got out, things heated up. A local right-wing rag called *Tocsin*—the pronunciation says it all—attacked the clerkship appointment because of my leftist leanings and activities. As the school year went on, this attack was picked up and echoed. Fulton Lewis, Jr., a reactionary columnist, fulminated. Congressman Tuck, of the House Committee on Un-American Activities, put something in the *Congressional Record*. The redoubtable James J. Kilpatrick wrote an editorial, "The Lady and the Tigar," for the Richmond, Virginia, *News-Leader*.

Apparently, the Supreme Court was not accustomed to this sort of controversy, particularly when abetted by the FBI. During the spring of 1966, as my law school graduation approached, people in Washington were busy. The FBI was providing information to Justice Brennan about my real and alleged political activities. Justice Fortas was a conduit for some of this material, as was Attorney General Ramsey Clark.

One day in the late spring, as I was later told by a Brennan clerk for the 1965 term, Brennan walked into the office where his clerks were sitting and said, "The Chief told me to fire Tigar." The "Chief" was Chief Justice Earl Warren, who had been governor of California before President Eisenhower appointed him to the Court. Warren had no doubt been talking with Justice Fortas and to his political contacts in California. According to Brennan, Warren was worried that the clerkship furor would influence the 1966 California gubernatorial election, perhaps helping the campaign of Ronald Reagan. Fortas had also heard from FBI Director J. Edgar Hoover's right-hand man, Clyde Tolson.

Reagan faced a challenge from San Francisco mayor George Christopher in the Republican Party electoral primary. He had decided to focus much of his campaign on allegedly subversive political activity on the University of California campuses. His allies included J. Edgar Hoover, John McCone, who had served as CIA director until 1965, and the California State Senate's Fact-Finding Committee on Un-American Activities. The FBI, CIA, and the

Committee were busy gathering information by lawful and unlawful means about the political views and activities of students and professors. This coordinated activity was not aimed at me, but I and the clerkship became a target of opportunity.

Of course, Reagan was well ahead in the polls. As a rational matter, my clerkship could not have an important influence, and Chief Justice Warren ought to have known that.

Brennan called Professor O'Neill and said he needed to meet with me. By this time, it was early June. I had graduated from law school and had arranged to lease a house in Washington, D.C., on Capitol Hill. Professor O'Neill told me to go to Washington that night, and arranged for an air ticket. I took the American Airlines "red-eye" from Los Angeles to Dulles Airport. I was afraid and alone. I can remember getting on that 707 jet plane at Los Angeles International Airport. Pam's mother had given me a sleeping pill just in case I wanted to get some sleep on the six- or seven-hour flight. I don't think I took the pill. I do remember going into the airplane lavatory, in a cold sweat, sometime in the night, and throwing up.

The plane landed at Dulles Airport about six in the morning. The people-mover took the passengers to the Saarinen-designed terminal. In the men's room, I washed my face, brushed my teeth and shaved. I am sure I looked a mess. Then I took the shuttle bus to downtown Washington, 12th and K Streets. I got a taxicab to the temporary home of Sanford Kadish, a Berkeley criminal law professor who was on leave in Washington working on some project or other. We ate breakfast and waited until it was time to go to the Supreme Court for the 9 a.m. appointment with Justice Brennan. I am not sure, looking back, why Kadish went along. I don't think I asked him to. Maybe Professor O'Neill thought it was a good idea.

This was my first visit to the Supreme Court. Chief Justice William Howard Taft had a major role in designing it. I walked up the broad front steps and under the lintel that said "Equal Justice Under Law." Inside, the building was quiet. Kadish and I were taken back to Justice Brennan's chambers.

Mary Fowler, the Justice's secretary for many years, greeted us at Brennan's outer office. Brennan's first wife, Marjorie, died in 1982, after a long battle with cancer. Justice Brennan and Mary Fowler were married in 1983 and the joy she brought to him added years to his life.

As we waited, Ms. Fowler was handling telephone calls. Attorney General Ramsey Clark was on the line for the Justice. Ms. Fowler put the call through. In a few minutes, Justice Brennan came out and greeted us. That greeting, looking into your eyes as he shook your hand, was not only a trademark—it was emblematic. It seemed to symbolize his power on the Court—the Justice who strove relentlessly to put together five-Justice majorities to advance a humane and decent vision of the law. I had read many Brennan opinions. Professor Hans Linde, visiting at Berkeley Law from Oregon, had sat in my Law Review office during the 1965–66 school year conducting a one-person seminar on Justice Brennan's work.

Memory may serve me ill, but I believe on that morning we also ran into someone who was just finishing up clerking for Chief Justice Warren. This man was to become a Berkeley Law professor, and he arrogantly criticized Brennan's search for majorities as dishonorable, as though constitutional judging can take place without a context. Of course, English judges to this day deliver their opinions individually, one by one, and then one counts the votes for a result. The U.S. Supreme Court started out working that way, but when John Marshall became Chief Justice in 1801, he began the practice of having an opinion "of the Court" authored by a Justice in the majority. This device was one mechanism by which Marshall imposed his own personality on the Court, but it also favored the development of consistent and coherent constitutional doctrine. In any case, I was privately contemptuous of this fellow's arrogance—he was a little young to be putting on those airs.

Brennan asked us into his private office. He sat behind his big desk and began to show me letters he had received, and communications about the congressional responses to news of my clerkship. One envelope was addressed in a spidery scrawl to Justice Brennan, The Supreme Court, Washington, D.C. Inside was a greeting card like you can buy at the drugstore, with an embossed lacy pattern and the words "To Hope You'll Soon Be Well." Inside the card, the same spidery penmanship proclaimed, "You must be sick, you senile fool. You coddle the criminals and let the Reds take over America." I thought Brennan's bemusement at the card, and even his showing it to me, boded well for our interview.

Then things got serious. He reviewed the press stories and the rumblings in Congress. He reminded me that ever since the school desegregation decision, reactionaries in Congress pushed legislation every year to strip away the Court's power in civil rights cases. Such legislation would be of doubtful constitutionality, and perhaps that had helped to ensure that these efforts never succeeded. But the threat had been and remained real.

Then, the Justice turned to the alleged "facts." He went briefly over some of the public reports of my political activities. He then asked, "Weren't you at a Communist Party training camp in Paterson, New Jersey?" The question startled me. It startled Professor Kadish, who was sitting beside me. Why did I think that I felt Kadish easing his chair away from mine, like the lawyer who begins to see his client in a new way?

I peered across the desk at the Justice. I tried to organize the thoughts that tumbled around in my head. "First," I said, "I have never been in Paterson, New Jersey, and I have never been to a Communist Party training camp at any time or any place." Then, thinking that the call from Ramsey Clark might have had to do with me, I added, "This sounds like some of that FBI gossip that the Court addressed in the loyalty-security cases, such as *Greene v. McElroy,* and your dissent in the *Cafeteria Workers* case. Second, your question raises a serious issue for me. I have regarded my political views and associations as my private business, and I applauded the Court's decisions that agreed with this view. You probably know that when I was a first-year law student I led a campaign to take the unconstitutional loyalty oath off the California Bar student application."

I paused, trying to see where this was going. "I don't mean any disrespect," I went on, "but I really admired what you did in your own Senate confirmation hearing, refusing to answer Senator McCarthy's questions." I had gone too far. Kadish looked apoplectic. The Justice looked nettled, and he said, "It is important for you to remember that I am the Justice and you are the clerk."

"Well, sir," I began, "I think that the relationship of clerk and Justice is as confidential as could be imagined. If you lack confidence in me for any reason, you shouldn't hire me. I am willing to answer all of *your* questions, on any subject. I am just unwilling to make, or to allow anyone else to make, a public exhibition of my private views." I struggled to be calm, in visible control of all that was going on inside me. I needed to grab hold of my own moral compass, to forget how badly I wanted this job and how much losing it would mean to me and my career. And I needed to be very clear about what I was doing and why.

That seemed to mollify the Justice, but not Kadish, who was looking more uncomfortable. "All right," the Justice said, "I want you to write out your complete political history—everything you have done, every organization you have joined. I want you to call me Sunday morning—two days from now—and read it to me. Then, I'll decide what to do." He gave me a copy of AO Form 79, which all Court employees were to fill out. This included an oath to support the Constitution and other affirmations that I read and found consistent with the constitutional law principles I had been taught.

The interview was over. Kadish and I walked outside. He grumbled that I had not shown the Justice proper respect. I was hardly listening. I had work to do. I got to a phone and called Professor O'Neill. He told me to fly to San Francisco and come to the home of Professor Mike Heyman, another law faculty member.

Heyman had been a good friend; he would later serve as chancellor of the

University of California at Berkeley and then secretary of the Smithsonian Institution. I flew to San Francisco. I was worn out, and I slept. Saturday morning, at Heyman's house, Professors Cole and O'Neill joined us. They began to echo some of Kadish's concerns that I had been less than respectful toward the Justice. I had a duty, they said, to the law school to make this thing work.

Of course I wanted the clerkship. It is as big an honor as a law student can get. Sure, there were several thousand other law students who could serve equally well—this clerkship business is a little like winning the lottery. My ego didn't let me dwell too long on this thought. But I was worried. I had told so many people I had the clerkship. I had rented a house in Washington. Our stuff was in boxes, ready to go into our VW bus. I felt pressured. I called Al Bendich and asked him to join us. When he walked into the living room of the Heymans' Berkeley Hills home, he radiated energy. Al listened to my story of events. He made a right fist and slammed into his left hand. "Well," he said, "let's get to first principles. We can't compromise the First Amendment right of private political belief. Right?" Cole, O'Neill, and Heyman looked blank. Bendich continued: "Nothing in this situation asks Mike to change his beliefs, nor should it. Can't we agree on that?"

The others seemed to agree, or more precisely acquiesce, drawn along by Al's infectious energy. I sat down at the typewriter and banged out a long letter, giving the information the Justice requested. At the end, I wrote that this was for his eyes only. I would, if asked by any public body—such as a congressional committee—for a political autobiography, decline on First Amendment grounds to provide it. I called Pam, told her what was going on, and read the letter to her.

Bendich and the professors read the letter. I did not sleep well that Saturday night. Justice Brennan had given me his home number in Washington. I waited until it was 11 a.m. there and called. Slowly, in cadences learned from my years as a radio announcer, I read the letter. "That's it, sir," I concluded.

There was a silence. It seemed longer than it no doubt was. Then Brennan's voice, chipper and strong, "You're my clerk!" "Thank you, sir," I said, and hung up the phone. I don't remember if I wept then with relief, or later, alone.

Back at my in-laws' house in Sherman Oaks, we packed up our VW bus for the trip to Washington. We had bought the bus in September 1965, when our daughter Katie was born and our old Mercury died. It was as basic as you could get—the Kombi model, without insulation or floor mats—a metal box. I bought carpet and made a floor liner. I installed an insulated headliner. Inside went Jon, who was three and a half, and Katie, who was nine months old, and

most of our possessions. We sent some boxes—files on legal research topics—
on to the Supreme Court in Washington, to be held for my arrival.

Heading east, I remember stopping at public campgrounds every night,
until we reached Lawrence, Kansas. Former neighbors from Berkeley were
living there while studying physics at the University of Kansas. Phone messages awaited us. Justice Brennan's office had called. He was in California
visiting friends but would return to Washington within days. Hurry up and
get to Washington. Something has come up.

We had planned to take more time on the trip, so that we would arrive in
Washington just as our lease began on the house we had rented. But we hurried, arriving with about $10 in our pockets and one credit card—a Wilshire
Oil Company card that would be accepted at Holiday Inn and Gulf Oil stations. We checked into the Holiday Inn on North Capitol Street. That first
morning at breakfast, a woman was mugged in the parking lot and staggered
into the dining room, blood streaming from cuts on her forehead.

I went to the Court. Justice Brennan was grave. "I have been thinking this
over. I want your permission to give out your personal political history to
anybody I choose. That will be a condition of your employment. Take a day
or so to think about this." I didn't know quite what to say or do. Some of the
1965-term clerks were anxious to help. Jerry Falk, Justice Douglas's clerk,
told me that he had called Douglas, who was in Goose Prairie, in the state of
Washington, where he spent the summers, and told him what was happening.
Douglas told Jerry that he could use the Douglas chambers as a meeting place
on this issue, for me and for other clerks in the building. "I heard about this,"
Douglas said. "People sent me letters about it. Obviously cranks. I ignored
them."

From the other clerks, I learned of the pressures under which Brennan
was operating. Yes, Warren was concerned because of California politics.
But the main pressure seemed to come from the FBI, encouraged by Justice
Fortas, who maintained close ties to the Johnson White House while he was
on the Court. The FBI reports were overblown, largely inaccurate, the results
of the bureau's efforts to discredit the American left. I was a small player in
this drama, but the FBI was busy creating files on many civil rights leaders
and antiwar activists.

The next morning, at about ten, I answered the phone in our motel room.
"One moment, please, Justice Brennan calling." I assumed it was Mary Fowler,
putting the call through. "Mike, this is Justice Brennan. I have been thinking
this thing over. I am sorry, but no matter what you decide about your statement, we can't go through with this. I am withdrawing the clerkship."

"Yes, sir. Thank you for calling." I hung up the phone. OK, there it was.

One off-brand credit card, ten bucks, a VW bus not yet paid for. Married, two kids. A lease on a house, with the rent soon due. I could borrow some from my parents and my in-laws, but the immediate future did not look too good.

Looking back, I believe Brennan feared that if he expended political capital to keep me as his clerk, he might be less able to forge majorities for cases before the Court. He had authored the Court's most powerful decisions defending the civil rights movement and its leaders. Yet his biographers relate that from his first months on the Court, he was sensitive to his colleagues' opinions about him. Decades later, talking to his biographers, Brennan continued to defend his decision. He recalled the political attacks on the Court's civil rights and civil liberties decisions. He said that he feared a congressional investigation, at which he and I would be subpoenaed to testify. He said he did not want to put me through such a thing, as though that was his choice to make. I continue to believe that judges and Justices with life tenure guaranteed by Article Three of the Constitution should be of sterner stuff. A rational voice reminded me that some of the Court's recent decisions had accepted too easily the arguments about national security and alleged subversion.

At another level of analysis, lessons from the Brennan episode helped me to write the brief and to argue David Gutknecht's draft case. The voices speaking of national security and raising an army were strong enough that we were not going to win that case by a direct attack on the war. As an advocate, I upheld and supported David's principled position. At the same time, the brief and argument offered a narrower—nonetheless principled—ground of decision.

I spent the next two weeks looking for work. My friend John Griffiths, who was clerking for Justice Fortas, arranged interviews at Yale Law School. Dean Lou Pollak offered me a one-year teaching contract. I had in mind that I would one day be a law teacher, but felt that without some experience representing people I would not have much to teach. As word trickled out, I got letters from law firms in California, renewing job offers that I had declined because of the clerkship.

Our friend Dick Prosten, whom I had met in connection with the Youth Festival, offered us a place to stay. Dick worked at the AFL-CIO headquarters in downtown Washington, and had a two-bedroom apartment on Vermont Avenue. He and his wife opened their doors to the four of us for the ten days until our house was ready. For this loving support, I have never properly thanked them. Professor Kadish called. He wanted to help me find work, so he arranged an interview at Shea & Gardner, then, as now, a top law firm in Washington. I decided instead to seek a job with Edward Bennett Williams (the story is in chapter 4).

Within a few days, the story of my clerkship hit the front page of the *Washington Post*. I had decided that I would not speak to the press about any of these events. But Jack MacKenzie, the *Post*'s Supreme Court reporter, happened upon the story. He was in the Supreme Court cafeteria and saw Abe Sofaer, a recent law school graduate. Sofaer said he would be clerking for Justice Brennan. MacKenzie asked what happened to Sofaer's clerkship with Judge J. Skelly Wright of the U.S. Court of Appeals for the District of Columbia. "Well, Brennan had a sudden vacancy so he asked Wright if I could work for him," Sofaer reported. MacKenzie went around the building and put the story together. The *Post* article led to several phone calls. One morning, I answered the phone and a voice said, "Michael Tigar, this is Ralph Nader."

"Sure," I said, "and how is your Chevy Corvair? [A reference to Nader's auto safety book *Unsafe At Any Speed*.] Really, who is this?"

"I *am* Ralph Nader. I want to say I think you have been treated shabbily. And I want to meet you." I agreed to meet this person the next morning at the Dupont Plaza hotel for coffee. He was late, and I began to think that I had been hoodwinked. But Nader eventually arrived, and we talked about politics and Washington and my admiration for his work.

The Brennan affair was not really closed. Andrew Kopkind wrote a *New Republic* article about it. When Bob Woodward and Scott Armstrong were writing their book on the Court, they came to see me. My FBI file, which I got in much-edited form under the Freedom of Information Act, contains several snide and self-congratulatory passages about my losing the clerkship. From a FOIA request to military intelligence, I got a report that was not declassified until 1978. It reported on my pending appointment, in 1969, to the UCLA law faculty, and looked back at the Brennan episode.

The intelligence report, from the Sixth Army HQ, was titled, "Oliver!":

> Oliver Twist won the awed admiration of his fellow orphans when he had the supreme audacity to take his empty porridge bowl back to ask for more. Oliver, apparently, has his counterpart among our young radicals. In 1966, Michael TIGAR was a candidate for the post of law clerk to U.S. Supreme Court Justice William J. Brennan, Jr. The appointment fell through when Brennan was apprised of TIGAR's left-wing background.

The report then cites an earlier dispatch, which I never received, titled, "Tigar in the Courts—Almost" and dated July 1966. The 1969 report concluded:

> TIGAR may still be as radical as he ever was, but even if his political position has changed, he may find that his widely publicized left-wing

activities as a young man will plague him far into the future. This is a bitter lesson many of today's young radicals may have to learn.

During this time, friends and acquaintances, and people I did not even know, wrote to me. I rejected calls to make some sort of public stink about it. I had a new job and was moving into work I wanted to do. I wrote a letter on July 28, 1966, and sent copies to everyone who had written or called. First, I wrote, please don't mount a campaign. I did not want my political views to become an issue. "I would like to retain my personal satisfaction at having kept the political faith in the sense of not having disclosures" of my political views and associations.

Second, I said, "Justice Brennan is not an evil man." After all, he had in his own career stood up to personal and political attacks, and had championed great constitutional causes. The episode was more about the political climate than about Justice Brennan. "The oaths, disclosures under pressure, security apparatus, and suspicion and hatred of the McCarthy heyday are still with us. The lesson of this affair is that we must be cognizant of forces great men find they must bow to, and not that we must think men small who bow to these forces." Finally, I said that I continued to feel an obligation to the Justice: "He has not, by word or deed, intimated that my conduct is other than honorable."

I did not want to become a source of public attention, as a kind of symbol of injustice. There were plenty of those. I wanted to resume the path I had chosen—to be a part of the struggle against injustice and not simply an object lesson. I thought about Clint Jencks. After his trial, appeals, and eventual vindication in the courts, he could have gone on the speaking circuit. He chose instead to move forward and to rejoin the larger struggle for social change.

The next year, after I had begun law practice, I received a letter from Justice Douglas, inviting me to submit a résumé for consideration as Douglas's law clerk. I called his secretary, Nan Aull, whom I had met during the Brennan episode. She told me that Justice Douglas wanted to make things right for me. I thought deeply about this, and talked it over with Ed Williams. I decided that my legal career was well underway, and that I did not want to relive any of what had happened.

Nine years later, in 1976, the Court decided a very bad First Amendment case, *Greer v. Spock*, restricting freedom of expression in and near military bases. Justice Brennan dissented. I had already argued and won three cases before the Court. But Brennan's dissent had an edge of disappointment to it. I felt that I should not write to Brennan about my feelings because I had a case at the Court that term. Maybe I hesitated because I did not know what to expect in reply. On July 7, 1977, however, I summoned my courage and wrote

him a letter. I said I thought his opinions were compelling and wondered if
he was discouraged by the conservative turn the Court had taken. I was surprised to get a two-page handwritten reply two weeks later:

Dear Mike,

Your most generous note of July 7 has just reached me here at Nantucket.
I'm deeply touched that you wrote me—far more than I can say. I confess
to periods of discouragement at times but they quickly pass—particularly when views of those I respect express their support. When the next
Term is underway, won't you telephone me and come in for lunch in
Chambers. I've followed your progress with keen interest and would like
to hear much more.

   With warmest personal regards & again my grateful thanks.

                                                   Sincerely,

                                                   —Wm. J. Brennan, Jr.

I took him up on the invitation and visited in early 1978. Sam Buffone and
I had opened our own law firm, Tigar & Buffone. We had an opening party
at the Washington Palm restaurant. Ed Williams showed up and wished us
well, as did Michael Rodak, Clerk of the Supreme Court. We had taken on
the highly publicized case of David Truong, a young Vietnamese accused of
espionage on behalf the Socialist Republic of Vietnam. The case was pending
in federal court in Alexandria, Virginia. During our meeting—lunch in his
chambers at the Court—Brennan commented that the case seemed headed
for the Supreme Court.

In *Truong*, the government had disclosed warrantless electronic surveillance, but had claimed that in a foreign national security case, no warrant
was required. This was to be a central issue. We had subpoenaed Attorney
General Griffin Bell—who was appointed by President Jimmy Carter—to testify about how, why, and when he had approved the surveillance. Brennan
recalled that Bell, an Atlanta lawyer, had been a judge on the United States
Court of Appeals from 1961 until 1976, when he resigned to work on the
Carter presidential campaign.

In 1966, then-Judge Bell had co-authored an opinion upholding the
Georgia House of Representatives decision to deny civil rights leader Julian
Bond the seat to which he had been elected. The basis for excluding Bond
was his opposition to the Vietnam War and the military draft. The Supreme
Court had unanimously reversed the lower court. Brennan remarked on Bell's
appearance in our case, recalling the *Bond* decision.

"I remember Bell's decision in *Bond*," Brennan said with a grin. "I thought

Hugo Black was going to come out of his tree." Justice Black, from Alabama, was the Court's First Amendment champion.

As we sat in Brennan's chambers, ate lunch, and talked, Brennan was affable and outgoing, seeking news of my doings and commenting on some of the certiorari petitions pending before the Court. Speaking of *Gelbard v. United States*, which I had argued in 1972, he joked, "You don't know what trouble I had getting five votes in that case. I thought Byron [White] would never see it."

Cordial as it was, the conversation seemed a little artificial, for we did not broach the subject of the clerkship. I saw the Justice again in the mid-1980s at a judicial conference. We also met for lunch in his chambers several times in the 1980s. Our lunch consisted of sandwiches sent up from the Supreme Court cafeteria in the basement. We would talk over issues before the Court, and he would inquire about what I was doing and about my family. We exchanged a few letters.

At one of those visits, I took a mild initiative. I asked him for an autographed picture of himself. He discovered there were no photos in chambers, so he sent one a few days later. The letter with it read:

February 2, 1989
Dear Mike:
I'm much flattered that you should want the enclosed. It goes with my best wishes for your continued magnificent success. Please drop in again very soon, even at the cost of that delightful cuisine.
All the best.

Sincerely,
—WJB, Jr.

The photo was inscribed "To Michael Tigar, whose tireless striving for justice stretches his arms toward perfection." The "cuisine" was the soup and sandwiches served in chambers by the Supreme Court cafeteria.

I finally decided on a somewhat more direct approach. I knew that Brennan had selected Steven Wermeil to write his biography, and had given Steve unprecedented access to his papers, as well as spending many hours in conversation with him. Steve, at the Justice's suggestion, contacted me to ask what I remembered. I gathered that the 1966 episode was still in Brennan's mind, an impression I had first gained several years before as people told me of things he had said.

In the fall of 1990, after Brennan had retired from the Court, I wrote a letter to him. I said simply that my respect for him and his work had grown throughout the years, and I admired his contribution to the cause of human dignity and freedom. I hoped that nothing I had done or said during that 1966 period had seemed to him improper. He wrote back:

> November 19, 1990
> Dear Mike:
> That morning in June 1966 is a date I shall never forget. I've often wondered whether I overreacted. I must say in all candor that, given the circumstances, I probably did. It's been you who have made it possible for me to justify myself. I hope we shall always remain the friends we have become.
> All the best.
>
> > Sincerely,
> > —Bill

I saw him again shortly before he died, at a conference on the death penalty. Clear of vision and speech though in a wheelchair, he was passionate for justice to the end.

His widow, Mary, invited me to the small memorial service held at the Supreme Court some months after Brennan died. After some of Brennan's (actual) clerks gave short talks, we went into the Court's reception room, where other Justices' law clerks and court personnel joined us for coffee. Justice Antonin Scalia came up to me and said, "You know he was the most influential Justice of the twentieth century. A lot of guys up here don't want to hear that."

Yes, I thought. And I am talking to one of them.

CHAPTER 4

Washington—Unemployment Compensation

FINDING A JOB, AND A MENTOR

Taking the story back to that 1966 day when Brennan withdrew the clerkship, there I was without a job. I wanted to practice law, to try cases, to do work that made a difference. I was seeing that the Supreme Court set out a sharper understanding of the Bill of Rights—free speech, free press, rights of the accused, the right of privacy. Being a lawyer gave one a ticket to that arena—as participant and not spectator. How could I gain entry and still support my family? I had already missed the deadline for the summer 1966 bar examination—I had thought there would be time for that after my clerkship. So I was not worth quite as much as a lawyer who had taken the bar exam.

In my third law school year, I had written to Edward Bennett Williams, saying that I would be clerking for Justice Brennan and would like to meet him and perhaps interview with his law firm when I was in Washington. I don't think he replied. Williams was a distant but persuasive ideal. He had represented Frank Costello, Senator Joe McCarthy, James Hoffa (in the first trial, when Hoffa was acquitted), Congressman Adam Clayton Powell, and other famous figures. More important, he had written widely and wisely about the lawyer's obligation to represent clients, and the client's right to competent and aggressive representation. He had argued leading constitutional cases before the Supreme Court.

In discussing my job prospects with Professor Kadish one summer day at an outdoor restaurant eating Italian food, I confessed my interest in Williams's law firm. Kadish had made his reputation writing and teaching about criminal law. His answer surprised me, and put a crimp in our relationship for the ensuing years. "You don't want to work for Williams," he said. "He represents criminals. You want to be in a law firm like Shea & Gardner where all the lawyers are law review editors."

I did not mention that Williams had graduated at the top of his class, and had taught criminal law at Georgetown. I simply said that I felt that the Williams firm offered a chance to do what I found most important.

Funny, isn't it, in how many different ways you can define yourself? The definition, and its perspective, can lead to quite different approaches to life. Yes, I had been first in the class and editor-in-chief. But I did not define myself by these things: I strove for them to have a better chance at doing what I really wanted to do. They were a means to achieve a self-definition. The work I did, and what I learned along the way, better equipped me to serve in the way I wanted to. I did not want to be co-opted into a world of law practice that did not represent the values and priorities I had struggled so hard to define.

One of my law professors had been a law clerk at the Williams firm, and he called to set up an appointment for me. The firm was then Williams & Wadden, with nine lawyers on one and a half floors of the old Hill Building, at 17th and I Streets. Williams's secretary, Lillian Keats, showed me into a huge office, where Williams sat behind a desk. He was over six feet tall, with brown hair that hung loosely over one side of his forehead. He had one of the most expressive and mobile faces I have ever seen. He stood and extended his hand. We sat.

"What can I do for you?" he asked.

"Well, sir, I sent you a letter and a résumé last year, and I find myself looking for a job sooner than I thought."

"A letter?" He shouted to his secretary, "Mrs. Keats, did we get a letter from Mr. Tigar?" She found the letter. Williams glanced at it. "What happened?"

I told him the story of my clerkship—winning it and losing it. He looked at me with an expression that I imagined he used on witnesses. "Bill Brennan is one of my best friends. He wouldn't do something like that."

"His telephone number is EXecutive 3-1640. You could call him and ask him what happened."

"Maybe I will." Another pause, while Ed looked out the window—later I would know this as a trademark gesture. "I wasn't thinking of hiring anybody." The interview was not going well, it seemed to me.

"Well then, sir, if you are not hiring then I guess you shouldn't hire anybody. I am not seeking charity. I am not the United Way." A voice inside told me I was getting defensive and a little arrogant. OK, more than a little.

I continued. "I want to work for you. My résumé is there. I think I am qualified. I respect what you do and have for a long time. That's why I'm here."

Williams nodded. "Let me think about it. Does Mrs. Keats have your number? No? Leave it with her on the way out." He came around the desk and we shook hands.

I walked back to the apartment where we were staying, about six blocks. I was talking to Pam about the interview when the telephone rang. "Mr. Tigar, this is Lillian Keats. One moment, please, for Mr. Williams."

"OK. If you want a job, you've got it. Show up next Monday morning at nine o'clock. Mrs. Keats will have an office for you. I don't know what we'll pay you, but I'll call over to Covington & Burling and whatever they pay is probably about right. Is that OK with you?"

"Yes, sir."

"See you Monday."

Before I showed up for my first day of work, John MacKenzie's article, "Law Firm Hires Rejected Clerk," appeared in the *Washington Post*. The story had a photo of me.

An elderly man in Pennsylvania with a legal problem read the story and called Williams over the weekend. When I came in on Monday, I had a case to work on. The matter was an administrative proceeding, and it had come to Williams because the client had read about my hiring and admired Williams for it. I remember taking my family along to the Pennsylvania horse country to do the initial client interviews.

In this first "real" case, I had to learn how trotting horses are bred. When a trotting horse is born, the rules of the sport provide that it becomes one year older on January 1. It is therefore good that the mare foals in early January. It is not good that she foals in December because the colt would have to compete against horses born nearly a year older. Veterinarians want the mare to conceive at a time that will likely produce the foal in January. Horse semen cannot be, or is not (I forget), frozen like bull semen. Artificial insemination of horses requires that a trained person palpate the mare's ovaries to check ovulation. This is done rectally, wearing a long latex gauntlet. If the mare is ready, then stallion semen, which has been collected in a large condom by making the stallion sexually excited, is inserted into the mare's female orifice. And so on; these are the details as I recall them. In any event, the U.S. Trotting Association had accused this man of having falsely represented that foals were born in December rather than January.

I returned from visiting the horse farm. Mrs. Keats had furnished my office and hired a secretary from the local Catholic secretarial school. I dictated my notes. My secretary sat at her desk with earphones on, becoming more and more agitated as she listened to my description of the marvels of horse conception. About halfway through the tape, she rose from her desk, collected her belongings, and went upstairs to Mrs. Keats's office to resign. I never knew if it was horse sex or the idea of condoms that horrified her.

Ed Williams became my mentor and friend, for all the rest of his life. We developed a special bond, and he appreciated the quirky way in which I sometimes looked at legal issues. Lois Romano of the *Washington Post* reported in 1995:

> The late renowned Washington lawyer Edward Bennett Williams, for whom Tigar . . . worked intermittently in the '60s and '70s, used to tell people that he wished he could walk behind his protégé with a basket to catch his discarded ideas.

The other lawyers in that office also shared their time and talent. When I returned from working on the horse case, I found case files and research requests on my desk that took me from arcane evidence points to Fourth Amendment theory, to the basics of criminal law and procedure.

The term "mentor" has taken on many shades of meaning. One of Ed's biographers called some of us who came through the law firm his surrogate sons, and surely he treated a handful of us young male lawyers with all the love and protective instinct of a good father. But the image does not quite capture the relationship, except perhaps in one way. Ed had these special ties to young male lawyers. He did not deal with female lawyers as fully his equals.

When I came to the firm, I was the tenth name on the letterhead. Two of those already there were Judith Coleman Richards, later to marry Bob Hope's son Tony, and Barbara Babcock. I spent a lot of time with Judy and Barbara. They shared their knowledge of law and of Ed's way of practice.

Not too long after I arrived, Barbara left to join and then lead the Public Defender Service. Through her work as a trial lawyer, her example of leadership, and her writing, she exercised great influence on generations of lawyers. She was the first woman to be appointed to the regular Stanford Law faculty, She passed away in 2020 at the age of eight-one. Judy moved to Los Angeles when she married. Ed could not see either of these good lawyers in the same way he viewed the males. They were not part of the same inner circle. Ed's own idea of our relationship is captured in a series of pictures and letters. On my wall are two reproductions of courtroom sketches—one of the Bobby Baker trial in 1967, and the other from the John Connally trial of 1975. Ed inscribed the first one "The Baptism of Michael E. Tigar, from his Godfather Edward Bennett Williams," and the second "The Graduation of Michael E. Tigar, from his Godfather Edward Bennett Williams." In the years from 1966 to Ed's death in 1988, I had the occasional note from him, sometimes signed "Goombah," invoking the Italian godfather image.

What was it to be in Ed's circle in that way? First was the law. It was all about living the law's challenges and its stories, for both were important. It is not simply some Irish-Catholic eccentricity that Ed had a story for every case, and for every situation in every case. He was trained in classical rhetoric and knew the importance of story. He had tried case after case as a young lawyer, focusing on the story in every one. He was a raconteur and he hung out with great storytellers like Ben Bradlee of the *Washington Post* and humorist Art Buchwald. The law's challenge was and is to put the story into a mold, the form of which was dictated by legal rules—either rules that now existed or that you would argue must be recognized.

The law was simply a framework within which to see events. The framework included legal rules and principles, but also the courtrooms, judges, and juries that were the places and means by which the law would be applied.

BOBBY BAKER

The case of Bobby Baker was full of stories and challenges. Robert G. Baker had been secretary to Senate Majority Leader Lyndon Johnson during the 1950s and 1960s, when Johnson was among the most powerful men in America. Baker helped Johnson manage the political deals that kept Democrats in the majority and Johnson's legislative program on track. Johnson did not invite Baker to share in his vice presidential duties; nor did Baker join the White House staff when LBJ became president. I have often wondered what mental reservation LBJ had that led him to trust others to help him put his key programs through Congress in those later days.

There was no question, though, that Johnson trusted Baker and that Baker in turn exercised great power, albeit mostly vicariously. So when in 1965 Baker's financial dealings became a major Washington scandal, the Baker story was front-page news for months. An ambitious set of federal prosecutors, whom neither LBJ nor Attorney General Nicholas Katzenbach restrained, pored over Baker's financial records and finally came up with a nine-count indictment.

The principal charges were two: first, that Baker had collected more than $100,000 in political contributions from California savings and loan executives, ostensibly for Democratic Senate candidates, and then kept the money while not paying taxes on it. Second, that Baker had used his political power to solicit monthly retainers from people seeking political favors, but had routed the money through a lawyer named Wayne Bromley and had therefore not properly reported it on his tax returns. Then, there were unrelated charges that for two successive years Baker had underpaid his federal income tax by a few thousand dollars. The variety of charges stretching over years was a central, though ultimately unsuccessful, focus of the defense attack, for it seemed to us that a severance of the case into its constituent parts would have been fairer.

By the time I arrived at the firm, the pretrial motions had been filed. One significant issue was the government's admission that Baker had been the subject of unlawful electronic surveillance. Baker was a friend of a powerful Washington lobbyist named Fred Black, who had a suite at the Sheraton-Carlton hotel near the White House. The FBI rented the adjacent suite and drilled a hole in the baseboard. It put a "spike microphone" through the hole and picked up all the noises in the Black suite. Agents worked shifts and recorded everything, then FBI clerks transcribed the tapes. This intrusion was illegal, done without a judicial warrant. Baker had often used the Fred Black suite, and was overheard and recorded.

Black had been convicted of income tax evasion. He lost on appeal, and petitioned the Supreme Court for certiorari. After certiorari was denied, Solicitor General Thurgood Marshall informed the Court of the illegal surveillance and requested that the conviction be set aside and that the case be sent back to the district court for a hearing on the extent, if any, to which Black's defense was prejudiced by the unlawful surveillance. The government's disclosures in Black's case were followed over the next several years by similar revelations in dozens if not hundreds of cases.

The government had long engaged in unlawful electronic surveillance, but the extent of its use multiplied under the Kennedy administration. Agents of the FBI and the IRS installed dozens, perhaps hundreds of telephone interceptions (wiretaps) and covert microphones (bugs), targeting alleged organized crime figures, alleged tax evaders, and political dissidents, and even some embassies of foreign countries in the United States.

The hearing on the hotel overhearings was my first experience of Ed's courtroom demeanor. The first witness was an FBI clerk who had been assigned to monitor the spike mike. Ed stood near the end of the empty jury box and began to put questions. As he asked each question, he took a small step forward until he was looming over the witness. The prosecutor objected: "Mr. Williams is intimidating the witness." Judge Gasch asked the witness, "Is he too close?" In a surprised and strangled voice that revealed his nervousness, the witness replied, "Well, if he could move back a little..."

Ed stepped backwards a bit at a time with each of his next questions. How did he know what was behind him? I asked myself. He had, in this as in all courtrooms, memorized the space so that his decisions to place himself within it were deliberate but seemingly natural.

The Baker case showed me the value of meticulous research, and gave me an introduction to the world of FBI illegal activity. From that introduction, I have become involved in dozens of cases involving unlawful electronic surveillance, each time returning to those lessons. Indeed, I continued to be involved in the Baker case even after I left the firm in 1969 to teach at UCLA. Ed called me in Los Angeles and asked me to argue Baker's second appeal, which dealt entirely with the fruits of FBI bugging and wiretapping.

The Baker case was only one of many I worked on that involved unlawful electronic surveillance. The Williams firm was at the center of several significant cases dealing with the disclosure and use of such surveillance, and I was involved in all of them. When the government confessed to illegal surveillance, defense counsel first challenged the extent of disclosure, seeking to ensure that the record of government illegality was complete. Then, one had to determine whether any of the government's evidence was the "fruit of the poisonous tree," that is, whether the prosecutors had used any of the unlawful surveillance results as evidence in the case or as the basis for obtaining evidence. As it happened, the leading Supreme Court case on the "fruit of the poisonous tree" doctrine was *Wong Sun v. United States*. Ed Williams had briefed and argued that case, by appointment of the Court.

Williams called me to his office one morning and explained what I was to do about the Baker case. "Counts three through seven of the indictment are in the alternative," he began, telling me what I already knew. "They charge larceny and larceny after trust for the same two sets of funds that Baker got from the savings and loan executives.

"Larceny," he continued, "consists of a trespassory taking and carrying away with the intent permanently to deprive the owner of possession; that is, caption, asportation, and *animus furandi*. Surely they taught you that in law school." I thought of what Professor Collings had tried to teach me in law school, but I nodded. This description of the elements—based on the old common law—was not Ed showing off; it was his methodology for every claim or defense in litigation.

As I learned, it was his style for every element of every case. When we talked about a cross-examination he was outlining, he would rehearse aloud the points at which leading questions were important. He would divide the examination into its parts: "I start by clearing away the underbrush. Short, focused questions to make sure we have the basic facts, such as when he came to Washington, where he stayed, whom he met. Keep the documents in front of the witness. Put a leash on him. Get him under control. Then, in the second part, I can swing a little wider, give him a little room." Or, discussing a Supreme Court argument, he would set out the main points in the order he was to make them by way of introduction, then go on to plot the structure of the argument as a whole.

I was learning that the intellectual discipline I was taught as an undergraduate was valuable as I approached a lawsuit. One had to see the structure of evidence and legal principles, and to decide where the result might be, contingent on what evidence the lawyer was able to marshal, and on the lawyer's ability to present witnesses and evidence in a persuasive way. In a criminal case, this work took place within the structure of the offense that was charged. That offense was defined by a penal code. But, as Ed had reminded me, the statutory definition of an offense could often be traced to its historical origins.

The procedural context of a criminal case was defined by rules concerning pleading and proof. These rules were devised and applied in a context provided by constitutional provisions relating to search and seizure, due process, the right to counsel, the right to be informed of the "nature and cause of the accusation," and so on. Williams put every case into a matrix of analysis that comprehended all of these elements. He was, in short, the most self-aware and disciplined advocate I have ever known. He talked to us with a double purpose. We were expected to contribute ideas and even to challenge his approach, leading to changes and refinements. Ed even remembered to note the ethical limits on what an advocate could do in given circumstances. And we, his acolytes, had the benefit of the best practical legal education that we could possibly have.

This method, which is the best use of the term "mentoring," is too often missing in litigation offices and firms, public and private. Young lawyers have both too much and too little responsibility. They have too little because they are assigned only pieces of cases, such as a motion to write, discovery to draft, a memorandum to prepare for the litigating partner's attention. Young lawyers used in that way do not see the case as a whole, and therefore they may fail to see the relationship between their work and the overall goal.

By the same token, the lawyer doing piecework has too much responsibility, in the sense that memoranda or discovery or motions done without knowing the whole case are likely to be overdone, just to make sure you are not missing anything. The young lawyer wants to make sure it is all in there, and thus overbills the case, even to the point of arguable misconduct. In my observation, much of the excessive discovery and motions practice in litigation is caused by litigation partners permitting young lawyers' work product to pass into the system unedited. Several years ago, working with a major law firm on a case I thought one of the associates did superb paper work but lacked litigation judgment, even though he had been practicing for several years. When I asked the firm's senior partner about this, he indignantly replied, "What do you mean, lacks judgment? Why, he billed 3,000 hours last year!" I replied that this seemed to prove my point.

I sought to see "the law" and "the evidence" in every case in this holistic way. However, I also strove to take the analysis to another level, and to apply what I had learned from studying the work of Sweezy, Mills, Baran, and others. Particularly in criminal cases, but not only there, the law is an instrument of a given system of social relations. The likelihood of any given range of possible results in any particular case is determined by what that system is prepared to tolerate. Williams did not share this radical vision of law and society, but his method of analysis led there if one followed it to its logical end.

The model of work I have described represents a kind of ideal. Successful operation of the model depends on the lawyer having time and resources to research the law and the evidence, on the honesty of prosecutors and police, and the integrity of judges. We have learned in recent years, with revelations of wrongful convictions, how the model may be distorted. We have seen that the right to a defense is undermined by underfunding of overworked public defender systems. And, in the systems of policing and charging, there is pandemic racial bias.

However, the model is not, for these reasons, useless. When lawyers fulfill the obligations of careful research and preparation, they maximize the chances of overcoming in each case, and for each client, the barriers to fairness that the system that calls itself justice puts in their way. In short, as I have written in *Mythologies of State and Monopoly Power*, they are able to bust the mythologies that surround that system. In every case where I have ever been lead counsel, I have followed Ed's example and seen that all the lawyers, paralegals, and investigators on the case meet together so that everybody sees the whole picture.

For the Baker case, I had three main jobs. First, I was to help Peter Taft, who had been with the firm several years, research the law and facts about unlawful electronic surveillance. Second, Ed gave me primary responsibility for running down all available evidence concerning Baker's alleged underreporting of income on Count One of the indictment, income tax evasion. Third, I was to try to corroborate Baker's story about what he did with the money that the California savings and loan executives had given him.

There were other lessons in the case. Brilliant tax lawyer Boris Kostelanetz was Ed's co-counsel. Their styles were so different that I think Ed never again would let anyone share the limelight in that way. At one point in the trial, Boris put his partner, Jules Ritholz, on the stand for half a day to discuss the legal theory that Baker had used on his tax return. Ritholz's testimony was complicated and something less than riveting. The direct examination seemed like a conference in Boris's office rather than an effort to reach a middle-class District of Columbia jury.

Some of the testimony dealt with capital gains versus ordinary income. The next morning, the marshal in charge of the jury, which was sequestered, told us that on leaving court one juror had said to another, "Who is that Captain Gaines they're talking about?" And the other replied, "He's going to testify tomorrow."

THE WILLIAMS FIRM EXPERIENCE

The atmosphere in the Williams office consumed me. We worked a half day on Saturdays, followed by lunch at Duke Zeibert's restaurant if Ed was in town. The corner table in Duke's front dining room, or sometimes a big table in the back, were the gathering places of Williams's salon. He had the most eclectic coterie of drinking and dining friends of any person I ever knew. His ability to swap stories with all of them was one measure of his success with juries. Some weekends, Washington Redskins quarterback Sonny Jurgensen would be at lunch—one of the greatest passers in National Football League history. One Saturday, Jurgensen carried my son Jon, who was then five years old, on his shoulders all the way from the office to Duke's.

He regaled Jon with a story: "Jon, I ate a dozen oysters last night. But only ten of them worked. Do you understand that?" Jon did not.

The Williams table at Duke's attracted journalists, broadcasters, and social commentators. Gamblers that Ed had represented, like Julius Silverman and Joe Nesline, came by to talk. Ben Bradlee of the *Washington Post* sometimes showed up.

The firm had an apartment in New York, at 55th and Lexington Avenue. There, and in the back room of P. J. Clarke's saloon on the corner of 55th and Third Avenue, the New York characters could be found: actor Don Ameche, publisher Billy Hearst. The palpable excitement of those days and nights, coupled with the cases on which I was working, sent adrenaline through my veins. But though all of this work was exactly the introduction and education I had craved, something was missing. This world of Ed's was both mine and not mine. It was mine because of its intellectual challenges. It was mine because Ed Williams was like my father in that he had come from a family without wealth. He was like my father in his energy. The booze and cigarettes were part of an environment that held fascination. It was not mine because this "café society" was a long way from my experiences growing up.

The café society side of Williams's life has transfixed more than one person. His biographer, Evan Thomas, was so taken with researching it that he wrote a foolish book that failed to capture Ed's brilliance as a trial and appellate lawyer. I can remember upbraiding Thomas about this when the book was in galleys, and then finding that I was not alone in this view. By running up big bar bills, Thomas managed to interview people who had dined or drunk with Ed. Thomas's pseudo-biography repeated stories of Ed's penchant for drink, of which we all knew, for we shared it. Thomas deliberately ignored Ed's unparalleled brilliance as an advocate for constitutional principles, even after I and others responded to Thomas's requests for research that he then disregarded.

At that time, in the late 1960s, I worried that the litigation life as Ed lived it carried too many dangers for me. I had little in common with most of these folks-I was meeting. The Vietnam War was heating up, and there were increased draft calls. The poor and Black in Washington were clearly ghettoized and marginalized. Unless I listened to those voices, and tried to put forward their demands for justice, I feared that I would become a well-to-do and skilled, but irrelevant, lawyer.

I am not saying that Ed lacked principle. He had stood for the right to counsel, and had argued the most important Fourth Amendment cases in recent years. He had supported my work on pro bono cases on firm time and with firm resources. But I needed to begin to make my own way. I began to search for cases I could do on my own, outside the office but with Williams's at least tacit blessing. Indeed, that showed another part of his character: Although the work I wound up doing was not what he would have chosen, he supported me all the way.

I thought my work at Williams & Wadden, later Williams & Connolly, was a perfect preparation for doing cases on my own. The criminal cases the firm handled paid well enough so that the young lawyers could research and write every potential motion, and run down every potential argument. When we went out to do our own cases, we carried that idea of preparation with us. I tell this because I have met so many young lawyers who feel trapped and underused in the jobs they find on leaving law school. I am not talking about the lawyers who work in public defender or legal services offices. They get plenty of responsibility as soon as, or more quickly than, they can handle it. But in the medium to large firms, a young lawyer is likely to spend several years doing discovery work and writing motions before ever getting a chance to see how their work plays out in court.

Bottling up young and talented lawyers in the library to handle litigation paper, and never letting them handle cases on their own, is bad for them and bad for the future of the firm. Thirty and more years ago, even the largest law firms had a docket of smaller cases that associates were given to try. That is the way the young Edward Bennett Williams learned trial work. I had this idea in some workable form in 1967 and 1968.

Like every lawyer, I remember my first solo trial. I have yet to meet a lawyer who does not have such a memory. For all of us, the recollection, though perhaps softened by time, still drives us in some important way. For me, my first case was also a response to my sense of injustice. I was choosing how to use my legal skills, rather than accepting a choice made by the law firm.

GOING TO COURT

In our Capitol Hill neighborhood, a young African-American, James Wilson, was arrested for threatening a woman with a knife. The arresting officer, Burns, also African-American, was the one who walked the beat past our house, though I didn't know that until later. Ms. Jacobs, who ran the local community center, called me because Wilson sometimes volunteered there. His court-appointed lawyer had not moved to get him out on bail, and he was in danger of losing his job if he continued to miss work.

I prepared a bail motion and ventured down to the General Sessions court, where all relatively minor criminal cases were tried. Since 1970, there has been a District of Columbia Superior Court, which handles the bulk of District of Columbia civil and criminal litigation. In those days, the really serious cases were all heard in federal district court. The Court of General Sessions was a kind of colonial backwater, a typical urban court staffed mostly by politically connected judges. There were notable exceptions to this rule. Judge Howard, an African-American, tried to care about the cases before him. Judge Tim Murphy wrote scholarly opinions, including one holding that merely calling a police officer a "son of a bitch" was not disorderly conduct. Of course, the police continued to use their discretion to arrest suspicious characters for bad words, but the police reports began to allege that the defendant had called the officer something that would colloquially but accurately describe Oedipus—a word that Judge Murphy had said would merit arrest.

General Sessions was where Ed Williams had started. It was a place to learn the craft of lawyering. Ed used to tell a story about his early days, before there were Xerox machines. He staggered into the courthouse one day with books under each arm to argue a legal motion. An old lawyer, a courthouse habitué, looked at him and drawled: "Get rid of those books, son. Get yourself a witness!" The story may have been apocryphal, but its lesson was not. The old lawyer and dozens like him lined the halls looking for business. Some of them had no offices, and simply printed the courthouse payphone number on their cards.

I wound up in front of Judge McIntyre, lean and dyspeptic. "Why are you here?" he demanded.

"I have filed a bail motion," I said.

"I know that. I mean why are you here when this man has counsel appointed? You think you are better than what the court can provide?"

"I am not saying that," I said, biting back my feeling I was being insulted. I wanted to win this motion. "The local community center has contacted me, and this is a case where bail would really help this young man. He has the kind of community ties that the bail legislation was designed to honor."

"Well," the judge said. "I am not appointing you. If you want to enter an appearance, you can come in as retained counsel." That was fine with me. I would be retained, but would not get a fee. That was the only way to displace the appointed lawyer. Judge McIntyre groused a bit more but granted release on personal recognizance and set a trial date.

I interviewed the young man at some length. He said that he and his girl-friend had been arguing, and that he had indeed said some harsh words. He denied brandishing a knife, but admitted that the knife taken from him by the police officer was his and that he had it in his pocket. He was charged with CDW—carrying a dangerous weapon. The government had to prove that he had used the knife in a threatening manner. The police officer would testify to seeing him wave the knife toward the young woman. The young woman refused to talk to me, probably because the prosecutor or police had told her not to. This was a routine tactic in those days.

Wilson would have to be ready to testify. I spent hours on the case. On trial day, I heeded the advice of other lawyers and got to court early. The assignment system was everything I was told it would be—loud and seemingly disorganized, but underneath this exterior like a cattle or tobacco auction. The courthouse regulars knew the assignment clerks, and their pushing and shouting was designed to get their cases continued, shifted, or directed toward particular courtrooms.

Wilson and I had decided that if we could get before Judge Howard, we should waive a jury. With any other judge, we would not take that risk. So I shoved my way to the front of the pack and shouted my case name and number. "*U.S. v. Wilson*. We'll waive jury trial if Judge Howard has calendar room." This mantra worked, and was my first introduction to the assignment system that prevails in urban criminal courts.

Outside the assignment court, I met the prosecutor who had the Wilson case. He was a young assistant U.S. attorney named Bob Bennett. Years later,

he was President Clinton's counsel. That day, he was an overworked prosecutor who had barely read the file and planned no doubt to use the police
report as his direct examination notes. This was not, for him, a big case. He
would not, however, take a plea for time served and a disposition that would
let Wilson clear his record if he successfully served a probationary sentence.

By this time in our short discussion, he had given me a copy of the police
report—which he was not required by law to do until after the officer and
the alleged victim testified. I sat down and looked at it. Even the Xerox copy
showed me what the officer had done. I wondered if Bennett had caught it.
Officer Burns, whom I now remembered as the young cop in our neighborhood, had initially charged Wilson with PPW—possession of a prohibited
weapon. He had begun to write his police report on this theory. Only then
did he measure the knife blade and find it too short to qualify as prohibited.
So Burns erased PPW and added a sentence or two claiming that he had seen
Wilson brandish the knife— thus making the case CDW.

We waited our turn in Judge Howard's court. The alleged victim could
not be sure that Wilson even had his knife out of his pocket, but she was sure
their argument had been very loud and that harsh words were traded. As often
happens in domestic dispute cases, the alleged victim had by the time of trial
become a reluctant witness.

I cross-examined Officer Burns as I had learned from Ed Williams. Take
him through his booking procedure. Get him to explain how important
that police report could be: it would be the basis on which the case would
be charged and tried. Then confront him with the erasures, the change of
theory. Judge Howard sat back and let all this happen. I moved for judgment
of acquittal at the close of the prosecution's evidence. I was entitled to that, I
thought. But Judge Howard had another lesson to teach me.

Maybe I should have an acquittal. And if I did not get it, maybe I could
take an appeal and hope the court of appeals would see it that way. But there
was no jury here, for we had waived one. And Judge Howard was in charge,
just as were all those judges in their own courtrooms. He administered his
own law, mostly untouched by anything the court of appeals would ever say,
for most of the cases in his court never made it there.

"Mr. Tigar, I am denying your motion. Maybe this girl changed her mind,
and maybe the officer changed things around. But I am not going to grant
your motion. Not right now."

"Yes, Your Honor."

"The way I see it, you have only one witness you can put on if you have to
go forward. You can rest now and keep Wilson off the stand, or you can put
him on. I'm giving you that choice. But I sure would like to hear from him."

We all understand the right not to testify. But I was facing down a judge with an agenda of his own; not sure what that was, I took the risk. Wilson took the stand and denied any threatening conduct. Not guilty, said Judge Howard, even before Bennett had risen to cross-examine.

By this time I had been at the firm more than a year. Baker was convicted in February 1967; I helped to write the motions for a new trial, in arrest of judgment, and for acquittal. The new trial motion was based on the jury foreman's failure to disclose that he was a reserve police officer. As often happened in later years, I had high hopes for this motion and not enough appreciation of the legal system's inertia. This was the first motion I argued in a Williams & Connolly case. As I sat down after arguing, Ed whispered: "Good job. You made chicken salad out of chicken shit."

What had I learned in that year? What would I do with it? This profession presents us with choices, and we can truly reinvent ourselves by tracking different parts of it, and using our training in different ways. Some choices, as I have said, have to do with following the sense of injustice, and wanting to make things right. Other choices have to do with what part of the law we want to explore. I had learned the anatomy of a criminal case, how to take apart its substantive elements and how to analyze procedural issues, from search and seizure to electronic surveillance, to evidence, to criminal pleading, to jury selection, to getting a fair hearing. I had learned to do research and to write motions. I had worked alongside older lawyers in writing appellate briefs.

When Ed agreed to take on the appeals for the African-Americans convicted of killing Malcolm X, he assigned me to write the brief—after I had gone to a Harlem office to pick up the fee. The appeal was probably hopeless to start with, although the legal issues seemed compelling. When Ed argued the case in the Appellate Division in New York, one of the judges interrupted his first sentence and kept hammering him with rude and rather abusive questions. After a few minutes of this, Ed smiled and said, "Judge, we have another hour here together. May I suggest that we think of this time as though we were trapped together in an airport waiting room waiting for a delayed flight, and needed to make the time pass as pleasantly as possible." I have never had the chutzpah to address a judge in that vein, but Ed did get to make the rest of his argument.

I had watched Ed try complex factual motions, and a jury trial. I had seen him argue legal points. I had made arguments myself. I felt more prepared and experienced than I was, but that first trial whetted my appetite to follow my sense of injustice. So I worked on cases involving racism, on wiretap cases, and on antiwar issues. I was publicly and often identified with this or that cause. Some of this publicity caused discomfort at the firm, but Ed supported my work.

Ed displayed his sense of humor even when I went a bit too far in my enthusiasm. During my first stint at the Williams firm, from 1966 to 1969, I became friends with leaders of the local Students for a Democratic Society (SDS) in Washington. They inhabited rented space in a building near Dupont Circle. The realtor wanted to kick them out, disliking their avowed politics and their alleged lack of personal hygiene. He wrote a letter stating that the zoning for the building was limited to nonprofit corporations. I drafted and filed papers establishing the Washington chapter of the SDS as a nonprofit corporation in the District of Columbia. I did not notice that the incorporation papers were on Williams & Connolly paper. Columnist Drew Pearson picked up the story and attacked the firm for giving aid and comfort to radicals. The firm at that point had eight partners. The vote to fire me was 7 to 1, but Ed was the 1. He thought the whole episode funny.

From that representation, I met other SDS figures who were clients and comrades in later years. When in early 1968 I wanted to edit the *Selective Service Law Reporter* (SSLR), Ed insisted that I keep an office at the firm and said he would pay me a reduced amount just to be available to consult on firm cases. The reduced amount, when added to my SSLR salary, put me in a league with my peers in private practice.

As I began to do draft law and represent protesters, there were times that Ed expressed gratitude for my work. Sons of his friends and clients faced draft problems and I could help. Sons and daughters would from time to time be arrested in demonstrations for this or that cause, and Ed would ask me to represent them.

When Columbia University students demonstrated in 1968, part of the worldwide student protests that year, the daughter of one of Ed's good friends was arrested. I was dispatched to the New York Criminal Courts at 100 Centre Street. I had thought that D.C. General Sessions was dreary, but the dirty wood-paneled courtroom of Judge Weiss was a step beyond. There was never any doubt about the outcome of these Columbia cases as far as I was concerned. The police had arrested people without much regard to the elements of any offense such as trespass or disorderly conduct. The sheer number of cases made it unlikely that the DA's office could try everybody if they all insisted on a trial. In those days before smartphone cameras, the police would no doubt be confounded at any trial by failure to remember and write down what each defendant had done.

On arraignment day, the judge began by clearing the docket of nighttime arrests—sex workers, drunks, and the other business of a morning calendar. I sat next to my client and my eye traveled around the room. The American flag was behind the judge's chair and off to one side. In a forlorn attempt to save it from harm, a plastic bag was draped over it. The bag itself had yellowed and was streaked with grime. On the wall behind the judge an incomplete set of metal letters proclaimed: IN GOD WE RUST. Other defendants had their own lawyers, many of whom were from white-shoe law firms. I got my client's case dismissed.

When Martin Luther King was killed, on April 4, 1968, the District of Columbia, like many American cities, witnessed a great deal of violence. I was appointed to represent people charged with uprising-related offenses.

DEPARTURE

I left Washington in June 1969 to become a law teacher at UCLA. My legal experience had given me a perspective from which I could teach, write, and continue to represent clients to the limited extent that the law school permitted. I had been lead lawyer or co-counsel in cases ranging from sit-ins to murder. I had worked on complex civil cases involving civil rights and anti-war protests. I had written a book on draft law and several law review essays. I was preparing for my first Supreme Court argument. My ego had become, as one of my law students wrote on an evaluation form years later, "as big as the Asian continent." I thought that I would go to Los Angeles, teach and write about law, and find some sort of balance in my life. I was mistaken.

CHAPTER 5

Like a Bird on a Wire

EDWARD BENNETT WILLIAMS AND EAVESDROPPING

In his book *One Man's Freedom*, Edward Bennett Williams traced the history of unlawful electronic surveillance. He had argued some of the Supreme Court's leading cases on the constitutional protection against seizing the spoken word. When I came to Washington, in 1966, he was representing several Las Vegas hotel executives for whom he had filed a lawsuit against the FBI for unlawful wiretapping and bugging.

I stepped into the legal challenges to unlawful electronic surveillance, and for the next decades followed the issue in courts, law teaching, and legal writing. From the dictionary:

> Eavesdrop started off literally: first it referred to the water that fell from the eaves of a house, then it came to mean the ground where that water fell. Eventually, eavesdropper described someone who stood within the eavesdrop of a house to overhear a conversation inside.

Initially, telephone conversations were conducted over wires that carried voice communication. A "wiretap" interception required a physical connection to the telephone wire, which could be attached anyplace along the telephone line. Often the government agents would work with the local telephone company to set up the tap. In the Communications Act of 1934, Congress outlawed wiretapping The Supreme Court held that the intercepted communications, and evidence derived from them, could not be used in court.

Another means of gathering voice communication was to place a concealed microphone, the signal from which could be transmitted by wire to a listening post where a government agent was stationed. The listening device became known as a "bug."

In the twenty-first century, these descriptions seem almost quaint. The network of wired and wireless communication allows interception of communications and personal information by electronic means that do not require a physical connection. A smartphone emits a signal that allows internet providers and government surveillance to trace your movements, and gain access to your communications and data. Government agencies collect, evaluate, and use information by means that are ubiquitous and largely shielded from public view. Surveillance from satellites has become routine.

From the day I showed up in Washington, I worked with other lawyers to define the constitutional attack on electronic invasion of privacy, compel the government to disclose these intrusions, and hold the government accountable. For a time, it appeared possible to restrain and redress government intrusion, relying on federal statutes, the extent of the Bill of Rights Fourth Amendment protection of "persons, houses, papers and effects" and requirement of a judicial warrant "particularly describing the place to be searched, and the persons or things to be seized."

Although federal law forbade wiretapping, bugging with the consent of one of the parties was generally thought legitimate under the Fourth Amendment, although the laws of many states prohibited it. Most of the electronic surveillance cases until 1967 were resolved under traditional search and seizure principles dealing with invasions of physical premises and seizures of persons. In that year, the Supreme Court decided *Katz v. United States*, and held that a bug in a telephone booth violated the Fourth Amendment even though the telephone user had no traditional property interest in the booth. The Fourth Amendment, the Court said, "protects people, not places."

Bugging a telephone booth was inefficient unless a particular individual used the booth regularly. Usually, the police or FBI or IRS had to enter someone's home in order to install a bugging device. Until the Crime Control Act of 1968, there was no federal legislation that permitted tapping and bugging, even with a warrant. A tap or bug sweeps much more broadly than a traditional search for tangible objects such as guns or narcotics or even private papers. Thus, a generalized judicial authorization for tapping or bugging would resemble a "general warrant" that did not, as the Constitution requires, particularly describe the things to be seized. The 1968 Act attempted to get around this problem by requiring an exceptional degree of probable cause for issuance of a warrant to bug or tap, or else the consent of one of the parties to the conversation.

The lack of legislative authorization did not trouble several government agencies. The FBI had been doing unlawful electronic surveillance at least since the 1930s. When Robert Kennedy became Attorney General in 1961, he vowed to continue his crusade against Mafia influence on legitimate business. Kennedy and FBI Director J. Edgar Hoover had sharply differed on investigative priorities. Hoover had used the FBI as part of the apparatus that surveilled, infiltrated, harassed and prosecuted progressives. The prosecutions of Clinton Jencks and of Communist Party leaders were part of Hoover's agenda.

Hoover held fast to the view that the civil rights movement, and particularly the activism and direct action led by Martin Luther King and others, were "Communist-led" and "Communist-inspired." Kennedy had come to national attention working with legislators investigating alleged organized crime influence on labor organizations and the Las Vegas gambling industry. He put FBI agents and IRS special agents to work investigating the operation and finances of Las Vegas casinos.

The gambling palaces in Las Vegas operated largely on cash. Gamblers exchanged cash for betting chips. The cash receipts were counted on the casino premises each night. In the counting process, some cash would disappear from the casino records. This was the "skim," and it wound up in the hands of organized crime figures. The motion pictures *Casino*, starring Robert De Niro, and *Bugsy*, starring Warren Beatty, are generally accurate in depicting the organization and financing of Las Vegas casinos in their earlier days.

When Robert Kennedy became Attorney General, the FBI began its program of bugs and taps in Las Vegas. In late 1960 or early 1961, FBI agent Dean Elson met with the president of the local Las Vegas telephone company. The FBI leased 25 telephone lines under the name of a dummy corporation, Henderson Novelty Company. The bills for these lines would be paid in cash.

These leased lines allowed two types of surveillance. In order to install a bug in a hotel suite or office, the telephone company would induce a malfunction on a subscriber's telephone line. FBI agents posing as telephone company employees would show up to "fix" the problem, and would install surveillance devices, the signals from which would be carried over the leased lines to a location where the FBI could record and monitor what the bug overheard. The telephone company also cooperated by helping the FBI install interceptions—wiretaps—at its switching facilities, billing the "service" to Henderson Novelty Company.

In April 1963, Fremont Hotel president Edward Levinson decided to redecorate his office, and in so doing to move his telephone. A telephone company installer named Al Kee, who was up to that point unaware of the FBI deal with his employer, was assigned to do that work. Kee discovered the bug concealed in Levinson's phone, and helped trace the connection to one of the Henderson Novelty Company leased lines. Word of this discovery spread, and soon a number of other listening devices were discovered.

Levinson retained the Williams law firm. In early 1964, Williams filed a multimillion-dollar lawsuit against Elson, other FBI agents, and the telephone company. Ed filed the suit in Nevada state court, invoking a Nevada statute that prohibited interception of conversations without consent. There was at that time no federal cause of action available; the *Bivens* case, which recognized a federal cause of action, was not decided until 1971.

The Las Vegas interceptions, in addition to violating state law, were also clear instances of Fourth Amendment violation, because the agents had actually invaded protected premises to install the devices. Before the Supreme Court's *Katz* decision, this sort of invasion was the touchstone of Fourth Amendment analysis.

In fact, Ed had argued the leading case on this issue, *Silverman v. United States*, which was decided in 1961. Julius Silverman was a gambler. In the case that went to the Supreme Court, the police had installed a "spike mike" through the party wall connecting Silverman's Washington, D.C., row house to the adjoining row house. By this means, the police could listen in and gather plenty of evidence that gambling was going on. Using this evidence, they got a warrant and raided the place. It soon became clear that the warrant was based on the overheard conversations.

The Silverman story was already legend by the time I got to Washington, but I heard it retold during the Saturday lunches at Duke Zeibert's restaurant. Julius Silverman walked with a limp and was therefore known to his buddies as "Cripple Julius," just as another gambler was known as Fifi, though for reasons I never knew, and yet another as "Lefty," which was fairly obvious. The Silverman legend goes like this: Silverman called Ed from jail. Vince Fuller from Ed's office went out to the alleged crime scene and found evidence that the spike mike had made a dent in the heating duct on Silverman's side of the row house party wall: a ¼-inch "trespass" into Silverman's rented premises. Indeed, the duct helped the microphone pick up sounds from all over the house.

A day or so later, at lunch, Ed said, "Julius, you will be convicted in the district court, though you will probably get bail on appeal. The court of appeals will affirm your conviction. But the Supreme Court will hear the case and unanimously reverse the conviction and set you free."

Julius shook his head, "I don't think so. I think this time I am going to prison. Thank god this is a federal rap here in DC so I maybe get to Allenwood or something instead of at Lorton."

At this point, Joe Nesline, who had a record of allegedly running illegal card games in suburban Maryland and even right over a liquor store on Pennsylvania Avenue, chimed in, "Julius, if Eddy says he can do this, he can do it."

"Oh yeah?" said Julius. "How much you want to bet?"

"$10,000," said Joe. "Duke here can hold the money."

"OK," said Julius, and then added, smiling, "but it has to be what Ed said, 'unanimous.'"

Nesline winced at this condition but agreed. Duke held the money. The case dragged on for several years, through the district court and court of appeals. The Supreme Court granted certiorari. Ed argued, brilliantly, as always. Every Monday, Julius would drag himself up the marble stairs of the Supreme Court to hear if the opinion had come down. On Monday, March 6, 1961, the Court decided. Julius hurried out to a pay phone and called Duke Zeibert. "Duke, Duke, I won, I won!"

Duke paused and asked, "Yeah, Julius, but was it unanimous?"

"No, Duke, I am sorry for Joe's money, but it was not. Two of them did something they called 'concurred.'" Because Justices Clark and Whittaker had indeed joined the Court's holding without reservation, legal experts called it unanimous and Julius paid off. Or so the legend had it. As noted above, the Supreme Court's 1967 ruling in *Katz* expanded its Silverman holding.

Back now to the Las Vegas saga: These stories were not simply the stuff of lunchtime conversation. They were part of the fabric of legal education. Ed would always punctuate the discussion with citations to cases, and bits of doctrine. In this, by the way, his biographers never got it right. They captured the bon vivant and raconteur. They mostly missed the legal theorist, mentor, and educator. The day I first heard the Silverman legend, Ed turned it into a discourse on the history of FBI illegal electronic surveillance. Ed saw where this law had been and where it was headed. The Las Vegas litigation foreshadowed the legal arguments on which the challenge to government electronic intrusion would focus for the ensuing decades.

First, one had to find out what the government had done. The discovery of that first Las Vegas bug was happenstance. The civil lawsuit was designed to uncover the origin, nature, extent, and contents of illegal surveillance. Later cases would focus on the government's obligation to disclose surveillance. When the government put the extent and nature of surveillance behind a wall of secrecy, often invoking "national security," the revelations of whistle-blowers such as Edward Snowden and journalist Julian Assange would become important.

Peter Taft and Tom Wadden, the lawyers in the firm who were in charge of the Las Vegas litigation, sought to take the deposition of FBI agent Elson, and to compel him to produce relevant documents. The Attorney General ordered Elson not to comply. The Nevada trial court held that Elson would have to testify. The Nevada Supreme Court affirmed that ruling. The Court held that the Attorney General's invocation of privilege was subject to judicial review, citing the Supreme Court's statement that "judicial control over the evidence in a case cannot be abdicated to the caprice of executive officers." A claim of executive privilege could not shield admitted wrongful conduct from judicial scrutiny. The Court noted that FBI agents had already given interviews to national media about the bugs and taps.

ALDERMAN AND IVANOV

There was a related wiretap-related case in the Williams office when I arrived, and it wound up making law that remains a solid basis for the right to a hearing on government illegality. The United States had prosecuted three Las Vegas and Chicago figures, Ruby Kolod, Willie "Icepick Willie" Alderman, and Felix "Milwaukee Phil" Alderisio. Kolod was an executive at the Fremont Hotel in Las Vegas. Alderman had the reputation of being a hit man who dispatched his victims with an icepick in the ear. Phil Alderisio was in business in Chicago. Kolod believed that he had been swindled by a Denver promoter named Robert Sunshine. He sent Alderman and Alderisio to Denver to explain to Sunshine that he should refund Kolod's money. The explanations, according to Sunshine, included death threats—in person and by telephone.

Sunshine complained to the FBI. Kolod, Alderisio, and Alderman were prosecuted in Denver federal court for using interstate commerce to make extortionate threats. Williams tried the case. Among his theories was that there were not in fact any threats. If there had been, and if Kolod had indeed met with Alderisio and Alderman to discuss plans, at least some of this activity would have been recorded on the FBI-installed bugs. For that reason, Williams argued, the defense needed copies of all the bugged conversations. If there was no incriminating evidence in these, then that fact would be admissible as tending to show no such conversations took place.

So the case stood when I joined the firm in summer 1966. My first research project was on "negative evidence to prove a proposition." There are a number of good cases on that issue. For example, if the witness was at a party all evening and did not see Bill there, this is some evidence that Bill was not there. This is not a surprising idea, and perhaps not very interesting. The witness can be impeached by all manner of cross-examination about how big was the party, in how many rooms, how much alcohol was consumed, and so on. Williams was hoping that the judge would order the wiretaps produced, that the FBI would refuse, and that the case would therefore be dismissed.

This hope was founded on another line of authority that was to prove significant. In criminal cases, the government is required to produce certain of its evidence for the defense to inspect, copy, and use in hearings or at trial. Sometimes the government can avoid this obligation by a valid claim that the evidence is privileged and not relevant or important to the defense.

For example, the government need not always reveal the identity of an informer on whose word a search warrant has been obtained, or a warrantless search conducted. Because of this "informer privilege," the FBI often called illegal wiretaps and bugs by code names such as "Confidential Informant C-1." But this privilege only goes so far. A leading case, on which we were to rely, shows how this works. In the late 1940s, the FBI wiretapped Justice Department employee Judith Coplon and a Soviet agent. These illegal wiretaps allegedly showed Coplon helping the Soviet agent prepare to commit espionage. Coplon's lawyers moved that they be produced, so that they could show the government's case was tainted by this illegal evidence. Coplon was convicted. The court of appeals reversed, in an eloquent opinion by Learned Hand. He held that in order to discharge its burden of coming forward with evidence and proving that there was no taint, all the wiretaps would have to be produced. If the government was unwilling to disclose its illegal taps, then the court would dismiss the prosecution. The *Coplon* case was part of Ed Williams's basic understanding of wiretap law, and he would rely on it again and again. The U.S. Supreme Court had expressly adopted Learned Hand's reasoning.

Williams's legal arguments (and my research on them) did not do well before the trial judge, nor in the U.S. Court of Appeals for the Tenth Circuit. We filed a petition for certiorari in the Supreme Court, under the case title *Kolod v. United States*. While that petition was pending, Peter Taft was talking one night to an FBI agent in connection with the Las Vegas civil case. The agent let slip that in addition to the wiretaps and bugs in Las Vegas, the FBI had a bug in a Chicago store where Alderisio was known to hold meetings.

On October 9, 1967, the Supreme Court denied certiorari. The case was over, unless we could think of something else to do. I drafted a motion to stay the Court's mandate pending filing of a petition for rehearing. Such motions are rare. Rarer still are cases in which the Supreme Court grants a rehearing after denying certiorari. In the motion, I repeated that counsel had good, and new, evidence that Alderisio had been the subject of illegal electronic surveillance that might have tainted his conviction. Citing *Coplon*, I argued that the government had to disclose this surveillance and submit to a hearing on it.

I took the motion to the Supreme Court clerk's office, and met with Deputy Clerk Callinan. He gruffly asked, "Does Williams know you are filing this thing?"

"Yes, sir," I said. "That is his signature."

"I know it's his signature," he said. "I'm asking you if he read the thing before you got him to sign it. We don't grant these."

I assured Mr. Cullinan and he file-stamped the motion. I asked Ed about the experience and he told me that Cullinan was famously belligerent and famously bibulous, to the point of losing exhibits and misinforming lawyers about scheduled arguments.

A few days later, Acting Solicitor General Spritzer answered our motion. He did not deny that there had been illegal electronic surveillance. However, he revealed for the first time that a committee in the Justice Department reviewed all electronic surveillance cases and would make disclosure to the defense only if the committee concluded that the illegal surveillance was "arguably relevant" to the case. This memo put new light on the government's disclosures that had begun a year earlier, when then-Solicitor General Thurgood Marshall initiated a policy of disclosing illegal surveillance in selected cases.

We replied to Spritzer's pleading. We derided the notion that a committee of prosecutors had the knowledge or desire to evaluate whether unlawful surveillance had tainted a prosecution. Our criminal justice system is adversarial. In every comparable situation, judges, not prosecutors, are the arbiters of what is legal and what is not. Whatever privileges government may possess, it cannot foreclose inquiry into its own illegality by the secret deliberations and Delphic pronouncements of its own servants. The Court stayed its mandate pending our filing a petition for rehearing.

Our petition, filed in mid-October, was in the same vein. On December 4, 1967, the Court entered a brief order directing the Solicitor General to file a response to the rehearing petition "within thirty days." Our optimism was fueled.

Newly installed Solicitor General Erwin Griswold filed the response, and we did a brief reply. We had expected at most a briefing schedule, but on January 29, 1968, the Court issued a brief *per curiam* order, granting rehearing, granting certiorari, and directing the government to disclose electronic surveillance so that there could be a hearing on whether the government's case was tainted. If the government had conducted illegal surveillance on a defendant, the issue of its potential effect on the government's case would be heard by a judge.

The Court's order deeply disturbed the Department of Justice. Perhaps the Court did not know just how many bugs and taps the FBI, IRS, and other agencies had installed. The use of these devices was not limited to a few so-called organized crime investigations. Rather, wiretapping and bugging were the norm in national security cases; even before the Nixon administration they were extensively used against all manner of dissidents.

The Justice Department, including the FBI, was sitting on a cache of illegally obtained material, with targets as diverse as Martin Luther King and white antiwar protesters. The short opinion in *Kolod*, read literally, would require wholesale disclosure of that material anytime the federal government prosecuted someone who had been picked up on a tap or bug. This point became clearer to the government as we got the chance to turn up the heat.

In the fall of 1967, while the Kolod case was pending, Ed and I met with Martin Popper, a New York lawyer whose clients included the Soviet Union. He sought counsel for a Soviet citizen, Igor Ivanov, who had been convicted of espionage. Ivanov, a chauffeur for the Soviet trading company Amtorg, was arrested along with two Soviet diplomats at a meeting with an American engineer for ITT, John Butenko. The government's case was that Butenko had been passing secrets to the Soviets. The two diplomats, because of their official immunity, were simply kicked out of the United States. Ivanov had no immunity, so he was prosecuted, convicted, and sentenced. The court of appeals affirmed the conviction. Ed assigned me to write the petition for certiorari, which was due the first week in December 1967.

Because the Kolod case was pending, I put a footnote in the *Ivanov* certiorari petition: "No question is raised concerning illegal electronic surveillance, on the assumption that the Solicitor General will, if there was any, disclose its presence," citing our *Kolod* pleadings. Solicitor General Griswold, in his response, included a footnote citing the government's *Kolod* pleadings and saying that any surveillance not found by the Justice Department committee to be arguably relevant would not be disclosed.

I had hoped for such a response. The odds were against any Supreme Court review of the criminal procedure issues in a case where Soviet spies were caught red-handed (as it were). The electronic surveillance issue had potential.

I invoked a little-used Supreme Court rule, and moved to amend the *Ivanov* certiorari petition to add an additional question presented. This procedure permits a petitioner to add an issue that arises after the certiorari petition is filed, and avoids what would otherwise be an untimely presentation. If the motion is granted, the petition with its amended issue is deemed to have been filed on the original filing date. The additional question read:

Whether, when the Department of Justice has in its possession recordings

of a criminal defendant's voice—or of the voice of a co-defendant—
obtained through electronic surveillance, the Department may refuse
unqualifiedly to disclose the existence and contents of those recordings
unless in its untrammeled discretion, free from judicial control, it determines both that the surveillance "is or may be unlawful" and that "the
government has thereby obtained any information which is arguably relevant to the litigation involved."

The *Kolod* opinion came down. The Solicitor General, assisted by senior
Justice Department lawyers and by the Department's Internal Security
Section, moved to "modify" the *Kolod* order. By this time, Kolod had died, so
the case became *Alderman v. United States.*

In his motion, the Solicitor General obliquely conceded that electronic
surveillance had become a favorite government pastime. He claimed that the
national security would suffer if the government had to disclose surveillance
in espionage and internal security cases. He said that a surveillance of a Mafia
boss might record two underlings plotting against their chief; disclosure to
the chief might endanger lives. He hinted, with little subtlety, that government
agencies might resist disclosure or even be less than candid about what they
had done. This last argument might lead somebody to ask "Who is really in
charge here?" though one might not want to hear the answer. To deal with
these issues, the Solicitor General suggested that disclosure *in camera* to a
district judge was the preferred way to proceed. Adopting this suggestion, we
believed, would merely provide for a secret and uninformed *ex parte* judicial
decision.

The issue was thus rejoined. Whenever government has done wrong, the
temptation is to bury the illegality in the bureaucracy. The fox, who remains
in charge of the hen house, will then assure everybody that all is well. When
that gambit fails, the government's next position is that it should present its
views to a judge, in secret and *ex parte*—without the other side being present or being able to respond—and let the judge decide how to proceed. This
suggestion has an allure of reason, for judges are supposedly "neutral." But
nobody can decide anything fairly without hearing both sides. As Proverbs
has it: "He who answers a matter before he hears it, it is folly and shame to
him." The danger of a one-sided presentation is particularly acute in these
cases, where the opening premise is that the government has deliberately violated the law.

By the spring of 1968, as we were responding to the Solicitor General's
arguments, I had already participated in enough wiretap cases to share the
Williams firm's institutional knowledge. We were representing Fred Black,

whose conversations had been overheard by the same spike mike as those of Bobby Baker. Black's income tax evasion case was on remand to the district to determine the extent to which the evidence against him was tainted by illegality. The prosecutor resisted disclosing the surveillance logs, saying that an informant's life would be in danger. The judge asked to review the logs. He then asked the prosecutor how the conversation could possibly endanger anybody. "Well," the prosecutor backtracked, "disclosure would harm a financial interest, so it is an economic life." Even when honest prosecutors eschewed this kind of sophistry, the FBI would often hide relevant information from its own lawyers. In case after case, I have seen prosecutors double-crossed by FBI agents who fail to make relevant and required disclosures.

On March 18, 1968, the Court set the Motion to Modify for oral argument, in order to air the issues more fully and perhaps to reconsider its *Kolod* ruling. In a later order, the Court also asked the parties to brief and argue the issue of standing to suppress illegally obtained evidence.

On June 17, 1968, we received another piece of good news. In *Ivanov*, the Court granted the motion to amend the petition for certiorari and granted certiorari limited to electronic surveillance issues. Our strategy had paid off, helped by the Solicitor General sweeping *Ivanov*-related concerns into his motion to modify the *Kolod* order. I set to work drafting two Supreme Court briefs—one in *Ivanov*, and the other in *Alderman*. I have included a link to the *Ivanov* brief in the Notes and Sources section of this book. It bears signs of being the work of a lawyer just two years out of law school. All the right cases and citations are there, but the style lacks grace and maturity. I was still, it appears, somewhat in awe of the issues about which I was writing, and the tone is a bit stilted.

On October 14, 1968, Williams presented oral argument in the now consolidated *Alderman* and *Ivanov* cases. I reproduced his argument, in annotated form, in my book *Persuasion: The Litigator's Art*. The excerpt below is an example of Ed's style of argument, from which I learned by sitting beside him in Court and by working with him as he prepared:

> Now, first of all, it is our position, if the Court please, that the Fourth Amendment to the Constitution does not make a division among the various kinds of crime. It does not draw a line of demarcation, and the founding fathers, when the Constitution was written and when the American Bill of Rights was forged, understood quite clearly that there is a difference in the various types of crime.
>
> They gave recognition to this in Article 3, Section 3, of the Constitution when they defined treason, and they prescribed the quantum and quality

of proof necessary for a treason conviction, but they didn't make any exception in the Fourth Amendment with respect to spy catchers or subversive hunters.

It is next our position, if the Court please, if the Attorney General of the United States certifies to the Court that there is a national security consideration which should excuse the United States from making a disclosure with respect to the nature, the time, the place or the fruits of an electronic surveillance illegally conducted, we say he should be excused provided he consents to a dismissal of the prosecution under the time-honored principle of Coplon against the United States. . . .

Now, that case, and I think it is significant to note, has stood unassailed by the government for 18 years until argument was heard in this case last Term. . . . So, if the Court please, it is reduced to essence that the concept of national security should not be the talisman for a *pro tanto* suspension of due process of law or of any of the rights guaranteed to an accused in a criminal case.

If, in the conduct of relationships between governments in our time, it has become the custom or it has become a necessity to engage in wiretapping or eavesdropping or dissembling or purloining or burglarizing or even killing, it is not our argument in this Court today that the Executive Branch should be manacled or impeded or harassed in the conduct of relationships with other governments. It is our argument here today that at least the federal courts should be a sanctuary in the jungle . . . and that the fruits of this kind of conduct should not become evidence in a criminal case brought by the sovereign power against an accused, nor should those derived from these kinds of conduct be available to the prosecutor in a criminal case brought by the sovereign power.

This passage shows Williams acknowledging the government's national security concerns and then casting them aside by saying that the only price the government must pay for illegal surveillance is potential dismissal of a criminal case. Other possible consequences can be addressed in another case. Williams returned to this theme, once again dispelling the government's idea that grave consequences would follow a ruling in our clients' favor:

If we are driven to the unhappy conclusion that the alleged spy goes free, then I think we can draw some consolation from the history of the last three decades; that in the three decades of recorded federal jurisprudence, during which there were three wars, we have only one instance of an averred spy going free in this frame of reference, and she was the

defendant in the case to which I allude, the *Coplon* case, and I think we
can also get a measure of consolation from the fact that of all the crimes
in jurisprudence, the amount of recidivism that takes place in the area of
espionage is by and large defused.

The Court's decision in *Alderman/Ivanov*, handed down March 10,
1969, required that the government disclose electronic surveillance in
any criminal case. A court hearing would then compel the government to
discharge its duty of showing that its evidence was not "the fruit of the poisonous tree." If the government chose not to make the required disclosure, it
would suffer dismissal of the prosecution.

The Court did not reach the issue whether the surveillance that had captured Ivanov's voice, which was directed against Soviet diplomatic personnel,
and was subject to claims of national security, was lawful. That was an issue
for the lower court to address in the first instance. Hearings in the lower court
went on for months. Eventually the United States and the USSR reached an
agreement to repatriate Ivanov to the USSR, so the legality issue was left for
other cases.

WARRANTLESS "NATIONAL SECURITY" WIRETAPPING

The battle against electronic surveillance took a new turn in the summer of
1969. I was one of the counsel for eight defendants charged with organizing
and fomenting violent protests at the 1968 Democratic National Convention
in Chicago. As I recount in chapter 9, the substance of the charges against the
defendants raised serious First Amendment issues. In our pretrial motions,
we invoked the *Alderman* holding, demanding that the government disclose
electronic surveillance. Given the defendants' political views, it was certain
that the FBI had targeted them for electronic intrusion.

My family and I had left Washington in June, and were driving across
the country for my new job as law professor at UCLA. My law school friend
Dennis Roberts was working for the Center for Constitutional Rights, which
was also providing legal representation to the Chicago defendants. He left
messages asking me to call him: the government had filed a fascinating collection of legal and historical materials, seeking to justify warrantless electronic
surveillance of dissidents, including our clients.

I caught up with these materials when we reached California. The Nixon
administration's Department of Justice and FBI had decided to use the case
as a vehicle to obtain a judicial ruling that wholesale electronic surveillance
of dissidents, without a warrant, was lawful. The documents included orders

to conduct wiretapping and bugging, signed by presidents from Franklin Roosevelt to Richard Nixon. The FDR "authorizations" were directed at World War II spies and saboteurs. The later ones tended to focus on alleged domestic subversion, but based on the Cold War mythology that progressive views in the labor, civil rights, and civil liberties movements were fronts for, or under the influence of, Soviet-dominated groups.

These documents reflected the FBI's influence and mindset, which had in turn been adopted by the Nixon Justice Department. Nixon had enlarged its Internal Security Division, which was poised to initiate investigations and prosecutions of progressive individuals and organizations.

Dennis and I analyzed the government's claim that domestic national security concerns could trump the Fourth Amendment. We had the *Ivanov* Supreme Court brief as a good beginning. This case was, however, more compelling than *Ivanov* because there was no rational claim that the targets of surveillance were acting for, or controlled by, a foreign power. And, whatever President Franklin Roosevelt found it necessary to do during a declared war, against alleged agents of a combatant, seemed to us irrelevant in the present day.

More to the point, a secret and long-continued series of executive actions that dispensed with the Fourth Amendment could not logically be pleaded as legal justification. The belated discovery that the executive branch had been violating the Constitution for decades was not a "precedent" that the illegality could continue.

As we had argued in the Supreme Court, the Framers of the Constitution did not contemplate "executive warrants." Our argument was based on the same separation of powers analysis that was in back of our challenge to the Vietnam War. The president is commander-in-chief, but nothing in the Constitution authorizes him to usurp functions that are constitutionally committed to another branch of government.

The Fourth Amendment gives judges, and not executive officers, the power to issue search warrants. Behind the amendment's text lies important history. Two English cases from the late 1700s had held that executive warrants were unlawful. These cases involved political dissidents, so those who drafted the Fourth Amendment had recent experience upon which to draw when they insisted on judicial warrants. There are some exceptions to the warrant requirement, for exigent circumstances and in public places. There are even instances where the Fourth Amendment probable cause standard is relaxed, such as border searches. But nothing in our history justified the sweeping rule for which the government contended.

I came to Chicago to present argument on the issue before Judge Julius Hoffman. Hoffman was elderly, cranky, and irrational. His behavior on argument day foreshadowed what was to come later in the case. For example, in our brief I had argued that the government should not be able to invoke secret and unreviewable decisions about social danger to support its position. I relied on a long common law tradition of adversary argument in open court One champion of this idea was the nineteenth-century philosopher Jeremy Bentham, author of *The Rationale of Judicial Evidence*.

I had hardly begun my argument when Judge Hoffman interrupted. He spoke in a measured tone, enunciating each word in a reedy voice: "Mr. Tigar, apparently you are familiar with Jeremy Bentham. I know who Jeremy Bentham is. But your presence here today has brought many members of the media. They are sitting back there. So why don't you turn around and tell them who Jeremy Bentham is?" I stifled my sense that Hoffman was as unhinged as he eventually proved to be. I said I would rather face forward and argue to the person who had the power to decide. Hoffman ruled against us, as did several other judges to whom the government was making the same arguments.

Our argument finally found a favorable forum in the case of Melvin Carl Smith, an alleged member of the Black Panther Party. As Judge Ferguson wrote in his opinion:

> Melvin Carl Smith was found guilty in this court of . . . possession of a firearm by a person previously convicted of a felony. He was sentenced to two years in prison on each of the two counts, to begin and run consecutively. Defendant appealed his conviction on October 31, 1969. While the appeal was pending, the government disclosed to the Court of Appeals that it had searched its files and discovered that the defendant had participated in conversations which were monitored by electronic surveillance conducted by the federal government to gather intelligence information relating to the national security. In light of this, the circuit court granted the government's motion for a limited remand to this court "for proceedings required by *Alderman v. United States*."

Smith's trial counsel, Jean Kidwell, had asked me to brief and argue the issue. Jean and her husband, Frank Pestana, were progressive lawyers of the old school: principled, resilient, and careful students of the theory and practice of legal ideology. I pulled out the briefs that Dennis Roberts and I had written.

The facts and argument in *Smith* followed the pattern established in the Chicago case. The Department of Justice disclosed that the FBI had picked up Smith on warrantless electronic surveillance, justified by an asserted national security exception to the Fourth Amendment warrant and probable cause requirements. It also pointed to a section of the 1968 Crime Control Act that says "Nothing contained in this chapter" or in the Communications Act should be considered to deny the Presidential power to protect the country from attack by obtaining "foreign intelligence information," nor "deemed to limit the constitutional power of the President to take such measures as he deems necessary to protect the United States against the overthrow of the Government."

This time, however, the case was before Warren Ferguson, a principled and studious judge. Ferguson had been a state court judge in Orange County, California, when President Kennedy nominated him to a federal judgeship. In later years, he and his wife and daughters became good friends.

Ferguson's opinion in *United States v. Melvin Carl Smith*, on January 8, 1971, was the first judicial ruling that warrantless national security electronic surveillance violated the Fourth Amendment. Judge Damon Keith in Detroit made the same holding two weeks later, relying on Ferguson's reasoning, and his decision was affirmed by the Supreme Court. Ferguson held that the government must disclose the contents and details of its surveillance, and submit to a hearing on taint, or else suffer dismissal of its case.

Ferguson began by discussing a provision in the 1968 Crime Control Act, the legislation that regulated electronic surveillance and contained the statute under which the Chicago defendants were prosecuted. The Act renewed the law that wiretapping without a warrant was unlawful, but also said:

> Nor shall anything contained in this chapter be deemed to limit the constitutional power of the President to take such measures as he deems necessary to protect the United States against the overthrow of the Government by force or other unlawful means, or against any other clear and present danger to the structure or existence of the Government. The contents of any wire or oral communication intercepted by authority of the President in the exercise of the foregoing powers may be received in evidence in any trial hearing, or other proceeding only where such interception was reasonable, and shall not be otherwise used or disclosed except as is necessary to implement that power.

This statutory language was an effort to legalize the electronic intrusions against progressive individuals and groups that had been going on for decades, in addition to authorizing executive power going forward. Note that this was 1968, the Johnson administration. The Nixon Justice Department had simply taken the baton and was running with it.

Judge Ferguson held that neither this nor any other congressional statute could authorize the president to violate the Constitution. His analysis
was the same as that presented by Ed Williams in *Alderman/Ivanov*: the
Fourth Amendment does not contain an exception for "subversive hunters." Ferguson noted the relationship between First Amendment–protected
expression and the right to be free from unlawful surveillance. Whatever
power the president might have to deal with a foreign threat, the use of
warrantless surveillance against domestic dissidents was forbidden by the
Constitution.

Judge Ferguson ordered that the government disclose the contents of its
electronic surveillance of Mr. Smith, or suffer a dismissal of the case. I contended that the government should be given one week to make its decision. As
the law then stood, a dismissal might not have been an appealable order and
Smith would be released. However, Ferguson wanted to give the government
an opportunity to seek appellate review.

The government took the *Smith* decision to the Ninth Circuit court of
appeals, and Judge Keith's order to the Sixth Circuit court of appeals by
way of writs of mandamus. A "mandamus" is technically directed to the
district judge whose rulings are being challenged, and at that time courts of
appeals were quite liberal in encouraging the district judge to be heard. Judge
Ferguson asked Warren Christopher to represent him in the court of appeals,
thus setting the stage for a three-part oral argument featuring Christopher, me,
and Assistant Attorney General for Internal Security Robert Mardian (who
was later prosecuted for his role in the Watergate scandal).

The Nixon administration had greatly increased funding for so-called
internal security matters, in the Department of Justice and in the FBI. It had
set up the internal security function under a separate Assistant Attorney
General, rather than keeping it within the Criminal Division. This independence meant in practice that the Nixon White House agenda of unlawful
surveillance of political enemies went on unchecked. In later years, when
Nixon resigned and Gerald Ford installed a new Attorney General, FBI agents
who had participated in illegal break-ins were prosecuted.

Mardian's oral argument in the Ninth Circuit was surreal. He apparently dwelt in a world where everyone shared his paranoid vision of enemies
hiding everywhere, and his view was that only a secret and unaccountable
government establishment could protect us. He began by holding up a sealed
cardboard box and telling the judges that it contained national security information that would show why these taps were necessary. Judge Browning,
presiding, asked, "What are we supposed to do with that?"

"You should receive it and read it, and you will see," Mardian replied.

"Mr. Mardian," Judge Browning said patiently, "is that material part of the record of proceedings in the district court?"

"Oh, no, Your Honor, it is for this court's eyes only."

"Mr. Mardian," Judge Browning continued, "as an appellate court, we review the record below. We are not in the habit of receiving ex parte communications that the other side has not seen, and that even the district judge did not have before him. We will not receive your box."

Mardian continued his argument, mostly reading it from a prepared script. Judge Shirley Hufstedler asked him a question. He looked at her impatiently and said, "Ma'am, I'll be getting to that later on."

All of us at counsel tables, and the judges, visibly caught our breath. Judge Browning, affable but with a steely edge to his voice, said, "Mr. Mardian, you will answer *Judge* Hufstedler's question, and you will do it now."

I had been gratified that Judge Ferguson was not hypnotized by the invocation of national security and that the court of appeals did not seem to be. I am sometimes reminded of Lord Coke's dictum, "God send me never to live under the law of conveniency or discretion. For if the soldier and the justice sit on the same bench, the trumpet will not let the crier speak in Westminster Hall."

The court of appeals for the Sixth Circuit upheld Judge Keith's decision on April 8, 1971. The Ninth Circuit waited to see what would happen. On June 19, 1972, the Supreme Court affirmed. The Ninth Circuit had only to follow suit. The government would not disclose how it had invaded Melvin Carl Smith's privacy, and so the case was dismissed. In the wake of these decisions, dozens of cases against dissidents were dismissed because the government has never wanted to make an accounting of its wrongful conduct.

One such case was that of Leonard H., who had been a fugitive for almost a decade and had been working as a nurse in Washington. He was arrested in the 1970s, and faced state court rioting charges in Illinois dating from 1968, and federal charges in both Chicago and Cleveland.

When Leonard and I went to the Chicago criminal court for arraignment on the old state charges, two FBI agents met us, along with the state's attorney. They said that Leonard had better make a deal to testify against his old comrades, or else it would go badly for him. We almost laughed. All the charges against him were tainted in one way or another by illegal government surveillance. The possible exception was a minor charge of scuffling with a police officer, and even then there were eyewitness issues.

When the bluff did not work, the state's attorney agreed that Leonard could plead to one count of nonviolent disorderly conduct and get 24 months unsupervised probation, freeing him to go to medical school. This plea bargain became the pattern for returning fugitives from the insurgency of the 1960s. Leonard went on to medical school.

Melvin Carl Smith and Leonard H. were only two of the victims of FBI bugging and tapping. I went to New Orleans in 1970 to try the wiretap motion in the case of civil rights leader H. Rap Brown; we proved that the Louisiana authorities had consciously sought to intercept lawyer-client communications. The federal judge refused to find that the FBI had known of or encouraged the state authorities in doing this. This was, however, my chance to try an issue in the old federal courthouse in the French Quarter, where the district courts and the Fifth Circuit sat for many years. The judge was Lansing T. Mitchell, known as "Tut." Imperious and always impeccably dressed, he was the figure of a jurist.

I had the FBI agent on the stand and was about to pin him to an inconsistency in his report, when Judge Mitchell interrupted. "Mr. Tigar, I don't know if you know this, but I consider my years as an FBI Special Agent to be the proudest of my life." I had not known, but asked my questions anyway, to no great effect.

1968: SPECIAL GRAND JURIES, MORE WIRETAPS

Although we had won some victories against warrantless electronic surveillance, the Nixon administration turned to different means of intrusion. The Crime Control Act of 1968 contained provisions allowing electronic surveillance, with judicial authorization, for limited periods of time. However, the application to a judge was done in secret, and there would be no review of the authorization until and unless the government took action against the surveillance target. The Act also provided for special federal grand juries, which could be convened by federal prosecutors for a period of 18 months and then renewed.

The Act was trumpeted as providing prosecutors with new tools to fight organized crime. But as soon as it was passed, its provisions were used aggressively against dissidents. It worked like this: A government lawyer would present an FBI affidavit to a federal district judge, outlining alleged criminal subversive activity by one or more people. The judge would authorize electronic surveillance. Disclosure of the surveillance and judicial review of its legality, so the government contended, would not occur and unless someone who was subjected to surveillance was prosecuted. The Act contained a provision forbidding the government to use illegal electronic surveillance in any trial or hearing, and requiring prosecutors to affirm or deny the existence of illegal surveillance if asked. These two provisions proved to be important in unexpected ways.

The Nixon administration tactic was simple: Subpoenas would go out to a number of dissidents, on some flimsy theory about a conspiracy to violate the law. Subpoena targets would be chosen based on electronic surveillance. In the Philadelphia area, the targets were nuns, priests, and lay workers involved in peace demonstrations. In Arizona, people involved in an organization allegedly connected to a bomb plot were subpoenaed; this alleged plot turned out to be a figment of the FBI's imagination. The Arizona grand jury directed most of its subpoenas to people in the Los Angeles area. Predictably, those subpoenaed refused to testify, on First Amendment grounds. When these objections were overruled, they invoked their privilege against self-incrimination.

Using a provision of the 1968 law, the government gave these refusers "use immunity," meaning that their Fifth Amendment privilege evaporated, but their answers could not be used against them, except in a prosecution for perjury if the government disagreed with their version of events. So the witnesses had a dilemma. If they testified that they and their friends were innocent, they might be prosecuted in Arizona, far from home, for allegedly lying. If they implicated their friends, then those friends would be prosecuted.

Many of these folks refused to accept immunity and went to jail for contempt. Those who decided to testify quickly learned about the "perjury trap." The prosecutor would ask question after question about the smallest details of their conversations and activities. It became clear that the prosecutor had access to electronic surveillance, and thus could keep asking questions about conversations that the witness might only dimly remember but of which the prosecutor had a transcript.

It appeared that prosecutors were using electronic surveillance to formulate their grand jury questions, hoping by this means to obtain indictments that would be arguably based on evidence independent of any illegality that had occurred in the surveillance, and in any event to imprison witnesses for contempt or prosecute them for perjury.

Lawyers for subpoenaed witnesses struck back. They demanded that the prosecutors disclose electronic surveillance that was being used as the basis for questioning any subpoenaed witness, and that the court must determine whether that surveillance was lawful. This issue was being litigated in 1971. Forcing disclosure in grand jury proceedings, in addition to that required when charges were filed, would be a significant deterrent to prosecutorial misuse of the grand jury process. The National Lawyers Guild assembled a group of lawyers and law students to write and publish a handbook on the rights of grand jury witnesses and limits on the discretion of prosecutors.

The grand jury was devised by King Henry II in 1166 as an instrument of royal power. The Framers of the United States Constitution regarded it as a protection against executive authority, and required in the Fifth Amendment that in the federal courts a grand jury indictment was a prerequisite to any capital or other felony prosecution. Despite a few victories in the courts for witnesses and defendants, the federal grand jury was rightly seen as the prosecutor's playground. As a federal prosecutor famously remarked, "I can get the grand jury to indict a ham sandwich."

Lawyers were raising, and courts were considering, the issue of wiretap disclosure in dozens of cases. Two of these cases came to the Supreme Court in petitions for certiorari. In Los Angeles, a long-running investigation of alleged interstate gambling focused on clients I had been representing. David Gelbard allegedly had friends who were involved in gambling activities in which they used the telephone. Sidney Parnas was associated with the Caesar's Palace casino in Las Vegas, which was the subject of an investigation into alleged influence by organized crime figures. When Gelbard and Parnas received grand jury subpoenas, their counsel demanded that the government disclose any electronic surveillance that was being used to target them and to formulate questions to be asked before the grand jury. The government refused these requests. The court of appeals for the Ninth Circuit held that the government was not required to make the requested disclosures.

In Philadelphia, the government was investigating an alleged conspiracy among peace activists to kidnap a public official. The targets of this investigation included Catholic priests and nuns, among them Daniel and Philip Berrigan and Sister Joques Egan of the Sacred Heart Order. Sister Egan was subpoenaed to testify before a grand jury, invoked her privilege against self-incrimination, and was then granted a limited "use immunity," meaning that her testimony could not be used against her in a future proceeding, though the government could use it against others. She persisted in refusing to testify, demanding that the government disclose any electronic surveillance on which she had been overheard. The court of appeals for the Third Circuit upheld Sister Egan's claim. These conflicting decisions by two different courts of appeals—a "circuit split" in lawyer jargon—made the issue a good candidate for Supreme Court review.

I was retained to draft a petition for certiorari for Gelbard and Parnas. In the petition, I discussed the statutory and constitutional questions, but also took care to describe in some detail the new government tactics that were being used in cases against political activists as well as against alleged gamblers.

On December 14, 1971, the Supreme Court granted certiorari on the Gelbard-Parnas petition, and on the U.S. petition in Joques Egan's case. At that time, I was traveling in England, working on the book that became *Law and the Rise of Capitalism*. I had a publisher's advance, and a small foundation grant, but little else. I agreed to brief and argue the *Gelbard-Parnas* case for a flat fee plus expenses. That, along with the advance and grant, was enough money to live modestly in France for a year and do research and writing on the book, as I discuss in chapter 10. I wrote the brief in the American law section of Oxford's Bodleian Library.

In *Gelbard*, the individuals were petitioners and in the Egan case the United States was petitioner. This meant that at oral argument, I would argue first for a half hour, then the Deputy Solicitor General would have two back-to-back half hours, as respondent in *Gelbard* and petitioner in *Egan*; then Sister Egan's counsel would argue. In the brief and in oral argument, I needed to show that this case involved at least two stories. The government's story was based on a narrow statutory reading, bolstered by decisions that sharply limited judicial control over prosecutorial discretion in running a grand jury. The government's brief ignored the social context created by the Nixon administration's systematic evasion of limits on electronic surveillance.

Of course, we had a strong textual argument, but I have never thought that such arguments are enough, standing alone. When the text supports you, by all means argue it. You may pick up a vote or two. But the self-styled textualists have proven ready to abandon their faith to reach a result. Textualism permits results without regard to their consequences. Although I was arguing for David Gelbard and Sidney Parnas, I wanted the Court to see these cases in a broader perspective. Text for the textualists, context for the discerning.

The four years since the 1968 Crime Control Act was passed illustrated how one should never accept just a little erosion of due process in order to catch an arguably dangerous enemy. This theme has been sounded again and again, in literature and in law, but it is often and easily forgotten. I wanted to show how an expansive view of the grand jury's power permitted prosecutors to avoid limits on the legality of government conduct. The Framers of the Constitution had thought of the grand jury as a protection against arbitrary power; it had become an instrument of that power. I wrote in our brief:

> So here is a weapon, committed largely to the Attorney General's discretion, which reason tells us and experience demonstrates is susceptible of the most sweeping use in the service of any motive that can be cloaked in the name "investigation of organized crime." It is this power that brings accountants and revolutionaries, nuns and gamblers, organizers and poets, together to the bar of this Court.

We won 5 to 4. Several years later, in *Calandra v. United States*, the Court held 6 to 3 that the grand jury could hear unlawfully obtained evidence that did not involve electronic surveillance. And in 1992, the Court held that the prosecutor was not obliged to present exculpatory evidence to the grand jury. So our victory was narrow, and represented an outer limit of judicial control of the grand jury.

The *Gelbard* oral argument sounded a theme that we had been using since the earliest briefs in *Kolod*, and which has remained central to challenges to the national security state. It had been Williams's theme in the *Alderman/Ivanov* argument. The theme was accountability, based on disclosure of government conduct and the right to challenge that conduct in a judicial forum. My argument began:

> I seek in this argument to show, on constitutional and statutory premises, that the opinion below is an unwarranted assault on settled principles of personal liberty and would permit the government to violate the law without paying the price for doing so.

I had thought that the case would be 5 to 4 or at best 6 to 3. In the days before oral argument, I met with Peter K. Westen to map out a strategy. Peter was then at the Paul Weiss firm's D.C. office, and had just obtained certiorari in *Chambers v. Mississippi,* a pro bono case involving the defense right to present exculpatory evidence. He was a couple of years behind me at Berkeley Law, and had been editor-in-chief of the *California Law Review*. With Peter's help, I found one case authored by each of the five Justices whose votes I really needed, and resolved to cite each case in the opening minutes of oral argument. Justice White caught on to this tactic. As I cited the second case, he whispered in Justice Brennan's ear and held his hand with fingers outstretched. He then counted off the remaining citations, and when I got to five, he reached out and gave Justice Brennan a playful tap on the shoulder. But the theme of the argument, set out in the first sentence, was that government illegality had traditionally been held to have a price; the issue was when should that price be exacted, and what was it to be.

When arguing to an appellate court, the judges' or justices' interaction can often give valuable clues. Sometimes, the judge may use a question to argue with a colleague, or even to help an advocate who is in trouble. In the *Egan* argument, Deputy Solicitor General Friedman noted in an aside that the government had searched its records after the court of appeals decision and that there had in fact been no electronic surveillance of Sister Egan. One Justice wondered aloud if this mooted the case, but of course the answer was no because the issue was bound to recur in the same grand jury investigation.

When Sister Egan's lawyer was arguing, one Justice asked him to comment on the government's denial that she had been the subject of electronic surveillance. The lawyer was being driven to concede that if there had been no surveillance, then Sister Egan was not justified in refusing to answer questions. Therefore, she would properly be held in contempt and properly committed to jail. Sister Egan was in the front row of spectators in her habit. At the mention of jail, she took out a handkerchief and dabbed at her eyes. Seeing a nun cry was too much for Justice Brennan. He quickly asked the lawyer "just to clarify" if in fact Sister Egan was entitled to a new opportunity to go before the grand jury, and did not face any risk of jail. The lawyer agreed.

Justice Brennan wrote the majority opinion, holding that the statute required the government to disclose electronic surveillance, and that its language therefore overrode the historic disinclination of court to interfere with grand jury proceedings.

Experience belied the government's assurance that wiretapping and bugging would be used only in carefully limited circumstances. Judicial controls on surveillance were in practice loose, even when a warrant was obtained. In case after case, I was confronted with surveillance tapes made over months, involving thousands of hours of conversations. Inevitably, these overhearings swept up attorney-client communications, innocent social conversations, and moments of intimacy. In one celebrated case, the defendant achieved a kind of "hat trick" record by (1) having an innocent social conversation (2) about an attorney-client privileged issue (3) while engaging in a sexual act.

The ubiquity of electronic searches points up their inherent character as "general searches." The application for surveillance may describe in detail what the government hopes to overhear, but the actual search is a kind of strip mining. The gleanings represent only a tiny fraction of what the listeners amass. The pervasive sense that the government, or big business, can collect and use so many details of our private lives erodes our sense of independence and freedom. After all these years, we have government agencies that actually listen to us, and look where it's got us.

Even after the Supreme Court held that warrantless domestic national security electronic surveillance was unlawful, the Justice Department continued to assert that it could wiretap and bug at will so long as its target was a foreign national or the case involved foreign national security. The courts of appeals took inconsistent positions on the issue, and in 1978 Congress passed the Foreign Intelligence Surveillance Act. The FISA set up a special court to issue judicial authorization for so-called foreign electronic surveillance within

United States borders. The "court" is a bad joke. It meets in secret, issues secret decisions, and has never turned down a government request to authorize surveillance. And, while the government must claim that it is targeting foreign nationals on matters of international concern, the actual surveillances may pick up conversations of U.S. citizens, who may then find themselves prosecuted for purely domestic offenses based on what is overheard. Had the FISA not been passed, the Supreme Court would probably have agreed to hear one of the foreign surveillance cases. Neither the Supreme Court nor the lower federal courts have been inclined to address the Act's serious shortcomings.

DAVID TRUONG: NATIONAL SECURITY WRIT LARGE

The most significant prelude to the Foreign Intelligence Surveillance Act involved David Truong, a student and researcher from South Vietnam who had opposed U.S. involvement in the Vietnam War and, after the American withdrawal from Vietnam in 1975, had worked to normalize relations with the Socialist Republic of Vietnam. David was part of a group against whom the FBI and the CIA directed its investigative activity. The CIA was, in this respect, violating the mandate that limited it to foreign investigation. Its justification was that the investigation involved a foreign country, and so it recruited a Vietnamese woman to pose as a friend of those seeking better relations with Vietnam. This agent urged David and others to try to obtain secret U.S. documents about American policy.

David developed a friendship with Ronald Humphrey, a lower-level State Department employee. Humphrey copied State Department cable traffic and gave it to David, who passed it along to Vietnamese diplomats. None of these materials related to military activity, or indeed to anything other than policy discussion. David and Humphrey were charged with espionage, theft of government property, and mishandling classified information. John Mage, a brilliant lawyer who I had met in the case discussed in chapter 10, Virginia lawyer Marvin Miller, and I assembled a defense team. David's friends and allies in the antiwar movement raised money for the defense.

The breadth of these charges, coupled with the use of warrantless physical and electronic searches, pointed to a truth about the pattern of prosecutions we had seen since 1968. That is, the *substance* of repression is achieved with the *procedure* of repression. This duality should not have surprised us. The eighteenth-century English cases on unlawful search and seizure involved the rights of dissidents. The case of colonial newspaper editor John Peter Zenger was rife with attacks on Zenger's procedural rights, including his right to counsel. State power intent on overriding the Bill of Rights Fourth Amendment is unlikely to hesitate in running over the First, Fifth, Sixth and, at times, Eighth Amendment.

David's case had several interwoven stories of state power procedural and substantive overreaching. The United States, unrepentant for its errors in Vietnam, had turned against those who had opposed its policies. Rather than opening debate about matters affecting national security, it invoked draconian laws to maintain the wall of secrecy. Even if one thought that David had strayed over the line, and had no right to the documents he obtained, punishing him under laws designed to protect vital state secrets represented a dangerously overbroad reading of those laws. The CIA's agent had befriended several well-known activists to create the basis for prosecuting them.

The investigation had begun in 1976, when Gerald Ford was president. Ford's Attorney General, Edward Levi, was a well-known legal scholar who during his brief tenure brought real reform to the Justice Department. Levi resisted the FBI's efforts to conduct warrantless searches directed at David. When Jimmy Carter became president in January 1977, Carter named Griffin Bell Attorney General.

In May 1977, having returned from a weekend at the Kentucky Derby, Bell approved the FBI burglary of David's home to install a hidden microphone, as well as a tap on David's home telephone. The tap and bug operated for 268 days, all without a warrant. Bell also approved warrantless searches of David's mail. We moved to suppress illegally obtained evidence. We subpoenaed Bell. The trial judge refused to quash the subpoena. Bell testified that he had approved these searches because "I was trying to catch me a spy." He appeared innocent of any Fourth Amendment understanding.

The electronic surveillance did not produce much evidence of consequence, and so the issue did not make much headway. In David's case, the government's contentions were particularly disingenuous. The 1968 Crime Control Act expressly permitted the government to obtain a judicial warrant to conduct electronic surveillance, subject to modest limitations and protections. Bell's sole purpose in evading the warrant requirement was to forestall disclosure and meaningful judicial review.

I recalled that Warren Christoper, Deputy Secretary of State under President Carter, had argued in the Ninth Circuit against warrantless electronic surveillance in the Melvin Carl Smith case, where I was counsel for Smith and he was designated to defend Judge Ferguson's decision. I telephoned him. At least he took the call; he was abrupt to the point of rudeness. He supported the decision to proceed with this case.

Having assembled its evidence in disregard of the Fourth Amendment, the government manipulated events to have venue in the Eastern District of Virginia. This meant trial in Alexandria, on the "rocket docket" and to a conservative jury. In the District of Columbia, it would have been a different case, at trial and on appeal.

At trial, the disregard for procedural fairness continued: we battled for disclosure of prior witness statements, to which we were entitled in order to cross-examine—based on the Supreme Court decision in the Clint Jencks case. Almost every day the prosecutors would present another batch of discovery material that they had "just received" from this or that secret or semi-secret agency. We were at the bench one day, with the jury out of the room, quarreling over one such late and incomplete disclosure. The prosecutors were saying that they had trouble getting the CIA to give up documents. I turned to the courtroom and said in a loud voice, "Would the CIA lawyer please stand up." A lawyer stood up, realized he had been found out, looked sheepish, and then sat down. Judge Bryant called him to the bench to explain the agency's position.

Substantively, the government's prosecution theory was in three parts. First, the government contended that David's supplying the information to the Vietnamese Embassy in Paris was "espionage" because the information was "to the injury of the United States" and "the advantage of Vietnam." We presented evidence, including the testimony of a former National Security Council member, that the material was "diplomatic chit-chat," informative and interesting but not harmful to any legitimate interest of the United States.

The government's second contention was that David and Ron Humphrey had stolen the information. That is, the government was repeating the contention it had made in the Pentagon Papers prosecution of Daniel Ellsberg, that all of government has an intangible property right to all information in the possession of any government department or agency. A whistleblower in the Environmental Protection Agency, equally with a mole in the Pentagon, is guilty of theft without regard to whether the information is worthy of being kept secret.

An assertedly democratic government, with a firm commitment to public discourse, was invoking the property norm as a means to exclude the citizenry from information about government process, and using a legal rule crafted at common law from the writ of trespass. The law's command was no different in form from the restaurant owner saying, "Those hamburgers are my property; they are off limits to people of color." Several years later, I published an article on this topic.

Third was the government claim of mishandling classified information.

The trial judge accepted the government's position on items one and

two. On the third item, he held that there is no judicial review of an executive
branch decision to classify a document as confidential, secret or top secret.

We were reminded again just how powerful the ritual invocation of
"national security" can be. Many judges seemed to abandon their power
of independent thought when the government pronounced this talismanic
phrase. In American law, in cases as diverse as the World War II Japanese
relocation and Cold War loyalty-security proceedings, the supposedly independent judiciary seems timid.

The *New York Times* reporter covering the trial was David Burnham. He
told us that the Carter administration had considered embarking on prosecutions of journalists for publishing stories based on government whistleblowers'
revelations, but had decided not to do that, for the time being. Later administrations were not so skittish.. In any event, it was clear to us that the Carter
administration was using this case to reassert a national security agenda that
had been discredited during the Nixon administration.

We talked to David Burnham about the 1971 Pentagon Papers controversy.
Daniel Ellsberg released a 47-volume Pentagon study of U.S. involvement in
Vietnam. The government sued to block publication, and lost in the Supreme
Court. The *New York Times* and the *Washington Post* published the material, despite some members of the Supreme Court having suggested that a
post-publication espionage prosecution might be permissible. The Nixon
administration prosecuted Ellsberg and his colleague, but prosecutorial misconduct doomed that case.

The striking thing for us, looking at that history in light of David's case,
was that the Nixon administration's characterizations of the Pentagon Papers
was greatly exaggerated. The Solicitor General at that time, Erwin Griswold,
described his preparation to argue the case in the Supreme Court:

> I arranged to have three high officials, one each from the Defense
> Department, the State Department and the National Security Agency
> come to my office. I asked them to tell me what items in the 47 volumes
> were really bad—what items, if disclosed, would be a real threat to the
> security of the United States. This produced a total of about 40 items
> over which these officers expressed concern. I then read each of these
> items, but quickly came to the conclusion that most of them presented no
> serious threat to national security, and that there was simply no prospect
> that the Supreme Court would ban the publication of all of these items.
> Eventually, I reduced the list to a total of 11 items.

Despite the judge's limiting the scope of permissible defense, we attacked the government's evident desire to single out and punish people who had opposed the Vietnam War, exposed its consequences, and now sought a reasoned and responsible postwar policy that took account of what this war had done to Vietnam and its people.

The jury, drawn from that conservative Northern Virginia area, found David guilty. The trial judge revoked his bail and held that he would be imprisoned pending appeal. The court of appeals for the Fourth Circuit upheld the denial. The law clerk for one of those judges later told me that he thought I had made a winning argument. He said this to the judge at the time, who replied, "You don't understand. This is a spy case. He stays in."

Our next step was to present the bail application to a Justice of the Supreme Court. We were able to use a procedural rule for our David's benefit. The Circuit Justice for the Fourth Circuit, Chief Justice Burger, was out of town. We could, therefore, present the application to any other Justice. We presented it to Justice Brennan, who granted it in an opinion that still carries a powerful message about the constitutional right to bail. Justice Brennan noted that the important constitutional issue of warrantless electronic surveillance had been left open in Supreme Court decisions. He held that under Supreme Court precedent, he was to make "an independent determination" and not defer to the courts below. He noted that historic peace churches and organizations had offered to put up money for bail, and that David's application was supported by prominent members of the community.

The court of appeals expressed concern that the government's interpretation of the Espionage Act might have been too broad. It noted that the issue of national security surveillance had been addressed by the Congress in the Foreign Intelligence Surveillance Act and was unlikely to recur. It affirmed the convictions and David's 15-year sentence. He served five years and was paroled. He continued to write and speak on foreign policy issues until his death in 2014 at the age of sixty-eight. The *New York Times*, in his obituary, noted that the prosecution's claims about secrecy were contradicted by "independent intelligence sources," and the warrantless searches were even "more troubling," concluding: "The case revealed a tangle of personal, political and diplomatic complications involving the lives of Americans and Vietnamese in the aftermath of the Vietnam War."

THE SURVEILLANCE STATE

I am at times chagrined to see the extent to which we have accepted electronic surveillance as a fact of investigative life. I am the more concerned when I see the cavalier way in which investigative agencies undertake it, the extent of its invasions, and the ways that government resists disclosure and accountability. The Truong case raised deeper issues about the state's determination to hide information from the governed. David's "crime" had been to obtain information about how the United States government was prosecuting a deadly and illegal war in Vietnam, and its refusal to accept the result. The purported congressional authorization for military involvement was fraudulent, the justification for the United States taking over the French colonial role in Indochina violated customary international law and treaties, and the war had been justified by a series of falsehoods from government leaders.

Looking back over the cases and issues in this chapter, I can see that I encountered the principles that have directed my legal life in the first days of my work in Washington. I find myself looking back at Learned Hand's 1950 opinion in *United States v. Coplon,* which Ed Williams mentioned in our earliest meetings, and which he used to such effect in *Alderman/Ivanov.* I can, as can many of my comrades, recall the citation from memory. In later years, I met Judith Coplon and many of the other lawyers who were concerned with these national security issues as the Cold War got underway.

Words from Judge Hand's opinion come to mind:

Few weapons in the arsenal of freedom are more useful than the power to compel a government to disclose the evidence on which it seeks to forfeit the liberty of its citizens. All governments, democracies as well as autocracies, believe that those they seek to punish are guilty; the impediment of constitutional barriers are galling to all governments when they prevent the consummation of that just purpose. But those barriers were devised and are precious because they prevent that purpose and its pursuit from passing unchallenged by the accused, and unpurged by the alembic of public scrutiny and public criticism. A society which has come to wince at such exposure of the methods by which it seeks to impose its will upon its members, has already lost the feel of freedom and is on the path toward absolutism.

Here, it seems to me now—as it seemed to me then—is the heart of our lawyer job confronting the state. Behind the mythology of national security, and the factitious invocation of the state's alleged "evidentiary privilege" to hide its motivations and conduct, lies mendacity and illegality. The purpose of these stratagems is to confer impunity by shielding the unlawful conduct, imprisoning those who reveal it, and denying redress to its victims. Our job is to compel disclosure, and then to impose accountability. To do that we require a fair forum, something we may not always find. And, as we have seen, when the state fails even the test of disclosure and accountability, it loses its grasp on legitimacy, with predictable consequences.

As the Nigerian poet Wole Soyinka wrote: "The truth shall set you free? Maybe. But first the truth must be set free."

CHAPTER 6

Civil Wrongs

I f one were to ask, "Looking back at your study, practice, teaching and writing, what parts of these experiences relate to race and racism?" I would have to answer, "Almost all of them, in some measure or another." Hence, this chapter, which deals with racial justice and injustice, does not stand alone. Resistance to racial injustice has pervaded almost every aspect of my work. As I think back on the issues of free expression, or protests against an illegal war—each of which is the subject of later chapters — I am reminded again of how state and monopoly power that curtailed basic rights struck more harshly at people of color. When I think about arguing to jurors, I am conscious that the increasing diversity of jury panels brings the life experiences, sensibilities, and attitudes of different people into the process of decision. And, at the root of most issues of *international* human rights, is the racism that accompanied imperial conquest.

To put this chapter, and my own sense of injustice, into perspective, one can contrast two approaches that have showed up in the civil rights debate. First, the historical approach, as illustrated by Professor tenBroek's masterful book *The Anti-Slavery Origins of the Fourteenth Amendment*; and second, an analytical approach, as illustrated by the 1949 tenBroek and Tussman article, "The Equal Protection of the Laws," in the *California Law Review*. When one says "civil rights," that is only the beginning of discussion.

Analytically, one can approach equal protection cases as simply involving categories or classifications chosen by the state. One then asks whether the classification is rational in light of its avowed or intended purpose, and whether it is under-inclusive or over-inclusive with respect to that purpose. For example, if the state offers a benefit for poor persons, but excludes people of color or women from eligibility, the under-inclusiveness of the eligibility category raises equal protection issues. By using this kind of analysis, we can tell whether or not a law treats like things alike. The Supreme Court has superimposed upon this framework a set of categories of governmental activity. These were designed at first to respect state power to regulate economic activity, while restraining actions that seemed likely to result in or be motivated by invidious discrimination. The Supreme Court's decisions of the late nineteenth and early twentieth centuries had been hostile to economic regulation and quite generous in permitting state and federal action that discriminated against African-Americans and Asian-Americans.

These superimposed categories are phrased as "levels of scrutiny" of classifications. In recent times, laws respecting economic regulation receive very limited and deferential scrutiny. Racial classifications receive "strict scrutiny," while gender may receive "intermediate scrutiny." This sort of classification may be helpful as a shorthand way of seeing classification problems, but in the hands of reactionary judges it has become an instrument for holding back progress toward true racial justice.

In the days when segregation was written into the law of many states, race-based classifications served no legitimate purpose and were properly struck down. When states and the federal government sought to promote fair housing, access to public accommodation, and equal educational and economic opportunity, it was easy to use classification systems that forbade decision-making, by public or private actors, based on race. From there, it is deceptively easy to conclude that any classification system that uses race is illegitimate.

Not so, many—I among them—have argued, invoking a historical view of racism. The classification system arose in a discrete historical framework, to reflect the historic reality of Jim Crow legislation and patterns of overt discrimination. It is risky to disengage that system from its historical basis and to manipulate its categories as independent of their origins. The false and disingenuous manipulation of categories appears in the opposition to affirmative action programs designed to redress historic racist patterns. For example, when colleges adopt admissions programs designed to remedy patterns of past discrimination, reactionaries proclaim that taking race into account in admissions decisions denies equal protection of the laws.

To put matters another way, the analytical approach to classifications can be useful as a starting point. However, an arid and ahistorical—not to say covertly racist—use of the method leads to results that are inconsistent with the liberating purpose of the Fourteenth Amendment. TenBroek's historical analysis of the Civil War amendments sets one on the right track. The fact is that American society has been permeated with racial bigotry in ways that have disadvantaged many groups. The Constitution expressly recognized slavery. When the Civil War ended, systematic discrimination against African-Americans continued, resulting in the creation of a ghettoized underclass. In 1831, the Supreme Court decided *Cherokee Nation v. Georgia*, holding that Native Americans were incapable of forming social organizations that were entitled to recognition by the conquering European powers, and hence incapable of claiming political or property rights except as those might be recognized by the United States. Indian land rights and political rights hardly existed. In the latter half of the nineteenth century, the Supreme Court upheld federal and state legislation that discriminated against Oriental people from China and Japan. One can view these historic events in different ways, but if you believe that these decisions and actions were wrong, there should be a correlative duty to provide a remedy.

The people originally displaced are dead, as are those who took immediate advantage of them. The traces of wrong remain, however. We can see that in so many settings; for example, as we note that people of color are underrepresented in the upper reaches of our own legal profession. We might add that until fairly recently law school admission patterns were skewed against women and people of color. One cannot begin to fashion a remedy unless one understands the historical roots of the problem, and tries to envision what the disadvantaged class has lost as a group. Any remedy at that point would necessarily take race and gender into account, to redress the inequality produced by the old, discredited criteria of decision.

The dry analytical method rejects this reasoning. Under that view, race cannot be a factor, without some overwhelming justification that will almost never be present. Thus, equality as a concept for redressing past wrongs is pushed aside in favor of a mechanical analysis that precludes any such redress.

When I speak of analysis based on history, I am not retreating into some imagined "original intent" of the Constitution's Framers or the authors of the Civil War amendments. It is very difficult to get inside the minds of those who wrote those documents at the moment they were writing them. A more accurate view of their desires must be gathered from examining the entire historical context of their work.

There is one abiding certainty about the views of those who assembled at Philadelphia in 1787. They were not so arrogant or foolish as to think they knew everything there was to know about government, science, or the human condition. They believed it was a constitution they were drafting and not a set of fetters they were forging. They stood on the shoulders of those who had gone before them, so that they could see farther. They understood that we would go beyond where they had gone.

When thinking about history or precedent—in litigation or simply in formulating arguments about justice—I have tried to see "the law" in its historical and social context. "The law" is not a thing, a mere body of rules captured at a moment of historical time. The law at any given time is the product of a process.

The summer of 1964, after my first law school year, was Freedom Summer. The Mississippi Freedom Democratic Party challenged the official segregationist Mississippi delegates at the Democratic Convention in Atlantic City. My friend Dennis Roberts went to Albany, Georgia, to work with the great civil rights lawyer C. B. King. Thousands of students went south to work on civil rights. The record of violence visited on these young people, and on those whose struggle they had come south to help, is still cause for wonder. This was, you may remember, the summer when the students Andrew Goodman, Michael Schwerner, and James Chaney were murdered in Mississippi as they worked for civil rights.

I did not go south. I needed to earn money for my second year in law school. I wrote and broadcast a weekly KPFA/Pacifica Radio program called *Mississippi Report*. I continued to work at the *Civil Liberties Docket*. Memories of that time have somehow faded, and perhaps sensitivity along with them. In the 1990s the film *Mississippi Burning* retold the story of that summer. A court of appeals judge who is at least my age, and therefore in a position to remember, remarked that he found the film overdone and exaggerated. I pulled out my old scripts from *Mississippi Report* and sent him the statistics of hundreds of black churches burned, thousands of illegal arrests, and a pattern of terror and intimidation.

The official Democratic parties of Mississippi and other southern states proclaimed their continuing faith in segregation and what they called "states' rights." I attacked them on the air, recognizing that they might demand equal, but separate, time. President Johnson temporized but sought congressional and political support for some compromise that would seat some African-American delegates from the South at the Democratic Convention.

The pace of political change seemed so slow, despite the imminent passage of the Civil Rights Act of 1964. The Democratic Party seemed unwilling to welcome the African-American voters who were being registered in the South, and the Republican Party was not doing any better.

Civil rights lawyers had to consider how their bag of tools could bring about more and faster change. Arthur Kinoy and William Kunstler, and their colleagues at the Center for Constitutional Rights, were developing broad-scale injunctive strategies against efforts to shut down civil rights organizations. I wondered how the Johnson administration could be prodded into more decisive action. The investigations into Ku Klux Klan violence dragged on, and local FBI agents in southern field offices were too often allied with local law enforcement. The administration did prosecute in egregious civil rights violation cases, but more was needed. The southern states were obstructing the federal courts' orders.

By that time, the direct action movement that had begun in 1960 had expanded. Civil rights workers were picketing, boycotting, sitting-in, and challenging segregation in public transportation. Hundreds of them were being beaten, jailed, and sentenced to jail. Lawyers from the North came south to assist. The lawyer skills they needed were the traditional ones involved in criminal defense. As I studied and chronicled these events, I gained new perspectives on what a lawyer could and should do to confront racism.

I talked with one of my professors about the events in Mississippi. He suggested that I look at President Eisenhower's response to the 1957 Little Rock school desegregation crisis. I did so, and found a trove of information about presidential power to enforce civil rights. What I found is important to this day, for it supports a view of federal power and against so-called states' rights that a slim Supreme Court majority in the late twentieth and early twenty-first century has ignored. First, I read or reread the Reconstruction legislation that made civil rights a federal matter, conferred jurisdiction on federal courts to enforce them, and directed the Executive Branch to enforce these laws. True, the courts had rejected suits that relied on the mandatory language of this post–Civil War legislation. The courts ruled that despite a congressional command that civil rights violations be prosecuted, the Attorney General still retained discretion not to act. Despite such limiting constructions, the Reconstruction legislation and the environment in which it passed supported my view that the Civil War had resulted in a promise of liberation and equality for African-Americans, without the keeping of which the government became illegitimate.

I turned then to study, and report on, the 1957 events in Little Rock. Arkansas Governor Orval Faubus mobilized the Arkansas National Guard to obstruct compliance with the federal court desegregation order. Faubus asked President Eisenhower for an assurance he would not be arrested for his defiance. Eisenhower replied by telegram, "The only assurance I can give you is that the Federal Constitution will be upheld by me by every legal means at my command."

Eisenhower's Attorney General, Herbert Brownell, looked back at legislation that had been passed in 1791 to assist President George Washington in putting down the so-called Whiskey Rebellions, which were protests against taxation of spiritous liquors. Eisenhower, based on that advice, announced that a governor has no power to resist the authority of a federal court order, and that he as Commander-in-Chief had the power and duty to federalize the state militia and send federal troops to see that federal court orders were carried out. He did just that, and sent the 101st Airborne to Little Rock in September 1957. I had known about these events as they happened, but did not know the legal basis for Eisenhower's actions.

I recounted this legal history in *Mississippi Report* broadcasts. I drew the contrast: President Kennedy had refused in 1963 to use troops when Mississippi Governor Barnett defied a federal court order to admit James Meredith to the University of Mississippi. President Lyndon Johnson refused to use federal power in the summer of 1964, despite the dozens of beatings, burnings, and shootings carried out by the Ku Klux Klan, aided in many cases by local law enforcement agencies.

In this storm, brave judges of the United States Court of Appeals for the Fifth Circuit did their part. When racist district judges, many appointed by Democratic administrations, refused to enforce federal law, the court of appeals for the Fifth Circuit stepped in. President Eisenhower had appointed four judges who, being Republican, had no ties to the segregation-ist Democratic establishment. They were John Minor Wisdom, Elbert Parr Tuttle, Richard Rives, and John R. Brown. Their opinions, particularly those of Judge Wisdom, were eloquent testaments to the constitutional command of racial justice. When Presidents Kennedy and Johnson refused to send the massive federal force necessary to enforce desegregation, the Fifth Circuit did the best it could. It even cited Mississippi Governor Ross Barnett for con-tempt for violating one of its orders, though it later withdrew the citation over Judge Wisdom's dissent. From Judge Wisdom's perspective, Barnett was a lawyer who knew perfectly well that his segregationist constitutionalism was factitious.

Twenty-five years later, the Fifth Circuit held its judicial conference in Jackson, Mississippi. Governor Mabus invited us all to dinner at the Governor's mansion. I fell into step beside Judge Wisdom as we walked up the front steps. "Judge," I asked, "did you ever think you would be invited in the front door of this mansion?" He laughed and said no.

In those law school years, from where I sat—writing, studying, and broad-casting—my views on this struggle took shape. You cannot count on the government to do its job, when that job involves acting on behalf of people's rights. The initiative must come from a popular movement, which should not permit itself to be co-opted. Litigation strategies on behalf of the people's movement may welcome official support but cannot count on it. Finally, the movement for change is the primary motor of change, because in the final analysis only the movement's coherent demands stand any chance to convince a court.

Working for Ann Ginger, I saw the hundreds of desegregation lawsuits, which were doubly slowed: first by the litigation tactics of lawyers for segregated school boards and reluctant courts, and then—when "victory" was achieved—by orders that mandated a glacial pace of desegregation, such as "grade a year" plans. I saw that the innovative litigation strategies of the Center for Constitutional Rights had achieved wide-ranging injunctive relief in some cases. But I had two concerns: First, the federal courts, considered as a whole, were not prepared to use their power as expansively and creatively as we might wish. The present circumstances, and a look at judicial review in historical perspective, told us that. Second, trumpeting litigation strategies risked "overselling" the importance, work, and capabilities of lawyers, and by this means disempowering the movement for change.

THE DISTRICT OF COLUMBIA

Living in the District of Columbia gave me a new perspective on racism. We rented a house on Capitol Hill, seven blocks from the Supreme Court building. The gentrification of this neighborhood had already begun. After a year, we bought a house a little farther from the Capitol, in a neighborhood where more African-Americans lived.

At that time, the District of Columbia was governed by commissioners appointed by the president. It was a feudal enclave, without meaningful self-government and of course without any voting voice in Congress. Nothing more clearly showed the District's political situation than the condition of its schools. The Supreme Court had ordered desegregation of the District's schools in *Bolling v. Sharpe*, decided the same day *Brown v. Board of Education*. However, schools in predominantly white and affluent neighborhoods were fairly well-financed and equipped, while those in African-American and poorer neighborhoods were not.

The District's revered civil rights leader Julius Hobson filed a lawsuit challenging the way D.C. schools were run. Because the D.C. Board of Education was appointed by the U.S. district judges, Hobson named all of the judges as defendants, which disqualified them all from sitting. As a result, court of appeals Judge J. Skelly Wright heard the case. There could not have been a better choice. Wright had been a district judge in New Orleans, where his pathbreaking civil rights decisions quickly earned him the enmity of the

Louisiana establishment. President Johnson could not appoint him to the Court of Appeals for the Fifth Circuit, for the nomination would have been blocked by Louisiana's senators. So he named him to the D.C. Circuit.

Judge Wright was temperamental, often quick to anger. His opinions were concise and powerful. He had courage. His opinion in the *Hobson* litigation was an indictment of the racial bias that dominated DC politics. Judge Wright held:

> The basic question presented is whether the defendants, the Superintendent of Schools and the members of the Board of Education, in the operation of the public school system here, unconstitutionally deprive the District's Negro and poor public school children of their right to equal educational opportunity with the District's white and more affluent public school children. This court concludes that they do.

The *Hobson* litigation was being conducted by some lawyers who lived near us, with assistance from William Kunstler. One of the remedies being discussed was a judicial decree mandating expenditure of money for better schools in African-American neighborhoods. Could a judge order such a thing? I set to work and mined the old cases. In the nineteenth century, municipalities issued revenue bonds and then sometimes defaulted. There were old cases requiring assessment and levy of taxes to pay the bondholders. And a California case, as I recall it, had ordered a community to buy a school bus. So I wrote my brief and handed it in. It was a very small part of the entire litigation, but writing it and talking to people in the neighborhood gave me a chance to know the District's racial tensions firsthand.

Judge Wright's opinion provoked hostile comment from some legal scholars, including Yale Law School professor Alexander Bickel, who wrote in *The New Republic* that the opinion was a "jeremiad" and irresponsibly "hortatory." I wrote a response to Bickel.

The next year, I worked with the National Capital Area Civil Liberties Union, the D.C. area branch of the national ACLU. We sued on behalf of Howard University sociology Professor Nathan Hare and Howard law student Jeroyd Greene. They had been disciplined by the university for their part in civil rights and antiwar demonstrations. Howard University was founded after the Civil War to serve the African-American community. It was the premier African-American educational institution in the country, and many civil rights leaders. including Thurgood Marshall, had been students or professors there. Our key argument was that the interaction between Howard and the federal government meant that its action was "state action." Therefore, we argued, Howard was obliged to respect the First Amendment and to afford students and teachers due process hearings before acting against them. The Supreme Court's decisions of the 1960s, and quite a few lower federal court and state court decisions, supported our argument. But we lost. As a junior member of the litigation team, I learned a lot about civil rights pleading and practice, supplementing the criminal law and criminal procedure work I was doing at the law firm.

In this context, I met Ralph Temple, NACLU staff counsel, and Professor Monroe Freedman. Over the years, they remained friends and colleagues. Monroe, in addition to being a litigator, was a scholar whose work on legal ethics emphasizes the lawyer's duty to provide courageous and zealous representation.

From the Hare-Greene litigation, I was ready when the state action issue came around again. The Maryland suburbs around Washington, D.C., boast a necklace of first-rate golf courses. Most of these are private, and some are famous locales for political and business meetings. One such course was at Kenwood Country Club. Kenwood was not owned by its members. The Kenwood subdivision developer built the course and its associated facilities and offered "memberships" to those who bought houses, while retaining ownership of the club property. Several prominent Washingtonians lived in the Kenwood subdivision, including American Friends leader Tartt Bell, Michigan Senator Robert Griffin, Idaho Senator Frank Church, and CBS reporter Robert Pierpoint. Church was a leading Democrat and Griffin a Republican. If these folks knew that the club had a "no Jews or Blacks" policy, this fact had not impressed itself upon them.

Until, that is, two celebrated events rent the Kenwood calm. One day, Senator Barry Goldwater was playing golf as the guest of Senator Griffin. The club owner learned of this, and hurried out to the 10th tee. He ordered Goldwater off the premises. This made the papers, and Goldwater remarked that he was only half-Jewish and had only played nine holes. Not long afterward, *Washington Post* columnist Carl Rowan, an African-American, showed up at the club as an invited dinner guest. He, too, was turned away, and he made sure the world knew about it.

A few leading citizens of Kenwood called and asked me to a meeting at Tartt Bell's house. I worked with a team of lawyers representing Senators Griffin and Church, along with Bell and Pierpoint. The key issue was whether this was truly a private club. Our research showed that the developers of suburban subdivisions who agreed to enhance green space by including golf courses in their plans received substantial tax benefits. I am not sure that this tax policy is wise, for golf courses are notorious emitters of runoff that damages waterways. The clubs, however, slurped up the property tax largesse quite willingly. The state regarded them as having built a "green belt" around the District of Columbia. This was, we argued, a public function supported by public funds. The federal court in Baltimore agreed, and ordered the club desegregated. It even awarded us a modest attorney fee.

The racial issues in the District of Columbia obviously cut much deeper than people's rights to play golf or to have dinner at a country club. Every day, living where we did at the fringe of Washington's ghetto, I saw these issues. I saw another part of the racist structure in the local court. My wife, Pam, was active in community organizations. Our children went to integrated schools and day care.

On April 4, 1968, at about 6 p.m., a sniper killed Martin Luther King, Jr. News of the killing in Memphis spread quickly. We were home making dinner. Jessica Mitford was our dinner guest. As it turned out, she spent the night because the streets were quickly filled with rioting citizens protesting the King death.

In the aftermath of that night, I represented people charged with crimes related to looting. Reverend King had represented, particularly to African-Americans in the District of Columbia, a symbol of their particular aspirations. He had said that change would come by nonviolent direct action. He had stood in opposition to leaders who advocated or predicted violence. When he was killed, in the midst of a campaign against racism and in a southern city, the forces that held the community in some kind of equipoise simply dissolved. All the anger, focused and unfocused, burst out.

There was also, to be sure, plenty of opportunism on the streets that night. As police sirens mingled with the noise of people running and shouting on our street, our neighbor knocked at our front door. He was an African-American man of about fifty. We opened and he came in to our living room.

"I can't keep my nephews from looting," he said. "I've told them that they are going to be arrested and maybe killed, but they don't listen."

"I guess I could explain what happens if they get caught," I said, "but I don't know it would do any good."

"Oh," he said, "I don't want you to do that. I just thought that since they were going down there, do you need a new TV or anything like that?"

The April 1968 uprisings in cities all over America seemed to be part of a worldwide movement. I am not preaching any kind of conspiracy theory here. However, students in colleges acted out their frustration over the Vietnam War and the limits on academic freedom. Students and elements of the French left took to the streets and nearly brought down the French government. That summer young people demonstrated in Chicago against the machine-dominated Democratic Party Convention and against the Vietnam War. The uprisings triggered a response from the wielders of power. (I described the use of wiretaps and special grand juries under the 1968 Crime Control Act in chapter 5.) At the same time, the tone and tenor of judicial opinions in cases involving sit-ins, marches, leafleting and other instruments of social protest began to take on a more restrictive tone.

The deep divides in American society, which had been papered over in the McCarthy era, were now reappearing. The divisions were not simply of age, class, race, gender, or politics, although each of these things was involved. As I was working through my own position, I met a judge who seemed to embody the entire set of problems.

In 1968, a student at a local university came to me with his parents. He had been driving in Prince George's County, which adjoins the District of Columbia and is where the University of Maryland is located. He was with some friends, one of whom was smoking marijuana in the car. The police officer noted the odor and arrested everybody in the car for possession of marijuana. In those days, penalties for first-time marijuana possession were heavier than they later became, and the young man might have been technically guilty of possession but had an argument to make on that point. There was also a search and seizure issue about the vehicle stop.

I drove out to Prince George's County to talk to the prosecutor. In those days, law enforcement and judicial administration there was dominated by archetypical white southern attitudes toward race. The county police were notorious for ignoring the constitutional rights of suspects. In short, this was not the place to litigate a Fourth Amendment claim, nor the place to be tried for a narcotics offense.

The prosecutor, Ben, agreed that my client was a good candidate for something called probation without verdict. That is, he would plead guilty to possessing a small amount of marijuana. The judge would award probation. If the client completed the probation without incident, the case would be dismissed without a judgment being entered on his plea. He would not have a conviction on his record. It seemed to be a good deal. But, Ben explained, the judge would have to approve it.

So we went to see Sam, the judge. Sam seemed to be in his fifties, with a military-style brush cut. He invited us into his chambers, and began immediately to share a story of his trip to San Francisco, from which he had just returned.

"You know, Ben," he began, hardly noticing me, "I got selected to attend this program on sensitivity, out in San Francisco. Now, you know San Francisco is not my kind of place anyway, but you should have seen what they had there. This program was in a big auditorium, and they had state judges, federal judges, and then a whole bunch of ex-convicts. I mean, Ben, they had everything from cop-killers to queens.

"Well right off, they asked me to be part of a psychodrama." He pronounced the word one syllable at a time, with evident distaste. "I knew something was up. They had me up on this platform, and they had three chairs. They called one chair 'ego,' the next one 'superego,' and the third one was your uncon- scious self, maybe like your 'id.' So I stood up there and this black ex-con is up there and he gets right up in my face and says, 'You white judge, how come you don't treat black people with respect in your courtroom?'" Sam's voice, while repeating what the ex-con said, imitated his version of African- American street talk.

Sam continued: "So I sat in the chair marked 'ego' and I said, 'Hah, hah hah!' Then I sat in the chair marked superego, and I said, 'I am a judge and I decide every case on the law and the facts.' Then I sat in that id chair and I looked right at that ex-con and I said, 'You goddam nigger, who put you up to this?'"

Ben laughed obediently. I did my best to stay in my seat. Who was this judge? Why had Ben brought me here? And how would I avoid saying or doing something that would harm my client, who fortunately was not present? This was 1968, and we were only a few miles from the District of Columbia. I felt I had taken a wrong turn and wandered into a past time.

His Honor switched from his recollection to the case we had brought. "Ben, Mike," Sam began, acknowledging me at last, "I know what you want. I won't do it. I am not going to cut these dope-smoking kids any slack." I thought about pointing out some facts that made this a good deal for the pros- ecution, but a glance at Ben convinced me that this would not have been a good idea.

Outside, I reminded Ben that we had agreed this was not a case that should give this young man a criminal record. Ben agreed to uphold his part of the bargain. In Maryland, a prosecutor can "stet" a case, that is, take it off calen- dar. Ben agreed to do this for a year, and if my client stayed out of trouble he would dismiss the charges. So that's what we did. But my trip to PG County sticks in my mind, as a warning that racism and racist attitudes linger on.

CHAPTER 7

Draft Board Days and Nights

When I came to Washington in 1966, the war in Vietnam had become a topic not only of discussion but also of litigation. Draft calls increased, putting pressure on young men and their families. All of a sudden, parents concerned with their male children's well-being were taking notice of the escalating American military presence in Vietnam. The war had become more controversial.

The war raised issues that I had been studying since undergraduate days, and in programs we did at KPFA. I thought back to my conversations with Konni Zilliacus in London about the issue of collective security as reflected in the United Nations Charter. One of Zilly's favorite epithets about unilateral engagement in war was "Charter-breaking aggression."

I unbundled the issue of collective security. I say "unbundled" because "deconstruction" had not yet been invented, so far as I was aware. The United Nations at its inception was divided into two governing parts, the Security Council and the General Assembly. There is also a Secretariat, which has administrative functions. The UN Charter envisioned a postwar world governed by collective security. The five permanent members of the Security Council— the United States, USSR, Great Britain, France, and China—had to be in unanimous agreement on any important matter, including the use of force. To some extent, this meant that the great powers had opted out of any significant control over their actions, because they could always veto any Security Council resolution directed at them.

Significantly, the United States took the first steps to break down the Security Council's sole power. When the Korean conflict began, the Soviets would clearly have vetoed any Security Council resolution to send UN military force. The United States sponsored and achieved passage in the General Assembly of what it called the Uniting for Peace Resolution. This empowerment of the General Assembly has helped to change the face of international law. As the newly liberated colonies took their place in the General Assembly, their plurality passed more and more resolutions addressing even the conduct of the "great powers."

The UN Charter also envisioned regional alliances, although there is some question whether military alliances such as NATO are within the terms of that article. Regardless of interpretation, NATO and the Warsaw Pact were quickly formed as the Cold War began in the 1940s. However, regarding a dispute between the United States and Cuba as a legitimate subject of NATO concern seemed questionable to say the least.

As the United States took over military security concerns from the French in Indochina, it also formed the Southeast Asia Treaty Organization, or SEATO. This grouping was, it seemed to me, inconsistent with the UN charter. The United States is not a part of the Southeast Asia region, as a buffalo does not become a giraffe by sticking its neck out. As a matter of international law, therefore, I concluded that the use of force in Vietnam and the threat of force in Cuba was wrong. These were disputes that the United States ought to have submitted to the United Nations and resolved within the framework of that organization.

During my law school years, from 1963 to 1966, President Johnson escalated American military presence in Vietnam, and the war was a major issue in the 1964 presidential election. In addition to my concerns about international law, I studied the constitutional issues related to war-making. Later, we would litigate these issues in draft cases. Under Article 1 of the U.S. Constitution, the President is Commander-in-Chief and can of course order action to repel sudden attacks. However, the Congress is given budgetary control over military expenditures, and has the exclusive power to declare war and to authorize lesser belligerent activity such as "letters of marque and reprisal." Supreme Court Justice Joseph Story, in his *Commentaries on the Constitution*, wrote that war-making posed such threats to a republican form of government that it should only be done with the collective consent of all branches of government. In Story's view, the president could not conduct war on his own decision. He had not only to consult but obey the will of Congress. In such a view, the Supreme Court would stand ready to decide, in an appropriate case, that legislative and executive power was or was not being properly exercised.

My thoughts were not new or original. Senator Fulbright of Arkansas had expressed similar views, and a prominent committee of international lawyers had prepared a report containing a detailed analysis of American Vietnam policy as a matter of domestic and international law. I was frustrated once again by my law school, for there was nothing in the course offerings that permitted a detailed examination of these issues.

I turned my thoughts into a speech, which I delivered as valedictorian at my law school graduation. Presidential, and more broadly, executive branch decisions to make war, conduct unlawful searches, stifle dissent, and otherwise endanger rights ought in our system to be subjected to review by the other branches of government as well as being the subject of popular protest. Yet here was a war that had been approved by Congress only by the stratagem of false reports. I said:

> The course of this war imperils the American system of separation of powers. We witness the erosion of any Congressional check upon executive war-making activity.
>
> Article 1, section 8, clause 11 of the United States Constitution vests in Congress the power to declare war. The Constitutional Convention of 1787 considered giving the power to the Executive, where it had always rested under the British monarchy. But the Convention rejected this thought, and gave the President only the power to repel sudden attacks.
>
> A century and more ago, Joseph Story, distinguished lawyer and Justice of the United States Supreme Court and the greatest legal scholar of the 19th Century, wrote this of Congressional power:
>
>> The power of declaring war is not only the highest sovereign prerogative; but it is in its own nature and effects so critical and calamitous that it requires the utmost deliberation, and the successive review of all the councils of the nation. War . . . never fails to impose upon the people the most burthensome taxes, and personal sufferings. It is always injurious, and sometimes subversive of the great commercial, manufacturing and agricultural interests. . . . It is sometimes fatal to public liberty itself. . . . It should therefore be difficult in a republic to declare war; but not to make peace.

I urged graduates to take an interest in the developing law of the United Nations Charter and other domestic and international principles regulating armed conflict and its dangers. Half the audience stood and applauded and half sat on their hands. That was about the division of opinion that I would have expected.

In most of my reading, thinking, and speaking I focused on "the war" as a relatively distant object. But I remembered that millions of young men were facing decisions about their own participation in the war and in the protests against it. I recalled my own turmoil in my dispute with the Navy.

I looked at the legal framework within which young men were compelled to make decisions. A part of this framework was a provision of the 1967 Military Selective Service Act that required a young man who claimed conscientious objection to military service to demonstrate that his objection was based on "religious training and belief." In addition, the Act guaranteed a 2-S student deferment to any undergraduate but eliminated the largely discretionary practice by which students had been able to remain in college all the way through their graduate years without serious threat of induction into the armed forces.

The 1967 Act thus guaranteed that a young person whose family could afford to send him to college would be able to get a bachelor's degree. But upon graduation, he would be a prime target for induction because draft calls were supposed to be "oldest first." This preferential treatment tended to skew draft calls even more markedly toward people of color and those with low incomes.

The system of rules by which the Selective Service System operated was Byzantine to say the least. More than 4,000 local draft boards, each composed of citizens without legal training, made decisions as to whether a young man registered with them was to be classified 1-A, and eligible for service, or 1-O, and entitled to exemption as a conscientious objector, or 1-A-O, and eligible only for noncombatant service. The other principal exemptions and deferments included the 2-S student deferment and the 4-A ministerial exemption. All of these were the focus of controversy.

The local draft boards followed not only the Selective Service regulations that were published in the *Code of Federal Regulations*, but also a series of LBMs, or Local Board Memorandums, authored by the Director of Selective Service, General Lewis Hershey. These explanations of local board practices and procedures were often more important in practice than the regulations themselves.

Once the local board had made a classification decision, it communicated that to the registrant by letter and by issuing a card showing the classification. Thus, in theory, every young man between the ages of 18 and 35 was required to carry two documents. One was a registration certificate, showing the name and address of the local draft board where he happened to be registered. The other was the classification card. Failure to possess either of these, or destruction or mutilation of them, was a five-year felony. As the Prologue to this book recites, protests involving destruction or abandonment of one's "draft cards" also led to a summary order to report for induction.

Of course, conscription had been with us for a long time. Those familiar with American history will remember the "draft riots" that accompanied the imposition of conscription during the Civil War. It was fairly easy to avoid being drafted into the Union Army during the Civil War if you could pay someone to substitute for you. Also, investigation and pursuit of those who avoided service was lax to say the least.

The first truly organized system of conscription was established in 1917. The First World War draft treated inductees in a rather summary fashion. The statute provided that all persons drafted into the service of the United States shall, from the date of said draft, be subject to the laws and regulations governing the regular army—that is, from the moment you received your draft notice, you were a soldier. If you did not report, the Army rounded you up and court-martialed you as a deserter. Roundups of "slackers" occurred regularly. There is little formal record of the disposition of most cases resulting from such mass arrests. What we do have suggests that opposition to the war was centered in groups of political radicals and in some German communities. Thus, opposition to the war was reflected in the leaflets, demonstrations, and other activities that formed the basis of some of the Supreme Court's early First Amendment decisions sharply restricting the rights of Americans to criticize the foreign policy of their government during wartime.

As the Second World War approached, the Congress passed the Selective Training and Service Act of 1940. This was a significant departure from the the First World War experience. Enforcement was left to the civil courts and we had a draft system pretty much like the one that that obtained during the Korean and Vietnam wars. A registrant who claimed to be exempt or deferred from service would file an application with the local draft board. If the local draft board sustained the claim, then the registrant was deferred or exempt. If it refused it, the registrant had the right of appeal to a board that was also composed of volunteer citizens, but if that was exhausted unsuccessfully, the registrant was subject to induction in the order of oldest first.

There was, in most cases, no right of any pre-induction judicial review of these very important determinations. If a registrant showed up at the induction center when called and refused to take the symbolic step forward, signifying entrance into the armed forces, he would then be prosecuted for the five-year felony of refusing to submit. The Supreme Court held, in the waning days of the Second World War, that such a person could obtain judicial review of the draft board's classification as a defense to prosecution. The local board's decision was to be regarded as final, however, unless it had "no basis in fact" or was wrong as a matter of law. Alternatively, if the local board had failed to give the registrant some procedural rights, such as declining to give him a form on which to claim conscientious objection or denying him an appeal to which he was entitled, the induction notice was also void. In a trial for refusing to submit to induction, the judge and not a jury would determine if the order to report, and the classification on which it was based, were lawful.

One can see that the administrative process of the draft board and the regulations by which the board purported to operate were all-important. In 1966, I was largely ignorant of this law and lore, except for the limited personal experiences I have mentioned. However, it became clear by the end of 1967 that mounting resistance to the draft was creating a challenge for lawyers and others concerned with fairness in the operation of the Selective Service System. A few lawyers in cities around the country were studying the Selective Service regulations and advising registrants about their options. Some universities had established counseling centers where students could get advice about what faced them. The historic peace churches, such as the Quakers, advised those who wanted to claim conscientious objection for military service and spend time in some civilian capacity for a nonprofit organization instead of serving in the military. In addition, the Jehovah's Witnesses had reached a kind of standoff with the Selective Service System whereby members who devoted more than 100 hours a month to preaching could obtain exemption under the ministerial exemption. The Supreme Court also upheld the Jehovah's Witnesses claim that adherents to their creed were objectors to "war in any form," even though they did believe in the final conflict of Armageddon. These decisions helped to establish the principle that a conscientious objector need not be a pacifist; one could believe in using violence under certain circumstances, but reject the idea of uniformed warfare as an instrument of national policy.

SELECTIVE SERVICE LAW REPORTER

In the waning days of 1967 three friends of mine called and asked if I would be willing to edit a publication to be called the *Selective Service Law Reporter* (SSLR). They were Tom Alder, Charles Halpern, and Brian Paddock. Tom had been around Washington, working in a number of nonprofit organizations for many years. Halpern was an associate at the law firm of Arnold and Porter. Brian Paddock had a longtime association with peace organizations in his capacity as a lawyer. I agreed to edit SSLR and we hired a staff. Our job was to inform lawyers, draft counselors, and even registrants about the complex statutes, regulations, and decisional law that governed the rights and duties of young men from 18 to 35 years of age, all of whom were required to be registered with Selective Service.

We rented office space. We formed an advisory board of lawyers well known in the field of draft and military law, including Francis Heisler.

SSLR consisted basically of three parts. First we wanted the draft boards regulations to be public so that anyone could read them. It was fairly easy to copy the regulations published in the *Code of Federal Regulations*, but we wanted to go further. We thought that the Local Board Memorandums should be available to everyone and not just to the Board members. The Selective Service System took a different view and only on threat of litigation did it release to us the LBMs so that everybody could know the basis on which these life-and-death decisions were being made. Brian Paddock, a lawyer with draft law experience, and Bud Schoefer, who had been a draft counselor, brought their expertise to assembling the regulations so that we could reprint them, along with the statutes.

The second part consisted of judicial decisions, both those destined for inclusion in official reporters and the unreported decisions that increasingly formed the basis of the growing body of draft law. The third part was the most challenging. It was the *Practice Manual*, a treatise on the administrative Selective Service process, the prosecution of those who refused to report and for other offenses, and on the use of federal habeas corpus to get out of the military, assuming that you were already in. SSLR was a looseleaf publication, which allowed us to update its three parts monthly with revised statutes and regulations, new judicial decisions, and updates to the *Practice Manual*.

You can imagine the circumstances under which we began work. We began in earnest in the early months of 1968. The antiwar movement had become so strong and strident that it had threatened Lyndon Johnson's presidency. It was to lead to his refusal to seek a second full elected term. Robert Kennedy and Eugene McCarthy were poised to challenge Lyndon Johnson's renomination. McCarthy's speechwriter Sy Hersh asked me to write something McCarthy could use in a UCLA campaign speech, dealing with resistance to the draft.

The Democratic Party, riven by the disputes that had marked the 1964 Democratic Convention, had reorganized itself in a way that would grant increased floor time to dissident factions. The 1968 Democratic Convention was to be held in Chicago, political base of powerful Democratic Mayor Richard Daley. Demonstrations by antiwar groups were already being planned. The Vietnam War had become a centerpiece of student protest, though by no means its only element. Yet one could detect discontent about the escalation of the war, and the increased draft calls that were one result of it. The military draft touched the sons of families from all parts of society, even as it affected the poor and people of color most harshly. Lawyers in the law firm where I worked began to hear from their neighbors, asking how to protect their sons from being drafted.

Up to that time, nobody had written a comprehensive treatise on draft law. Some lawyers were gaining experience in these cases and developing their own forms. Organizations such as the Central Committee for Conscientious

Objectors and the Jehovah's Witnesses had their specialized publications for religion-based exemptions. The issues were also beclouded by the Military Selective Service Act of 1967, which recast significant portions of draft law.

In early 1968, I wrote the administrative section of the *Practice Manual*. LEXIS was in its infancy, and modem speeds of 300-baud made online research impossible. But I wanted a crash course: I took out *United States Code Annotated* and turned to the Selective Service law sections in Title 50. I read every case in the annotations. I then copied out West Publishing's key numbers from those cases, and went back to read every case decided under older versions of conscription law, dating back to the Civil War.

I wanted to see patterns of legal development, and to make sure that nothing escaped me. I am convinced that this method of research, tiresome though it is, is the best means to "capture" a complex subject. In these electronic days, law students are learning to rely too much on computer-assisted research. They think up a query and plug it in. The cases the machine spits out define the borders of their galaxy of thought. They have no idea that the boundaries might be different than they believe, or of where their chosen galaxy lies in the universe of legal ideology. Simply put, computer research alone is incomplete. It confines thinking. It misses important citations. It is not very helpful in finding analogies, which are a key element of common law reasoning.

Before focusing on particular aspects of a problem, one must examine all of its details and then form an impression of it that takes in the whole. I use, when talking to lawyers, the example of Claude Monet, who sometimes painted the same scene over and over, each rendering giving a different impression. If you read Justice Douglas's opinion for the Supreme Court in David Gutknecht's case, you will find that he annexed to the opinion a history of the delinquency regulations; that history is taken from the brief I wrote. I wanted the Court to see how arbitrary and baseless the process had become.

For me, learning conscription law was only the beginning. The local draft board's errors in construing draft law might indeed invalidate its actions. But if we were to help lawyers shape the law, we needed to overlay three more bodies of knowledge. These were administrative law, criminal procedure, and civil procedure—all as applied in the conscription context.

The Selective Service System had functioned for too long as a law unto itself, outside the mainstream of administrative due process. Yet several Supreme Court decisions had recognized the System's obligation to respect its own procedural rules. The System was exempt from the Administrative Procedure Act, but surely there were relevant notions of administrative due process that could be invoked at the local board level, and then referred to in the event of litigation.

The need to understand criminal procedure was obvious as well. To challenge an erroneous order to report for induction, the registrant had to show up, refuse induction, and then defend a criminal case. For years, draft advice was given mostly by lay counselors. The lawyers who were entering the field were in many cases innocent of any knowledge of federal criminal practice. I was lucky. Williams & Connolly had introduced me to complex federal criminal litigation.

By early summer I had the administrative section done. In the summer of 1968, I took a family vacation in California for a month. For three weeks of that month, I sat down at an electric typewriter every day and worked on the criminal practice section of the *Practice Manual*. I drafted at speed, noting the need for footnotes and authorities with cryptic notations. Once the text was finished, I went back and put in the footnotes, drawing on the conscription cases I had read and my knowledge of criminal law.

In those days before the word processor, the three-ring binder was the height of technology. I typed the draft with large margins on three-hole punched paper. This kept the pages in some kind of order. When it came time to do the footnotes, I typed them on separate pages and then cut and pasted them so they would be at the bottom of the correct page.

I look back fondly at those sections of the *Practice Manual*. Sometimes lawyers of my generation will mention SSLR and its role in their professional lives. Sometimes younger lawyers will remember that their lawyer or draft counselor had a copy. You can find SSLR in law libraries to this day, and digitized versions exist as well. I also look back at the reviews of our work, including one in the *Yale Law Journal* by Judge J. Skelly Wright.

In 1968, 1969, and 1970, I crisscrossed the country, talking to bar groups, law schools, and draft counselors. In the debate about the Vietnam War, our work was controversial for its own sake. Many people thought it disloyal to be telling young men how not to serve in the military. I got some of this sentiment from lawyers at Williams & Connolly, where Ed Williams was still paying me well to work part-time. Their criticism was muted when well-heeled clients called and asked if their sons could come in and consult with me.

Our work helped to put into the field a cadre of trained lawyers and counselors. With their efforts the conviction rate in draft refusal cases plummeted and even those convicted were getting lighter sentences. Although there were no published statistics, lawyers and counselors also achieved a creditable record of success before the local draft boards. The downside of these developments was that the burden of military service tended to fall more heavily on those without access to counsel and information. That group was disproportionately young men of color. For that reason, I did not inveigh against the institution of conscription, but rather against the pursuit of national military policies that were used to justify it.

Among the most strident attacks on draft advising were mounted by segments of the organized bar. For years, non-lawyers had been the best experts on the draft, generally working from church-related groups such as the Central Committee for Conscientious Objectors. With the advent of SSLR, and the increased need for reliable information on the draft, non-lawyer counselors began to work from civic organizations, colleges, and political groups. Bar associations claimed that these folks, most of whom were not charging for their services, were engaged in the unauthorized practice of law. In some instances, bar associations sought injunctions.

The theory of unauthorized practice is that non-lawyers are not competent to interpret the law, and the public must be protected from them. Behind these noble words often lurks a desire to keep the profession's monopoly intact, by requiring that only lawyers perform services that non-lawyers could do just as well or better, such as real estate closings. In this instance, there was no financial motive at work. Most lawyers did not know draft law, did not care to practice it, and would not have taken on the job of counseling young men for free. "Unauthorized practice" became a screen for political motivations, rather like the attacks on lawyers in the South who were trying to encourage African-Americans to join civil rights cases.

I also helped young men who were having trouble with the draft. In all of this work, I saw—and tried to get others to see—the unity of legal theory and practice, in itself and in a social context. In order to do a good job as a draft lawyer, you had to understand administrative law. You had to see how concepts like free expression, religious tolerance, and due process overlay the more technical aspects of advising draft registrants. And if the draft board denied relief, and the administrative process did not work, you had to defend the ensuing criminal case with both technical proficiency and a broad view of what your client stood for.

For example, in most of the conscientious objector cases, victory at trial came because the draft board had denied the registrant some procedural right, or misapplied its own regulations. Yet it was necessary in every case to stress the client's sincerity, and even to challenge the legality of the war in which he had been summoned to fight. The Supreme Court, over a dissent by Justices Douglas and Stewart, refused to consider these legal challenges to the war itself, but the legal arguments helped fuel opposition to American foreign policy. That opposition brought changes in draft law and eventually an end to the war. The activism spilled over into the Chicago conspiracy trial of 1969 and 1970.

At a time when the apparatus of repression was becoming more overt, the movement against the war and the draft was gaining ground. Looking back, the sole criticism that one might have is that this movement focused almost entirely on how and whether American youth were being sent to war, and not on the injustice of the United States' imperial ambitions in Southeast Asia, the death toll among people who lived there, the irreparable environmental harm wrought on their countries.

I opened this memoir with my first Supreme Court argument, a draft case. I represented many young men who were indicted for various alleged crimes related to the draft and the war. The draft was not only a means to raise an army for Vietnam. As I wrote in the Prologue, Selective Service Director Hershey had authorized local draft boards to help curb dissent against the war by issuing draft notices to dissentient registrants. Looking back, of course, there was finally amnesty for the draft offenders during the Carter administration, but that came only after the judicial tide had turned and conviction rates were down. A few stories will paint the picture.

RICK

Rick lived in suburban Maryland. I remember him as frail, bespectacled, with a wispy beard. He dressed in dark colors, neatly. He had grown up as part of the Washington-area Jewish community, traditionally a strong center of social justice concern.

It came as no surprise, therefore, that when he reached eighteen and registered for the draft, he applied for conscientious objector status. He was articulate. He was able to show his local draft board that he had a basis in religious training and belief to claim that he was conscientiously opposed to war in any form. The Supreme Court had helped by interpreting the Selective Service laws to avoid a God-based test that would have fallen afoul of the First Amendment by "establishing" religion. His local board classified him I-O, conscientious objector to all participation in war.

With his I-O classification, Rick was ready for the two years of alternative civilian service that the law required. He was not ready for the vindictive attitudes of his local board and the Selective Service System. He was ordered to report for work at a Baptist social service center in Mississippi. During his first week on the job, the overt anti-Semitism of his supervisors was combined with hostility to his "draft-dodging." He quit the center and came home. When he was, in due course, indicted in Mississippi federal court for refusing to perform civilian work, he came to see me.

This was a case about objectives. Rick wanted to do civilian work. He was not interested in risking, much less going to, federal prison. The federal court in Mississippi was a legendary harbor of reactionary sentiment. Appellate review in the United States Court of Appeals for the Fifth Circuit—which included Mississippi—was much more likely to be unfavorable than in the District of Columbia Circuit.

For Rick, therefore, the goal was to get him into some civilian work that would not be a punishment for his views, and to avoid the stain of a criminal conviction on his record. In those days, in the District of Columbia federal district court, you could plead your client guilty before any district judge who would agree to take the plea. So if your client was a gambler, you had a good idea which judge to choose, and if a white-collar criminal, a different judge. I approached Judge William Bryant, and told him about the case. He agreed to take a guilty plea, but with no promise of what he would do about sentence.

Next, I negotiated a transfer of Rick's case from Mississippi to the District of Columbia under Federal Rule of Criminal Procedure 20, which is designed to let a defendant who wishes to plead guilty to do so in a district of his choice.

I thought, naively, that once the case was before Judge Bryant all would be well. I could not imagine a judge with compassion, and a background in criminal defense and community law, sending Rick to prison. I reckoned without the pressure that other judges would put on a relatively new appointee to the bench, and without Rick's own misguided judgment.

On the day appointed for sentence, Judge Bryant's secretary called me and asked me to come to court immediately. I was not to wait for the afternoon calendar call. The judge was furious. Rick, in a gesture of love, had sent the judge a bouquet of flowers. He did not mean any harm, and he had not asked my advice. It was a nutty thing to do.

As Judge Bryant vented his anger at me, our conversation turned to what he was going to do about sentence. "I won't do it today," he said. "I am too angry. But let me ask you this: What am I supposed to do? Here is a young man who gets everything the system has to offer. He gets his CO classification. He just can't stand the pressure down there in Mississippi with those Baptists. I don't necessarily buy that. I am a black American, and I have lived with hostility all my life one way and another. Why can't this kid grow up?"

I thought about this. "Well, Judge, the decision is yours. This is not an isolated case. Thirty-seven percent of the Harvard graduating class says they would not serve in the Vietnam War. What do we tell those young men? What do we do about the draft boards being hostile to conscientious objectors? These young people are not dropping out. Almost all of them recognize some obligation to serve their country in some way that does not involve killing. So why not figure out a way to tap in to that desire?"

"Well," the judge said, "that's not all. The other judges around here are not happy about your client. I am getting some pressure to make an example of him."

"I can't answer for that," I said. "I know what you are saying, and I can only hope you will listen to our sentencing plan." The prosecutor was not there, and I did not want to descend into an argument for a particular result in this *ex parte* setting.

I left chambers and got a new sentencing date. Our proposal was that Rick be sentenced to probation on condition that he perform alternative civilian service with a community group I had found. We asked that he be sentenced under the Young Adult Offender Act, so that when his probation was finished his conviction would be expunged. That would put him more or less back where he would have been if the local board had not sent him to Mississippi. I went to talk to the Assistant U.S. Attorney, who had children of his own. He would not consent to this plan, but did agree to stand mute at sentencing— that is, to let Rick and me make our case and not comment one way or the other. Rick got his probation.

LOUIS

I don't remember how I met Louis. No doubt somebody told him about this young lawyer who had written a guide on trying draft cases. He was, I remember, from Louisiana. He had asked his local draft board to be classified as a conscientious objector, but the local board didn't do that sort of thing. In his hometown, there wasn't much war resistance going on, nothing to affiliate with. So he and his girlfriend drifted north. Lou was by no means a leader. He was just one of the tens of thousands of young men who were saying no to the Vietnam War and to the draft.

In Washington, he joined a group that was demonstrating in front of Selective Service headquarters. In view of the television cameras, he took out his Selective Service registration and classification cards and tore them up: two five-year felonies right there.

The theory of this requirement to carry the cards was presumably that if a nuclear war erupted and wiped out the Selective Service records, the military could round up enough able-bodied young men to get the fighting done. Prosecutions under these sections were very few in the mid-1960s. However, once draft-age young men began to burn, tear up, or refuse to carry their cards, prosecutors began bringing more cases. The Selective Service System even adopted the delinquency regulations at issue in David Gutknecht's case.

Louis's protest was on the cusp of these changes. A guard picked up the pieces of his cards and sent them to the FBI. I had been admitted to the bar for about a year, and this case might be nicknamed "pathways of illusion." I had learned how to pick apart, and move to dismiss, an indictment that did not spell out the offense with enough detail and certainty. I had learned the value of a "bill of particulars" to refine the indictment's allegations: Under the case law and Federal Rule of Criminal Procedure 7(f), a prosecutor was required to give the defense details of the charge—and variances between those details and the proof at trial might be seized upon to obtain dismissal or acquittal. Too, the prosecutor was required to give discovery.

Beyond these procedural issues, I wanted to address the meaning of this statute that authorized punishment of anyone who "alters, knowingly destroys, knowingly mutilates, or in any manner changes" a draft card. The Supreme Court had held that such action did not qualify as protected speech, but rather as unprotected expressive conduct. Surely one could argue that the First Amendment dictated a narrowing construction of the statute. Lou had torn up his card, but with a little Scotch tape it would be as good as new.

All of these were good theories. I hoped that, given my status as associate in Washington's premier criminal defense firm, I would receive the same respectful attention that Ed Williams observably received in the local federal court. I had trouble imagining the visceral hostility of older conservative judges—and some not so conservative ones—to the protests against the Vietnam War and to the often unruly and ill-dressed protesters.

I wrote motions to dismiss, for particulars, and for discovery. The case was assigned to Chief Judge Edward Curran, an aging Irish-Catholic with a reputation for dealing softly with gamblers and white-collar defendants. The prosecutor was Assistant U.S. Attorney Earl Silbert, later to become U.S. Attorney and to have some difficulty figuring out what really happened in the Watergate burglary. Earl was bright and able, but with a very short fuse.

For this hearing on legal motions, Lou did not need to be present. It was just as well. I began my argument on the indictment, and I thought I ably criticized a case decided by the U.S. Court of Appeals for the Second Circuit, which covers New York and Vermont.

"What's wrong with the Second Circuit?" Curran demanded.

"Well, Your Honor, it is clearly less concerned with defendants' rights than our own D.C. Circuit," I ventured. The frown on Curran's face showed that he had doubts about the D.C. Circuit's innovative criminal procedure holdings.

"Maybe that's not all bad," said Judge Curran. "How many motions have you filed?"

"There are five, Your Honor," I said, and began to name them.

Judge Curran held up his hand with fingers outstretched. "OK," he said, counting on his fingers, "denied, denied, denied, denied, denied. Let's set a trial date." So much for my legal theories.

Before Lou's trial came up, a group of protesters was arrested blocking the entrance of the National Selective Service headquarters on G Street N.W, two blocks from the White House. In 1968, this sort of thing would not have attracted much attention, except that this demonstration was led by Lea Adams, daughter of one of Selective Service Director Lewis Hershey's top assistants, General Adams. General Adams was the only African-American in a leadership role at Selective Service.

The demonstrators were hauled off to jail for blocking the sidewalk. At that time, the misdemeanor court, the Court of General Sessions, held night court. The idea was to get bailable offenders out of jail, and to clear up minor cases with on-the-spot plea bargains. Our misfortune was that Judge Charles Halleck was sitting that night. He was the son of a prominent Republican congressman. In later years, he found love and tolerance and let his hair grow long. But that had not happened yet.

My friend Spencer Smith and I came downtown to represent the protesters. We thought we should move for bail first. If we could get everybody out on their own recognizance, then we could ask for a long continuance and maybe things would calm down and the U.S. Attorney would drop the case. If bail was too high to meet, we didn't want these young people in the old D.C. Jail, so we might ask for trial within a couple of days.

Speedy trial in a case like that can work for the defense. The police haven't had time to compare notes. They may not have found some good photographs to study, and may be confused about who sat where and when. Cross-examination can raise that reasonable doubt.

These protesters were really making the same complaint that drove Louis. The Selective Service System was probably the most uncommunicative part of government—leaving aside agencies like the CIA that dwelt in a world of their own. It tried to keep its regulations and procedures a mystery. At every stage, it sought to make its decisions unreviewable by never giving—and perhaps not even having—a reason for saying that this young man would go to war and this other one would not. General Hershey, the longtime Director and symbol of the Selective Service System, ran the agency like J. Edgar Hoover ran the FBI—in a highly personal way that tolerated no dissent or interference. So a jury might well decide that this sit-in on a sidewalk did not so incommode the passersby that their message should be punished.

These were our thoughts as we faced Judge Halleck. "If the court please, we would like to get the issue of bail settled for these young people and then get a trial date," I said.

Halleck grinned and stroked his crew cut. "Not so fast, Mr. Tigar. First a trial date, then I'll think about bail."

Time for Plan B. "In that case, Your Honor, we would request a trial as soon as possible. We are ready."

"OK, Tigar," the Judge said, dropping the honorific "Mr.," October 31. How'd you like to try these creeps on Halloween?"

My mouth moved more quickly than my brain. "That depends on whether Your Honor was thinking of a trick or a treat."

Judge Halleck did not think this funny, but he set bail fairly reasonably. A few days later, we came to court for trial and managed to get the case away from Judge Halleck. The defendants went to trial and were found not guilty.

Louis's case was much more serious. The median sentence in draft cases was around three years, but because D.C. did not have an induction center where men actually refused to enter the armed forces, we did not have sentencing figures for the District's federal judges.

The case was assigned for trial to Judge Howard Corcoran, who was appointed by President Lyndon Johnson. He was brother to Tommy "the Cork" Corcoran, a premier Washington insider since the FDR days. Edward Bennett Williams called Tommy and people like him "rainmakers," by which he meant that they would confide, as inside information, that it would rain or that it would not. Since they had at least a 50 percent chance of being right, their reputations grew. Tommy claimed influence over Howard's appointment. Judge Corcoran's politics were surely not conservative, but Louis was, after all, protesting Lyndon Johnson's war.

Judge Corcoran was patient, though. I had not much trial experience. I made a lot of objections to admissibility of evidence. Some were thin, to say the least. But he treated me as though I knew what I was doing. All of these objections meant a lot of conferences at the bench, so the jurors would not hear. I thought of "going to the bench" as part of what lawyers did. Louis and his girlfriend Mary thought differently.

Mary was a sketch artist. She produced a drawing of Louis in the foreground, pensive, sitting at counsel table. In the distance sat the judge, with me and the prosecutor huddled with him arguing some legal point. The jurors sat off to one side in shadow. The memory of that picture, which Mary and Louis kept, has stayed with me. Here is somebody on trial for their liberty, and the important issues are being thrashed out, off in the distance, in conversations they do not hear. The sense of alienation that every defendant feels must be heightened by such doings, as though the law's studied unconcern can be crueler than deliberate vengeance.

The jurors, too, must resent being excluded from important decisions in so visible a way. If the conferences are frequent and long, the interruptions become part of jurors' overall resentment at the waste of their time. "It is the privilege of the rich," says the poet Stevie Smith mockingly, "to waste the time of the poor."

I have tried to learn this lesson. I make fewer objections, and try to make them in a way that does not interrupt what is going on unless absolutely necessary. I propose to trial judges that "speaking objections" and bench conferences be limited, and that lawyers and the judge deal with such matters before the jury arrives or at recesses. I make a file for every possible evidentiary and legal issue that may arise, so that I can draft a two- or three-page memorandum on short notice. I try to phrase objections so that the jurors and everybody else can see what is going on. For example, "Objection," not "I object," to the hearsay. Most people know that hearsay is not a good substitute for direct testimony.

I also object to excluding my client from most chambers conferences with the court. Sometimes, these objections are not successful. A criminal defendant need be present only at "critical stages" of the case, and some legal conferences are not thought by judges to be "critical." Defendants whose life and liberty are at stake understandably disagree.

I had not learned all those lessons then. Judge Corcoran would not agree that tearing up your draft card was not "mutilating" it, even if the card fragmenrs could be reassembled. The evidence against Louis was straightforward. Several police officers saw him tear up the cards. The local CBS affiliate obediently gave its film to the FBI, so that Louis's actions could be projected on a screen. This was a case that a prosecutor could not possibly lose.

So why not fold our hand right then and plead guilty, perhaps reserving for appeal a legal issue about whether the card was really "mutilated"? One practical answer was that we didn't think Judge Corcoran would give Louis more jail time if he went ahead and had a jury trial.

Hidden in this case, and the participants' reactions to it, is a profound debate about what Louis had done. Was it "civil disobedience," such that he should acknowledge that he had broken the written law and accept his punishment? This is the view popularly ascribed to Socrates in his dialogue "The Crito." Socrates has been condemned to death by the Athenian equivalent of a jury, for corrupting the youth. He has a chance to escape, but refuses. He speaks instead of his continued obligation as a citizen to accept the judgment, having accepted to live in Athens and enjoy its benefits.

I understand this view. I have never agreed with it. Some protesters want a sort of martyrdom, and they are entitled to try for it. The perceived injustice of jailing or executing someone who has acted on principle may indeed help to bring about change. And the imprecations heaped on someone who escapes punishment by a "technicality" are real, as though enforcing some constitutional claim to freedom or fairness, or obtaining a jury acquittal, were "technical."

There are many good reasons to disobey a law that one believes is unjust. Sometimes disobedience is a purely personal statement and being punished for violation is a part of the process that the protester finds congenial to the statement he or she wants to make. Such cases are rare. The disobedient one more usually wants to make a statement—to speak truth to power as the Quakers have it. Sometimes these truths are spoken to a prosecutor who declines prosecution. Sometimes to a judge who dismisses the charges, or a jury that acquits. An appellate court may reverse a conviction, or moderate the jail time.

The protester is seeking to strike a responsive chord. The tide of protest against the Vietnam War moved prosecutors, judges, and juries to acquit more and more protesters, and to moderate sentences for those whose convictions were upheld. This phenomenon had historical forebears. Prohibition did not work because so many people paid no attention to it and the courts were notoriously lax in dealing with offenders. In a much earlier time, the English Quakers led by William Penn were acquitted by their jury in 1670, thus making a statement about the right to demonstrate for one's beliefs and the independence of the jury. The prosecutors would inveigh, "The defendant takes the law in his own hands." To which a logical, though perhaps unspoken, reply would be, "They are better hands than those that have been holding it."

John Brown was convicted and sentenced to death, but he made of his trial a convincing story of slavery's evils. As the song has it, "His soul [went] marching on." In 1873, Susan B. Anthony violated the law by voting—a right reserved by the law to males— to make a statement about what the Fourteenth Amendment ought to mean. She was prosecuted. Woman suffrage protesters, angered that President Woodrow Wilson reneged on his promise to support a suffrage amendment to the Constitution, chained themselves to the White House fence, provoking political turmoil that helped get the amendment ratified. In each of these cases, I would not expect the defendant to accept blandly the court's judgment and go down to jail or death.

The lawyer must remember that the choice of approach is the client's to make, after the lawyer has explored and explained the alternatives. The lawyer commits an ethical violation by overriding the client's judgment. In cases where the client's choice is being influenced by a group with which he or she has an affinity, the lawyer must champion the client's right to choose. Louis had chosen to make his protest. He also chose to address —or to have his lawyer address—a judge and jury to make the case that the legal system should endorse, or at least excuse, his conduct.

Louis's act of tearing up his cards was, in my opinion, justified by the way he had been treated. And the way he had been treated mirrored what was also happening to tens of thousands of young men. So Louis had something to say, and maybe his saying it could make a difference. We had not convinced the prosecutors, nor Judge Corcoran, but we were not done yet. As we look back on that time, the stand taken by people like Louis was part of a national movement against the Vietnam War that changed the face of American politics.

Louis took the stand and faced the jury. We were going to do what my mentor Edward Bennett Williams thought was a very bad idea: we were going to put some politics into this trial. Ed was a Roman Catholic, devout in his way. He had little patience for the Catholic movements that encouraged civil disobedience, or for that matter for most of the Vietnam War protests that were on the fringes of the law. When Dr. Benjamin Spock, Reverend William Sloane Coffin, Dr. Marcus Raskin, and others were indicted on January 5, 1968, for encouraging young men to resist the draft and turn in their draft cards, the American Civil Liberties Union staff counsel asked me to approach Ed Williams to see if he would represent the defendants pro bono.

I went to see him on a Saturday. He said, "Being out of the office would cause real financial problems here. Can they at least pay something?"

"I think so," I said, sensing that this was not really the issue.

"Well, will they take direction? I need client control. I wouldn't want them mouthing off about the case."

"Ed, their political lives are centered in being in the public arena. It is a little difficult to think that they would be muzzled." I was losing this battle, I could tell.

"And at the trial, I suppose they all want to get on the stand to make speeches about the war in Vietnam. Right?"

"I think they want to tell their story and the reason for their actions."

"Well then," Ed replied, although with the trace of a smile, "they don't need a lawyer. They need a toastmaster." So Dr. Spock was tried, convicted, and his conviction reversed on First Amendment grounds under the brilliant leadership of lead lawyer Leonard Boudin. The court of appeals decision in *Spock* became the centerpiece of arguments about the use of conspiracy law in political cases, including my work for Angela Davis.

I did not think I was Louis's toastmaster. It was important how his story came out. I wanted to have a conversation with him, in the jury's presence. We were treading close to the line. He was entitled to tell the jury his story so they could judge his intent. He was not entitled to make a frontal challenge to the judge's legal opinion that tearing up a card was mutilating it.

The testimony of a criminal defendant who takes the stand—and by no means all of them will or should—is in three strophes. This respects the Greek rhetoricians' theory that "triplets" are the most persuasive form. The three are: "Who am I?" "What did I do?" "What is a just and fair way of looking at what I did?" The defendant may always be introduced to the jury, and may introduce himself. Judges can limit these presentations in terms of time and content, but may not curtail them altogether. So the jury can know the defendant's upbringing, background, and basic attitude toward life. The more central that state of mind is to the result, the more latitude the defense will have.

"What did I do?" presents a counterpoint to the prosecution's version of events, or at least a more ample context. When I make an opening statement, I will begin with a discussion of what happened, rather than starting with a long introduction of the defendant. This is because the jury has just heard the prosecutor's opening, with a graphic statement of what the defendant allegedly did. The jury is ready to hear the defense counter this, and not an explanation of who this defendant is and what he stands for. So, in the opening statement, we usually start with only a brief introduction of the defendant, then go into the facts and then return to look at the defendant's life in more detail.

"What is a just and fair way of looking at what I did?" is the most diffi-cult part. In most American non-capital cases, the jury does not sentence the defendant, so there is usually little occasion for him to discuss a mild versus harsh sentence. However, there are sometimes lesser charges on which a jury can compromise, and a defendant's statement of intention can lead a jury to acquit outright.

Louis took the stand. His quiet, gentle manner was very much in evidence. The jury wanted to meet this young man who had been seen only in the pros-ecution's version and on news film. Because we knew that Louis would be testifying, I had introduced him during opening statement, but this was the real thing and not some lawyer's version. Like all trial events prefigured in opening statement, this was the time when jurors could see if I was telling them the truth.

He had grown up in a middle-class home. He was successful in school. The Vietnam War, with its escalating demand for soldiers, was a big topic of conversation at his high school and in his community.

The jurors watched Louis carefully. Their median age was between 35 and 40. Most of them were African-Americans. In their communities, these discussions had also taken place. I continued asking Louis questions:

Q: Did you make a decision about the War?

A: Yes. I thought that we had no business there, that we were fighting for an unjust regime. I did not want to be part of that.

Q: What did you do about that?

A: I was registered with my local draft board. I knew about people who left the country to avoid service. I did not want to do that. The guys in my high school, some of them were enlisting, others were being drafted.

Q: So what did you do?

A: I got a book about the draft and read about what it means to be a conscientious objector.

Q: What did that mean to you—to be a conscientious objector?

A: It meant that you would serve just like you had been drafted into the military. But you would serve the community in some other way—some way that did not involve killing or war.

Q: Did you think you were a conscientious objector?

A: I knew I was opposed to war, and that I wanted to serve. To be what the draft board calls a conscientious objector, you have to fill out a form showing that you are opposed to any form of war. You have to show some religious belief.

Q: Did you think you met that test?

A: As I read about it, I did.

Q: What did you do about that?

A: I filled out the form, and I went to the local draft board for an interview.

Q: What happened?

A: They treated me like I was a communist, a disloyal person.

Louis continued by telling about the local draft board refusing to classify him as a conscientious objector, and then the draft appeal board upholding that decision. He was barely twenty years old. He had taken a stand in his community for what he thought was right. And, as happened to literally thousands who had taken similar stands during all the time we have had the system of conscription for military service, he was rebuffed by petty officials in the rudest possible way.

He had not started out to resist the law; he started out to obey it, to serve his country in the manner provided by the laws and the Constitution. It was his local board who were the lawbreakers, and there was no way to take them to court for their lawbreaking except by risking a felony conviction. That is, he could wait and get a notice to report for induction, and refuse to submit. Then a judge would rule on whether his conscientious objector claim was valid. The local board would probably dwell in ignorance of how his case came out—and would keep on interpreting the law as it wished.

In this system of non-accountability, Louis chose from among the limited alternatives. He hit the road. He had no clear idea of where he would end up. He wanted to be near people who shared his ideals. As things turned out, he made the right choice. Had he stayed home and refused induction, he would have faced trial in the most hostile federal court system in the nation, with the slimmest possible chance of victory and a long prison term if he lost.

Louis continued his story, right up to the day he tore up his card. We took the card, which was in evidence, and put it back together as though the fragments were puzzle pieces, so that the jury could see it was basically all there. Why did he make this public protest?

A: I wanted—I want—people to know that the War is wrong. I want them to know that whatever you think about the War, the draft system is unfair.

The jurors listened carefully. Then came final arguments and the judge's instructions. We ran into a little luck. Assistant U.S. Attorney Earl Silbert had, as I say, a short fuse. In his summation, he laid out the evidence. He knew that the judge would tell the jury that to tear up a draft card was to mutilate it. This was, he told the jury, an easy case.

In my summation, I mostly ignored the legal instructions the judge would be giving. I did say that the term "mutilate" was an ordinary English word that they could figure out for themselves—almost, but not quite, contradicting the judge. The instructions were not helpful, except for the ones on reasonable doubt and on the jury's role.

In the end, members of the jury, this case is not so much about events as about a human being. It is about Louis [in the summation, I used his last name too], his journey. To be young, and to face decisions about war and peace, life and death, taking life or preserving life—is almost too much to bear. To have answers to those most basic and personal questions dictated to you by people who refuse to listen—that is so humiliating. For the young, in the face of injustice and intolerance, all journeys are uncommonly long and all roads suddenly uncommonly straight. So they may act out their beliefs. . . .

Louis expected that the draft board would obey the law. That it would listen to and read what he had to say. That it would not rush to judgment. We are, it is true, engaged in a war. Young men like Louis are asking "What are we fighting for?"

I was deliberately provocative. If there were a few jurors ready to send a message to the Selective Service System, I hoped to arouse their interest. This jury included people who had been the victims of racism, and who had perhaps struggled against it. I also thought that Earl Silbert would have trouble keeping his temper.

Silbert's rebuttal was, as one of his colleagues later said with understatement, "problematic." He attacked Louis for disloyalty. He invoked the spectre of men dying on foreign battlefields. The judge overruled my objections to this line of argument, saying that I had "opened the door."

The jury was out for many hours, but finally came in with a guilty verdict. The judge, after a pre-sentence report, sentenced Louis to three years in prison. We got bail pending appeal, so Louis remained at liberty.

I arrived early the morning of oral argument on the appeal. The U.S. Court of Appeals for the District of Columbia Circuit sits in the same building as the district courts. In those days, back in 1969, you did not know which judges would hear your case until the panel of three came on the bench. As we waited for court to begin, I spoke with Tom Green, the Assistant U.S. Attorney who would argue for the government. He smilingly said that he had rebuked Silbert for his rebuttal summation.

In the real world of appeals, a prosecutor's misconduct in summation will seldom produce a reversal. But if the court is troubled about the case for other reasons, this is a good basis for decision because such cases are so fact-intensive and therefore have little effect as precedent.

The judges took the bench. I began my argument with a brief statement of the facts and of our central contentions. I had not been speaking for long when Judge Wright said, "Mr. Tigar, is it clear from this record that this young man is sincerely a conscientious objector?" I said I thought so. The judge continued, "So where this all starts is that he wanted to do civilian service and the local board said no?" I said yes. This case was being argued after we had begun publication of the *Selective Service Law Reporter*, which Judge Wright had reviewed in the *Yale Law Journal*. Most law clerks were young males, and they would all have been sensitive to the issues that underlay the case.

"Mr. Green," Judge Wright asked, "does the government agree that this young man was sincere?"

Tom got to his feet and stuttered a bit. This oral argument was not like any he—or I—had witnessed. "I have no reason to doubt what Mr. Tigar is telling you," he finally said.

"Then," the judge said, "if he is willing to do civilian alternative service, shouldn't the district judge have considered sentencing him under the Young Adult Offenders Act? That way, he would do civilian service as a condition of probation, and his conviction would be expunged at the end of that time." We had asked Judge Corcoran for this, and our request was in the record. But Corcoran had refused.

It was by now clear that the judges had talked about this issue before taking the bench. So Judge Wright continued, "There are several difficult issues presented by this record. However, it may well be that Mr. Tigar and his client would be satisfied with a Young Adult Offender sentence. We will hold this case in abeyance and remand to the district judge to reconsider the sentence. If the defendant is not satisfied with the sentence on remand, he can bring the case back up and we will decide it."

A couple of days later, the court's formal order to that effect came in the mail. Silbert and I went to see Judge Corcoran in his chambers. He was furious. "They don't have the power to do this. Sentences within the term allowed by law are not reviewable on appeal. This is blackmail." I sat quietly. The goal was clear—get that sentence—and provoking Judge Corcoran would not get us there. A chastened Earl Silbert urged the judge to go along with what the court of appeals had suggested.

"Very well," Judge Corcoran finally said, "on the government's suggestion, which is a change of position from when you asked me to give him hard time, I will re-sentence."

So Louis wound up where he had wanted to be. He did his alternative service as a teacher, had his conviction wiped away, and wound up in teaching and counseling as a career. He called me some twenty years later to tell me how he was doing. Of course, to get "where he wanted to be" he had to risk prison and live on the fringe. His solace was that in processing his case, the legal system was forced to stop and think about what it was doing to young men like him.

LARRY

The son of a San Antonio, Texas, businessman, Larry took his conscientious objector stand after reading deeply in religious texts. His draft board was not convinced. He had filed his CO application before the Military Selective Service Act of 1967 was passed. Under the pre-1967 procedures, the FBI investigated all conscientious objector claims and filed a report with the local draft board. FBI reports that supported claims of conscientious objection were rare—I don't remember hearing of one. Thus, in challenging the draft board's decision, one had to deal with the one-sided FBI report. As I tried more federal criminal cases, I became familiar with the FBI Form 302, "Report of Interview," prepared by the agent or agents from notes that they often destroyed. 302s are notoriously economical with the truth, and invariably slanted.

By 1969, when I was retained, Larry had refused induction, and had been convicted, and sentenced to three years in prison. I took his appeal to the United States Court of Appeals for the Fifth Circuit. That was my first oral argument in that court. The case came to me through some San Antonio lawyers who became friends and colleagues over the years: Maury Maverick, Jr., Bernard Ladon, Jesse Oppenheimer, and Herb Kelleher, who was later CEO of Southwest Airlines and was an even better airline executive than he was a lawyer.

At oral argument at the federal courthouse in Houston, Larry and his family sat in the spectator section. The Assistant U.S. Attorney arguing for the government adopted a high-dudgeon style. At his rhetorical apogee, he said, "And you know, this young man is not a Christian pacifist at all. The evidence shows he believes in the Karl Marx theory of Communism!" Pretty strong stuff, I thought.

In rebuttal, I gestured toward Larry and his family. "You know," I said, "I need to answer this Karl Marx business, here before [Larry] and his parents. That allegation shows up in the FBI report, from an anonymous person that [Larry] never had a chance to confront or answer. Probably some hostile neighbor."

Judge Homer Thornberry looked down at me. "You mean to say that this is one of those FBI anonymous neighbor things, and never tested or verified?"

"That's right, Judge Thornberry."

The judge looked with disapproval at the prosecutor. "Oh, my goodness!" he said. The lesson is there for every litigating lawyer. You can lose the judge or jury with a single burst of over-the-top rhetoric. If you want your decider to come to a conclusion, you can't push them there with imagery. The court of appeals reversed the conviction.

ROSALIO

Rosalio Muñoz was a student at UCLA, where I taught at the law school. He was student body president, and leader of the Chicano Peace Movement, active in opposition to the Vietnam War. Chicano youth had a particular complaint against the Selective Service System, as they were drafted, sent to Vietnam, and killed in a larger percentage than Anglo youth. There were many reasons for this disparity. Lack of educational opportunity meant that kids in the barrio did not go on to college and therefore benefit from the automatic four-year student deferment. Young Chicanos had less access to information and counseling about their options with respect to the draft. And there was certainly a great deal of anecdotal evidence that conservative Anglo draft boards favored Anglo youth in making up their draft calls and deciding exemption and deferment issues.

To be opposed to the war did not mean, however, that one was a conscientious objector, opposed to "war in any form." Rosalio wrestled with this question, but did not file his conscientious objector application until he had received an induction order. Under the law, that was too late—unless the local board actually considered the application and rejected "on the merits," as opposed to simply refusing to hear it. The courts had held that the local board could itself waive any objection to late filing by its own conduct. What constituted review on the merits was a difficult and sometimes technical issue.

Rosalio came to see me in my law school office in the fall of 1970, after he had been indicted for refusing to submit to induction. He knew that I had written a book on draft law, spoken on the issue, and trained lawyers and draft counselors. He also knew that I was representing my colleague Angela Davis.

In Rosalio's case, and later for Fernando Chávez, I had support from the Mexican-American Legal Defense & Education Fund, MALDEF. In the late 1960s, there were only one-third as many Hispanic lawyers as a percentage of the Hispanic population as there were African-American lawyers as a percentage of the African-American population. The historically black law schools had played some role in getting African-Americans into the legal profession. There were not equivalent law schools for the Hispanic population. Partly for this reason, MALDEF did not have Hispanic draft lawyers to call upon. The Muñoz case and later the Chávez case were sponsored by MALDEF, and I received a fee from them of $375 for each one. They paid some expenses as well.

Rosalio and I showed up one morning for arraignment at the federal courthouse on Spring Street in Los Angeles. Along with dozens of other defendants, Rosalio would stand before the arraignment judge, hear the charges read, and say he was not guilty. I would file a paper saying I represented him. The clerk would spin a wheel and announce that the case was assigned to this or that judge.

We were not prepared for Judge Andrew Hauk. Bellicose, quixotic—and not a little taken with his power as a life-tenured federal judge—Hauk was an equal opportunity autocrat. He verbally savaged prosecutors and defense lawyers, and both sides in civil cases. That morning, Rosalio and I wandered in to a concatenation of hostilities that was to endure for nearly two years.

I was not a member of the California Bar. I had been admitted to the bar in the District of Columbia. I did not think much of this; because this was a federal criminal case, I would be serving almost pro bono, and there was a local district court rule providing that lawyers licensed in other jurisdictions could practice in federal court, *pro hac vice*, for this time only.

Judge Hauk saw it differently. When I announced my appearance, he demanded whether I was a member of the California Bar. I said no. He read aloud the local rule, which said that a non-California lawyer who maintained an office for the practice of law in California could not practice in federal court. This rule was designed to protect the fees of California lawyers from competition, and raised some serious constitutional issues that we would have to argue later. I simply said that I did not have an office for the practice of law. I was a law professor. The rule's anti-competitive animus did not cover my situation.

"Nonsense," said Judge Hauk, "I am not going to let you appear." He was to boast of this moment for years afterward, despite the eventual outcome. Judge Hauk was, it turned out, filled with personal hostility to the kinds of cases I was doing and the political positions I was taking. "Mr. Muñoz, how do you plead?"

Rosalio looked at me imploringly. This was not going as expected, but he thought his rights were being violated and he wanted to make some protest. I whispered that he could say that because he was being deprived of his right to counsel, he would stand mute and not plead. He did this.

In eighteenth-century England, standing mute would have entrained serious consequences. A defendant called upon to plead was supposed to say, "Not guilty, my Lord," and then when asked "how will you be tried?" he was to say "by God and my country, my Lord," meaning that he would "put himself upon the country," which was another way of saying that he wanted a jury trial. If a defendant stood mute at this juncture, he would be taken away, stripped, and laid on a table. Boards would be placed on his body, and weights added to the boards until he either agreed to say the magic words or expired. This sort of thing went on as late as the 1770s, and was called *"peine forte et dure,"* which was Norman French for "hard and strong punishment," or colloquially, "gosh, that hurts."

In these modern days, the Federal Rules of Criminal Procedure provide that if the defendant stands mute a not guilty plea will be entered for him. That happened, and the clerk announced that the case was assigned to Judge

Jesse Curtis. This seemed like good news to us, for we thought that surely Judge Curtis would show a little more reason. I had forgotten the solidarity of the judicial robe-wearers. By this time, the prosecutors as well were enjoying making our lives difficult.

A couple of days later, Rosalio and I appeared before Judge Curtis. I asked Carol Krauthamer to come with us. Carol was a trial lawyer of skill and distinction, with a lot of experience in Selective Service cases. Before Judge Curtis, we were going to apply to have me allowed to represent Mr. Muñoz. It was at best awkward and perhaps even unseemly as a matter of ethics for me to argue my own qualifications and character. Carol agreed that we could make a better record if I went on the witness stand under oath and she asked me a series of questions. That way, Judge Curtis and the prosecutors could put any questions they liked, and even present any contradicting evidence We would have a "record," and if they chose not to challenge us on the facts, so much the better.

I got on the witness stand. Carol led me through my biography, with emphasis on my draft case and federal court experience, and the pro bono cases I had done on a *pro hac vice* basis. Rosalio affirmed that he wanted me to represent him. We argued the law. There was precedent. In one case, a California lawyer had given federal antitrust advice in New York. The client refused to pay, saying that the lawyer had violated New York ethical law by practicing law in New York without a New York law license. The U.S. Court of Appeals, no doubt having considered giving the client a chutzpah award, held that a lawyer admitted in any jurisdiction has a right under the privileges and immunities clause of the federal Constitution to give federal law advice in any other jurisdiction.

In a more recent case, arising from the civil rights movement in 1964, lawyers from the North had come to Mississippi to help represent young people who had been tossed in jail as the result of demonstrating for civil rights. The local Mississippi judges refused to let these out-of-state lawyers appear in state courts, even with a local lawyer present. Given that few Mississippi lawyers would dare to represent civil rights protesters, these decisions effectively denied defendants their right to counsel. The U.S. Court of Appeals for the Fifth Circuit, in *Lefton v. City of Hattiesburg*, held that out of state lawyers had the right to appear and the demonstrators had the right to their services.

Judge Curtis listened to our presentation and without hesitation said that I could not appear in his court. He gave Rosalio a week to find another lawyer. We were ready for this. We quickly finished drafting a petition to the court of appeals for a writ of mandamus, ordering the judge to permit my appearance, and got an expedited copy of the transcript of proceedings. Ordinarily, if a defendant is wronged by the trial court, he or she must wait until the trial is over. If convicted, an appeal will then lie to the court of appeals and all the claimed errors will be reviewed at once.

But sometimes an early trial court error is so serious, so clear, and so easily remedied that the court of appeals will reach out and tell the trial judge what to do. This may avoid a long trial that would simply have to be done over if the trial judge was only later held to be wrong.

We wanted immediate relief, so we presented our petition to a court of appeals judge with chambers in the same federal building where the district courts were sitting. In those days, things were done a bit more informally than is the norm today, and we made an appointment directly with the judge rather than going through the clerk's office.

Judge Walter Ely agreed to see us, and he invited the prosecutors to be present. Walter Ely was from Texas. He had been a good friend of Lyndon Johnson. His easy Texas manner did not disguise his deep concern for justice. He listened to us. He asked his law clerks to bring him the books containing the cases we cited.

"All right," he said at last, "I am not going to decide this myself. I will confer with at least one other judge and we will get you a decision soon." Two days later, Judge Ely and Judge Shirley Hufstedler issued an order. They cited the *Lefton* case, and quoted the local rule. To avoid a constitutional issue, they said, it would be best to construe the local rule to allow Mr. Muñoz the right to counsel of his choice.

At Mr. Muñoz's next appearance before Judge Curtis, we presented the order and expected all would be well. Not so.

Judge Curtis said, "I see this order. A copy has come to my chambers. But the order has not been spread upon the record." I had a mental picture of an order coming packed in a jar, like peanut butter, perhaps with "NEW" and "MORE SPREADABLE" on the label.

"When will the order be spread?" I asked, not knowing just what this might entail or how it was done. To avoid contretemps like this, the present rules provide clearly that the district court is to obey the court of appeals order when that order is received.

"This will happen in due time. The court will be taking certain measures with respect to this issue. Until this is resolved, this case is off the calendar."

I was beginning to understand. Judge Curtis was going to force a show-down to try to keep me out of his court. That morning, as I came into the courtroom, I had run into my old friend Joe Ball. Joe had been president of the California Bar, a courageous fighter for defendants' rights, and a warm friend of Ed Williams. I asked Joe what he had going, and he said that he was there to represent Judge Curtis. I thought it was a joke, based on Ball's decades of experience in that courthouse.

No, it was serious. The Los Angeles County Bar Association had decided to provide lawyers to keep Rosalio Muñoz from having the lawyer of his choice, and to protect their monopoly. As this battle wore on, another agenda surfaced as well.

I protested that Mr. Muñoz's speedy trial rights were being endangered, to which Judge Curtis replied that he could have a trial with another lawyer. So we left it at that. Joe Ball and two other stalwarts of the bar establishment filed a brief in the Ninth Circuit attacking Judge Ely's and Judge Hufstedler's ruling that I should be admitted.

A panel of three judges issued a new opinion, saying that the earlier ruling had been precatory in tone but of unmistakable intent. Judge Curtis was to admit me. This put the district judges into a mode of full resistance. All but two of the district judges in that courthouse—which at that time housed all the Central District of California judges—signed a statement supporting Judge Hauk's and Judge Curtis's actions. They added gratuitous and insulting statements that I had a reputation for representing disruptive and radical defendants and that the combination of my representation and Mr. Muñoz's "temperamental" nature would endanger the chances of a fair and orderly trial. This personal attack was without any cited basis in any court record. But it made a deep impression in several quarters, as I later found out.

Stalwarts of the organized bar continued to file briefs. The court of appeals stuck to its guns. The judges' lawyers petitioned the court of appeals for a rehearing by all of the judges—not just the panel of three that had said I should be admitted. Unfortunately, all this legal talent was unable to get their petition filed on time. In fact, it was six weeks late. The court of appeals denied it. They then went to the U.S. Supreme Court—with these volunteer lawyers paying the costs—seeking a writ of certiorari to keep me off the case. The Court denied certiorari. I heard later from Michael Rodak, the Clerk of the Supreme Court, that there was some sentiment among the more conservative Justices to address this issue, but that the untimeliness of the application proved an insurmountable obstacle.

In the meantime, Rosalio was awaiting his fate—still under the cloud of indictment. When the Supreme Court's denial of certiorari came down, I filed a motion to disqualify all the judges from hearing the case, except the two who had not signed on in support of Hauk and Curtis. They had all expressed personal opinions about me and Rosalio, based on "extrajudicial" knowledge—that is, on information not contained in any court record. This at least presented the "appearance of bias."

I later found out that Judge Curtis was planning to deny the recusal motion and try the case anyway. But one of the two "dissenting" judges, Warren Ferguson, saw Judge Curtis at lunch and said, "Jesse, do you want to keep up this fight, or do you want to get this case tried? If you want it tried, just send it over to me. You don't have to grant the motion or admit you are biased, but just reassign the case." Curtis did so, and we wound up in front of Judge Ferguson.

I had already appeared before Judge Ferguson in the Melvin Carl Smith case. He had admitted me to practice in that case, knowing of the controversy that had arisen before Judges Hauk and Curtis. Judge Ferguson's older son, Jack, who had enlisted in the Marine Corps, had been killed in Vietnam. Whether despite this experience, or because of it, Judge Ferguson listened carefully to the defense in Selective Service cases. When the defendant was convicted, he was willing to impose some sentence other than jail time if the defendant would perform community service. On the district bench, and later on the court of appeals, Warren Ferguson was always compassionate, intelligent, and articulate. He embodied all the qualities that a federal judge should have.

Rosalio waived a jury—one of only two times in all my years of practice that I have advised a defendant to do that. The government consented to the waiver: even though you might think that jury trial is the defendant's right, the Supreme Court has held differently for almost all cases, and government consent is required as well as that of the court. The reasons are wound up with the same history as the *peine forte et dure* mentioned earlier.

My reasoning on the waiver was this: If Judge Ferguson convicted Rosalio, we would have the same legal issues on appeal as if a jury had done so. If Judge Ferguson acquitted, the government could not appeal that acquittal. If we had a jury that convicted, and Judge Ferguson granted a post-verdict acquittal, the government could appeal that ruling. All in all, it seemed the best choice.

The government's case was, then, fairly simple. The prosecutor presented the draft board records, including Rosalio's request for conscientious objector status. The case then boiled down to a legal argument as to whether the board had actually considered the application so as to "waive" the alleged untimeliness. We also presented evidence of the induction patterns in the San Gabriel Valley where Rosalio lived, showing that Hispanics were being drafted out of proportion to their numbers in the population. This, we claimed, invalidated the ethnically biased orders to report for induction.

Judge Ferguson heard the evidence and listened to our legal arguments. He started by referring to the issue of discrimination by local draft boards. He continued: "G. K. Chesterton once said of the English judges, 'They're not cruel, they just get used to things.' Well, I feel like that. I have heard many of these draft cases, and I have entered judgments of conviction in cases rather like this one. But no lawyer has pointed out to me, until Mr. Tigar did so today, that the local board cannot rely on the lateness of one of these applications if it goes ahead and denies it on the merits. When it does that, it is not relying on its procedural rights, it is making a decision about some young man's sincerity. And the law says that when the board does that, it has to give the young man the right to an administrative appeal and cannot issue an induction order until that appeal is over. The defendant is acquitted."

The prosecutor stood up and said, rather belligerently, "But Judge Ferguson, the court of appeals has clearly held that when the registrant files his claim—"

Judge Ferguson interrupted, firmly but softly, "Mr. Fox, do you understand that in that case, there was no consideration of the merits?"

Undeterred, the prosecutor continued, "But, Your Honor, in that case—"

A little more firmly, Judge Ferguson said, "If you don't understand that, Mr. Fox, you are not likely to understand anything else I might say. We are in recess." And he strode off the bench.

For Rosalio, the case was over. He could resume his life and his involvement in social struggle. He has continued to be a leader in the Chicano community. The *Los Angeles Times* reported the acquittal on February 17, 1972, noting that Judge Ferguson took seriously the allegation that the Selective Service System had committed "a terrible injustice against Chicanos." I went back to my mother's house in the San Fernando Valley to gather up my things. I had been there only a couple of hours when the phone rang. "For you, dear," my mother said.

"Mike," said a voice that I recognized, "this is Walter Ely. I just wanted to tell you on behalf of myself and Judge Hufstedler how proud we are of how you conducted that trial."

"Thank you, Your Honor. I appreciate the call."

I was left by this brief exchange to wonder what conversations, fears, and expectations had swirled around in the courthouse. The disruptions in trials during the 1960s and 1970s were hysterical and largely one-sided toward lawyers representing dissident defendants. I surmise that some of this lawyer-bashing rhetoric had created a fear that Rosalio and I would try this case some way other than to try and win it. Or perhaps the fear was that we would speak uncomfortable truths to judges who would resent hearing them. At any rate, I appreciated the call.

FERNANDO

César Chávez was for decades leader of of the United Farm Workers, the labor organization that sought to represent agricultural laborers, mostly in the American Southwest. Founded in the Central Valley of California, the UFW had faced stiff and often violent opposition from growers' organizations and other unofficial and official minions of the Valley's establishment.

As part of the farmworkers' struggle, César developed and practiced a philosophy of nonviolence. All these things I had known since my undergraduate days, when we supported the farmworkers by petition drives, volunteer efforts, and some meager financial help. My law school classmate Jerry Cohen went to work for the union as its general counsel. In the summer of 1968, Jerry called to say that César's son Fernando had a problem with the draft. Fernando wanted to apply for conscientious objector status. I advised Jerry on what Fernando should do to file for CO status, and how to take any necessary administrative appeals.

The local draft board—this "little group of neighbors"—did not have any members identified with the UFW or notably sympathetic to its goals. They denied Fernando's application outright, and the appeals board predictably affirmed. Once Fernando's student deferment expired, he received an order to report for induction.

Fernando, in order to challenge the local board's order, refused to take the step forward at the induction center. He was indicted for his refusal. He could defend his criminal case on the basis that the board had committed one or more of the three kinds of errors I discussed above: that the board's classification of him was so wrong that it lacked any basis in fact; that the local board had made a demonstrable error of law in classifying him; or that the board had committed a significant procedural error. Under the law, the decision on these three issues was for the trial judge to make. The jury would decide only whether he had indeed refused to step forward.

Nonetheless, we did not waive a jury. This decision was the subject of much debate in the draft defense community, but it seemed to Fernando and me right for this case. Rosalio had waived a jury, under the peculiar circumstances of his case, but Fernando would be tried in Fresno, California, the heart of the Central Valley agricultural area. The trial judge would be the conservative M. D. Crocker, who had been an FBI agent, a prosecutor, and a state court judge before President Eisenhower appointed him to the federal bench. The prosecutor was William Allen, who had come to the U.S.

Attorney's office from a stint as Assistant District Attorney in Bakersfield, another Central Valley community about 100 miles south.

Fernando's case was bound to excite press attention. Every juror would know who he was, or least who his father was. Jurors have the power to vote for acquittal for any reason that seems right to them. We would challenge the rule that limited the jury's function, if only to save the issue for appeal. We would seek to introduce evidence about the legality of American involvement in Vietnam, and request jury instructions on those issues. We would do as William Penn and so many others have done—challenge the jurors to vote their consciences, having aroused their concern by our evidence and argument. Or so we hoped. And thinking back to Louis's draft card cases, we might in our flurry of motions on legal and procedural issues find a way to derail the case, in the trial or appellate court.

Cynics say that trying to discuss complex and controversial social issues with the average juror is nearly always futile. I have never believed that. Reading Clarence Darrow's summations—those masterful webs woven of history, evidence, and law—left me thinking that every jury presented a challenge that could be overcome if I cared enough, thought enough, and worked hard enough.

The prospective jurors were a sort of cross section. A young man from the community showed us how to research the names on the jury list to find their voter registrations and any initiative or referendum petitions they had signed, all from the public record. We did not have law enforcement files on them—the sort of thing the FBI gives to prosecutors and that few judges will make them share with the defense. We knew from their answers where they worked, and something about their families.

Judge Crocker denied our motion to dismiss from the jury all employees of the major growers who had been openly hostile to the UFW. We had four of those on the jury and four more identified with grower interests, though less directly. They all said they could be "fair." That generalized assurance, often accepted by judges, tells one nothing about whether the juror will listen carefully to the evidence, and respect the rule about reasonable doubt. I spent a week in Fresno before the trial, in a local motel in the mid-price range. I listened to the most popular local radio stations, watched local television, and read all the local papers. I wanted to know as much as I could about the community, and about the attitudes and ideas that our jurors would have.

One afternoon before the trial began, Fernando came over and we sat out by the motel pool. I had not spent more than a few hours with him up to that time. I had worked on legal theories with Jerry Cohen, and with some others on our small team, but I did not feel I knew Fernando's story. The root questions—who are you, and why have you taken this risk—had eluded me. It was

as though he had dwelt in shadows cast by his father, and by the legal consequences of his decision to resist the draft and the war.

Don't get me wrong. I knew the "story," as Fernando had sketched it and
as Jerry Cohen had told it at some length. Fernando was away at college in
San Jose, at the southern end of San Francisco Bay. He had shown little interest in his father's work. One day, his mother called him and asked him to
come home. His father César had begun another fast to protest an injustice
against the farmworkers. Because of César's frail health, Mrs. Chávez feared
the fast would do permanent injury, and would perhaps be fatal. Fernando
drove home to Delano, a small community near Bakersfield, determined to
talk his father out of it.

Father and son took a long walk through the fields. When they returned
home, César was still on his fast and Fernando had determined that he was a
pacifist. He told César that he wanted to refuse military service. César said,
"If you are sincere in this belief, and have the courage to follow it through, I
will support you in every way I can." We have read and heard of such epiphanies, usually the product of accumulated experience that suddenly comes
together to produce a qualitative change. In every religious tradition, these
stories teach powerful lessons. In the Vietnam War era, many young men
faced with an imminent draft notice discovered their opposition to war. Local
draft boards were suspicious of these belated changes of heart. I worked with
so many of these folks and found that they were mostly sincere. At 18 or 21
years old, they had not thought about these issues in any coherent way until
confronted with them.

That evening's father-son conversation in Delano had led to Jerry Cohen
calling me.

Fernando and I sat outside my motel room on the eve of trial. We revisited
that walk in the fields. Tears formed in Fernando's eyes as he told me what his
mother had said. As he recalled what his father told him, he began to cry. He
had grown up in that house, amid the daily dramas of farmworker organizing,
and yet he had never really listened to his father's story. Like so many other
young people, what his father did was in a sense alien to him. On that walk, he
was drawn into his father's place in an important chapter of history.

His father did not preach, nor make himself the center of events. It was the
sort of patient and moving account that was the hallmark of César Chávez's
eloquence. By the time Fernando's account was well underway, he could
hardly continue. I stopped him.

"That's enough," I said.

"Enough? There is more."

"I know there is more. And I will ask you to tell the jury all of it. But I don't want to make that moment of telling any less effective by having heard it all now. I want you and I to be talking about this as though it was the first time." So we changed the subject and went over the kind of cross-examination that William Allen could be expected to do.

The government's case went in quickly. The local board representative identified the induction notice. A government witness testified that Fernando had not taken the symbolic step forward at the induction station. The judge denied a motion for acquittal at the end of the government's case. He sustained the government's motions to keep out of evidence any of our attacks on the legality of the Vietnam War.

As in every case, we were entitled to present evidence of Fernando's intent and actions through his own testimony. His intent may be formed by a sense of perceived injustice. The court may rule that the injustice, if any, is not the jury's business, but the defendant's reasons for acting are always the jury's business.

Fernando took the stand. I stood over near the jury box. Judge Crocker did not put shackles on the lawyers, as do so many judges these days. Within reason, I could stand wherever I wanted to when examining a witness. This business of standing where you want to is more important than most lawyers think it is. When you stand, you occupy space. If you stand close to a prosecutor, you occupy some of her space. If you move close to the witness box, you and the witness are seen as "in the same space," and this makes any conflict between you sharper and any cooperation more intimate.

I did not want to be in Fernando's space. He was going to tell his story. Yet I wanted to have this conversation with him, in as natural a tone as possible. So I stood at the far end of the jury box. That way, the jurors could easily see one of us at a time, by turning their heads back and forth. I leaned forward slightly. I had just a few notes on a yellow pad—nothing to take away from the sense that we were talking about something that interested both of us. I went through the introductory material.

Q: Did you get a call from your mother while you were at the college?
A: Yes, I did.
Q: What did she say?
The Prosecutor: Objection, Your Honor. It's hearsay.
Mr. Tigar: He's telling us why he felt this way, Your Honor. Not offered for the truth.
Judge Crocker: Yes, overruled. Go ahead.
Q: Tell us what your mother said.
A: She said that my father was going on a fast, and that the doctor told him that—

The Prosecutor: I'll object to that.

Judge Crocker: Overruled. It's the same issue. Go ahead.

Q: You can tell us, Mr. Chávez.

A: The doctor said that the fast could hurt him. That he might die. [Fernando begins to choke up.]

Q: Did you go home?

A: Right away.

Q: Did you see your father?

A: Yes, I did.

Q: Did you talk to him?

A: Yes.

Q: Tell us about that. What happened?

A: We took a walk together. I told him what my mother and the doctor had said. I told him that too many people needed him. [Fernando's words are punctuated by labored breathing. He is struggling for control. I am having trouble with my own voice. Four jurors dabbed at their eyes. His telling of the scene is more vivid than the words can convey.]

Q: What did he say?

A: He began to explain to me the farmworkers' struggle. He talked to me, for the first time I can really remember, about his faith and his example.

Fernando continued the account, tracing their walk and his eventual understanding. He shed tears as he described that long conversation with his father. He spoke then of filling out and filing the conscientious objector form with the local draft board.

As he spoke, all the jurors watched him carefully, only taking their eyes away to glance at me as I asked a question. Direct examination is funny that way. The witness cannot use narrative, and the lawyer cannot use leading questions. Yet when we tell stories to each other in the world outside the courtroom, the teller often narrates and the listeners often probe with leading questions. But somehow this artificial method of discourse in the courtroom can bring a sense of immediacy and drama that narrative lacks.

By the time Fernando finished, at least eight jurors were tearful. Prosecutor Allen's cross-examination was short, devoted to exploring just how recent Fernando's "conversion" had been.

We next called César to the stand. Allen had attacked Fernando's assertions of belief as recent fabrications. His hostile cross-examination had opened the door to César's full account of the event, for its own value and to strengthen Fernando's credibility. We were entitled to rebut. Contrary to all the rules, including my own, I put César on the stand with no more than a few minutes' conversation; he had not had time to meet with me, so Jerry Cohen had prepared him. In this farming metropolis, his name and face were known to every juror. His presence ensured media attention for the day of his appearance. It was a surprise to me just how diminutive he was "in real life."

César told the story of his and Fernando's walk and talk. He spoke calmly, slowly, as if reliving each part of the event so as to evaluate it in his mind. César Chávez was, in a small room like a court, the most charismatic person I had ever met. Despite themselves, the jurors seemed drawn to him. He was, for many of them, an ogre, a troublemaker—but one that they had never seen in person. And he was telling a story about his son, whom he clearly loved very much.

William Allen did not like this turn of events. He reacted in apparently the only way he knew. He attacked. Of course, cross-examination is about attacking, but foolish lawyers assume this means high dudgeon (is there such a thing as medium dudgeon?) and an aggressive manner. Allen no doubt thought of Chávez as several kinds of evil—he was up there vouching falsely, like a mother giving her bank robber son an alibi. He was just what Allen's conservative friends said—yes, a troublemaker.

After a few preliminary sarcasms, Allen warmed to his task:

Q: You are telling us, Mr. Chávez, that you are a pacifist? (He deliberately pronounced it CHAH-vez, in the manner that Anglos do—either from ignorance or in an effort to be insulting.)
A: I am a pacifist.
Q: And does that go for your whole union?
A: I cannot speak for all of them. Our philosophy is to resist evil with nonviolence.
Q: Well, Mr. Chávez, what if a Russian soldier were raping your wife. What would you do about it?

This question was so off the wall that you could hear a collective intake of breath. The effect was magnified by Allen's tone of voice and his manner. It was as though he was back in misdemeanor court in Bakersfield, cross-examining some hapless wrongdoer caught in the act. We have all heard of questions like this being put to pacifists. There is, for example, the famous First World War draft hearing in England of Lytton Strachey, the gay author and critic.

Q: And what would you do, Mr. Strachey, if a German soldier were raping your sister?
A: Why, sir, I should interpose my own body.

César was unfazed. He leaned forward in his chair and peered at Allen for perhaps thirty seconds. That is a long silence. Long enough that the prosecutor became anxious and fiddled with his notes.

Then César spoke:

A: I am sorry. I have forgotten your name.

The Prosecutor: Allen. William Allen—

A: You see, *Mr. Allen*, the farmworkers' struggle puts poor people with only strength of numbers against powerful interests—

"Your Honor, I object to this speech." Allen interrupted.

Judge Crocker smiled. "Counsel, come to the bench." We did.

"Your Honor," Allen protested, "this is just a political speech. It's the very thing you have already ruled inadmissible."

"You're right, Mr. Allen," the judge replied, "I did grant your motion. But then you had to go and ask that damn fool question. So now you and the jury and everybody else is going to hear the answer—however long that might take. Understand?" Judge Crocker turned to César. "Mr. Chávez, you go ahead with your response."

César traced the farmworkers' history, and put his walk with Fernando in context. I do not think any of the jurors will forget that day, as César sat and looked at them, taking them all in with his eyes and his voice. When he was done, Allen had no more questions. We rested, the government had no rebuttal, and we made the pro forma motion for judgment of acquittal, which Judge Crocker took under advisement.

That night, we worked on more proposed jury instructions, focusing on expanding the jury's role beyond merely deciding if Fernando had failed to step forward. If the judge would not give such an instruction, I could in any event tell the jurors of their unreviewable power to acquit. We thought that the images of Fernando and César lingered in the courtroom, at least enough that two or three jurors might hold out for acquittal and hang up the jury. If that happened, the government might not retry the case. Given the government's unbroken record of success in Fresno draft cases, we thought this result might not only help Fernando but send a message about other cases as well. The court reporter shared our hopes and he wore a shirt with a subtle Mickey Mouse pattern, to show the prosecutor, he said, what he thought.

Judge Crocker had other plans. At 8:00 the next morning, we were in Court, ready to get the jury instructions settled and to argue to the jury at 9:00. Judge Crocker took the bench.

"The Court has reread the various brief and legal arguments, and is of

SENSING INJUSTICE

the opinion that the local board committed a legal error in processing Mr. Chávez's claim for conscientious objector status. The motion for judgment of acquittal is therefore granted. The defendant is acquitted and he is free to go."

Outside the courthouse, picketing farmworkers set up a cheer. My jury argument notes were now unimportant.

Twenty-five years later, I was at the Ninth Circuit Judicial Conference and I saw Judge Crocker. I asked him if he remembered the case. "Of course I do," he said, as though insulted that I would think that age had taken his memory. "You probably think you won that case."

"Well, yes . . ." I started to reply.

"You didn't. That dumb son of a bitch Allen lost it."

I did not take this comment with humility—which would in any case be out of character for me with respect to a case where the client won. I took it as confirmation of what we thought—that Fernando and César, helped by Allen's bad manners, had made enough of an impression on the jury that Judge Crocker decided to short-circuit things.

And Fernando? He went on to law school and continues to care about human rights. In 2018, Fernando came to Austin, Texas, to speak at the dedication of an archive of my work and writing. He spoke movingly about that evening's conversation with his father. He said that it was the first time his father had opened up to him about these basic issues of faith and struggle, and he reaffirmed the nature and sincerity of his father's support.

MORE DRAFT ISSUES

Beyond the constant effort to provide draft counseling to young men, and to explain the deferments and exemptions to which the system entitled them, and beyond the prosecutions for refusing induction, there were two hot draft law issues as the 1960s drew to a close. The first was pre-induction judicial review. If a young man claimed exemption or deferment from induction, why should he have to refuse to submit to induction and then face a criminal prosecution in which he could finally get a court to consider Selective Service error? The statute was unclear, and the Supreme Court had never squarely held that pre-induction review was not available.

The other issue was Selective Service Director Hershey's determination to use Selective Service local boards to punish those who protested against the Vietnam War. In 1967, the U.S. Court of Appeals had enjoined a local draft board from revoking student deferments of students who had been kicked out of school for holding a peaceful sit-in demonstration. The court's theory was that the students had a statutory right to their deferments, and a constitutional right to express themselves. A local draft board could not invade those rights without triggering an immediate right to judicial review.

These two issues intersected at the point of accountability. The draft system did not have impunity from due process and free speech rules. In our constitutional system, an invasion of rights opens the doors of federal courts to provide a remedy. This basic principle had been sounded by Chief Justice Marshall in *Marbury v. Madison*. Upholding it has been the central battle of human rights lawyers ever since *Marbury* was decided in 1803. Federal judges, whose powers derive from Article 3 of the Constitution, have often been squeamish about exercising their powers when doing so confronts the executive branch in its war-making and foreign relations modes. Yet, to repeat, it is precisely those executive activities that are most in need of judicial scrutiny, for war and national emergency become powerful excuses for invading or ignoring individual rights.

In 1968, the Supreme Court confronted the issue of judicial review. In *Oestereich v. Selective Service Local Board No. 11*, a slim majority of the Court held that when a local draft board improperly denies a ministerial exemption from service, that decision is subject to immediate judicial review. However, in *Clark v. Gabriel*, that same year, the Court majority held that a decision to deny conscientious objector status was not immediately reviewable, because a decision that involved the exercise of board discretion and CO classifications did not occupy the same clear place in the law as ministerial exemptions. In short, there was no clear Supreme Court majority for reining in the draft boards.

For its October Term 1969, the Supreme Court agreed to hear two cases that would settle some of these issues. Warren Burger had replaced Earl Warren as Chief Justice. *Oestereich* had drawn dissents from Brennan, Stewart, and White—three Justices that a civil liberties litigant might need in order to prevail. Justice Harlan, by a concurring opinion in *Oestereich*, had shown he was "on the fence." Justice Fortas had been a Lyndon Johnson adviser and had publicly denounced civil disobedience.

One of the two cases was *Breen v. Selective Service Local Board No. 16*, and presented the questions that the Second Circuit had decided in *Wolff*— pre-induction review and student deferments. The other was *Gutknecht v. United States* (discussed in the Prologue).

I had been following these cases from my two offices in Washington, at the *Selective Service Law Reporter* and at Williams & Connolly. Early in the summer, ACLU staff counsel Melvin Wulf called me. He had argued *Oestereich*. He said, "I have a deal for you. If you will write the briefs in both *Breen* and *Gutknecht*, you can argue *Gutknecht*." I accepted. I was to begin teaching at UCLA Law School in the fall, and this was a perfect summer project.

The *Breen* brief was straightforward. The Supreme Court had considered the judicial review issues in other cases, in a variety of contexts. I traced the history of Selective Service judicial review, and wrote a brief to be argued by another lawyer, in what turned out to be a winner.

Gutknecht was more difficult. Yes, the fragile *Oestereich* majority—from which Brennan, Stewart, and White had dissented—had suggested that the Selective Service System should not behave lawlessly. The Solicitor General, Erwin Griswold, had refused to present the government's position. It seemed to me, however, that the Court would not wish to confront the Selective Service System in a head-on constitutional collision. The constitutional issues of free expression, due process, and nonjudicial imposition of punishment lurked, but I wanted to chart a course that avoided them. I turned to the history of conscription in America. I noted that during the First World War, a notice to report for induction meant that you were from that moment in the military. The idea of local civilian draft boards began in 1940 as America prepared for possible war, and the idea was modified somewhat in the Military Selective Service Act of 1967. In all of this history, Congress had never given local draft boards the power and duty to punish registrants for not having their draft cards. These boards were created to decide cases of deferment and exemption, and to provide a mechanism for fulfilling induction quotas if that was necessary. The entire "delinquency" system was an invention of General Hershey and his staff.

I began to think of other instances in which the Warren Court had confronted possibly unconstitutional administrative action and had held that the agency had exceeded its statutory powers. For example, in *Greene v. McElroy*, a civil servant was fired for alleged disloyalty. He had never been able to confront and cross-examine those whose allegations were the basis for his firing. In those days, it was difficult if not impossible to get five Justices to hold that the loyalty-security program violated due process of law. Chief Justice Warren wrote an opinion showing how unreliable was the evidence against Greene, and how he would surely have been helped by being able to cross-examine his accusers. This right of cross-examination, Warren wrote, is so important that we will not presume that Congress intended to let the agency dispense with it. Unless the authorizing statute clearly says "no procedural rights," the Court will hold that those rights must be afforded.

The Court had used the same reasoning in *Kent v. Dulles*. The State Department denied a passport to Rockwell Kent, a dissident artist, based on his political views. The Court avoided the First Amendment and "right to travel" constitutional issues by holding that the Congress had not authorized the Secretary of State to withhold passports on such grounds. So this became the keystone of the brief. We would chart the constitutional issues, and then show the Court a way to navigate around them to our result. I consulted with Mel Wulf often, and he endorsed the content and approach of the two briefs.

It worked. The Court's opinion traced the history of Selective Service law and held the delinquency regulations invalid. A later decision confirmed that the others who had been drafted under these regulations, and who had refused induction, would be released.

<h2 style="text-align:center">GONE AWAY</h2>

Many young men, faced with hostile draft boards, left the United States in the 1960s and early 1970s. Some of them went to Canada and Sweden. In their absence, they were ordered to report for induction and then indicted when they didn't show up. From 1974 until 1977, when the Carter administration issued an amnesty that covered all nonviolent draft offenses, I worked on obtaining dismissals of pending indictments so that these young men could come home. I let it be known that I would represent anybody who was abroad and who was the subject of a draft indictment. I thought that if I could get some of these cases decided, then other lawyers would step in and take on some of them.

In some cases, the local U.S. Attorney agreed that the draft board had behaved illegally and would dismiss the case. In other instances, the prosecutors and the draft board would team up not only to deny any relief but to refuse to honor the defendant's written consent that I could examine the young man's draft file to see if there were any errors.

My legal theory was this: The defendants in all of these cases had never appeared in court. They had, therefore, never been arraigned nor asked to plead guilty or not guilty. That plea, in federal procedure as at common law, is known as "pleading to the general issue." Before the federal rules of criminal procedure were adopted, and still in many states, the defendant must make all motions addressed to the face of the indictment before entering a plea to the general issue. Failure to make those motions might be considered a waiver of the right to make them. This technical waiver jurisprudence no longer exists, but I argued that a defendant still had the right to move for dismissal of his indictment before being arraigned and therefore without actually appearing in court. I then argued that draft board errors presented purely legal questions that could be raised and heard on motion rather than at a trial.

The authority for this mode of argument was, as you may gather, old and thin, although there was an in-chambers opinion by Justice Douglas that supported my position. Prosecutors invoked the "fugitive disentitlement doctrine," by which someone who does not appear forfeits the right to be heard. This doctrine applies, however, to someone who appears and then runs away. My argument was that there needs to be some check on prosecutors who simply obtain invalid indictments against people who are not in the country, with no way for those people to challenge them without submitting themselves to arrest.

Some district judge agreed with this analysis, and the case law was building nicely when the 1977 amnesty mooted the issue. This is an example, it seems to me, of looking beyond the text of legal rules to their background and context. Speaking of civil procedure reform, Maitland said, "The forms of action are dead, but they rule us from their graves." He meant that law forms persist across generations, and even across historical divides such as social revolution. They are invested at different stages with different content, but understanding the historical continuity of forms gives you new and creative ways to think about the law.

ASSESSING

The tide of resistance to the war and the draft rose from the '60s into the '70s. Mostly, we were representing one resister at a time, in the draft board system and in the courts. There are two lessons here. Young lawyers ask me whether handling one case of injustice at a time is a worthy endeavor. I say yes, it certainly can be. Over and over, we see that the accumulated weight and reasoning of the cases we try reaches a kind of critical dialectical force. You will find other examples in this memoir. The second lesson, however, is that one must remember that we lawyers are not the movement for change. To repeat, "We lawyers do not stand at the center of all the events by which the world is moved." Moreover, the battles in which we may win significant victories are chosen for us by people who are experiencing injustice.

CHAPTER 8

Military Justice Is to Justice . . .

S omebody wrote a book subtitled *Military Justice Is to Justice as Military Music Is to Music*. That was about it. I was mostly a spectator to the '60s and '70s military cases. The law of courts-martial, and of judicial review of military decisions, was of academic interest. I worked on some ACLU cases about military prosecutions. but I was not trying them. I handled some discharge matters, helping young people in the military assert conscientious objector claims like the one I had made so long ago, and then filing federal habeas corpus actions if the military denied the discharge claim.

I did not try my first court-martial until 1996, and I rediscovered all the issues that had held my attention in the 1960s. An Air Force major, Debra Meeks, came to my office at The University of Texas Law School. She was stationed at Lackland Air Force Base in San Antonio, Texas. She was about to be charged under the Uniform Code of Military Justice with "sodomy" and "conduct unbecoming an officer." Conviction would ruin the career she had spent twenty-two years building, and might forfeit the pension she had earned and even send her to prison. The felony of sodomy, under the Uniform Code of Military Justice (UCMJ), included any oral-genital contact between people of the same or opposite sex, whether married or not.

The Air Force proposed to charge that the major had carried on a two-year relationship with a civilian woman, Pamela, who lived in her home. When the relationship cooled, so the allegations went, the major demanded that the woman move out. When the woman refused, and instead threatened legal action, the major allegedly brandished a pistol and threatened her.

The major's two lawyers, one military and one civilian, had urged her to consider a plea bargain. These lawyers rightly saw that the testimony of the alleged lover was, if believed, conclusive. The lover/victim, Pamela, had made consistent statements to civilian law enforcement officers about the alleged assault, and after several sessions with Air Force investigators had told the story of the alleged sexual liaison in great detail. What did I think? Would I represent her? I agreed. I am able to relate the story of Major Meeks's case, and the issues it presented, because Major Meeks has consented to my doing so. The defense took place in four stages, directed at four different audiences.

First, the Clinton administration had announced a policy of "don't ask, don't tell" about homosexuality in the military. One announced goal of this policy was to protect service members' privacy about their sexual orientation and activities, so long as one's actions did not interfere with military discipline or intrude on the rights of others. An example of the latter concern would be a service member importuning someone lower in the command structure. I called the Department of Defense general counsel, whom I had known in private practice. She said that "don't ask, don't tell" was just a sort of precatory admonition, not truly a policy or directive. Well, I thought, that's the Clinton administration again—keeping the word of promise to our ear and breaking it to our hope. Once again, as in the civil rights struggles, it fell to individuals willing to assert their rights and take the attendant risks to get the job done.

Second, we could not let this case be handled away from public view in a little courtroom on a military base. Those bringing and hearing this case should have to do their work in the light of day. Also, there was a chance that someone in the chain of command, having read about the case, would call a halt. I called a *New York Times* reporter. I did not want publicity for myself, nor to expose Major Meeks's private life. The reporter understood, and wrote a sensitive article that described the case in the context of service members' rights and the obduracy of some military commanders, The story ran prominently, and was picked up by the local San Antonio paper.

Third, we addressed motions to dismiss to the military judge hearing the case. Our case theory was not "we are representing a gay person and asserting her rights." It was, at this point, that the sodomy section of the UCMJ was unconstitutional because private sexual conduct of any kind should not be subject to criminal prosecution. And, if we went to trial, the prosecutors would have to prove that sexual conduct of any nature had occurred.

This was 1996. The Supreme Court did not decide *Lawrence v. Texas*, striking down statutes like the UCMJ sodomy provision, until 2003. Major Meeks did not want to be a test case; she wanted her case to be dismissed by the military judge, or if that did not succeed, to gain an acquittal.

Our motion to the military judge raised the legal issue later decided in *Lawrence*: private consensual sexual conduct is none of the government's business. We also had detailed figures showing that the military—with rare exceptions —prosecuted oral-genital sexual activity only when committed

between people of the same gender. That is, everybody in that little courtroom might have been doing the forbidden acts with their spouse or friend
of the opposite sex, but only Major Meeks was being prosecuted. The apparatus of prosecution was discriminatory and denied equal protection of the
laws. The prosecutors presented a chart that, they claimed, cast doubt on
the statistics we presented. We did some research and found that their chart
was inaccurate. When we pointed this out, the military judge rebuked us for
maligning the prosecutors. The judge denied our motions. We were going to
trial: the fourth audience.

In a general court-martial of an officer, the "court," which acts as a jury,
consists of up to nine officers who outrank the accused. We would see colonels and lieutenant colonels. Each of these career officers would have a college
degree and some postgraduate work. Each would have served in the Air Force
for at least twenty years. They would all have some interest in military history
and customs. They would look across the courtroom and see the major, in uniform with her medals, and see reflected a distinguished service record. The
military base being a fairly tight community, and the case having been covered
by the media, they might already have some idea of the issues. We could also
be sure that the court members were aware of the "don't ask, don't tell" policy.
Some of them may have wondered why this case was being brought.

In 1996, I was spending most of my time in Denver preparing for the
Nichols trial—the Oklahoma City bombing case for which the venue had
been changed. (The story of that litigation, its people and issues, is in chapter 13.) I went to a Denver bookstore owned by a gay woman, and browsed
books dealing with gay female relationships. I had no particular idea where
this inquiry might lead. The owner had heard of the Meeks case, and offered
insights. I should not have been surprised that I would learn from someone
so far removed—geographically—from San Antonio. In litigation, we step
into communities of people with lives, goals, and ideas that may differ from
our own. We would be presenting the case to deciders from different backgrounds. I should have known that the Meeks case would arouse interest in
gay communities, and that some observers would have insights to share.

The bookstore owner asked me about court-martial procedure. I told her
that colonels and lieutenant colonels would be the "jurors."

"Will there be any nurses? You know, female officers?" she asked.

"Perhaps," I said.

"Odds are one out of three they're 'ours,'" she said with a smile.

The standard of proof, as in a civilian trial, was "beyond a reasonable
doubt." We might have made the classic defense error of analyzing the weaknesses of the prosecution's case, deciding how best to reveal and emphasize

them, and stopping there. That would have been a mistake, as it is always a mistake for a defendant to rely solely upon weaknesses in the plaintiff's case. The jurors will, one must assume, apply the burden of proof. However, they will want a context—a how and a why.

The Air Force assigned three prosecutors to the case. The lead prosecutor, Major Flannery, was balding, a little overweight, and had a high voice and a nervous manner. Another prosecutor was a "squared-away"—to use the military jargon — young man with a buzzcut. The third had a feckless air; we dubbed him "Gomer Pyle," after a television character. The military defense counsel assigned to Major Meeks was Major Dawn Eflein. Dawn gave invaluable assistance, giving insights into our adversaries, finding important information on the Air Force policies on prosecuting sexual behavior, and being a source of knowledge on court-martial procedure.

The heart of the prosecution's case would be testimony by Pamela, the alleged "victim" and sexual partner. Pamela described in detail a sexual liaison with the major in Virginia, followed by Pamela's moving to San Antonio to share the major's house and bed. The prosecution would produce letters and cards allegedly from the major to Pamela. Some of the letters were affectionate. One card was rather explicit, and spoke of tongues. A handwriting analyst was scheduled to testify.

In addition, the Air Force investigators who interviewed Pamela would produce a prior consistent statement if necessary; a San Antonio police officer would testify that Pamela had called and complained that the major had brandished a gun at her. A former (and perhaps now) lover of Pamela's would say that she saw the major and Pamela being affectionate and that the major said at a public gathering that she was going to "marry" Pamela.

Pamela was the only person who could claim to have witnessed Major Meeks commit any unlawful act—from engaging in sexual conduct, to brandishing a firearm. If we undermined Pamela's credibility, we could win. We would also have to deal with the corroborating evidence. It would not be enough merely to show that Pamela had some animus, that is, a motive to falsify. It almost never is. All witnesses are biased, if only in favor of their own prior version. That prior version becomes "their truth." We must show why the witness is not to be trusted on a point—we must develop a reason.

As we pondered, we received a gift. The prosecution produced Pamela's journal for the year in question. The journal corroborated the brandishing charge—for it contained an account consistent with Pamela's present story—but it proved the prosecution's undoing. Here in Pamela's hand was nearly a year's worth of reflections—the year of living in the major's house and a few weeks beyond. In the diary, Pamela confessed her hatred and resentment of Major Meeks. She described her life's ambition of being able to live off someone else's earnings. She explained that she wanted to live in the major's house rent-free until she could get around to applying for medical school, and that by having a Texas residence she would avoid out-of-state tuition. She described filing a false insurance claim. She wrote of forging Major Meeks's signature on a medical school recommendation letter. She wrote of threatening to ruin the major's career by "exposing" her as a lesbian. The diary was written in a hand that resembled in many ways the handwritten portions of the more salacious correspondence Pamela claimed the major had authored and sent.

The trial began with voir dire of the prospective members of the court. We found that some of them had religious beliefs that might signal homophobic bias. Others said that they indeed had religion-based beliefs concerning homosexuality, but convinced us that they would judge the case based on the evidence. We wound up with nine officers; the senior officer, a Colonel Stewart, became foreperson by virtue of his rank.

We had to undermine Pamela's credibility, but we needed to do that while maintaining Major Meeks's dignity as a military officer. We, including Major Meeks, decided that she would not testify. This was an acceptable option, tactically and legally. Her presence in the courtroom, dignified and in uniform, was a visible symbol of our case theory.

In opening statement, I told our story. The major, having served for more than twenty years, was being accused by Pamela Dillard. Pamela Dillard's story does not make sense, is contradicted by her own diary, and is motivated by a demonstrable desire to inflict hurt. Perhaps knowing that Ms. Dillard's story is not convincing, the prosecutors will bring other witnesses, whom they claim add to Ms. Dillard's version. Not so. Everything these witnesses say depended on Ms. Dillard's credibility. Ms. Dillard's friend repeated what Ms. Dillard told her, using the excited utterance hearsay exception. A police officer summoned by Ms. Dillard days later could not repeat Ms. Dillard's story, but admitted that Ms. Dillard did not ask him to search the house for a gun, nor did he do such a search. He did check and see that in fact the major did not have a gun registered in her name. Photographs of Ms. Dillard and the major do not show them in any compromising positions, and the only one slightly suggestive showed the major, fully dressed, with her arm around a man.

The handwriting expert from the Texas Department of Public Safety would not, I said, be able to add anything. I left that part vague, because the "expert" had minimal qualifications, and his report was riddled with errors that we would bring out on cross-examination. Recall that we were going to show that Ms. Dillard's journal acknowledged that she forged Major Meeks's signature.

Ms. Dillard's direct examination was predictable—describing alleged sexual encounters with the major, and purporting to tell the story of their living together. Cross-examination took longer than the direct. I took Ms. Dillard one by one over the relevant parts of her diary: her anger, fraud, and forgery. I kept the tone matter-of-fact, letting Dillard's words speak for themselves, and allowing the court members to gauge her anger and hostility. Some cross-examinations follow a general rule of keeping questions short and sharp, calling for very brief answers. This was a cross-examination in which witness control was achieved by having this lengthy prior statement in hand. I could let the witness roam, and exhibit mannerisms and behavior that the triers of fact would evaluate.

Relying on our theme, I cross-examined Ms. Dillard on her admitted hatred, her admitted threats, and her admitted wrongdoing. I examined the officers who had questioned her on her delay in making the central accusation, and from the police officers Dillard had called I brought out that Ms. Dillard had not sought to have the major's house searched. From Ms. Dillard herself, I showed that after allegedly being threatened, she continued to live in Major Meeks's house.

The prosecutors called one of Ms. Dillard's friends to testify about a party in Virginia at which the major supposedly told the guests that she was going to marry Ms. Dillard. There were some pictures of the party, which showed fully clothed people of both sexes smiling. The friend had not told this story to investigators the first few times she spoke with them, but presented and embellished it in later meetings.

I wondered why Pamela and her friend bore such evident animus toward Major Meeks. We assumed they were gay, so why would they be willing parties to enforcing a law that made consensual homosexual activity a felony? I concluded that this prosecution resembled, in some respects, a nasty divorce. Major Meeks and Pamela had lived together in some kind of relationship. They parted rancorously, and Pamela bore a grudge and convinced some of her friends to help her bear it.

The handwriting "expert" did not do well for the prosecutors. He had mixed up the handwriting samples, showing some as being both the major's handwriting and also not identifiable. He had made elementary errors in evaluating the handwriting sample given by the major. He had to acknowledge that the most provocative writings, on greeting cards that Ms. Dillard claimed the major had sent, were done with a different pen and in a different style—hand-printing rather than handwriting—than the letters from the major to Ms. Dillard. The letters and cards had been given to the prosecutors by Ms. Dillard, and he was influenced in forming his opinion by her claims that Major Meeks had written them.

All in all, he was what I sometimes say a hired expert is: someone who was not there at the time but who for a fee will gladly imagine what it must have been like.

Eventually, in closing argument, I wanted to argue that Ms. Dillard and not the major had written the inscriptions on the cards, but I did not ask the expert about this. After all, handwriting comparison can be done by the lay fact-finder as well as by expert witnesses. A prosecution expert was not likely to agree with our assessment of the writing.

To find a theme for summation, I cast my mind back to *Pro Murena*, an oration of the Roman advocate Marcus Tullius Cicero. Cicero defended General Murena on charges of corruption. His themes were military versus civilian accusers, and the dignity of military service. Of course, any civilian accuser may destroy a military career with a true tale of wrongdoing. But Ms. Dillard had threatened the major's military career with extortionate demands for money and lodging long before she told a story of a lesbian affair. The parallel with Murena's case, where civilians jealous of the general's power had made their accusations, seemed clear.

In any jury case, one wants to have a theme with which the jurors will identify. One casts the case as championing a set of agreed values against an adversary who threatens those values. Sometimes the values are simply those of fairness, burden of proof, and neutral application of accepted principles. In the major's case, the ill-motivated civilian accuser was one strong element. Another element was the threat to military careers from allegations so easy to make and so difficult to dispel. If statistical evidence is any guide, most of the officers on the panel would at some time have had sexual relations other than with a spouse. It was also likely that most of the officers—in or outside their marriages—had engaged in some form of oral sex. The Uniform Code of Military Justice provision criminalized as "sodomy" all oral-genital contact, consensual or not. A sexual partner would therefore have a powerful weapon—the threat to report that he or she had been kissed below the belt.

The major's case illustrates all the decisions you must make in choosing the trial narrative. The basic decision must be based on the theory of minimal contradiction. This theory has different names: KISS (Keep It Simple, Stupid), don't assume a burden of persuasion that you do not have, everybody on the other side is not a damn liar, and so on.

The jurors come into court with a set of intuitions, sensibilities, and points of view. We might call these prejudices, and if any juror possesses them to an unacceptable degree we challenge for cause or peremptorily. We are fortunate to have voir dire and challenges, for these tools give us far more control over who decides the case than a speaker before a public assembly in ancient Greece or Rome—or even a candidate for office or member of a deliberative assembly.

For the jurors who are selected and sworn, we dignify their presuppositions by calling them common sense, or we work to identify them and show how they cannot properly be applied in our case. Thus, the first canon of minimal contradiction is that our narrative should be one that jurors are ready to accept. Ideally, you will not challenge their basic assumptions—or not all of them. In the major's case, we had to accept that the jurors assumed sodomy to be a crime, and that some of them thought it an abomination against God. The military judge would instruct on the first of these principles, and voir dire revealed the second. We might have put the issue directly, and asked for a nullifying verdict. This is an honorable tradition in criminal cases, but it takes a jury convinced that a certain stance is so morally right that one ought properly to defy the judge's interpretation of strict law. We decided not to pursue this strategy—it would have been foredoomed.

But the legal rules about sexual conduct were not the only principles in play. There was also the idea of reasonable doubt—of the prosecution's burden. The principal witness was a civilian, accusing an officer with a distinguished career. So rather than confront the prosecution's and jurors' principles head on, we counterpoised them to another set of equally compelling ones. Jurors are mindful of their oath. And they understand that they do represent a particular community—in this case, a military one. The members of a court-martial take an oath to respect the law, the facts, and their conscience.

A second form of contradiction is with the story being put forth by our adversary. Both sides are working with almost the same body of data. Why and how must our story differ from the adversary's? To refer again to Claude Monet, different renderings of the same scene evoke different impressions in the viewer.

As we work toward a theme, we must first examine all of the adversary's evidence, and all the witnesses on their side, for material favorable to us. "Even their witnesses tell us," "even their documents say" are refrains we begin to develop. Perhaps my desire to mine the other side's ore in civil as well as criminal cases has its basis in my criminal defense practice, where the "reasonable doubt" standard and conventional wisdom often make the defense presentation of "its own" witnesses truncated or absent. But I am convinced that it has more general application. You are looking for the minimum perceptual shift that brings the entire story in line with your viewpoint.

We were, after all, asking the jurors to take a step across their own prejudices against gays, and against a certain view of military discipline and order. We do not usually expect juror epiphanies of the character of religious conversion. When the jurors say "aha!" it is because they have been willing for a time to see reality from a certain perspective that is not so very different from the one they brought to court.

The closing argument was really asking the court members if they wanted to end the major's military career on the word of Pamela Dillard. I said something like this:

> I know that many of you have studied military history, and therefore you probably know about the case in ancient Rome of General Murena. General Murena was accused of corruption by a bunch of civilian witnesses. For his lawyer, he chose Cicero, the most brilliant advocate and orator of his time. In speaking to the tribunal, Cicero contrasted the profession of lawyer with that of general. General Murena had brought riches to Rome, and helped to guarantee the liberty of its free citizens. By contrast, and in his address Cicero was quite mocking in word and gesture, lawyers are all tied up with their technicalities, their pettifogging. And by this means, Cicero pointed out the importance of honoring those who serve in uniform and make their career doing so, and protecting them against the baseless charges that ill-motivated civilians might bring.
>
> Members of the court, I became a lawyer because I believe in human rights. But I'll tell you something. These days, there are a lot of times when we lawyers run out of words. And that's when we call you. The finest hours of your service today, when you best fulfill the oath you took, are in defense of human rights where they are endangered in so many places in the world.
>
> You know, in voir dire we talked about religious beliefs and upbringing. I was raised a Baptist, and was therefore taught that the story of the loaves and the fishes is, quite literally, historically true. But whether or not you believe that, there is a powerful image there, a powerful message. And that is that there are two things that do not diminish, but grow greater as they are given away, and those are God's love and human justice.

I sat down. The lead prosecutor, Major Flannery, leapt from his chair and approached the court. His voice betrayed his anger and excitement. He looked like the actor Wallace Shawn on amphetamines. He picked up a letter that was in evidence.

"It's all a smoke screen, what Mr. Tigar is putting up here! A smoke screen!

Just look at what Major Meeks wrote to Pamela: 'I can't wait to see you face to face. Or face to dot dot dot.' You know what 'dot dot dot' means? It means vagina! Sodomy? You betcha!'"

We at counsel table had difficulty not laughing. Some court members struggled to hold back their own reaction. Flannery had not only reminded us all that the claim of authorship was doubtful, but had graphically brought to mind an image of sexual congress with which most of the court members were probably familiar in their own lives.

The court members went out to deliberate. In a court-martial, the senior officer, as foreperson, directs deliberations, and calls for a vote only when satisfied it is time to do so. The court members vote once. If two-thirds vote for conviction, the verdict is guilty; otherwise it is not guilty. Every time the court members need a break, the court must reconvene, with the judge, lawyers, and defendant. The senior officer announces that the members want to eat dinner or go to the toilet, or even that there is a verdict.

They deliberated for nearly six hours, with several short meal and rest breaks. At each such break, our nervous anticipation increased, as we tried to see body language signs of which way things were going. I was confident that the senior officer, a colonel, understood that no good would come from convicting the major. But it was hard to read the rest of them. For those hours, the defense team sat in an office and told bad jokes to pass the time and keep our minds off our fears and hopes.

Finally, late that night we had a verdict: Not guilty. A few weeks thereafter the major was offered promotion to lieutenant colonel, but chose instead to retire. She did not want to hang around for a few more years and risk having to go through another experience like the one she had just survived.

In an ironic twist, the commanding officer who had instigated the prosecution was soon thereafter relieved of his command. It seems that in a speech to a local business group he made some unkind and intemperate remarks about the wife of his commander-in-chief. Somebody had a tape recorder running. So it is indeed true that in the military, you have to be careful what you do with your mouth.

CHAPTER 9

Chicago Blues, Seattle Times, Free Angela

The presidential race of 1968 seems at times so far away. It is, for the law students I teach, "history." "What was it like," one of them asked, "to live in history?" "He's history," people say, meaning that somebody is no longer relevant. Such an expression could find currency only in a society that devalues the lessons of the past.

In 1968, President Lyndon Johnson decided not to seek a second elected term. The debate over Vietnam and the civil rights movement had riven the Democratic Party and the country. In an emotional speech, on national television, he announced his decision. But the Democratic Party regulars continued to embrace the failed politics that led him to that speech. When Johnson defeated Barry Goldwater in the 1964 Presidential Election, the Vietnam War was a major issue. Johnson voters believed that LBJ would keep his promise to end the war and bring the troops home. Instead, and despite impressive actions in domestic policy, he repeatedly heeded military advice and continued to escalate American involvement.

The year 1968 had seen nationwide demonstrations against the Vietnam War, including a huge protest centered in Washington, D.C. Thousands of demonstrators ringed the Pentagon Building just across the Potomac in Virginia and predictably many were arrested for minor offenses such as trespass and disorderly conduct. A group of us lawyers had set up a legal command post to give advice on constitutional and other aspects of direct action law, and to coordinate representation of those who might be arrested. The Johnson administration's Attorney General, Ramsey Clark, had indicted leaders of the draft resistance movement.

There were two sidelights on this intense work. After the weekend of Washington protests, a thin bearded young man came to my office at the Williams firm. Police had stopped him in Lafayette Park, across from the White House. He had been picking a chrysanthemum. The police officer gave him a ticket, on which was written "picking flowers." There was no statute or rule prohibiting picking flowers in public parks. The ticket recited a statute that punished "harming" the flora.

I did not and do not think one should pick the flowers in our parks. I suspended my moral judgment and agreed to help the young man. I did not have the benefit of Jacques Brel's song about chrysanthemums, and he had probably not even sung it yet. However, a gardener friend told me that picking the flowers encourages the plant to put out more of them. There you are, I thought: the defendant was not *harming* the flowers, he was *helping* them to grow more beautiful. I called the U.S. Attorney's office and spoke to the Assistant who would be handling the case. When he finished laughing, he agreed to dismiss the case.

As another outgrowth of protests, the Secret Service and FBI became very concerned that somebody would try to harm President Johnson. Their fears led them to initiate prosecutions of alleged threats that were either patently ridiculous or clearly protected by the Constitution.

One day, another young man showed up at my office. Again, as seemed to be the fashion of the times, he was very slender, bearded, and somewhat ascetic in appearance. He had received a subpoena to appear before a federal grand jury, which according to the subpoena was investigating threats on President Johnson's life.

The young man explained that two Secret Service men had visited him a week before, and told him they had intercepted a postcard sent to him from California that contained a threat on the president's life. He said he had not received any such card. The agents said they had intercepted it and were holding it as evidence. He told me he was a pacifist vegetarian, and did not wish the president, or any other sentient being, harm. He did not know why anyone would send him a threat in the form of a postcard.

We went on the appointed day to the federal building and met Assistant U.S. Attorney Don Smith. I asked what this was about. Smith, sitting with the Secret Service agent, said that this was very serious indeed and that my client would find that out when he went before the grand jury. I said if that was all the information Smith wished to give, the client would invoke his privilege against self-incrimination. Smith said in that case he would charge me with obstruction of justice for giving that advice. I laughed and said he would do no such thing, as the client had the right to be silent and the right to my advice on that score.

Smith yielded. He agreed to read me the text of the offending card. I could see it in his hands, a hand-printed message addressed to my client, but I could not read the words from across the table. "It says," Smith began, "'Antonin Artaud had it right. Things are getting worse.'" Smith stopped to say that the Secret Service would be investigating this Antonin Artaud person. "'Lyndon's war is sicker and sicker. Murder is the name of the game.'"

Smith intoned this last bit sepulchrally. He added, "And the guy who wrote it does not even know how to spell 'murder.' He spells it M-E-R-D-E." It took me a minute or so to control my laughter. I explained that "*merde*" is the French word for shit, and that Antonin Artaud was a writer. Smith withdrew the subpoena.

CHICAGO BLUES

On the main stage of national politics, Hubert Humphrey, who had served loyally as vice president, was anointed the regular Democratic candidate. Humphrey, long considered liberal, but acceptably so, by the Democratic Party machine, eagerly prepared to accept the nomination. The ferment that had caused President Johnson not to run was, however, unabated. Two major challengers emerged in the primaries. JFK's younger brother Robert had moved to New York and won a Senate seat. From that base, he mounted his campaign. Senator Eugene McCarthy of Minnesota, literate, articulate, and dovish on the Vietnam War, declared his candidacy.

In June 1968, Robert Kennedy was assassinated in Los Angeles. McCarthy's campaign could not best the tide of money and fixers that was sweeping Humphrey along. The Democratic National Convention in Chicago became a battleground of many skirmishes. Groups of protesters from the civil rights and antiwar movements massed in Chicago to demonstrate against the rigged nomination process and the political views it was designed to vindicate. Chicago Mayor Richard Daley put the police on the streets to help keep the convention on its appointed track.

The results were on national television for all to see. Inside the convention hall, objections to the Humphrey nomination and the process leading to it were gaveled down. Outside, police and demonstrators clashed.

The Chicago police had arrested many hundreds of demonstrators for disorderly conduct and related offenses, and had mercilessly beaten those arrested and others as well. The state court cases filled the dockets. More ominously, U.S. Attorney Tom Foran convened a federal grand jury to investigate the leaders of groups that had come to Chicago to demonstrate. This was my first personal involvement in the process.

I knew some of these leaders, and had represented them and their organizations in various ways. This was 1968, and I had been a member of the bar for little more than a year. But I was in Edward Bennett Williams's law firm, and had learned something about federal criminal law and procedure. In the fall of 1968, therefore, two activists who had helped plan the convention demonstrations called me. Foran had subpoenaed them to the federal grand jury.

I went to Chicago and met with the two—let's call them Joe and Jim. Bill Kunstler had flown in from New York. Kunstler was famous; I was not. He had been a lawyer for two decades; I had not. I had met him when I first came to Washington. His brilliance, commitment, and charisma at first enveloped me. All the rest of his life, until he died in the 1990s, I never lost my admiration for him, his work, and his courage. There were, however, times when he was simply the most brilliant unprepared lawyer I knew. His tactical judgments were sometimes innocent of any study of the applicable law. Then there were those cases for which Bill recruited me, and then somehow had a schedule conflict as the trial date approached, so I was left to fend for myself. All that said, there were so many ways in which Bill inspired and delighted all of us.

I think this Chicago trip was the first time that all of these concerns about a new wave of repression began to come together. Foran's grand jury was, we all knew, forerunner to a prosecution of movement leaders. The Chicago police excesses were not in Foran's sights. Joe and Jim, with their subpoenas, were a test case, the canaries in the coal mine.

Tactically, however, we were in a weak position. A federal grand jury has a wider power to investigate than the government has to prosecute. Although the Supreme Court's 1970s' cases reaffirming that power were some years off, I doubted our chances to derail the grand jury investigation, even though it was provably politically motivated and designed to invade First Amendment rights. This was, for young me, heady stuff. Bill's vision was of motions to quash, and a court hearing that would expose Foran's political agenda.

I kept pushing at the edge of this vision, to the time when the judge would rule, and perhaps refuse to quash these subpoenas. Late at night, we all confronted that prospect. If the judge ruled against us, and Joe and Jim refused to testify, they would be jailed for contempt of court. Maybe the court of appeals would let them out, and maybe not.

As the vision moved from courtroom postures to an image of Joe and Jim being led away in handcuffs, they took a more active role in the discussion. "Are you fucking crazy?" was their opening strophe. They felt they would be more useful to the movement for change outside, rather than inside, jail. With their concurrence, our strategy was this: We would move to quash the subpoenas, raising all the First Amendment issues. If the motion was denied,

Joe and Jim would go before the grand jury but refuse to answer any questions beyond their names, citing their privilege against self-incrimination. The decision of whether to assert the broader claims, and the extent to which those arguments would be advanced, was the clients', not the lawyers'.

"Taking the Fifth" might seem dishonorable to some misguided souls, but it guaranteed they would not spend much time in front of the grand jury. It was clear that Foran was bent on indicting somebody. The grand jury is secret and inquisitorial. The prosecutor usually runs it, and was certainly running this one. A potential defendant almost never gains anything by letting the prosecutor question him before the grand jury. The prosecutor gets a preview of the defense case, and often indicts not only for the main offense but for perjury for telling an allegedly false exculpatory story.

The next morning the federal judge heard and denied the First Amendment claims. Joe and Jim went into the grand jury and gave their names. When asked their addresses, they invoked their privilege. I had a quick heated discussion in the hall with an Assistant U.S. Attorney who claimed that it was improper to plead the privilege against compelled self-incrimination to a question about one's address. There were in fact two federal court of appeals cases right on point and in our favor. One's address could be a link in a chain of incriminating evidence, and the Fifth Amendment privilege is therefore available.

Perhaps because of this initial experience, I got another phone call when Foran finally obtained indictments in the spring of 1969. The main charge was that the eight defendants had conspired to travel, and had traveled, in interstate commerce with the intent to foment civil disorder, in violation of the Rap Brown Law, 18 United States Code, section 2101. The "Law" was part of the 1968 Crime Control Act.

The Rap Brown Law took its title from H. Rap Brown, an African-American revolutionary. The law is based on the idea that just one person, crossing a state line with the intent to do or participate in mischief, is dangerous enough that he or she ought to be prosecuted. And how will the state know of this forbidden intent? By his or her writings or speech, duly intercepted, or by the compelled testimony of erstwhile comrades. One is reminded that in the bad old days in England, it was a crime to "compass," that is, to imagine the death of the monarch.

The eight were a disparate group: Aging antiwar activist David Dellinger, Black Panther leader Bobby Seale, SDS co-founder Tom Hayden, Youth International Party leader Jerry Rubin, peace and student activist Rennie Davis, irrepressible madcap leftist Abbie Hoffman, and two surprise additions. The two were chemistry graduate student John Froines and organizer Lee Weiner. The other six were all nationally known figures in the antiwar, student, and civil rights movements. John and Lee were less well-known, and the trial evidence would hardly connect them to the major events of that Chicago summer.

It is not unusual for a conspiracy indictment to include some relatively minor players. Conspiracy law is so sprawling and elastic that prosecutors can make a credible case against many a marginal figure . Justice Robert Jackson called conspiracy "the darling of the prosecutor's nursery." *Conspiracy*— the word has a sinister sound. The original conspirators gave themselves that name. *Conspirare*, in Latin, means to kiss or to breathe together. In the eleventh century, the Catholic Church abolished the ritual embrace and kiss among parishioners at the end of the Mass. Rather, the senior prelate would kiss a ritual object. The more general kissing was regarded as denying the hierarchy of the secular and religious feudal order. "Conspiracy" became an ecclesiastical offense, and later migrated into the common law.

The nascent bourgeoisie, who did indeed deny those feudal ecclesiastical hierarchies, embraced, kissed, breathed together, to symbolize their belief in equality. Their heresy was the symbol of their treason against things as they were. For centuries, ecclesiastical tribunals railed against this and other apostasies.

When I look at the government's 1960s and 1970s assaults on the movement for change, I am reminded of the centuries-earlier official reaction to heretics. The Nixon administration particularly brings to mind that earlier time. It reestablished an independent "Internal Security Division" in the Department of Justice, and multiplied its resources fourfold. Internal Security prosecutors and their FBI outriders were caught breaking the law again and again: illegal wiretaps, opening people's mail, burglary, putting informers into legal defense teams, and so on. All this was done with a perfect sense of rectitude and a naive vision that youthful protest was dangerous to the Republic.

The Chicago indictments were brought, and then prosecuted, with a fervor of this flavor. The defense camp—and "camp" was more than once the word of the day—resisted with displays of law and theater that further taxed official patience. The defendants, or some of them, thought of me as contributing to the legal defense, not the theatrical one. I had known Tom Hayden since 1960, when he was editor of the *Michigan Daily* and an undergraduate student leader. I had met the other defendants, except for Froines and Weiner, at meetings concerned with war, the draft, and racism.

Ironically, Froines was the first to call me. He respected the defendants' decision to mount a joint defense, but he wanted me to make sure all the legal issues were raised. He and I knew that Arthur Kinoy, Bill Kunstler, and a host of others would be working on the same issues, so I was flattered that somebody thought I had something to contribute.

The case was assigned to Judge Julius Hoffman. I do support life tenure for judges, but robe fever quickly infects many of those appointed. Thomas Jefferson became so angry when one of his own appointees ruled against him that he had his Attorney General, Caesar Rodney, write a philippic that decried "the leprosy of the bench." Jefferson had himself written of judges as "a subtle corps of sappers and miners." But when a judge appointed under the Constitution's Article 3 sees and seizes the legitimate power to protect individual rights, there are few sights more inspiring. I have seen it happen, as judges and Justices thought to be predictable followers of this or that line have proven courageous and independent. Warren, Brennan, Stewart, Stevens, Souter all come to mind. Judge Hoffman suffered from no such contradictions. He was arrogant, and usually sure that threats to his established order of things were dangerous.

I sat at my typewriter and wrote motions addressing the legal issues. Lawyers at the Center for Constitutional Rights were also drafting motions. One basic contention was that the indictment did not clearly describe the defendants' conduct in terms that showed it to be beyond First Amendment protection. This was, of course, to be a theme of the trial. But there were quite a few judicial decisions holding that an indictment touching upon First Amendment protected areas must be detailed and precise, so that a reviewing court can determine that the prosecution is not seeking to punish free expression. It became important, though at the time I did not know it, that I wrote and signed these motions on behalf of all the defendants. Each defendant had his own chosen lead counsel: Bill Kunstler for some, Len Weinglass for others, and Charles Garry of San Francisco for Bobby Seale.

I also filed a motion for disclosure of any electronic surveillance that might have been done on these defendants (I discussed the litigation of that issue in chapter 5). Hoffman denied all the motions, and set the case for trial in early September. In August, Bobby Seale's lawyer, Charles Garry, fell ill and needed gall bladder surgery. He moved for a brief continuance of the trial date. Hoffman denied the motion. Seale protested that Garry had been his counsel in several cases, and alone among lawyers was prepared to provide an effective defense.

Hoffman responded by observing that four lawyers, me among them, had entered appearances for the pretrial motions. The other three were Dennis Roberts and Michael Kennedy of San Francisco and Gerald Lefcourt of New York. We four had, for that limited purpose, represented all the defendants. Hoffman decided that he would not recognize a "limited appearance." He therefore held that the four of us would—and did—represent Bobby Seale. He entered an order that we come to Chicago and try the conspiracy case, which was expected to last several months. Len Weinglass called me from Chicago to tell me of the order. I was getting ready to teach my classes at UCLA Law School, and later in the fall to argue my first Supreme Court case.

"Len," I said, "Bobby Seale's chosen lawyer is Charlie Garry. I am not going to participate in some charade that has the effect of denying Seale counsel of his choice. Hoffman's order is clearly wrong. He is crazy. Will he really provoke a confrontation over this? Won't Foran and his assistant Dickie Schultz warn him that he is making a fool of himself?"

"Well," said Len, "on the front lines here we are not so sure. Hoffman does not appear to have many limits, and the Foran-Schultz team is more interested in goading him on than in trying to keep him within the law."

"Well," I said, "I am not going to come to Chicago. Hoffman has no lawful power to order me."

I knew that, usually, anybody ordered by a federal judge to do something must comply, or else get the order set aside by an appellate court. Unlike the situation in many state courts, one cannot disobey the order and defend a contempt citation on the basis that the order was invalid. There are some exceptions to this rule, but they are few and narrow. This order seemed exceptional enough to me, and in any case I had not been served with it.

The next day, Weinglass called again. "Hoffman has issued a warrant for your arrest."

"What!"

"He has ordered that Kennedy, Roberts, Lefcourt and you be arrested and brought to Chicago to represent Bobby Seale."

I called my friend Neil Herring and asked him to represent me. Neil quickly drafted a writ of habeas corpus attacking the arrest warrant, which we had not seen. Kennedy and Roberts were doing the same thing in San Francisco and Lefcourt in New York. I told the law school dean's office that I would likely miss the first meetings of my civil procedure class, and my seminar on repression of dissent.

Neil and I went downtown to the United States District Court on Spring Street to file the petition for writ of habeas corpus. As we entered the clerk's office, a beefy cop-type approached and asked, "Which one of you is Michael Tigar?" (Ah, the joys of youthful anonymity!)

Neil and I stepped up to the clerk's counter. "File this, please," Neil said.

"I am a deputy United States Marshal," the cop repeated. "Which one of you is Tigar?"

The clerk stamped the petition as filed. "I am," I said.

"I am Deputy Marshal Ray Smock. You are under arrest. You have the right to remain silent," he began, and continued with the rest of the *Miranda* litany. Smock agreed that I could remain with Neil while the paperwork was being done. An Assistant U.S. Attorney showed up and took the service copy of the petition. We all went upstairs to the courtroom of Judge Harry Pregerson, to whom the case had been randomly assigned.

I knew Judge Pregerson by reputation. He was a Marine Corps veteran, who had been decorated for valor. He had been a community lawyer in the San Fernando Valley area of Los Angeles. There was a courthouse story that he had presided over a draft case when fairly new to the bench, convicted the defendant, and sentenced him to prison. Before the time to reduce the sentence expired, Pregerson began to think about the defendant's claim of conscientious objection. He got in his car and drove to the federal prison in Lompoc, 200 miles away, to talk to the young man. He came back and reduced the sentence to probation on condition that the defendant perform community service.

Neil presented our case: the order was illegal, Seale has the right to counsel of his choice. Assistant U.S. Attorney Brosio argued that Hoffman was just trying to hold unruly defendants in line. Judge Pregerson then got all technical, and when that started I knew that no good was likely to come of this. Habeas corpus, he said, is a limited remedy. (Where have you been, I said to myself, while the Supreme Court has been deciding a series of cases saying that habeas is a powerful tool in defense of liberty?)

"Mr. Tigar," Pregerson continued, "your remedy is before Judge Hoffman. My only duty is to see that the arrest warrant is valid on its face. I cannot inquire into its background and rationale."

(Judge, my internal monologue continued, in American history the first major use of habeas corpus involved one court testing the validity and motivation of process issued by another court. I was thinking of Thomas Jefferson's failed efforts to round up alleged associates of Aaron Burr and hold them in military custody. The analogy was not perfect, but in my internal monologue there was no adversary to point out weaknesses. And I had a desire not to be in jail.)

"So, Mr. Tigar, you can obey Judge Hoffman's order or be arrested."

I thought about this, and was to rethink my decision over and over in the ensuing 48 hours. First, I was disappointed that Judge Pregerson would not look behind the paperwork and see what was happening in Chicago. I knew that Charles Garry had brilliantly defended Bobby Seale in one politically motivated trial after another. I did not know, but would later find out, just how many illegal steps the federal government was then taking against Seale and the Black Panther Party, but I had a sense that this was going on. All right, so I would be arrested. Being arrested in defense of a principle is not so bad; I spent much of my law practice defending people who had made that choice or had it thrust upon them. I thought about Pete Seeger and the Quaker hymn "How Can I Keep From Singing."

In prison cell and dungeon vile
Our thoughts to them are winging
When Friends by shame are undefiled
How can I keep from singing.

In court, I stood at the lectern. "Judge Pregerson," I began, "the order directed to me is invalid. It is an effort to deprive Bobby Seale of his right to counsel of his choice. I do not think I can be part of any such effort, nor contribute to it by any action of mine. You tell me that there are risks to me if I take this position. I am moved to think of Lord Brougham's defense of Queen Caroline, when he was reproached that his defense might endanger the British crown itself."

I quoted from memory a passage I had often read:

I once again remind your lordships, though there are some who do not need reminding, that an advocate in the discharge of his duty knows but one person in all the world, and that person is his client. To save that client by all means, and at all hazards and costs to all others, and among all others to himself, is his first and only duty. And in performing this duty he must not regard the alarm, the torments, the destruction which he may bring upon others. Nay, separating the duty of patriot from that of an advocate, he must go on, reckless of consequences, though it should be his unhappy fate to involve his country in confusion.

Judge Pregerson was not moved, and in retrospect I was taking myself rather too seriously. He ordered the marshals to take me to Chicago. Deputy Marshal Smock recruited a retired Los Angeles Police detective to help him. That's right. Two armed guards. They left the handcuffs off, based on my promise not to escape. We took the TWA red-eye flight to Chicago, me in the middle seat with these two beefy guys on either side. When I had to take a pee, one of them would go with me. The flight attendants averted their eyes at the sight of an older guy taking a younger guy into the lavatory.

I wanted to call home and let my family know where I was going and when I would arrive. This was, Smock told me, forbidden. It seemed that in the 1930s, somebody let "Baby Face" Nelson tell somebody where the marshals were taking him and the Dillinger gang intercepted them. At some point, I learned that the federal judge in San Francisco had held Hoffman's arrest warrant invalid, and liberated Roberts and Kennedy. Still no word on Lefcourt.

In Chicago, other marshals met us and drove me to the federal building. The courthouse lockup is on a high floor. The cells adjoin a corridor, and out the windows I could see boats riding on their moorings at the marina as the sun rose. Sometime later, Bobby Seale was brought in from wherever they kept him overnight. Then Gerry Lefcourt arrived. The judge in New York had refused to quash the warrant but told Lefcourt to go to Chicago on his own.

So there we were, Seale, Lefcourt, and me, sitting in jail together waiting for court to begin. The marshals took us all down into the crowded courtroom. Media people whispered back and forth about what must have happened. Gerry and I sat flanking Bobby Seale, and the other defendants sat with Bill Kunstler and Leonard Weinglass. They all smiled at us.

I don't remember much about that day in court. There were pretrial proceedings. Judge Hoffman was irascible. I wasn't sure what I was supposed to do. At first, I thought that I must be a lawyer in the case because the judge had ordered me to be that. So I started to participate in conferences with the other lawyers and the defendants. A marshal looked at them all sternly and said, "Don't talk to the prisoner"—meaning me. So I just sat there; the marshals took the three of us us back to the cell at each recess. Lunch was bologna on white bread. "Tigar," Seale told me, "this is not a gourmet restaurant."

Sometime in the afternoon, Tom Sullivan showed up to represent Lefcourt and me. Tom is a hero. He was a partner at Jenner & Block, a big Chicago law firm. Years later, in the Carter administration, he was U.S. Attorney for the Northern District of Illinois and he enforced the highest standards of professionalism and decency you would ever find in a prosecutor's office.

Late in the afternoon, Tom, Gerry and I were seated in Foran's office, along with Foran's acolyte, Richard "Little Dickie" Schultz. "It's easy," Foran said to Lefcourt and me. "You get Seale to waive his claim about being denied counsel of his choice, and then you go free." Sullivan said it was outrageous to hold us hostage to force Seale to waive a perfectly good constitutional argument. Lefcourt and I said we wouldn't be a party to such a thing.

"Up to you," Foran said. "In a couple of hours, court will be over for the day. We don't hold prisoners in this building. You will go to the Cook County Jail for the weekend, and we'll see what happens to your white ass over there." I found this a little scary.

Next stop was the courtroom. At the courtroom door, I spotted Irwin Weiner, a Chicago bail bondsman. He called out that Vince Fuller from the Williams & Connolly firm had asked him to be ready to post a bond if

Judge Hoffman granted bail. I waved and said thanks. In the courtroom, Tom Sullivan introduced himself as our counsel and moved that we be released on bail. Hoffman flew into a rage. He appeared demented in his fury, like the Red Queen.

"No lawyer who tries to horse this court," he intoned, his voice rising in pitch and volume with every syllable, "will ever be granted bail! Mr. Marshal, take them away!" I looked around at the spectators, the lawyers and defendants. Everybody seemed frozen in time and space, arrested (as it were) by what they had just seen and heard. As the marshal put a hand on me, I raised my right arm with my fist clenched, a spontaneous gesture of defiance.

Upstairs in the cells, Lefcourt and I sat and let the adrenalin dissipate. In a few minutes, Bill Kunstler came along the corridor and stood outside our cell.

"Well," Bill began, "they are filing an emergency application for bail in the Seventh Circuit, so let's hope we can get you out of here." We nodded our agreement. "Gerry," Bill continued, "I have to get back to New York. Did you leave your car at LaGuardia?"

"Yes."

"Well, just in case you are in jail over the weekend, I could pick up your car. You don't want it in the parking lot all that time."

"Thanks, Bill," Gerry said. He fished in his pockets and handed over the car keys. It occurred to me that the marshals had not searched us and had not taken our stuff away.

"And, Gerry," Bill continued, "I really need to be in the city this weekend. Could I camp out at your apartment?"

"Sure, Bill," Gerry said, handing over another set of keys. Bill shook our hands through the bars and called for the marshal. Then he was gone. Gerry cocked his head after a long, thoughtful pause.

"Do you know what just happened?" he asked me.

"Yeah," I said.

"I am in fucking jail. That's one of my lawyers. He is going to get in my Mercedes convertible and drive to my apartment. He is going to take off his pants and probably get laid in my bed, and I am going to spend the weekend in Cook County jail."

I was agreeing that things did not look good for us when a deputy marshal came along to the cell door. "Tigar," he said, "there is a man named Irwin Weiner here to see you."

"Oh, great," I said.

The marshal looked surprised, then said in a voice tinged with respect, "You know him?"

"Yes," I said.

"Well, it is really past the time when we are supposed to let anybody in here, but come this way." He unlocked the cell door and led me to an interview room. On the other side of the wire mesh screen was Irwin Weiner and a younger man who looked like a bodyguard.

"Irwin," I said, "thanks for coming. I really appreciate it."

"Vince Fuller called. I came right over. Mike, this is Angelo Pugliese."

Angelo said, "Hi."

Some explanation may be needed. In chapter 5, I discussed the cases of Ruby Kolod, "Icepick Willie" Alderman, and Felix Antonio "Milwaukee Phil" Alderisio, and the Supreme Court decision in *Alderman v. United States* that resulted from that work. Phil was from Chicago, and for some reason he often traveled with Irwin.

"Listen, Mike," Irwin continued, "if the court of appeals sets a money bond, it will be posted no matter what the amount. And Phil says that you can come to his house and have dinner, because he is cooking fettucine. Or you can have an airline ticket to wherever, and I mean wherever, you want."

"Thanks," I said. "If I get out of here, I will catch the first plane home. I don't think I need to run from a contempt citation."

"OK," said Irwin. "Now, if you don't get bail, they are going to take you to Cook County jail. I guess you heard some bad things about that place?"

"You could say that."

"Well, don't worry. Some people we know are already waiting for you if you show up there. When you get there, a guard will come and ask you what you want for dinner. Steak, quail, lobster—you name it. They'll bring you dinner and make sure you are OK. Only thing is, when they do something for you, give them a tip. You got any money?"

I reached in my pocket. "I've got some twenties," I said.

"Oh no, that's too much. Use ones and fives. Angelo, ones and fives!" Irwin snapped his fingers. Angelo pulled out a roll of bills and peeled off a few. He handed them to Irwin who slipped them through the wire mesh.

"You smoke?" he asked. I said yes; at that time I did.

"Regular or menthol?"

"Menthol."

Again Irwin snapped his fingers. "Angelo, menthol," he said. Angelo came up with a pack and Irwin pushed it through the mesh. "Good luck."

The marshal came and led me back to the cell. About half an hour later, a judge of the court of appeals signed an order releasing us, on condition that we show up Monday morning for court. So I never found out what would really happen at Cook County jail. I just went to the airport and paid what Continental Airlines charged to take me home.

Sunday night, I flew back to Chicago. Michael Kennedy and Dennis Roberts had flown in from San Francisco, and Gerry Lefcourt from New York. Monday morning, there were picketers in front of the federal building protesting our arrest; I saw that they included law professors from several schools including Harvard. Over the weekend, Judge Hoffman had apparently reflected on the excesses of his position. He seemed, at any rate, to be a rather different person. Foran had also reconsidered. The four of us—Kennedy, Lefcourt, Roberts, and Tigar—stood before the bench. Tom Sullivan was beside us. Judge Hoffman entered the room. The clerk called the case.

After some preliminary verbal skirmishing with Tom Sullivan Hoffman ruled:

> The Court: Agreeable with the motion and suggestion of the government, the contempt proceedings against the two lawyers who were here and the other two lawyers who were not here—you have their names, Mr. Clerk?
> The Clerk: Yes, your Honor.
> The Court: . . . will be vacated, set aside, and leave will be given to them to withdraw.

Apparently, the sideshow was threatening to overtake the main event; and Hoffman and the prosecutors wanted to get on with the trial. The trial began. Judge Hoffman severed Bobby Seale's case and sentenced Seale to jail for contempt, having had him bound and gagged during the early parts of the trial for continuing to protest the violation of his rights.

The jury's verdict on February 18, 1970, acquitted Froines and Weiner and convicted the other defendants on some but not all charges. Judge Hoffman held all defendants and their lawyers in contempt for their unruly behavior during the trial. I rejoined the team to assist with the appeal brief. The court of appeals upheld the constitutionality of the Rap Brown Act, so it remains a weapon that federal prosecutors threaten to use again.

However, the court of appeals reversed the convictions. The judge had conducted an inadequate voir dire of potential jurors in this highly publicized case, and his and the prosecutors' conduct deprived the defendants of a fair trial. The court set aside the contempt convictions, because Hoffman's bias and self-interest were evident.

Due to my momentary burst of fame, I was invited to speak at programs addressing the trial and the conduct of the defendants, their counsel, the prosecutors, and the judge. Stalwarts of the bar inveighed against defense counsel. I could not then agree that defense counsel bore any blame for the disruption at trial, and with the perspective of years still do not.

Yes, some of the defendants' antics were silly and counterproductive: I see this in context. The politics of Vietnam and the civil rights movement had sapped confidence in the political and judicial systems. The prosecution was designed from the beginning as a show trial, not by the defendants but by United States Attorney Foran and, as January 1969 dawned, the Nixon administration. The Rap Brown Act was a calculated assault on direct action as a means of social protest.

Judge Hoffman not only ruled against every significant defense position, he derided the defense, in the jury's presence, and made clear that he was not paying attention to any of its contentions. He adopted a supercilious and mocking attitude from the first moment of being assigned the case. I was there for the pretrial motions, before any defendant or defense counsel had uttered a single disrespectful word, and I saw and heard it.

Hoffman's treatment of Bobby Seale was particularly horrific. The escalating disorder of the trial was mostly a reaction to Hoffman's and Foran's continuing provocations. I was reminded again of Queen Caroline's trial, this time of Lord Erskine's speech, as a decider and not as counsel: "Proceedings of this kind, my lords, have never been tolerated save in the worst of times and have afterward been not only reversed, but scandalized."

In 1979, Judge Pregerson was appointed by President Carter to the Ninth Circuit court of appeals, where he served until his death in 2017. He and his wife, Bernardine, a college teacher, loved to take car trips. One day in the 1990s, as I was teaching civil procedure at Texas, the classroom door opened and the Pregersons strode in. The judge looked nearly the same as decades before, but in a leather jacket and chinos. I smiled and introduced my class to "Harry Pregerson, a wise and principled federal judge who once threw me in jail." The class applauded the judge, who retorted, "It was your own fault, and you know it."

In 2013, my son Jon Tigar was sworn in as a U.S. District Judge for the Northern District of California. Soon thereafter, he sat by designation on a panel of the Ninth Circuit court of appeals. Presiding on the panel was Judge Pregerson: he commented wryly that he had known Jon's father in another context. He told Jon that sending a Tigar to jail was a once-in-a-lifetime experience that he would not repeat.

As I look back at my arrest and brief detention, my sense of resolution is reinforced when I consider the law under which the Chicago prosecution was brought. H. Rap Brown (now Jamil Abdullah Al-Amin), a civil rights activist, had traveled from state to state. Some said that he was a powerful leader against racist political and social institutions. Others, including those who sponsored this law, said he was a carpetbagging troublemaker who stirred up riots. The Rap Brown Law does not require that the traveler's actions pose any clear and present danger of lawless action: it punishes the desire to participate in unlawful conduct. It therefore flunks the Supreme Court's clear and present danger test as reaffirmed in *Brandenburg v. Ohio*, where the Court overturned a venerable criminal syndicalism statute.

The Chicago case was a perfect example. Most of the defendants had planned that there would be demonstrations, and had even participated in them. Some of their plans and even their actions might be termed disorderly conduct. The reaction of Chicago's police to demonstrations at the 1968 Democratic Convention—even lawful demonstrations—was more violent and unlawful than what the demonstrators were doing. Local authorities would not and did not prosecute police officers. Federal officials could not use the Rap Brown Act against the police, if only because that Act punished only those who used an interstate facility. That is, the Act burdened the right of interstate travel as well as the right of free expression. Of course, the U.S. Attorney was not interested in prosecuting the police in any event.

SEATTLE

The actions of protesters in Chicago, like many events in history, were replayed in different versions in other places. The most immediate of these were the student and youth demonstrations to protest the guilty verdicts of the Chicago case.

In college towns across the country, student groups had been preparing for TDA—"the day after" the verdicts. Given Judge Hoffman's rulings, everyone expected that the defendants would be found guilty. In Seattle, the local SDS chapter and affiliated groups picketed the federal courthouse in protest against the trial and verdicts. When the verdict came, on February 18, 1970, so did the protests.

The Seattle demonstrations turned violent. Demonstrators painted slogans on the federal building and broke windows. The U.S. Attorney, Stan Pitkin, responded by indicting eight young activists under the Rap Brown Act. None of these young people had been born in Washington State, they all had to have travel, interstate to get to Seattle. The fact that some of them had arrived years before, and could not conceivably have had the forbidden intent at that time, did not deter the government. These were the leaders and the violent demonstrations would be blamed on them.

The indictment was issued in mid-1970, while I was teaching at UCLA Law School. The defendants were Susan Stern, who had a graduate degree in social work; Michael Lerner, an assistant professor of philosophy at the

University of Washington, Jeff Dowd; a high school graduate from New York; Michael Abeles, who had briefly attended Cornell University; Roger Lippman, a Reid College chemistry student who had dropped out to do political organizing: Charles "Chip" Marshall, a recent Cornell graduate; and Joe Kelly, Marshall's friend and also a Cornell graduate. Also indicted was Michael Justesen, a University of Washington freshman who decided to become a fugitive. The Seattle 8 became the Seattle 7. Jeff Dowd was the son of economist Douglas Dowd, and stepson of Paul Sweezy.

The defendants were all affiliated in one way or another with the Seattle Liberation Front (SLF), an anti-racist, antiwar organization that focused on community issues and community organizing.

One of the defendants' friends called me and asked if I would join the defense team. She had been prompted to call me by Jeff Steinborn, a Seattle lawyer who had recently been admitted to the bar and had struck up a friendship with the defendants. This woman was married to a draft resister who had benefited from the Supreme Court's decision in *Gutknecht v. United States.*

I met the defendants; they were articulate. They saw the February demonstration as more than a response to the Chicago verdict. Rather, they viewed the Chicago case as one more evidence of a tide of repression that aimed to maintain the Vietnam War and to roll back the gains made by the civil rights movement's direct action campaign. They had forged ties with the labor movement in Seattle and with community organizations.

I agreed to be part of the defense team. I learned a great deal in the months that followed. Our team also included a prominent African-American lawyer from Spokane, Carl Maxey, and Lee Holley, who had experience representing draft resisters and demonstrators. The local American Civil Liberties Union made office space available to us in Smith Tower, an old downtown building.

Defending a complicated conspiracy case, or a complicated case of any kind, requires a team devoted to organizing the files and exhibits. We also needed legal research help. Law students came aboard to help us, and members of the defendants' organizations provided paralegal help. We did not find out until later that one of these youthful paralegals was in fact funneling all our defense information to the FBI and the Justice Department. This infiltration was organized by the local FBI, abetted by a senior Justice Department lawyer named Guy Goodwin. Goodwin had a lot of responsibility in those Nixon administration years; he was caught pulling similar stunts in several prosecutions of political dissidents. He had been responsible for some of the most odious misuse of the federal grand juries convened under the 1968 Crime Control Act. He was a slightly stocky, shortish chap with salt-and-pepper hair. He was always impeccably dressed, and spoke softly and in a slightly affected way. Behind his back, his prosecutor colleagues mocked him as effeminate and regarded his work as sloppy. He was snide. When I criticized him in the Seattle case for a "shotgun" approach to the evidence, he said evenly, "With your clients, I would use a squirrel rifle."

Our trial judge was George Boldt, an aging conservative jurist with no sense of humor and little patience with the exuberance of youth. Boldt put the case on a fast track for trial, but did agree that the trial would be set for December so that I would not have to miss many of the law school classes I was teaching. Despite my meeting all my classes, I was back and forth to Seattle a lot. California's then-governor, Ronald Reagan, seized upon these absences to demand that the UCLA Chancellor fire me. At the monthly meetings of the University Board of Regents, he urged my dismissal. He was angry because I was also helping my colleague Angela Davis.

The trial team was organized so that two defendants would represent themselves, while Carl Maxey and I would alternate in lead roles as defense counsel for the others. Maxey left the pretrial preparation to the team we had assembled in Seattle. We challenged the constitutionality of the Rap Brown Act. Boldt predictably denied the motion.

U.S. Attorney Stanley Pitkin was one of those Republican civil lawyers who get appointed when the Republicans have the Presidency. He appeared to have swallowed whole the Guy Goodwin/FBI theory that my clients were dangerous revolutionaries. In the end, this delusion was the government's undoing. He had lost that essential skeptical detachment from the official ideology.

An example came early. Pitkin called one day and said that he had an item of evidence to show me, and would I please come to his office immediately. I rounded up two of the defendants, Michael Abeles and Jeff Dowd, and we went to the federal building. Pitkin was in his office with the FBI case agent. In hushed tones, they said that they wanted to to show us this evidence before they considered bringing more serious charges. They led us to a room. The FBI agent carefully opened a wooden box. "This," he intoned, "was found at the scene of the demonstration."

"This" was a World War II hand grenade body, the classic pineapple shape. It was empty of any explosives, no doubt having come from a war surplus store. It was painted baby blue. An alligator clip, such as electricians use, was soldered to the top of it.

Abeles and Dowd began to giggle. "It's a roach clip," one of them finally sputtered.

"What's a roach clip?" Pitkin asked, mystified.

"Ask your teenagers," Dowd replied.

The harmless grenade body had been configured by some unknown person to hold the end of a marijuana cigarette, known as a "roach," so that the smoker could get the last hits from a joint.

This episode captured the essence of this case. This had been a protest demonstration during which some slogans were spray-painted, a couple of windows were broken and people tussled with police. Whatever one thought of it, it was not markedly different from thousands of protests that had taken place in U.S. history. But Goodwin and Pitkin had decided to cast the event as part of a larger conspiracy to create disorder and to topple the present social system. This was the same sort of reasoning that had dominated the most repressive judicial decisions of the McCarthy period. By focusing on the defendants' ideology and ultimate social goals, the state justified the severity of its reaction.

The Rap Brown Law reflected this state-sponsored mythology. Protest demonstrations are not dangerous because of what happens; they are dangerous because of what the demonstrators allegedly want, and what might in some unpredictable future actually occur. Therefore, the state must punish the incipient action coupled with the forbidden desire. By placing the moment at which the law is violated at such an early time, the state also claims the power to investigate and arrest long before any social harm might realistically be threatened.

As the trial date approached, the defendants made public speeches about their views and activities. We were getting discovery from the government in the form of video footage of the demonstration. Some of this had been taken from an FBI van. The case agent told us, humorlessly, that the van was known in Bureau lingo as a "creepy peepy."

The actor Donald Sutherland took an interest in the case. He and his wife, Shirley, were outspoken supporters of dissident individuals and groups. At a party in their Beverly Hills home, Don and I talked about the Seattle case. He arranged for me to join him on Dick Cavett's late-night television talk show. On the day set for my appearance, ABC censors tried to bully Cavett into keeping me off the show, but he courageously held to his position. On the show, we bantered about possible uses of the Rap Brown Law. Noting that the Law dealt not only with interstate travel but also with the use of the mails, I imagined an elderly woman collecting radical literature sent to her post office box and exclaiming "Right on!" in the post office. That would satisfy all the elements of the crime.

I am sure that Judge Boldt began to wonder what a Seattle jury would do about these defendants, when the evidence turned out to be rather less inflammatory than the indictment suggested and the government had loudly

and publicly stated. He ordered that the case would be tried in the Tacoma
Division of the federal oourt, rather than in Seattle. This meant that we would
have to commute 30 miles each way to and from Seattle during rush hour, in
the wet weather of a Washington December. It meant that instead of the urban
jury we would see in the Seattle federal courthouse, we would have more suburban types, government employees, and people from rural areas—and less
racial diversity. We filed a petition for mandamus challenging Judge Boldt's
unilateral and unexplained action, but lost 2 to 1 in the court of appeals. The
Sixth Amendment guarantees only a trial in the "state and district" wherein
the alleged offense was committed. Many larger districts are divided into
"divisions." The potential jury pool in each division can be quite different.
We thought, and the dissenting judge agreed, that the trial judge should not
have unlimited discretion to move a case.

As we prepared for trial we faced the most significant issue in any conspiracy case: the element of agreement. Our eight defendants were from different
political groups and held different political views. They were activists. They
strongly believed that if their message about civil rights, the Vietnam War, and
free expression were repeated enough times in enough forums, the listeners
would demand social change. Their belief ran headlong into two canons of
criminal defense.

First, evidence that the defendants met together many times would tend
to support an inference that they were discussing illegal objectives. If the
defendants took the stand and with other defense witnesses described how
they had worked together, the jurors might not see this as simply a lot of protected associational activity. There was a tension between the desire to help
the jurors understand these defendants and the tactical unwisdom of seeming
to support the government's conspiracy theory.

This was not an insoluble dilemma. Jurors will accept counterintuitive
propositions. They will come to analyze the facts without regard to their own
preconceptions. In a long trial, such transformations are more likely, because
unfamiliar ideas become commonplace as the trial wears on. Clarence
Darrow's trial strategies and jury arguments provide illuminating examples.
There is no guarantee of this happening, however. In our case, a Tacoma jury
would be less likely than a Seattle one to accept our invitation to see the world
through the defendants' eyes.

The second issue involved public statements. There is no such thing as a
public forum any more. Public forums existed in fourteenth-century towns,
where it was possible to reach almost the whole populace by standing up and
shouting. By the eighteenth century, one might reach a fair number of people
by broadsheets and leaflets. Today, our information is filtered through the

media, whose editors decide what to print and broadcast. People congregate in shopping malls, which are privately owned and unreachable by picketers and leafleters. The Seattle case began in 1970, so there was no internet to speak of.

For our Seattle clients, therefore, my message was that their actions and activities would be seen by the public only to the extent and in the manner dictated by dominant print and broadcast media in our market. We had to think about the content of our messages, and the way in which they were presented. Did I think about the legal ethics of media contacts? Of course. But this was not an ordinary case. It involved a number of public issues, including but going beyond the right to demonstrate for one's views. The fact that the government had chosen to try these defendants did not rob them of their First Amendment rights. Nor could the charges be a valid reason to halt their participation in the ongoing debate over the Vietnam War, racism, and government accountability for its misdeeds.

The defendants' and my views were soon to be tested. I learned a great deal, and I think they did as well. During jury selection, defendant Chip Marshall was questioning a prospective juror:

Q: What do you do at that company?
A: I make nuclear missiles.
Q: (with genuine surprise) What do you do that for?
A: About fifteen dollars an hour.

We seated a jury in Tacoma. In opening statements, the prosecution lost no time in branding the defendants as interlopers who had come from the East to disturb the tranquil precincts of Puget Sound with their radicalism and disorder. Where had these prosecutors been, I wondered to myself. The State of Washington had been the organizing ground of radical unions from the Industrial Workers of the World (the Wobblies) down to Harry Bridges's International Longshore and Warehouse Union.

Carl Maxey, Michael Lerner, Chip Marshall, and I each gave opening statements. In my opening, I took a page from Darrow's opening in an Industrial Workers of the World case in adjacent Idaho:

Yes members of the jury, it is true that I am not from here. I am from Los Angeles, California, where I live and work. And, like most of you, I would rather not be here today. I would rather be sitting by a quiet and free-flowing stream near my home. But I am here because hundreds of people gave what little money they could afford to see that this case was defended. Now there is injustice being done in many courtrooms across this country, and I would be in every one of those if I could. But I cannot. I am here, in this courtroom. And I do not apologize for that, because I know that together we are going to find out the truth about what happened in Seattle on that day.

I also talked about "conspiracy," the idea of punishing people for thoughts.

After some preliminaries, the government called its first major witness, "Red" Parker. There was a frisson as the bailiff announced his name and he came into the courtroom. Red Parker had joined the local Students for a Democratic Society chapter. He was a part-time student. He worked in a paint store. He always had a radical, violent suggestion about proposed action. He spoke often of imminent violent revolution.. He offered to provide explosives. He had brought cases of spray paint to the demonstration and urged people to deface the federal building.

On direct examination, and then on cross, he owned up to all of this. Our defendants were at the center of youth and student radical activity in Seattle, but their organizing had been lawful. Red Parker had been recruited by the FBI to join SDS, and to try to set it on a different course. The FBI paid him. The FBI told him to encourage violence, to see who would rise to the bait. They told him to see who would want to practice with a rifle. And because the FBI did not approve of theft, they gave Red the money to buy the spray paint for the demonstration.

Chip Marshall waited for his turn to cross-examine Parker. In a multi-law-yer case, you always hold your breath because the other lawyers are bound to ask questions that you deliberately did not ask. You did not ask them because you didn't want to give the witness a chance to explain an answer, or to curry favor with the jury with a self-serving speech. Having obtained a good answer, you don't ask the same question again, to give the witness a chance to back-track. Marshall was innocent of this lore. And he was having a good time questioning his old buddy Red. His cross-examination was magnificent, as he took risks in questioning that yielded impressive concessions from Parker.

Chip plowed on where few lawyers would dare:

Marshall: You are willing to go, as you say, to any length to get us?
Parker: That's correct.
Marshall: Do you still feel that way?
Parker: Yes
Marshall: You're willing to lie to get us?
A: Yes.
Marshall (to the jury): That's what he said.

The government's case was coming apart. Fearful that they would not win on the merits, the prosecutors changed tack. They began to complain that the defendants were speaking to the press and were making too much noise in court, and in and around the courthouse. Every morning at trial, one or more defendants would saunter in late, so the judge and prosecutor began to make more of an issue of this tardiness. As the evidence revealed more government dirty tricks, the defendants' comments became louder and more frequent. Judge Boldt's impatience also increased, leading to this exchange ourside the jury's presence:

> The Court: Mr. Tigar, this gentleman is one of the Deputy Marshals. Tell him what you have.
>
> Mr. Hanson (Deputy Marshal): I watched Jeffrey Dowd place this on the wall and asked him to take it off and he gave me the finger, and on the elevator and on the walls we have seen them. They don't come off when they dry (holding up a broadsheet about the trial events).
>
> The Court: Mr. Dowd is your client, Mr. Tigar, and I expect you to take appropriate action to see that this does not occur.
>
> Mr. Tigar: The only evidence we have is this one label and I take the position that I am this man's lawyer and I have an obligation to explain your Honor's wishes and I have an obligation to explain what the law is, but I don't believe I have the obligation to control his conduct or behavior, even assuming that I wanted to or that I could. He is his own man and will take the consequences.

Later, the exchange went on:

> Mr. Tigar: My thinking is that I represent two defendants in these proceedings, Jeff Dowd and Roger Lippman, and we will have conversations throughout the course of this trial about their legal liability and obligation for things they have done. Those conversations are covered by the lawyer-client privilege. My job is to advise those defendants about consequences of actions they may contemplate taking and actions they may have taken in the past.
>
> The Court: I take it that you will do that now in connection with this incident?
>
> Mr. Tigar: Judge, the conversations I may have with them you may be assured will be in accord with my consideration of my responsibilities. I cannot talk to you about my professional client-attorney relationship.

The Court: I only ask you to advise them about this type of conduct and what it may lead to.

Mr. Tigar: I will inform them of your Honor's views, certainly.

The Court: If you will do that, that is all I am asking you to do.

As Professors Dorsen and Friedman said in their book *Disorder in the Court*, I was trying to express the lawyer's duty when placed under pressure to become an associate enforcer of the judge's ideas of decorum. As they note, "A criminal lawyer should no more be obliged to announce that he has cautioned his client against disruption than an antitrust lawyer should be obliged to announce that he has cautioned his corporate client against price-fixing." Whatever one may think of rules, we owe our clients undivided loyalty within very broad limits. As the Dorsen/Friedman book documents, courtroom disorder was a major topic of discussion in the 1970s. I thought the debate somewhat overwrought, but I was sure about my own stance. I had accepted the representation of these defendants, against whom all three branches of the federal government had set their hands. I was not going to become an agent for one of their assailants.

A day or so after Parker self-destructed on the witness stand, some of the defendants were late again. They were late because some of their number tried to see the judge before court to protest the treatment of spectators who had come to see the trial. Word of Parker's appearance had gotten out, and many people with the look and dress of those who might support the defendants had lined up outside the courthouse to gain admittance to the trial. The marshals refused to process them, claiming security problems. Marshals randomly took people out of the line and searched them. Outside, where this was happening, a freezing rain was falling. The defendants took umbrage.

When court began, the defendants wanted to make a record of their objections to the treatment of spectators. Judge Boldt took the bench and read a generalized and somewhat rambling critique of their conduct and held that all but one of them had been in contempt. He set sentencing for four days later. There was to be no trial of the details of the alleged contempts, he said, because he had seen enough of their actions that he needed no other information to make a decision.

Since the contempts were in his presence or "near thereto," he was, so he claimed, entitled under the rules to proceed summarily. The court of appeals later held that he did not have the power to punish people based on conduct he had not personally witnessed, such as the activity outside the confines of his courtroom at times when he was on the bench. For the time being, however, he was doing it his way.

Some of the defendants tore up their contempt citations. Others made their displeasure known in other ways. The judge also declared a mistrial in the case, which meant to him that the government could begin again at its pleasure. The defendants' reactions to all of this led to a second round of contempt citations.

Let us pause to consider this state of affairs. These young people—Lerner, Marshall, Dowd, Abeles, Stern, Lippman—had no doubt engaged in a demonstration at the federal courthouse. Television footage showed it. Some of them arguably had done some property damage during that demonstration. For this they were charged with conspiracy to commit and committing several felonies that carryied heavy potential prison terms. They were required to post bail, and were about to incur heavy expenses of trial preparation. Their own resources being insufficient, they raised money from other sources. When they got to trial, they found that the FBI had planted an informer in their midst who tried to provoke unlawful activity. The prosecution was directed from the "Justice" Department of President Richard Nixon's administration, by personnel later found guilty of felonies for their unlawful actions, and who used methods later denounced as part of the impeachment hearings against Nixon.

In a broader context, the President and his men were continuing a war that the majority of Americans disapproved of, and plotting in other ways—as congressional hearings later disclosed—to undermine the democratic process.

In this setting, what were these young people to do? Were they to remain silent and powerless as the system that calls itself justice unwound itself, and to wear the badge of accused felon all the while? Their courtroom comments, and their marks of disrespect for the process, seemed to me defensible. I choose that word carefully. I would have welcomed contempt citations from Judge Boldt that offered the defendants a trial where they could defend their courtroom behavior. The conditions would be these: The case would be tried by jury in Seattle, where their political base existed. There would be full discovery of the government's ignoble role in invading the defense camp. There would be full discovery of government infiltration of their lawful political activities. Then, let a jury as representative of the community decide the issue. By "defensible," I mean just this: I would defend them in a fair fight on fair terrain.

I saw firsthand how the marshals manhandled the defendants' supporters who sought entry to the trial. And the chief marshal of the district singled me out as well. One Friday night I walked down the jetway with other passengers to board the plane back to Los Angeles for the weekend. There stood the United States Marshal for the Western District of Washington, Charles Robinson. He put me up against the jetway wall in full view of all the passengers and did a thorough search, making sure to feel all my pockets and squeeze hard where he knew it would feel uncomfortable.

Thinking of Judge Boldt, I am reminded of meeting my mentor Edward Bennett Williams one night at the Washington Palm restaurant, just after he had lost a jury verdict in front of Judge Gerhard Gesell. He was later to win a new trial and an acquittal due to jury misconduct. I asked him how he had gotten along with Judge Gesell. He replied, "I will meet that SOB on any field of human endeavor, in a contest of his choosing, and under rules of his devising. So long as the SOB is not also the referee." Williams was, in his own eloquent way—both of us being somewhat the worse for drink—saying what Lord Coke had held in 1608: no man shall be judge in his own cause.

In any event, the mistrial and contempt scene was dramatic. In a few days we would go back to hear the sentences the judge was to mete out. But that afternoon, Carl Maxey and I and the other lawyers repaired to a bar near the airport, so that Carl could be ready to catch a flight back to Spokane.

With the bravado of the truly inebriated, I decided to drive back to the home of Michael Rosen, the ACLU lawyer who had lent me a bedroom in his house. I was doing just fine with all the controls and such, but I did not see a Stop sign near Rosen's house. A Seattle policeman pulled me over and asked me for my driver's license. I saw him register who I was, and I thought I was in serious trouble. The cop looked from my license to my face, and said, "You're the lawyer for those defendants in that trial, aren't you."

I said yes.

"Well," he continued, "is it true what they said in the paper, that the FBI bought the spray paint for people to use in the demonstration, and all the rest of that?"

"It's all true," I said. "Their witness admitted it on the stand."

"I'll be damned," the cop said. "That really pisses me off. You know, we local cops had to go down there and wrestle with that crowd, trying to protect that federal building. It was really crappy duty, let me tell you. And now we find out that the goddamn feds were actually helping make it happen. I'm glad you were able to bring that out."

I felt better, but he continued. "Sir, you not only went through a stop sign but you appear drunker than owl shit, if you don't mind me saying so. How far do you live from here?"

"A couple of blocks." I gave the address.

"OK, I want you to follow me, real slow. There are no Stop signs between here and there, but I want you to watch my tail lights and take it easy. I'll get you home before you hurt somebody."

A few days later, Judge Boldt had all the defendants back for sentencing.

This was before the days when all federal and many state courtrooms feature metal detectors. The courthouse scene was ominous. More deputy marshals than I could count patrolled the outside and inside of the courthouse. In the courtroom itself, more than a dozen deputy marshals sat or stood, all in black turtleneck sweaters, some with black jackets and some also wearing black gloves. Outside and inside, the marshals hassled potential spectators who looked like they might support the defendants, by intrusive searches and by pushing them around.

Carl Maxey sat beside me at one of the counsel tables. The judge took the bench and called upon counsel to speak. We had agreed that Carl and I would split the argument. Our main contention, then and on the appeal we later won, was that the judge could not proceed summarily and was so personally embroiled in the dispute that he should turn the case over to another judge. Whatever these defendants might have done, and with whatever intent they might have done it, the determination should be made in a hearing before a neutral tribunal with all the rights that the adversary system guarantees. Judge Boldt ruled against us.

Then, one by one the defendants exercised their right of allocution, to say why they should not be sentenced. It came to be Susan Stern's turn to speak. Susan was about five feet tall, and weighed perhaps 100 pounds. She was no physical threat to anyone, and she had to stand on tiptoe to be seen over the lectern.

She began quietly enough talking about what young people had come to feel about a government that was distant, hostile, and uncaring. She rebuked those who stood aside and would do nothing about injustice. Evoking the passivity of those who watched Hitler's rise to power and did nothing, Susan spoke of "good Germans." Judge Boldt either did not understand the reference or chose to feign ignorance, for he said heartily, "Well, let me tell you something. There is not a drop of German blood in my veins. My people are all Danish!"

Susan could not resist. "Well, then, your Honor," she said, "there is something rotten in Denmark." Perhaps the Judge had not read *Hamlet*, but he snapped that Susan should stop talking and sit down.

"I am not finished with my statement," she said. "We are entitled to be heard."

Again came the order to sit down, and a very large deputy marshal stepped up and grabbed Susan from behind. He pinned her arms behind her and she grimaced in pain. I lost my temper. I stepped behind the deputy and tried to pull him off Susan. This was not a particularly wise move. Another deputy stepped behind me and grabbed me. He tossed me against the wall, and my head snapped back against the unyielding paneling. As I opened my eyes, the deputy sprayed something in my face. I got dizzier and my eyes burned. I am not sure what happened next, but I can remember being carried out of the courtroom by two deputies. I opened my eyes as we all reached the courtroom side door and saw U.S. Attorney Stan Pitkin standing there agape.

"Mike, what's going on," he said, unnecessarily, as he had been there all along.

"Tell these guys to put me down," I said.

He did and they did. The courtroom melee soon quieted down. The Judge had retired to his chambers to write up more contempt citations.

I have reflected many times on that day's events. I used to hear rumors that the whole episode was captured on videotape and that some judges had seen the tape. I could never pin that down. I thought then and think now that the marshals showed up spoiling for a fight, and that they had begun the day with gratuitous exercises of force against relatively harmless civilians. Somebody in power must have evaluated the case and concluded it was not worth pursuing, for I never had so much as a whisper that I might be prosecuted for an assault on a federal officer.

Judge Boldt sentenced the defendants. He said that "Divine Providence" had revealed to him a method for dealing with trial disruption. He denied bail pending appeal. Nine days later, on December 23, 1970, the court of appeals ordered Boldt to grant bail. Initially, he announced that the court of appeals order was wrong and that he would not obey it. After a couple of days, he reconsidered and freed the defendants on bail.

The court of appeals reversed the contempt convictions on November 17, 1971. By that time, I had finished my work in the case and other lawyers had stepped in. I had resigned from teaching at UCLA Law School and was exploring next steps in my life. The case had roiled my life as much as the defendants' lives.

Because the court of appeals' decision left open the government's right to retry the defendants for contempt, they agreed to plead no contest and were each sentenced to brief jail time with credit for time already served. Finally, in 1973, U.S. Attorney Pitkin dismissed the conspiracy indictment. He explained that among the four confidential informants on which the government was to rely at trial, one had been compromised by infiltrating the defense camp, and the others had what he charitably described as credibility issues.

ANGELA DAVIS

I met Angela Davis in September 1969. She had been appointed Assistant Professor of Philosophy at UCLA. Ronald Reagan was governor of California. Right-wing newspapers, politicians, and commentators protested her appointment. She had a distinguished academic record, including study with Herbert Marcuse. As she later said, "Herbert Marcuse taught me that it was possible to be an academic, an activist, a scholar, and a revolutionary."

At that time, all faculty on all campuses of the University of California were required to sign a loyalty oath, avowing among other things that they were not members of the Communist Party. Angela set a date on which she would announce her decision about signing the oath, and invited law professors Ken Karst, Hal Horowitz, and me to her press conference. I expected her to say that the oath offended the First Amendment and was invalid under several Supreme Court cases. She did that, and went on to say that she would not sign the oath because she was in fact a member of the Communist Party.

On September 19, 1969, the University Board of Regents fired Angela because of her Communist Party affiliation. California Superior Court Judge Jerry Pacht held that the firing was unconstitutional. The Regents fired her again on June 20, 1970, because of her denunciation of Regents policies toward demonstrators and because she had allegedly used "inflammatory rhetoric" in speaking against police misconduct.

Angela was active in support of prisoners at Soledad State Prison, a maximum security facility in California's Central Valley notorious for harsh and racially discriminatory treatment of prisoners. Angela developed a friendship with George Jackson, a Soledad prisoner. Racial tension among prisoners was high. In early 1970, prison officials began to allow African-American and white maximum security inmates to exercise together, knowing that some of the white inmates were white supremacists, and were fully expecting violence. Predictably, on January 14, 1970, there was a fight in the prison yard. A guard shot and killed three African-American inmates; two other guards participated in reprisals against African-American prisoners. Four days later, a prison guard was killed. A note near his body read "one down, two to go." George Jackson and two other inmates were charged with the guard's murder, and transferred to San Quentin Prison, which is in Marin County, north of San Francisco.

On August 7, 1970, Soledad prisoner James McClain was on trial in the Marin County Courthouse for stabbing a guard. Three other Soledad inmates were waiting to testify in the case. George Jackson's seventeen-year-old younger brother Jonathan stood up in the audience, pulled a rifle from under the raincoat he was wearing and took charge of the courtroom. His announced purpose was to compel the release of his brother George. McClain and the three Soledad witnesses joined the effort. They took hostages, including the trial judge Police arrived and began shooting. By the time the shootout was over, four of the Soledad inmates, Jonathan Jackson, and trial judge Harold Haley were dead of gunshot wounds. The prosecutor was gravely wounded. One of the Soledad inmates, Ruchell Magee, was also wounded; he was later to be charged along with Angela.

On August 14, a Marin County judge issued a warrant for Angela's arrest for conspiracy, murder, and kidnapping: capital offenses at that time. She avoided capture until October 13, 1970, when she was arrested in New York. John Abt led a team of lawyers challenging her extradition to California, advancing the themes that were to guide the defense: Yes, Angela supported the Soledad Brothers and all political prisoners. Yes, she was a Communist, committed to a struggle against a system that fostered racism. Yes, she had lawfully and openly purchased the guns that were used in the shootout. California law permitted gun purchase. Angela legitimately feared for her own safety. Yes, others probably knew she had guns in her home and had access to those guns. No, she did not have any role in, or advance knowledge of, the courthouse events. In December 1970, the New York courts authorized extradition to California.

At that time, the Seattle conspiracy case had ended in a mistrial and in the contempt sentences of defendants. I was working on an appeal of those orders, going back and forth from Los Angeles to Seattle in order to take care of my obligations at UCLA. In addition, my marriage was falling apart due mainly to my inattention to Pam, Jon, and Kate. I received a telephone call from Margaret Burnham, a New York civil rights lawyer who was also Angela's longtime friend. Would I help the defense? I said yes, recognizing that whatever I might do would be part of an effort that would involve a large legal team, but more important, would require political organizing and media contact to help dispel the press campaign against her by Governor Reagan and President Nixon and their allies.

If there was ever a teaching moment in my life, this was it, although I saw it only in hindsight. I wanted to be part of this effort, but clearly I was not indispensable to it, and would not have been criticized if I said no. I was under many personal pressures. When I asked my son about this issue, he said, with fifty years of perspective, "Dad, you were a rock star." There is a great deal of meaning that one can gain by reflecting on the many meanings of that phrase.

Angela was arraigned on January 5, 1971, in the Marin County court-house. She was being held in solitary confinement and not even allowed to have books. In California at that time, there were procedural rules that helped us see and combat the case against her. First, the prosecutors had chosen to proceed by indictment, rather than to file charges and have a preliminary hearing. They were therefore required to give the defendant the transcript of the grand jury proceedings. Second, the grand jury could receive only such evidence as would be admissible over objection at a trial—unlike the federal grand jury which could indict based only on hearsay provided by an FBI agent summary witness. Third, in reviewing the grand jury transcript, the court could not consider evidence found to be the fruit of an unlawful search. Finally, the reviewing court could take into account exculpatory evidence readily available to the prosecutors but withheld from the grand jury.

We applied these legal principles by making a motion under California Penal Code Section 995 to dismiss the indictment. We divided our analysis of the prosecution's case into two parts. The first part was evidence of Angela's alleged actions that were claimed to support an inference of involvement in the courthouse events. These actions were all lawful, and the evidence in support of them was questionable, but the prosecutors claimed that Angela had done them in furtherance of the planned courthouse attack.

I recruited a brilliant law student, Tom Horn, to help write the Section 995 motion. As for alleged acts, the prosecutors alleged that several of the guns Jonathan Jackson brought to the shootout had been purchased by Angela over a period of two years: a pistol, two rifles, and a shotgun. Angela had purchased the four guns that were offered in evidence to the grand jury.

The claim that these were weapons recovered at the crime scene was dubi-ous, as the chain of custody—the proof that each gun was marked at the scene and securely kept thereafter—was uncertain. And even if these weapons were found at the crime scene, they were items that Angela was entitled to purchase under California's liberal firearm laws, and that Jonathan Jackson, who was Angela's friend, could have obtained without Angela having provided them. Angela's purchase of firearms was understandable given the threats that she had been receiving ever since arriving in Los Angeles.

The prosecutors also produced a white eyewitness who said she had seen someone who looked like Angela near the courthouse a couple of days before the shootout. This cross-racial identification was already shaky in the grand jury; at trial it collapsed utterly. We would argue that the identification was unreliable.

The grand jury heard evidence of Angela's departure from California on the day of the shootout, and that she had remained unavailable to authorities until captured. We noted that the California courts and the U.S. Supreme Court had held that flight was not necessarily evidence of consciousness of guilt, and might simply betoken a fear that one would be a victim of state-sponsored injustice.

The grand jury heard extensive testimony about Angela's concern for political prisoners, including the Soledad Brothers, and in particular George Jackson.

The prosecutors regarded these lawful actions as circumstantial evidence that Angela had joined a conspiracy to kidnap and kill. I had long been fond of quoting from Arthur Conan Doyle's Sherlock Holmes story "The Boscombe Valley Mystery":

> "I could hardly imagine a more damning case," [Watson] remarked. "If ever circumstantial evidence pointed to a criminal it does so here." "Circumstantial evidence is a very tricky thing," answered Holmes thoughtfully. "It may seem to point very straight to one thing, but if you shift your own point of view a little, you may find it pointing in an equally uncompromising manner to something entirely different."

In court, I have taken the image further: circumstantial evidence is like a stick on the ground. Where it points depends on which end of it you are standing. We argued that the prosecutors had the wrong end of the stick.

In the Section 995 motion, we denounced the prosecutors' invocation of constitutionally protected beliefs and conduct:

> To have even introduced such evidence before the grand jury reveals the prosecutor's Orwellian turn of mind. To transmute Angela Davis's advocacy of legal defense for the Soledad Brothers into proof of guilt in a conspiracy forcibly to release them turns the matter on its head. As we show below, the law is clear that only "relevant" evidence before the grand jury is to be considered in support of the indictment. The fact of "relevance" is "the tendency of an item of evidence to prove a fact in issue.". . . If advocacy of legal defense proves anything at all, it proves disinclination to use extralegal means. Moreover, such advocacy, being protected by the First Amendment, is not admissible in support of a prosecution for conspiracy. See *United States v. Spock*, 416 F.2d 165 (1st Cir. 1969); *Castro v. Superior Court*, 9 Cal.App. 3d 675 (1970).

The *Spock* decision held that in a conspiracy with both lawful and unlawful objectives, an alleged adherent could not be found guilty based solely on evidence of his or her protected conduct. This principle was significantly eroded in later years, as will be apparent in the discussion of Lynne Stewart's case in chapter 15. However, the *Spock* analysis had been used in Justice Otto Kaus's opinion in the *Castro* case. In *Castro*, Mexican-American students and community activists had been charged with conspiracy and other offenses in connection with protests against discrimination in the Los Angeles public schools.

Our motion concluded:

> Angela Davis is a Black woman and a Communist. She has advocated the release of the Soledad Brothers. She has lived her life as scholar, teacher, activist, and advocate in the glare of hostile publicity. Now the State seeks her life, and struggles to turn against her the open and honest way she has carried out her political goals: speaking out when she was concerned, caring for the lives of others, and buying guns when she had reason to fear for her safety and indeed for her life. But these things are not crimes. If they can be made crimes by the exuberance of prosecutors and the acquiescence of judges, the freedom of none of is safe.

There were many public meetings to protest Angela's indictment. Her mentor Herbert Marcuse came to Los Angeles; he and I spoke at an outdoor rally. We talked about her case and the conditions in which she was being held.

On March 16, 1971, I argued the Section 995 motion in Marin Superior Court. Contra Costa County Superior Court Judge Richard Arnason had been assigned to the case as all of the Marin judges were recused.

A year later, the California Supreme Court struck down California's death penalty law. Angela was released on bail in time for her trial. I recall, however, how the prospect of death hung over the courtroom on that day. The lead prosecutor in the case was Albert Harris, an Assistant Attorney General designated by Governor Ronald Reagan to lead the prosecution team. Although our hearing was devoted only to legal motions, he made a grandstand press play by wheeling in a shopping cart laden with guns connected to the crime, but not necessarily to Angela Davis. Since neither side could present evidence at this hearing, the shopping cart was simply a prop.

I thought that if posturing were the order of the day, the court should be reminded that this prosecution, on this evidence, had a political motive. So I began my argument, "May it please the court. I am going to show that with Albert Harris as the engineer, the Marin County grand jury is America's only working railroad." I then went over the evidence and law in detail and at length.

Harris made his argument, and as he finished he walked across the small courtroom to stand in front of Angela. He concluded that not only was there enough evidence to sustain the indictment, but enough to put Angela to death. Judge Arnason denied the motion to dismiss. We had, however, laid out in a public forum the contentions that would guide the case from that point on. My part had been only to raise issues in the pretrial motions. The trial team was led by Leo Branton, Doris Brin Walker, and Haywood Burns.

The events of the struggle to free Angela, who was acquitted by a jury on June 5, 1972, after just 13 hours of deliberations, are brilliantly captured in the documentary *Free Angela and All Political Prisoners*.

CHAPTER 10

Connecting Life, Law, and Social Change

It was 1971. I was thirty years old. I had helped write the brief on appeal for the Chicago case. The Seattle defendants' contempt convictions had been reversed. I had done my assigned part in the Angela Davis case. I resigned from the UCLA law faculty. My law review articles on judicial review had been published in the *UCLA* and *Harvard* law reviews. Rosalio Muñoz and Fernando Chávez had been acquitted. Members of the SDS Weatherman group had become fugitives from charges of riot, believing that they would not receive fair trials. Federal grand juries, and prosecutors armed with wiretap warrants, attacked progressive people and organizations. The *Selective Service Law Reporter* had played a role in the liberation of draft resisters. Pam and I had separated. I was tired and more than a little confused.

I had spent so much time with protesters, resisters, and other courageous opponents of war, racism, and economic injustice. Young lawyers and their clients were asking, "What is the good and useful of what we have been taught? The 'law,' we were told, has given us tools to battle injustice. But against this wave of repression, these tools seem inadequate." For some, the expression was more terse: "Law is bullshit." When I confronted judges' refusal to honor basic guarantees of freedom and fairness, this view made sense; the law was indeed not what it said but what it was doing. And yet, we were winning some of these encounters with state and monopoly power.

I believed that if we were going to make any progress at all toward human rights, we had to be better lawyers than the ones on the other side. We had to develop a deeper understanding of the law's limits and possibilities, and in our work have a scrupulous attention to detail.

I had come to law school admiring the work of advocates who invested their arguments, to judges, jurors and public audiences, with the historical and social context in which the issues arose. Jacobus tenBroek and other professors had challenged me to see law in this way, not as a collection of rules to be learned, but as part of a dialectical process of social control, progress, and repression. If you follow some of the links in this book's "Notes and Sources," you will see written and oral arguments that I tried to place in historical context.

At this same time, some were saying that the present tide of repression, and the resistance to it, heralded some imminent and fundamental change. I thought of Shelley's words: "The cloud of mind is discharging its collected lightning, and the equilibrium between institutions and opinions is now restoring, or is about to be restored."

I could break the inquiry into three questions: First, where are we? By "we" I meant narrowly the progressive movement in the United States, and more broadly the progressive and liberation movements in the world. Second, how did we get here? I understood in a general way how the present system of social relations had come into being. I did not have a deep understanding of the role that lawyers and legal ideology had played in that process. Third, in the light of a dialectical and historical examination of these questions, what ought lawyers to be doing, and with what prospect of success? I was concerned also about how a movement, or more accurately movements, could come together, resolve contrary views, and approach fundamental social change.

I concluded that I could better understand where we were, how we got here, and what we ought to do and were able to do, by examining the role of lawyers in the social change that brought the present system of social relations into existence.

On the basis of an outline of a proposed book, I had obtained an advance and foundation grant. I had assumed that the displacement of feudal social relations by the rising capitalist class could be traced to the merchant capitalists of the sixteenth century. My initial research proved me wrong: The legal system under which we were living in 1971 was based on legal rules and ideas that could be traced at least to classical Roman law. I ought to have seen this, as my research and writing in my law school days had taken me back to Roman law in search of the origins of just one procedural rule. In the first edition of *Law and the Rise of Capitalism*, I quoted Pollock and Maitland: "We are made aware that 'such is the unity of history, that anyone who endeavors to tell a piece of it must feel that his first sentence tears a seamless web.'" I had to see legal history as a continuous and dialectical process that could be seen in periods or eras only for the historian's convenience.

The more important insight, however, was that most of what passes for legal history scholarship is avowedly or implicitly teleological Of what was this "web" to be woven? The recognized scholars of Western legal history had written in a sort of magisterial style. They wrote to explain and justify the legal ideology of their own time. They sought to invest that ideology with the sanction of immemorial usage, in order to give it an air of legitimacy. Or, confronted with a usage or principle that seemed wrong, the historian might argue that this was a departure from prior principle. For example, the legal writers of seventeenth- and eighteenth-century France wove unifying themes into a legal argument that the French monarchy could and should unite the regions of France, and that its rule was founded on principles drawn from Roman times and from immemorial customary usage. The seventeenth-century Dutch legal writer Hugo Grotius built a structure of legal thought to justify Dutch imperialism. Lord Edward Coke's attacks on monarchial and feudal strictures were couched as reaffirming the old principles of Magna Carta. These writers wrote about the law as though its operation and effect could be understood by studying what jurists and judges had written.

In the writings of these legal scholars, history marches from one expression of a legal idea to another. So here I was, seeking to understand the legal events of my own time, and discovering that the literature from which I proposed to learn would not help me. I would broaden my search.

I wanted to study history in order to empower makers of change, not to justify acceptors of things as they are. I got a sidelight on the persistence of old discredited stereotypes when I accepted a lunch invitation from Fenner Brockway. He had been a Labour Member of Parliament, famed for his anti-war stance, and had been elevated to the peerage in 1964. It was an honor and a pleasure to meet with him and hear his ideas about the state of world politics. He was now Baron Brockway. As we were finishing lunch in the Lords' guest dining room, Baroness Barbara Wootton, a leading criminal law scholar who had also been appointed a life peer, joined us at the table. She had been having lunch in the Peers' dining room, where by tradition one sat at any empty seat even if it meant dining next to a disagreeable person.

She had been seated next to an unregenerate Tory peer, who was upset with the government's policy on Rhodesia. She quoted him: "It is all wrong. They should let the white people of Rhodesia decide the issue. They're the ones who have to live there."

With a tentative outline of the book, and some assurance of financial support, I spent a day with Eduard Goldstucker at his home near the University of Sussex in Brighton. Eduard had been my colleague for a summer at the Center for the Study of Democratic Institutions. He was Czech, a scholar of

German literature who had suffered for his political views. He was one of the world's leading scholars of Kafka's work.

In 1939, he fled Czechoslovakia due to the Nazi occupation and was active during the war in the government in exile in London. He returned to Czechoslovakia after the war; in 1951, however, he was a defendant in the infamous "Slansky Trial" in Czechoslovakia and served three years in prison. He was "rehabilitated" in 1955, and became head of the writers' union and a member of Parliament. In the 1960s, he became a member of Alexander Dubcek's reformist government. That government was displaced by a Soviet-led invasion in 1968–69. Once again, Goldstucker was compelled to move. He accepted an invitation to the Center for the Study of Democratic Institutions, where I met him. He remained a convinced socialist, saying only that the Soviets had misapplied socialist norms.

He read my outline. I felt like a student summoned to a tutorial with a singularly wise and gentle don. He thought the outline made sense. He shared, based on his study and his personal experience, the sense of people making history by means of battle against perceived injustice. "To tell this story," he said, "you must study the work of three people. The first of course is Marx, for insight into the relations between a system of social and economic relations and the rules that govern it. Second, by way of contrast, is Max Weber, who was writing about some of the same events that concerned Marx. And third, Karl Renner." I knew of Marx and Weber.

"I had not heard of Karl Renner," I said.

"He was an Austrian socialist. Look up his book *The Institutions of Private Law and Their Social Functions*. You already have grasped the principles and history of civil law. Renner will help you continue that journey." Of all the conversations I had about the book I wanted to write, and the understanding I was seeking, this was the wisest.

I had begun work on the proposed book with Madeleine Levy. She and I went on from Brighton to France. We rented a small house in the hills near Grasse, in the Alpes-Maritimes about 20 kilometers from Cannes.

I had an introduction to the English writer John Collier, who owned a large house near Grasse. Collier wrote novels, short stories, and screenplays. He was a co-author, with James Agee and others, of the screenplay for the movie *African Queen*. Much of his work featured a dry wit with a wicked edge. His house—really a mini-chateau—had been built about 1805. The property had several hectares of gardens, which John had planted in vegetables for the table.

On many Sundays, John hosted a midday meal where expat writers gathered. Some of these writers had been blacklisted in Hollywood during the

McCarthy period. John was a magnificent cook. The discussions at these lunches ranged over literature, history, and politics—and food.

On one Sunday. John looked at the cheese plate; he put a finger on one of the pieces of cheese. "Harriet," he said to his wife, "the cheese has been in the refrigerator. It should be kept in the big crockery thing that has a little dish of vinegar inside to keep things fresh."

"John," she replied, "I am tired to throwing out cheese that has been in there too long. After all, at the market in Peymeinade, they put the cheese in the refrigerator every night and bring it out in the morning; I am just doing the same thing."

"Harriet," John said, "I see no reason why, having dragged Christ down off the cross, one should nail him back up there again."

As the December holidays approached, someone said that the local butcher had hung up the carcasses of young goats for those who wanted to have a holiday barbecue. "And there they were," the guest remarked, "all those little kids hung up on hooks."

"Oh yes," John said with a wicked grin, "I love children."

The region where we were lucky enough to live evoked thoughts and images that were to form the structure of *Law and the Rise of Capitalism*. The streets, the fortified walls of villages, old churches and their decorations, and even the landscape that rose from the seafront into the pre-Alps evoked the growing commerce carried on by bourgeois merchants and traders from the medieval period onward. The South of France has a mild climate; documents from the medieval period survive.

I soon learned that the French approach to legal study begins by introducing students to a panoramic view of history from antiquity to the present. Every student begins by reading a series of books titled *Histoire des institutions,* by Jacques Ellul. I read those books, but found that Ellul had written history from "top down." He, like so many legal historians, focused on "institutions" and not the people subject to institutional commands.

I have had a book of Brecht's poems for decades. One of my favorites is "A Worker Reads History." It begins:

> *Who built the seven gates of Thebes?*
> *The books are filled with names of kings.*
> *Was it kings who hauled the craggy blocks of stone?*

I discovered the work of two historians, and then met their contemporary disciples. Marc Bloch was my first discovery. In the 1920s, he founded the Annales school of historical research, which sought to understand history by examining economics, sociology, and geographical influences. I read his work on French rural history and feudal society. Bloch had taught at several French universities. While he was teaching at Montpellier in 1942, he became active in the French Resistance, somewhat tardily given that the Nazis had rolled into France in 1940. The Nazis captured him in Lyon in 1944, and tortured and executed him.

Bloch had great influence on historians of French law and legal history. I turned also to the work of Roger Aubenas, a legal historian who spent much of his career at the law faculty of Aix-en-Provence where I was later to teach as visiting professor.

In a local bookstore, I found a study by Pierre-André Sigalas, *La Vie à Grasse en 1650*, somewhat later than the period in which I was mainly interested, but based on a careful study of archival material. I wrote to Sigalas, and he invited me to meet. He was a retired judge who had indulged his interest in history by writing the book as his doctoral thesis. He and his wife and daughter lived in one of those magnificent apartment buildings in the foothills of Nice. He introduced me to professors at the Nice law faculty, Paul-Louis Malaussena and Marie-Louise Carlin. These scholars were applying the historical methodology of the Annales school to the study of legal institutions beginning in the 1100s, the earliest period from which significant caches of documents were available.

It appeared that the conversation about "law" in the faculties of law was self-consciously seen as situated in a historical process, a tension between change and stability.

Beyond the scholars and teachers, memories of May 1968 were still fresh in many people's minds in 1971–72. As the *New York Times* recalled:

Just six weeks after France's leading newspaper, *Le Monde*, pronounced that the country was "bored," too bored to join the youth protests underway in Germany and in the United States, students in Paris occupied the Sorbonne, one of the most illustrious universities in Europe.

The day was May 3, 1968, and the events that ensued over the following month—mass protests, street battles and nationwide strikes—transformed France. It was not a political revolution in the way that earlier French revolutions had been, but a cultural and social one that in a stunningly short time changed French society.

"In the history of France it was a remarkable movement because it was truly a mass movement that concerned Paris but also the provinces, that concerned intellectuals but also manual workers," said Bruno Queysanne, who, at the time was an assistant instructor at the École des Beaux-Arts in Paris.

I had gained a glimpse of the European student movement in 1969. Karl Dietrich Wolff, former president of the German Socialist Students Federation, came to the United States in January 1969 and spoke at colleges and public forums about the student movement in Europe. He was engaging and articulate. Predictably, the FBI followed him around and reported on his activities.

In March, the Senate Internal Security Subcommittee, chaired by Senator Strom Thurmond, subpoenaed him to testify. Someone told Wolff to call me and we appeared on the appointed afternoon. The idea of a Senate investigating committee with a roving commission to investigate leftists was strange to Wolff, who became increasingly restive as the afternoon wore on. I was reminded of Bertolt Brecht's appearance before the House Committee on Un-American Activities, a recording of which I had heard. Brecht's English was not very good, and neither was that spoken by the translator he brought with him. An additional complexity was that the Dixiecrat committee chairman also had a limited vocabulary, and at one point wanted to know if Brecht believed in the "class struggle between the petroleums and the bergewarsie."

As our hearing began, committee counsel Jay Sourwine asked Wolff if he swore to tell the truth. Wolff whispered that he preferred to affirm than to swear to a deity. I repeated this. "What?!" Thurmond exclaimed. "He won't take the oath? He has to take the oath."

"Senator," I said, "he would prefer to affirm. He has the right not to invoke a deity."

Thurmond persisted, "He is in contempt if he won't take the oath."

I asked for a recess; Jay Sourwine and I talked. Sourwine then chatted with the senator and we resumed. Wolff affirmed.

Sourwine then went through a series of questions about Wolff's visit to the United States and his speeches to student groups. Wolff deflected the questions with complaints about being harassed, as he was simply exercising his right to speak and respecting his listeners' right to hear. At one point, Wolff spoke of the legal problems that the Black Panther Party was having, and blamed the Committee for helping cause those troubles. Sourwine interjected, "You mention panthers. You have been talking about people, and now you talk about panthers. Panthers are an animal species, are they not?"

This was too much for Wolff. He replied, "I tell you one thing, Mister. I prefer panthers to pigs." The dialogue became even less informative from that point on, and after a few more questions Wolff got up and left the hearing room. I followed. The Committee issued a new subpoena, but it was never served, as Wolff returned to Germany.

Wolff's critique of the state's repressive apparatus was woven of the same cloth as the Paris protests and the events in the United States. A transnational generation saw the prospects of struggle and transformation in similar ways.

In short, the people I met and the places I walked somehow gave me a context to write about the sweep of social history from the tenth century, when the first battles against the feudal system were waged, and the present day. The book began to take shape. If I am to do any lengthy piece of writing, I have to see the project as a whole. I have to be able to describe the theme in a relatively few words.

To tell the story of social change and the lawyers' role in it, I divided past time into historical periods, and within each period related stories about social struggle. As the nascent bourgeoisie—literally "city dwellers"—made demands on holders of state and economic power, its demands and activities were written down.

Lawyers were among the relatively few who were literate. We have the contracts they drafted, and the documents that reflect the formation of business entities. When the merchants of a particular place came together to form a community, we have the document describing the system of social relations they were establishing.

I worked on the book almost every day. From conversations with other Americans living in France, I learned that in order for a U.S. citizen to be married in France, he or she had to obtain a *certificat de coutume*, from a lawyer approved by the U.S. consulate, attesting that he or she was eligible to be married under U.S. law—that is, not already married or under some other legal impediment. I registered at the consulate in Nice, which brought in some of this and other legal business. I also registered with the local court as a *conseil juridique*, authorized to engage in a limited consulting law practice.

The phone would ring. The caller would say that he or she wanted to get married, usually very soon. I would take my typewriter to a hotel or home. One such evening, the American man and a French woman had fallen in love in Monaco, at the Hotel de Paris. Would I come and help them take the step toward getting married by the sea? I obliged. On another occasion, an American woman of a certain age wanted to marry a Frenchman who had retained his noble title as "count." He was willing, provided she signed a document in English and French disavowing any claim on his assets or title. I drafted the document. After we had lived in France for a year, Madeleine and I were married.

The consulate referred other business, including tax issues of expatriate writers and artists. Because French law recognized handwritten wills, I gave some advice on that topic as well, helping people draft wills that would be valid in France, where they were made, and also made dispositions recogniz-able under U.S. law.

One day, I got a call asking me to come to the port of Antibes, where Otto Preminger was filming an altogether forgettable movie starring Peter O'Toole and with a cameo appearance by former New York Mayor John Lindsay. A disagreement had arisen with the film crew and Preminger needed to revise their employment agreements in order to avoid a work stoppage. There was no time to call in the lawyers from Paris. I sat all day with my typewriter draft-ing new agreements.

A younger consular employee in Nice seemed to be the person who would refer potential clients. I was only one of two lawyers certified to issue *certifi-cats de coutume*. The other was a dyspeptic gentleman decades older than I.

In the village of Le Tignet, where Madeleine Levy and I were living, and in the neighboring towns, I was seen as another expat American working on a book and speaking passable French. Some of my friends shared a concern for social justice and knew I was a lawyer. One day, my friends Jeannot and Jacqueline Massaguen came by with a young Tunisian man who had been summoned for an interview at the gendarmerie, the French paramilitary police station. The young man had fallen in love with the daughter of a butcher in Grasse. The butcher was angry that his daughter was dating an Arab.

At that time, there was a building boom along the Mediterranean coast. Many of the construction workers and the lower-paid workers in the new buildings, resorts, and restaurants were from Tunisia, Algeria, and Morocco. Racist sentiment abounded. When underpaid workers demonstrated in the streets, local mayors responded with tear gas and water cannons.

The butcher complained to some of his friends in the gendarmerie about his daughter's boyfriend. Three officers in uniform arrested Ali. He had his girlfriend's name tattooed on his forearm. One officer took out his cigarette lighter and burned off the tattoo.

A few days later, Ali complained to the commanding officer. He described the lighter that his assailant had used. The officer summoned a platoon of his men and ordered them to turn out their pockets. One of them had the lighter that Ali had described. A few days after that, Ali received the summons to be interrogated. He was worried that this was payback time. I explained that my right to practice law in France was limited, and probably did not extend to providing counsel during official interrogations.

I concluded that this would not be the first time I had wandered into situ-ations where officials thought I did not belong. I went with Ali. The officers were adamant. He was to be questioned and had no right to counsel of any kind, particularly a lawyer who was not French.

Ah yes, I explained, but Ali is a citizen of Tunisia, and thus his right to counsel is a question of international human rights law, particularly given the European Convention on Human Rights. I am a *conseil juridique*; I want only to counsel him. I was making some of this up as I went along. The officers huddled. They offered to question Ali in a room on the ground floor of the gendarmerie, with the door open. I could stand just outside the door and listen.

Perhaps the controversy dulled the interrogators' ardor. They asked a few questions about the attack that Ali had suffered, and then let him go. A few days later I was in my study working on the book. A military jeep pulled into the driveway, blocking the entrance. The driver jumped out and opened the passenger door. A man in uniform, of middle height and military bearing, dressed like Claude Rains in *Casablanca*, stepped out, came on to the terrace, and knocked on the study door.

I invited him in. He was, he said, Commandant Marion. He understood I was interested in international law. I said I was.

"Very interesting. I also am a student of international law. I am enrolled at the law faculty in Nice. Do you expect to be involved in international law while you are here in France?"

"Not really," I said. "I am working on a book on legal history."

"Ah," he said, "that is good work to be doing. Ah, well, I just wanted to pay a brief visit. Enjoy your sojourn in France." He stood, and walked out to the jeep. His driver opened the door for him, and drove away.

I called my friend on the law faculty. Commandant Marion was not enrolled. I understood the message he was sending.

A few weeks later, I invited the young official from the American consulate to dinner at my house. I thanked him for introducing me to Americans who might have legal business. He enjoyed my cooking, and got sloppy drunk.

"You know," he said, "we were told to keep an eye on you."

"Who told you?" I asked.

"Our people," he said. "You know what your problem is? It's your left ear."

I wasn't sure what this meant, but he said it earnestly as though he was making sense. He burbled a few more thoughts about my politics, wobbled to his car and drove away—nicking the driveway gatepost on the way out.

In January 1972, the news from the United States reported that Angela Davis's case was set for trial. On a fine January day, I stopped for lunch at the Colombe d'Or hotel-restaurant in the hill village of St.-Paul-de-Vence, above Nice and Antibes. I must have felt that my fee in the *Gelbard* case allowed the financial indulgence. James Baldwin and Simone Signoret were seated at a nearby table.

I introduced myself and told Baldwin that Angela appreciated his support. He asked me to sit at his table. Baldwin wanted me to go over the issues in Angela's case, much in the way—as it turned out—that I had parsed them in the pretrial motion to dismiss. He was especially interested in the state's use of constitutionally protected resistance to oppression as a basis for inferring willingness to join with others to commit serious crimes. When a discriminated social group organizes to resist, people will make different choices about whether to break the law. The state's use of conspiracy charges tends to lump all the resisters together, substituting—as one court has said—a feeling of collective culpability for a finding of individual guilt.

Somehow, in the conversation, I revealed that my thirty-first birthday would be on January 18. Baldwin said he would cook a birthday dinner at his house down the road. Signoret joined us for dinner. Baldwin cooked a superb dinner, and conversation ranged over the political events through which we had been living.

Among the dinner topics was the Slansky trial in Czechoslovakia, in which Eduard Goldstucker had been a defendant, and during which the prosecutors had alleged that the World War II Czech government in exile in London had been subjected to anti-Soviet influence by Konni Zilliacus. Signoret and Yves Montand had recently completed *L'aveu* (*The Confession*), a Costa-Gavras film about the Slansky trials and their aftermath. They knew Goldstucker, and knew of Zilliacus. Signoret and Montand saw the film's story and the characters they portrayed as emblematic of the political commitment they shared. It was a wonderful evening.

As I worked, one of the most valuable sources was a book of maps of Western Europe, charting the political, demographic and economic events of periods from 400 CE to 1900 CE. I could visualize the social disintegration of the post–Roman Empire latifundia system, and the formation of secular and religious feudal institutions. I could chart the establishment of communes— merchant enclaves—along the routes of trade from the Eastern Mediterranean, northward and westward.

In hundreds of communities, a rising merchant class confronted feudal and royal power. To express their commercial agreements, they were using forms of words based on compilations of Roman law. One could see these formulations in the surviving contracts. In towns where merchants gained power, they would draw up charters reflecting principles of governance—*coutumes*, or collections of custom.

Though forms of words for contracts and town charters were passed along the routes of trade, it could not be said that there was some overarching ideological framework of a united merchant class. Rather, the system of social relations was fundamental and primary. The "law" was superstructure. The similarity of legal forms was the product of the same system of social relations being replicated in place after place.

The struggle against injustice moves from the particular toward the universal. People living in the same or similar social conditions come to see the injustices that beset them. They band together. In resistance, they unmask the processes by which these injustices are inflicted and move together toward change. Any legitimate "idea" of human rights is a distillation of human experiences.

I was writing a book of history, and achieving my personal goal of understanding what lawyers do about social change: the power of, and the limitations on, their insights and knowledge. A lawyer's job was to seek out and assist those elements in the struggle for change that seem most adapted to resisting injustice and most capable of bringing a new society into being.

By the fall of 1973, I had almost finished a working draft, and I could foresee the book being done. I was restless. Some years later, I was talking to therapist Anya Rylander-Jones in an effort to save my third marriage and perhaps understand what drove me so hard. Anya tried to get me to focus on what was happening now, and what was possible to make happen. I still carry some little sayings around that address this issue:

> Don't push the river; it flows by itself.
> I am doing this now and it's enough.

Anya's other way of describing my condition was to describe two archetypes—the warrior and the scholar. The warrior battles; the scholar ponders. I have both of those in me—maybe we all do. I am convinced that the great litigation lawyers think deeply about the context and consequences of their work. The warrior and the scholar need to talk.

My scholar was under some serious pressure from my warrior. Yes, I was doing some law practice. Yes, I had argued the *Gelbard* case in the Supreme Court, and taken a couple of months to go to California to litigate search and seizure motions. I had not, however, cured the restless energy that had propelled me in the past. My children, Jon and Kate, had visited me in France. I had spent time with them in California, but I wanted to see them more often. Madeleine Levy and I had gotten married in France. She wanted to go back to the United States and perhaps enroll in law school; she had begun legal study by clerking in a New York law firm in the 1960s. I was also learning what many husbands learn in second marriages, the tension with children of the first marriage. This was to prove a major element in Madeleine and I splitting up a few years later.

As though my discomfort went forth on the ether, I received a call from Dave Scribner in New York. Dave had been a leading labor and civil rights lawyer since the 1930s. He was a founder of the National Lawyers Guild. He had more energy at his then-age—sixty-five or so—than I at thirty-two. He wanted to visit me in France, to talk about a case. A week later, he arrived, energetic and rubicund, with a trimmed white beard and spectacles. We sat on my front porch, looking down some 20 kilometers to the bay at Cannes, drank coffee, and talked.

Dave was representing a group of rank-and-file steelworkers. The Steelworkers Union president, I. W. Abel, had signed a new contract with the ten largest steel companies, the key feature of which was an "Experimental Negotiating Agreement." Under this ENA, the union and management would negotiate for a time when the contract ran out, and then submit any differences to binding arbitration. The right to strike would be a thing of the past.

To me, it seemed foolish for the union to give up its heftiest bargaining tool. In labor history, the right to take concerted job action had been won at great cost. Merits aside, the ENA was wrong because it had been forced upon the membership without any semblance of democratic procedure. There was no membership consultation, much less a vote. The deal looked like another high-handed action of Abel and his group, who were already being challenged for leadership positions by people who had more support among the rank and file. Abel would argue that the companies gave up the right to lock out the workers, but even this was lopsided; the companies could still lock out on "local" issues, while the workers could not strike on such issues.

Dave said he was going to file a lawsuit challenging the ENA. We discussed theories. The plaintiffs would be rank–and–file leaders from the big steel towns—Gary, Cleveland, Pittsburgh, Youngstown.

This was a case that embodied many of the principles and ideas that had energized my work on *Law and the Rise of Capitalism*. Already by that time, steel workers were being marginalized by the big steel companies. And now their union was giving away its most effective weapon—the right to strike. Dave spoke of these issues in a language that reflected a theory of history that I shared, and with a far deeper knowledge than I had. I was reminded of my father's union work all those years ago.

As Dave and I talked, we both saw the story of the case, but we needed a legal theory. For that, we turned to the Labor-Management Relations Act of 1959, the Landrum-Griffin Act. This was a difficult choice, because Landrum-Griffin was enacted to curb union power, and to impose more limits and restrictions than its predecessor, the Taft-Hartley Act of 1947. Taft-Hartley, in its turn, was an attack on the union rights conferred by the

Wagner Act of the New Deal era. Indeed, Taft-Hartley was passed over President Truman's veto.

Some parts of Landrum-Griffin, such as those regulating union elections, did not confer a right to sue individual union members. Only the Secretary of Labor had standing in the first instance to bring such a lawsuit. But other sections gave our clients claims we could litigate. The law guaranteed freedom of expression, in the context of union democracy, and it required union leaders to be fiduciaries for their members.

I was not a labor lawyer, but I had done some work for unions and had a general idea of what this was all about: Union democracy and members' rights echo familiar themes from other parts of my practice and experience. Dave had brought some of the basic legal material with him. We roughed out a lawsuit, sitting there on the terrace overlooking the bay at Cannes. Several weeks later, I was sitting in Dave's office in New York ready to begin work. In the office was a lawyer my age who was also volunteering to work on the case, John Mage. John and I became friends, and later law partners.

John was—is—my age. From that 1974 morning to the present day, we have been together in cases representing outcasts and rebels. John has become a leading figure in *Monthly Review* magazine and press, where I have published two books and several articles. He sees legal issues in a richly studied historical context.

For the next few weeks, my warrior and scholar personae lived in happy harmony. The scholar met Staughton and Alice Lynd in Chicago. Staughton was a social historian, son of famous sociologists. He had moved to Chicago and was attending law school, so he brought legal theory together with economic history into our discussions. When he graduated law school, he began practicing labor law in Youngstown, Ohio. In Pittsburgh, I met Jim Logan, a labor lawyer and activist who would play a key role in the case. We decided to file in Pittsburgh, in the U.S. District Court for the Western District of Pennsylvania. This was the historic "steel town," and was in the Third Circuit, where court of appeals precedent seemed to favor us.

In New York, I met Professor David Gordon, of the New School for Social Research. David died a few years later, very young. He was among the most articulate and progressive scholars of labor economics of our generation. I sat and listened, sometimes contributing a thought or two, with Mage and Scribner and Gordon. We ranged over the history of American labor, from the labor struggles in the early 1800s through the statutory reforms of the 1930s, and down to 1974.

In the 1806 *Cordwainers' Case*, Pennsylvania courts upheld the convictions of striking workers for a "conspiracy in restraint of trade." All concerted job action was, under this view, a crime. From the eighteenth century onward, and throughout the nineteenth century, this idea held sway. Union organizing was incitement to lawlessness. As America became an industrial nation, and its workforce was joined by European immigrants schooled in a radical tradition, the anti-strike rhetoric of establishment forces increased in fury.

During the 1887 Chicago strikes that led to the infamous Haymarket trials, Tom Scott, the president of the Pennsylvania Railroad, proclaimed, "Give those strikers a rifle diet for a few days and see how they like that kind of bread." The *Indianapolis News* proclaimed, "If the workingmen had no vote they might be more amenable to the teachings of the times." The *Chicago Times* thundered: "Hand grenades should be thrown among these union men who are striving to obtain higher wages and less hours. By such treatment they would be taught a valuable lesson, and other strikers could take warning from their fate." Not until 1932, with the Norris-LaGuardia Act, did federal law limit the judicial role in union-busting and give limited protection to the right to strike.

If a major industrial union were to abandon the strike as a weapon, such a concession should be made only after the membership as a whole had been consulted, informed, and had made a deliberate decision. Gordon agreed to be our expert witness, to present a historical panorama about workers' rights. At the same time, we did not want to embrace a legal theory that would weaken the power of union leaders to confront powerful management on behalf of a unified workforce. We did not want to make law that would permit management to fracture the fragile unity of the union membership. Union decisions were entitled to membership respect, and not a proper occasion for disruption or "dual unionism." But the only decisions entitled to such respect were those democratically arrived at.

Our legal theory had to incorporate these historical truths. Union democracy, as somewhat guaranteed by Landrum-Griffin, was only a part of the story. The abstract entity known as the union represents the members in name only—the "representing" is done by the union leaders. On the shop floor, the union rep who will present your grievance is the "shop steward." That name, blessed by long history, says a lot. Union leaders have an obligation of stewardship.

To express this theory, we turned to Title 3 of Landrum-Griffin, which simply stated that union officers have a fiduciary obligation—they are trustees. There was some case law holding that this statute applied only to union financial assets. The better view, or so we thought, was that it applied to the whole range of union member rights. This would include the right to fair representation, the right to strike, and the right to be consulted. Our view of fiduciary duty had good support in decisions concerning the obligations of corporate officers and directors to the corporation and its shareholders.

My sense of purpose was enlivened by meeting the clients. In Gary, Indiana, many of the steel mills were already closing down. The town as a whole suffered the malaise of so many industrial cities in what came to be known as the Rust Belt. I will always remember my first meeting with the group of rank-and-file activists who were to be our Gary clients. Their leader was Alice—"Brother Alice" as she was fondly known. In steel union lingo your fellow workers were your brothers, and in 1974 little attention had been paid to finding a gender-neutral way of speaking.

We met at the mill, and then went on to a Catholic social hall. A local priest—who seemed young even to my thirty-something self—let us in. He spoke to us of the social problems of the decaying city. The struggle to reclaim the union from I. W. Abel was, it seemed, part of some larger idea to revitalize this community.

In Cleveland, George was our host—a tough and gray-haired veteran of the mill. For George, the right to walk off the job was central to his way of thinking. George even pointed out how wildcat strikes—those not authorized by the contract, or at least openly, by union leadership—were playing an important role. He recounted how worker protest had ended some unsafe working conditions in several plants.

My soldier and my scholar were united in Youngstown. There, rank-and-file candidates committed to union democracy had won elections and were running the local. Local leaders John and Jim and the others were not only going to help us in this lawsuit, but they regarded it as part of a broader strategy to democratize the union as a whole. We spent long evenings talking through short- and long-term strategies.

We filed our complaint with a motion for a preliminary injunction blocking the ENA pending a full trial. This was the quickest way to get our case into court, and put the maximum pressure on the other side. Our defendants were Abel, the Union, and the ten steel companies. With adversaries like that, we could not afford to get into a major discovery battle. We needed to find out quickly if the lawsuit would have staying power.

Staying power in the courts was not our only objective, and for many of our clients was not the major objective. This case could be a rallying point for Abel's opponents, for those who wanted to democratize the union and return it to core principles in which they believed. The ENA had been adopted in a hurry, and after negotiations that were mostly secret. The lawsuit was a focus for publicity and protest.

In Pittsburgh and other steel towns, rank-and-filers stood every night at the plant gates passing out leaflets about the issue. Our case plan was simple. We would present the testimony of rank-and-file leaders about how ENA was adopted, and then the expert overview from Dr. Gordon. Staughton Lynd helped with research and worked with witnesses.

There was no jury. We wanted, however, to impress Judge Teitelbaum and the media that we represented genuine union member voices. Every day of the hearing, the courtroom was filled with steel workers. Since they were all our clients, directly or as members of the plaintiff class, we subpoenaed them to appear as potential witnesses and asked the judge to waive the rule and permit them to remain in the courtroom. Their union contract provided for days off with pay so long as they remained under subpoena.

Our rank-and-file witnesses showed a greater understanding of steel company finances and organization than our opponents thought possible. They withstood condescending cross-examinations. In the end, Judge Teitelbaum ruled against us. But we had worked alongside those who were organizing rank-and-file activity and opinion in the union locals and in the international union, which in turn led to election victories for our clients in union politics. We had served a purpose that lawyers can serve.

Something else: standing up in court alongside Dave Scribner, examining and cross-examining witnesses, and arguing the issues of law and fact, brought back that sense of participation that had impelled me. Maybe I was, as Anya Rylander-Jones had said, a kind of "intensity junkie." If so, perhaps I could control and channel that energy.

And "the book"? I took the completed manuscript to Random House, actually to its Pantheon imprint and editor André Schiffrin. We met one evening in New York. He didn't like the book. Random House/Pantheon relinquished any rights they had under the contract. I would keep the modest advance. I don't think I listened carefully to his reasons. I was distressed and angry.

I cannot recall who suggested that I take the manuscript to Monthly Review Press. Leo Huberman, Paul Sweezy, and Harry Magdoff read it. They approved the title *Law and the Rise of Capitalism*, brushing aside my concern that this might be seen as hubris, given the fame of R. H. Tawney's book *Religion and the Rise of Capitalism*. Actually, the difference in titles reflects the different emphases of the two books, Tawney having embraced a theme and theory that Weber would find agreeable, and my emphasis on Renner and Marx.

John Mage read the manuscript. Susan Lowes of Monthly Review Press painstakingly and wisely edited it. The book, to use an overtaxed expression, "speaks for itself." It has been translated into Spanish, Portuguese, Greek,

Chinese, and Turkish. It was reviewed favorably by Christopher Hill in the *New Statesman,* though less favorably elsewhere. I meet academics and political figures in foreign countries who have read it. This recognition is owed to Monthly Review Press: No other publisher commands such international attention and respect.

CHAPTER 11

By Any Means Necessary

Justice Brandeis wrote: "Government is the potent, omnipresent teacher. For good or for ill, it teaches the whole people by its example. . . . If the government becomes a lawbreaker, it breeds contempt for the law; it invites every man to become a law unto himself; it invites anarchy." I think government is the most dangerous criminal. When government commits offenses, or more exactly when people commit crimes in the name of government and with its power, they can wreak more harm than any individual. Government is also a recidivist. If not stopped, it repeats its crimes. It seldom repents for wrongs; its spokesmen think up new justifications and excuses.

Suing the government civilly for wrongdoing is daunting. Government agents have qualified immunity from lawsuits. The state and federal governments, as entities, claim a broad and absolute immunity. The Supreme Court has made it harder for lawyers to get legal fees when they sue the government and win. Public officials and sovereign entities can move to dismiss the complaint on immunity grounds, and if the trial judge rejects their legal position, they can take an immediate appeal. The Supreme Court has held that the official defendants may be able to appeal more than once in a single case, putting the day of reckoning off even further. The government is a repeat player in the legal system; it has a staff of lawyers skilled in managing litigation and keeping the plaintiff from bringing it to closure. The marginal cost of one more lawsuit is relatively small, compared to the resources that a plaintiff must expend.

The defense of criminal cases provides significant opportunities to expose and correct government overreaching. However, that process provides those opportunities only when the government has behaved badly by prosecuting an innocent person or by using foul tactics. The defendant in such a case endures torments that can often never be redressed, as well as risking loss, jail or even death.

I have tried to choose cases that permit me to litigate government account- ability, and particularly that of the intelligence services such as the FBI and CIA. These agencies not only threaten democratic rights of individuals, but their conduct and operation can undermine the right to organize and to par- ticipate in public decision-making. Many of the cases I discuss in this book are examples. And it may well happen that government misconduct affects well-heeled clients as well as poor ones. This is in one sense a good thing, for I have been able to pay my rent all these years and put my children through school.

Some of these cases are studies in judicial courage, or the good sense of juries. Cameron Bishop, Francisco Martinez and John Demjanjuk are three examples.

CAMERON BISHOP

In the middle of 1975, I was visiting John and Nellie Connally on their ranch South of San Antonio. It was just after John had been acquitted in the case I will discuss in chapter 14. I took the chance to ride with him on horseback and by jeep over the Texas Hill Country. Somehow, a lawyer in Denver man- aged to get the ranch number and track me down. Cameron David Bishop had been arrested. Cam was charged with having used dynamite to blow up four electrical power towers in the Denver area in 1969. He had, however, been unavailable for trial—a 'fugitive," in the government's opinion—until he was arrested in Rhode Island in 1975. Would I come to Denver and discuss representation?

I said I would come. I went back to Washington and told Ed Williams that I was thinking of doing the case. The family could pay expenses, but not a fee. Ed peered over his glasses and said, "How about I get you a communist bomber in Baltimore to represent, then maybe you could come back and bill a few hours on weekends?" I demurred and he gave his rueful blessing.

Cam Bishop was from a southern Colorado farm family, sheep ranchers by trade. He had been part of the student movement against the Vietnam War in college and active in the Students for a Democratic Society. The indict- ment charged "sabotage," and each of the four charges carried a thirty-year jail term, on the theory that the electrical power supplied defense facilities along with other customers.

The case brought at least one stroke of good fortune. I met Hal Haddon, who agreed to be co-counsel, along with me and John Mage. Hal had just started in private practice after heading up Colorado's statewide public defender office. He is one of the world's great trial lawyers and champion friends.

The trial was set before Chief Judge Albert Arraj, stern but practical. It is ironic that when I stepped into the Denver federal courthouse more than twenty years later to try the Nichols case, that was the second bombing case tried in that building, and again the presiding judge was Chief Judge of the district. Arraj knew of the Williams firm, for he had been trial judge in the Kolod-Alderman-Alderisio case.

The government presented evidence that Cam had assembled a cache of dynamite and had worked with others to blow up the towers. We had one miraculous scene in which the FBI said it had found his fingerprint on a piece of dynamite wrapper found at the scene, right near the center of the blast. We did not have the forensic resources to debunk this evidence. We subpoenaed a man from DuPont, who said that this type of wrapper did not exist at the time of the bombings, but first began production a year later. We also showed that it was possible to fake a fingerprint. I focused on this evidence in summation.

We also had experts jousting over whether blowing up one power tower in an entire grid could pose any danger to power supplies, given the way in which the system was interconnected. The government proved, without contradiction, that defense facilities were located near Denver and did use electricity from this power grid. And because one of Cam's former friends had been given immunity in order to testify against him, we had the standard sort of cross-examination about testimony obtained in such a way.

Given that Cam made his own opening statement, and given all the small doubts that we might sow, we thought it possible to get a hung jury. At the core of the case was the government's decision to charge Cam with "sabotage," rather than destruction of property. The sabotage charge required the government to prove that the defendant had acted during a time of war or of national emergency declared by the U.S. president. This element escalated the case from a property crime punishable in state court to a major-league federal case. In 1969, no war was in progress, for Congress had not declared one in Vietnam. What was the "national emergency"? Government Exhibit 600 provided the answer. It was a beribboned and gold-sealed copy of a proclamation by President Harry S. Truman concerning the Korean War in 1950.

1950? Yes. No president had "undeclared" the Korean War national emergency, and therefore the prosecutors claimed it was still pending. This did not make sense, we thought at first. Then, we began to look at the statute books. Dozens of federal programs and presidential activities were continuing under various authorizations that depended on the continued existence of a national emergency. Presidents Truman, Eisenhower, Kennedy, Johnson, Nixon, and Ford had not wanted to issue a new proclamation of national emergency, and the Congress had not taken action to require them to do so.

Such a fiction might serve to preserve funding for executive branch programs, or maintain an executive prerogative to authorize some military action. But it seemed ludicrous that this old proclamation could provide an element of a federal felony. I went to see Adrian "Butch" Fisher, then Dean of Georgetown University Law School. Dean Fisher had been law clerk to Justice Brandeis and to Justice Frankfurter. He had begun his career in public service in World War II, and by 1950 was Legal Adviser to the State Department. I liken this job to being Solicitor General. The Legal Adviser is not, or should not be, simply an instrument of administration policy, but rather must give independent advice about the legal powers and duties of the United States.

Fisher agreed to be a defense witness. He thought it absurd to claim that the Korean War was still going on. Then the question arose, on what basis could he testify? He had personal knowledge of the national emergency declaration, Exhibit 600, and the events that led to it. He had maintained his role as a leading international law scholar, teacher, and practitioner.

But was pendency of a national emergency a "fact" element of sabotage, such that the jury would decide? Or was it a "jurisdictional" element, on which the judge would make a finding and instruct the jury? The law on this subject has moved in the ensuing years, and today it seems more likely that the Supreme Court would hold that this element is for the jury. We were ready to argue it both ways.

Dean Fisher came to Denver. With the jury in the box, he took the stand. The two prosecutors looked at each other, and at their FBI case agent, but none of them knew who Fisher was or why we might be calling him.

Q: Will you tell the jury your name, sir?
A: I am Adrian Fisher.
Q. What is your business or occupation, sir?
A: I am Dean of Georgetown University School of Law, in Washington, D.C.

We continued, through his clerking, his public service, his tenure as General Counsel of the *Washington Post*, and his teaching and writing.

Q: I show you now what has been received in evidence as Government Exhibit 600, and I ask you, sir, if you have ever seen it before?
A: Yes, I have.

Q: Who wrote it?

A: I did.

Q: How did you come to write this, sir?

A: President Truman decided that the Korean hostilities required that he declare a national emergency. I researched the precedents concerning the various military conflicts short of actual war in which the United States had been involved, and I drafted this for his signature.

The prosecutors were looking at each other like rabbits in the headlights. Judge Arraj, knowing incipient roadkill when he saw it, leaned forward and said to them, "Don't you want to object now?" The lead prosecutor obediently stood and said, "I object," without stating a ground.

"Sustained," said Judge Arraj.

I asked that we be permitted to make an offer of proof, of what Dean Fisher would have said, but in the form of questions and answers out of the jury's presence. Judge Arraj excused the jurors. Dean Fisher told us a brief history of the Korean conflict and how the proclamation came to be. He then said that the Korean War was over no later than the mid-1950s. Up to that point there had been some stray shots over the border between North and South Korea.

Hal, John, and I tried the case to conclusion. A juror later told us that three jurors wanted to acquit, but after Judge Arraj called them back several times to urge them to reach a verdict, a compromise was reached. The jury convicted on three of the four counts. Some jurors were horrified to learn later that each charge carried a potential 20-year sentence.

The prosecutors moved to revoke Cam's bail, noting that he had been a fugitive for nearly six years. We then saw a human side of Judge Arraj that we had not seen. I cited to him Justice Jackson's opinion as Circuit Justice in the Communist Party Smith Act cases. These leaders had been denied bail, but Jackson set them free. His main argument was that the case involved core issues of political freedom, and what a reproach it would be to our system if the defendants were jailed and it turned out that their First Amendment challenge to their convictions was sustained on appeal.

Judge Arraj listened to our arguments, and heard that Cam's family would put up their property to secure his presence. He granted bail, saying:

One of the impressive sights in this trial has been that Mr. Bishop's family has been here every day. Some days, his children have been here as well. It is heartening to see this kind of family support, and I believe that Mr. Bishop would not disappoint his family by running out on this case and causing them to lose almost everything they own. There is something else. I am confident that my rulings in this case are correct, but suppose the court of appeals thinks otherwise? These young people would rightly suffer some loss of confidence in the judicial system.

I returned to Washington and did a first draft of the appeal brief for Hal and John to review, revise, and improve. The oral argument in the court of appeals foreshadowed its decision. The morning of argument, I was having coffee with Hal Haddon and his partner Bryan Morgan. Bryan rode the bus to work, and he told us that two young men, whom he assumed were law clerks, were talking about our case on the bus. The tenor of one clerk's remark was how ridiculous it was to contend that a national emergency declared in 1950 could still be going on.

Some oral arguments seem to turn on a single question from the bench. The prosecutor argued that a national emergency lasted until it was "undeclared." A judge asked:

Q: If President Lincoln had declared a national emergency for the Civil War, and no later President had revoked that declaration, would that emergency still be going on, so as to permit a sabotage prosecution instead of one for simply destroying government property?

The prosecutor hesitated and that rabbit in the headlights look came over him again. The judge continued, "That has to be your position, doesn't it?"

"Yes, I suppose so," the answer finally came.

The court of appeals could have approached the issue from a number of perspectives. If it had held that Judge Arraj erred by excluding the evidence, we would have been back for a retrial, perhaps on some lesser charge. The court held, however, that the sabotage statute as applied violated due process of law, for how could anyone know that the Korean War was still going on? In effect, the court held that there was a knowledge requirement with respect to the element of national emergency that could not possibly be satisfied. We took this as an acquittal on appeal, foreclosing a retrial, at least in federal court. Given that the statute of limitations had run on any state charges, Cam was almost free.

We were not, however, quite finished. The United States has the right to petition for certiorari from an adverse court of appeals judgment. I called Andy Frey, the Deputy Solicitor General who handled criminal cases. He was agitated. "This decision is indefensible. Maybe you can argue that the evidence should be admitted, but declaring the sabotage statute unconstitutional is really too much."

"Andy," I said, "this is all because the government decided to use a draconian law when it could have used a milder one that did not create these problems. And when you think of it, the government's theory about the Korean War looks a little silly."

Our conversation turned to pending legislation, soon to pass, that did away with any pending national emergencies and regulated how future ones might come and go. Andy was sure that since the Congress would soon resolve the underlying problem, the Supreme Court would not want to inject itself into the issue. And the United States does not petition for certiorari unless it is pretty sure the Court will take the case.

Cam was truly free. It was a story like the fable of the fox, who had a bird in his mouth and was walking over a bridge. He saw his reflection in the water, and thought there was another bird down there. So he dropped his real bird and went for the reflection, thus losing everything.

FRANCISCO MARTINEZ

Francisco "Kiko" Martinez grew up in Alamosa, Colorado, near the New Mexico border. This is ranching country on the lower elevations, and then you get into the magnificent San Juan Mountains over by Pagosa and Durango. Alamosa is about 200 miles west of Rocky Ford and La Junta, where Cam Bishop had grown up.

Kiko attended the University of Minnesota Law School, and went to work in a legal services program near his hometown in the early 1970s. Kiko's legal efforts for farmworkers and his radical politics angered a lot of people. Somebody torched the legal services office. As conflict escalated, somebody sent letter bombs to a right-wing biker group, perhaps in retaliation for the arson. The government alleged that Kiko had sent the bombs. They indicted him. Fearing that he would not receive a fair trial, Kiko fled to Mexico, where he lived under the name Jose Reynoso-Diaz for seven years. In 1980, he was crossing the border at Nogales, Arizona, when a border guard became suspicious and began to question him closely about who he was. Kiko attempted to leave the crossing point, but was arrested and jailed. He gave the name Jose Reynoso-Diaz. The government held him in custody, and was about to deport him to Mexico in the belief that he was not a U.S. citizen. However, a routine fingerprint check revealed that Francisco Martinez and Jose Reynoso-Diaz were the same person. He was sent to Colorado to stand trial on the bombing charges.

The defense obtained a severance of counts of the indictment, so that there would be three separate trials, one for each alleged sending of an explosive device. The trial had generated such publicity that federal judge Winner moved it to Durango, Colorado. After the third trial day, Judge Winner met secretly in his hotel room with prosecutors and law enforcement people. He said that he thought the case was being badly tried and that the government should provoke a defense motion for mistrial. Judge Winner said he would grant the motion. The judge and the others discussed strategies to provoke the defense. Sure enough, the defense made a motion, the prosecutors feigned reluctance but consented, and the judge granted it.

However, a television reporter had seen people going into Judge Winner's room, and told the defense. This led to litigation to find the facts, at the end of which the court of appeals held that the government could not retry Kiko on the charges being tried in Durango. The government persisted, however, and brought the severed charges on for trial. Kiko was acquitted on the second set of charges. The government then dismissed the third set, and Kiko and his family thought the case was over.

Two weeks later the government brought a new case, this time in Tucson, Arizona. They resurrected the border crossing incident, and indicted Kiko for falsely telling the border guards his name was Jose Reynoso Diaz, and for falsely swearing to a magistrate that this was his name. The magistrate charge related to the hearing at which he was given appointed counsel and had to tell his name.

Kiko called me. Would I represent him? I recruited some law student help and went to Tucson. Judge William Browning dismissed the indictment as being a vindictive retaliation for the government's loss in the earlier case. The court of appeals reversed and sent the case back for trial. In Tucson, Antonio Bustamante and Fernando Fajardo agreed to help. A new team of students stepped forward as well. We all thought that Judge Browning would be angry at having been reversed and that he would still harbor good feelings about Kiko. We therefore prepared a statement waiving a jury, thinking that Judge Browning would see how flimsy these charges were.

The morning of trial, we looked at the waiver. There is this old story about the trial lawyer who said he knew jurors were prejudiced, but so is everybody in one way or another. He said he would rather have twelve prejudiced people than just one. If Judge Browning wanted to help Kiko, he could do so with jury instructions and in a dozen other ways. So we did not file the waiver.

Judge Browning took the bench. The government moved to exclude all evidence that we might present that Kiko faced unfair government tactics in Denver, so that we could not tell the jury why he took the name Jose Reynoso Diaz. To our surprise, Judge Browning quickly granted the motion. I put the jury waiver form in my briefcase. This judge was not inclined to do us any favors.

The trial took only a few days. Kiko had indeed used the name Jose Reynoso Diaz, and had identification permitting him to live lawfully in Mexico under that name. So what? we said. Leonard Slye had become Roy Rogers, Marion Morrison was John Wayne, Gary Hartpence was Gary Hart. Kiko was not charged with trying to deceive the Denver authorities, for there would not have been venue for that. And by claiming to be a Mexican citizen, he was not deceiving the border guards with an intention to gain unauthorized entry into the United States, for he was entitled to come in because he was in reality a U.S. citizen.

The prosecutor sought to suggest that Kiko was an international terrorist, taking advantage of our inability to show the facts of the Colorado cases. He tried to introduce evidence that Kiko had been to Cuba, even going so far as to staple a document to that effect to the back of another exhibit in the hope we would not see it.

The jurors figured that something odd was going on, even if they did not know exactly what it was. In my summation, I stressed the jury's role. The prosecutor had said the case was quite simple. Kiko was not Jose Reynoso Diaz and therefore he was guilty.

I said something like:

[The prosecutor] talks to you like this case is open and shut, like there is nothing really for you to decide. Then when the lawyers are done arguing, the judge will give you instructions, in a very matter-of-fact tone. Don't be misled by all that. We all take an oath to do what we do here. The prosecutor takes one to uphold the law. I took one to be a lawyer. The judge takes one to be a judge. You took two oaths. One to tell the truth when we talked to you on voir dire, and another one to well and truly try this case. So don't let the attitudes that you might think the prosecutor or the judge have keep you from doing your job. This case is too important for the prosecutor to decide. It is too important for the judge to decide. It is so important that we asked you to give up time from your work and family and come in here and decide it.

Our textual argument was that the hearing before the magistrate had been addressed to a single issue: whether the defendant was indigent and therefore entitled to appointed counsel. A defendant might say, "I am indigent and my name is Mickey Mouse." The only relevant matter was whether he was indigent, for if so a lawyer would be appointed no matter what his name was. Our real argument was that this case was part of a dishonorable agenda, mostly hidden from the jurors, but that they could infer from all they saw and heard.

The jury was out three days and came back with a split verdict. Not guilty of false statements to the border guards, but guilty of perjury for swearing to a false name before the magistrate. There was a reason for this split verdict. The false statement charges required the jury find that the statements were material, and the jurors no doubt concluded they were not. However, in those days, before the Supreme Court decided to the contrary, the issue of materiality in a perjury case was for the judge to decide. Judge Browning told the jury that with respect to the perjury charge they had to assume the statements were material. The Supreme Court has since held that the jury decides this issue.

Kiko had been out on bail during the trial. But now Judge Browning, without much urging from the prosecutor, revoked Kiko's bail and ordered him committed to jail while an appeal was pending. He set bail at $250,000. We were stunned, and glad indeed that we had not waived a jury given this judicial attitude. Kiko's wife was crying quietly.

At that moment a Tucson lawyer who was in the courtroom, and who had been watching the trial, came forward. I had met him briefly in a coffee shop, but knew him only by reputation as a civil trial lawyer who litigated pro bono cases. "Your Honor," the lawyer said, "you know me. I have a firm downtown. I'll put up the bail." The judge argued with the lawyer for about ten minutes, saying that there might be an ethical problem putting up bail for a client.

"Mr. Martinez is not my client and never has been, Your Honor. I am putting up bail money because I think there was error here and because I trust him."

So Kiko spent a few hours in the Marshal's office while the lawyer got the money together. On appeal, the court of appeals noted that the trial judge had not received, nor had the government offered, any evidence of how the Jose Reynoso Diaz name was material to the magistrate's inquiry. Conviction reversed, with directions to acquit.

After fifteen years Kiko was free and within the year readmitted to the bar. He went to work providing pro bono representation to prisoners and to people in his community. He and Cam Bishop are among the tens of thousands of young men and women dealt with unfairly, to one degree or another, or chilled in their activism by an atmosphere of repression. I grieve sometimes at how much America lost by silencing and punishing the energetic desire of these young people to help make a more just society. That has been a major theme of the work I have tried to do. By litigating test cases, by defending those accused, I hoped to be doing more than helping these clients. I wanted to free up their power to make change.

A similar, and perhaps more dangerous, form of repression is at work now in the day-to-day operation of the criminal law system. In the past decades, the rate of incarceration in the United States has increased geometrically, so that we now imprison five to eight times as many persons as a percentage of our population as do Western European countries and Canada. This toll falls most harshly on people of color. The atmosphere of repression and the attitude of over-criminalization that produces these statistics results also in decimating families and communities. Young people caught up in this system for relatively minor first offenses are shunted into overcrowded prisons and derailed from meaningful participation in society. They face great hurdles resuming a productive life. We are wasting that energy.

JOHN DEMJANJUK

The Demjanjuk case was not about youthful energy, but about government fraud and vindictiveness. In 1977, the United States sued John Demjanjuk, a Cleveland auto worker, claiming that he had fraudulently obtained his citizenship when he immigrated to the United States after World War II. The government sought to denaturalize him. It claimed that Mr. Demjanjuk, born Iwan Demjanjuk in the Soviet Ukraine, had in fact been the notorious "Ivan the Terrible" of the Treblinka death camp. According to the government, Ivan was a Soviet soldier, captured by the Germans and recruited into the Nazi guard forces. As Ivan, he allegedly supervised the murder of tens of thousands of concentration camp victims—dissenters, gypsies, homosexuals, and Jews.

There was never any question that such a person existed, and that he was savagely cruel even by death camp standards. The camp survivor stories, corroborated by postwar Soviet interviews of other collaborators, proved that beyond doubt. But was this man, living in his suburban home with his children, that Ivan?

The case was brought by the Office of Special Investigations (OSI), a unit of the Department of Justice Criminal Division, established and funded for the express purpose of hunting down Nazi collaborators and denaturalizing them. It was clear in 1977 and as a result of government studies is clearer now that tens of thousands of Nazis and Nazi collaborators gained entry to the United States and were helped to gain entry to other countries after World War II. It was official United States policy to exclude such people. It was also official United States policy to help some of them gain entry. If a Nazi could help us build rockets, root out leftists, or otherwise might be useful, he or she would be assisted. Stories of American complicity in protecting Nazis are legion. American intelligence services protected Klaus Barbie, known as "The Butcher of Lyon" from capture for many years until finally the Bolivians helped the French bring him to trial. In the process of admitting and protecting Nazis, many agencies generated millions of pages of classified documents, which two decades ago were at last beginning to be reviewed and released.

OSI, like many other single-purpose agencies, sometimes lost sight of its broader obligation to make sure that its work was done fairly. And when it was discovered to have acted wrongfully, it not only refused to admit culpability but doubled down in its pursuit of its goals, claiming a kind of immunity from the ordinary rules of fairness due to its rather hypocritical claim to be an avenger of the Holocaust.

John Demjanjuk came to trial in 1981. A federal judge in Cleveland accepted the government's proof and held that he had been Ivan the Terrible. The Sixth Circuit court of appeals affirmed. OSI began deportation proceedings, and at the same time cooperated with Israeli authorities to extradite Demjanjuk to Israel for trial. All his appeals done, Demjanjuk was sent to Israel in 1987. The Israelis put him in a solitary confinement cell, where he was to remain for nearly seven years.

The Israel trial was televised to the world. Treblinka survivors gave emotional testimony that they recognized Demjanjuk as Ivan the Terrible. The trial court rejected arguments that these eyewitness identifications were tainted by suggestive photo arrays that had been shown to the witnesses. The court rejected Demjanjuk's testimony that after he was captured by the Nazis he spent the war in various POW and work camps. It discounted the testimony of an expert that the German identification card claimed to be his did not bear his signature and was irregular in appearance. The court sentenced him to die by hanging, and he waited in his cell while a scaffold was built in the prison yard.

After the Israel conviction, Demjanjuk's son-in-law, Ed Nishnic, and his son, John, Jr., called me and asked if I would go to Israel and handle the appeal. In Israel, an appeal of such a case could take months, as the Supreme Court would review all the evidence over many days of proceedings. I said no. I was not interested in going to Israel for that length of time, and the issues of eyewitness identification and forensic testing did not seem to me as important as some of the other cases I was working on. Israeli counsel were doing a first-rate job.

Within months, however, the case changed. Ed and John Jr. had from the beginning known that their best hope was to find the real Ivan. Against the combined forces of American and Israeli prosecutors they stood little chance with a reasonable doubt defense. They therefore invested all their energy in trying to find that person. They went to Europe to interview people. They became suspicious that OSI had not turned over all its evidence during the

American proceedings. They started a Freedom of Information Act proceeding that yielded clues to exculpatory evidence. Thinking that perhaps the OSI lawyers were discarding material that might be relevant, they stationed themselves outside the OSI offices in Washington, D.C., and raided the trash cans. They took shredded paper from the trash and reassembled documents that showed the OSI had indeed concealed exculpatory evidence. When the former Soviet Union began to fall apart, Ed and John Jr. gained increased access to investigative files located in that territory.

From all this effort, they pieced together the relevant history. Ed and John Jr. proved that Ivan the Terrible was a man named Ivan Marchenko, and they could document this by witnesses and photographs.

John Sr.'s Israeli lawyer, Yoram Sheftel, introduced the new evidence before the Israel Supreme Court. As the media covered the story of John Jr. and Ed's work, the court of appeals judges who had upheld sending Mr. Demjanjuk to Israel became concerned that OSI had misled them. After all, some of the new evidence consisted of Soviet interview reports, called "protocols," that had been in OSI's hands from 1979 onwards.

In January 1992, the Sixth Circuit judges directed the court clerk, Len Green, to send a letter to the Department of Justice asking for an explanation of how exculpatory evidence had been withheld from the defense and the court. When that happened, Ed and John Jr. called me again. I said that I knew something about U.S. federal procedure, and that sending an innocent man to his death based on false evidence was an issue on which I could work. I asked them to call me if the court of appeals took further action, and even if it did not we could discuss what other proceedings might be filed to help restore the old man's citizenship and contribute to a good result in the then-pending Israel appeal.

By June 1992, the Department of Justice still had not answered the court's letter. The judges—Chief Judge Merritt and Judges Lively and Keith—were irked at being ignored. They issued an order directing the Department of Justice to produce evidence and to file a brief explaining its position. The court appointed the Federal Public Defender for the Northern District of Ohio to represent Mr. Demjanjuk and directed his office to file a brief as well, with whatever evidence had become available to the Demjanjuk family. Ed and John Jr. called me.

I had been scheduled to try a complex antitrust case, but it was settled during jury selection. I had been working with students at the University of Texas Law School on appointed criminal appeals, but those involved supervising briefs and an occasional oral argument. I was winding up my responsibilities as past chair of the ABA Litigation Section. I want to be candid here. I won't take a case if it goes against my grain, but sometimes I am moved by restless energy. I agreed to work with the Federal Defender as appointed counsel, if he would agree to that arrangement. He agreed. I agreed to recruit law students to help.

It is difficult to describe the love and devotion that John Jr. and Ed lavished on this case. John Jr. was eleven years old when it all started. Ed had married into the family in 1980. By the time I met them, they had put their careers firmly in second place. No sacrifice of time or energy was too great for them, even as the press reviled the old man as a mass murderer.

In June and July 1992, the Federal Defender and I studied the evidence and worked on a brief.. The court set oral argument for August 8. On August 7, I was in San Francisco at the ABA Annual Meeting, planning to take the red-eye overnight to Cincinnati. I ran into Kenneth Starr, who was then Solicitor General, at a meeting. We were standing with Myron Bright, a judge on the U.S. Court of Appeals for the Eighth Circuit, and author of some really good articles on appellate argument. I asked Ken whether he would be arguing in Cincinnati.

"Oh, no," he said. "Patty Stemler will be arguing for us. Bill Bryson and I have been getting her ready for weeks now. Our case is solid. We are going to clean your clock."

Myron Bright rasped, "Ken, if your case is so goddam good, why don't you argue it yourself."

I stumbled off the Delta red-eye and to a hotel in Cincinnati to shave and change clothes. Patty Merkamp Stemler was and is a formidable lawyer. That day, she had a hard time with a tough panel of judges. And she made what I think is a fatal error for an advocate. She refused to concede the obvious problems with her own position. "Mistakes were made" was the best she could to, and the passive voice and halfhearted tone simply angered the judges.

Ed Marek, the Federal Defender, did the first part of our argument. He focused at length on factual detail. When it was my turn, we did not have much scheduled argument time left, but the court let me present a full position. Yes, I said, you have the inherent power to recall the mandates you issued in the denaturalization and extradition cases. You have jurisdiction regardless of the passage of time because fraud on the court can always be redressed under Federal Rule of Civil Procedure 60(b)(6), as was the case at common law. And you always have what the Supreme Court called "jurisdiction to determine jurisdiction." That is, you can compel parties to produce evidence and argument to determine if there was fraud that you would in turn have the power to recognize and remedy.

What should the court do, the judges asked. I said that a panel of three appellate judges was not the most efficient fact-finding body. You should, I said, appoint a special master to take testimony and make recommendations. The argument then turned to the more general subject of fraud on the court. Why, Chief Judge Merritt asked, why would government lawyers do the things of which we accused them? Why would they hide documents, mislead witnesses, and tell lies to the court and their adversaries? In my mind, I thought of the self-righteous attitude of these lawyers.

I answered Judge Merritt this way: "I do not know *why* these lawyers did these things. I only tell the court what they did and how they did it, based on the evidence we now have and that we confidently expect to produce. Perhaps this case illustrates Ruskin's maxim, 'No more dangerous snare is set by the fiends for human frailty than the belief that our own enemies are also the enemies of God.' "

A few days later, the court of appeals named federal district judge Thomas Wiseman of Nashville as Special Master and we embarked on the next phase of our adventure. For the next ten months, our team of lawyers and law students took depositions and held hearings, in Nashville, Boston, Los Angeles. and Washington. We exchanged thousands of documents with the OSI lawyers.

The key witness was George Parker, who had been an OSI lawyer in 1979 and 1980 in charge of the Demjanjuk litigation. In early 1980, Parker prepared a memorandum to his superiors. He typed it himself. He reviewed the evidence, including some recently obtained Soviet protocols. Despite eyewitnesses who placed Demjanjuk at Treblinka, documentary evidence cast significant doubt on that claim. Parker wondered if the OSI's position would be a "ruse." John Jr. and Ed had heard about this memo, and had repeatedly asked the Department of Justice to produce it. The Department had officially denied that such a memorandum existed.

We put a subpoena on George Parker, and he called to say that he had kept a copy of his memo when he quit, or was removed from, the Demjanjuk case. That had happened in the spring of 1980, after his views about the case, and about the government's professional responsibility, were largely rejected by his superiors in OSI. In our 1992 hearings, the Department of Justice lawyers at first tried to say that Parker's copy was not authentic, or that he had not in fact sent it. They retreated from this position as the evidence mounted.

The Parker memo centered on several Soviet protocols that the United States had received in 1979. The Department of Justice first took the position that these had simply been misfiled, and never intentionally withheld from the Demjanjuk defense. This version paled when a former Assistant U.S. Attorney took the stand. He had kept copies of the protocols when he left government service. I pause here to say that Xerox was a wonderful invention, for it made copying quick and easy. The xerographic fusion of powder to paper has got more people in trouble than many other inventions, for the human desire to keep a memento has frustrated many efforts to get rid of difficult documents.

This witness admitted that the protocols were not in some file cabinet during the 1981 Demjanjuk trial, but in a government lawyer's briefcase in court. So when the government lawyers told the federal judge they had turned over all the exculpatory material, and that the only documents they had further inculpated Mr. Demjanjuk, they were not telling the truth. These documents discussed someone who was of a different description and at different places than the person who was Ivan the Terrible.

Another, though not the only other, item of significant evidence concerned one of those eyewitness identifications. In December 1979, OSI attorney Norman Moskowitz went to Germany and interviewed a former concentration camp guard named Otto Horn. Initially, Horn could not identify a photo of Demjanjuk as having been Ivan the Terrible. Moskowitz then presented Horn with another set of photographs that were different, except that the Demjanjuk photo was also included. He left that set on the table in front of Horn with Demjanjuk's photo on top. Horn, after Moskowitz prodded him, got the idea and identified the Demjanjuk photograph. Horn had a motive to cooperate because he had clearly collaborated with the Nazis and did not want trouble. Later, Moskowitz noticed Horn's deposition in Germany and with Demjanjuk's counsel present asked him if he could identify Demjanjuk from a photograph. He did so. Moskowitz then asked him if he had previously identified the same photograph, and Horn said yes. When Parker resigned, Moskowitz became lead trial counsel in the 1981 denaturalization case.

On that first trip to Germany, Moskowitz had been accompanied by two OSI historian/investigators, Garand and Dougherty. They saw this suggestive identification procedure and each made a separate memorandum noting—and questioning—it. Moskowitz was shown as receiving a copy of these memoranda although he denied ever reading them. Somebody at OSI threw a copy of them in the trash in the late 1980s when the Demjanjuk case was still going on in Israel. Ed and John Jr. recovered them, and they became important items of evidence in our proof that the OSI had defrauded Demjanjuk and the courts.

During the year of hearings on our fraud claim, I went to Israel with Deputy Public Defender Michael Dane, to see Mr. Demjanjuk and to get his signature on interrogatories posed by the government. At that point, the government was still clinging to a theory that there were two "Ivans" at Treblinka, one of which was Mr. Demjanjuk. Later, they conceded that this variant was untenable.

Knowing and working with Mike Dane was one of those unalloyed plea-
sures in this kind of law practice. There are lawyers with whom I would share
a counsel table, and those with whom I decidedly would not. This decision,
for me as for any lawyer, is quixotically personal. But the decision to be co-
counsel involves the kind of camaraderie that one also hears about in military
campaigns.

I went to Israel by flying to Paris and then catching the Delta flight to Ben
Gurion Airport. It was January 1993, during a cold winter in Paris, but staying there overnight was nonetheless a kind of inspiration. Of all the cities I
have visited, Paris has her magic for me. Walking the streets of the Left Bank,
peering into and visiting the antique booksellers, sometimes buying an old
edition of French law books, having dinner at Allard, are all a connection to
the history of those principles of struggle and ideology by which our views on
human rights are shaped.

Mike Dane and I arrived in Israel in the afternoon on separate flights. That
night, I walked up to the Arab city of Jaffa and had dinner. The next morning, Mike and I had breakfast at the hotel with Yoram Sheftel then went to see
Mr. Demjanjuk. He was under the sentence of death that would not be lifted
until July 1993. He was in solitary confinement. His cell was perhaps 8 feet
by 12 feet, and included a partially partitioned area with a shower and toilet.
The entire length of the cell's front was barred. On the other side of the bars,
a guard sat at a desk. Against the wall on the guard's side was a cot. A guard
sat at that desk at all times. Facing the guard, on his desk, was a small television set. To speak to Mr. Demjanjuk, we sat in his cell with the barred cell
door locked. He had pasted on the walls many of the cards he had received
in the nearly six years he had been there. He had by some means fastened a
cardboard box about 12-inches cubed, to the wall in the corner of the cell. On
the front of the box, he had drawn the image of a TV screen and tuning knobs.
He had asked for a television set in his cell or at least visible to him. Not only
was his request denied, but a TV set was issued to the guards, who pointedly
watched it with the screen turned in their direction. The cardboard "TV set"
was a silent protest.

When he arrived in Israel, Mr. Demjanjuk had been repeatedly interrogated by Israeli police and lawyers, who used sleep deprivation and threats
among the measures to seek a confession. None ever came. He always denied
collaborating with the Nazis. To try to establish rapport with his guards, he
taught himself basic Hebrew conversation.

Mike Dane and I talked to the old man at length. At times, there were tears
in his eyes. At one point he looked at us and said, "Not for you, I am a long
time hanging in the yard," gesturing toward the area where a scaffold was to be

built. Our business done, the old man insisted we stay for lunch. He had been afraid to eat the food prepared in the prison kitchen, and had therefore conducted a hunger strike until the authorities agreed to let him prepare his own food. So the guard brought a table and set it just outside the cell. On the table were cans of food, a can opener, bowls, and eating utensils. Mr. Demjanjuk could reach between the bars and laboriously open cans and prepare a simple meal. We shared what he made for us.

After that day, I did not want to stay in Israel. Early the next morning I went to Ben Gurion airport. A security guard opened my suitcase and my briefcase, and called over a more senior guard who had a big gun and some insignia of rank. She began to take file folders from my briefcase and read the contents. I said, "I am a lawyer. Those are private legal files."

She said, "I know. I can see that." And kept on reading. After what seemed a long time, she looked up and said, "These are about this man Demjanjuk."

"Yes," I said.

"You are his lawyer."

"One of them."

She looked at me appraisingly. "You are going to clear his name?"

"I hope so," I said.

"Good!" she replied, and snapped my briefcase shut.

After the hearings before Judge Wiseman, he wrote an opinion that disappointed us greatly. While agreeing with almost all of our factual submissions, he held that the government's conduct was not so bad as to require any relief. So the matter stood as the summer of 1993 began. We challenged Judge Wiseman's findings.

Then in late July 1993, while our challenge to Judge Wiseman's order was pending in the court of appeals, the Israel Supreme Court issued its opinion acquitting Mr. Demjanjuk. A few days later, the Court also upheld the Israeli Justice Ministry's decision that there was not sufficient evidence to prosecute him for having served at other camps than Treblinka, including Sobibor. In our view, such charges would also have been barred by the doctrine of specialty, which says that if you are extradited to stand trial on one set of charges, you may not then be tried for something else.

Demjanjuk's acquittal raised a new problem. The judgment denaturalizing him was still in effect. He was not a United States citizen. The USSR had fragmented, so perhaps he could claim Ukrainian nationality. He did not want to go to Ukraine. A Department of Justice spokesman told the press that Ukraine was his most likely next stop, and that he would probably be tried there and shot. In Israel, crowds had gathered to protest the Supreme Court judgment and the Demjanjuk family feared for the old man's safety.

Our team prepared and filed an emergency motion in the court of appeals. For more than two hundred years, American law has given the executive branch nearly complete power over the admission and exclusion of aliens. We thought it futile to seek an order directing that he be admitted to the United States. Rather, we requested an order that the government not interfere with him entering the country, that is, that the government not interfere with his liberty—a small textual difference with a big consequence. We were also concerned that if he were to stop in a third country between Israel and the United States, he might be held there and tried.

Our efforts to get him back into the United States drew publicity. My University of Texas teaching colleague Michael Churgin, an expert on immigration law, told me we had little to no chance in the court of appeals. However, they set us down for argument the afternoon of August 3, 1993. I flew to Cincinnati. As our team had lunch, I had a message to call Alan Ryan. Alan had been my colleague at Williams & Connolly, then went to the Solicitor General's office, and in 1980 had become head of OSI. In that last capacity, he had negotiated a deal with the Soviets whereby they were supposed to produce all relevant material on Mr. Demjanjuk. Alan was by 1993 in private law practice, but he had been a witness in our proceedings and kept track of the case.

Alan asked if we would be willing to accept a deal, if he could broker it. The deal was that Mr. Demjanjuk would be admitted to the United States. The government would consent to restoring his citizenship. The government might then file a new suit seeking to denaturalize him, alleging service at Nazi camps other than Treblinka. If he lost in the district court and on direct appeal he would leave the United States without taking further legal action. If he won, that would be it.

The deal sounded good to us. It would reunite him with his family, put an end to the litigation over fraud on the court, and give him a clean shot at clearing his name for good. We talked it over and said we thought we could convince the old man to accept it. Ryan promised to call Deputy Attorney General Philip Heymann and try to get him to consent.

We walked across the plaza from the hotel to the federal courthouse. The press was on hand. We sat in the spectator section of the courtroom waiting for the clerk, Len Green, to tell us the judges were ready. As we sat, we chatted with the *New York Times* reporter. The reporter then recognized a Justice Department lawyer and asked him, "Hey, Bob, are you going to argue this today?"

"No," said Bob, "Doug Wilson will argue it. I am just here to help out."

"How do you think it's going to turn out?" the reporter asked.

"I don't know," Bob said. "But whatever happens, you will have a decision before five. Chief Judge Merritt wants to see his kisser on national TV."

At that moment, a woman sitting just ahead of us turned around and looked at Bob. "Excuse me," she said, "I am Mrs. Gilbert Merritt. And my husband will not be pleased when I tell him what you said."

I was reminded of the bumper sticker "Be sure brain is fully engaged before putting mouth in gear," a remnant of the days before automatic transmissions.

The oral argument was challenging and enjoyable. Everybody knew the procedural facts. The issue was whether the court had any authority to get Mr. Demjanjuk out of danger and back into the country. Oral argument on the merits of the case was a month away.

I began by noting that we had an uphill battle, and cited a new Supreme Court decision that the government had not mentioned, that might seem to strengthen the government's position. You might ask why I did this. If the court of appeals ruled for us, the government might well have challenged its ruling in the Supreme Court. I wanted the court of appeals to take account of all the adverse precedent, so that the government could not later argue that it had missed something.

The case turned, I said, on the historic power of federal courts to control the custody of those who were seeking relief. Chief Judge Merritt asked if this referred to habeas corpus *ad subjiciendum*, known as the Great Writ. This version of habeas corpus is the one we hear most about. This is the writ federal courts use to liberate state prisoners from unlawful confinement. It can be used to enforce an order for release on bail. But the scope of this Writ has been limited by Congress and the current Supreme Court.

No, I said. We are seeking a writ of habeas corpus *cum causa*, which has a narrower function but is equally enshrined in English and American legal history. This is the writ that compels the jailer to bring a litigant to court so that his case may be decided, and so that no harm comes to him while the court is considering his fate. This writ does not require a decision on the merits as to whether the litigant is ultimately entitled to relief. It seeks to protect the prisoner and the court's jurisdiction to provide meaningful relief. Chief Justice John Marshall had held that federal courts have the inherent power to issue it. Again, I thought this narrower ground of relief more defensible.

I noted that of course the executive branch had said that the court had no power to do anything at all. Judge Keith interrupted to say, "Well, Mr. Tigar, they come in here and say that several times a week, but that doesn't usually stop us."

As the argument continued, Judge Merritt asked me what kind of an order I thought the court should enter. At that point, I felt the panel was really with us. The discussion of fairly technical historic distinctions among common law writs had engaged the judges' attention. Judge Lively, in questioning the government lawyer, seemed particularly concerned that he had written an opinion sending Mr. Demjanjuk to Israel, but that the government had misled him on the facts.

Late that afternoon, in a decision that was not published in the official reports, but is available on Westlaw, the judges granted our request. If we could get Mr. Demjanjuk to the border of the United States, the government would have to let him in. Ed and John Jr. got the old man on an El Al flight to New York and then by plane to Cleveland. He was home. Picketers assembled on the sidewalk in front of his home, shouting epithets, but he was home.

On September 3, 1993, I argued the merits of the case. On November 17, the court ruled that the United States had defrauded the courts by concealing exculpatory evidence and creating a false trail. Judge Lively's opinion for the three judges began:

> The question before the court is whether attorneys in the Office of Special Investigations (OSI), a unit within the Criminal Division of the Department of Justice, engaged in prosecutorial misconduct by failing to disclose to the courts and to the petitioner exculpatory information in their possession during litigation culminating in extradition proceedings, which led to the petitioner's forced departure from the United States and trial on capital charges in the State of Israel. For the reasons stated herein we conclude that OSI did so engage in prosecutorial misconduct that seriously misled the court.

The court's opinion analyzed the false representations that OSI had made, and catalogued the exculpatory evidence that it had hidden from the court and the defense. Some time later, I was invited to speak at the Sixth Circuit court of appeals conference. I was seated at a luncheon table with Judge Lively, a conservative Kentuckian. He described his feelings of anger and betrayal at OSI's having lied to him and then refusing to acknowledge their wrongdoing.

The United States sought to have all the Sixth Circuit judges rehear the case, but was rebuffed. Now the question was whether the government would ask the Supreme Court to overturn the decision. I called Solicitor General Drew Days, and asked for a meeting in Washington so that we could argue that the United States should not seek Supreme Court review.

Our team met with Solicitor General Days, Deputy Attorney General Heymann, and other Department of Justice lawyers. I began by saying that

I was surprised that the government was still litigating this case. I reminded everyone that Alan Ryan had proposed a deal that would have avoided the Sixth Circuit excoriation of the government. Solicitor General Days said he had not heard of any such proposed deal. Heymann looked flustered and mumbled that he had not thought the deal was worth pursuing and had not told anybody about it. He had simply rejected it. This news seemed to upset Days. My friends in the media told me that Heymann's penchant for going his own way was angering Attorney General Reno and that his tenure at Deputy Attorney General would not be long. This turned out to be true.

I contended that the government should now simply leave this case alone. Its position was surely arguable, but using Mr. Demjanjuk as the means to test the law seemed unfair after sixteen years of litigation that had impoverished and taken a great emotional toll on him and his family. Shouldn't the government say to this old man that it was sorry for its behavior and allow him to live out his life?

Our arguments did not prevail. I have often observed the same government attitude that we saw that day. The Solicitor General's office is staffed with bright lawyers, many of them recent law graduates. Their job is to represent the United States in the Supreme Court and to supervise government appellate litigation. They are concerned with establishing judicial precedents that favor the United States. Very occasionally, as occurred in David Gutknecht's case, the incumbent Solicitor General will rein in federal prosecutors. The basis for such intervention is almost never some consideration about injustice to a particular litigant, but rather a possible outcome that is considered legally unjustified.

Experience has taught government lawyers throughout the system that they need not worry unduly about overreaching, that even if rebuked, they will be free to pursue their intended targets.

Days sought certiorari, which the Supreme Court denied, but only after a further complication. I ran into Days a year or so later, at a memorial service for Justice Brennan. I had been talking with Jack McKenzie, who had just retired from the *New York Times* editorial board, and Days came to sit beside us. He had returned to law teaching, and I remarked that our last meeting had been about the Demjanjuk case.

"Tell me about that," Jack said.

"Well," Drew said, "I thought the Sixth Circuit had applied the wrong standard—a kind of reckless fraud on the court—and that the Supreme Court should set them right. So I went ahead and petitioned for cert." It should be noted that an impressive number of the Solicitor's petitions are granted.

Drew continued: "We routinely distribute the printed petition to all the lawyers in our office. A couple of days later, one of the lawyers came to see me. He had been in the SG's office for nearly twenty years, a specialist in tax. His eyes were rimmed with red. He had not slept and he had been weeping. He laid the petition on my desk and said, 'I know about this case. In 1980, I think it was, I talked to a lawyer in this office who was about to go to work at OSI.'"

By inference, it seemed likely that that lawyer was Alan Ryan, who did move from the SG's office to OSI at about that time. Days continued, "So this lawyer went on 'I asked what cases he would be working on and he said Demjanjuk. But that there was some evidence they had the wrong man.' I asked him if he was going to reveal this to the other side and the court and he said no."

McKenzie, ever even-tempered and even-spoken in public, said, "Oh, my goodness. That is what Max Frankel used to call 'a turd in your pocket.'"

Days smiled. "A turd in my pocket? A turd on my table. A big one. Here I am litigating against Tigar and now I get this news."

I cut in. "Drew could have kept his to himself, but instead he told me about it and wrote a letter to the Court. He probably doomed his chances for certiorari, but in my book his candor set him apart from the other lawyers who worked on this case."

After the Supreme Court denied certiorari, I was involved in other cases. I tried to find a law firm that would represent the family in the next phase, getting the denaturalization judgment overturned. It seemed obvious that this should be done, and that seeking this relief would not be expressing a view for or against the OSI as an institution or Nazi-hunting as a process. No law firm I approached would touch the case. Partners at the big firms candidly said they wanted nothing to do with it. They knew I had been attacked for representing Demjanjuk, and that I had replied forcefully that exposing government fraud that almost sent someone to his death did not seem even controversial.

Federal Defenders Mike Dane and Debra Hughes stepped back into the case, and won a ruling restoring the old man's citizenship and dismissing the denaturalization, though "without prejudice." So matters stood until December 1998, when OSI wrote to the Demjanjuk family and said they planned to sue the old man again to take away his citizenship. This time, they said, they had solid evidence that after he was captured by the Nazis he agreed to be a camp guard and had served at several concentration camps, including Sobibor in occupied Poland. No live witness had ever seen him serve as a guard. The records on which OSI based its case were contradictory and fragmentary.

The family called me again. The Federal Defender could no longer serve. For more than two years, Ed, John Jr., Jane Tigar, and I sifted through more than 100,000 pages of documents and a dozen CD-ROMs, each the

SENSING INJUSTICE

equivalent of several boxes of material. We went to trial in May 2000. The judge ruled we were not entitled to a jury trial.

As the trial preparation wore on, we became more and more convinced that the government's case was too thin to meet the standard of "clear and convincing evidence," almost beyond a reasonable doubt, which the law requires. More seriously, I voiced a concern with what I called "trial by archive," that is, digging up old documents from ill-maintained Soviet archives and dispensing with proof that could be cross-examined. The tactic reminded me of the loyalty-security purges of the 1950s, when FBI archival files were used indiscriminately.

The government's case included testimony of a documents expert who said that an identity card claiming to carry Demjanjuk's photograph was authentic. He was later indicted for giving false testimony in another case. The judge refused us permission to conduct independent testing on the card. The government's expert admitted that it was possible that documents like this would still have fingerprints of the person to whom it had been issued, especially on the inside pages. He told the court of cases in which such evidence had been obtained by spraying a mist of ninhydrin on the card or using laser technology. The government declined to conduct such tests on its Demjanjuk evidence.

The government presented a summary of evidence from archives in the former USSR and Poland. When World War II ended, the USSR forces had collected evidence from the areas that they had conquered. The summary was more than 100 pages long, with more than 300 footnotes. The testifying expert who submitted the report admitted that he had never visited these archives, that he did not speak or read Russian. He relied on OSI lawyers and researchers to find relevant evidence and then to translate and summarize it.

There is a common law rule of evidence called the "rule of completeness," which is codified in Federal Rule of Evidence 106:

> If a party introduces all or part of a writing or recorded statement, an adverse party may require the introduction, at that time, of any other part—or any other writing or recorded statement—that in fairness ought to be considered at the same time.

We were foreclosed from relying on that rule because we had no access to the archives that the OSI had visited.

Over our objections, the trial judge admitted the evidence of the government's proffered experts. He held that Demjanjuk should be denaturalized. A few years later, after Mr. Demjanjuk had died, we uncovered FBI documents that had been created around the time of his denaturalization trial and that directly questioned the reliability of the government's evidence in support of its new theory. The government argued that Mr. Demjanjuk's death made the matter moot.

Having obtained a denaturalization decision, the government handed Demjanjuk—now nearly ninety years old—over to the German government. Germany charged him as an accessory to the murder of all the more than 50,000 people who perished at Sobibor death camp. This prosecution, it seemed to me, was an exercise in hypocrisy, and in legal and factual error.

The hypocrisy was exposed in a book by historian Mary Fallbrook. She found that although up to a million people—mostly Germans—are believed to have actively participated in the extermination of millions of Jewish people during the Holocaust, only around 20,000 were ever found guilty of crimes, and fewer than 600 received heavy sentences.

Even if one accepted all the German prosecutors' contentions, Demjanjuk's activity was that he carried a rifle and patrolled the borders of the camp. He was a Soviet POW, among the millions who were subjected to inhumane treatment by their German captors and given the choice of death or carrying out menial tasks. The message of this prosecution was that the death camps were run by Ukrainian and other POWs, and not really by Germans.

The German prosecution's evidence was based on the same photographs and documents of questionable authenticity and relevance. There was probably a man named Demjanjuk who was at that camp. But that is a common surname, and indeed in Demjanjuk's home village there was another Iwan Demjanjuk of about the same age and similar appearance.

But again taking the prosecutors' factual contentions as valid, Demjanjuk's alleged role was not sufficient as a matter of German law or international human rights law to make him guilty of the offense of murder. I wrote a long legal memorandum summarizing the relevant law. I relied on a decision of the International Criminal Tribunal for Yugoslavia, and on the basic principles applied by the International Criminal Court. The German court convicted Demjanjuk. He died while his appeal was pending.

The controversy has continued. In 2019 and 2020, OSI has claimed in a television documentary and a new book about the Holocaust that perhaps Demjanjuk really was Ivan the Terrible at Treblinka—despite the federal court having found this allegation fraudulent and mendacious.

One should not wonder at this persistence in asserting error. Consider the experience of the Wrongful Convictions Legal Clinic at Duke Law School, and many another group engaged in the same work. Diligent investigation reveals that the prosecutors withheld exculpatory evidence, and that someone in prison or even on death row is in fact innocent of the crime of which he was convicted. The prosecutor not only refuses to take this new evidence seriously, but even when the court has set aside the conviction vows to retry the defendant. Or, when there is a serious and credible allegation that defense counsel did not provide effective assistance, the prosecutor and that erstwhile defense counsel often join forces to keep the defendant in jail. Defense counsel's decisions to reveal lawyer-client confidences have been reined in by amendments to the Federal Rules of Evidence, but the problem persists.

I repeat: The state, when it offends, has more power to do harm than any private actor. The state resists accountability by means of secrecy and mendacity—as is illustrated by more than a dozen cases discussed in this book. Even when its crimes are exposed, the state continues to deny responsibility for providing redress to the victims. Only rarely do the offending police and prosecutors receive discipline.

CHAPTER 12

Speech Plus

AN IDEA OF FREE EXPRESSION

Freedom of speech, press, and assembly were dominant themes of my study and experience from Berkeley days onward, from Jacobus ten-Broek's class to KPFA, through law school, and then in the Brennan episode. When I began law practice, these free expression issues followed me. Defending civil rights usually involved securing the right to protest. The Vietnam War protests dealt as much with the right to oppose the war by various means as with the wisdom and legality of the war itself. The Chicago and Seattle cases dealt with First Amendment issues arising from the congressional statute that sought to punish interstate travel for the purpose of protesting. When government wishes to pursue a policy without interruption, it often seeks to chill expression by its opponents, and to that extent speech is bound up with all sorts of substantive policy issues.

I have not often been asked to advise government about such matters, but one case makes the point. During the 1970s, the Federal Trade Commission was considering restrictions on advertising directed at children. FTC lawyers asked me and my law partners to help in this endeavor. We declined. We thought that such ads were quite improper. But we reasoned that rules to restrict them were inherently overbroad and subject to abuse.

This has proven, in my view, to be so. Enforcement of "kiddie porn" laws has swept up exploiters of children, but has also led to prosecution of researchers and of those whose private conduct poses no public threat. And like all censorship laws, enforcement techniques drift quite easily into entrapment, as the Supreme Court has noted. We also thought, for example, that high school students' free speech rights should not be curtailed, and that the First Amendment problems in drawing lines between different types of speech directed at minors were insurmountable.

There is another issue of choice here. I don't have time or resources to defend everybody's speech, so I choose the battles in which I will engage. In America today, those without money have a hard time having their voices heard. I have preferred to represent progressive folks who lack access to a money-controlled market in expression. In the same vein, I do not agree with current Supreme Court teaching that "money is speech." The current doctrine of state and monopoly power wielders is that in order to be free to speak widely and with effect, you must own, or otherwise have access to, the means of producing speech: a printing press, a newspaper, a piece of ground on which to stand. And, as we see in the government attacks on whistleblowers, information itself has been made a kind of private property. I have written elsewhere:

> The First Amendment to the United States Constitution guarantees freedom of speech and press. Today, moneyed interests dominate electoral politics, drowning out less well-financed voices. The sensible citizen wonders if campaign finance reform would help even things out. That citizen even asks whether the dominance of money so erodes the freedom of speech that government has an affirmative duty to see that all voices can participate in the process.
>
> That citizen, reading current Supreme Court decisions, will be disappointed. The Court has held that limits on individual contributions to influence elections, and contributions to officeholders for increased access, are forms of speech protected by the First Amendment. Only few and ineffective restraints on money in politics are found to be constitutional.
>
> Thus, the Supreme Court sees the First Amendment through the prism of bourgeois ideology. Money, the universal commodity, enables speech. It pays for the means by which a message is delivered. Therefore, money and speech are in a sense equivalents.

My choice of free speech cases means that I get to meet very interesting people. If making a pile of money is not your first concern in law practice, this is a very good organizing principle. Think about it. I have already listed some of the protesters whose paths crossed mine. The gay beat poet Allen Ginsberg retained me for a time on a matter that I don't quite remember; he sent me a little money and an autographed collection of his poems with a nice drawing and a long inscription.

ROBERT F. WILLIAMS

Many federal cases illustrate the connection between racial justice and the rights of free speech, press, and association. The Supreme Court upheld the right to demonstrate; it struck down efforts to intimidate civil rights workers by compulsory disclosure; it upheld the right of organizations to recruit and provide legal services to victims of racism. Robert F. Williams's lawsuit to vindicate his right to send information through the Postal Service was one such case.

Williams led the NAACP chapter in Monroe, North Carolina, in the 1950s and early 1960s. He worked to integrate the local library and swimming pool. He came to national attention. He formed an NRA chapter to arm African-Americans in the defense against racial violence. His 1962 book *Negroes With Guns* influenced leaders in the Black Panther Party and other organizations.

During a 1961 racial protest in Monroe, a white couple was traveling through town and were threatened by a group of demonstrators. Williams took the couple into his home for their protection. He was charged with kidnapping them. The charge was wholly factitious, but Williams rightly feared for his safety and he left Monroe with his family. He first went to Cuba and then in 1965 to China. Williams published provocative articles and made radio broadcasts. In 1969, he returned to the United States. He was arrested on the kidnapping charge, and acquitted.

While Williams was in China, he mailed copies of his writings, including the newsletter *The Crusader*, to people and organizations in the United States. The Postal Service banned the May 1967 *Crusader* issue from the mails and refused to deliver it. The ACLU recruited me and Sanford Jay Rosen to represent Williams. We assembled a group of writers and Lawrence Ferlinghetti's City Lights bookstore in San Francisco as class action plaintiffs, along with Williams, and sued in the District of Columbia federal court.

In a unanimous 1965 decision, *Lamont v. Postmaster General*, the Supreme Court had held that a statute that required the Postmaster General to detain and deliver only upon the addressee's request unsealed foreign mailings of "communist political propaganda" violated the First Amendment rights of recipients.

The statute we challenged authorized the Postal Service to block mail that advocated arson, murder, or assassination. When the Postal Service believed that domestic mail contained the forbidden advocacy, the sender received notice and was given an administrative hearing. In the case of a foreign sender, however, the non-mailability determination was made by the Postal Service General Counsel. There was no provision for a hearing. The General Counsel's determination resulted in the questionable material being seized.

Our lawsuit alleged that the statute was unconstitutional. Regardless of the contents of the mailed material, excluding it from the mails without a hearing

violated the due process rights of senders and addressees. Moreover, written
material that advocates violence is protected by the First Amendment unless
it creates a clear and present danger of imminent lawless action.

Because our lawsuit sought to enjoin the operation of the offending statutes, it was heard and decided by a three-judge federal court. We won. The
court recognized and applied the *Lamont* holding that the potential recipient
of information and advocacy has a First Amendment "right to hear," that is as
well-grounded as the right to speak and publish.

The *Lamont-Williams* holdings point up a principle that is relevant to
cases where the government seeks to punish whistleblowers and leakers who
reveal information about government wrongdoing.

James Madison wrote:

> Knowledge will forever govern ignorance. And a people who mean to be
> their own governor must arm themselves with the power that knowledge
> gives. A popular government without popular information or the means
> for acquiring it is but a prologue to a farce or tragedy or perhaps both.

John Adams wrote:

> And liberty cannot be preserved without a general knowledge. But besides
> this they have a right, an undisputable, unalienable, indefeasible divine
> right to the most dreaded and most envied kind of knowledge, I mean of
> the characters and conduct of their rulers.

TRUTH AND ITS NEAR RELATIONS

When I came back to the United States in January 1974 to work on the steelworkers' case, I took the time to hunt around for a longer-term job. I met with
Edgar and Jean Cahn at Antioch Law School, and discussed the idea that I
would teach there. The school, based as it was on clinical legal education, was
a fascinating and challenging place, though riven by internal dissension even
then. I also had reservations about full-time teaching. I had been a lawyer for
less than a decade, and wanted a setting in which to improve my skills. A commitment to social change can guide decisions about one's professional life.
But the clients one agrees to help will depend on the advocate's knowledge of
how the system works and how to confront it.

Coincidence helped to resolve the matter. I called Ed Williams to say hello
and he invited me to lunch. We sat at Duke Zeibert's restaurant with some
of the lawyers I had known in the firm and talked inconsequentially about

memories. A lawyer who had joined the firm since I left, Earl Dudley, was working on a bribery case and we batted around First Amendment issues about the difference between lawful campaign contributions, which are a form of protected expression, and illegal bribes and gratuities.

Ed and I walked out together, past the headwaiter's table where Mel Krupin alternated with Duke as captain of the place. Ed turned and spoke softly. "We've got a new case coming in. It would be nice if you and I could work on it together." We parted, and only later did I wonder if I had just been offered a job.

The next day I called and asked what he had in mind. Did I want to come back to the firm, on a fast track to be a partner? And, by the way, the case concerned the impending indictment of John Connally, former Texas governor and Treasury Secretary, for allegedly accepting an illegal gratuity from the milk producers. So when the steelworkers' case was over, I returned to France to pack up.

I was back in the old firm, in the same building at 17th and I Streets, NW. I had a corner office, and freedom to work on draft cases left over from the Vietnam War. The firm, which was Williams & Wadden when I joined it in 1966, and then became Williams & Connolly, had become Williams, Connolly & Califano. Joseph Califano had jumped from Arnold & Porter.

The law firm had changed in five years. When I left in 1969 to teach at UCLA, there were about 15 lawyers. By 1974, not only were there 35 lawyers and a lot more office space, the atmosphere had changed. Lawyers my age were concerned that the old, informal way of doing things would give way to a bureaucracy that would change working relationships. More important, for many, Joe Califano seemed to be seeking clients whose cases would change the firm's approach to the law.

The law firm governance issues were being debated by the lawyers of my generation. The name partners Williams, Connolly, and Califano each had "super-percentages" of the firm's income. For all the partners after them, the younger partners wanted to have a lockstep system that would prevent year-end fights over money. They wanted to encourage retirements by capping profit shares by the time a partner had been practicing a certain number of years. They hoped to preserve the camaraderie of the place. After all, we were accustomed to drop in to each other's offices and talk about cases and issues. We would head out for lunch together in small groups. By 1976, the new plan was in place.

This sort of informal discussion is essential to any litigation practice. Every well-run law firm encourages it. I think of public defender offices with their regular meetings to talk about cases. When Sam Buffone and I opened our law firm, we vowed never to be larger than would fit a table at the Palm Restaurant, and that we would meet at least once a week while everyone talked about every case in the office.

A firm grown as large as Williams, Connolly & Califano could not fit every lawyer at a restaurant table, but it could maintain something nearly as useful. The firm had installed a lunchroom on the first floor, open to all the lawyers. Williams's idea was that you could talk about a case in that room without being overheard by a potential adversary. The food was pretty good, too. There were a couple of smaller rooms where you could lunch with a client in privacy.

The lawyers my age were right to be concerned about the firm's future. Its operation showed signs of tension. Califano had joined the firm on condition that he get a bigger share of the pie than Paul Connolly was getting. Ed Williams retained his even larger share, but it seemed to me that in a law firm where there was plenty of money for everybody, Joe's need to show that he could "outdo" Paul was unseemly. Paul was a founder of the ABA Litigation Section and a first-rate trial lawyer. We sometimes disagreed on ideological issues, but despite our disagreements he went out of his way to help me make a name in the profession. He did this for many others as well.

There were other ways in which Joe's view of law practice seemed at odds with what this litigation law firm ought to be doing. Joe had attracted a major client who had litigation and other issues as well. Joe pitched the idea of "fully servicing" this client by helping draft administrative regulations concerning batteries or some such thing. Drafting regulations is good lawyer work, but litigators might not be good at it. If you hire lawyers to work on the regulations, then you would need to keep that regulatory work coming in to feed those lawyers.

Joe's other innovations were continual sources of frustration. He hired two retired noncommissioned officers he had known during his days in the Pentagon during the LBJ years to be office managers. He had originally named their quarters on the fifth floor "the control module," but Williams balked at that. By the time I got there, the operation was called "Executive Services" and included a typing pool, central file repository and retrieval, office supplies control and related functions. That name was dropped as well, after some of us saw leaflets posted near the office advertising a downtown massage parlor called "Executive Services." Among the organizational innovations was off-site file storage. In one test, some of us asked for retrieval of fourteen case files related to an issue on which we were working. Executive Services was able to find only five of them.

Litigators are famously antagonistic to bureaucracy. We prefer a kind of organized chaos. We count on good people and not the assumed perfection of systems. Because our work is about people's problems, and our jurors are dawn from all walks of life, we are aware that systems of control consist only of people. Joe Califano did not understand that if you bureaucratize a litigation law firm, you will kill its spirit.

More significantly, the delegation and sub-delegation inherent in Joe's organization model may produce a lot of billable hours, but it plays hell with effective litigation strategy. Joe's and my disagreement on this surfaced soon after I rejoined the firm. His secretary called and said that Mr. Califano wanted to talk with me. I said, "I'll be in my office all day." She politely said that this was not the point, and made clear that I had been summoned. I went.

Joe began by saying, "Williams says you are pretty good. We need to see about that." Not a good beginning. "I've got a case for you. The other side is being handled by my old firm, Arnold & Porter. This is sort of a grudge match for them." And for you, too, I thought. He told me about the case—a libel suit against *Army Times*, a publication for people in military service. *Army Times* had published an exposé of insurance sales directed at military people; the insurance company had sued. If the company was a public figure—which it surely was—then whatever minor errors might be in the article were no doubt protected by the Supreme Court's decision in *New York Times v. Sullivan*.

Joe and a team of firm lawyers had drafted a motion to dismiss the complaint, which the district judge in San Antonio, Texas, had denied in a scathing opinion from the bench. Judge John H. Wood, Jr., was a crusty, opinionated autocrat. A discovery battle loomed. I winced. In civil cases, you don't need much detail to state your case. Had Joe and his team fixed the judge's mind that this case needed to be tried?

Joe told me how he thought the case should be handled. "I can give you one-fourth of the time of one lawyer, one-half of another one, and maybe one-half of yet another." He kept on, until the total reached about two and a half lawyers.

"I don't want that kind of help," I said. "I would like the full-time help of one lawyer, Kevin Baine. I don't want any paralegals from downstairs. Kevin and I will use our own secretaries for any paralegal work. That is the way I would like to do it."

Joe seemed mystified by this approach, but acquiesced. "Well, this is your case now, so handle it the way you want."

I leapt into the facts. The reporter had done a valuable service, based on months of investigation. The story had merited an artist's drawing on the cover, depicting a smooth con man bilking a GI. At the same time, the other side alleged that the story was flawed in both concept and details. This promised to be an exciting trip, defending one voice in an important debate.

There is a temptation to over-lawyer complex litigation, especially when the client is paying by the hour. It happens for other reasons as well, when the lead lawyers are taking on too many projects, handing off too much work, or are insecure about their own abilities. Using too many lawyers makes case preparation unfocused and unwieldy. It leads quickly to overuse of discovery devices, which runs up the cost even more.

In this case, plaintiffs' counsels were being paid by the hour, and they staffed the case that way. At our first meeting with them, two junior partners and an associate showed up. A senior partner and more associates were available if need be. They presented a list of *Army Times* employees whose depositions they wished to take. As to some senior executives who had nothing to do with the challenged story, we said nothing doing. From the remaining names, the plaintiffs' lawyers proposed a punishing schedule that would set all the depositions in a row over a three-week period. We agreed to that.

The author, editor, and illustration artist gave their depositions first. At each one, the plaintiff was represented by at least two partners and one associate lawyer—the combined bills just to take those depositions must have been enormous. The lawyer asking questions followed a detailed script that was in a notebook that had no doubt been prepared by a paralegal. The questioning was long, tedious, and antagonistic.

From questioning by plaintiff's counsel at the author's deposition:

Q: You use the word exposé to describe your story. Isn't that a loaded word?

Author: It doesn't seem so to me.

Q: Well, have you ever heard of an exposé that was favorable to somebody? [The interrogator's voice rose to a crescendo.] Have you ever heard of an expose of a *saint*?

Mr Tigar: In the answer, would you like the standard elements of sainthood—temptation, miracle, and martyrdom?

Q: I withdraw the question.

Plaintiff's counsel also deposed the cover artist, who was a skilled painter but nearly incoherent when asked to explain the reason why he depicted characters in a certain way. All communication requires some connection between speaker and hearer, and in this deposition there was next to none.

Q: And did somebody from *Army Times* call you?

A: Yes.

Q: Did they ask if you were free?

A: What?

Q: [Impatiently reading from the deposition notebook] Did they ask if you were free?

A: They wouldn't do that. I don't work for free.

After the initial three depositions, the other side called and said it would not be taking any others for the time being. Not so fast, I replied. We want to move this case, and you told us you wanted that also. We promptly noticed the depositions of all our witnesses, on the same schedule the other side had set and then abandoned. We made the complete record of how the story was conceived, researched, written, and edited. The other side showed up and said each time that they had no questions now but would have some at some indefinite future date.

If we had to try this case to a jury, I wanted a way to get inside the head of an investigative journalist. People in that line of work tell harsh truths if they are doing a good job. If they are sloppy or malign, they tell hurtful falsehoods. I am not a friend of libel law. Once, at a dinner with Justice Hugo Black late in his life, I listened as one of the other guests at this small gathering went on and on about his libel suit against *Time* magazine, and the harm the offending article had done him. The lawyer's rant was discourteous to the Justice, who bore it politely, interrupting only to repeat his long-held credo that the First Amendment was designed to forbid private libel actions as well as government suits alleging seditious libel or "libel on government."

I have often thought Justice Black's view was right, and cannot think of filing a libel suit myself, at least against the media. My view is often tested in practice by the spectacle of irresponsible journalism. In my line of work, however, the fault is as much or more with the government "sources" who use their journalistic contacts to plant false stories in an effort to influence pending cases.

In our *Army Times* case, for our summary judgment motion to the judge and for an eventual jury trial if we lost that motion, the issue was intensely practical. I have believed, and written for trial lawyers, that a good expert witness is like a mid-trial summation. But what expertise would we need here? Not an insurance expert. The plaintiff's case was about insurance. Our case was about journalistic integrity and freedom of expression. The plaintiff was an insurance company; let them try to get the jury to identify with their problems. Our client was a newspaper; we wanted the jury to identify with us. *Army Times* had only recently turned to investigative journalism, to better serve its readers by discussing such issues as insurance targeted at the captive military market. This was our story.

I asked around. Where could I find a journalism professor who really understood how reporters think and work. I wanted somebody who identified with investigative journalists. I thought first of my old journalism teachers, Pete Steffens and Alan Temko. Neither one seemed right for a San Antonio jury. I called Sidney Roger, a labor journalist of the old school who had been a commentator on Pacifica Radio, and had taught at Berkeley. Sid might not be the best person for San Antonio either, although in the waterfront towns of East Texas I would have used him in a heartbeat.

Sid told me of Roy Mac Fisher, who had been editor of the *Chicago Sun-Times*, a tabloid, and was now Dean of the School of Journalism at the University of Missouri. This was an education for me. Sid told me that Missouri and Columbia were the best journalism schools in the country, with Missouri having an edge in print journalism and Columbia in broadcasting.

I got Fisher's résumé and made an appointment to see him. I asked him to sit with the reporter who wrote the story and pretend that he was the senior editor. I asked the two of them to take the challenged story and number every factual statement in it, sentence by sentence and paragraph by paragraph. There were more than a thousand statements.

Then I asked Fisher to interrogate the author about the source of every statement and decide whether the author's use of sources was in accord with good journalistic practice. In journalism, as in the rest of life, we are often less than entirely sure about things. Journalists, like anybody else who is talking in public about other people, have a responsibility not to monger unreliable information. Indeed, they have a special responsibility to their readers because of the position of authority they assume. Did this journalism meet those standards? And could Roy Mac Fisher say that it did based on his decades of practical experience and the best academic standards he could use?

He could, and did. If we ever tried the case to a jury, I wanted to tell two stories. The first would be about the plaintiff's insurance business, for that was what we had been sued about. But I wanted also to tell the story of how an investigative reporter works, researches, uses sources, and then puts it all together. If the jurors identified with the reporter, as a working person trying to do a job, then we would win even if the jurors thought he made an error or two. That said, we stood by the story.

We finished the discovery we wanted to take and moved for summary judgment. There was, we claimed, no genuine issue of fact. I finally got to meet Judge Wood. The courtroom was full of lawyers. It was a calendar call for all pending motions. Wood took the bench in a foul mood.

When our case was called he said, "I see that the defendants have filed one of these motions for summary judgment. It looks like the same sort of thing that this fellow 'California.' or whatever it was, put before me months ago." I assumed he meant "Califano."

"Oh, we agree entirely," said the plaintiff's lawyer.

"If Your Honor please," I ventured, "we filed this motion only after a lot of discovery. It is a new motion. The plaintiffs don't like it, and maybe you won't like it either. But we feel about our motion like the mountaineer said about his pancakes, 'No matter how thin I make 'em, there's always two sides.' "

Lawyers in the courtroom laughed. That scared me. Most judges like to originate the humor. Wood smiled. "Oh you mean it's like the little boy who was asked what was the score in the baseball game and he said, 'We are behind 25 to zero,' and the man asked him, 'And you ain't worried?' And the boy said, 'No sir, we ain't had our ups yet.' " The courtroom lawyers laughed again, thankfully louder this time.

Judge Wood set a hearing date, and the other side argued that they needed more time to take additional discovery before making a full response to our motion. Judge Wood was only mildly impressed. "You say there is something out there that gives you a case. All right, you have forty-five days to take discovery and find it. If you don't, I am inclined to grant this motion. Now, court is adjourned, so come back and let's have some coffee in my chambers."

In those days, Braniff Airlines had a one-stop flight from San Antonio to Washington, D.C. But you had to get it about 3:30 in the afternoon, and the airport was on the outskirts of town. The other side's lawyers said they had to leave to catch a plane. We said we could use some coffee. No, we did not talk about the case *ex parte*, but we did visit with the judge about my representing his friend John Connally, and he showed me his signed picture of Connally. This litigation had been hard-fought, and I think the judge resented the other side's rejection of his efforts to get the lawyers in his chambers. It is a Texas tradition: the lawyers see the judge in an informal setting and the judge can discreetly evaluate the prospects of settlement. Of course, he had just finished rejecting their position, but that is the very time when one should seem ready to continue the fight.

Judge Wood was controversial. He had even made some remarks from the bench showing that the racial and ethnic biases of his South Texas upbringing were alive and well. But he had been a superb jury lawyer, representing defendants in civil negligence and product liability cases. He no doubt thought the "liberal media" needed policing. So our task was to explain our case as a principled, fact-based defense. If we could do that, we might introduce cognitive dissonance into Judge Wood's preformed views about the media.

This, to repeat, is the same approach one always makes to a decider. The decider carries around a bundle of preconceptions. Some of these represent fundamental values about fairness and hearing both sides. Others are less benign. We try to find a reason that appeals to that decider why we should win the case. This is not pandering, it is simply recognition that humans decide cases and that all humans have prejudices.

By Monday of the next week, the other side was ready to extend an olive branch, and to reach a settlement that was acceptable to our clients. Joe Califano was pleased, and I got another libel case.

REBOZO

Ed and Joe asked me to represent the *Washington Post* and its investigative reporter Ron Kessler. Kessler's *Post* article alleged that Charles "Bebe" Rebozo, a friend and confidant of many political figures and owner of a Florida savings and loan, sold stock that he knew had been stolen. The stock had been stolen, but Rebozo denied knowing this. The article had run in the aftermath of Richard Nixon's resignation as president. Rebozo's name had figured in the Nixon investigation; there had been allegations that Rebozo helped the Nixon campaign raise and spend money in questionable ways.

Ron Kessler was a formidable investigative reporter with interest and expertise in financial matters. He was proud of his story. However, Rebozo had filed suit on his home turf in Miami, and had beaten back the *Post*'s claim that it was not subject to suit in Florida. In addition to Ron Kessler, I had the chance to work with the *Post*'s legendary editor Ben Bradlee, and even to meet Katherine Graham. In Florida, we had the help of Sandy d'Alemberte, the great Florida lawyer who was later ABA president.

We worked the same basic theory as with *Army Times*. We retained Roy Mac Fisher to interview Kessler. In the meantime, we confronted Rebozo's claim that he was not a "public figure" within the meaning of *New York Times v. Sullivan*. Public figures cannot collect for a false and defamatory story without proof by clear and convincing evidence that the author knew the story was false or acted with reckless disregard of its truth or falsity.

To prove Rebozo was a public figure, I asked a researcher to copy and clip every media reference to him beginning about 1950. In that year, Rebozo had first come to press attention as a friend and supporter of George Smathers, a conservative Florida political figure. This being 1975, before the days of internet search, the researcher pasted each reference to an index card. I arranged these in some sort of order. We noticed Rebozo's deposition. The deposition began affably but went downhill. I turned over card after card and asked Rebozo to acknowledge that he had been at this or that public function, or played this or that public role in business or politics. He became increasingly irritable as the second deposition day began and I was still turning over cards. Ron Kessler sat beside me and passed notes.

Several hours into the second day Rebozo turned to Kessler and said irritably, "Who are you? I don't know you."

Kessler introduced himself. Rebozo looked stunned. "You mean you are the hooligan who wrote that story?" He turned to his lawyer: "Why do I have to sit in this room with this hooligan?" From this exchange, I had the sense that having Rebozo under examination during a jury trial might be fun.

Even after being confronted with all of this, Rebozo refused to concede he was a public figure. We filed a motion for summary judgment nonetheless based on his deposition and on the factual research that showed a basis for Kessler's story. But I wanted to nail down that public figure status and I thought there was one person who could confirm it authoritatively, and that was Richard Nixon.

I told Ed Williams I wanted to take Nixon's deposition. He doubted the wisdom of doing this, and said I would have to get Katherine Graham's personal approval. Ed and I met her and Ben Bradlee in Bradlee's office at the *Post*. She dismissed concerns that taking Nixon's deposition would cause trouble. She recalled the threats that John Mitchell had made in the Watergate days. I glimpsed in that moment Katherine Graham's courage and managerial style. Her tone was soft, but her air of command unmistakable. She would make this decision, as so many others, based on her principles and not on any idea of convenience.

As it happened, I did not take Nixon's deposition because we got summary judgment shortly thereafter. The judgment was reversed in part, though not on the public figure issue, after I left the Williams firm. The court of appeals noted that the First Amendment–based preference for summary judgment in libel cases had been disfavored by the Supreme Court, and the case was decided before the Court clarified the law and tilted it back toward the media. The case dragged on and later I heard that it was settled without Rebozo collecting any money.

PATRICK CUNNINGHAM

The First Amendment also led me into the world of New York politics. In late 1975, New York Governor Hugh Carey authorized an investigation of New York Democratic Party Chairman Patrick Cunningham, who was also party leader in the Bronx. The investigation was to be conducted by the notorious Office of Special Prosecutions, and was clearly an effort to unseat Cunningham from his party positions.

The regular Democratic Party in New York was politics in the old style, with an organization that rewarded the faithful with public jobs. Over the years, I came to respect Pat Cunningham's political judgment and to value his friendship. I litigated and won cases for him, and lost the last one when the action moved to federal court and jury found he had evaded tax on his income. In the earlier skirmishes, however, I thought that regardless of my disagreements with the regular Democrats the use of state criminal charges to settle political fights was a bad idea.

In the first act of this drama, the special prosecutor summoned Pat to a state grand jury, and demanded that he waive his Fifth Amendment privilege against self-incrimination before testifying. Under New York law at that time, unless he waived, he would have immunity from prosecution for whatever he disclosed. Pat refused to waive. The special prosecutor then invoked New York Election Law Section 22, which said that if any party officer refused to waive the privilege, he or she was automatically stripped of his party position.

We convened a three-judge federal court, which held that this statute violated the First and Fifth Amendments. A political party had the right to choose its leader, within certain broad limits, and the politician had the right to serve as leader. Conditioning political participation on giving up your Fifth Amendment rights violated settled Supreme Court law and trespassed on the First Amendment.

The state appealed the decision directly to the Supreme Court. I argued the case in the spring of 1977. As I prepared for oral argument, I was conscious of some parallels between this case and my own situation. If a Supreme Court Justice could reject a law clerk for a good reason, a bad reason, or no reason at all, why could New York not regulate who would be a political party officer? The answer was obvious, because political parties are voluntary associations with rights of their own, and this law was dictating to them who they may and may not have as a leader.

The parallel had also occurred to Chief Justice Burger, who referred to it in oral argument. I said in reply, "The power of public officers with respect to those whom they choose to be their confidential aides may be greater" than the Constitution permits states to exercise in this context. Justice Brennan smiled and I went on. The Court held, with only Justice Stevens dissenting, that New York Election Law Section 22 violated the First and Fifth Amendments. Justice Stewart did remind me during argument that he believed I should be more precise in citing the Constitution. I had said "privilege against self-incrimination."

Potter Stewart: There is no privilege against self-incrimination in the
Constitution. There is a privilege against compulsory self-incrimination.
Michael Tigar: That is true, Mr. Justice Stewart.

Alone among the Justices, Stewart always insisted that the words *compelled*
or *compulsory* always precede the word *privilege* in discussing self-incrimination, as a nod to the history of compulsion to testify.

More than ten years later, I was seated on the dais at a luncheon where I was
to speak. Justice Stevens sat next to me. I had a flashback to the *Cunningham*
argument. I said, "Justice Stevens, I have wondered if I failed to answer the
question you asked me in oral argument, about the *Nelson* case." He smiled,
and looked at me quizzically: "What the hell do you care," he said, "you won,
didn't you?"

Back in New York, Cunningham was charged with having wielded his political power in violation of the law. He was charged with extortion for allegedly
telling a newspaper editor that the Democratic Party would not run ads in the
paper if the editor continued to attack Cunningham's policies. He was charged
with an offense akin to bribery for favoring a judicial candidate who had contributed to the party's coffers. There were other, similar charges. We won them
all. Politics is not polite, and heated controversy is not extortion. The First
Amendment shields decisions about candidates, or newspaper advertising, or
many other things from attack by means of criminal statutes. The use of criminal sanctions in the arena of speech is fraught with special dangers, for general
criminal laws tend to be so vague and broad that they sweep protected conduct
within their terms and fail to give fair warning of what is prohibited. This is, as
the cases teach, the vice of vagueness in the First Amendment context.

Pat's law partner was indicted also in some of these cases, and was represented by Louis Nizer. Nizer was one of the great trial lawyers. Even in his
later years, he was a formidable negotiator. When I represented the producers
of *One Flew Over the Cuckoo's Nest* in a threatened antitrust suit against United
Artists, Nizer took personal charge of the case for UA. We held a meeting in
his New York office, and he showed an impressive command of the issues in
our case and of the movie business. He also made clear from the beginning
that he had authority to settle. In a single meeting, we resolved the dispute and
walked away with serious money and major concessions, as well as preserving
a valuable business relationship. This last point may bear emphasis. Often,
litigators forget that the clients may have good reason to deal with each other
in the future, and that too much hostility can destroy that prospect.

In the criminal case, however, Nizer should not have appeared. He had
written his argument out in longhand, with red pen marks on it for emphasis.

As he stood at the lectern, his associate crouched beside him so that when he lost his place the associate could help him find it. As litigators, we should pray that someone will be kind enough to tell us when to hang up our weapons.

DOMINIC GENTILE: LAWYERING IN THE MEDIA SPOTLIGHT

Lawyer speech has often had loftier expression than some of these accounts would suggest. In 1761, the British colonial authorities used general warrants called writs of assistance to search for goods on which protesting colonists had not paid tax. John Adams was at that time a young lawyer in Boston. Another lawyer, James Otis, made a speech on the Boston Common against the writs of assistance. Of those events, Adams later wrote "then and there was the child Independence born." When the young Adams was retained to represent John Hancock in a forfeiture proceeding, his contentions and later a text of his undelivered argument were thoroughly aired in the press of the time, along with running commentaries on the legal issues. When John Adams was in Philadelphia on July 3, 1776, waiting for the next day's events, he looked back at those times and wrote that these court cases and the controversy around them were "the Commencement of the Controversy, between Great Britain and America."

Lawyers are qualified by training to speak on public issues. Their participation in major litigation qualifies them further. As my friend John Mage has written, "In the U.S. system, all significant political and social questions are given legal form." For this reason, lawyers are valuable participants in public discourse, even when they are also litigating about the judicial resolution of the same issues on which they are speaking in public.

Because I see things in this way, I was honored when Dominic Gentile called and asked if I, along with Sam Buffone, would take his case to the Supreme Court. Dominic was a successful Las Vegas defense lawyer, former faculty member of the National Criminal Defense College and published author. His client was Grady Sanders, who owned a private storage company. The Las Vegas police rented lock-boxes from Sanders' company, and used the boxes to store money and narcotics for use in a sting operation. The police omitted to tell Sanders what they were doing.

The money and narcotics disappeared, and the ensuing public outcry occupied the media for months. Eventually, the district attorney indicted Sanders, the police having unpersuasively denied guilt. Dom went to court and got a trial date six months in the future. The night before, he had carefully studied the rules of professional responsibility to see what press comment he could make about the case.

After the arraignment, Dom held a press conference, which he had the good sense to videotape. He kept within the bounds of proper comment as he saw them, and he said that the evidence showed that the Las Vegas police were probably the ones who had stolen the money and drugs. At the trial, no prospective juror remembered Dom's press conference, although some jurors recalled the police and DA public statements. Dom presented evidence to support his theory and the jury acquitted Sanders.

Shortly after the trial, the Nevada bar sent Dom a letter saying that his press conference violated Nevada Supreme Court Rule 177, relating to lawyer public utterances, and that he was subject to discipline. A justice of Nevada Supreme Court had initiated the complaint. Dom put on a thorough defense at the bar disciplinary hearing, including testimony on his own qualifications and the opinions of a media expert and a criminal defense lawyer.

The bar held that his conduct violated Rule 177, holding that Dom's comments created the possibility of interfering with the fairness of Sanders's trial. the Nevada Supreme Court affirmed, despite the absence of any evidence that Dom's press conference had any effect at all on the trial. The punishment was a private reprimand, which would do no great harm to Dom's reputation, but he chose to challenge the decision. We filed a petition for certiorari, making three basic points. First, we said that lawyer speech should be protected unless it poses a clear and present danger to the administration of justice. Second, we argued that the Nevada Rule under which Dom was punished, based on an ABA Model Rule, was unconstitutionally vague and broad, indeed contradictory. Dom was found to have violated Section 2(d) of Nevada Rule 177, which proscribes uttering "any opinion as to the guilt or innocence of a defendant or suspect in a criminal case." Section 3(a) of the same Rule, however, states that, notwithstanding the prohibitions of Sections 1 and 2, counsel "may state without elaboration: a. the general nature of the claim or defense." Third, we argued that on the facts Dom's press conference was not only harmless but performed a public service.

This third point, being factual, is not the sort of thing the Supreme Court is said to care about. Its jurisdiction extends only to deciding federal law issues when reviewing a state court judgment. It was clear to us, however, that one's attitude toward lawyer press conferences in general, and this one in particular, could well drive this case. The story here was the relentless press barrage from the police and DA, and Dom's modulated response, undertaken only after careful study. As we looked at the cases on lawyer speech and gag orders, an interesting pattern emerged. The only lawyers who were disciplined for comments prejudicial to the fair administration of justice were defense lawyers. Prosecutors and police never seemed to be sanctioned, even though in my own experience they are the most potent and deliberate source of prejudicial press leaks.

Few defense lawyers have a pipeline to media sources. On the other hand, in every media market there is a "police beat" that keeps in daily contact with the prosecutors and police. Over time, reporters develop relationships with these law enforcement sources. In every major criminal case in which I have been involved, the prosecutors have been responsible for prejudicial press comments. These comments have ranged from premature release of information to prejudicial rumor and speculation. In a case that continues to excite media attention, by the time we see the prospective jurors they have internalized the media reports and it is difficult if not impossible to unearth and examine their preconceptions on voir dire.

We did find one celebrated case where a prosecutor was disciplined. He had tried a murder case that was then reversed. He said publicly that the case should not be retried, and the district attorney brought disciplinary charges.

We could not know how Dom's story would impress the Justices. The case would be close either way, and it was Justice Souter's first term on the Court so he was an unknown quantity. So we had another story, rooted in the writings of John Adams and James Madison and other lawyers whose public speeches had fueled the drive for American independence. After all, I argued, if the Las Vegas police had stolen money and narcotics, it was a matter of public concern quite beyond the Sanders trial. The public's business may be done in one forum at once. To restrict lawyer speech because a trial was pending in one forum would cripple the debate in the forum of public opinion.

I thought that an argument based on this constitutional history might interest the orginalists and textualists on the Court, principally Justices Scalia and Thomas. As it turned out, I was much too optimistic. In the final tally, five Justices held that lawyer speech about a pending case could be restricted or punished if it poses a substantial threat to the fair administration of justice. The Court rejected cases holding that only a clear and present danger standard was proper, saying that those rules applied only to non-lawyers, including clients and the news media. This holding did not do us much harm, for reaffirming the client's right to speak has proven valuable in high-profile cases.

The tone of this part of the majority opinion was quite hostile to Dom and his actions. These Justices had, it seemed, taken this case in order to clamp down on lawyers, and the opinion reflected that view.

A separate five-Justice majority, led by Justice Anthony Kennedy, held that the disciplinary rule under which Dom had been punished was unconstitutionally vague and overbroad, in that it provided no discernible standard for telling what speech was permitted. This opinion contained helpful language about the lawyer's right to speak. Justice Kennedy also noted, but did not have five votes for doing so, that once the Court had decided that Dom's punishment, and the rule under which it was imposed, were unconstitutional, it had no business reaching out to decide the broader issue.

Even with that split outcome, *Gentile* has put a barrier in the way of those who would draft restrictive rules for lawyer speech, for drafting narrow and precise rules in this area is difficult.

At oral argument, I was struck by how much opposition the Court's members had to my position. The historical argument simply was not resonating with Justices Scalia and Souter, and Justice Thomas was quiet as usual. Justice White was positively hostile. In any case involving a constitutional rule, the battle is usually over when you decide who has the burden of proof. That is, if my opponents had the burden of justifying a restriction on speech, in light of history and the decided cases, they would probably lose. On the other hand, if I were compelled to find a case that upheld a clear and present danger standard for lawyer speech, I would lose.

Justice White made clear that he thought I had the burden. I resisted these suggestions, and in my rebuttal argument he returned to the attack. "Has this Court ever held . . . " his question began, his voice rising with each word. My daughter Elizabeth, then eight years old, was sitting in the front spectator row and her little voice said, "Mommy, why is that man yelling at Daddy?"

It became clear to me that Justices O'Connor and Kennedy were the keys to a majority here. Justice Kennedy had taken a consistently pro–First Amendment position, and I thought it likely he would do so again here.

Justice O'Connor was going to be a key vote. At that time, she was often the leader of a five- or six-Justice majority. A few minutes into the argument, she asked the key question:

Sandra Day O'Connor: Well, Mr. Tigar, here we're dealing with, I suppose, Nevada Supreme Court Rule 177.
Michael E. Tigar: That's my understanding, Justice O'Connor.
Sandra Day O'Connor: And Part 1 of that says that a lawyer shall not make an extrajudicial statement if the lawyers know or reasonably should know that it will have a substantial likelihood of materially prejudicing an adjudicative proceeding. Now, do you take the position that that provision is invalid as a matter of constitutional law?
Michael E. Tigar: Yes, Justice O'Connor, we do. We take that position because we agree with the American Bar Association, which doesn't support the outcome here but supports the rule, that it doesn't embody the clear and present danger standard. . . .

Sandra Day O'Connor: And is this provision, Part 1 of Rule 177, rather typical of what many States have in their rules governing attorney conduct?
Michael E. Tigar: Yes, Justice O'Connor, it is typical of what many States have done.
Sandra Day O'Connor: So they're all invalid?
Michael E. Tigar: Any rule that does not embody the clear and present danger standard would be invalid under our view, Justice O'Connor. And I think it is important to point out that this would not be the first time that the Court has had to say to the bar that the First Amendment doesn't stop short of its door. Again, however, the problem, Justice O'Connor, is not simply a facial invalidity. It is not simply overbreadth but vagueness.

Arguing the Gentile case helped me to put my own views about lawyer speech into perspective. I am not a fan of lawyer advertising, because I think it cheapens the profession, but I can't see a constitutional basis for barring it. I was called for jury service in Austin, Texas, some years ago and the lawyer asked if anyone on the panel knew him or his name. One juror said, "I saw your TV ads." The lawyer brightened and said, "What did you think?" The juror replied, "I think that sort of thing makes a piss-poor impression."

I also believe that restrictions on lawyer solicitation should be limited by the First Amendment. In the civil rights days, the Supreme Court struck down such restrictions as applied to the NAACP and to labor organizations. Today, in the wake of a mass disaster such as an air crash, insurance company and airline representatives are on the scene talking to victims and their families, to get statements and make settlements. That is the time when those folks need lawyers, and there must be some way to let them know that they have that right.

The major lawyer speech issue remains the one I have faced in almost every case I talk about in this book: Regardless of whether the lawyer has the right to speak, should he or so do so? I will routinely seek a gag order preventing discovery material from reaching the media. This material is often not admissible in evidence and it can have a prejudicial impact on prospective jurors. We got such orders in the Nichols case and I successfully argued in the court of appeals that they were valid.

In general, I don't trust the media. These reporters have their own agenda. They may tape or interview for thirty minutes and choose a snippet or two that fits the theme of their story of the day. I also think that jurors do not appreciate lawyers who grandstand for the press. Lawyers who do that hurt themselves, often by creating expectations that the admissible evidence will not fulfill. It has been said of a lawyer I know that the most dangerous place to be is between him and a TV camera. Actually, it has been said of more than one lawyer I know.

That said, media people have been very helpful over the years. Often prospective witnesses will talk to a reporter when they will shut the door on an investigator. Media people have resources to run down leads. Their reportage can help us prepare. Then, there are media forums where the public interest aspect of a case can be discussed in an intelligent way. I learn to trust certain reporters, and certain forums. In some cases, the decision to prosecute, or to appeal, may be in the hands of public officials. These officials pay attention to media coverage. There are, in short, no iron-bound rules, only the exercise of judgment.

If I am lead counsel in a case, then I must be in charge of media contacts. I will respect media confidences and expect mine to be respected as well. In most cases, when there is a phalanx of reporters on the way to court, I will confine myself to a brief statement on what we expect will happen, and be sure to say something like "we respect the jurors so much that we think they should be the first to hear the evidence." If I am representing a political figure, the rules may be different. Politicians must explain their conduct to the media, to maintain contact with the electorate. Case law firmly holds that the defendant, particularly one who holds or aspires to public office, has a broad right to speak. However, this right and opportunity can too often be misused. If a case is pending, we can often put the client's position into pleadings filed in court, which the press can then have and from which the client can read.

It is important to keep those media contacts short and controlled. I remember in the early 1980s representing Congressman Ron Dellums. The Reagan Justice Department had leaked a false story that somebody in his office was dealing narcotics. The leak was timed to hit the evening news. I had only a limited chance to confer with Dellums and his staff before the news deadlines, so I was surely not going to spin some story that later events might contradict. I stepped before the cameras and said, "We deny the allegations and we are trying to find the allegators," and then went back inside Dellums, office. After six months of investigation, an official report concluded what we had found within 24 hours—there was no evidence to support such allegations and none was uncovered in a diligent investigation.

Because the media is insatiable, it will keep on hammering at the story. Letting your client make a detailed statement before you know the facts is therefore almost always perilous. One of our duties as lawyers is not to believe our clients. We are supposed to have our crap detectors strapped on and working. Letting our public figure clients lead with a story that later proves false can do more harm than confessing. If President Clinton and his lawyers had followed these precepts, the course of history would have been quite different.

The final media debate concerns televising trials. Some states do it, and the Supreme Court has given the practice its constitutional blessing. The Court has refused, however, to allow televising its own proceedings. I oppose television of sensational trials. Even though the camera may be hidden, it has a pervasive influence. Jurors are aware it is there. Witnesses know they are on television, and their celebrity status can influence their testimony. Direct and cross-examination are by nature intimate, a relationship among witness, lawyer, jurors, and judge. When the witness feels that he or she is performing for a larger audience, this intimacy is broken. Then, too, television broadcasts of snippets on the evening news adds to the sensationalism of media coverage and makes it harder for jurors to avoid it. We have enough trouble convincing judges not to sequester juries into the hands of obliging pro-prosecution bailiffs without this added distraction.

In sum, when one thinks about the First Amendment and trials, it is important to distinguish between what the Constitution may permit and what it might be wise to do.

CHARLESTON FIVE

Charleston, South Carolina, has been an important seaport since colonial days. In modern times, it ranks with New York and New Jersey, Baltimore. and Jacksonville, Florida, as one of the most important destinations for containerized cargo ships. Containerization—loading items into huge steel boxes that can then be transported on ships, railcars, and trucks—has changed patterns of production around the world. While containers vary, 40 feet long and 8.5 feet high is a usual size.

Before containerization, items transported by ships were unloaded a few at a time by longshore workers. Today, the containers are packed and then loaded on the ship by large cranes. Containers can be stacked seven or eight high. The impact on the global workforce has been enormous. As I had learned while researching and writing a paper in my undergraduate journalism course, it is now possible to load and unload containers of automatic automobile transmissions cheaply and efficiently enough that importing them from low-wage areas rather than having them built in the United States makes economic sense—to the manufacturers. Containerization is one major engine of globalization.

In 2001, I was invited to fulfill a sort of cameo role in a labor struggle on the Charleston docks. As at other East Coast ports, the union was the

International Longshoremen's Association. The case had become known as the Charleston 5, after the five union members charged with riot after a confrontation between a peaceful ILA protest march and 600 armed officers from seven different departments.

I knew the the Charleston port from several perspectives. In December 2000, Jane Tigar and I had traversed it on our way down the Intracoastal Waterway in our new boat. It is difficult to navigate the harbor. Currents are swift and there are unmarked shallows. In later years, we would sail offshore, entering and leaving the port into the Atlantic.

I also had a human perspective. My friend Armand Derfner and his young partner Peter Wilborn represented ILA Local 1422, led by Ken Riley. Armand and I are about the same age. We met in Washington, where we were both starting law practice in the 1960s. Armand later went to the American South and became a leading figure in voting rights and other significant litigation. Armand is affable, studious, intense, eloquent, and very smart. Peter Wilborn had worked on international human rights issues before settling in Charleston to work with Armand.

The dock workforce in Charleston is racially integrated. Three ILA locals— 1422, 1771, and 1422-A—cover the waterfront, with members involved in loading, checking, and maintenance.

The events I am about to describe, and their context and consequences, are brilliantly captured in Susan Erem's and Peter Durrenberger's book, *On the Global Waterfront: The Fight to Free the Charleston 5*, published in 2008 by Monthly Review Press. The authors have given me permission to quote from and rely upon their work. They hope, as do I, that you will buy their book.

In January 2000, South Carolina was the scene of civil rights marches to demand that the Confederate flag over the state capitol be taken down, primary election campaigning by George W. Bush and John McCain, and the political maneuverings of South Carolina Attorney General Charles Condon. Condon built his popular support by attacking labor unions as a violation of an individual worker's right to negotiate with an individual multinational employer, advocating more capital punishment, opposing civil rights, and other bits of demagoguery.

Most of the shipping companies on the Charleston docks used union labor. Nordana, a Denmark-based firm, did not. The night of January 19, 2000, ILA 1422 and the other locals planned a protest march and picket directed at the Nordana dock. These protests had been a regular occurrence.

That afternoon, however, Ken Riley heard that 600 police in riot gear had assembled to confront the picketers. By mid-afternoon, this armed force had assembled with its vehicles, dogs, and equipment. Riley and the presidents of the other locals presided over a meeting at the union hall. The union members voted not to hold their scheduled march—for the time being. Let the cops mill around waiting for something that was not going to happen, they thought.

Later in the evening, however, the consensus was that there had to be some demonstration of power and solidarity. "We are going to stand up for our jobs tonight," one longshoreman said. Dozens of longshore workers, some with picket signs, left the union hall and headed toward the docks. The police blocked their path. A few workers walked up to the police line. Workers shouted at the police, "What are you doing here? We are here to protect our jobs!" A few workers moved in past the first row of police.

Workers and community members threw rocks and railroad ties toward the police. For the next few hours, longshore workers clashed with the 600-strong police force. Police with nightsticks began to beat picketers. They fired beanbag projectiles, tear gas, and concussion grenades. A police SUV ran into a demonstrator. Ken Riley took a blow to his head that required twelve stitches. A police official, using a bullhorn, ordered the workers to disperse.

The next morning, and for the next several days, the political forces in and around Charleston reflected on events and reviewed the extensive video recordings made by media and police. The local consensus, supported by the video images of police violence, favored the longshore workers' version of events. Somebody in state government had called out an armed force to provoke a confrontation.

Attorney General Condon began a press campaign that was to continue for twenty-two months. "Rioters," he proclaimed, vowing punishment: "jail, jail and more jail." Meantime, local police and sheriff's office officials found little if anything to prosecute. Eight union members were charged with misdemeanors, but ten days later a local magistrate reviewed the evidence and dismissed the cases. Local Charleston officials, including business leaders, did not want these events to disturb the orderly and profitable operation of the Charleston port, where $2.2 billion in imports and exports crossed the docks every year. They were unwilling to join Condon's crusade.

Condon was not deterred. He took over the case, convened a grand jury and obtained indictments for felony riot against five union members: Kenneth Jefferson, Rick Simmons, Peter Washington, Elijah Ford, and Jason Edgerton. The five were placed under house arrest. Ken Riley sought and obtained support from the the national AFL-CIO and from longshore union locals on the West, East and Gulf coasts. Charleston's mayor said that Condon should turn the case over to local prosecutors. Charleston's chief of police said he thought the charges were too harsh.

Condon kept up his media campaign. After September 11, 2001, he compared the Five to those who had attacked the World Trade Center. He acknowledged that although prospective jurors would hear and read his comments, he thought they could be "fair."

The union recruited lawyers for the Five. Andy Savage, one of Charleston's premier defense lawyers, would represent Kenneth Jefferson and Jason Edgerton. Lionel Lofton, a former federal prosecutor from McClellanville, South Carolina, would represent Rick Simmons, Peter Washington, and Elijah Ford. Local 1422's lawyer, Armand Derfner, coordinated defense and organizational efforts with Ken Riley and other union leaders.

Ken Riley sought support from other unions and from the national AFL-CIO. The Charleston 5 became a major topic of union campaigning. Many union leaders and members realized that if the longshore workers in the port of Charleston could be defeated and discredited, their own efforts would be undermined. Longshore unions around the world planned to support the Charleston 5, if necessary, by shutting down port operations, disrupting billions of dollars in trade.

In early September 2011, Armand called me. He shared his view of the case, its history, and the political forces at work. A pretrial hearing was set for October 12, trial for November 12. I agreed to review the pleadings that had been filed. The charge was riot, defined in the Anglo-American common law as:

A concerted action: (1) made in furtherance of an express common purpose; (2) through the use or threat of violence, disorder, or terror to the public; and (3) resulting in a disturbance of the peace.

Riot was a common law crime in South Carolina; it was not defined in a statute, but by history and judicial interpretation. Federal law proscribes common law offenses; there are no federal common law crimes. However, some states still have a few of them in force.

South Carolina's riot offense had been upheld against a facial First Amendment challenge in 1970 in a case involving civil rights leader Ralph Abernathy. However, that old case was decided by the federal court of appeals; the state court was free to make its own decision. We would probably have more success in taking the same approach as in Angela Davis's case and others: As applied to the charged conduct, the defendants' actions were protected by the Constitution. Given the abundant video coverage, "charged conduct" included not only what was written in the indictment but the undisputable evidence that could be presented to the court.

Armand and the rest of the team recognized that this case was being driven by Condon's political ambition. If Condon could be pushed aside, things might, as Ken Riley said, "get a little better." Ah yes, I told Armand, as my grandmother used to say, "If you want to clean the creek, you have to start by getting the pigs out of it." Of course, my grandmother never said any such thing, but I like the expression.

I thought back to the *Gentile* case, and to the revised rules about lawyer comment on pending cases. Condon's statements had created a substantial likelihood of prejudice to a fair trial. He had almost admitted as much. I put together a collection of Condon's public statements and an analysis of his ethical violations. His inflammatory utterances not only violated the rules on lawyer comment, they demonstrated a conflict between his professional obligation as prosecutor and his personal political agenda and ambition.

Armand, Andy Savage, and Lionel Lofton filed this supplemental material on October 5. They asked me to come to Charleston and participate in the October 12 motion hearing. On October 11, the legal team met in Andy Savage's office. We were each assigned our roles. The *Charleston Post and Courier* for October 11 reported:

> Accusing labor unions of creating a "sly smoke screen" to divert attention from last year's waterfront riot, S.C. Attorney General Charlie Condon Wednesday transferred prosecution of the so-called Charleston Five case from his office to a Dorchester County solicitor [S.C. version of a district attorney]. Condon wrote a letter to 1st Circuit Solicitor Walter Bailey giving Bailey "full authority and complete discretion to make all prosecutorial decisions." Condon added, "This appointment to you removes the focus from the person who is prosecuting the case and returns the focus to where it belongs—the true facts of the case."

The morning of October 12, we arrived at the courthouse and were told to meet in Judge Victor Rawl's chambers. Rawl was from the Low Country of South Carolina, and understood the people, politics, and economy of Charleston. It turned out that Rawl and Walter Bailey were classmates. Judge Rawl held up a copy of the newspaper. "Walter," he said to the prosecutor in a slow drawl, "in my court a lawyer who wishes to withdraw from a case does so by filing a motion. He does not do it by holding a press conference. Very well. He's out. But Walter, he is not coming back. He is no longer welcome here, is that clear?" This seemed a good start to the day.

Every seat in the courtroom was occupied. Andy Savage spoke first. He laid out the basis for dismissing the charges, telling the story of how the police assembled their forces and attacked the workers. He attacked Condon's misconduct, and focused on the way that Condon had for his own purposes escalated the disgraceful actions of the police into this attack on the union and its members. His argument had gained power by Condon's departure, and the arrival of Walter Bailey who was not from Charleston. Savage quoted the South Carolina Supreme Court: "The grand jury is not the prosecutor's plaything."

It was my turn. Erem and Durrenbeger described the scene:

> The most substantive arguments were still to be heard. The very constitutionality of South Carolina's riot statute was in question, and the defense was well aware of the long list of cases that had challenged it before and lost.
>
> Here Michael Tigar took over. His reputation preceded him. This was the man whose defense of Oklahoma City bombing conspirator Terry Nichols led to an acquittal of the murder charges against him, the man whose rapport with that case's jurors allowed him to shed tears during his closing argument as he told them, "This is my brother, and he's in your hands."
>
> Tigar lived up to his reputation that day in Charleston as he took Judge Rawl, the prosecution, and the packed courtroom through the maze of two centuries of case law as if he were giving a tour of his own home.
>
> First Tigar reminded the court of the incredible breadth of the indictments. Each man was charged that he did unlawfully and willingly "unite, combine, conspire, confederate, agree, have tacit understanding, or otherwise participate in a combination" for the unlawful purpose, that being "instigating, aiding or participating in riot, as defined in Count II of the indictment."
>
> Count II charged them with "participating in . . . a tumultuous disturbance of the peace, by three or more persons assembled together, of their own authority, with the intent mutually to assist each other against anyone who shall oppose them, and putting their design into execution in a terrific and violent manner, whether the object was lawful or not." Then he facetiously referred to the end of the indictment as having "two multiple choice clauses" or what might be considered a laundry list of possible crimes.
>
> "The purpose of the assembly, or of the acts done or threatened or intended by the persons engaged, was . . . to resist the enforcement of a statute of this state, or the United States; or obstruct a public officer to this state, or of the United States, in serving or executing any process or other

mandate of a court of competent jurisdiction, or in the performance of any other duty; or the offender carried, at the time of the riot, firearms, or any other dangerous weapon or was disguised."

In other words, Tigar argued, the state had thrown the book at these men, and had never bothered to tell them what page they were on. Tigar explained one case after the other that spoke to a defendant's right to know the specific charges against him. He then moved on to explain why the riot statute, adopted in 1968, was itself "suspect." It allows people to be convicted for showing up or being present at a riot without any proof of involvement. Finally, he argued that the statute was unconstitutional because it applied to events where both lawful and unlawful behavior could occur, and one couldn't tell which one the person charged had been involved in.

Anticipating the prosecution's argument with the Abernathy case, Tigar explained the limits of that case. It didn't address the definition of "rioter" and it didn't involve applying the rioting charge to both protected (lawful) and unprotected behaviors.

"The South Carolina riot/rioter framework, therefore, appears to allow punishment of an individual merely because he belongs to a group, some members of which commit acts of violence," Tigar argued. "Not only is the citizen left without guidance, but prosecutors are armed with excessive discretion." In fact, this case was proof of that, he said, because while local police charged the men with trespass, the attorney general upped the charges to riot on all of them in a day, with no indication that he knew anything more about them than that they had been present.

Armand Derfner, replete with colorful disheveled clothes and a magnifying glass on a lanyard around his neck, alternately hunched, reading and sifting through piles of paper, and stood to finish off the motions and summarize for the defense. Having him in the courtroom lent an auspiciousness to the occasion. As he cited one case after another, it became obvious that if he hadn't been directly involved in a case he was citing from thirty-six years ago, he had been sitting in the courtroom, and if not in the courtroom, then later discussing it over a glass of wine with the attorney who *had* argued it. He, Tigar, Lofton, and Savage stood on solid legal ground, but Derfner and Tigar could make the ground sway with their eloquence.

Young Peter Wilborn sat in awe, watching his superheroes perform right there, just for him. Indeed, it was more of a performance *for* attorneys *by* attorneys.

"It was dramatic if you knew all the details," Derfner modestly admitted later. "It was dramatic in the way Shakespeare can be dramatic if you know English and you've read the play." But the end goal was always in sight: free their clients.

After the courtroom arguments, we were summoned to Judge Rawl's chambers. The judge began by addressing the prosecutor. "Walter, you know that somebody ordered up 600 police and troopers, well before there were any marchers or picketers. Remember when we were in college and law school. During all of those antiwar protests, nobody ever thought there should be a military-type force like that. Walter, we have labor peace in this town, and mostly we have racial peace. Those things are important to us. I am concerned that if you take this case to trial, I and everybody else are going to find out who it was that ordered up that police action that night. I don't want to know that. And Walter, there is something else. When something like this happens, you can't just put the riot label on it. By tomorrow, I want you to make a list of everything you have on these five defendants that is not conduct protected by the First Amendment."

"But Judge," Bailey replied, "under the rules, the defendants are not entitled to a bill of particulars at this time."

"Walter," the judge said, his voice rising, "I am not talking about those rules. I am talking about what I just ordered you to do. It surely looks like these men started out that evening to hold just another picket line down at the docks."

Rawl was lecturing Bailey as though talking to a first-year law student. He was giving a short course in how the state's mythic idea of riot, when deconstructed, was a collection of assaults on free expression. Rawl had already shown a keen appreciation of the union's right of peaceable assembly; in an earlier case, he had denied the employers' request for an injunction against the picketing of non-union docks.

Walter Bailey was slow to take the hint. He affirmed that the trial would go forward on November 12. Charleston public figures raised their voices against the prosecution. Armand called several times to discuss the issues. Any agreement to settle the case had to achieve several goals. The Charleston 5 would not accept any agreement that harmed the interests of their union and fellow workers. They would not plead guilty to anything that would give the non-union shipping companies an advantage in civil litigation involving labor issues on the docks. They could not plead guilty to any offense that under post-9/11 legislation would bar them from working on the docks. They would not admit to being rioters. The defendants also rejected Bailey's demand that they apologize.

Finally, an agreement was reached: each of the Five would pay a nominal fine, and plead "no contest"—nolo contendere—to taking part in an "affray"; that is, they were involved in a disturbance. Their record of being convicted of this petty offense would be expunged in due course.

One might ask whether the defendants ought to have taken the case to trial. The probability of acquittal was high. However, they ended the case at the moment of a huge surge in public support for them and for their union. Attention could then turn to the rights of all dockworkers in the Charleston port and elsewhere.

For the next fifteen years, until Jane Tigar and I at last sold first our sailboat and then the small Nova Scotia trawler we bought to replace it, we visited Charleston almost every year. We visited with Armand Derfner, his wife, Mary Giles, and Peter and Cappy Wilborn. Every once in a while, Armand and I exchange emails and talk on the telephone about cases on which we are working.

CHAPTER 13

Death—and That's Final

BUCKLEY AND RISOTTO

O ver the years, I debated capital punishment, and other issues of criminal justice, with William F. Buckley, Jr., several times. In a 1989 program, he intoned, "A society that takes ten years to execute Ted Bundy is a society whose legal processes are not working well enough." We could start there.

Buckley was an impassioned, eloquent spokesman for his ideology. He lived just off Park Avenue in a lovely duplex apartment, where one is greeted by sounds of him playing the harpsichord. Before one taping of his program *Firing Line*, he invited me to lunch with him. This is an honor, I was made to believe, accorded to few. I arrived at the restaurant a few minutes early to find it shuttered. Apparently, Buckley and I were to be the only lunchtime guests. The Buckley limousine arrived, and he greeted the owner in a flurry of Italian conversation. Inadequate linguist was I.

Seated at the table, Buckley and the owner continued their discussion. At last, in English, the owner asked me what I would like to eat. "I only caught a word or two of that," I said, "but if you indeed have risotto, I would like that. Perhaps risotto con funghi," thus nearly exhausting my knowledge of menu Italian.

A few minutes later, lunch was served. Mine was a lovely looking rice with mushrooms. Buckley was served a plate of plain white rice. He looked pained, and asked in English why his rice was different from mine. "But, *signore*," the owner protested, "that is what you ordered."

The battle of egos continued as we faced off during the program. Buckley was at his most arch, and at one point he interrupted my argument to say, "Oh, Mr. Tigar, now you're being fatuous." I replied, "Well, I thought it was my turn."

At one point, Buckley summed up by saying that laws passed by legislatures mandated a death penalty for cold-blooded murder. He continued, "Those laws, in my judgment, are now being frustrated as a result of the cool resources of very bright people who walk into the situation with an ideological predetermination to render the law nugatory."

I argued, "If I'm retained as a lawyer and there's a human life at stake—one of course is gone, that's why there's a murder charge—the question is, shall the state be entitled to take this other life, this life, now, deliberately. As a lawyer I've got the obligation to go out and walk the mean streets and find the facts, to check that alibi out, to check the defendant's mental condition, to hire an investigator. How can I do that if I'm in, for instance, a state like Georgia, where the only thing I can get for my fee is $500 . . . and where the pressure of my other business makes it impossible for me to do a decent job?"

Over the years that I knew Buckley, he often spoke up on behalf of people convicted of murder when he thought they had been treated unfairly and that there was evidence they were wrongly convicted. One such case was that of Charles Culhane and Garry McGivern, convicted of murdering a deputy sheriff. They were at first convicted and sentenced to death, won a retrial, and were again convicted but given long prison terms. I represented them on appeal and in post-conviction proceedings, though without success. Eventually, Governor Mario Cuomo granted them parole. They became spokesmen for prison reform and against the death penalty. Buckley was even a member of a support committee that also included Pete Seeger. I claimed to have brokered that deal by getting Bill to agree not to sing progressive folksongs and Pete to agree not to espouse right-wing politics.

Culhane and McGivern were sentenced to death in the shooting case, but were re-sentenced to 25 years to life when the death penalty was held unconstitutional. While on death row in New York, they acted out life-affirming violations of prison rules. They were forbidden to have a garden, so they swept the dirt in the recreation yard into cracks in the brickwork, and planted grass seeds that people sent to them in prison mail. They asked a female who visited them to give them a pair of her panties, which were bright orange-yellow in color. This was contraband, and when it was discovered in a search of their cells, they were hauled before a prison disciplinary board. Culhane spoke: "You have caught us. We confess. We were going to use hot water to moisten our bedsheets and then bend the bars on the window. Then, under cover of darkness, we were going to go to the prison wall and crouch there. And just before dawn, we were going to pull the panties over our heads and go up the wall, disguised as the rising sun."

This quality of compassion points up the contradiction in Buckley's point of view, and in that of others. He began the television program of which I speak by talking about a notorious confessed multiple murderer. Yet I had with me a newspaper clipping recounting that Buckley had asked the archbishop of New Orleans to intercede on behalf of a Louisiana man who had been on death row for nine years. Had the law acted with the celerity for which Buckley seemed to contend, his act of charity would have been impossible, for its object would have been killed.

In that same program, Buckley excoriated New York Governor Hugh Carey for vetoing a capital punishment bill, saying that Carey was wrongly frustrating popular will. Carey said that if the bill passed, and anyone were sentenced to death, he would feel duty-bound to commute the sentence. A week later, Buckley wrote, "You were your usual brash brilliant self, but plainly wrong on the Hugh Carey matter. How does it feel to be wrong every now and then?" I wrote back, "Given other experiences with him, I would be pleased to see proof that Hugh Carey did something wrong. Proof that he promised to spare someone from the executioner in the manner provided for by the New York State Constitution doesn't quite do it for me." I went on, "I will plead guilty to being brash. I am taking your letter home tonight to show my mother, and she will thank you for 'brilliant.'"

Tucked into this exchange are almost all the issues in the death penalty debate as I have observed it. As I said, summing up on the television program, "If we're going to have this penalty, which I acknowledge I oppose and you acknowledge that you favor, I take it that it's common ground between us that the state should never be able to exact it without making sure that the system that led to it is fair and just and decent and right and accurate."

In 1972, in *Furman v. Georgia*, the Supreme Court invalidated almost all capital sentencing statutes in states and in the federal system, on the ground that those laws did not sufficiently narrow the number of cases in which a death sentence could be obtained, and permitted arbitrary exercise of judge, juror, and prosecutor discretion in determining who would live and who would die.

The Congress and the state legislatures went to work, and beginning in 1976, the Court upheld many of the newly devised capital sentencing schemes. Justices Brennan and Marshall concluded that the process could not be made rational, and that the death penalty was under all circumstances a "cruel and unusual punishment" that violated the Eighth Amendment. Justice Blackmun, for different reasons, came eventually to conclude that the death penalty could not be fairly administered.

The 1976 Supreme Court rulings were a great disappointment to the community of lawyers engaged in death penalty litigation. They had hoped to convince a majority of the Justices that this system could not be made acceptably, constitutionally, fair. From 1976 on, the legal battles focused on narrowing the cases in which the death penalty could be sought or imposed, developing standards for effective assistance of counsel, and uncovering police and prosecutorial misconduct. The Court refused to consider the persuasive evidence of pervasive racial bias in the administration of the death penalty. There was a grim irony at work: Capital cases arise out of crimes that may shock the community and trigger calls for vengeance. Police, prosecutors, and judges want to reassure the community, and in their haste and desire to do that they are willing to ignore basic rules about procedural fairness.

A Columbia Law School study in the 1990s found fundamental legal error in two-thirds of the capital cases tried in the United States since 1976. Most of those errors involved police officials hiding exculpatory evidence, prosecutors and police denying the accused basic rights in the criminal justice system, and judges who overlooked those errors. Many of these judges, particularly in the "Death Belt" states of the American South, are elected in campaigns designed to fire up the vengeful spirit of the majority community. This Columbia study reaffirmed what has been clear for so many years, and is borne out by looking at the racial composition of death rows. Crimes committed against whites by African-Americans are far more likely to be prosecuted as capital than those committed in any other combination of victim and killer. It is easy to see why a system so dominated by racial disparity would tolerate the other errors that the Columbia study found.

As for the right to counsel, the *National Law Journal* did a study of appointed counsel in capital cases in 1990. Given what is at stake, one would expect that only the most-qualified lawyers would be found adequate to the task. By now, almost everyone has read the anecdotal evidence that this is not so. The classic story of the Texas-appointed lawyer who slept during his client's capital murder trial has made the rounds. The trial and penalty phase lasted just 13 hours, and the lawyer did not even make objection when the prosecutor said the jurors should sentence the defendant to death because he is gay.

The *National Law Journal* found:

- "the trial lawyers who represented death row inmates in the six states were disbarred, suspended, or otherwise disciplined at a rate three to forty-six times the discipline rates for lawyers in those states"
- "there were wholly unrealistic statutory fee limits on defense representation"
- "nonexistent standards for appointment of counsel"

- "capital trials that were completed in one to two days, in contrast to two-week or two-month long trials in some states . . . where indigent defense systems were operating"
- In short, the right to effective counsel is ignored in the cases where the stakes are highest, and error rates are demonstrably high. Although the Supreme Court has on several occasions overturned death verdicts because of ineffective counsel, the lower federal courts apply those decisions narrowly and grudgingly.

TEXAS RESOURCE CENTER

I arrived to teach at the University of Texas School of Law in 1983. I had married, for the third time, to Amanda G. Birrell. Our daughter, Elizabeth Torrey Tigar, was born shortly before we moved to Texas.

Then as now, Texas had one of the largest death rows of any death penalty state. I was teaching classes, working with students to provide pro bono representation in criminal appeals, writing articles and serving in various posts in the ABA Section on Litigation—mainly related to capital punishment, white collar crime, and international criminal law.

In 1988, the Congress allocated funds for several "Resource Centers for Capital Litigation," one of which was located in Austin, Texas. The lawyers who set up the Austin Center asked me to be chair of the Board of Directors. I met and worked with these brilliant and dedicated young lawyers, whose main tasks were to advise trial lawyers and to provide direct representation in post-conviction collateral review of death sentences. A capital case defendant has the constitutional right to counsel in the trial and direct appeal. Once direct appeals are exhausted, the defendant has the right to seek "collateral review" of the conviction and sentence in federal court by filing a petition for writ of habeas corpus, having first made sure to exhaust any state post-conviction remedy that might be available. The Supreme Court held that the state may not carry out an execution while this process goes through the post-conviction phase, including the federal trial court and court of appeals.

However, the Court also held, in 1989, that the inmate has no constitutional right to counsel in this state federal court post-conviction phase. The Resource Centers were designed to fill the need for counsel in that setting. Under the Center's auspices, I argued appeals in several capital cases. At this time, the ABA Litigation Section was also helping to recruit lawyers to represent death row inmates.

My tussle with William F. Buckley gives a hint of how important the post-conviction process can be. If the inmate has a new and diligent counsel, a fresh look at the record may reveal errors of fact and law, including ineffective trial counsel, racial bias in jury selection, and prosecutorial failure to turn over exculpatory evidence. By 1989, law schools and lawyers were establishing "innocence projects" to investigate capital cases; the delay of execution dates occasioned by the right to collateral review allowed time for investigators to uncover evidence of innocence. Indeed, in the very case in which the Supreme Court held there is no right to counsel in collateral review, the defendant—Joseph Giarratano—was able to find a volunteer lawyer who assembled evidence of innocence. Years later, this lawyer, Stephen Northup, helped me represent Jomo Davis, former Black Panther Party Minister of Justice, and gain Jomo's release from a Virginia prison. The law school innocence project and wrongful conviction clinics have obtained exoneration of hundreds of death row prisoners.

From the beginning, the Center drew hostility from politicians who wanted the death penalty carried out more surely and swiftly, and from judges who for one reason or another resented the zeal the Center exhibited in every one of its cases. Some judges spared no chance to criticize Center and volunteer lawyers, sometimes in published opinions. When a lawyer for a large corporation, with lots of money at stake, takes every procedural step to protect his or her client's interest, that is called aggressive lawyering and is praised. When these lawyers invoked every procedure to forestall executions, they were criticized.

A Fifth Circuit judge publicly rebuked a volunteer lawyer for unduly delaying the litigation process. I spoke in defense of that lawyer and others who were doing the same work. The *New York Times* reported this exchange of views. That evening, I was at a meeting with another Fifth Circuit judge. With a smile, he said, "Ah yes, Tigar mano a mano with Judge X."

The Supreme Court and the courts of appeals had made clear that if a capital defendant did not raise a given argument at the earliest possible moment, the argument might well be waived. Knowing this, I often said to groups of lawyers that capital case representation in the court of appeals was different from other cases. In the ordinary case, one must choose among arguments, rejecting weaker ones to focus on the main chance. But in a capital case, who would want the responsibility for jettisoning an argument that might turn out in later caselaw to be victorious? Therefore, I said, put all your arguments in. After one such talk, a court of appeals judge stopped me in the hall and said, "Goddamn it, Mike, why do you tell these lawyers to gum up the works with all of these arguments?" I said I thought their doing so was the fault of a system that penalized their clients if they did not do so.

At every Fifth Circuit judicial conference, the attorneys general of Texas,

Louisiana, and Mississippi would circulate written attacks on the resource centers and their work. I would meet with supportive judges and try to organize responses. Even our supporters at times expressed anger at the youthful enthusiasm of some Center lawyers.

One Center lawyer had made a press statement after an adverse ruling from a district judge, doubting that the judge had paid attention. I confess I have picked public fights with judges, but have tried to do so only when there seemed to be some point to it. This sort of remark did not seem to serve any purpose, but the lawyer surely had a right to make it. A court of appeals judge telephoned me at the law school. "Come to my office," he said. I did. He showed me the offending newspaper article. I began to say, "Well, of course, this lawyer had a First Amendment right—" That was as far as I got. The judge thumped his desk. "I am not talking about the First Amendment! I am talking about what people are allowed to say!"

The Center helped make some good law, winning some and losing some. I lost three that I can remember. A young mentally retarded man named Marquez had been on trial for murder. Every day, the deputies led him past a phalanx of TV cameras and lights on the way to and from court. Resenting a remark one TV reporter made, he spat. The judge responded by ruling that this gesture meant young Marquez was dangerous, and ordered him shackled in the jury's presence during the penalty phase of his trial. The jury sentenced him to death. The court of appeals rejected arguments based on mental retardation and on the evident prejudice of being shackled by court order when the jury is deliberating whether you are "dangerous." It did so not on the merits, but because trial counsel had not made an adequate record.

I twice argued in the Supreme Court on the issue whether youthful age is so clearly a mitigating factor that jurors must be instructed to consider it. Most states provide for such an instruction, but Texas does not. I lost both cases 5 to 4. In the first one, *Graham v. Collins*, the majority held that the issue had not been raised by trial counsel and therefore could not be raised on appeal. The next term, in *Johnson v. Texas*, the Court had the issue squarely presented and rejected my argument 5 to 4. I thought Justice Kennedy's opinion for five Justices failed to keep the promise of what he had earlier written, about the need to guide the jury's decision. After all, as even Justice Scalia has said, jurors have life experience that permits them to evaluate evidence. They have no life experience with legal concepts, including concepts about what they are to do with the facts as they find them.

At oral argument, I knew which Justices would not vote for life. I said at one point that youthful age has been a mitigating factor since antiquity. Justice Scalia interjected, "What in antiquity?" I noted a Roman law principle from several centuries before the Christian era. Justice Scalia asked a question about this principle, more it seemed to see if I knew what I was talking about than from any interest in the issue. Justice Scalia, after writing at least one solid opinion on the importance of mitigating evidence, came to reject the entire Supreme Court doctrine of special procedures for capital cases. He did not, in this instance, care what history might teach us, even though in other cases he had been assiduous to discover rules for today in the experience of the distant past.

Justice White was also plainly hostile. He had written an opinion reversing the death sentence in *Morgan v. Illinois*, holding that a juror must be willing to listen to mitigating evidence and give it effect in order to sit on a capital case. I thought that *Morgan* said something important about the principle we were asserting. So I cited *Morgan v. Illinois*. Justice White said, "Flattery gets you nowhere." I replied that I was taken aback. Justice White said that was his intention. At that point Justice Stevens, seated to White's right, chimed in, "I would still like to have you tell me, because I'm not as familiar as some of the others are, why is the *Morgan* case relevant." I replied, emphasizing the importance of guiding jury discretion in capital cases.

I was traveling in England when I heard news that I had lost the *Johnson* case. I wept in my anger and frustration, as much for myself as for the young African-American whose life I had not been able to save. I could not think of a way to protest, except to stop eating the flesh of dead animals, so I did that for several years.

A few years later, this issue of youthful age came back to the Supreme Court, in challenges to sentencing youthful offenders to "life without parole." At that time, more than 2,300 people were serving life without parole sentences in U.S. prisons for crimes committed before they were eighteen. This put the United States first among nations; Israel was second, with seven such cases. Justice Kennedy apparently reconsidered his *Johnson* views, and wrote that these punishments raised serious constitutional issues. By that time, Dorsie Johnson had been put to death.

Working with the Center lawyers, I was reminded of three important insights. The first was that the death penalty was only one element of the vindictive and racially biased mechanism of punishment in the United States. When we attacked capital punishment, we were exposing the system that called itself "criminal justice" as a whole. From 1980 to 2006, the number of people incarcerated in the United States climbed from 100 per 100,000 population to nearly 700 per 100,000. The United States has more than 20 percent of the world's prisoners and just 4 percent of the world's population. African-Americans are 13 percent of the population and 40 percent of the prisoners. As we exposed the injustices in the capital punishment system, we helped to shine light on the system as a whole.

Second, the abolition movement was worldwide. By 2020, 142 countries had abolished capital punishment, by statute or in practice. Once abolition occurs in a given country, support for the death penalty seems gradually to dissipate. Even in countries where the death penalty was in force, there were limits on its use against people under eighteen and those with mental retardation. The U.S. Supreme Court took those principles into account in decisions limiting the death penalty as a matter of Eighth Amendment law. I discuss the international law issues below.

Third, the basic strategy of anti-death penalty litigation was being vindicated in ways that had not been fully anticipated. In case after individual case, the federal and state appellate courts of appeals, and the Supreme Court, were handing out limited victories, requiring adequate counsel, a full exploration of mitigating evidence, and enough procedural means to raise legal and factual defenses that include claims of innocence. Prosecutors, judges, and Justices complained at how the system was being slowed down.

In well-tried capital cases with competent counsel, there were fewer death verdicts year by year. One felt that this tendency was influenced by jurors, having learned of wrongful convictions, being reluctant to make a decision that was irreversible. Prosecutors were finding out that litigating through the appeals and post-conviction process was in many cases a waste of public resources.

At a conference at the Barreaux de Paris in 2001, to observe the twentieth anniversary of France's abolition of the death penalty, several of us noted that the publicity surrounding wrongful convictions was a principal reason for juror reluctance to impose death. This despite the fact that jurors are not instructed that "residual doubt" may play a role in their decision.

Here, it seemed to me, is an important lesson as to why the state refrains from being as repressive or punitive as it is able to be. We, in the struggle for change, and especially the lawyers among us, are making it too expensive for the state to behave as unjustly as is theoretically possible.

Reluctant budgetary-driven concessions to justice have also been obtained in prison litigation. Over-incarceration has led to prison overcrowding and to the imposition of inhumane conditions on prisoners. Courts have ordered remedies. Rather than paying the increased costs of compliance, states have begun to release prisoners serving outrageously long sentences or convicted of nonviolent offenses.

Knowing that competent counsel could make a difference, I welcomed an initiative led by Fifth Circuit judge Patrick Higginbotham to obtain financing for and to hold training courses for capital defense lawyers. I taught at several of those. Higginbotham had famously observed that a capital inmate had received ineffective assistance of counsel: "The state paid defense counsel $11.84 per hour. Unfortunately, the justice system got only what it paid for." Some months later, in another decision, he said he had reconsidered and that the justice system did not get what it paid for.

Congress abolished the Federal Resource Centers in 1996, and passed a statute titled the Anti-Terrorism and Effective Death Penalty Act, or AEDPA. I wondered at the term "effective death penalty." I had thought the death penalty was effective, in that even in religious chronicles nobody who was executed had come back to corporeal life. But that is probably not what is meant.

OKLAHOMA CITY

I had been involved in death penalty work for many years when the phone call came about the Oklahoma City bombing case. On April 19, 1995, at 9:02 a.m., a white nationalist named Timothy McVeigh detonated a truck bomb in front of the Murrah Federal Building in Oklahoma City. The bomb consisted of ten or twelve plastic barrels filled with a mixture of ammonium nitrate and fuel oil and perhaps including some nitromethane to create a more powerful explosion, linked together with blasting caps. At least 167 people died in the explosion, hundreds more were injured. Property damage ran into the millions. McVeigh was arrested ninety minutes later by a highway patrolman, for not having a license plate on his getaway car, and for possessing an unregistered firearm. Within a day or so, the authorities had evidence that he had set the bomb, using a rented Ryder truck. The FBI also found out that McVeigh had a friend, Terry, who lived in Herrington, Kansas, and whose association with McVeigh raised suspicions. The FBI interrogated, then arrested Nichols—first as a material witness and then as a co-defendant.

A couple of days after the bombing, I was in Washington, D.C., waiting for a flight home to Austin. I called home to check in. My daughter Elizabeth told me that a "Judge Russell" had called from Oklahoma City. Would I call him back? Russell had appointed Stephen Jones, a lawyer from Enid, Oklahoma, to represent McVeigh. The Federal Public Defender office had declined to represent Nichols, because their office had suffered damage in the bombing and their staff members knew many bombing victims. Other lawyers in Oklahoma demurred, for various reasons.

I thought, why me? Judge Russell has told different versions of his decision to call me. In his most colorful version, he recalled his visit to the Smithsonian Institution in Washington, where he saw a videotape of my closing argument in a mock death penalty case. Every summer, the Smithsonian holds a "folk-life festival" on the Washington Mall. In 1986 the American Trial Lawyers Association set up an outdoor courtroom and held a program on lawyers as storytellers. They invited thirty-two lawyers and judges from around the country to hold forth, a few at a time. We told stories, did mock direct and cross-examinations and summed up to juries composed of spectators. We got good crowds and good press, letting folks know what trial lawyers do.

In the telephone call, Judge Russell also mentioned having consulted a court of appeals judge. On a hunch, I called Judge Higginbotham's chambers and asked to speak to the judge. He came on the line chuckling and admitted that Russell had called him and that he had mentioned my name. It turned out that in the Federal Judicial Center in Washington, lawyers involved in supporting capital defense had drawn up a list of counsels who might be appointed in capital cases.

I asked Judge Russell for 24 hours to think the matter over. I took that time to talk with other lawyers who might agree to join a defense team. My friend Ron Woods agreed to be co-counsel. Ron is about my age. He had graduated from the University of Texas Law School, had worked as an FBI agent, a state prosecutor, and an Assistant U.S. Attorney. He had been appointed U.S.Attorney for the Southern District of Texas by President George H. W. Bush. We had faced each other in cases he was prosecuting and I was defending, and then we had been co-counsel for the defense in cases after he went into private practice.

Having urged lawyers to take on pro bono and appointed cases, and having put forward the idea that capital cases required defending, I could not refuse this appointment. I said yes. In one of those coincidences that exercise a kind of silent influence on decisions, Amanda's and my marriage was in serious trouble, and was soon to end in divorce.

I recruited law students to begin research on legal issues. Ron and I hired paralegal assistants and eventually some top-flight investigators. Other lawyers joined our team, including Reid Neureiter, who had been a Texas law student and had worked on the Demjanjuk case, and Adam Thurschwell, who had been co-counsel with me in a Supreme Court case that I will discuss in chapter 14. We found experts in chemistry to help us analyze the forensic evidence from the bomb site. We set up an office in Oklahoma City with the help of lawyers we knew. Our work on the Nichols case has been chronicled in books, some of which are cited in this book's Notes and Sources, so what follows is a partial account from my viewpoint and experience.

It is important to emphasize our mode of work. We were a team. Ron and I wanted everyone on the team to share the knowledge that each team member

had obtained, and to feel free to contribute ideas. We devised a system of
central files that recorded evidence and events, all on computer media and all
protected by password. We held office meetings regularly. An example of how
this system works: one morning, Cathy Robertson, a paralegal, strode into the
central part of our office suite and said aloud: "Terry Nichols was building a
life, not a bomb." I used that phrase in opening statement, as it expressed a
basic theme of our defense.

The federal death penalty statute had been reworked by the Clinton
administration. The number of offenses for which one could be sentenced to
death was increased. When a defendant was charged with a crime that might
carry the death penalty, a committee in the Department of Justice would
review the case and decide if the penalty would be sought. The trial would
proceed in two installments: a first phase for a jury determination of guilt or
innocence, followed by a penalty phase if the jury found guilt of a "death-eligi-
ble" crime. The law gave the defense broad leeway in presenting and arguing
for mitigating factors. The most important feature of this part of the law was
that each juror could give any mitigating factor such weight as that juror felt it
should have. If we got to a penalty phase, we would be paying close attention
to the attitudes and values of each individual juror. To find out those attitudes
and values, we would need the broadest possible opportunity to question
prospective jurors.

Our first responsibility was to understand Terry Nichols. He was not a
racist or white nationalist. He had become McVeigh's friend during their
military service. His relationship with McVeigh was complex, but we based
the defense on the facts that Terry was not in Oklahoma City on the day
of the bombing, and that the government's proof of Terry's involvement in
McVeigh's plans was thin and inconsistent.

McVeigh and Nichols were held in federal custody while the federal grand
jury considered the case. I moved Judge Russell to release Terry on bail. We
did not expect to win that motion, but the bail hearing gave us insights into
the government's strategy.

One morning in August 1995, the grand jury indictment was filed in court.
McVeigh and Nichols were charged with conspiracy, arson, use of a weapon
of mass destruction, and eight counts of murder of federal agents. The federal
agent deaths were the only homicides that could be tried in federal court;
years later, the state of Oklahoma tried Nichols for the remaining deaths.

The case was randomly assigned to Judge Wayne Alley. Judge Alley, a
former military officer and military judge, had chambers in the federal courthouse near the Murrah Building. The ceiling of his office had collapsed due
to the bombing. He had attended funerals of bombing victims.

Judge Alley called me that morning. "Mike, I guess you know that the indictment has come down and the case assigned to me."

"Yes, sir," I said.

"Well, I am entering an order denying your motion to recuse me," he said.

I replied," Judge, I have not made a motion to recuse you."

"But you will file one, and I am just saving time."

We filed our motion to recuse Judge Alley. He denied it, again. We filed a petition for a writ of mandamus with the U.S. court of appeals. We asked McVeigh's lawyer, Stephen Jones, to join us in this effort. He declined. He was willing to try the case in Judge Alley's court. This was our first real contact with Jones, who had some reputation as a Republican Party activist and candidate, and who relentlessly sought publicity for himself in his role as appointed counsel. Ron and I had decided that we would speak to the media sparingly and on our terms. We began to see that at some point we would want to separate the Nichols and McVeigh defenses.

We argued not only that Judge Alley should be recused, but also that there was a risk that *any* Oklahoma judge would feel he or she had a stake in the outcome. The court of appeals agreed. In a ruling on mandamus that the Nichols team sought, it disqualified all Oklahoma federal judges. Acting under a statute permitting the court of appeals chief judge to name a trial judge, Chief Judge Stephanie Seymour selected Richard P. Matsch, chief judge of the U.S. District Court for Colorado.

Matsch had a solid reputation as a trial judge who respected the adversary process. He came to Oklahoma City to preside over our motion to change venue. The government argued that publicity about the case had been nationwide, and that jurors in any potential trial location would have been subjected to intense media coverage. Our argument was that the people of Oklahoma had a special kind of interest in the case. Oklahoma Governor Keating had publicly said that the defendants would get a fair trial before they were executed, which did seem to encourage prejudgment. During the venue hearing, we found that the federal courthouse cafeteria was selling bombing memorabilia. The marshals guarding Terry Nichols had allowed the media to take his picture, shackled and in a bulletproof vest, as he was led from the jail. Judge Matsch would never have allowed his home courthouse to be used in this way.

There is also an unspoken but observable phenomenon in cases where a judge comes in from out of town in a major case. For Judge Matsch, his assignment to Oklahoma City would have him trundling back and forth to Denver during months of pretrial litigation, and then for months of trial. We found that in several major cases, the out-of-town judge found for one reason or another that the case should be heard in his home city.

Getting the case moved out of Oklahoma City was the second of our three most significant defense victories, the first having been to recuse the Oklahoma judges. The arguments we made and evidence we presented on this issue have provided guidance in later years for lawyers seeking a fairer forum.

Scott Armstrong, a journalist who had worked for the *Washington Post* and had written several important books on aspects of the legal system, provided important evidence in the venue hearing. Armstrong observed that media editors serve their readers and viewers. When a tragic event happens, it may be national or even international news. But the community immediately affected has a special interest in a special kind of coverage. That community wants "justice" and "closure." Its members are more concerned than outsiders with the tragedy's effect on particular community members and groups. These special concerns can be seen in print and electronic media, as editors serve their local market. As a result of this kind of coverage, there is a high risk that community members develop attitudes that make fair and impartial consideration of trial evidence more difficult. In the language of lawyers, the sort of community sentiment that Armstrong identified is called "implied bias."

I explored these themes, arguing to Judge Matsch:

Two roads diverge before us, gathered as we are, with the decades of constitutional liberty piled so high, the anguish of the victims close at hand. To one of those roads we are beckoned, from sadness, to anger, to vengeance. Governor Keating beckons us along that road by what I suggest is deliberate design. The media have beckoned us along that road, simply by their desire to serve their market. The other road, I suggest to the Court, is the one the Framers laid out for us while the memory of unfair trials in distant forums was fresh in their minds.

We neither dishonor nor deny the grief and anger of the victims, nor even their cry for vengeance. Your Honor, this is my 30th year in the law, and I believe, more than ever, that when we summon someone, anyone, Terry Nichols, into court, to find out whether he's going to live or die, that it is our job to construct, where we best can, a kind of sanctuary in the jungle.

One obvious question, and government counsel asked it rhetorically, is why voir dire is not an adequate remedy to explore juror attitudes and eliminate those whose minds are made up. Many cases deny change of venue motions on the theory that juror attitudes can be explored on voir dire. To this concern, which Judge Matsch expressed in a question, I replied:

Nothing I have said, Your Honor, diminishes the power of advocacy nor the abilities of judges to ferret out bias and get at the truth, but my mother always told me not to eat my soup with a fork. Forks are good implements, but there are some things they're just not designed to do.

Our third victory was to get separate trials for Terry Nichols and Timothy McVeigh. We found that at the time the Constitution was adopted, separate trials were the norm in capital cases. Witnesses, including the celebrated capital case lawyer Bryan Stevenson, testified that the individualized consideration of punishment that is the hallmark of capital case decisional law cannot occur when the jurors must weigh the evidence for more than one defendant.

When multiple defendants are tried together in a conspiracy case, the fact that they are seated in the same space, and that their counsel are seen to confer with one another, lends credence to the idea that they must have conspired with one another. In our case, McVeigh's counsel Stephen Jones had already shown that his defense theory was shifting and ill-defined, his rhetoric tended toward bluster, and his remarks to the media were not helpful. In a joint trial, we would be compelled to agree with McVeigh's counsel on jury selection. Judge Matsch granted a severance. McVeigh's case was tried first, in the spring of 1997; the jury sentenced him to death.

Terry Nichols's trial was set for September. We had decided that we would try our case to the jury and not in the press. When the press assembled outside the courthouse after hearings, Ron Woods or I would say only that the judge and soon the jurors were entitled to be the first to hear our evidence and arguments, and we would not preview those in the media. Ron and I did appear on one or two television programs where the host made, and kept, a promise to focus on the legal issues in the case. Journalists did profiles on the defense and prosecution team members.

Judge Matsch decided to follow the same procedure as in the McVeigh case: the clerk of court would draw 1,000 names for potential jury service. The jurors would go in groups of 500 to the Colorado state fairgrounds on the outskirts of Denver to fill out questionnaires on their qualifications, attitudes, and media exposure. Both sides had submitted draft questionnaires and the judge had crafted one from parts of both submissions. From these questionnaires, some prospective jurors could be eliminated based on evident unshakeable bias, hardship, or other reasons. In our proposed jury questions we focused not only on the juror's exposure to media coverage, but also membership in organizations that would give us a clue to social outlook, as well as favorite sources of news and entertainment.

However, McVeigh's lawyers did not demand that their client be present as the prospective jurors filled out their questionnaires. We took the view that these mass gatherings were part of jury selection, a critical stage of the trial process and that Terry therefore had a right to be there. The law provides that he could not, in such a setting, be shackled or in prison dress. Matsch grumbled at our request, but had to yield. So the jurors saw him seated a few feet from the judge, with Ron Woods and me, wearing a sport jacket, slacks, and an open-neck shirt with a turtleneck under it. He did not look at all like one would imagine a mad bomber would look.

We knew that the jurors would seek to understand their job from the moment the case began. They would make an initial judgment about Terry Nichols. Federal judge Bernice Donald tells of a narcotics case over which she presided. Defense counsel approached the assembled prospective jurors and asked, "Who knows what a dope dealer looks like?" About half of the prospective jurors raised a hand. They then looked over at counsel table, to see an African-American defendant who for many of them "looked like" what they had in mind. After this demonstration of initial bias, the lawyer and the jurors could talk about the need to get beyond our prejudices.

Once the jury list had been pared down, voir dire began. One at a time, prospective jurors came into the courtroom and took a seat in the jury box. Judge Matsch, one of the prosecutors, and either Ron Woods or I asked detailed questions about what they had seen and read, and what if any conclusions they had formed.

We also focused on whether the juror would automatically favor the death penalty if there were a conviction, rather than following the judge's instructions about weighing aggravating and mitigating evidence. We needed to root out and move to disqualify any "automatic death penalty" juror.

Under the Supreme Court's decision in *Witherspoon v. Illinois*, every juror in a capital case must aver that he or she is willing to follow the court's instruction and under some circumstances to vote for a death penalty. There is a dispute among social scientists as to whether the resulting exclusions from jury service skews the pool of potential jurors in favor of the prosecution. I agree with those who say that it does, based on having observed jury selection in many capital cases.

All our jurors would, therefore, have accepted in one form or another the mythology of the death penalty: that it is a deterrent, which it is provably not; that it brings closure to victims' families, which it demonstrably does not; that it can be reliably administered, which has been proven not to be so. All jurors, at least in their mental imaginings, were willing to see another human being as the "Other," unworthy to live. Our task would be, if there was a penalty trial, to bring these mental attitudes into the law and evidence of a real-world set of events. Some have said that this process involves "humanizing" the defendant. My friend and colleague Rob Owen wryly notes that the defendant is already quite human enough. Our job is to wake jurors up to that fact.

Then there were jurors who said at first that they would not under any circumstances vote for a death penalty. The government challenged them for cause. We questioned them at length, trying to get a concession that yes, under some conceivable circumstances they would vote for death. When this line of inquiry succeeded, the government either had to use a peremptory challenge to remove the juror, or take the risk that if he or she was on the jury there would be no unanimous vote for death.

The trial was held in a large courtroom. In the spectators' section, there were rows of wooden benches, rather like church pews. As one entered the "well" of the courtroom, the jury box was on the right wall. Counsel tables for prosecution and defense were perpendicular to the jury box. Across the front wall was the judge's bench, with the witness chair on the right end of it, so the witness and jurors could see one another.

In the Nichols case, however, our team consisted of several lawyers and paralegal assistants other than Woods and me. We asked that we have a counsel table that permitted Ron, Terry, and me to face the jury, and another table perpendicular to that for our other team members. As with the initial jury selection gathering at the fairgrounds, we focused on the semiotics of courtroom arrangement.

In the McVeigh trial, the prosecutions table had been placed right up against the rail of the jury box. Assistant U.S. Attorney Vicki Behenna sat in the chair closest to the jurors. During emotional testimony she would silently weep and sniffle. McVeigh's lawyers had not objected to this behavior. As the Nichols trial approached, we asked Judge Matsch to order that she not sit at the prosecution's table. He denied our request, but cautioned the prosecutors and ruled no one could sit in the chair closest to the jurors.

At our counsel table facing the jury, Ron Woods and I sat on either side of Terry. Whenever a prosecutor mentioned a death sentence, one of us put a hand on Terry's shoulder. The implicit statement was "to get to him, you will have to get past us." Terry dressed as he had at the fairgrounds and listened carefully to the evidence with a neutral expression.

After five weeks of questioning, 12 jurors and 6 alternate jurors were selected and seated. All had sworn to listen to and fairly judge the evidence and to follow the judge's instructions if there was a penalty phase of trial. The trial of guilt or innocence took almost three months. We were able to show that the FBI's forensic examination of the bomb and bomb residue was deeply flawed and had been carried out by incompetent lab personnel. We showed how FBI agents "adjusted" their recollection of important events when their original version had become inconsistent with the government's developing theory of the case.

There was, to be sure, evidence that Terry Nichols and Timothy McVeigh had associated with each other over the relevant period of time, and that Terry had access to ammonium nitrate. To challenge the government's version of events, we called more than a hundred witnesses in our defense case, to build up an alternative version of events.

Arranging for these witnesses to come to Denver, stay in a hotel, and then be available when called was a difficult task. We needed the help of someone with relevant experience, and who would be better than someone who had supervised the arrival and billeting of Air Force recruits at Lackland Air Force Base? With Judge Matsch's approval, we hired retired Major Debra Meeks to do that job.

One theme of our defense was that the FBI had decided, once Terry Nichols and Tim McVeigh were in custody, to stop investigating other potential people and case theories. As Ron Woods said in opening statement: "If it please the Court, counsel, Mr. Nichols, members of the jury, the evidence will show that in conducting the investigation right after the bombing that the FBI did an excellent job—for a day and a half."

There was plenty of evidence that McVeigh had an accomplice, perhaps more than one, other than Terry Nichols, in planning the bombing. Yet the FBI decided to ignore all the evidence that someone other than Terry Nichols was involved. They had more than a thousand latent fingerprints from the agency where McVeigh had rented the truck and from a motel where he stayed. At those two locations, eyewitnesses said he was accompanied by someone who was not Nichols. Yet the FBI failed to check those fingerprints.

A government witness, Sergeant Wahl, testified he had seen a pickup truck that looked like Terry Nichols's truck—dark blue with a white camper top—at the state park where McVeigh mixed the bomb in the back of the rented Ryder truck. We challenged Sergeant Wahl's version of events. The government called Christopher Budke, the FBI agent who had interviewed him. Budke testified that Wahl had consistently said he saw a dark blue pickup truck.

I took Budke slowly through his meetings with Sergeant Wahl, asking at each juncture whether Budke had made a written record or note or summary of their conversation. My cross-examinations usually begin with this search for the witness's prior written or oral statements. Finally, Budke admitted he had written a "lead sheet." We were two and a half years into this case and three months into the trial. We had not heard of "lead sheets." It turned out that in addition to the typewritten 302 forms that agents made, copies of which had been given to the defense, they had also been making handwritten notes. We later learned that the government had withheld some 35,000 of these from the defense in the McVeigh and Nichols cases.

After some dispute, Judge Matsch ordered the prosecutor to give me Budke's lead sheet. He said he had written it while talking to Sergeant Wahl or immediately afterward. The lead sheet did not mention a blue pickup truck. I continued:

Q. So what it says is [Sergeant Wahl] observed a Ryder truck and a gray Chevy pickup truck parked at the lake. Isn't that what you wrote?
A. That's what I wrote.
Q. And that's what he told you?
A. He told me it was a dark-colored pickup truck, possibly gray.
Q. Sir, do you see the words "dark-colored" anywhere on this document that you wrote?
A. No, I don't; but that's what he told me.
Q. Is it your habit, sir, to write down something different from what witnesses tell you when you're conducting investigations?

This episode was only one of many where the government visibly fell short of fulfilling its promises. After the trial, several jurors focused on these events during interviews with the press. They said that they had come to their job with faith that the government, and especially the FBI, was a competent, capable, and on the whole honest organization whose work and word could be trusted. When this mythology was challenged, these jurors were at least willing to examine the evidence from a new point of view. And if we did not win an outright acquittal, perhaps jurors would hesitate to vote for a sentence of death.

I borrowed one theme in summation from the movie *A Few Good Men*, adapting Jack Nicholson's outburst to say of the prosecutors, "They can't handle the truth." The jury deliberated over several days. One of the jurors had told a friend about what was going on in the jury room. It seems that at one point, the jurors were 10 to 2 for acquittal on all counts. The verdict was an evident compromise. Not guilty of arson, not guilty of use of a weapon of mass destruction, not guilty of first degree murder or second degree murder of federal agents, but guilty of conspiracy and of involuntary manslaughter of the federal agents.

The verdict encouraged us. We argued that there should not now be a separate penalty trial to consider a possible death sentence. The Supreme Court had held that only first or second degree murder were serious enough

SENSING INJUSTICE

crimes to warrant a death sentence. The conspiracy count of the indictment did not allege that causing death was an object of the conspiracy. Judge
Matsch disagreed. The jurors were to return to court after a few days off, and
the government could make its case for death.

There was another, quite different reaction from the victims' group whose
members had been attending the trial, and others of whom had been watching
it on the live video transmission to Oklahoma City, which had been mandated
by special congressional legislation. In the same legislation, for which the
victims' group had lobbied, the Congress passed AEDPA, one part of which
would have the effect of limiting any appellate review of a death sentence.
The victims' group held public meetings at which speakers expressed anger
at the jurors, Terry Nichols, and defense counsel. In 2012, law professor Jody
Madeira published a book, *Killing McVeigh*. Based on hundreds of interviews
with survivors and victims' families, she documented this anger.

We felt the anger. Some members of the victims' group were heard to
make death threats against defense counsel. As it happened, my mother was
in Denver during this time, and it was the holiday season. Judge Matsch
assigned an armed female U.S. Marshal—in plain clothes—to accompany my
mother as she did holiday shopping in the crowded mall.

In the penalty phase of a capital trial, prosecutors are entitled to present
"victim impact evidence," testimony from family and associates of a homicide
victim about the trauma caused by this death. In the McVeigh penalty trial,
the defense did not object to emotion-laden testimony that we thought could
overwhelm the jurors' rational consideration of the evidence. For example,
in the McVeigh case, one witness gave a heartbreaking account of how she
kissed her son's feet and legs at the funeral home because his head and face
were so badly injured. We focused on the Supreme Court's direction that the
penalty decision must be a "reasoned moral response" to evidence about the
offense and the offender.

Judge Matsch cautioned the government not to repeat its McVeigh trial
tactics and warned he would intervene if necessary, without the defense having
to interrupt emotional testimony and thus incur juror disfavor for doing so.

Why did Matsch impose these limits? In the Nichols trial, our defense
benefited from some rulings that gave us more fairness and more leeway
than had been the case in McVeigh's trial. I believe, and so do the many trial
observers who have written about these cases, that it was our consistent legal
and factual arguments at every conceivable juncture that compelled Judge
Matsch to consider and rule upon trial rights issues that the McVeigh lawyers
had not raised.

Very soon after I was appointed by Judge Russell, I met with the law

students I had recruited; we discussed legal issues that we could foresee arising in the case. They put together a notebook of legal research, to which we
added as time went on. When trial began, I got up every morning at about
four, and went to the office. I thought about the legal and evidentiary issues
that we might confront that day in court. I would write a brief legal memorandum on one or more of these issues and send it to be filed with the court so
that Judge Matsch would see it first thing in the morning, These memos not
only presented the law; our filing them was a reminder that we were going to
insist on every procedural right that the law claimed to provide.

On reflection, I believe that Judge Matsch recognized that the government's case against Terry Nichols was weaker than the case against Tim
McVeigh, and that an appellate court would allow him less leeway in the event
of a conviction and death sentence.

Despite Judge Matsch's warnings, most of the victim witnesses in the
Nichols penalty phase were angry with the jurors for having delivered so
many acquittals, and showed it in their demeanor on the witness stand.
Family members of the dead federal agents were particularly outraged. The
courtroom spectators clearly, though silently, shared these emotions.

Almost every time a lawyer calls a witness, the lawyer and witness have met
beforehand and discussed what will be asked and what will be the answers.
The lawyer counsels the witness, within ethical limits, to achieve a desired
effect from the testimony. The desired effect of impact testimony is to encourage the jurors to vote for death. For a time, the Supreme Court held that such
testimony was too fraught with danger to the fairness of a penalty trial, then
decided to allow it.

The prosecutors' emotional jury speeches in the penalty phase were based
on the same idea of stirring up emotion-laden recollections of the bombing.
We had known all along that this would be their tactic. In my opening statement in the first phase of the trial, I said:

We do not contest that Timothy McVeigh did indeed conspire with several other people to blow up that building. We agree and understand and
stipulate and concede that at least 168 people died from that crime, that
the crime visited enormous harms on the hundreds of others. There's no
dispute about that. The dispute is can they overcome the presumption in
law that Terry Nichols had nothing whatever to do with it.

But I want to warn you: The prosecutors may choose not to accept
the reality that we accept. They may choose to put before you graphic,
emotional, tragic evidence of the devastation on April 19. These evidence—these events, I repeat, are—they're not in dispute. We understand

that there's not a joy the world can give like—like that it takes away. The prosecutors may replay these terrible images over and over as if to say that somebody has to be punished for these things. That, of course, is not the question. The question for you at the end of the evidence will be who; and that is a question to be answered, we trust, in the light shed by the evidence and the law and not in flashes of anger.

If the prosecutors present this evidence, our concern will be to show how it fits the picture that we have drawn and not theirs. We will cross-examine all the witnesses who come here, even those who have lost so much. By doing that, we mean them no disrespect. To the living, we owe respect. To the dead, we owe the truth.

As we approached the penalty trial, we decided that none of us—counsel or witnesses—would raise our voices above a conversational level, and that we would emphasize calm deliberation in every word and gesture. We could predict that the prosecutors would present impact evidence that to some greater or less extent would tell the jurors that their verdict was wrong. We did not predict that the prosecutors would present a penalty case that had all the fervor that they would have used if they had obtained a conviction on all the charges. Looking back, I believe that this overwrought view of events alienated some jurors. The jury foreperson, a nurse, had said on voir dire that she was wary of lawyers "manipulating the system." It is almost never possible to impose one's fervor on jurors. These jurors had shown by the time and care of their deliberations, and indeed in the answers on voir dire, that they would not be hurried along to judgment.

In closing argument, I reviewed the emotionally charged evidence the jury had heard:

> I feel now, when I think about that evidence, as though I'm standing before you and trying to sweep back a tide of anger and grief and vengeance. And I'm given pause by the fact that I feel that way, and I wonder if sometimes you might feel that way. But when I think that, then I think also of the instructions that the Judge is going to give you, because those instructions, as we contemplate this tide of anger and grief and vengeance, can get us all to higher ground, because the instructions will tell you that neither anger nor grief nor vengeance can ever be a part of a decision reached in a case of this kind.

Later in the summation, after talking about the evidence and the judge's instructions, I said:

When I concluded my earlier summation, I walked over to Terry Nichols and said. "This is my brother." And the prosecutor got up and reminded all of us, thinking that he would remind me, that there were brothers and sisters and mothers and fathers all killed in Oklahoma City. Of course, when I said, "This is my brother," I wasn't denying the reality of that. I hope I was saying something else. I was talking about a tradition that goes back thousands of years, talking about a particular incident, as a matter of fact. You may remember most of us learned it I think when we were young: the story of Joseph's older brothers, Joseph of the many-colored coat, now the *Technicolor Dream Coat* in the MTV version. And they were jealous of him, cast him into a pit thinking he would die, and then sold him into slavery. And years later, Joseph turns out to become a judicial officer of the pharaoh, and it happens that he is in a position to judge his brothers. And his brother Judah is pleading for the life or for the liberty of the younger brother, Benjamin; and Joseph sends all the other people out of the room and announces, "I am Joseph, your brother." That was the story, that was the idea that I was trying to get across; that in that moment, in that moment of judgment, addressing the very human being, his older brother Judah, who had put his life at risk and then sold him into slavery, he reached out, because even in that moment of judgment he could understand that this is a human process and that what we all share looks to the future and not to the past. . . .

I won't have a chance to respond to what the prosecutor says, but I know that after your 41 hours of deliberations on the earlier phase, you're all very, very accustomed to thinking of everything that could be thought. My brother is in your hands.

After days of deliberation, the jurors announced that they were deadlocked on the threshold question of Terry's intent toward resulting death. We read the federal death penalty statute as requiring jury unanimity for every phase of a penalty trial. In the ordinary criminal case, if the jury fails to agree there is a mistrial and the defendant may be retried. However, we argued that this law provided that if the jury were not unanimous then there could not be a death sentence. Put another way, every juror had to sign the verdict sheet for death, if such a sentence were to be imposed.

The government saw it differently. They argued that a jury deadlock meant that we would impanel another jury and they could once again seek a death verdict. The lead prosecutor moved for a mistrial. The judge said he had not decided how to read the statute. This presented us with a classic dilemma, made more painful by the fact that Terry's life was at stake. We thought the jury would never agree to a death penalty, but we could not be sure. If we were wrong, the stakes were too high. So we joined the motion for mistrial, but expressly conditioned our motion on our view that the judge should decide here and now that the jury had rejected death.

That was in the late afternoon. The next morning Judge Matsch called counsel to the bench. He said he had thought about the issue overnight and "I am going to take this verdict." He was calling a halt, ruling that the non-unanimity was a vote for life; the Supreme Court later held unanimously that this is the proper reading of the statute. Two of the prosecutors, as they heard this ruling, embraced each other and wept. They were weeping because they had not been able to get a death sentence. Their arguments for death, laden with emotional reminders of the carnage wrought in Oklahoma City, had not been rhetorical devices much less intentional excess. They had bought into the ideology of what they were doing.

I do not necessarily fault them for that. I simply observe that for many prosecutors seeking a death penalty is not the performance of an unpleasant duty but a step on a righteous crusade. I think it is dangerous to wield the power of the state with such fervency, for one is more easily led into the serious errors that scholars and lawyers and judges have found in capital cases.

The effect of the jury's decision was to give Judge Matsch the power to impose sentence, but not to impose a death sentence. Matsch sentenced Terry to life without parole, calling him "an enemy of the Constitution," whatever that meant. I asked on what statutory authority such a harsh sentence could rest. Matsch replied that he was applying the federal sentencing guideline for felony murder. I asked what the predicate felony was. Matsch replied that it was the conspiracy charge. I pointed out that, at common law, conspiracy was a misdemeanor and therefore as a matter of interpretation could not be the basis for felony murder. That crime required a completed felony offense, in the course of which someone was killed.

The court of appeals performed interpretive legerdemain and upheld the sentence. It seemed to us that our trial victories had given us all the justice that the system was willing to allow. We had, however, shown that with adequate resources and a committed trial team we could beat back the mythology that surrounds the wielders of prosecutorial power.

Prosecutors and politicians in the state of Oklahoma were dismayed by the jury's failure to impose a death sentence. In media interviews, books, and articles, people in the victims' groups excoriated the jury, Judge Matsch, and our defense team. Seeing that there might be a state court trial in Oklahoma, Judge Matsch agreed that our defense team could index and box all of our trial-related materials—hundreds of boxes. When that state trial came to be,

Brian Hermanson and Barbara Bergman led the defense. The jury convicted of more than 100 counts of first degree murder, but did not impose a death sentence.

RELATIONSHIP AND FORENSIC EVIDENCE

From my appointment to the Nichols case in April 1995, through the verdict and appeals in 1999, our defense team included several dozen people who were part of the effort for various periods of time. Ron Woods was the perfect colleague, as he brought unique skills and experience, including the insight gained during his service as an FBI agent and prosecutor.

More significantly, I met Jane Blanksteen. She was a law student at Columbia, having enrolled in law school after careers in journalism, media work, and even in her family's insurance business. Columbia has a requirement that all students perform forty hours of pro bono work sometime before graduating. Jane has relatives in Oklahoma City. One of her law school class-mates had met me while working as a summer intern at the Texas Resource Center for Capital Litigation. Jane wrote and asked if she could do pro bono work on the Nichols case.

She joined the team first using her media experience on our motion for change of venue. When her forty hours were done, she asked to continue to work with us. She used knowledge gained in the Columbia prisoners' rights clinic to work on Nichols's conditions of confinement, specifically the right to family visits. She offered to consult with Professor James Liebman at Columbia—a formidable expert—on constitutional issues presented by the federal death penalty statute.

She found her work on the defense team a worthwhile challenge. She declined two federal judicial clerkships and joined the team when she gradu-ated from Columbia in June 1996. On the team, she worked on preparing material for cross-examining the prosecution's forensic expert witnesses. At this time, the FBI's forensic laboratory, which had processed all the bomb res-idue and other related evidence, was under attack. Dr. Frederic Whitehurst, who worked at the lab, had revealed the incompetence of the lab's direc-tors, and the pro-prosecution bias of lab personnel. He was plaintiff in a whistleblower lawsuit related to his allegations. In sum, we had ample reason to investigate the provenance and reliability of the government's proposed expert witnesses.

Finally, in an effort to cleanse its crime scene findings, the prosecutors asked the leading British bomb site analyst, Linda Jones, to review the case and to testify as the prosecution's lead forensic witness. Because Jones had testified in UK bombing cases, we consulted Gareth Peirce, the solicitor who had worked on many such cases, and went to London to observe Jones in court. In 2019–20, we were fortunate to be working with Gareth again—in the Assange matter, as I discuss in chapter 16.

At trial, we had the same courtroom arrangement as during voir dire. Terry Nichols, Ron Woods, and I sat so we could see the jury box. Other counsel, paralegals, and investigators whose work was relevant to that day's proceedings sat at the perpendicular table. When Ron or I was addressing the judge or examining a witness, we stood at counsel's lectern. Neither of us likes to be interrupted when speaking, so we put an inbox on the table where our team was sitting, and gave each team member a stack of index cards, in a different color for each team member. Thus, if a team member wanted to communicate, he or she would write a note on a card and put the card in the box.

Over two or three days in mid-trial, the prosecution called more than a dozen forensic expert witnesses. As I rose to cross-examine each such witness, I had the notebook that Jane had prepared with the witness's prior statements and other materials to use in questioning. Jane's index cards were purple; she would be sending me notes as I did the examination. On the second morning, the court clerk told us that jurors had been observing the inbox and cards. One of them had said to another, "Did you notice that when Mrs. Tigar puts a purple card in the box, that Mr. Tigar is about to beat up on the witness."

Jane and I had been married by a Denver judge, in a ceremony in the defense offices. When the trial was over, I did not want to return to Austin. I had a dream that I would explore the Atlantic Intracoastal Waterway from its origins in the Chesapeake Bay to its end in Florida. Jane was game. We bought a Beneteau 321 sailboat, and found a house in Annapolis, Maryland, near the water.

I was hired to teach at Washington College of Law. On weekends we became familiar with sailing our boat, *Lady Jane*. In the fall of 2000, we began to sail south, and I had my sixtieth birthday dinner in Marathon, Florida—at Porky's Bayside restaurant—"Swinin' and Dinin.'" We traded the Beneteau a couple of years later for a Hunter 420, a 42-foot center cockpit sloop. When we had time off for the next decade and more, we sailed from Long Island to the Keys and out to the Bahamas.

For this past quarter-century, we have worked and lived together for the clients whose stories it remains to tell.

SOUTH AFRICA, MITIGATION, AND THE KENYA EMBASSY BOMBING

I have turned the Nichols summation over and over in my mind, wondering what was in it that might have struck a chord with jurors, and helped them to look beyond the devastation of the Oklahoma bombing. In the summer of 2001, a New York federal jury refused to impose a death sentence on two men convicted in the Kenya U.S. embassy bombing that took more than two hundred lives. A defendant in that case, Khalfam Mohamed, had been arrested in South Africa on his arrival there from Tanzania. A South African immigration officer and an FBI agent cooked up a story that Mohamed had demanded to be sent to the United States to stand trial on the bombing charges. He was quoted as saying that he wished to be with his comrades even if that meant facing a death sentence.

The South African authorities obligingly put him into the FBI's hands and deported him to New York. Had he demanded formal extradition, South Africa would have imposed a condition that no death penalty be sought. Such a condition is mandated by South Africa's constitution, as interpreted by the unanimous Constitutional Court. The same condition was imposed as to another defendant extradited from Germany in the same case.

David Ruhnke, Mohamed's lawyer, helped to initiate proceedings in South Africa seeking a judicial declaration that Mohamed's removal was unlawful. Given U.S. Supreme Court case law, a favorable decision in South Africa would not bar the U.S. courts from trying him. Our courts, with some cogent dissents, still hew to the now-discredited view that it does not matter how the prisoner is brought to the forum, even if doing so violates international law.

However, Ruhnke argued that a declaration by the South African courts that Mohamed should not as a matter of South African law face the death penalty would be a mitigating factor on which the judge in New York might instruct the sentencing jury. Mohamed's lawyers lost in the trial court and lodged an appeal with the South Africa Constitutional Court. As it happened, Jane and I were in South Africa the week the case was to be argued. We had lunch with Justice Richard Goldstone in his chambers.

Justice Goldstone asked me to read Ruhnke's affidavit and the rest of the appeal record, and to help his clerks research whether or not a South African decision would make a difference in the American courts, or whether the case was mooted by Mohamed having been deported. I did as he asked.

In late May 2001, the Constitutional Court decided the case. It recognized that South Africa would have attached a condition to any formal extradition. It held that when a country sends someone from its borders—by deportation, extradition, or whatever—into the hands of another country, the sending state bears a responsibility to ensure that the person will not be subjected to invasion of his or her rights in the receiving state. Because the Constitutional Court had held that the death penalty violated South Africa's post-apartheid constitution, deporting Mohamed risked his being executed in violation of South African law.

I emailed the decision to Ruhnke as soon as it arrived. He convinced Judge Sand to instruct the jury that as a matter of South African law Mohamed would not face a death penalty, and that the jurors must consider this as a mitigating factor. He and his team also assembled a picture of the client's background and personal experience, documenting the perceived injustices that motivated him to act. The jury deadlocked, resulting in a life sentence. This was not such a stretch of mitigation law. The statute and the Constitution give the defense wide latitude. In *Nichols*, for example, we had asked Judge Matsch to tell the jury that one mitigating factor is that "Terry Lynn Nichols is a human being." The government argued that we were trying to smuggle anti-capital punishment sentiment into the case. Judge Matsch gave the instruction.

The life verdict in that case is a tribute to David Ruhnke's brilliance as an advocate. One measure of that brilliance is his ability to weave the South African decision into a narrative about justice. In the life or death struggles of capital litigation, we welcome these reminders that advocacy can make a difference, and that judges and jurors can see through and beyond mythologies about vengeance and portrayals of some "other" humans as unworthy of full respect.

ORLANDO HALL

In early 2000, Rob Owen asked me to help in a post-conviction challenge to a federal death penalty sentence. In 1994, Orlando Hall, a young African-American from South Arkansas, participated in the kidnapping, rape, and murder of Lisa Rene. The crime was linked to an interstate marijuana distribution operation in which Hall was involved. The crime took place near Dallas, Texas.

Hall was tried in federal court in Fort Worth, Texas, and sentenced to death. The Fifth Circuit affirmed his conviction in 1998. Rob Owen and Marcy Widder began a post-conviction challenge to the conviction and death sentence. They had evidence of racial bias in venue selection and jury selection, in the decision to seek the death penalty, and in the overall administration of the federal death penalty. They challenged Orlando's treatment on death row, and the lethal injection protocol intended for use in the execution chamber.

Rob and Marcy asked me to review the transcript and give an opinion whether Hall's appointed counsel had been constitutionally ineffective. Over the years, I—like other older lawyers with experience—have given written and oral testimony on this issue. Criteria for performance of the defense role may be gathered from experience, as well as from authoritative works such as the

American Bar Association's *Guidelines for the Appointment & Performance of Defense Counsel in Death Penalty Cases,* which have been cited in some Supreme Court opinions.

I found that Orlando's counsel had not done meaningful investigation until shortly before trial, and so was not able to find witnesses and other evidence such as what an investigator might find. More egregiously, counsel did not do a thorough investigation into Orlando's troubled childhood and the brutal treatment he had received as a child. They did not search for, and therefore did not find, the many witnesses who from personal experience could have given significant mitigation testimony. In fact, four days into the trial phase, the mitigation specialist appointed by the court complained to trial counsel that they had done virtually nothing to investigate crucial aspects of potential mitigation evidence. I provided an affidavit as an expert witness.

The trial court rejected all of these claims, refusing even to hold an evidentiary hearing. The court of appeals affirmed; the Supreme Court denied certiorari. By now, it was 2007. Orlando Hall was on federal death row. Rob and Marcy, with the help of Owen Bonheimer from the firm of Steptoe & Johnson, filed a Petition Alleging Violation of Human Rights with the Inter-American Commission on Human Rights. IACHR is established by and hears matters arising under the American Declaration of the Rights and Duties of Man. My affidavits became part of the record before the IACHR. On October 29, 2010, I testified at the IACHR. Rob Owen's argument that day focused on the ways in which Orlando's case raised issues under the Declaration, and under general international law, beyond the violations of U.S. law.

In my testimony, a cameo appearance in the larger context of this case, I identified the right to counsel in international human rights principles developed over centuries and recognized in treaties, state practice, and the opinion of jurists. I discussed counsel's historic obligation to bridge the intellectual, social, and cultural gap between the defendant and the triers of fact.

Barack Obama was president when the hearing was held. I expected that the Obama administration government lawyers would at least be respectful of our contentions, and of Orlando's situation. Not so. They were dismissive and snide. One of them intoned nasally, "Not *everybody* can have a lawyer like Mr. *Tigar,* you know!"

On January 18, 2019, IACHR sent a draft copy of its report to the U.S. government, asking for a response within two months. The United States did not respond. On June 10, 2019, the Commission issued its report.

In 15 single-spaced pages, the Commission upheld all of Orlando's claims. It traced the history of racism in the administration of the death penalty. In summary:

On the basis of determinations of fact and law, the Inter-American Commission concluded that the State is responsible for the violation of Articles I (life, liberty, and security), II (equality before the law), IV (freedom of expression), XVIII (fair trial), XXV (protection from arbitrary detention), and XXVI (due process) of the American Declaration.

The Commission sent its decision to Secretary of State Pompeo, demanding that he provide relief. Pompeo and Attorney General Barr ignored the decision and ordered Orlando executed before a new administration could take office. Orlando was executed on November 19, 2020.

Our only solace is that the IACHR decision is one more element in a worldwide movement to abolish the death penalty, and to expose the racism in its administration

Rob, Marcy, and Owen succeeded in defining and extending the international human rights principles that have so far been honored by the countries that have abolished the death penalty. IACHR spoke to the basic idea of "human rights," which is that it is at its core an idea about "humans."

I continue to respond, to the extent I am able, to requests to assist lawyers involved in this work: writing, consulting, teaching. My daughter Katherine McQueen is a physician specializing in addiction medicine and internal medicine. She has been an expert mitigation witness in the penalty phase of capital cases, explaining to the jurors that adolescent drug abuse can impair the ability to make good decisions, and that a life sentence will give the brain a chance to heal. She and I have team-taught this topic at capital defense seminars.

CHAPTER 14

Politics Not as Usual

Considering many of the cases and issues in this book, you may wonder how a lawyer can make a living with so heavy a pro bono docket. There are several kinds of answers to this question. Once I was representing a corporate executive during a grand jury investigation. He said, "I heard that you represented Angela Davis." I said yes, I had. "Well, how is it that you can represent me and her, given that politically we have nothing in common?" I asked him what his biggest problem was at the moment. He said, "This prosecutor seems hell-bent on messing up my life."

"That's interesting," I said. "That was Angela's problem too."

He then said, "Yes, but did you charge her what you are charging me?" I thought this uncharitable of him, because his legal fees were being advanced by the corporation as permitted by Delaware law. But I answered, "I represented her without a fee."

"How does that work?" he asked.

"She was an underdog. I represent a lot of underdogs. I make it up by charging market rates to the overdogs. That's you." He seemed happy to be an overdog.

In the same vein, a congressman under indictment sat in my office with his longtime friend, a very conservative lawyer. Indeed, this lawyer had been a prosecutor of whom Ed Williams had said, "He gets up every morning and pisses on the Bill of Rights."

The lawyer said to the congressman, "OK, you don't have to worry. I'll protect your right wing and Tigar here will protect your left wing."

"Wings, hell," the congressman said, "it's my ass I want protected."

The lesson here is that you can represent controversial clients and still get "ordinary" business. The smart clients, and the firms that refer litigation, want a certain kind of representation and they respect those who battle for underdogs. There are exceptions: Two days after the press reported that I had been appointed to represent Terry Nichols, a major corporation for whom I had been litigating fired me.

When Sam Buffone and I started our law firm in January 1978, we made sure that one-third of our billable hours were pro bono. We still made a good living. That brings up the next point. If you wish to get rich beyond your dreams, then sell cocaine or become an investment banker. Of course, you stand some chance of going to Club Fed if you make that sort of career choice. By the same token, I am saddened to see our very best law graduates opting for large law firms where they will be required to bill inhuman hours and will have neither meaningful pro bono work nor great responsibility for litigation. That sort of environment provably leads to burnout and alienation, or puts you on a ladder that you need to keep on climbing to support the lifestyle you acquire.

I find it hard to sympathize with the young lawyer, let's call him Bob Cratchit, told by the partner to stay in on Christmas Day to draft one hundred more interrogatories, if he is making six figures and signed up for this with his eyes open. I am not condemning Cratchit's choice, only saying that there are other choices out there.

Smaller litigation firms still get good business and do a good job, often better than the leviathans. When a major client asked me to head up a litigation project, I kept the team as small as possible. When I think of the behemoth law firms and their approach to litigation, I am reminded of the Texan who got off an airplane at Shannon Airport in Ireland and rented a car. He drove into the countryside and stopped to talk to a farmer who was standing near the roadway. "Tell me," the Texan asked, "how big a spread do you have here?"

"Well," said the farmer, "it goes along this stone wall to that hedgerow, and then up to the top of that rise where the sheep are standing, then along over to that line of trees."

"Is that all?" said the Texan. "Back where I live, I get in my car in the morning, and I drive and I drive and I drive, and by sundown I still haven't got to the edge of my ranch."

"Oh," said the farmer, "I had a car like that once."

In sum, it is possible to do well enough and to do enough good. It is possible to practice law, or at least the kind I like to do, in a setting that satisfies. Over the years I have managed to blend practice and teaching in this sort of way. Candidly, it is harder to find a job that includes a heavy dose of public service than it used to be. The cuts in legal services funding have seen to that, as have law firms' reluctance to take on pro bono work. On that latter point, I used my position as Chair of the ABA Litigation Section to lobby firms along these lines: Doing pro bono helps your bottom line. It tunes up your associates by giving them challenging work. It gives you good publicity.

All of this fails, however, to answer the question, "What kinds of cases ought one to take and what kinds should one shun?" I have made choices some have disagreed with, but have tried to develop a working way to answer this question. My answer will not be right for everyone. That is as it should be. The personal decision to take or decline a case resides with the lawyer. For the representation to work, the lawyer and client have to connect at some point. You must find the client's story compelling at some level of abstraction.

You can think of this from the standpoint of the jurors (or judge) who will try your client's case. If you are suing for $100,000, the jurors don't think of their decision as a "zero sum" matter, in which $100,000 is subtracted from one side's assets and placed with the other. They believe that they are adding to the net store of justice in the world, and they should be helped by lawyer argument to see it that way. So you have to ask, in the first moment, "where is the injustice in this case?" If you can't answer that, maybe some other lawyer can, and that case should go to that lawyer and not to you. When Ed Williams joked that the ideal client was "rich as Croesus and scared as hell," he captured the image obliquely. Whatever has scared that client must be seen as a kind of actual or prospective injustice.

In law practice, as in the rest of life, we may not be presented all at once with a cosmic decision as was Faust, or Jabez Stone in the American version, where the devil offers us a bargain for our soul.

The image of the devil fighting for the soul pervades our literature. Images from Stephen Vincent Benét's *The Devil and Daniel Webster*, or the cadences of Milton's *Paradise Lost*, enliven our speech and our perceptions. The devil, we say, is in the details, or in the bottle in front of us. For, as we know,

> Malt does more than Milton can
> To justify God's ways to man.

In lawyer circles, there is the story of the young law student standing in front of the career services bulletin board and shaking his head. An older gentleman appears beside him. "Why the frown?" the older man inquires.

"There are no jobs in public service," the young man laments. "To make money and pay off your law school debt, you have to sell your soul."

"And what," asks the old man, "is wrong with that?"

"Well for one thing you go to hell when you die."

"That's not so bad."

"Oh, come on!"

"No, really. I'm the devil, and I know."

"Oh, sure! The devil."

"You don't believe me. Come with me for a while. I'll have you back before your next class."

And with that, the young man was spirited away to a sort of paradise. Soft breezes blew. There were refreshing drinks and good things to eat. Beautiful young men and women swam in the lagoon. The young man spent several days there, and then by some magic was back where he had been standing— and hardly any time had passed.

So he sold his soul. He became successful, and wealthy. Unlike some who followed in the same path, the United States Attorney never bothered him, and he certainly did not go to Club Fed.

As it must to all mortals, death came to him. And he went to hell. It was a fiery furnace. The noise and stench were unbearable. The cries and groans of eternal anguish rattled around inside his head.

After a few days of this, by his reckoning of time, he demanded to see the devil. There was a wait, but his wish was granted. There in an air-conditioned office sat the older gentleman who had recruited him.

"Look," the fellow said. "When you and I made the deal, I came down here. It was beautiful, peaceful—nothing like what's out there."

"Ah, yes," said the old gentleman, "you must have been in our summer associate program."

No, I don't worry too much about that kind of bargain, though it has in various forms been the subject of popular literature, including the movies. As a lawyer, I may make metaphorical use of the Faustian legend, as I defend the life or liberty of someone committed to my care. But in my life, my own piecemeal bargains, the legend lives as well. I say to myself, fearful of my own failures to heed my fellow creatures' calls for justice: What if I wanted some day to sell my soul to Mephisto. I might see him at a distance, that old gentleman. Quickening my step, I catch him by the shoulder and he turns to look me in the face.

"Mephisto, old man, remember me? I am ready to sell you my soul."

And he looks at me, finally recognizing who I am. "*Your* soul?," he says with that smile of his. "I already have it."

Wishing therefore to find cases that enrich in all the right ways, including the way that pays the rent, I have been led down some wond'rous paths. I take up this theme again in chapter 17, titled "Envoi."

LEERY OF LEARY

In 1973, I took a break from writing *Law and the Rise of Capitalism* and came to California to represent Michael Randall. He had been charged in state court with a batch of felonies for possession and distribution of marijuana and LSD. He was said to be a leader of the Brotherhood of Eternal Love, a group of hippie dope-smokers who more or less followed the teachings of Dr. Timothy Leary. Indeed, Leary had dwelt among the Brotherhood until his arrest and imprisonment on California state marijuana charges.

Leary had escaped from his California prison on September 13, 1970, and was rumored to be in Algeria, or Gstaad, or somewhere. However, prosecutions of his erstwhile associates continued. I packed up and moved into a rented house in Laguna Beach, California, and drafted a batch of motions to suppress the evidence against Randall and his co-defendants.

The state's investigation of the Brotherhood had been sloppy. The police had seldom bothered to get warrants, and the probable cause was thin for their warrantless searches. Why should I get involved in all of this? I never tuned in to the "dope culture." I thought "drop out" was a cop-out. The social problems of racism, poverty, and war were not going to be solved by living up in the canyon and tending marijuana gardens. These folks even lacked the sort of coherent worldview that characterized intentional communities like the Quakers, Shakers, and utopian socialists.

But defending the Fourth Amendment against police misconduct seemed a good fight, and ultra-conservative Orange County seemed the right place to do it. At that time, California law conferred "standing" to challenge an illegal seizure upon any defendant against whom the evidence was to be used, even if the search was of somebody else's person, car, or house. The federal law limited standing to the actual "victim" of the illegal search, and the Supreme Court had expressly rejected the California rule. The liberal standing rules in California state court meant that I could file more than a hundred motions to suppress evidence for Randall, based on almost every conceivable Fourth Amendment issue.

We were lucky. Our trial judge was Raymond Vincent, who thought it was his job to enforce the Constitution even on behalf of unpopular defendants. We were winning about two-thirds of the motions to suppress. I was working with San Francisco lawyer Michael Kennedy. While we were litigating these motions, Timothy Leary was arrested in Kabul, Afghanistan, and brought back to Orange County jail. He would face federal passport charges, in addition to his alleged role in the Brotherhood case being tried in Orange County and of course his escape from California state prison. I had met Leary only once, back in 1966 when he came by radio station KPFK in Los Angeles for an interview with another staff member. Michael Kennedy had represented him in the California courts. Leary, through another lawyer, asked that Michael and I come to see him.

This was a lawyer-client conversation, but Leary's later behavior has blown the privilege, so I can tell the story. Leary looked gaunt, but his blue eyes sparkled. He began to talk. He had been in Switzerland, and some member of the Afghan royal family had urged him to visit Afghanistan where narcotics were plentiful. Before Leary could get there, the old royal family was displaced. He was met at the airport by American drug enforcement agents and escorted back to the United States.

Simply put, Leary wanted Michael and me to represent him in the Orange County cases. We said we already had a client, Michael Randall, and could not do that. Leary tightened his lips. His expression became slightly demented. He looked at Kennedy and said, "Michael, if you don't represent me, I can make things very tough for you." Michael shrugged and we left.

A couple of years later, Leary struck a bargain with the federal and state authorities, and offered to give testimony against his former wife, Rosemary, his former lawyers, and others. For a time, the Justice Department tried to sell those cases to local U.S. Attorneys in various parts of the country. Nobody was buying. I represented one of the targets of his proposed testimony, whom the government proposed to charge with helping Leary to escape from prison.

"You know," the Justice Department lawyer said, "Leary has waived his attorney-client privilege, so we can subpoena all his former lawyers if we want to."

"A waiver, to be valid, must be made by someone in possession of his faculties. Where did he send the waiver from," I asked, "Pluto?"

One of the proposed cases went so far as to land on the desk of William Browning, the U.S. Attorney for the Northern District of California. Browning was a Republican appointee, a civil trial lawyer from the Peninsula. He had prosecuted Patty Hearst, and had bested F. Lee Bailey.

I sat in his office with the Justice Department lawyer. "You know," I said, "this DOJ lawyer has never tried a major case in his life. I want to talk to you about his idea that you should use Leary as your main prosecution witness. Leary has written a book admitting that he has told seventeen different stories of his prison escape. So if your direct examination takes two hours, I have thirty-four hours of cross. In one of his stories, he said that he was having LSD flashbacks and that he thought he was a Buick and that every other prisoner was a Chevrolet, and he just had to get away. Leary is so far out that his testimony would really be a story from the center of Uranus."

Browning smiled, but did not commit. Two weeks later, he sent word that the grand jury had refused to indict based on Leary's story. Rumor was that Browning had frankly told the grand jurors the problems with these cases. I respected Browning for his actions. Unlike so many prosecutors, he saw the weakness of the bargained-for testimony and evaluated the case without yielding to the political pressure to charge somebody.

JOHN CONNALLY

I used to have a picture on my wall, drawn by a courtroom artist, of the Connally defense table; the picture is now at the Briscoe Center for American History. I am sitting between Ed Williams and Connally. Connally had been Treasury Secretary in the Nixon administration. He was a Democrat, and had been governor of Texas. Most people recognized him because he was riding in the car with President Kennedy on Assassination Day, and was himself seriously wounded.

Connally had always supported the cause of agribusiness, and openly opposed plans to cut milk price supports. The issue arose in 1972, and the dairy farmer associations were awash with well-paid lobbyists. One of these, an Austin, Texas, lawyer named Jake Jacobson, was Connally's longtime friend.

When the Congressional and Special Prosecutor investigations of the 1972 Nixon reelection campaign uncovered the milk lobby's financial records, suspicion focused on the Jacobson-Connally relationship. The milk lobby group, Associated Milk Producers, Inc. (AMPI) had given Jacobson $10,000, and its records suggested that this money was for Connally, as a "thank you" for his support.

Jacobson admitted he had received the money. He said he offered the money to Connally, who refused it. Jacobson repeated this story several times under oath. He said that he had kept the money in his safe deposit box, and he indeed opened his box and produced $10,000 in cash. This gesture simply increased suspicion, because several of the bills were signed by George Schultz, who had succeeded Connally as Treasury Secretary. It was, of course, impossible that Jacobson could have received those bills from AMPI while Connally was Treasury Secretary.

The Watergate Special Prosecutor indicted Jacobson for lying about Connally refusing the money. The indictment was dismissed because the prosecutor's grand jury questions had been inept and Jacobson could plausibly claim that he did not deny giving the money. Jacobson was asked in effect, "Is it your testimony that you did not give the money?" He answered, "Yes."

And indeed, that was his testimony. It might have been false, but it was his. So he had told the literal truth, and under Chief Justice Burger's opinion for the Supreme Court in *United States v. Bronston*, that meant he could not be a perjurer. The prosecutors persevered, however, and Jacobson eventually pleaded guilty to giving Connally money. In exchange for this testimony, the prosecutors forewent any more perjury charges, dismissed Texas indictments charging Jacobson with looting three savings and loan associations of millions of dollars, and agreed to help Jacobson keep his law license.

The Watergate Special Prosecutor's office had achieved a formidable reputation for integrity and success. They had won all their cases but one. That one, an acquittal of agribusiness magnate Dwayne Andreas, had come in a case defended by Ed Williams.

By the time the Connally case was brought, Leon Jaworski had become Special Prosecutor. Although Jaworski recused himself from the Connally matter, his years-long antagonism and rivalry to Connally and the Vinson-Elkins-Connally law firm fueled some suspicion that this was a grudge match. That suspicion was not, however, widespread. The media were nearly unanimous in putting the case in the best pro-prosecution light.

That attitude palpably changed during the trial. Ed's cross-examination of Jacobson was classically brilliant. I had traced every one of the bills that Jacobson had turned over, and the government's theory came apart. Jacobson had indeed received $10,000 to give to Connally, but soon afterward had applied just that sum to his own mounting pile of debts.

Connally's testimony showed all the characteristics that had brought him success and that commended him to me as a friend in later years. He was measured and firm, and radiated a sense of confidence. This was difficult, for the trial bore down upon him, as he struggled to maintain his air of command in the face of family and friends.

Character witnesses took the stand one after another. The expected strong white males, such as Ambassador Robert S. Strauss, Jack Valenti, Robert McNamara, and Dean Rusk. Barbara Jordan, the African-American member of Congress who had led the impeachment proceedings against Richard Nixon, surprised us all by agreeing to testify for Connally. When she had been a state senator in Texas and he was governor he had behaved honorably and she was there to recognize that despite the passage of time and despite Connally's defections, first to Nixon and then to the Republican Party.

Reverend Billy Graham was a character witness. Ed asked him, "What is your name?" "I am the Reverend Doctor Billy Graham" came the booming reply. "What is your business or occupation?" "I preach the gospel of Jesus Christ all over the world," the witness declaimed. "Amen!" exclaimed Juror

No. 5, an African-American woman who carried a Bible in her purse and read from it during breaks in the action.

My favorite character witness was Lady Bird Johnson. We sat one weekend in the 8th-floor conference room just off Ed's office and talked about being a character witness. Bob Strauss sat with us, as a longtime family friend and counselor. Mrs. Johnson said she was nervous about testifying.

"It really is a formula," I said. "Ed will ask you how you know John Connally, and then put the two questions permitted of character witnesses. He will ask your opinion of his character for integrity, and then what you know of his reputation for integrity. Then he will ask the same two questions about the attribute of truthfulness, since Connally has testified and his honesty is relevant."

"Yes," Mrs. Johnson said, "but I am not sure how I should be, if you know what I mean."

"Mrs. Johnson," I said, "when I first came to Washington in 1966 and your husband was president, you were very active in establishing parks where children could play. I lived on Capitol Hill then, in a racially mixed neighborhood, and I remember you coming to dedicate these parks. The people on this jury are just like the parents of those children who came to hear you speak."

On the stand the next day, Mrs. Johnson was her usual poised self. She answered the ritual questions, and then, with no question pending, turned and looked right at the jury. "You know," she said, "there are a lot of people who don't like John, but there's nobody who says he isn't honest." This was a perfect comment in so many ways. It counterbalanced Connally's evident arrogance, a quality that turned off voters. It was heartfelt.

When the case went to the jury, it was early afternoon. Bob Strauss was there, and he predicted that the jury would be back in time for dinner. He had ordered all the ingredients for a victory party delivered to his Watergate apartment. Strauss was right, and we celebrated that night.

Back in 1967, when I first came to Washington, I had been junior lawyer to Ed Williams in the defense of Robert G. "Bobby" Baker, the secretary to the Senate majority. We lost. As the Connally jury came in, I was sitting next to Ed at counsel table. The foreman stood to announce the verdict. Ed's hand tightened on my leg. "Not guilty." Twice. Ed had tears in his eyes. "Well," he murmured, "that makes up for the last time."

I got a lot of criticism for participating in the Connally defense, from old friends and comrades on the left who wondered how I could represent somebody like that. I liked Connally personally, and thought the deal for testimony that had been struck with Jacobson was lousy. The case was worth defending.

As Connally's personal fortunes declined, and I had moved to Austin, I continued to help him and his family.

In a more general sense, there is something pleasing about representing conservatives charged with crime. Indictment gives them cognitive dissonance, for their previous suspicion about defendants' rights is first challenged and then evaporates. One can only hope they hold on to the lesson. Connally certainly did, and lent his voice to attacks on grand jury abuse and unfair plea bargains.

In a related vein, during one trial of a political figure, we were sitting in the office after court one day. The client suggested that we call as a defense witness a once-powerful but now disgraced and convicted political ally in order to establish a fairly marginal point. Ed and I argued against this course. The client persisted. Finally, Ed said with some exasperation. "It will create a diversion. It will be like blowing up the courthouse." The client replied heatedly, "Well, you know, they have done everything they can to get me in this case. They have spent ten million dollars if they've spent a dime. They have gone to every one of my clients and friends. I am sunk even if I'm acquitted. I say let's blow up the courthouse." I looked at him and said, "You know, you are the second client I've represented who said he wanted to blow up the courthouse." Ed chimed in, "Yes, but the other one said it before he was indicted."

JOAN IRVINE SMITH

In Orange County, California, early in the twentieth century, James Irvine assembled more than 90,000 acres into the Irvine ranch. By 1975, there were some 88,000 acres left, but control had drifted into the hands of a foundation controlled by major corporate interests, with the Irvine family holding only a 22 percent stake. The foundation proposed to sell its interest to Mobil Corporation for $123 million.

For years, Joan Irvine Smith, the founder's granddaughter, had battled against the foundation. Indeed, she had lobbied for the legislation that forced it to divest. She thought the Mobil deal grossly undervalued the ranch, and she did not like Mobil. She wanted to see a leveraged buyout whereby the family could regain control. In fact, due to our litigation victories she was able to make that deal.

I got the case early in 1975. Chuck Robb, who was later Virginia governor and U.S. senator, was the associate initially assigned. Our job was to enjoin the proposed deal, whereby the foundation would sell its stock in the Irvine Corporation. The foundation was a California entity. The corporation had been formed in West Virginia. Joan lived in Virginia. We could piece together a diversity action to be in federal court, though we did not have a federal question that would survive analysis.

In those days, there was no federal courthouse in Orange County. We would be litigating in downtown Los Angeles before a judge who might or might not know or care about the impact of 88,000 Orange County acres—including prime beachfront—passing into the hands of an oil company. So we filed our lawsuit in Orange County Superior Court, during a month when the regular probate judge was handling preliminary injunctions. He was careful and scholarly, and understood fiduciary duties from several perspectives.

Lawyers sometimes choose a forum automatically, marching into federal or state court, or filing in a state with only marginal contacts, without thinking through the consequences. A hasty forum choice can condemn the client to years of litigation that never touches the merits. We needed to get this case heard.

Our theory was that a dominant majority shareholder in a closely held corporation owes a fiduciary duty to the minority shareholders to get a fair price when it sells out. The law in support of this view was not uniformly in our favor. However, this majority shareholder was a nonprofit corporation, subject to regulation by the state of California. We convinced the attorney general that the price was inadequate, so the State joined us as plaintiff, in its capacity as parens patriae. Not only did we get a valuable ally, but I was able to argue that the court should consider denying our motion for preliminary injunction and granting the state's motion. The state did not have to post a bond.

Mobil invited Joan to a meeting to lay out its real estate plans for the property, hoping to gain her support. The meeting was on February 14, 1975, and when the Mobil lawyer wished her Happy Valentine's Day, Joan said between her teeth, "Yeah, the massacre."

In discovery, we found that the corporation had enough cash flow and liquid assets to make a leveraged buyout possible. But that merely meant that we were not asking for a remedy that would do no good. Our story was that of the Irvine family being frozen out of their patrimony, and a big chunk of Orange County passing into the control of Mobil. The foundation's lawyer argued at length that the case law did not support us.

When it was my turn, I discussed the cases that were on our side, then turned to a broader theme:

This court sits, as Your Honor knows from long experience, in equity. The consolidation of law and equity in code pleading has not abolished the unique role of the court of equity. The chancellor of England got his legal principles from a different source than did the common law judges. He relied on rules derived from the canon law and ultimately Roman law. Indeed the term "fiduciary" is a corruption of a Latin word, *fideijussor*, meaning bearer of rights.

Now, Mr. Privett has cited a lot of cases, essentially arguing that because in certain older cases majority shareholders could behave in a certain way, it must be all right here. I am reminded of Pope Urban II, of the eleventh century, who received a letter from a peasant complaining that the lord was grinding him down by unfair exactions. Gregory asked the lord to explain, and he said he was doing no more to these peasants than was permitted by the custom of that place. Gregory replied, and I would say to Mr. Privett, "The lord thy God hath said my name is Truth; he hath not said my name is Custom."

We won a preliminary injunction and the Irvine family at last took some control of their patrimony. I am not sure I approve of the development that has taken place on those acres, but one bright spot is a progressive law school that is part of the University of California system.

EDWARD HUDSON

Ed Hudson was an engineer by profession. He and his company had built major oil and gas projects in the United States and abroad. He was honored by the French and Algerian governments for his role in building pipelines in North Africa. Politically, he was somewhere over on the right. He had been a good friend of old H. L. Hunt, the reclusive and unorthodox Dallas oil magnate. This friendship brought him into touch with Hunt's two sons, Herbert and Bunker. These two were later to amass and then dramatically lose a fortune in a foolish effort to corner the silver market.

Back in 1975, the Hunts were mainly in the oil business. Like their father, they tended to be secretive and suspicious. Their suspicions led them to hire an investigator to wiretap some of their employees. This was illegal. The investigator was clumsy: he was caught climbing down a telephone pole on the outskirts of Dallas, where he had been servicing a wiretap recording unit.

The government charged and convicted the investigator under the federal wiretap statute. But the prosecutors suspected that the Hunts had paid the wiretappers, and they pursued this suspicion before a federal grand jury. The Hunts were apparently worried about this investigation. Ed Hudson entered the picture.

According to the government's allegations, the Hunts asked Hudson to retain famed criminal defense lawyer Percy Foreman to represent the wiretappers, in the hope that Foreman would induce them to refuse to testify about who hired them to do the wiretap. Hudson was not a lawyer, and saw nothing particularly wrong with carrying money and instructions from the Hunt boys to Foreman. After all, the wiretappers were going to get a lawyer, and they wouldn't have to pay Foreman's fees.

This sort of thing often happens in the pro bono world, where an organization pays legal fees to someone under government attack. The difficulty arises when the payor wants to influence the choice of lawyer, or worse yet, wants the lawyer to represent the payor's interests rather than devote his undivided loyalty to the true client. The government obviously thought that the Hunts were paying Foreman to keep the investigators quiet rather than simply provide representation. Ed Williams tried unsuccessfully to talk Justice Department lawyer Guy Goodwin out of naming Hudson in the indictment. Ed asked me to take over the case. The government indicted the Hunt brothers, their general counsel, Ed Hudson, and Percy Foreman. The case was assigned to Judge Halbert Woodward, whose chambers were in Lubbock but who also sat in Dallas, which is part of the same judicial district, the Northern District of Texas.

One joy of working this case was that I met lawyers with whom I formed lasting friendships. Representing Ed Hudson along with me was Mort Susman. Mort had been U.S. Attorney for the Southern District of Texas, and was one hell of a trial lawyer. We were co-counsel in other cases.

The Hunts' general counsel Ralph Shanks was represented by Patrick Higginbotham of Dallas, but when Pat was appointed to the district bench, Shanks's case was severed and never tried.

The Hunts were interesting co-defendants. Bunker in particular seemed a little out of place, no matter where he was. The first day in court, he took care to introduce himself and shake hands with everybody inside the bar of the court, including the marshals, clerks, and prosecutors. As he made the rounds of the astonished court personnel, one lawyer on the team drawled, "Bunker's pancakes never did get quite done."

Even though Guy Goodwin had obtained the indictment, he showed up only for the first few months of pretrial wrangling. U.S. Attorney Jim Rolfe and Assistant U.S. Attorney (and later U.S. Attorney) Mike Carnes represented the government, though with some diffidence because they thought little of the case and less of Goodwin.

The government evidence included some notes that Ed Hudson had made of his conversations with the Hunts about the reasons for hiring

Foreman. These might be viewed as suggesting that Foreman would be more loyal to the Hunts than to his clients. Foreman was recorded as having said he would refund the fee if the investigator did not invoke his privilege against self-incrimination. Hudson had the habit of making notes of conversations as a reminder of what he was to do. He kept these notes in his desk drawer.

In addition to hiring a lawyer for the investigators, the Hunts had tried to find them jobs in their chosen field of endeavor. Investigator Kelly had worked as a security guard; Hudson needed a guard at his plant and offices and hired Kelly. Kelly's other chosen field had, of course, been illegally obtaining evidence; his wiretap conviction was his résumé-builder on that score. Kelly spent part of his night shift at the Hudson Company rifling the files. When he found Mr. Hudson's notes, he took them to the government and traded them for a reprieve on his wiretap conviction.

Guy Goodwin eagerly agreed to use the stolen notes, and to give Kelly the benefit he sought. In so doing, Goodwin doomed the entire case against all the defendants. The notes were ambiguous, but they clearly referred to dealings between the Hunt brothers and Hudson. Under the Supreme Court's decision in *United States v. Bruton*, these written statements by Hudson could be used against him in a separate trial, but not in a joint trial with the Hunts and the other defendants.

I filed a severance motion for Hudson, seeking a separate trial. The government was hard put to oppose the motion, given the *Bruton* decision. As the prospect that the case would become untriable loomed, Goodwin sought to salvage what he could. He offered Hudson a free pass if he would testify against the Hunts.

Hudson scoffed at the idea. The case was ridiculous, he said, and he would not cooperate with somebody like Goodwin. It was interesting. I disliked Goodwin because of my Seattle experience and because he had been caught violating the Constitution. Hudson simply didn't trust him. Goodwin asked that Hudson come to the U.S. Attorney's office and hear the offer in person.

One Dallas morning, we paid that visit. Goodwin, down from Washington, had borrowed an office. He said that if Hudson would testify against Percy Foreman and the Hunts, he would drop all the charges against him. Hudson, gruff and blunt-spoken at age seventy-two, said, no thank you and prepared to leave.

"Just a minute," Goodwin said primly. "Mr. Hudson, didn't Percy Foreman represent your wife in your divorce case? And didn't he get the largest cash settlement in Texas history from you?"

"Yes," Hudson said carefully. "So what?"

"Well," said Goodwin, "this is your chance to get back at Percy Foreman." Hudson looked at Goodwin with a mixture of puzzlement and distaste. "You don't understand a thing about it," he began. "I had been trying to divorce that woman for years. Every time we would get close to settlement, she changed lawyers. So one day I read in the paper that she has hired Percy Foreman. That morning I went down to the Rice Hotel where he always had breakfast and sat at his table. 'Percy, how much?' I said. 'Thirteen million,' he said. I said, 'Done!' And he kept his word. So I have nothing against Percy Foreman, even assuming I wanted to make a deal with you to take care of it." Then, turning to me, he said, "I've had enough of this. Let's get out of here." As we walked out, Hudson turned to me and said in a voice that could be heard in Abilene, "Tigar, am I wrong or is that man a damned faggot?" So there you had Ed Hudson, reactionary and homophobic, but targeted by the same government in the same unfair way that had befallen my "politically correct" clients. There was no social harm in freeing him, and a great deal of social good in confronting and beating the government, and especially Guy Goodwin.

How did it turn out? Goodwin abandoned ship and went back to Washington. Rolfe and Carnes prepared to try a case that did not include Hudson, who had been given a separate trial. They would also be without Percy Foreman, who was always too ill to come to court and whose brilliant lawyer, Mike Johnson, got him severed out as well.

Carnes and Rolfe were no strangers to Texas juries, and they knew their case was looking a little thin. On the eve of trial, under pressure from Judge Woodward to get the matter settled, they offered the Hunts a deal: the charge was obstruction of justice, a felony. If the Hunts would plead guilty to "aiding and abetting misbehavior so near to the court as to obstruct the administration of justice," that would settle the case. Nothing doing, said the Hunts' lawyer. Carnes and Rolfe then agreed that the Hunts did not have to admit they were guilty of anything. They could plead nolo contendere and pay a $1,000 fine each, making clear that this was a petty offense on a par with a traffic ticket. The deal was done.

I went off to Los Angeles for the premiere of a movie that had been made by Fantasy Films, another one of my clients. I had a message to call Judge Woodward. He was cordial, but he asked frankly, "Mike, were you thinking of forcing the government to try Mr. Hudson?" I said that had crossed my mind. He said that it was none of his business, but that Mr. Hudson could have the same deal that the Hunts had received, and that it was surely not a big deal to pay a fine. I got the message. Ed and Mort Susman and I flew to Lubbock one fine day—in Hudson's plane—to plead nolo contendere. In recognition of Hudson's alleged lesser involvement, his fine was only $500. This is what Guy Goodwin's case had come to.

ROBERT MANN

One night in my Dallas hotel room, while working on the Hudson case, my friend Seagal Wheatley came to see me. Seagal was a trial lawyer in San Antonio, a former U.S. Attorney. I have done a few cases with Seagal and we have come out on top in every one. We had met in the *Army Times* libel case.

That night, Seagal brought with him Robert Mann, a banker from Waco who was charged with conspiracy to misapply, which is a polite way of saying steal, the funds of his bank, the First National Bank of Waco. This case gave me a fascinating journey through the Texas banking system and the many ways in which property rights can be defined in the system of finance capital. There were plenty of good reasons to be involved in it.

I had litigated in Texas beginning with the Wingerter draft case in 1969, which had been referred by one of San Antonio's oldest law firms. From the Connally acquittal and the *Army Times* libel case onward, I built a reputation in Texas that gave me good trial experience, brought business to Williams & Connolly, and when I started my own firm put us on a solid "pay the rent" foundation.

The Mann case was right for me, because it raised issues that needed to be aired. I also got to work with my friend John Mage, whose knowledge of economic theory proved decisive in our trial. It was a chance to bring together law, economics, and regulation.

The year was 1975, long before national banks leapfrogged across state lines. Texas prohibited branch banking, which meant that every bank stood by itself, limited to one place of business plus a remote location for automobile banking. In such a banking system, small banks needed to form relationships with larger banks in order to service their customers. If the small bank had a customer who wanted a larger loan than the small bank could provide, it could enlist the aid of its big city associate. These small bank/bigger bank arrangements were known as correspondent banking relationships.

John Mage took on the task of chronicling the history and operation of this type of loan and banking relationship. Typically, the relationship was cemented, and the small bank's customers assured of a warm welcome in the big city by the small bank putting a fairly large demand deposit in the larger bank. The larger bank could use this money to increase its lending power. At that time, demand deposits of this kind did not draw interest. This state of affairs produced something called the compensating balance bank stock loan.

A compensating balance loan is a familiar phenomenon. Almost anybody who borrows substantial sums of money, for example for a mortgage, has one. If you keep a balance on deposit at the bank, they are more willing to lend you money because they are making a profit two ways. First, they lend out the money you deposit for a higher interest rate than they pay you. Second, they charge you interest on what you borrow.

The compensating balance bank stock loan, in 1975, was a variation on this theme. Mann, who already owned a couple of small banks, purchased more than 90 percent of the stock of the First National Bank of Waco. To finance the purchase, he pledged the stock as collateral for a loan from Bank of the Southwest in Houston, which was one of Texas's major banks. He paid only 2.9 percent interest on this loan. The day that deal closed, Mann caused the First National Bank of Waco to place a $4 million demand deposit in the Bank of the Southwest, which was about the amount of his bank stock loan.

The government indicted Mann and the corporate entity Bank of the Southwest. The theory was that Mann had appropriated to his personal benefit the financial leverage/advantage of the demand deposit. That is, it was alleged that he personally got a lower interest rate because the bank's money was up in Houston at no interest. There were a number of ways one could analyze this transaction from the government's point of view, but they all focused on Mann taking a personal benefit from corporate assets. The case had been brought by a Justice Department prosecutor who was following up on a Treasury Department study of these bank stock loans, and on congressional hearings concerning them.

A correspondent banking relationship, we found, was full of intangibles. Sure, you could look at the demand deposit that the little bank put in the big bank and figure the lost opportunity cost to the little bank, that is, the amount it could have made by lending the money at interest. You could then add up the "other side" of the balance sheet and compute a value for the services the larger bank gave to the little bank and its customers—handling foreign transactions, arranging loan participations, and so on. John Mage and I read a batch of articles on correspondent banking. It was impossible to put a value on these services. Should you price them at average cost, marginal cost, or the fully distributed cost, which would include a share of everything including the polish on the bank's front door?

In addition, there were intangible aspects of the relationship that could not be measured at all. If a Waco customer wanted tickets to a Houston football or baseball game, the Waco bank could call somebody at the Houston bank and get some help obtaining those. This little service might ensure customer loyalty in Waco, the value of which is impossible to measure. In one study, the author found that the big bank had helped one of the little bank's customers buy a pet alligator.

In sum, the government had decided to define the allegedly lost opportunity to get interest as a form of "property" belonging to the bank as an entity and to its shareholders, and to quantify that opportunity as the difference between the interest Mann paid and the market interest rate he would supposedly otherwise pay. In this calculation, the customary rights and benefits of the underlying banking relationship were simply factored out of the equation. This was the bourgeois property norm in modern dress. Indeed, it was an instance of using money as the universal commodity, monetizing yet another aspect of human relationships.

These small-town one-location banks in Texas were usually closely held, by one or two families. Their stock was not publicly traded, and hence was difficult to value for estate or resale purposes. The bank stock loan inevitably put a value on the stock because the big lending bank had to determine value in a way that satisfied federal regulators that its loan was backed by sufficient collateral. The compensating balance bank stock loan was therefore a principal means of making bank stock marketable.

This research was fascinating, but we would rather be lucky than smart. We were lucky. One author of articles that supported the value of these loans to depositors and shareholders was a Dr. Edward Knight, who worked at the Federal Reserve Bank in Kansas. Another author, of an article that was even better for us, worked alongside Dr. Knight. We found out that Dr. Knight was in Houston, helping the prosecutors put their case together. We devised a strategy to force the government to put him on the stand so that we could put John Mage's research before the jury during the government's case.

The case was assigned to Judge John V. Singleton, a fair-minded but combative and cantankerous judge. The court of appeals opinion that remanded the *Mann* indictment for trial had been written by court of appeals Judge John R. Brown, who had chambers in that same federal courthouse building in Houston. One day early in the trial, Judge Singleton called the lawyers into chambers after lunch and said, we thought jokingly, that he had seen Judge Brown at lunch:

"I asked him right out if the court of appeals intended to say that your clients were guilty. And you will be relieved to know that he said no, they could still be acquitted and it would be all right with him."

The corporate co-defendant, Bank of the Southwest, was represented at trial by Mort Susman and lawyer from Leon Jaworski's Houston law firm. We had a little trouble with jury selection because the corporate lawyers from Jaworski's firm did not understand that this was a criminal case and that we wanted jurors whose outlook would make them suspicious of the government's actions and motives. I remember one tense discussion among lawyers, as Mort Susman and I explained to one of Jaworski's partners that we would not exercise peremptory challenges to exclude all the African-American jurors. Our general reasons were two: first, it was racist and we would have nothing to do with it even though the Jaworski partner said it was his practice to do it. Second, the backgrounds of African-American jurors gave them insights into police and prosecutorial behavior that may not be shared by whites. We had a specific reason as well. One African-American juror, that this partner wanted to exclude because of his race, held a PhD in Economics and would be uniquely situated to interpret the evidence we planned to present.

For the trial, the bank chose to have a vice president sit at counsel table as its representative. I wished they had chosen somebody else, for he looked too much like the archetypical heartless banker, austere in his three-piece pin-stripe suit that seemed out of place in a warm Houston summer. He was also unaware of his duty to help us make a good initial impression on the jurors. I began my opening statement and heard a noise behind me: "click, click, click." I glanced back; the bank vice president had taken out a fancy clipper and was clipping his fingernails.

Mort Susman delivered his usual ebullient and brilliant opening statement. I was listening to it most impressed until he said, "And members of the jury, all these things I have told you will be shown to you by Mr. Mann's counsel, Michael Tigar."

I didn't need the plug, and winced at the idea that jurors would expect me to carry a burden of proof that we did not possess in this criminal case. But I understood that we did have a story to tell, even though we would try to tell it by cross-examining the government's witnesses. We had not planned to put Mr. Mann on the witness stand. This was not a reflection on him.

Robert Mann was and is an articulate and honorable banker. In fact, when I was appointed to represent Terry Nichols in 1995, I had not seen Robert for nearly twenty years. The Oklahoma federal judge to whom the case was initially assigned, Wayne Alley, said we would try the case in the little town of Lawton, Oklahoma. We of course won a change of venue to Denver when Judge Matsch was assigned to replace Judge Alley. But we were plenty worried about how that Lawton community would receive us. One day, Robert Mann called me to say that he guessed that I was concerned about Lawton. I said yes. He said he had spoken to a banker friend of his in the community and that while there was a lot of sentiment about our client this banker would make sure that the trial team was welcomed and could find the facilities and services it needed. This sort of gesture arose no doubt from Robert's own experience, which back at trial time in 1976 weighed upon him.

As I noted earlier, there had been thousands of these loans. The government targeted Robert Mann as a test case. This "test" was to consist of convicting him of a felony and putting him in jail. His civil lawyers had sought to head off the attack, and by the time I came aboard he had been battling for several years at great financial and personal cost. Waco is a small enough town that when the bank president is charged with a felony everybody knows about it. Living under that cloud had taken its toll on the Mann family.

In the end, and without revealing confidences, I can say this. Often somebody who has been targeted in this way is unable to be the most persuasive witness for himself or herself. Their anger and frustration seems ready to burst out and overwhelm the jury. A solid merits case then becomes personalized in a way that diverts attention from the real issues. And so I have been economical about defendants taking the stand, often against the advice of my mentor Ed Williams.

The government's case would have to include a summary witness, to give an overview of the transaction and to try to show how the compensating balance loan benefited Mann personally. The government had to prove that Mann and the Bank of the Southwest had agreed to injure or defraud the First National Bank of Waco. They had also said we would hear from at least one senior official of the Federal Deposit Insurance Corporation. Our defense was that Mann did not intend to injure or defraud his bank. That the bank was not in fact harmed, that he relied on the fact that this was the normal method of financing small bank acquisitions in Texas. This last point gave us a fine line to walk. It is never a defense to say that "everybody else did it too," although a jury that hears that fact may acquit from a sense of fairness. Rather, we needed evidence that Mann was aware of this common and lawful practice and of its approval by regulatory authorities until the Treasury Department switched its outlook. But if Mann was not going to testify, how would we do that?

We assembled speeches and articles about compensating bank stock loans, and managed to get government witnesses to admit that these were widely circulated among bankers. Mann had to have seen them.

The government's first major witness was a senior Treasury Department accountant named Shockey. His direct examination at the hands of prosecutor Hank Novak seemed wooden. As is our custom, Mort and I moved for production of any of Shockey's prior statements before we began the cross. The government resisted, saying that one key document was not Shockey's prior statement at all, but government lawyer "work product," done while preparing him to testify. We cited the Supreme Court's then-recent decision in *Goldberg v. United States*, and Judge Singleton ordered the paper turned over.

The document was in question-and-answer format. It contained the full, literal text of each direct examination question and each of Shockey's answers. We had witnessed a memorized recital. The document was entirely typewritten. There was, however, no answer typed in for the first question. Mort went first, so he got to spring that trap.

Q: Mr. Shockey, this whole thing contains all the questions and all the answers that the jury just heard, is that right?

A: Yes.

Q: Except that for the first question there is no answer, do you see that?

A: Yes.

Q: The first question is "What is your name?," correct?

A: Yes.

Q: Well, my question is, did they not know who was going to be the witness, so they left it blank and that way anybody who showed up could read off these answers?

A: No, that's not it at all.

In the general merriment, the answer went unheard.

In my cross-examinations, I kept seeking ways to build our factual record on the ubiquity of these loans. And I asked every witness whether they knew the work of Dr. Knight. If the witness said yes, I went on to ask if they thought well of his work. They all said yes. And I asked if it wasn't true that Dr. Knight was right here in Houston, working on this case. Would Dr. Knight appear as a government witness?

Whether or not this pressure led the prosecutor to call Dr. Knight I do not know, but he did. Dr. Knight was a scholarly and rather smug fellow, but he clearly knew the theoretical side of banking. Mort Susman, in his cross, dwelt on the doctor's lack of practical experience at lending money and protecting bank assets. That had been one of our themes. Building a correspondent relationship is not just a matter of counting and calculating, as we kept asking the government witnesses to affirm. There are intangible aspects of customer service and financial stability, and these pose decisions that a community-oriented banker is best qualified to make.

For my cross-examination, I took Dr. Knight carefully through the literature that John Mage had assembled on compensating balance bank stock loans, and on the larger subject of correspondent banking. You might think this sort of thing is not cross-examination fodder in a jury trial, but I would disagree. Our job as lawyers is to help the witness teach the jurors. Even when cross-examining an opponent's expert, we want to keep the witness at a level of discourse that bridges the gap between his or her discipline and the experiences of jurors.

Finally, I reached for the articles that Dr. Knight and his colleague had written. He explained how these bank stock loans promoted liquidity of bank stock and helped the small bank's customers. He acknowledged that it was hard to give a numerical value to a demand deposit on one hand, and the services provided by the correspondent bank on the other. I took a risk:

> Q: Doctor Knight, in sum you are saying that the transaction for which Mr. Mann is on trial here was in fact beneficial to the stockholders and depositors of the First National Bank of Waco?
> A: Yes.

Dr. Knight and the prosecutor tried to qualify or minimize that answer on redirect, and the jury did take more than two days to acquit. The rather lengthy deliberation time was due, we later heard, to the stubbornness of a retired railroad engineer from Conroe who didn't like us.

Dr. Knight was the last witness that day. As we got into the elevator to leave the building, the junior prosecutor on the team stepped in with us. My ego treasures this moment. He looked at me with wide eyes and said, "How in the hell did you do that?"

I tried the Mann case barely ten years out of law school. Its lessons were important to me. Jurors care when the government is unfair to people. Jurors care that the defendant tried to do a good job in whatever profession he chose. Jurors' desire to do justice leads most of them to be intellectually curious, and to welcome the chance to follow you into a complex area in order to understand it.

BEN AND RICHARD

Ben was from San Antonio and, as an accomplished gemologist, dealt in watches and jewelry. Richard sold oil field pipe, and was damn good at it. So far as I know, they never met, but they are joined together in my mind. In both of their cases, I had to explain to a jury how a responsible businessperson could become so befuddled by addiction to alcohol that he lost track of what he was doing. Their cases taught me valuable lessons, some of which I did not appreciate at the time. The trial lawyer lesson in each case was how difficult it can be for jurors to put themselves in another person's place, and how hard we must work to make that happen.

Ben made a trip with business associates to Hong Kong. While there, he bought $300,000 worth of gemstones. He called back to his office in Texas and had them add the purchase to his insurance policy, which was some evidence that he did not intend to conceal them. He became ill in Hong Kong and started taking medication. He was also emotionally troubled by a telephone quarrel with his wife. On the flight from Hong Kong to San Francisco, he drank at least 12 ounces of vodka, a bottle of wine, and some cognac. He had the gems in various pockets of his clothing, consistent with his practice of not carrying them all in the same place. When he stepped off the plane in San Francisco, he handed the customs agent a partially filled-out form that he had not signed. The agent asked him to sign the form, which did not include the gems. The agent then ordered a search and the gems were found.

At this point, Ben's traveling companion, a corporate lawyer, advised him to cooperate with the customs agents. Ben obligingly sat down and wrote out a statement admitting to smuggling the gems. He was of course indicted. The trial judge refused to suppress the confession.

It was clear to me that Ben had been in an alcoholic haze, that he had begun to fill out the declaration on the airplane but had lost track of things. The customs agents testified at the suppression hearing, and would at trial, that he appeared normal and in control of his faculties.

How could we help a skeptical jury to understand Ben's condition? Expert opinion testimony is essential in almost every litigated case, to help the trier of fact see the issues in context. A physician testifies that the injured worker needs a certain kind of treatment, costing a certain amount, to recover from workplace injuries. An economist testifies about the differential in wages paid to male and female employees. In the steelworkers' case, Robert Gordon and Staughton Lynd provided essential evidence on the history and importance of labor rights.

On the other hand, thousands of unjust convictions and sentences have been set aside, as it is discovered that prosecution forensic evidence—ballistics, DNA, blood type, and so on—has been given by biased, unqualified "experts," working in forensic laboratories operated on unscientific principles, and based on false or incomplete evidence fed to them by police and prosecutors.

In Texas, a capital case sentencing is asked to determine whether there is a risk that the defendant, if not sentenced to death, will commit crimes of violence in the future. For years, Dr. James Grigson, a forensic psychiatrist testified in dozens of cases that a defendant was indeed a danger. His bias toward death was evident, his method of prediction did not have a firm scientific foundation, and his opinions were based on minimal acquaintance with the defendant's social history. In the Nichols case, our cross-examination of the government's forensic experts helped to undermine juror confidence in the government's case.

But a well-qualified expert can be an invaluable asset. He or she can give the trier of fact a helpful context in which to see the issues and personalities in the case. I asked Dr. Bernard Diamond, the founder of modern forensic psychiatry, to examine Ben, to help the jury understand how he had not been in charge of his own thoughts and actions. But fearful that jurors would react negatively to "shrink" evidence, I also called Dr. Arthur Burns, professor and chair of the department of pharmacology at the University of Texas Health Science Center.

Dr. Diamond had been a trial witness in many cases. His testimony was authoritative and compelling. He rebuffed the prosecutor's efforts to trivialize or undermine his conclusions.

Dr. Burns was also a magnificent witness. He explained the synergistic effect of alcohol, medication, and altitude on people. He said that there is a state of intoxication, at about three times the minimum legal definition, in which a person can appear normal and go through an entire evening talking and interacting with people. He or she will then go home to sleep and the next morning not remember a thing. It is fugue state. Burns turned to the jurors and said, "This has happened to one in three Americans. I know it has happened to me." Three jurors nodded in agreement.

We had Ben's friends as witnesses as well, to help the jurors know about what he drank and how he felt. When the customs agents took the stand, I tried to get as much evidence as possible of Ben being somewhat "out of it," but also stressed his entirely cooperative demeanor. I asked the jurors how they thought the customs service should behave. Several of them were working-class folks, and several were people of color who had shown some suspicion as the customs agents testified. In summation, I said:

> This is not just an issue about the airport in San Francisco. It deals with the border crossing at Tijuana and the roving checkpoints along the highways. When they stop you, should they try to trick you into signing something, or try to help you make sure that all the items are checked and the proper duty paid. If they cared about the revenue, and not about just making cases, the taxpayers would sure some out ahead in cases like this one.
>
> Now the prosecutor points a finger and says that our witnesses are Ben's friends. Sure they are. If ever it happens to you, and I pray that it does not, that you are 1,500 miles from home and a bunch of cops take

charge of you, you will give thanks that you had some friends or family with you so that they can tell what happened.

The jury hung 9 to 3 for acquittal on the main charge. The three dissenters were women from the suburbs, about Ben's age. I thought they had probably heard the "Honey, I got drunk and screwed up" story in their own lives and were not prepared to be charitable. That view, for which I had no particular evidence, influenced in preparing for Richard's case.

Richard was charged with understating his income by about $7 million on his personal returns over four years. He had been in the oil field pipe business with an offshore corporation, but bad tax accounting resulted in all the income being taxable to him personally. We could and did show that he paid tax on all the income that he actually spent. He lived fairly modestly. As a matter of the government's tax accounting, he was liable for half the total business income. His business partner, who had made a deal and was not indicted, had simply taken the money and spent it on airplanes, fancy homes, and other pleasures. Even if tax accountants might say Richard should pay tax on half the money, fairness in this criminal tax evasion said Richard did not intentionally violate a known legal duty to pay.

Richard was a recovering alcoholic. For the four years of the business, he was one of those people who function very well during the day and are drunk every night. He sold a lot of pipe, but did not keep track of the money.

To tell Richard's story, we asked a physician who ran a treatment center to help us. In this way, we could show the jurors that he was seeking help and not simply hiring some doctor to try and beat the rap. I did not think the defense would be credible unless Richard acknowledged his problem enough to seek help for it. The doctor had never testified for a criminal defendant. He had testified in favor of suspending licenses of impaired doctors, and had twice been appointed by courts to examine defendants in celebrated cases. He looked and sounded credible and qualified.

To introduce the themes of his testimony, I borrowed from a suggestion made by Chief Judge David Bazelon: "Doctor, when someone like Richard here comes to you as a patient, do you find that their family has a hard time understanding why they are behaving as they do?" "Do you ask the family to come in so you can discuss the condition that Richard is suffering from, and what can be done about it?" "Do you sometimes find that family members are fearful, or skeptical, or even maybe a little hostile, about what you do, and about Richard himself?" "Doctor, I want you to imagine that the jurors and I are Richard's family, and that we have come to ask you for an explanation of why he has been behaving as he has. Would you do that?"

However, in line with my experience with Ben, we also had a "hard" scientist, a neurologist who presented pictures of brain scans showing what alcohol had done to Richard's brain.

This medical evidence would not have carried the day with a skeptical jury. We called Richard's former wife, a nurse, to say with dignity and compassion that she had loved him but that his drinking drove her away. The jurors told us later that they voted her "best witness." They were told not to deliberate about the case until it was over, so they kept a score sheet on witnesses.

We also presented evidence of Richard's partner's profligacy, to such an extent and effect that the government did not dare call him as a witness. A Nieman-Marcus employee told of the fur coats the partner bought for young women; an accountant told of hauling cash in suitcases; an oil company employee ruefully confessed to receiving bribes and kickbacks. The government ought willingly to have produced this evidence of their witness's wrongdoing, but they did not. Every day, we would file a motion seeking more such information, and every day the judge would turn us aside. But as we were able to piece together some of the story, the judge finally relented. One afternoon he said, "A federal judge is supposed to listen. And sometimes a bell goes off. I have denied repeated defense requests, but today the bell went off. The defense motion for production of impeachment material is granted. Produce it tomorrow morning here in court."

The prosecutor said, "Your Honor, the documents are in New Orleans." The judge replied, "I am not talking geography, I am talking about my order. Tomorrow morning."

The jurors, however, reserved their "worst witness" award for the government's summary witness, an IRS special agent who had a chart of Richard's unreported income. He had, without apology, based his chart on the testimony of the liars and thieves on whom the government relied. This proved again the adage that an expert is someone who was not there when it happened but who for a fee will gladly imagine what it must have been like. Even when faced with governmental assurances that its experts are worthy of trust, the jurors can reject those assurances if cross-examination deconstructs the claimed expertise and its lack of evidential basis.

As we spoke to the jurors after the verdict, I learned again an important lesson about the team sport of litigation. My son Jon, then on summer break from college, had worked with us in the courtroom, keeping track of exhibits in this document-heavy case. One of the jurors said, "We figured out that this was your son, and we said what a good relationship the two of you have." The way your team looks in the courtroom, and the mutual respect they show one another, makes an impression on the ever-watchful jurors.

ANTITRUST

I have hesitated at times to take on corporate clients. When it was a criminal case, there was a chance to move the law in a constructive way. In civil cases, I tried to be sure that I could embrace the issues with passion and concern. If I could not, then I would not be a good lawyer for that case.

The general counsel of an oil company called me. He told me that his company and others were defendants in an antitrust case. It had been to the court of appeals and back. It had been pending for fifteen years and they wanted to get it over with. It seemed that so much discovery had been done that there was a database on Lexis, accessible by password. That must mean that every fact in the known world had been discovered, and just for this case. I said, "How about a trial?" The general counsel said that this idea had not been suggested. I said that in my experience setting an early trial date would get the case over with by settlement or otherwise.

I am not exaggerating. Many corporations, and their outside counsel, buy the idea that when you get sued the object is to prevent resolution of the case as long as possible. I think this is usually a bad idea, for it keeps contingent liabilities alive. As a matter of policy, this tactic also chews up too many scarce judicial resources.

When I looked at the case, I thought the plaintiff's theory unrealistic. I quickly learned how some large firms spend the clients' money in high-stakes litigation. Of course, we had droves of lawyers at every meeting. The defendants had already, before I came on board, agreed to share the cost of mock minitrials and jury research. We did a couple of those at a cost of hundreds of thousands of dollars, and got nothing I thought very useful. I hired jury consultant Hale Starr to help our team, for a modest cost, and sharpened our themes and theories.

The pressure of a quick trial date worked wonders. The plaintiffs agreed to a mediation process that was on a parallel track with the trial. This helped them to get a realistic view of their potential recovery.

I do not believe in haste for its own sake. I say this partly because a judge may read this book and I don't want it cited against me when I move for a continuance. I am in this respect reminded of Judge Lucius Bunton. On the bench, he became famous for "moving the docket." A cleaning crew left a spray bottle near his bench. He filled it with water and aimed it at lawyers and witnesses who droned on too long.

He asked a lawyer in a civil rights case, "How long will this trial take?" The lawyer did not know—or perhaps did not appreciate—Bunton's passion for speed. "Well, Your Honor, I would say about three weeks."

"Very well," Bunton replied, "we'll set it for a weekend in August in Pecos, Texas. It'll seem like three weeks."

This was not an idle threat. There is a federal courthouse in Pecos, Texas. There is also a small airstrip. My friend Gerry Goldstein reports that he could not use the phone booth there because there was a rattlesnake in it, trying to escape the sun.

In time, Bunton became the longest-serving judge in the Western District of Texas, which stretches from El Paso to Austin, some 600 miles. That meant he was Chief Judge. He was fairly new to that title when Walter Smith was appointed a federal judge. At Judge Smith's first judicial conference, he was sitting with me and some others having breakfast when Bunton approached.

"Walter," Bunton said in terms that could be heard all over the dining room, "what the hell are you doing?"

"What do you mean?" Smith replied.

"Taking five days to try a half-day case," Bunton exclaimed.

"Well, Lucius," said Smith evenly, smiling as he said the first name, "if it's the case I'm thinking of, it was sent back for retrial by the court of appeals after you did it the first time. I think they call the other four and half days 'due process.'"

That is not the sort of haste of which I speak. In our antitrust case, just a few weeks before trial, the plaintiffs moved to have the courtroom wired up for CD-ROM video presentation of documents. I object to that sort of thing because I want the witness to handle the actual papers they wrote and the jurors to see them do it. Our plaintiffs said, "Judge, we need this because we have 20,000 exhibits."

I replied, "They are lying, Judge. Nobody has ever tried a jury case with 20,000 real documents. I have read their exhibit list, and at least four out of five items on it are not admissible. So I think we should get a pretrial order on exhibits before we go wiring up the courtroom."

The judge agreed. As we kept the pressure on, we drove the case to a settlement even as we were selecting a jury. Over the years, using basic litigator moves has settled more than one complex case that was mired in discovery and motions. In a complex case, one can be overwhelmed by detail and fearful of bringing the case to trial.

MITCHELL AND THE EXPERT

The Mitchell brothers, Jim and Art, were producers of pornographic films in San Francisco. On February 27, 1991, Jim Mitchell went to Art Mitchell's house in Sausalito to deal with what he thought was Art's drug- and

alcohol-fueled frenzy. Art's girlfriend Julie Bajo had called Jim. Jim was carrying a .22 caliber rifle. As Jim entered Art's house, he saw Art in a dark hallway
holding what appeared to be a gun, but was in fact a bottle. Jim fired eight
times, killing Art. He was charged with first degree murder. Represented by
Nanci Clarence, Dennis Riordan, and Michael Kennedy, Jim was convicted in
Marin County Superior Court of the lesser offense of voluntary manslaughter,

One witness for the prosecution was Dr. Harry Hollein, presented as an
expert on forensic acoustics. Dr. Hollein examined the audiotape of Julie
Bajo's call to 911. Hollein testified that he could hear, on the tape, the eight
rifle shots. He opined that the shots were fired with a certain measurable inter-
val of time between each shot. This testimony supported an inference that Art
had had time to think about how many shots he was firing. Hollein said that
he was sure that some of the popping noises he heard on the tape were shots
being fired, and that other popping noises were not gunshots.

On appeal, I was asked to brief and argue the contention that Dr. Hollein's
opinion was not based on reliable factual information and that his claimed
expertise was junk science. Dr. Hollein had reached his conclusions by performing an experiment at his home in Florida. He had not used the .22 caliber
rifle that Jim had used, but another one that he said was similar enough. He
did his experiment in his own hallway, which he said was probably similar
enough to Art's hallway. To make sure he did not damage his walls, or shoot a
neighbor, he put stacks of wet newspaper at the end of his hall and fired into
those. The acoustics of all of this were, he said, similar enough.

Our panel of California Court of Appeal judges included Anthony Kline, a
judge with a good reputation for listening to defendants' arguments. I mocked
Hollein's alleged expertise. Judge Kline had questions. I said:

> Let me illustrate. One day long ago, the chief rabbi of Minsk came into the
> street and cried, "The chief rabbi of Pinsk has died." A few days passed,
> as news was slow to travel in those days, and it turned out that in fact the
> chief rabbi of Pinsk was alive and well. But the chief rabbi of Minsk is still
> revered, because it is a hell of a thing to be able to see from Minsk to Pinsk
> even if you get it wrong.

The court held, in forty carefully reasoned pages, that it had been error to
admit Hollein's opinion. Then, in a conclusory couple of paragraphs, it held
that the error was harmless, the conviction was affirmed, and the opinion was
not to be published.

I saw Judge Kline some months later at a Bar Association luncheon, and
we had a testy exchange of views. It seemed to me that regardless of ultimate

result, a closely reasoned critical view of criminal case forensic evidence should see the light of day. He disagreed.

ABA

I first learned of the National Lawyers Guild from Ann Ginger, when I was in law school. The Guild was founded in 1936 by New Deal lawyers, as an alternative to the American Bar Association. The ABA excluded African-Americans and had admitted only a token few women. It was notoriously anti-Semitic. Its leading expert on legal ethics, Henry Drinker, addressed the ABA annual meeting in 1929, and openly decried the "Russian Jew boys" and "other foreign Jews" who had joined the bar and seemingly lowered its ethical standards. The *ABA Journal* was a forum in the 1950s for attacks on the Warren Court and its civil rights decisions.

By contrast, the Lawyers Guild lawyers I knew had staked out the path I was trying to follow, with their principled representation during the McCarthy period. Guild lawyers had been among the early and dedicated group that stepped up to work on draft cases.

In 1974, when I rejoined the Williams firm, Paul Connolly told me that he and some friends were going to start a "Litigation Section" of the American Bar Association, that would reach out to lawyers of all political views and practice settings. The Section would have a quarterly publication, *Litigation*, with articles and essays by and for practicing lawyers. Although Paul's cases for the firm were not the ones on which I wanted to work, I respected him greatly. He was a naval officer in 1945, and the first U.S. military officer to enter Hiroshima after the bombings. "I was ashamed to be an American," he told us.

I wrote an article in the first issue of *Litigation*, reviewing a book on defending political trials. The Litigation Section grew. I became an active member. I enjoyed meeting other trial lawyers. When Sam Buffone, John Mage, and I started our boutique litigation firm in 1978, my work in the Section gave me an introduction to lawyers who referred interesting and remunerative cases to us. Indeed, I spoke on a Litigation Section program in the early 1980s, and a lawyer in the audience came up afterward and said he had been indicted for campaign finance fraud, liked what I had to say, and wanted me to represent him.

By the mid-1980s, the Section had grown to 40,000 members. It was influencing ABA policy in a progressive direction. We were recruiting lawyers to assist in death penalty post-conviction litigation, and working on the establishment of forums to hear and decide international human rights cases.

I was surprised to receive a phone call from Benjamin Civiletti, chair of the Section. Ben had been Attorney General in the Carter administration, and had returned to private litigation practice. Would I be willing to be a candidate for chair of the Section? he asked. I said yes.

Ben sponsored my candidacy. I was elected Vice-Chair for 1987–88, which put me on the road to be Chair-Elect 1988–98, and Chair 1989–90. By that time, the Section had grown to 60,000 members.

The Section has dozens of committees devoted to practice areas, such as product liability, employment law, and criminal law, and to professional issues such as legal ethics. These committees hold programs, publish newsletters, and encourage member involvement. As I had done, lawyers seek to be chair of a committee for professional satisfaction and professional advantage. The Chair-Elect appoints committee chairs, co-chairs, and vice-chairs for three-year terms. Thus, I wold be able to make nearly a hundred discretionary appointments. I looked at the existing roster and found, disproportionately, white males. I chose qualified women and people of color for more that half of the appointments.

To allow lawyers with family responsibilities more opportunity to participate in our work, we provided child care at every meeting. We would book a meeting room and make a contract with a local insured and bonded provider. We called these rooms "Camp Litl'Gator."

The leadership team we assembled took other progressive steps. My friend Bernardine Dohrn founded and led the Section's Children's Rights Committee that has for thirty years dealt with significant issues including juvenile incarceration.

I found that lawyers in "ordinary" law practice will come forward and take a role in upholding rights, if given an opportunity and shown the way. At that time Congress had legislated restrictions on the kinds of cases that federally funded Legal Services offices could provide for poor people. Notably, the legislation forbade participation in impact litigation such as class actions to address and redress a significant injustice with a broad remedy. Our team established the Litigation Assistance Partnership Project and hired a coordinator. LAPP receives requests from Legal Services offices and finds law firms willing to take on, pro bono, the tasks that the Legal Services lawyers cannot. Law firms accepted these challenges, as a means of providing meaningful experience to their own lawyers and gaining recognition for "doing good."

I cannot take credit for the outpourings of energy that we saw in the Section's work. Younger and older lawyers accepted and welcomed the opportunities to say and do something about injustice.

I looked around for other ways of seeing the progressive, even iconoclastic, role that courageous lawyers sometimes play, and also to signal the limits on lawyers' power faced with state power. I wrote three plays on legal history with the same idea. The first was about the trial of John Peter Zenger, the colonial newspaper editor who was tried for seditious libel and acquitted by the jury in 1735. Andrew Hamilton of Philadelphia, who was Benjamin Franklin's lawyer, came to New York to provide a defense after the colonial judge had disbarred local lawyers for criticizing him. Zenger had criticized an autocratic colonial governor. His trial was a celebrated step on the road to American independence from Britain. Gouverneur Morris, a signer of the Declaration of Independence, said much later that "the trial of Zenger in 1735 was the morning star of that liberty which subsequently revolutionized America."

I admit that I liked writing the play in part because I was to perform in it at its opening, during the ABA Annual Meeting in August 1986. A troupe of actors from Austin played most of the parts. I was Andrew Hamilton. My daughter Kate played Hamilton's daughter Margaret. Scott Armstrong, the journalist, played Zenger. *The New Yorker* wrote up the performance in its "Talk of the Town" section, and dashed my hopes of an acting career by writing that "Mr. Tigar went well beyond ham. He went whole hog."

The Trial of John Peter Zenger has since been performed by bar groups, theater groups, and college drama departments. An excerpt was performed at the New York Historical Society in 1990, and I reprised the role of Andrew Hamilton. Pictures appeared in *Newsday* the next morning. That day, I had an oral argument in the Second Circuit, and my opponent gave me an offhand and grudging compliment. Judge Pratt said, "Ah yes, but you should see him as Andrew Hamilton!"

For the ABA meeting in Chicago, I wrote *Haymarket: Whose Name the Few Still Say With Tears*. The action was set against the 1886 trial of labor activists led by Albert Parsons for a bomb explosion on Chicago during labor strife in the city. I used the play to frame a debate between Parsons's widow Lucy and Clarence Darrow about the limits on law's power to combat injustice.

In 1989, I teamed up with the actor Kevin McCarthy to write *Warrior Bards*, in which one or more actors portray five Irish-American lawyers. Kevin performed it in San Francisco.

RICO AND THE LAPTOP

Edward Bennett Williams gained national prominence in the 1950s for representing Frank Costello, the alleged Mafia leader. I met Costello in the late 1960s, wearing his trademark silk turtleneck and smoking English Ovals cigarettes.

Over the years, beginning with my time in the Williams firm, I have represented people charged with alleged Mafia involvement. These cases seem to bring out the worst in prosecutor and police behavior. Reversals of convictions are rare in the U.S. Court of Appeals for the Second Circuit, which hears appeals from the New York federal courts where many of the big cases are tried. Many years ago, reversing conspiracy convictions, that court of appeals warned against substituting a "feeling of collective culpability for a finding of individual guilt," but that warning has largely gone unheeded in later years. Indeed, conspiracy law has been stretched in Second Circuit case law further than in any other court I can think of. I say this ruefully because one of its most troubling cases involved my client, the Puerto Rican independence leader and human rights lawyer Roberto Maldonado. The Second Circuit affirmed his conspiracy conviction in connection with the 1983 Connecticut bank robbery committed by Puerto Rican nationalists. Roberto was charged with and convicted of a role in planning the robbery.

A small detour: Roberto suffered from a medical condition that required treatment. He was therefore sent to the federal prison medical facility in Fort Worth, Texas, to serve his sentence. As I was then teaching in Austin, I visited him. When he became eligible for parole, I came to Fort Worth to assist. Judge Hiram Cancio from Puerto Rico and the prison chaplain both attested to Roberto's character and to his work in the prison with other inmates. The government lawyers said that Roberto would not get parole unless he revealed the names of his comrades, including those who were fugitives.

He declined to do that, and so he served his entire sentence. When the day came on which he was to be released, those lawyers showed up again. They demanded a hearing before the U.S. magistrate judge, to argue that Roberto should be kept in prison until he had either paid his fine or submitted to a detailed examination of his resources and associates to demonstrate indigency.

Things turned out well. As the court session opened, the judge welcomed me and said that his son, a Texas law student, was enjoying the criminal law class I was teaching. He listened to the government lawyers. We presented evidence of Roberto's work in prison, and of the way that the government had behaved.

The judge lectured the government lawyers on the unwisdom of trying to pile on the punishment beyond what a court had imposed, and suggested that the lawyers were out of touch with the way things worked in his court. Roberto was free to go. He returned to Puerto Rico and resumed his political activism. He was readmitted to the Puerto Rico bar. He died in 2020.

Returning to the organized crime conspiracies, one example of the way these cases are brought and tried was in what started as the Salerno case and became the DiNapoli case when Salerno died. My friend Gus Newman had called and asked me to represent Vincent DiNapoli on appeal. Gus was one of the world's great lawyers and great friends. If he tried a case and lost, which was not often, he would bring in another lawyer to do the appeal. That way, he said wisely, somebody can grade his paper and feel free to raise any issue that he might have overlooked. I have never found an issue that he did overlook: a Gus Newman record is a pleasure to read.

Vincent DiNapoli was convicted of racketeering offenses after a 14-month trial involving many defendants. The case involved price-fixing, union bribery, and other allegations. The evidence about Vincent and his brother Louis was all heard in about three months of trial. They sat there for the rest of the time without any visible or audible connection to the case. In such a megatrial, fairness goes out the window. The most careful jury couldn't possibly keep all the evidence straight.

As is usual in cases like these, there had been months of electronic surveillance, resulting in thousands of hours of tapes. These had been mishandled by being turned over to a retired police officer to study. There were dozens of issues on appeal, including a report by some jurors that the judge and the marshal had tried to pressure the jury into reaching a verdict.

The court of appeals panel was headed by Judge George Pratt, whose fair-mindedness led him to schedule an entire morning of oral argument. All the lawyers could be heard, the court could ask its questions, and all the issues could be aired. After a remand for hearings on the jury issue, the panel reversed the convictions. It reached only one issue. The government had called two men, Bruno and deMattei, before the grand jury, where under grants of immunity they had given testimony that tended to exonerate the DiNapolis. When trial came around, the government refused to turn over the grand jury testimony to the defense, much less give Bruno and deMattei new grants of immunity so that they could testify to the trial jury.

The court of appeals acknowledged that the law did not require the trial judge to force the government to grant immunity, but noted there was something unfair about using the grand jury to find exculpatory evidence and then allow this evidence to be buried if the witnesses later decided to invoke a privilege. It held that the trial court should have admitted the Bruno-deMattei grand jury testimony in evidence.

Having been denied bail on appeal and sentenced to 24 years in prison, the defendants were now out on bail, at least for the time being. The government filed a petition for certiorari, which the Supreme Court granted. The court of appeals theory for admitting the grand jury testimony was certainly arguable, although there were other theories on which it could have reached the same result. Therefore, my major tactic was to convince the Court that the result was fair even if the Justices disagreed with the reasoning.

The Justices seemed skeptical. During argument, I held up the transcript of Bruno's and deMattei's testimony—which was in the record—and criticized the government for trying to suppress it. I was echoing Judge Altimari's criticism of government counsel during the court of appeals argument. Justice White broke in and asked, "Do you expect us to read all that?"—as though the content of this testimony were irrelevant to the result. I said yes, and noted that under the Court's precedents "you can affirm the court of appeals on any ground, even if it was not raised or considered below." To which Chief Justice Rehnquist remarked, "But only if we want to." Here was another example of the Court sometimes taking a case to decide the issue it has chosen, if necessary by skipping over uncomfortable facts.

The Court, in an opinion by Justice Thomas, reversed the court of appeals. But as a clerk to the Justice explained to me, there was a paragraph in the opinion that held out plenty of hope for us on remand. The court of appeals was invited to reconsider how this testimony might be held admissible. The opinion rejected only the reasoning and not the result.

On remand, the panel of three judges again reversed the convictions, but the en banc court—all of the court members—set that aside. However, the en banc court noted that there were a half-dozen issues yet to be resolved. In sum, the panel could reverse the convictions again. At that point, Gus Newman stepped in and negotiated an end to hostilities on favorable terms.

Representing alleged leaders of the alleged Cosa Nostra can have desirable side effects. One day in the 1990s, I was standing at 88th and First Avenue in New York, trying to hail a cab for the airport. As I waited, a garbage truck rumbled up the street with a dumpster hanging on its side. The dumpster broke loose and careened toward me. I pushed my companion out of the way, and jumped aside as the dumpster approached. It rolled over my laptop case and into a parked car. My computer was broken in half.

I gathered my wits and took down the names and addresses of witnesses. I copied the name and phone number of the garbage company from the side of the dumpster. Later, I called the number and told the man that his trash truck had ruined my laptop computer. He was quite rude, and said I could not prove that his truck did the damage.

I called a former client, and told him what had happened. The client said, "That's terrible. No wonder they say the garbage business is run by gangsters. I will call this gentleman and explain his obligations." I soon had a new computer.

POLITICAL COMMENTARY

Another Ed Williams legacy to me was the representation of political figures—understanding the First Amendment and speech and debate constitutional issues, the media pressures, and the ways the public and therefore the jurors see such people. Those were good lessons when Sam Buffone and I represented Congressman John Murphy, charged in the ABSCAM cases with having taken a bribe in exchange for offering to help a fictitious Arab sheik. The cases were part of a sting operation conducted by FBI agent Anthony Amaroso and a professional con man named Mel Weinberg. In an effort to sanitize Weinberg's testimony, the prosecutor began by having him list many of his misdeeds. I objected, and the judge said, "Mr. Tigar, there is no ground for objection. After all, you were going to bring all of this out on cross-examination, were you not?" "Indeed, Your Honor," I said. "I object on the ground of stolen thunder."

The jury became wary enough of the FBI and the con man that, of all the defendants in the ABSCAM cases, only Murphy was found not guilty of two-thirds of the charges, including bribery and racketeering. The trial judge gave him the same sentence as the others, however.

I make no apologies for losing one-third of that case. I am convinced, however, that two reasons we lost were that voir dire was compressed into a morning and that we were yoked for trial with another member of Congress whose lawyers pursued a different strategy. On the voir dire issue, I ran into one of the jurors a couple of years later at a restaurant. He said hello and reminded me that he had served, and then said, "We knew your client was guilty of something, but we had a hard time figuring out what it was."

Then, in 1993, while I was on the University of Texas law faculty, I was propelled into another political case. I was at home one evening when Dean Mark Yudof called me. He said, "In a few minutes, you will get a telephone call from Senator Kay Bailey Hutchison. She is an alumna of this law school and played a very important role in reorganizing our alumni association. She will ask you a question. The answer is yes."

I had already read that Senator Hutchison had been indicted for misusing her office, charges dating from her tenure as Treasurer of the state of Texas, a statewide political office. The Travis County DA, Ronnie Earle, had conducted a publicized raid on the Treasurer's office to get computer hard drives that he said would show that Kay had used state employees to raise political funds for her candidacy.

Senator Hutchison did call and I did say yes, joining a defense team led by Dick DeGuerin, with Ron Woods as co-counsel. I have seldom agreed with

Senator Hutchison's political positions, but this case did not smell right. I knew Ronnie Earle, and had seen the way his office cavalierly dealt with capital cases. I knew that he harbored political ambitions, and indeed had his eye on the Senate seat that Kay then held. I also knew that Texas law is wide open when it comes to raising campaign funds. I regret this latitude, but it had certainly well served some of my favorite people, like Ann Richards and Bob Bullock. The raid to get evidence that could just as easily have been subpoenaed was a grandstand play, and gave us a solid motion to suppress evidence.

For months we litigated pretrial motions, finally forcing Earle to delete any allegation that Kay had destroyed documents and to admit there had never been any evidence of that. We moved to recuse the Travis County judges, as being political allies of Earle and opponents of Kay. We then had good fortune. Retired Judge John Onion was assigned to the case. Judge Onion was a scholar and teacher as well as a judge. He was regarded as nonpartisan and fair by everybody we met; this is quite a feat in a state that elects judges on partisan lines.

Judge Onion granted a motion for change of venue to Fort Worth, Tarrant County. As trial approached, we put subpoenas on state political officers for their fundraising records, to establish that Kay's activity was consistent with the best political practices. These officers resisted the subpoenas and boxes of responsive records piled up in the courtroom waiting for Judge Onion to rule.

We brought our motion to suppress on for hearing, but Earle said he was not ready to try the issue. He consented that the motion would be deferred until the challenged evidence was offered at trial. This was a fatal error, for which he later blamed the judge.

In Fort Worth, we began jury selection. Kay sat with her husband, Ray, and was as attentive and skilled an analyst of prospective jurors as I have ever seen. At one point, the prosecutors objected to Kay and Ray holding hands in the presence of prospective jurors. Judge Onion thought this motion was nonsense, and underscored this by saying that they could hold hands but could not kiss.

Judge Onion also rejected media efforts to televise the proceedings. After he ruled, the lawyer for the TV station asked him to hurry up and sign an order denying relief. Judge Onion smiled and said, "You're going to try and mandamus me, aren't you." The lawyer said, "It had crossed my mind."

"Well," said the judge, "I am not going to let you take me up there without some findings on the record. Mr. Tigar and Mr. Earle, please submit proposed findings and conclusions so that I can do a short opinion." This was a good thought. In the Nichols case, when we wanted a sealing order we always made sure to build a record so that Judge Matsch would be protected on appeal. Even then, the media argued, though unsuccessfully, that he should have made more detailed findings. I characterized this in oral argument as saying in effect that Judge Matsch should stay after school and write a hundred times on the blackboard, "I find that the balance favors nondisclosure."

A week before the trial, the *Fort Worth Star-Telegram* carried a big picture of Ronnie Earle, above the fold, with a story of how he planned to win this case.

Jury selection was almost finished one afternoon. The next morning, Earle asked to see us all in the judge's chambers. He said, "Judge, I move to enter a *nolle prosequi* in this case"—that is, a voluntary dismissal. If that were granted, he could start over again in Travis County and hope to get a different judge; he could then rethink his tactical decisions.

We said we opposed this, recognizing that the DA has discretion to discontinue a case. "Mr. Earle," Judge Onion said, "there are more than one hundred prospective jurors out there and it is all over but the peremptory challenges. If you have a motion, you file it on paper and I will hear it. But I am not going to inconvenience those people that you have caused to be here."

We went into the courtroom and exercised peremptory challenges. Earle presented a written motion. Kay, whose courage I salute to this day, stood firm that she wanted her case tried and not dismissed. Judge Onion called us to the bench. Dick stated our client's position. Judge Onion said, "I'll hear this motion later this morning. Right now we are going to swear the jury. Mr. Earle, I know you are ready for trial because I read that story in the paper." Earle looked stricken. When the jury was sworn, jeopardy would attach.

The jurors were in the box, the prospective jurors excused. Judge Onion gave them the oath, and his initial instructions. He looked over at the prosecutor's table and said, "Who will open for the State?" Earle and two other prosecutors looked down at their table. Judge Onion said it again, "Who will open the for the State? Mr. Earle?"

Earle stood and said, "Your Honor, we have a motion."

Judge Onion said, "I know you do. But this is the time for opening statement. Will you make an opening statement or not? The law requires that you do so."

"No," Earle said at last.

"Very well," said Judge Onion, "the State rests and closes." He turned to the defense table. "Counsel approach the bench."

At the bench, Dick moved for directed verdict of acquittal. Texas practice, unlike that in federal court, ascribes real meaning to that motion. A judge cannot enter judgment, but rather must instruct the jurors and let them reach a verdict. In open court, Judge Onion said, "Members of the jury, in Texas the law requires that the prosecutor make an opening statement, setting out what the State intends to prove. If he does not, he rests without presenting evidence. Therefore, the part of the trial that I told you about, where the evidence comes in, is over. Please retire to your jury room while I prepare a jury charge and form of verdict."

Judge Onion then wrote out instructions to the effect that since the state had a burden beyond a reasonable doubt and had presented no evidence at all, the jurors should return not-guilty verdicts on the charges. He prepared verdict forms for their use. Then, the jurors trooped back in to hear the instructions and receive the forms.

A new form of agony began. They were out five, ten, fifteen, twenty minutes. Finally they came back in. They had taken their job seriously, so they elected a foreperson and read all the papers carefully. The foreperson read out the verdict. Kay was not guilty.

Earle blamed it all on the judge, saying that he had been sandbagged by the ruling that the legality of his search would be litigated only after the jury was sworn. But his own consent had created that situation. In truth, I believe somebody with more political sense told him that it was dangerous to start this kind of a case.

Senator Hutchison has remained a friend. And she does have a piece of paper signed by twelve jurors saying she is not guilty. The other 99 senators have to ask that you take their word for it.

CHAPTER 15

Human and Global Rights

FIRST GLANCES

My earliest encounters with international law concerned issues of war and peace, for example, in my law school valedictory address and in representing young men facing the military draft. As time went on, I became concerned with the "globalization" of human rights. As a journalist in England in 1962 and 1963, I covered the early work of Amnesty and other organizations involved in the founding of the European Court of Human Rights. I covered the debates over Third World economic development, as the former colonies put forward ideas of social and economic rights. During law school, Ann Ginger spoke often of the international human rights movement. These forces have today become much stronger. The basic rights to political expression, religious freedom, and due process have been expressed for more than three hundred years. They are enshrined in our Bill of Rights. They are the "first generation."

After World War II, such documents as the Universal Declaration of Human Rights recognized a "second generation" of rights, to self-determination, subsistence, education, health care, and generally to a just distribution of national wealth for certain basic necessities of living. Today, one speaks as well of a third generation of rights, dealing with the environment and responsible development.

While the concept of rights, thought of as entitlements that every state must recognize and enforce, has developed, the autonomy of nation-states has eroded. That is, it was once thought that every sovereign could, within its borders, recognize or deny rights as it wished, without interference from other sovereigns or from international bodies. This positivist theory, on which

Jeremy Bentham wrote extensively in the late eighteenth century, dominated legal thought in the nineteenth century.

Throughout the nineteenth century the theory of sovereign right came under increasing pressure, however, first with international opposition to the slave trade and then in other areas as well. The two world wars changed the face of international legal thought entirely, and the Nuremberg trials firmly established that sovereigns, state actors, and individuals would not have immunity, or impunity, from crimes against humanity and crimes against the peace. In the years since World War II, there has been a growing consensus that sovereign states must also respect at least first-generation rights.

There is a tension: the tendency of nation-states to mouth respect for human rights while accepting or even perpetuating their denial. I recall the Belgian socialist Emile Vandervelde mocking the Belgian colonial claim that imperialism is "the work of civilization." The military and other U.S. interventions in country after country have been done in the name of democratic rights. Jean Bricmont has written a persuasive study, *Humanitarian Imperialism: Using Human Rights to Sell War*.

Validating human rights lawyering is, in my view, little different from validating any lawyer work. It is ennobling to speak grandly of human rights, provided one has begun by talking at length with humans who, in their daily lives, experience injustices that must be portrayed in narratives about rights. The lawyer's basic task is to find a forum in which to hold accountable the perpetrators of these injustices. This point may seem obvious, but it has not proven to be so. We see the same debate as occurred in the civil rights movement in the years after *Brown v. Board of Education*. The demands for justice, phrased in terms of human rights, were not honored widely or speedily enough. People began direct action and resistance movements. The lawyers had new tasks defending human rights advocates.

Regardless of forum, our root principle is accountability, to be distinguished from immunity or impunity. We had argued the illegality of the Vietnam War in many draft resistance cases, to no effect. Our victories were on narrower grounds.

In 1976, I was propelled into a more direct part in the human rights struggles by a terrible event.

CHILE

I had watched with concern and horror the 1973 military coup in Chile that brought an end to the progressive civil government of President Salvador Allende. General Augusto Pinochet and his colleagues embarked on a pattern of killings, tortures, and disappearances, all with the apparent support of American military and intelligence agencies. I befriended Chilean exiles who were struggling to restore democracy in Chile. One such exile was Orlando Letelier, who had been Foreign Minister and Ambassador to the United States in the Allende government.

On September 21, 1976, in Washington, D.C., a bomb exploded in Orlando's car, killing him and his assistant Ronni Karpen Moffitt, and injuring Ronni's husband, Michael. Orlando had been working at the Institute for Policy Studies, a think tank organization in Washington. The FBI quickly descended on IPS demanding information and documents in a purported effort to see if leftists had killed Orlando.

It was obvious to Orlando's colleagues that the most logical suspects were agents of General Pinochet, who had publicly branded Orlando a traitor. Within hours of the killing, people at IPS called me and asked for my help. That "help" drew me into the Letelier case for the next sixteen years, and then into the broader fight to bring General Pinochet to justice.

I called a friend at the Department of Justice. We set up a meeting with Attorney General Edward Levi. Levi took us seriously. I said that I thought the FBI was using the investigation as a pretext to investigate IPS and Orlando. A couple of years later, a congressional committee reported in detail that the FBI and other agencies did indeed keep track of foreign dissidents in the United States and report on them to their oppressive home governments. Finally, in the year 2000, the United States government released documents showing that the FBI had reported to Chilean secret police about the actions of anti-Pinochet activists, and that at least one such report had led directly to the arrest and killing of an activist.

Back in 1976, our concerns were based on experience and intuition. I said to the Attorney General that I thought the bombing would not have been done by Chilean agents personally, and that the question was who would they recruit in this country. The most likely suspects were Cuban émigrés. That group had already claimed credit for bombings at the Cuban UN mission. And where, I asked, would evidence of their actions be? At CIA headquarters in Langley Park in the custody of CIA Director George Bush.

"Tell you what, General Levi," I said, "you back one truck up to IPS and one up to the CIA. IPS will produce documents at the same rate as the CIA." He laughed and said he would take care of the CIA angle, and that the FBI would be reined in. For the next two years, the FBI investigation zigged and zagged, and I began to study what else might be done to redress Orlando's death.

By this time, I had met Sam Buffone, and we were planning the law partnership that we formally established January 1, 1978. Sam proved to be as

good a friend and as good a law partner a person could have, and after I left
Washington in 1984 he continued to pursue the Letelier case until our judgment was finally paid. Starting our law firm with work on the Letelier-Moffitt
case was one of several interconnected events. In my personal life, in my marriage to Madeleine Levy, there had been tensions about my desire to have a
relationship with Jon and Kate, the children of my marriage to Pam, among
other issues. We had very different ideas about building a life in the law. We
agreed to divorce.

By the summer of 1978, the FBI had officially determined that Orlando
was killed by Cuban émigrés recruited and paid by Chilean intelligence
agents. It captured two of the agents and made plea bargains with them,
and the government indicted the émigrés. One beneficiary of a plea bargain was Michael Townley, the principal architect of the assassination plot,
who recruited the Cubans, and assembled the car bomb. Townley was an
American-born agent of Pinochet's secret police, the Directorate of National
Intelligence, or DINA. The U.S. government put Townley in the Witness
Protection Program.

Sam and I drafted a civil federal court complaint on behalf of Orlando's
widow Isabel, his four sons, and the Karpen and Moffitt families. The Foreign
Sovereign Immunities Act (FSIA) had been passed in 1976. It contained a
provision that foreign states were not immune from suit in the United States
for certain torts committed in this country. This statutory language seemed
straightforward to us, so we sued the individual perpetrators, the head of the
Chilean secret police, General Contreras, the Chilean secret police agency,
and the Republic of Chile.

Our suit provoked criticism from the established international bar. The
FSIA tort provisions were, they wrote, designed for automobile accidents and
not for alleged human rights abuses. It is hard to imagine in today's atmosphere that our suit would be controversial, but we were regarded as oddities
for filing it.

We were granted an audience with Griffin Bell, President Carter's Attorney
General, to ask for Justice Department help with our lawsuit. Bell was testy,
arrogant, and unhelpful. Isabel Letelier said to him, "Mr. Attorney General,
we are asking for your help. What shall I tell my and Orlando's sons about
whether or not you will do anything?"

Bell replied condescendingly, "Well, little lady, people get killed in
Washington every day and I can't be expected to pay more attention to one
case more than another."

The Chilean government filed objections, in the form of diplomatic notes
to our complaint. The individual defendants chose not to appear. When the

judge rejected Chile's official claims of immunity, we tried the case. Just as when one sues the United States, one cannot get a default judgment against a foreign state without proving the case to a federal judge. Judge Joyce Hens Green heard the evidence and arguments. She was clear and decisive. The Chilean government never quite admitted the killing, but argued that even if they were guilty, it would be "discretionary act" from which they were immune. Judge Green curtly reminded them that whatever discretion a foreign sovereign might possess, it did not extend to blowing people up on the streets of Washington. Her rejection of the argument could not mask the arrogance of the Chileans having made it.

We won a judgment against the Chilean government and against the individual defendants. Over the next few years, Congress passed statutes restricting American military and diplomatic cooperation with Chile until the judgment was paid. We sought to collect by seizing a LAN-Chile airliner in New York, but had to give the plane back because the court of appeals said LAN-Chile was sufficiently independent of the Republic of Chile that its assets could not be seized. In short, we combined court work with the clients' political organizing around the issues.

Finally, in 1991 President Pinochet stepped aside. The new civilian government agreed to set up an international tribunal that would look at the Letelier case. The American and Chilean governments took this step because Senator Edward Kennedy was about to introduce legislation that would have let us. Sam Buffone brilliantly handled this situation, and the judgment was paid—some four million dollars. One must note that you cannot get punitive damages against a foreign sovereign. The tribunal awarded legal fees to Sam and me. I used mine to establish Letelier-Moffitt human rights scholarships at the University of Texas and Berkeley Law.

Orlando's son Juan Pablo became a Senator in Chile; Orlando's son Francisco became an artist whose work depicts aspects of the struggle for justice. The Letelier case—and the fact of winning against Pinochet—encouraged and emboldened progressives in Chile.

SOUTH AFRICA

I enjoy teaching and writing about advocacy skills; a half-dozen of my published books bear witness. I have participated in advocacy teaching events ranging from one-day seminars to week-long intensive courses that allow students to practice jury argument and witness examination.

In 1987, I was in North Carolina with my family. I taught a summer course at the University of North Carolina Law School, and worked on my book about federal appeals. I had dinner one night with my friend Ken Broun. Ken teaches at the University of North Carolina Law School and writes about the law of evidence, and has written about the apartheid-era trials of Nelson Mandela and others. He told me of a project in South Africa that he and our mutual friend Jim Ferguson were doing. Jim is an African-American civil rights lawyer. We would also be working with Charles Becton, an African-American North Carolina lawyer and judge whom I had also met in the NITA setting. Ken described the exciting methods they would be using to train black lawyers in South Africa to represent people in civil cases, discrimination cases, and political trials.

I wanted to raise money for this project through the ABA Litigation Section, and to have leaders of the Section participate. To do this, the ABA Board of Governors would have to approve. That proved difficult. The ABA Individual Rights Section opposed our request. They doubted that the apartheid government would give us visas. Mainly, however, they wanted to be the first ABA group to go to South Africa, to conduct what they called a "needs assessment."

I maintained calm. In my mind, I was shouting, "A needs assessment? What they *need* is liberation, and what we are doing is working with the lawyers who are helping the movement to achieve that." The Board, by a divided vote, approved our plan.

Ken, Jim, Charles and I agreed on a schedule for our trips to South Africa. I applied for a visa. A polite person from the South African embassy in Washington called and asked pointed questions about my view of apartheid. Maybe, I thought, the naysayers were right, and I would not get a visa. After a few tense phone calls with the embassy, the visa came through. In August 1988, I flew from the ABA Annual Meeting in Toronto to Johannesburg to participate.

The work that Ken, Charles, Jim, and I were doing was sponsored by the Black Lawyers Association, affiliated with the Pan-African Congress. The next year, we broadened our approach and also worked with the National Association of Democratic Lawyers, affiliated with the African National Congress.

Apartheid South Africa was chilling, but underneath the repression one could feel the pulse of change. I dined one night with a white South African lawyer who represented major oil companies. As we drove to his house, he pointed out the signs that the racial barrier was crumbling. When we met with the black lawyers in suburban Johannesburg, two white judges participated and helped with the teaching. The law school at Witwatersrand was integrated, as was that at Natal, in Durban.

The organized bar had managed to keep most Blacks out of law practice, but we thought our work might increase the number. From Johannesburg, we went to Umtata, the capital of Transkei. Transkei was one of the "homelands" established by the apartheid government. Blacks were to be citizens of a homeland and not of South Africa itself, where they had no social or political rights. The homelands were, in short, a cruel joke if said to be sovereign, and an instrument of apartheid policy. Only Israel recognized them as viable political entities.

One of the judges I met in Johannesburg was Richard Goldstone. Richard had already decided a leading anti-apartheid case called *Govender*. Govender was prosecuted as a non-white living in a white group area, which was a criminal offense. Upon conviction, she was evicted from her home. Goldstone wrote an opinion holding that under the statute as he read it, she could not be evicted unless there was equivalent housing available. Under this modest precedent, it became so difficult to evict non-whites that housing segregation in Johannesburg began to break down. In later years, Justice Goldstone would head a commission to investigate police violence against anti-apartheid activists and would serve as prosecutor at the International Criminal Tribunal for Yugoslavia. Later, he was appointed a Justice of South Africa's Constitutional Court.

I recall sitting in a law office in Umtata—in the so-called homeland of Transkei—and reading the official magazine of the South African Law Society. An editorial complained that domestic and foreign critics were urging the Law Society to take a stand against apartheid. The Law Society disagreed. Our job, it said, is to take and apply the law as we find it, and not to try to change things. This bit of nonsense was galling for several reasons. First, the system of apartheid was imposed in the early 1950s by the National Party, which "changed things" by purging the voter rolls of non-whites and forcibly evicting non-whites from their homes. Second, there were plenty of examples of progressive lawyers working to "change things," if only to make rules that would ease the inevitable transition to a post-apartheid society.

In one sense, the editorial was only a symptom of the world in which the white rulers dwelt. The first day I arrived in Johannesburg, police were scooping up all copies of a newspaper that had dared to violate the law by printing a picture of police beating Black protesters. I attended a public meeting on a possible new constitution for post-apartheid South Africa, but we could not publicly utter the name of Albie Sachs, the constitutional scholar who had written on this subject. Albie was in exile, a "banned person." Indeed, the apartheid government had tried to kill him with a car bomb as he worked in exile in Mozambique. One of our Black Lawyers Association colleagues had

been arrested and charged with a felony for having a book by Nelson Mandela
in his car; he was acquitted when he explained that he needed the book
because he represented clients charged with treason for supporting Mandela
and the ANC. I was reminded of the Robin Williams routine, in which he
portrays former Alabama Governor George Wallace, and intones:

> P. W. Botha [the South African President] to a white courtesy telephone
> please. P. W. Botha to a white courtesy phone. Say, P.W., this is George
> Wallace. Listen here, Sparky, do you understand that you got six million
> whites and somethin' like thirty million blacks in your country? Does the
> name Custer mean anything to you?

One of our mock trials for training advocates was a treason case.

The case file assumed that the principal witness against our clients was
tortured into confessing and then offered a life sentence in exchange for testimony. Torture was routine police behavior in South Africa, not to mention
outright political killings. I was asked to demonstrate how one would cross-
examine such a witness.

> Q: Ms. Mqubele, do you want to die?
> A (hesitantly): Why, no.
> Q: I want you to look around this courtroom and tell his lordship [there
> were no juries in South Africa] who it is in this room who has the most to
> say about whether you will live or whether you will be hanged by the neck
> until you are dead?

The rest of the examination could go into the circumstances of her capture
and questioning, but I thought this was a good way to get the court's attention. It was important for all of us involved in the teaching to stress the need
for vigorous advocacy, that one must not be intimidated by the atmosphere of
repression. In this we were supported by our South African colleagues, one of
whom was a living example of such courage.

Godfrey Pitje had been a lawyer in the offices of Oliver Tambo and Nelson
Mandela. When Tambo was exiled and Mandela jailed, he kept on practicing
law. One day, he refused to sit at the small table reserved for non-white lawyers. He insisted on sitting where white lawyers sat. For this he was tried and
convicted. For some months, he was under a restriction that he must remain
in his house, but could not meet with more than one other person at a time.
His wife and children took turns having their meals with him.

On that 1988 trip, we went to Durban, on the East Coast. My friend

Charles Becton, an African-American judge and lawyer, was in the group. One morning, we walked out to look at the beach. Signs restricted the best beach for the "white racial group." Bec wanted to take a photograph, but there were also signs making it a felony to take a picture of the signs. Ken Broun said that the previous year, he had been walking along the beach and asked a passerby, "Is this the Indian Ocean?" The man replied in a shocked tone, "Oh, no sir! This is the white ocean. The Indian Ocean is 200 meters farther on."

I came back to South Africa in 1989. On that trip I met Dullah Omar, who was one of Mandela's lawyers and was later to be Minister of Justice in the first nonracial government. Dullah confided that the summer of 1989 would see demonstrations against apartheid all over South Africa, led by an umbrella group called the Mass Democratic Movement. The MDM was new enough that the government had not got around to banning it. Dullah said there would be mass arrests at these protests, and he wanted us to work with young lawyers and teach them what we knew about cross-examining police in such cases. He predicted that Mandela would be out of jail within a year. Seeing the repressive state of things, we doubted him—or at least I did—but he was right.

The next time I came to South Africa, Dullah was working with the ANC people who were drafting a new constitution for the country. We talked about the legal status of the homelands, and about the African National Congress's desire and promise to move from "legality to legality." This form of transition meant, for example, that the life tenure of judges appointed during the apartheid era would be respected. Of the 100 or so judges on the higher courts, 99 were white and 99 were men. The new government would move as quickly as possible to diversify that group, as judges retired or died.

But, Dullah and others were thinking, can we really trust those old judges to fairly interpret the new laws? South Africa would have a constitution that included the most advanced bill of rights in the world. I gave a lecture at the University of the Western Cape titled "Old Judges and New Laws." I suggested that the ANC study the Western European experience and establish a court with exclusive jurisdiction over constitutional issues. Such a Constitutional Court would have its judges all named by the new regime. This suggestion came from others as well, and was adopted. A multiracial Constitutional Court sits in Bramfontein, near Johannesburg, and its decisions are widely respected. Its members include Albie Sachs, Richard Goldstone, and Arthur Chaskalson, three white leaders of the anti-apartheid struggle.

In my 1990 visit, I lectured on constitutional principles at the historically Black law schools in Umtata, Cape Town, and Fort Hare (where Mandela went to law school). I can remember at Fort Hare my surprise when my talk drew a crowd of about 600; there were only 200 law students. The evening began with the group singing a freedom song that was a felony to sing only months before.

Even though a transition was in progress at that time, the old white government still ran things. The week after my visit to Fort Hare, 27 students were gunned down by the security police. And as I left Fort Hare by car for Umtata, with my two ANC comrades, uniformed military police with Uzis stopped our car. They asked us to get out and lie on the ground. We did so and they searched the car. My friends negotiated with them in Afrikaans and we were allowed to go on our way.

As I learned more about South Africa, I involved the Litigation Section more deeply in the changes there. Richard Goldstone visited with us on a trip to the United States. Dullah Omar spoke to our annual meeting. A Black Lawyers Association representative attended a Section Council meeting. We began to send books to Fort Hare Law School. We were invigorated by watching the changes being made in that society.

Ken Broun and I still meet for lunch or dinner every once in a while. We both look back on our experiences with a sense of having participated in a meaningful social struggle. Ken has written a compelling book, *Saving Nelson Mandela*, focused on the Rivonia treason trial of Mandela and other revolutionaries. We reflect that Mandela's release was provoked by the regime's realization that all of its guns, torture, police, and hangings would not stop the movement for change.

The point is illustrated by the dual nature of our advocacy teaching. We were preparing lawyers to assist in ordinary civil and criminal cases, seeking to replicate such victories as the *Govender* case. However, the idea that apartheid could be litigated or legislated out of existence had long been exploded. We were training lawyers to defend people in the armed—and peaceable—direct action struggles. We had before us the example of the trial in which Nelson Mandela and others were convicted of treason, but in which the state was unable to obtain a death sentence. Ken has written reflectively and brilliantly on that trial. He describes the political coalition that came together around the trial, and the political alliances of that defense.

I also see the corruption and neoliberal economic policies of the post-apartheid governments, and reflect that the struggle for human liberation is a permanent one. The dialectic of history includes an interpenetration of opposites, by which old forms and attitudes persist even after a fundamental change.

PERSPECTIVES FROM AIX-EN-PROVENCE

In the 1980s, the University of Texas School of Law had an informal exchange arrangement with the law faculty of Aix-en-Provence, France. That law school has been in existence since the 1300s under various names. For a time if was Faculté de droit et des sciences politiques, of the Université Aix-Marseille. Later, in an idea no doubt born of marketing—a word taken into French by the consumerists—it was the Université Paul-Cezanne, after Aix's Post-Impressionist painter.

The program had been dormant. I proposed to revive it. I would go to Aix in the spring for three or four weeks and teach classes to their students. Aix would send someone to Austin for an equivalent period. Three weeks in Provence, in the spring, and be paid.

In Aix, the faculty asked that I teach classes, in French, on capital punishment and on freedom of expression. I returned to Aix several times. In later years, I taught in a seminar about French medieval history, noting the archaeological evidence of significant events in the history of French law.

Each year, I was asked to give a public lecture on a legal topic. I chose to discuss France's prosecution of those who had committed war crimes and crimes against humanity during World War II. I regarded the study of this topic as an essential part of my own understanding—and perhaps that of others—of the importance of accountability for human rights abuses, and the difficulty in making people and institutions own up to those abuses. At the time of my first visit to Aix we were still trying to collect the Letelier judgment, so the issue was on my mind.

For many years after World War II, and the Nuremberg trials, groups of former Resistance fighters and deportees, and their families, had advocated that those who collaborated with the Nazis should be tried and punished. I traced some of this history in a 1995 article. Finally, in 1964, France amended its Penal Code to define and punish genocide and the crime against humanity.

The movement from legislation to prosecution proved difficult, impeded by Cold War hypocrisy and convenient collective amnesia.

The hypocrisy was evident when the French sought to try Klaus Barbie. He had been head of the Gestapo in Lyon during the war. After the war, the West German, American, and Bolivian governments recruited him to help with their anti-Communist intelligence operations. Finally, he lost the protection of these governments and was sent to France for trial. He was represented by left lawyer Jacques Vergés, who sought to gain Barbie's acquittal by proving that France had committed genocide and crimes against humanity in its former colonies and thus was unworthy to sit in judgment. Barbie was convicted.

Prosecutorial attention turned to Paul Touvier, who had ordered the execution of Jews in 1944 in his capacity as an officer of the Vichy France paramilitary group the Milice. Prosecuting an agent of the Vichy regime raised the specter of amnesia. Many French people held on to the view that the Vichy regime was, in the words of one judge, "a constellation of good intentions." The fact that the regime's agents had done the Nazis' bidding and had rounded up, deported, and killed thousands of people, was conveniently ignored. French courts allowed the Touvier prosecution to proceed, on the theory that he had actually done the Nazi regime's bidding. The courts required that, in order to convict of the crime against humanity, the prosecution must prove that the accused acted "as agent of a hegemonic government." The courts indulged the fiction that the Vichy government was independent of the "hegemonic" Nazi regime.

The next chapter in this saga was the prosecution of Maurice Papon, who had been Secretary for Jewish Questions in the Gironde, in Vichy France, and had a distinguished postwar career in the Gaullist government. He was finally brought to trial in 1997.

Papon had signed orders ordering that Jews be rounded up, interned, and sent to concentration camps. His lawyers argued that he had done all of this as an officer of the Vichy government not the Nazi occupation power, and that the statute therefore did not apply to him. The French trial and appellate courts rejected this argument. Papon was aware of the Vichy government's anti-Jewish policy and had indeed been one of its architects. He was not, as Touvier claimed to be, a foot soldier just following orders. And, the courts said, Papon acted with knowledge of the Nazi regime's actions and motivations. He could therefore be an accomplice even though he did not share the Nazi ideology and was not a member of any Nazi organization. This result corresponded with the general law of accessory—"aider and abettor"—criminal liability in France and for that matter in the United States' and other legal systems.

For my first public lecture in Aix, I discussed the Barbie and Touvier cases, with a brief mention of the Demjanjuk litigation. Aix law professor Gaétan Di Marino, an expert on criminal law, commented. He criticized the Touvier case as an improper exercise of the prosecution function. Law and history, he said, are not necessarily good companions. This surprised me, because I had observed that the two of them had been getting along pretty well for a couple of millennia, although at times they misunderstood one another.

I returned to the theme several years later, and focused on the Papon case, and the way he was welcomed into postwar high government positions despite his Vichy record. I retraced the debates that led to the 1964 Penal Code amendments. Di Marino came to the microphone and said with emphasis, "*J'aveu. La France, elle etait collaboratrice.*" France, she was a collaborator. The discussions of Barbie, Touvier, and Papon helped to illuminate this ongoing question of accountability for human rights abuses.

I enjoyed discussions with law professors in Aix. I also met three students who later enrolled in the University of Texas LL.M. program: Isabelle Giordani, Sophie Fanelli, and Robin Mardemootoo. Sophie and Isabelle were French, Robin was the son of a Mauritius lawyer. The three of them collaborated with me on an article, "Paul Touvier and the Crime Against Humanity."

Sophie worked on the Nichols defense team, doing legal research and becoming familiar with United States law. After the case concluded, she took the California bar exam and went to work for the ACLU.

Robin brought me into the decades-long litigation over the rights of the Chagossian people, forcibly expelled from their island home to make way for the U.S. military base on Diego Garcia.

CHILE, THE FIRST SEQUEL

The Letelier precedent played a role in 1998: a brave Spanish lawyer, Juan Garcés, brought a private criminal action against former Chilean dictator Augusto Pinochet, and Spanish judge Balthazar Garzon began judicial proceedings on the application. In Spain as in many other countries, counsel for victims can commence a criminal prosecution. Garcés's clients were victims of Chilean military torture and their families. All in all, Garcés presented more than a thousand cases of torture, disappearance, and murder, out of the thousands of such instances during the junta's rule in Chile from 1973 to 1991.

Garcés and Garzon fought back several legal challenges in Spain. Garzon issued a warrant for the arrest of General Pinochet. In the fall of 1998, Pinochet went to London for medical treatment, thinking himself immune from trouble on these charges. The British authorities acted on the Spanish warrant and arrested him. He claimed immunity from prosecution, and resisted extradition back to Spain. Many people in the human rights community thought that this case would go nowhere. I did not agree. I was therefore pleased to get a telephone call from the English barristers who were representing the British government, and by extension the Spanish judicial authorities, in the extradition proceedings as they made their way to Britain's House of Lords.

These lawyers asked if we could advise them on the immunity issues that we had litigated and won in the Letelier civil case. I said yes, and the law school approved travel for two law student research assistants. Jane and I paid our own way, and were on the next plane to London. The main issues were two: first, was the president of a country, even one who had achieved power by military coup, immune from prosecution for complicity in tortures, disappearances, and murders? Second, did Spanish courts have the power to try and punish Pinochet for his crimes, since most of his acts were done in Chile? A subsidiary issue was purely factual: Did the evidence show that Pinochet either ordered these abuses or know of them and encouraged their commission? On that factual issue, the European Union treaty does not permit the prisoner to present evidence in the extradition court; the issue is to be tried in the demanding state if the prisoner is sent there. Nonetheless, it was important that the extradition court in Britain have a comfortable sense that the prosecution theory of complicity was well founded. In any event, it was important to tell the story of what Pinochet and his regime had done.

For us, however, there was a further question. This was a case brought by Spain, former colonial ruler of Chile. Pinochet, despite no longer being president, had support within the Chilean military and with right-wing elements. Did the Chilean left, which had suffered under Pinochet, believe that this case was politically wise and not a danger to their movement? That is, a grand idea of human rights accountability should not obscure or replace the interests of those most directly affected.

Juan Pablo Letelier and a group of Chilean activists flew to London and we spent a long evening discussing the case. Yes, they agreed, the matter should proceed, to be followed up later with actions in Chile.

The second Pinochet issue was that of jurisdiction. Traditionally, a nation's criminal law is enforced against acts within its territory—the principle of territoriality. This principle may be expanded to cover actions done outside the borders but knowingly directed at the territory with the intent to cause a result there. For example, an illegal business combination in Central America may violate U.S. antitrust laws if it is designed to produce an anti-competitive effect in our market.

A nation may also, under a traditional view, punish criminal acts against its citizens and nationals, no matter where those acts occur—for example, by an attack on American citizens abroad. This is the principle of passive nationality. In Pinochet's case, some of the victims were Spaniards, and this principle would apply. The criminal law may be brought to bear on conduct by American citizens and nationals done anywhere in the world, if the legislature specifies that the law is to have extraterritorial effect, a principle known as active nationality.

However, there is a group of crimes that are regarded as being committed against all humanity, and therefore prosecutable by any state where the alleged offender may take refuge. This notion was firmly established by the end of the eighteenth century, with respect to the offense of piracy. It is known as "universal jurisdiction" and today is applied to crimes against humanity, genocide, torture and other violations of international peremptory norms. A peremptory norm may be defined as one that is so well established that no nation may opt out of it and claim it is not applicable to its conduct.

Universal jurisdiction has been controversial. Henry Kissinger has denounced it, and the official United States position toward it has alternated between caution and hostility. After all, conceding the principle would give a Chilean court the power to try Henry Kissinger for plotting the kidnapping of a pro-democracy Chilean general, or former CIA Director George H. W. Bush for supporting the tortures, disappearances, and killings done by the Chilean military intelligence apparatus with CIA support. In the Pinochet case, an aspect of universal jurisdiction was important. A state where the prisoner is found is obliged to try him or extradite him. *Aut dedaere, aut judicare*—either deliver the wrongdoer or prosecute him — is the maxim of the law.

The House of Lords held that Pinochet had immunity as former president of Chile for only some of the charges against him, removing one barrier to extradition, The case went back to Magistrate's Court for a decision on whether extradition would in all other respects be lawful.

The extradition hearing, which Sam Buffone and I attended to assist Juan Garcés and the English lawyers, was quietly dramatic. The hearing took place in the Bow Street Magistrate's Court, a blocky 1960s-style building near Covent Garden. Today's court is just across the square from where Sir John Fielding sat as Bow Street magistrate in the eighteenth century. Sir John was the younger brother of Henry Fielding, who preceded John as magistrate. The two of them established London's first professional police force; Henry wrote the novel *Tom Jones*.

Dozens of Chilean victims of the Pinochet regime stood with signs outside the courthouse, and filed in to hear the proceedings. In the evenings, we gathered at a local pub with them and with British human rights supporters, including Jeremy Corbyn, who vocally and actively supported the cause.

In the courtroom, charge after charge detailed the record of Pinochet-directed oppression, torture, and murder, and nothing in the rather stilted and boring speeches of his lawyers could change the evident course of things. These lawyers took the absurd position that Pinochet could not be liable for crimes if he were not personally present when the victims were tortured and killed.

For me, the most exciting moment was the procedurally routine testimony of a Scotland Yard inspector who had arrested Pinochet. He described going to a house where Pinochet was staying, being made to wait, and then being taken to a sumptuous drawing room where "the prisoner" was sitting, wearing a silk shirt and holding a silver-decorated cane, and saying:

Augusto Pinochet Ugarte, I arrest you for the crimes of torture, genocide and conspiracy. I caution you that anything you say may be taken down and given in evidence against you. Anything you may later decide to say may permit a comment on your silence. And he looked at me and said, "I do not recognize your authority. I will not respond to these charges."

Because the magistrate, Roland Bartle, was known to harbor conservative views, the Pinochet lawyers thought he would rule in their favor. They went so far as to encourage leading conservative politicians to make press statements in favor of Pinochet's cause. This strategy backfired. Bartle wrote a stinging denunciation of efforts to influence him, and reaffirmed the idea that the growing human rights movement was on its way to producing "one law for one world," an astounding sentiment from that source. He began his opinion by noting the various human rights and international criminal law treaties that have come into existence. He continued:

These Conventions represent the growing trend of the international community to combine together to outlaw crimes which are abhorrent to civilised society whether they be offences of the kind to which I have referred or crimes of cruelty and violence which may be committed by individuals, by terrorist groups seeking to influence or overthrow democratic governments or by undemocratic governments against their own citizens. This development may be said to presage the day when, for the purposes of extradition, there will be one law for one world.

Bartle ordered that the extradition could proceed. However, the Blair government caved in, and Home Secretary Jack Straw decided Pinochet was too ill to stand trial and sent him home to Chile, where courts there reached a similar result.

The litigation had, however, fractured what was left of Pinochet's perceived invulnerability in Chile, as we were to discover as we continued to work with Juan Garcés.

UNROW

That London trip in 1998 brought an interesting perspective. I had been tempted to see the end of the Nichols trial, in January 1998, as a signal to step back, slow down, teach and write. Others did not see the agenda quite that way.

On January 16, 1998, the State of Texas and the largest tobacco companies reached a settlement in a lawsuit seeking damages and other relief. In 1995, Texas Attorney General Dan Morales had retained five Texas lawyers—Walter Umphrey, Harold Nix, Wayne Reaud, John O'Quinn, and John Eddie Williams—to bring a lawsuit focused on the harm caused by cigarette smoking. Up to that time, the tobacco companies had been sued 800 times for the health harms of smoking and had never had to pay a penny in damages. The five lawyers agreed to take the case for a contingent fee. They came up with a new theory, that the tobacco companies were liable for the increased health care and associated costs caused by marketing cigarettes and other tobacco products. That is, they focused on the epidemiological evidence of harm, rather than on individual decisions to smoke cigarettes. They contended that tobacco companies had not only caused harm, but had lied about the potential harm in their advertising and to legislative entities. The complaint was based in part on the RICO statute, which provided treble damages, nationwide service of process, and attorney fees.

The ensuing complex litigation resulted in a docket of more than 2,000 entries in the federal court in Texarkana. The five lawyers spent more than $50 million of their own money to conduct the case. The case had been set for trial in January 1998, and the tobacco companies caved in. The settlement provided for a payout to Texas over time of more than $17 billion, in addition to restrictions on marketing.

The settlement was barely announced when predictable political and financial motivations entered the battle. Texas governor George W. Bush denied that the contingent fee contract was enforceable, and that the lawyers—all big donors to the Democratic Party and known as litigators for injured workers and consumers—would receive a fee and reimbursement, if any, if and when the Republican legislature decided to award one. The newly elected Republican Attorney General, Morales's successor, John Cornyn, alleged that the lawyers must have paid a bribe for the honor of representing Texas and spending all that money.

Looking back, we chuckle at the irrationality of Bush's and Cornyn's position, but at the time they were earnest. The tobacco lawyers asked Jane and me to represent them. Jane bore major responsibility, first for the ensuing five years of intense litigation, and then for the occasional bursts of activity thereafter. In summary: two federal grand juries and several state courts looked into the retention and conduct of our clients. They found nothing amiss and every reason to laud their work. The settling defendant tobacco companies agreed to pay a court-approved legal fee, and reimburse most of the out-of-pocket litigation costs.

However, an Assistant U.S. Attorney in Austin, Sharon Pierce, found a case to pursue. In 1997, when it became clear that the lawsuit might actually be successful, Attorney General Morales asked the five lawyers for several hundred thousand dollars in campaign contributions. He did not intend to run for reelection, and under Texas law he could keep this money. Our clients said no.

Undeterred, Morales directed that his friend Marc Murr be added to the roster of counsel for the state of Texas. Our clients resisted. So Morales began to develop a false paper trail of Murr's purported work on the case. When the settlement was announced, Murr and Morales engaged in a phony arbitration that awarded Murr more than $100 million in fees.

Sharon Pierce and an FBI agent followed the paper trail. Our clients responded to subpoenas and requests for interview. Morales and Murr were indicted. Morales pleaded guilty and was sentenced to four years.

By mid-2000, Jane and I were having some success battling back the attacks on our clients. At the same time, Robin Mardemootoo had written from Mauritius to ask if we would help with the Chagos litigation. Juan Garcés had written from Madrid to ask our help in suing Michael Townley, the assassin of Orlando Letelier and Ronni Moffitt, for having murdered a Spanish diplomat, Carmelo Soria, in Santiago in 1976. Finally, Isabel Letelier called from Chile to ask if we would seek justice for the family of General Rene Schneider, who had been kidnapped and killed in 1970, with U.S. connivance and support, in an effort to destabilize the government of President Salvador Allende.

All of these were worthy projects. We recalled how excited the law students had been to work on the Pinochet extradition. I was on the faculty of Washington College of Law, which was founded in 1896 by two women who wanted to break down the barriers to women seeking to enter the legal profession. WCL's faculty included Elliott Milstein, a pioneer of clinical legal education, and a clinical faculty that included Richard J. Wilson and Ann Shalleck.

I suggested that WCL should have an international human rights clinic, where students would work on cases like those being suggested to me. Elliott, Rick, and Ann were skeptical, concerned that students would play a "law clerk" rather than a lawyer role in complex cases. More immediately, there was the cost of student travel to distant forums, and the associated costs of such litigation.

The issue of student learning and participation would have to be worked out in practice, and my faculty colleagues were open to the experiment. For the money, our tobacco clients had been talking about giving us a bonus on top of the hourly fees we had been billing. They agreed that instead of paying us, they would give a total of two million dollars to the law school as an endowment, the income from which would provide funding for human rights litigation to be done by and with law students.

We named it the UNROW grant, from the first letter of the clients' last names. As I write these words, more than two decades on, the UNROW income has enabled students to work with and learn from clients and lawyers in the United States and a half-dozen other countries. Elliott, Ann, and Rick have become convinced that this work fits the model of clinical education they champion. Students who participated in human rights work have gone on to good careers in law—or more to the point, careers in good law.

After Jane and I had led the clinical seminar for a few years, we took a less active role. Ali Beydoun, a formidable lawyer and inspiring teacher, took on the responsibility, and others followed.

CHILE, THE SECOND SEQUEL

Between Salvador Allende's election as president of Chile in 1970 and the 1973 Pinochet coup, Henry Kissinger and the CIA directed millions of dollars into efforts to destabilize the Chilean government. On October 22, 1970, using submachine guns supplied by the CIA, a far right Chilean group kidnapped General Rene Schneider, the commander in chief of the Chilean armed forces. General Schneider was wounded during the kidnapping and died two days later. In 2000, declassified U.S. State Department cable traffic revealed how Kissinger and CIA director Helms had orchestrated the kidnapping, provided the weapons, and paid the kidnappers.

The students began to assemble a picture of the kidnapping, using the cables and other information. Edward Korry had been U.S. ambassador to Chile from 1967 to 1971. He had agreed with the anti-Allende U.S. policy. However, he denied having supported the Schneider kidnapping and said he had come to Washington around that time to make that point to Kissinger and Nixon.

In mid-1971, he was interviewed at length on the CBS news program *60 Minutes*, and gave a firsthand version of events that was corroborated by the cable traffic. I called him, and he agreed to having the law students interview him. I went with two law students to Charlotte, North Carolina, where Korry lived. The students interviewed him over two days and did a detailed memorandum of the conversation. Korry was in poor health, and he succumbed to cancer a little over a year later.

Using the Korry interview and the documents they had obtained, the students drafted a complaint on behalf of General Schneider's children, naming Henry Kissinger and Richard Helms as defendants. The Federal Rules of Civil

Procedure allow for a "short and plain" statement of the court's jurisdiction and the plaintiff's claim. However the students wanted to let the defendants, the court, and the world at large know that we had solid evidence of the defendants' complicity.

The students arranged for a process server to serve the complaint on Kissinger and Helms in a public setting, because their counsel would not agree to accept service. Kissinger's lawyers called me to express indignation at the lawsuit. I referred his call to the students.

Predictably, Justice Department lawyers took over the case for the two defendants. They moved to dismiss the complaint, arguing that due to the national security rationale for the kidnapping, the case involved a "political question," that is, sensitive issues of foreign policy unsuitable for judicial determination.

Our first hearing, on the government's motion to dismiss, was before U.S. District Judge Henry Kennedy. Law student Brittany Benowitz argued eloquently and with poise. Judge Kennedy upheld the government's position, as did the court of appeals.

The government's "political question" argument was complicated nonsense. The factual issue in the case was "Did Henry Kissinger arrange for the kidnapping of General Schneider by an armed gang, and did these circumstances create a high and foreseeable risk that deadly force would be used?" The legal issues were: "Did this conduct constitute complicity in murder under Chilean law?" and "Did the planning within the United States to carry out the kidnapping, given the high risk that death would result, constitute conspiracy to murder under applicable U.S. laws that had in the past been applied to U.S.-based conspiracies to assassinate foreign political figures?" The documentary evidence, and Korry's testimony, made a strong case. No lawyer for Kissinger challenged our factual recitals.

The judges' real concern was more prosaic, as indifference to injustice often is. They were concerned with the hoary old "open the door" issue. For example, in 1979, the Supreme Court heard the case of Warren McCleskey, an African-American who was sentenced to death for having killed a white Atlanta policeman. He presented evidence that an African-American charged with killing a white person was more than four times as likely to receive a death sentence than a white person. He argued that this racial disparity should invalidate his sentence.

The Supreme Court rejected the argument, 5 to 4. The majority said that the statistical study did not prove that there was racial discrimination in McCleskey's case. The decision is an infamous example of judicial refusal to face facts about the system that calls itself "criminal justice."

In dissenting, Justice Brennan commented, "The Court next states that its unwillingness to regard petitioner's evidence as sufficient is based in part on the fear that recognition of McCleskey's claim would open the door to widespread challenges to all aspects of criminal sentencing. . . . Taken on its face, such a statement seems to suggest a fear of too much justice."

Sometimes the judges fear the "door" and sometimes they conjure up "opening the floodgates," but the reasoning and result are the same. If a door were opened to view all the times that Henry Kissinger had advocated, planned, supported, applauded, or rewarded kidnapping, torture, or murder, the judicial system would have a lot of work to do. We know that when human rights abuses committed by state actors are revealed, usually after years of concealment and lies, the state is reluctant to acknowledge the wrong much less redress it.

And, as I will discuss below, the state's first reaction when a courageous journalist blows the whistle is to prosecute the messenger.

At the Schneider family's request, the law students took the Schneider case to the Inter-American Commission on Human Rights, which has yet to decide it.

CHILE, THE THIRD SEQUEL

The next UNROW clinic case has had a more fruitful journey. Carmelo Soria, a Spanish national, was a United Nations diplomat. Michael Townley and two of his colleagues in the Chilean secret police agency known as DINA, kidnapped, tortured, and murdered him in Santiago in 1976. Soria's widow, Laura Gonzalez Vera, has been seeking ever since then to bring Townley to account. At Juan Garcés' request, the UNROW students filed suit against Townley, and served him through the U.S. Department of Justice in Washington. Although the murder had taken place in Chile, he could be sued where he lived. As expected, Townley did not respond to the suit, and the court entered judgment against him. The Justice Department refused to cooperate in locating Townley's assets to satisfy the judgment as he was not only still in the Witness Protection Program but also, so the Department averred, providing intelligence service to the United States. The Department ordered Townley to pay $75 per month toward the multi-million-dollar judgment.

Now the battle shifted to Chile. Laura Gonzales Vera's Chilean lawyer, with Garcés' help, filed suit in the Supreme Court of the Chile requesting that Chile seek Townley's extradition so that he could be tried for the Soria murder. In March 2015, Jane, Ali Beydoun, and I accompanied a group of law students to Santiago for a hearing before a Justice of Chile Supreme Court.

We met with a lawyer in the Ministry of Justice who had compiled a file on Townley. He told us the Ministry could prove that Townley had committed at least a dozen murders as a DINA agent.

On March 5, we sat in the chambers of a Supreme Court Justice and outlined the evidence against Townley. The Justice listened, then said that when Pinochet was leaving office, he had secured legislation granting him and all agents of the military junta, including the DINA, amnesty for a list of crimes including murder. I noted that under international law, a plea of amnesty or former jeopardy was invalid if obtained by legal fraud or in violation of fundamental rules of public order. The Justice nodded and said he would consider the matter.

Our team went out for coffee. We wondered if there were crimes that Townley had committed that were not on the amnesty list. I don't remember if I or the students made the first discovery, but within a few weeks the students had a memo, discussing articles 292 and 293 of the Chilean Penal Code:

Article 292: The formation of any association for the purpose of committing offenses against the social order, social conventions, persons, or property constitutes a crime.

Article 293: If the purpose of the association has been to commit felonies, the heads, anyone who has exercised leadership therein, and their instigators, shall be punished by long-term imprisonment in any of its degrees.

Judicial precedent established that the association must be shown to have a defined organizational structure and that the accused must have acted with knowledge of the illicit purpose and the intention to further it. This is somewhat like the law of aiding and abetting in common law countries, except that illicit association is a separate offense from the crimes the associates commit.

That is, Townley might have amnesty for murder, but not for the separate crime under Article 293. The Chilean lawyer filed a memorandum with the full Chile Supreme Court, embodying the students' work.

On May 16, 2016, the Supreme Court issued its opinion. Townley and his two confederates had committed the offense of illicit association, and did not have amnesty; Chile was requesting the United States to send them to Chile for trial. The "illicit association," the Court held was DINA itself, a holding that opened the way to prosecution of many other crimes of the Pinochet regime. We had not invoked a "thought crime." Townley and his DINA colleagues were all involved in threats, beatings, torture, kidnapping, and murder.

The United States has shown no inclination to send Townley to Chile, but the case remains a beacon in the law of accountability.

The Chile litigation reflects the judgment about international human rights that runs all through what I have been discussing: the need to keep the inquiry and our work focused on human needs and consistent with our understanding of history and society. Seeking to try Pinochet in Spain made sense because it was a means to support and empower the movement in Chile to hold the Pinochet regime accountable. It was a step toward the eventual result in Santiago.

In marked contrast, it seems to me, was the effort in Belgium to prosecute a government official of the Democratic Republic of Congo. In 1998, Abdoulaye Yerodia, the foreign minister of the Democratic Republic of Congo, publicly urged citizens to kill opponents of the government, who were mostly ethnic Tutsis. At that time, Belgian law asserted universal jurisdiction over genocide and crimes against humanity, and a Belgian court issued an arrest warrant for Yerodia. Congo sued Belgium in the International Court of Justice in The Hague, claiming that under international law a serving foreign minister was immune from the criminal judicial jurisdiction of a foreign country. On February 14, 2002, the ICJ ruled in Congo's favor and ordered the arrest warrant withdrawn. There was disagreement among the ICJ justices, three of whom dissented on the immunity question, and six on the question of remedy. The most apt opinion was that of Judge Bula-Bula, the Congolese member of the tribunal. His opinion can be characterized as exclaiming: "What! Belgium is to give lessons on humanitarianism to the Congo?"

Another example: Liberian President Charles Taylor was tried by a "Special Court for Sierra Leone," created by the United Nations and the government of Sierra Leone. The court premises are in Freetown, Sierra Leone. When it was decided to move the Taylor prosecution away from Freetown, The Hague was chosen. Was there not an available courtroom in, say, Cape Town, South Africa? There was no question of "jurors" being chosen from a "vicinage," as the trial court consisted of judges. But moving the case to Western Europe, and to a city in a former colonial power, was astoundingly insensitive.

I endorse the use of international human rights standards, and international tribunals, to try offenders. What we are seeing in some cases, however, is the erosion of generally accepted standards of criminal defense, reliability of evidence, unbiased choice of defendants, and interpretation of criminal statutes. In this, as in all our work, we must begin as we mean to go on.

I also recognize that international human rights standards can be brought to bear as arguments in debates about social change and in national courts.

The social change we seek is international. For example, in *Roper v. Simmons*, the Supreme Court held, 5 to 4, that the Constitution forbids executing someone for a crime committed before the age of eighteen. Justice Kennedy, writing for the majority, noted that state practice in the international community rejected execution of juvenile offenders, with the exception of only seven countries. He also noted that the Convention on the Rights of the Child forbade such executions. Justice Scalia, dissenting, derided this use of "foreign law," as though the United States was on a separate planet from the other members of the international community, and in professed ignorance of the dozens of cases in which the Court has looked to international norms for guidance.

CHAGOS

Robin Mardemootoo, who had been a student in Aix-en-Provence, had kept in touch. We told him about the UNROW-funded human rights law clinic. He proposed that our law students join an international team of lawyers who were representing the Chagos Islanders. To sketch the background: The British colony of Mauritius, a group of islands in the Indian Ocean, became independent on March 12, 1968. However, based on a secret 1966 agreement between the United States and the UK, the Chagos archipelago, a group of more than sixty islands, which had historically been regarded as part of Mauritius, was detached and retained by the UK as a colonial possession—the British Indian Ocean Territory or BIOT.

The U.S.-UK agreement was designed to make way for the construction of the U.S. military base on the island of Diego Garcia. At that time, the islands were home to more than 4,000 people who worked in the coconut plantations and engaged in fishing, farming, and other pursuits. Most of them lived on Diego Garcia. Their ancestors had first settled on the island from Africa in the eighteenth century, when the archipelago was a French possession. The British acquired the archipelago by conquest in 1815. The people on Diego Garcia had houses and household gardens, the title to which they held as a form of real property under French law, which remained applicable because the islands had been taken by conquest.

The United States and UK falsely stated to the UN and other groups that the islands were uninhabited. They set out to make that statement come true. Beginning in 1967, when a Chagossian left the island for medical care on the main island of Mauritius, or for a family visit there, he or she would be barred from returning to Diego Garcia. The UK halted imports of food and other goods. Finally, in 1971, they brought a ship into the Diego Garcia harbor, loaded the remaining 4,000 Chagossians aboard, took them to Port Louis harbor on the main Mauritius island and left them on the docks. Parties of UK and U.S. personnel went ashore on Diego Garcia and killed all the Chagossians' domestic animals.

By 2000, when we discussed the case with Robin, Richard Gifford, a UK lawyer, had been pursuing legal remedies in the UK courts for several years, with some success. The Chagos Refugee Group, the association of plaintiffs, was headed by Olivier Bancoult on the main Island of Mauritius. For the next several years, law students participated in the litigation in several forums.

The Chagossians' goal was to return to the archipelago, and to be compensated for their forcible removal. They were willing to accept that the Diego Garcia military base would remain. There were at least a dozen other islands that would be suitable for settlement and for economic activity such as ecotourism and fishing. They also noted that there are hundreds of civilian employees on Diego Garcia, from many countries, but that Chagossians are excluded from such employment.

The first task, however, was to see, and prepare to help others to see, this case from the Chagossians' perspective. What were their experiences? What was the proper remedy for the harm they were suffering? Law students went to Chagos, benefiting from the UNROW grant, to meet the clients and gather evidence.

Here, it seemed, was a case in which the trier of fact, in any of the forums in which the case might be heard, would be assisted by expert opinion on the lives, livelihoods, and aspirations of the Chagossians, or, as they are also called, the Ilois people. We believed that their story might best be told by a social anthropologist or sociologist. We consulted with Dr. Wojciech Sokolowski at Johns Hopkins and Philip Harvey at Rutgers Law School. Harvey and I had worked together on litigation several years earlier; he has a law degree and a PhD in economics.

We learned of Professor Shirley Lindenbaum at the City University of New York, who had worked with peoples in the Indian Ocean region. She had a brilliant suggestion: one of her doctoral students, David Vine, was looking for a dissertation topic. Perhaps he would take on this project.

In September 2001, we met David at a restaurant in lower Manhattan. This proved to be a collaboration and friendship that has continued over the years. David agreed to study the Chagossian community and its forcible exile. He would consult with our team to ensure that his methodology and conclusions would be admissible in evidence under prevailing rules on the reliability of expert testimony. He spent many months in Mauritius and in the Seychelles Islands, where some Chagossians had resettled. He learned the Bourbonnais

Creole spoken by the Ilois. His thesis, published as *Island of Shame: The Secret History of the U.S. Military Base on Diego Garcia*, has provided important insight into the issues in our litigation, and has been widely praised in its own right. David has since published important work on the more than 800 U.S. military bases around the world.

Our U.S. lawsuit, against present and former U.S. officials, was dismissed on "political question" grounds. Our students reached out to members of the Senate and House of Representatives, seeking support for the Chagossians, with very limited success. In the post–September 11, 2001 world, the military's interests were treated with deference. The official U.S. position was that the entire archipelago was off limits due to "security concerns."

Our students provided assistance to the UK lawyers. A UK trial court upheld a limited right of return. Rather than negotiate in good faith, the Blair government took steps that they expected would permanently bar the Chagossians from their homeland. They produced an environmental study that seemed to support denial of resettlement in the archipelago and even any fishing activity. When Chagossians ventured into BIOT in fishing boats, they were turned away. With this study in hand, the Blair government had the Queen issue "Orders in Council" barring the Chagossians. They claimed that the Orders in Council were royal acts not subject to judicial review.

The UK High Court held the Orders invalid; its decision was affirmed by the Court of Appeal in 2007. I read the Court of Appeal decision., written by Lord Justice Stephen Sedley. I had known a Stephen Sedley back in 1962-63 in London. He was the son of an East London solicitor who strongly supported the labor and peace movements. He was then in college, and I knew him from various political gatherings.

Yes, this was the same Stephen Sedley. He had been a brilliant barrister, and was appointed as a trial court judge in 1992 and an appellate judge in 1999. He had sat on the European Court of Human Rights. I wrote to him. Jane and I have since become friends with him and his wife, Tia Sedley; Stephen has welcomed our law students to his home for discussions of human rights issues.

Sedley's judicial opinion first held that all the monarch's orders are subject to judicial review. The UK is long past having an absolute monarch. This holding has been followed in notable cases since 2007. He then held that the Order was objectively unreasonable.

The United Nations Human Rights Committee stated that the UK "should ensure that the Chagos islanders can exercise their right to return to their territory and should indicate what measures have been taken in this regard. It should consider compensation for the denial of this right over an extended period." The Blair government chose instead to appeal to the House of Lords.

The Chagossians sent a delegation to London, led by Olivier Bancoult, for the week-long arguments before the five Law Lords. The arguing barristers were Sir Sidney Kentridge, Maya Lester, and Anthony Bradley. I sat with Richard Gifford and Robin Mardemootoo at the solicitor's desk behind the barristers.

Their lordships ruled against us 3 to 2. They all agreed that the orders were judicially reviewable, but found that the idea of a nature preserve throughout the Chagos archipelago was a reasonable basis for excluding the Chagossians. The Chagossians continued to campaign for relief in other legal and political forums.

We got a piece of good news from Wikileaks. On December 2, 2010, the *Guardian* published a cable that Wikileaks had obtained from a UK diplomat to his U.S. counterpart, saying that the UK was establishing a marine preserve in BIOT, but that the idea was based on political-military considerations without regard to any environmental concerns. In sum, the UK government had lied to the House of Lords.

UK government lawyers claimed in court that the cable was protected by the Vienna Convention and could not be considered. The UK court disagreed. Law students in the clinic sent a copy of the cable to the Defense Department and State Department asking, under the Freedom of Information Act, for any copy of it in those departments' records.

A clerk in the Defense Department replied that yes, they had the cable, but that it was secret and we could not have a copy, thus admitting the cable was authentic.

Through the years of litigation and political action, I wondered how the government of Mauritius was viewing these events. Robin Mardemootoo introduced me to the prime minister in 2001. Most of the Chagossian community lived in an impoverished part of the capital city, Port Louis. The UK decision to hold on to BIOT at the time of Mauritius's independence was another example of imperialist line-drawing.

In 2017, Mauritius took action. It rounded up overwhelming support in the United Nations General Assembly for a resolution asking the International Court of Justice to give an advisory opinion. The resolution, adopted June 22, 2017, asked the ICJ two questions:

(a) Was the process of decolonization of Mauritius lawfully completed when Mauritius was granted independence in 1968, following the separation of the Chagos Archipelago from Mauritius . . . ?; and (b) What are the consequences under international law . . . arising from the continued administration by the United Kingdom . . . of the Chagos Archipelago, including with respect to the inability of Mauritius to implement a program for the resettlement on the Chagos Archipelago of its nationals, in particular those of Chagossian origin?

This was a significant event. By moving in the General Assembly instead of the Security Council, Mauritius avoided the prospect of a U.S. or UK veto in the latter body. And, by having the General Assembly seek an advisory opinion, Mauritius could demonstrate the worldwide support for its position, a showing that was replicated with the number of submissions by nation-states to the ICJ.

Was there work here for law students in the clinical course? Yes. Robin sent Pooja Bissoonauthsing from his firm to Washington for a month. Pooja consulted with the Mauritius embassy in Washington and worked with the law students on suggestions that she would make to the lawyers for Mauritius concerning its submission to the ICJ.

The ICJ oral hearing was in September 2018. Robin was in The Hague assisting Mauritius's counsel. He called during the case to discuss one of the central issues: Was this an essentially bilateral dispute between the UK and Mauritius, so that it could not be the subject of an Advisory Opinion? The answer was clear: the General Assembly had referred to UN resolutions of a general character. More to the point, at a historical moment when the great majority of General Assembly members are former colonies, it was by now clear that relations between a colonizer and the colonized are not bilateral, but rather of concern to the entire international community.

On February 25, 2019, the ICJ issued its opinion. The court unanimously found it had jurisdiction to issue the advisory opinion; decided, 12 votes to 2—the U.S. judge and the Slovakian judge dissenting—to comply with the request for an advisory opinion; decided, with only the U.S. judge dissenting, "that having regard to international law, the process of decolonization of Mauritius was not lawfully completed when that country acceded to independence in 1968, following the separation of the Chagos Archipelago"; that "the United Kingdom is under an obligation to bring to an end its administration of the Chagos Archipelago as rapidly as possible"; and that "all Member States are under an obligation to co-operate with the United Nations in order to complete the decolonization of Mauritius."

On May 21, 2019, the General Assembly, taking account of the ICJ decision, voted 116 to 6 that the UK should end its control of BIOT "as rapidly as possible." The Mauritius representative said in debate: "One would have hoped that any country found to have engaged in an unlawful act would hasten to make amends." Negative votes were cast by Israel, Hungary, Australia, and the Maldives. Fifty-six countries abstained. The United States and UK have not, as of this writing, complied with the resolution.

LYNNE STEWART AND THE "BLIND SHEIK"

The case of Lynne Stewart, a progressive lawyer I represented from 2002 to 2005, raised all of the issues about the state's procedural and substantive overreaching, done in the name of fighting terrorism.

Lynne Stewart grew up in New York City, and began a career as a teacher. In 1972, she enrolled in Rutgers Law School in Newark, New Jersey. She commuted to law school on a motorcycle that her husband, Ralph Poynter, had restored. After admission to the New York Bar in 1975 she began practice in lower Manhattan, first in an informal law partnership and then on her own.

Her practice focused on criminal defense of poor people and people of color. She had a deserved reputation as able, aggressive, diligent, and caring. She would receive—and reply to—letters from past clients thanking her for her work on their behalf. She was defense counsel in high-profile cases.

In 1994, former attorney general Ramsey Clark convinced her to take on the defense of Sheik Omar Abdel-Rahman, who was indicted in New York federal court for seditious conspiracy and related charges for having been leader and spiritual adviser to a group that had allegedly carried out the 1993 World Trade Center bombing and planned to bomb the Lincoln and Holland Tunnels and other New York area landmarks, and had conspired to assassinate Egyptian president Hosni Mubarak.

The Sheik had been a leader of the "Islamic Group," a militant Muslim organization in Egypt. He was recognized as a leading scholar of the Quran, and spoke against Egypt's secular regime. He spent three years in an Egyptian prison in connection with the assassination of Egyptian President Anwar Sadat, although he was eventually acquitted in that case. He immigrated to the United States in 1990 and was leader of several New York–area mosques.

Lynne took on the months-long trial. The jury returned its verdict convicting her client and the other defendants on October 1, 1995. The judge sentenced the Sheik to life imprisonment. The court of appeals affirmed the convictions, in an opinion that failed to observe the constitutionally protected distance between speech and imminent lawless action. The court's opinion indulged many of the same fears of social danger that one had seen in the 1961 Supreme Court decisions about the Communist Party, and the same theory of conspiracy that motivated the Angela Davis prosecution. This time, the fear was not of a Soviet-dominated revolutionary movement, or of African-American protest against a savage prison system, but of an allegedly unitary worldwide band of Muslims all bent on terror—a harbinger of judicial attitudes to come.

Yes, there was an Islamic Group, IG, which existed in several countries and advanced an agenda based on its leaders' and members' view of Islam and Islam's role in the world. The actions taken in the group's name included political action in opposition to the Egyptian regime; some of those actions involved the use of violence. However, not all those associated with IG advocated or participated in violence. As in other contexts, the state projected a mythological view of a unitary entity, greatly exaggerating the social danger posed by speech and advocacy. We were seeing, again, the use of constitutionally protected speech and association as a basis for inferring adherence to an unlawful agreement. Here it was again, as Roland Barthes had described it: "Justice is always ready to lend you a spare brain in order to condemn you, not as you are but as you must be."

The Sheik had been blind since he was ten months old, and was otherwise in ill health. He served his sentence at three different federal prison hospitals, and died in 2017. As with all her clients, Lynne continued to monitor the Sheik's treatment in prison, and to visit him. Ramsey Clark, who had referred the case to Lynne, argued the appeal and took some steps to improve the Sheik's prison conditions. Clark was involved with a number of international human rights organizations; from time to time, he explored the prospect of the Sheik being returned to Egypt to serve his sentence, where he could be close to his family.

The Sheik's 1995 imprisonment coincided with a dramatic change in federal prison regulations: the introduction by the Bureau of Prisons (BOP) of Special Administrative Measures, or SAMs. As a Yale Law study reported in 2017:

> The BOP first promulgated the regulations establishing SAMs in 1996 to target prisoners who allegedly posed extraordinary safety threats to the public from within prison, for example, by directing acts of violence against witnesses or others.... The rules permitted the Attorney General to restrict prisoners' communications that she determined might pose a threat to national security or lead to "acts of violence or terrorism."

In practice, the BOP's determinations about national security seemed influenced by the prisoner's religion. For the blind Sheik, the prohibitions on his interaction with other human beings were especially onerous. Moreover, the prospect that, through the efforts of Ramsey Clark and others, Egypt and the United States might agree to his serving his sentence in Egypt depended on his not becoming isolated and "invisible." As Lynne and Clark saw it, this meant that news of the Sheik's concerns should be shared with the public, subject only to reasonable and constitutionally permissible limitations.

The April 1997 SAM provided that the Sheik "will not be permitted to talk with, meet with, correspond with, or otherwise communicate with any member, or representative, of the news media, in person, by telephone, by furnishing a recorded message, through the mails, through his attorney(s), or otherwise." Lynne argued with the prosecutors about these restrictions and was led to believe, as a result of those discussions, that the ostensibly blanket prohibition was subject to a "rule of reason." Based on that understanding, she signed an affirmation that she would comply with the SAM. In the event, the charges against her did not reflect or honor her understanding of the bargain she had made with the government.

Even as Lynne was negotiating with prosecutors over the SAMs, they and the FBI were engaged in a multi-country investigation focused on the Islamic Group and other organizations identified as centers of terrorist planning and action. After the September 11, 2001, attacks, and given congressional grants of surveillance power to the executive branch, the FBI faced no obstacles in its choice of methods and targets.

The government obtained a warrant from the Foreign Intelligence Surveillance Court to monitor telephone calls among alleged associates of the Sheik, including Ahmed Abdul Sattar, who had been a paralegal assistant in the Sheik's trial. Because Lynne was an American citizen, she could not be the subject of a FISA warrant, but it was lawful to record her conversations if she spoke with someone against whom a warrant was obtained. FISA has limited protection for lawyer-client conversations. The FBI also obtained authorization to video-record Lynne's prison conversations with the Sheik, during which she was accompanied by Mohamed Yousry, a translator who had also worked with the Sheik's defense team.

In all, more than 88,000 telephone calls were intercepted and recorded. Due to equipment inadequacies, many of these recordings were lost and could not be turned over to the defense.

On April 8, 2002, the grand jury indicted Lynne, Sattar, and Yousry. The indictment also named a London-based activist, Yassir al-Sirri. Al-Sirri was arrested in London but never brought to the United States for trial. He and Sattar were parties to many of the intercepted calls. The indictment's general allegation was that IG was a foreign terrorist organization (FTO),

an international terrorist group dedicated to opposing nations, governments, institutions, and individuals that did not share IG's radical interpretation of Islamic law. . . . IG considered such parties "infidels" and interpreted the concept of "jihad" as waging opposition against infidels by whatever means necessary, including force and violence.

Sheik Omar Abdel Rahman was alleged to be IG's leader, and all its activities in every part of the world could, so the government alleged, be attributed to his leadership. From the time he was imprisoned, those who helped him keep in touch with the outside world were in effect his surrogates and shared responsibility for all of IG's violent actions. Sattar was alleged to be "an active IG leader who serves as a vital link between Sheik Abdel Rahman and the worldwide IG membership." This was a theory of global conspiracy that replicated the state's contentions in the old and discredited Communist Party cases.

Count 1 of the indictment charged all three defendants with conspiring to provide and to attempt to provide material support and resources to a foreign terrorist organization. (Yes, this is a double inchoate crime—a conspiracy to attempt.) Count 2 charged that they had provided such support and resources. Count 3 charged Sattar, and Al-Sirri, but not Stewart or Yousry, with soliciting persons to engage in crimes of violence. Count 4 charged Sattar, Stewart, and Yousry with conspiring to defraud the United States, by working to evade the SAMs. Count 5 charged that Lynne's written agreement to abide by the SAMs was a false statement.

The indictment envisioned a trial at which all of the violent acts, and possible violent acts, that Sattar discussed with Al-Sirri and others on the telephone would be presented to the jury, with Lynne's role as an English-speaking lawyer unfamiliar with those activities folded into the mix. The trial judge would remind the jurors that this or that item of sensational evidence was to be considered only as to Sattar. We shared Justice Robert Jackson's view that believing such instructions are effective is a "naive assumption" that "all practicing lawyers know to be unmitigated fiction."

Lynne was arrested at her home in Brooklyn, and soon released on bail, as was Yousry. The judge denied bail to Sattar. The FBI, armed with a warrant, raided Lynne's law office and removed correspondence, financial records, and client files. The trial judge, John Koeltl, appointed a special master to take custody of the seized materials and determine which constituted lawyer-client or attorney work product material and could not be given over to the government. I knew and had worked with John Koeltl when he was a lawyer in private practice.

I met with Lynne and her partner Ralph Poynter. She asked me to accept a court appointment to lead a defense team; I agreed. After pretrial issues were resolved, the trial began in May 2004. The jury returned its verdict February 10, 2005, after 13 days of deliberations.

Lynne's defense team for the pretrial motions included Stephen Ragland and several law students. As trial approached, Jill Shellow-Lavine became co-counsel and worked through the trial and beyond.

Opinion about Lynne from journalists, lawyers, and public figures was divided. Some, most of whom did not know her work, denounced her as the tool of terrorists. Others saw her as a lawyer of courage and commitment, who was being targeted for representing her client's interests. From the first, our client-centered task was to help the judge and an eventual jury see the Lynne Stewart whose life and work we knew.

The first legal task was to file pretrial motions asking Judge Koeltl to restrain the indictment's overbroad substantive allegations, and to address the procedural mess of a multi-year, multi-defendant congeries of allegations that would make a trial unfair to each individual defendant, and particularly to Lynne.

Upon examination, the government claimed that the "material support" and "resources" alleged in Counts 1 and 2 were "communications equipment" and "personnel." The communications equipment consisted of the telephones the defendants used to make phone calls. The personnel were themselves. That is, in addition to whatever crimes were committed by making phone calls, and by doing other acts, additional decades of punishable conduct occurred by using one's own telephone and by, well, being oneself. The statute under which these counts were brought arguably permitted this expansive allocation of criminal liability.

We contended that Counts 4 and 5 depended on the validity of the SAMs. If, as we argued, the SAMs represented an overbroad curtailment of speech and association, then one should not be prosecuted for allegedly violating them.

We also noted the years-long sweep of the indictment's allegations and argued that it did not provide the constitutionally required specific notice of the "nature and cause of the accusation.

We attacked the use of FISA, with its relaxed standards for warrants and restricted judicial review. Granted, most of the overheard conversations involved foreign nationals, but all the conversations took place in, or included a person located in, the United States. The government had no valid reason not to use the procedures in the 1968 Crime Control Act, including the time limits and disclosure obligations we had enforced in other cases.

Finally, we focused on the markedly different conduct alleged against each defendant. Sattar was charged, along with Al-Sirri, with being a central figure in an international conspiracy. His telephone conversations with people in the United Kingdom and Egypt concerned detailed plans that allegedly included violence. These calls were with people Lynne did not know, and whose language she did not speak. Given the evidence rules about conspiracy cases, jurors and the trial judge would have an impossible task in separating evidence about one defendant from evidence admitted as to all. A similar argument existed as to Yousry, whose job had been to translate.

Our arguments on pretrial motions consumed most of a day. On July 22, 2003, Judge Koeltl issued a 21,000-word opinion. Judge Koeltl held that the statute under which Counts 1 and 2 were drawn was unconstitutionally vague; he dismissed those counts.

Judge Koeltl rejected our attack on the SAMs. SAMs had been upheld in other cases. His principal point was that Lynne should have litigated the validity of the SAMs at the time they were issued, if she believed them to be invalid. Having failed to do so, and having agreed to abide by them, she forfeited her right to judicial review. This ruling, we thought, was "bait and switch." Lynne was willing to abide by the SAMs as she understood them. When the government indicted her, in effect rejecting her understanding of the SAMS, she should have been able to make an "as applied challenge." Judge Koeltl disagreed.

Judge Koeltl held that the indictment sufficiently informed us of what to expect at trial, which proved to be a triumph of hope over experience.

The judge denied our and other defendants' motions for separate trials. Under Federal Rule of Criminal Procedure 8, which requires that the charges be related to one another in order to be tried together, he noted that he was allowed—but not required—to accept the government's representations that the indictment's allegations really did make for one cohesive whole. He also denied relief under Federal Rule 14, which gives the judge some discretion to give separate trials. Yes, there might be some risk of "prejudicial spillover" of evidence from one defendant to another. Yes, the jurors might have trouble compartmentalizing the evidence as to the different defendants.

Judge Koeltl held that he would carefully instruct the jurors that certain items of evidence would be admitted and could be considered only as to one or the other defendants. I was reminded of voir dire in the Nichols case: A prospective juror assured Judge Matsch that although he had read much detailed and graphic media coverage of the bombing, he could "put it out of my mind." I politely asked him, "Where will you put it?"

In sum, a trial would be based on events taking place over many years in several countries, involving people speaking different languages and with different goals and interest, under an overarching government view of a multifarious but unitary conspiracy that was very scary. During the nine-month trial, Judge Koeltl gave hundreds of instructions about the limited admission of items of evidence. I asked him to go through the transcript at the end of the case and remind the jurors of each of these. He refused.

Immediately after Judge Koeltl's ruling on the pretrial motions the prosecutors filed a notice of appeal from the dismissal of Counts 1 and 2. Under a federal statute, any government appeal from a pretrial order must be authorized by the Solicitor General of the United States. I wrote to Solicitor General Theodore Olson, who had been a year ahead of me at Berkeley Law. I had edited his law review comment. After law school, he joined the law firm of Gibson, Dunn & Crutcher, and had offered me a job there after the Brennan clerkship fell through. I argued that the First Amendment princi-ples he had advocated as a law student were implicated in this case. I asked for a meeting.

Two weeks later, I got a call from Deputy Solicitor General Michael Dreeben, the Solicitor General's criminal law specialist. Michael invited me to a meeting at the Justice Department three days hence. In a conference room at the DOJ building in Washington, a dozen people assembled, all senior law-yers in the Criminal Division and the Solicitor General's office. We discussed Koeltl's ruling.

A few days later, Michael called to say that the government's appeal would be dismissed, and a new indictment obtained. That indictment came down on November 23, 2003. The statutes cited were different, but the theory and scope of the case was the same. Notably, the new indictment focused in more detail on Mohamed Yousry, alleging that he exchanged information about political plans and events with the Sheik in Arabic during prison visits. Koeltl upheld the new indictment and renewed the denial of separate trials.

We would try this case in lower Manhattan, within a mile of the World Trade Center. Our jurors would be drawn from Manhattan and surround-ing counties. For all of them, the events of September 11 were a recent and powerful memory. We asked the Judge for lawyer-conducted voir dire, so that we could question individual prospective jurors one at a time. Instead, Judge Koeltl did all the questioning of jurors, in groups of twelve.

The prosecutors on this case had offices adjacent to the courthouse. They too were no doubt thinking about the events of September in a fearful, per-sonal way. Preet Bharara was an Assistant U.S. Attorney in that office at the time of Lynne's trial, and became U.S. Attorney in 2009. He later recalled:

> I was fearful in the short term after 9/11. I had a four-month-old daugh-
> ter. My wife and I were living in the city, I was working at the Southern

District. And for days, I thought at any moment there could be another attack and we could die. And people we know could die and your sense of security was stripped away from you.

On many trial days, the proceedings consisted of government agents reading translations of Sattar's telephone calls, discussing plans for action and his views on permissible violence. The judge would often start proceedings before the jury an hour or more after the scheduled time of 9:00 a.m., to hear lawyer argument about admissibility of evidence, and then at the end of the day would order briefs on these issues to be filed overnight and taken up in the morning. This was an exhausting schedule for all, including our team.

After the trial, the National Lawyers Guild published an insightful monograph that agreed with our view of the case. The Guild lawyers had a little more distance from the case than I, and I appreciated that they witnessed the same case I did:

> At least 75% of the evidence at trial was not offered against Stewart or Yousry, but against Sattar. . . . Unbeknownst to Stewart or Yousry, Sattar was in contact with militant members of the Islamic Group in Afghanistan, London, Iran and around the world and had issued a false fatwa in the name of Sheikh Rahman to kill all Jews. The Court denied repeated severance motions both before and during the trial. . . .
>
> One of Stewart's defenses was that she had a good faith belief that notwithstanding the language of the SAMs she was permitted by ethical rules to release a press statement on behalf of her client. That statement was not a direct call to resume armed violence but rather to criticize the lack of progress of a peace initiative. . . .
>
> Critical to the case was the knowledge and intent of all three defendants.
>
> Consequently, the court allowed the government to present to the jury inflammatory evidence such as two videotapes of Osama Bin Laden, not "offered for the truth," but for Sattar's "knowledge, intent and state of mind." Repeatedly, the government gave the jury vitriolic statements by her client, Sheikh Rahman, regarding the burning and destruction of American buildings, planes and corporations. This, and newspaper articles found in her files, was offered against Stewart solely for "her knowledge, intent and state of mind."

I underscore this last point: the government wished the jurors to infer that if a person subscribes to publications that report on violent uprisings, this may show a desire to become personally involved. Even in apartheid South

Africa, such inferences were not indulged, as I noted earlier in this chapter in discussing the arrest of one of our Black Lawyers Association colleagues.

Another example from the trial also illustrates the problems we faced. On November 12, 1997, armed fighters killed 62 people and wounded more than 28 others at Egypt's Deir el-Bahari monument, a popular tourist site across the Nile from Luxor. Over our objection, Koeltl allowed the prosecution to present evidence of the attack, including eyewitnesses who described the events in detail. At the time, the attack was blamed on IG, though later evidence tended to show the attackers were a breakaway group. In any case, Lynne had nothing to do with the attack. Yousry and Sattar had discussed it, after the fact, as it was newsworthy. The Sheik understood that the attackers wanted to destabilize the then-existing truce in the dispute between IG and the Mubarak government. We did not have the resources to take on the government's attribution of the attack to IG. We could only sit while these details washed over the jurors.

This prosecution rested on the government's claimed power to place prisoners in isolation, shut off speech about public issues without showing any real risk of social harm, intrude into thousands of conversations, and intercept lawyer-client communications. Despite all the heated rhetoric, there was not a shred of proof that anything Lynne said or did caused harm. The government's legerdemain cloaked its aims and action by repeated reference to terrorist attacks, including one that the jurors vividly recalled.

Judge Koeltl's denial of a severance of defendants proved to be not only deeply unfair but also hugely inefficient as it affected Lynne. Her entire case could have been tried in six weeks. The entire Yousry case would take another six weeks. Then, without all the wrangling and judicial tergiversation about limited admissibility and special instructions, the Sattar case could be efficiently tried in two months. That is a total of five months, not nine. The judicial endorsement of liberal joinder of defendants and charges does little except help the prosecutors.

There was also the issue of juror fatigue. Lynne's jury was not sequestered in a hotel. Jurors were picked up near their homes and driven by government employees in buses to the courthouse basement. They sat all day in the jury box chairs. When they were not hearing evidence, their needs for food and drink were taken care of by court officers. Due to Judge Koeltl's way of proceeding, they spent a great deal of time in the jury room. They went home at night but were forbidden to read newspapers or discuss the case with others. After a time, with day after day of hearing witnesses simply read the text of phone calls, concentration and discernment are bound to suffer.

By contrast, in the Nichols trial Judge Matsch ensured—at our urging—that whenever the jurors were in the building, they should be hearing evidence. Hearings on evidence admissibility and other issues were held, if at all possible, before and after the court day and at recesses.

Lynne knew from the outset that she wanted to testify. She firmly believed that she had done no more than provide compassionate, zealous legal services. As we looked at the case, we wondered why Ramsey Clark, who had done as much or more to tell the world about the Sheik's situation, had not been indicted also. He later made that point to Judge Koeltl, in connection with sentencing, and he testified at trial.

Lynne took the stand. She talked about her growing up, her decision to be a lawyer, and the way she had decided to practice law. Her direct examination was a conversation. We had spent days together so that I could appreciate her and her work, and yet not turn the discussion into a scripted performance. Lynne did not mask her revolutionary political sentiments, but she was clear about the causes in which she would and would not enlist. She described in detail the conversations with prosecutors that led her to believe she was acting ethically and lawfully.

Judge Koeltl's instructions to the jury focused on the prosecution's duty to prove beyond a reasonable doubt that Lynne had "intentionally violated a known legal duty." I summed up for more than a day. The jury deliberated for sixteen days, and found Lynne guilty on all counts.

The trial had taken a physical toll on me. My physician insisted that I turn the work over to others for the next phase. Jill Shellow-Lavine organized lawyers and legal workers to assemble a presentation on sentencing. Joshua Dratel agreed to handle the appeal. Lynne remained free on bail. I joined Jane in Florida, on our boat, to rest, get my blood pressure under control, and recover from a hugely painful attack of shingles.

The colleagues, clients, community people and lawyers who had known and worked with Lynne helped to paint a picture of her life and work. In ruling on post-trial motions, Judge Koeltl held to the belief that the jury's verdict was reasonable; he rejected a call to investigate juror reports of having been subjected to various kinds of pressure.

The sentencing decision was another matter. On October 15, 2006, Judge Koeltl sentenced Lynne, Yousry, and Sattar. Yousry faced a maximum of 15 years; Koeltl sentenced him to 20 months. Sattar could have received a life sentence, but was given 24 years. The prosecutors argued that Lynne should be sentenced to 30 years, effectively a life sentence for a woman in her sixties who had been diagnosed with cancer.

Judge Koeltl explained his reasoning. He said there was "no evidence that any victim was in fact harmed" by Lynne's actions. He spoke of her 30-year career as court-appointed lawyer to "the poor, the disadvantaged and the unpopular" and that she did not choose cases in order to become wealthy. He concluded, "It is no exaggeration to say that Ms. Stewart performed a public service not only to her clients but to the nation." He sentenced her to 28 months incarceration. As I heard of the sentence I wondered again why, if Lynne's and Yousry's conduct differed so much from Sattar's, did we have a nine-month-long joint trial.

The sentence drew criticism from right-wing media and prosecutors. Joshua Dratel was lead counsel on the appeal, and he encountered judicial reactions that ranged from mild criticism to intense anger. Among the judicial complaints was that Lynne had not shown remorse for the actions, and in fact had said she would make the same decisions if she were again presented with a similar situation. She was also quoted as saying, in a courthouse-steps expression of joy that she could serve 28 months "standing on my head." On November 17, 2009, the court of appeals affirmed Lynne's conviction, revoked Lynne's bail, and sent the case back to Koeltl for resentencing. The court's consensus view signaled that a new sentence should be harsher but left Koeltl room to decide what to do. A team of lawyers and friends assembled to make a new sentencing presentation.

Once again, the prosecutors argued that Lynne should be sentenced to 30 years. At the court of appeals' suggestion, they combed Lynne's trial testimony and alleged that she had lied when she testified that she did not know the names of some of Sattar's contacts. I wrote to Judge Koeltl, saying that I had worked intensely with Lynne as she prepared to testify. I would not reveal any lawyer-client communications, but I was emphatic that I would not have elicited testimony from her that, based on my deep knowledge of the case, was untruthful. Koeltl did not reply, nor seem to take any account of what I wrote. Nor did he seem to credit much of the new sentencing presentation.

When he took the bench on July 15, 2010, to hand out a new sentence, he seemed grim. Lynne made a dignified statement, putting her earlier remarks in context. The prosecutors inveighed. Koeltl sentenced Lynne to 10 years. In the succeeding months, her health declined. Koeltl ordered her "compassionate release" on December 31, 2013. Home with her family, she died on March 7, 2017.

I had worked with John Koeltl in the ABA Litigation Section, and we were co-counsel in a large civil case when he was in private practice. I have wondered what shaped his sometimes inconsistent attitudes toward Lynne and the case. He has not seemed reluctant to make controversial rulings. In 2019, Koeltl, in dismissing a lawsuit about Russian interference in the 2016 elections, described Wikileaks' publishing activities as "plainly of the type entitled to the strongest protection that the First Amendment offers." This is a view later challenged by the indictment of Julian Assange. Was he affected by criticism of the original sentence from other judges in the courthouse? Was he offended by what he saw as Lynne's trivialization of his efforts to recognize her work?

CHAPTER 16

What to Do While
Enjoying Medicare

I became sixty-five in January 2006. I started receiving Social Security and signed up for Medicare. There is a social consensus that this is a time of life to reflect on next steps. I did that: teaching, writing. Some of the human rights cases discussed above were still going on. And I played a modest role in some of the same kinds of battles.

All of us who make it this far seek to do useful work while recognizing that leadership—its benefits and burdens—has passed to others. I am dismayed to see people my age occupying positions that younger people should have. This view is coupled with my sense that the new generation is poised to take meaningful action.

I did not want to be the person of whom people watching me work would say, "He used to be Michael Tigar." I reminded myself of a joke Ann Richards told me: "People ask me if I believe in the hereafter. Of course I do. I go from room to room in my house asking myself 'What am I here after?'" Yes, I was wondering: What am I here after? At the eye doctor, my old friend Ed Clark had the appointment before mine. He came out of the examining room and said, "Doctor says I can see more than I have the energy to do anything about." I was taken by what Samuel Beckett wrote: "Perhaps my best years are gone. . . . But I wouldn't want them back. Not with the fire in me now."

TEACHING AND TELEOLOGY

Jane and I had learned to love the coastal sailing areas from North Carolina north to New York and south to the Florida Keys and the Bahamas, but we wanted as well to be closer to people, events—and good medical care—a little farther inland. We had lunch one Saturday in early fall 2006 with Paul and Bessie Carrington. Paul had been dean of Duke Law School and was a leading writer and teacher of civil procedure. I said that at age sixty-five I was monitoring some human rights cases and doing some writing. Paul asked if I would help him teach a seminar on appellate litigation.

"I could do that," I said. "When would that be?"

"Monday," he replied.

"I am not on the Duke faculty."

"I'll work on that."

Duke gave me an office and a title, Professor of the Practice of Law. I taught criminal law and civil procedure, and seminars on appellate litigation and case theory. Duke is a private law school, one of the "Top 14" in a national ranking. Tuition is expensive. Most students will graduate with heavy loads of debt. The dominant career desire is to practice "big law" in a large firm. I wondered what social attitudes might accompany such desires and goals. Nonetheless, many students want the search for justice to be a part of their lives. They sought me out, as did faculty colleagues with shared interests. Duke's clinical programs offer students the opportunity to work as community lawyers in civil and criminal cases, and in matters involving LGBTQ discrimination.

I taught at Duke. I presented continuing education programs on advocacy to bar groups and judicial conferences. I sought to bring teleology into my teaching. As I learned in my first law school year, much law school teaching focuses on doctrine in the abstract. A lawyer must have command of rules and techniques. I tried to shape my teaching so as to put the study of every principle, rule and technique in the context of a sense of injustice and a determination to address it. It was not enough to grasp ideas well enough to pass the course, get through the bar examination, and get a job. I wanted students to glimpse what I had seen: the ways of using what we learn to advance the struggle for justice. Seeing the context helped students to better grasp the rules. Students who embraced this approach tended to do better on exams, which were graded anonymously. Some students thought that my approach was designed to sell them left-wing ideas, and wrote scathing anonymous "evaluations."

Thus, in the civil procedure class, we studied civil rights cases. In criminal law, we tried to see the way that offense definitions and enforcement policies served social goals.

TRIAL STORIES AND NINE PRINCIPLES

I had written books about advocacy. A legal publisher, Foundation Press, was doing a series of books under the name "Stories": *Torts Stories*, *Contracts Stories*, and so on. A book on *Trial Stories* would look at well-known cases and analyze how lawyers serve their clients' demands for justice. Would I edit the volume and perhaps write a chapter? My Washington College of Law colleague Angela Jordan Davis agreed to be co-editor. *Trial Stories* met my expectations, with chapters on the trial of Aaron Burr, Darrow's defense in the Ossian Sweet case, the O. J. Simpson trial, and more.

Still thinking about teleology, I wrote *Nine Principles of Litigation—and Life*. The book's theme was that with access to zealous counsel, a fair forum, and a judge who exercised independent judgment, rational discourse might allow for just outcomes. The first of the nine principles was "Courage," followed by "Rapport."

WRITING AND THINKING ABOUT TERRORISM

As I finished the first edition of this book in early September 2011, I added a coda to the manuscript. I wrote:

> I paraphrase the philosopher only a little when I say that those who do not understand history are condemned to repeat it. This is not a new insight. Every spring I say to law students, "Those who do not understand criminal law are condemned to repeat it." It was right to say this when they asked me to look back at the struggle for human rights these past 35 years. It is imperative to say it now. . . .
>
> In more modern times, however, we think of terror as organized but senseless violence, done in the name of an ideology. For example, in the town of Beziers, near Marseilles, in the year 1209, 15,000 men, women, and children were slaughtered to root out the Albigensian heresy. "Whom should we kill?" asked Philip Augustus's general. "Kill them all," the papal legate replied. "God will recognize his own." In Ireland, Bosnia, Chechnya, South Africa, and a hundred other places in the world, young people will point to this or that spot and tell you a story. Someone's grandfather's grandfather killed someone else's grandfather's grandfather right over there. And the killing is not yet fully avenged.
>
> We have in our country been mostly spectators of this sort of thing, and must now catch up to the rest of the world in understanding its causes and remedies. I say we have "mostly" been spectators. From 1872 to 1920 there were more than 4,000 lynchings in America. Some of us remember the Freedom Summer of 1964, when thousands of young people went south to Mississippi and other southern states. In Mississippi alone,

dozens of black churches were burned, and hundreds of civil rights workers beaten, brutalized, and even killed.

Calmly now, therefore, with as keen a sense of history as we can command, what are the causes of the kind of violence we have seen? In Ireland, to take an example close by, we can trace the path of English oppression, which robbed people of their homes and land and, in the interest of forced unity, forbade them to speak their language and practice their beliefs. Irish resistance is spoken of in songs and stories. The pent-up anger has for nearly two centuries taken the form of urban violence, of terrorism. If we can see the roots of that violence, we may more clearly understand what is now going on around us.

Our leaders' strident vow that terrorism is always illegitimate sounds cynical and hypocritical. After all, our own CIA has sometimes sought out practitioners of vengeful extremism. We have paid them and equipped them. We have sponsored them in the arts of assassination and bloodshed. Indeed, in the Islamic world many of the groups we today denounce as terrorist were funded and armed by the United States as counterweights to the Soviets. Many of the guns our troops face today were furnished to arm the opposition to the Soviet Army. Our leaders' failure to acknowledge this history puts us all at the terrible risk that it will be repeated.

There are two basic forms of terrorism, both equally criminal. One is state-sponsored terrorism, as practiced by the former repressive regimes in Chile and South Africa and still in use today in Afghanistan. The second form of terror, which usually takes the form of urban violence, often begins with insurgent groups fighting injustice. Then, at some point, a group of insurgents loses touch with the imperative need to embrace human values even in the struggle against inhumanity. Frighteningly, to those of us who watch the angry crowds on television, desperate people give their support to that kind of leadership. When I say desperate, I mean the kind of poverty and deprivation which we in this country can scarcely imagine. I have walked in villages littered with the shards of shattered lives, and I have seen that anger. The desperate followers of that kind of terrorist leadership are as much victims as those who perish in the attacks about which we read and hear.

Both state-sponsored terrorism and insurgent group terrorism are criminal. I have no doubt that there must exist the duty and the right and the power to investigate and to judge the killings of innocent people. But the legitimate right to conduct those investigations and to inflict that punishment lies only with those who accept the following obligations:

To use means that honor and do not trample upon the tradition of human rights;

To understand the reasons people will follow the lead of those who sponsor terrorism; and

To support the legitimate struggle of those people to live in dignity in accordance with those norms of human rights that have become norms of international law in the past three score years.

To put the matter another way, the only kind of justice worthy of the name is social justice. Social justice includes both process and legitimacy. It includes process because that has been the lesson of history for three millennia. It includes process because we have seen the cost of doing otherwise. We have seen how the arrogance of power has detained people without probable cause, refused or subverted impartial judicial review of detention, and drowned out calls for reason and proof with strident cries for vengeance. Hundreds of people, perhaps more, are being held right now while our government disregards these guaranties. The department that calls itself Justice is using this excuse to repeal dozens of guaranties of procedural fairness, not only in so-called terrorism investigations but also across the board. . . .

Yes, I am frightened by the terror that has rained upon our country and that continues to haunt us. I want those who commit and who would commit such acts brought to justice. I also know that with so much hatred and fear in the air, we are at risk of losing sight of justice. If you hold your hand in front of your eyes, you can say that it is bigger than the tallest mountain on the far horizon.

Fighting terrorism means stripping state-sponsored terrorists of their impunity and bringing them to justice. It means shining a light into the darkest corners of human existence, and bringing a real promise of human rights to all the world's people, so that desperate men and women are not driven to follow leaders whose only real message is vengeance. When we see that the struggle for human rights in all the world is the surest and best means to prevent and to punish "terrorism" properly so called, we then understand what progress we have made, and we will see where we need to go from here.

I looked back at Lynne's trial, and at the spate of congressional statutes, executive branch actions, and judicial acquiescence, all done in the name of a "war on terror." We were seeing events and the characterizations of events that replicated the past. Movements for change have often been accompanied by violent actions. Some of those actions might logically be termed "terrorist," in the sense that they are intended predominantly to sow fear rather than marshal willing social support. Even the distinction in the previous sentence could be faulted as not quite capturing the meaning of "terror" and "terrorism."

An editor at the American Bar Association Press asked me to write a book. I did: *Thinking About Terrorism: The Threat to Civil Liberties in Times of National Emergency*. In order to write the book, I read widely of the movements for change that had been given, or had adopted, the name "terrorism." I reread what Che Guevara and others had written about their own decisions to engage in, or refrain from, actions they considered terrorist. I reviewed what Richard Posner and others had written about the alleged need to defer to executive power. I did a first draft in six weeks.

The historical evidence that I examined permits one firm conclusion. "Terror," "terrorist," and "terrorism" are epithets applied by challenged holders of state power to those who seek to overthrow them. The terrorist label is the state's way of creating a mythology about social danger, to whip up support for repression.

Two examples follow, one from Mark Twain and another about the Mau Mau uprisings in Kenya. In *A Connecticut Yankee in King Arthur's Court*, Twain wrote:

> Why, it was like reading about France and the French, before the ever-memorable and blessed Revolution, which swept a thousand years of such villainy away in one swift tidal wave of blood—one: a settlement of that hoary debt in the proportion of half a drop of blood for each hogshead of it that had been pressed by slow tortures out of that people in the weary stretch of ten centuries of wrong and shame and misery the like of which was not to be mated but in hell. There were two "Reigns of Terror," if we would but remember it and consider it; the one wrought murder in hot passion, the other in heartless cold blood; the one lasted mere months, the other had lasted a thousand years; the one inflicted death upon ten thousand persons, the other upon a hundred millions; but our shudders are all for the "horrors" of the minor Terror, the momentary Terror, so to speak; whereas, what is the horror of swift death by the ax, compared with lifelong death from hunger, cold, insult, cruelty, and heartbreak? What is swift death by lightning compared with death by slow fire at the stake? A city cemetery could contain the coffins filled by that brief Terror which we have all been so diligently taught to shiver at and mourn over; but all France could hardly contain the coffins filled by that older and real Terror—that unspeakably bitter and awful Terror which none of us has been taught to see in its vastness or pity as it deserves.

Looking at Kenya, I found:

> The Mau Mau, called Muingi by the Kikuyu tribal leadership, was para-
> military in nature. Its members were armed mostly with spears, whips and
> machetes. It conducted deadly raids on white settlements. In the inter-
> national press, these killings were portrayed as the central element of the
> African uprising. This was not so. By 1960, when Britain began to yield
> to independence demands, the death toll from some 12 years of fighting
> stood as follows:
>
> - 68 white settlers killed, probably by Mau Mau forces;
> - Tens of thousands of African rebels killed by British troops, with the
>   British government claiming 11,503 and scholars saying it was at least
>   twice that; more than 1,000 alleged rebel sympathizers hanged after
>   trials that did not comport with recognized standards of fairness;
> - 63 British soldiers and police killed;
> - Slightly more than 2,000 African and Asian British sympathizers
>   killed.
>
> Most of the combat deaths occurred in military sweeps conducted not
> only against alleged Mau Mau rebels but also against other Kenyan rebel
> groups that were also fighting for independence.

As I thought about the way the "war on terrorism" label was being used
to market repression, I recalled an evening gathering in Austin a decade or
so back. The speakers were a deputy director of the FBI and the great Texas
storyteller John Henry Faulk. The FBI man painted a picture of threats facing
the country and called for law enforcement action that included surveillance,
infiltration and all manner of related activity. When it was his turn, John Henry
rose and said something like this:

> You know, not many people know this, but I was in law enforcement. I
> was United States Marshal. I was nine years old. My territory stretched
> along the banks of what is now Lake Austin, from the Faulk homestead
> and inland for a mile or more. So it was that Billy Johnson and I were
> patrolling one day, and we decided to check out the chicken house. We
> opened the door and went in, and the door slammed behind us. We did
> not notice that the latch slipped into place as the door shut.
>
> Billy felt around up in the nesting boxes above the height of his head,
> and all of a sudden he screamed, "Chicken snake!" He had put his hand
> up there and touched a snake. We ran for the door and, the door being

shut, we crashed right through it. We were hollering "Chicken snake! Chicken snake!"

You may well ask, me being marshal and all, where was my courage. It was running down my leg into my tennis shoe. Billy and I were scratched and bruised from our encounter with the door and the ground. Our hollering excited the attention of my grandmother, who came running out the back door. "John Henry, what on earth is going on?" she asked.

"Grandma," I said, "Billy found a chicken snake in the henhouse."

"John Henry Faulk," grandma said, "don't you know a chicken snake can't hurt you."

"Yes, ma'am," I said, "but it can scare you so bad you could hurt yourself."

Around that same time, I experienced firsthand the FBI's abilities. Back in the 1970s, I had represented Frank Rosenthal, a Las Vegas casino executive. Frank's life has been, with his permission, the subject of a book and a motion picture, *Casino*. In *Casino*, the character Ace Rothstein, portrayed by Robert De Niro, is Frank. As the movie discloses, Frank was the victim of an attempt to murder him with a car bomb, and other threats to his life from organized crime figures. By the 1980s, he was living in California in peaceful retirement.

Frank called me in my office at the University of Texas Law School. The FBI had told him that his life was again in danger. They wanted to provide FBI protection. Frank was not inclined to accept, preferring to make his own arrangements. He agreed to meet with a senior FBI agent to discuss the issue. The meeting would take place in a secure hotel room at Dallas-Fort Worth airport. Frank and I would arrive, be met by the FBI agent, and taken to the room.

We settled down in the room to talk. After a little time, it became clear that the FBI precautions had not included putting the Do Not Disturb sign on the door handle or telling the hotel to provide privacy. We heard the sound of the door latch clicking, and the door opening. The agent grabbed his gun from his briefcase and assumed a shooter stance. The door opened, and the maid came in. She saw the agent and the gun, screamed, and ran off down the hall. The agent left us and took a few minutes to calm things down.

When he returned, Frank said that he was declining FBI assistance.

My comrade John Mage and I worked on a *Monthly Review* symposium on the national security state, to which I contributed an article tracing judicial review of executive power to its common law roots. Wishing to learn from historical parallels, John and I wrote an article on the 1933 Reichstag fire trial, in which a united left movement aided by courageous lawyers turned back Nazi power—for an all too brief moment.

PARIS

Two anti-labor strategies of multinational enterprises are globalization and outsourcing. Globalization moves manufacturing processes to low-wage areas with minimal enforcement of workplace standards. This process is aided by a worldwide increase in the number of wage workers, most of which is occurring in the Third World.

Outsourcing consists of moving support functions out of an enterprise. For example, a hospital has been employing people to wash sheets, uniforms, and so on. In many settings, those employees have secure jobs with benefits that include health care. The enterprise fires those employees and sends all the laundry to a company that serves many enterprises and employs low-wage non-union personnel. The same tactic may be used to contract out food service in a company or college dining room.

The Service Employees International Union (SEIU), Teamsters Union, and Farm Workers Union have formed a coalition to organize workers in outsourced settings, to obtain better wages and working conditions. Their tactics have included seeking community support to compel employers to bargain. Employers have responded with lawsuits claiming that community organizing is a form of extortion, that forcing employers to pay a decent wage is criminal conduct that can be addressed by the federal racketeering laws. Yes, this is a crazy theory, and judges have dismissed most such lawsuits. *Mythologies of State and Monopoly Power* includes a more thorough discussion.

In 2011, the food service and facilities management company Sodexo, a major beneficiary of the outsourcing movement, brought a RICO suit against SEIU in a Virginia federal court. SEIU's general counsel Judy Scott decided to fight back with the weapons SEIU was using in other battles. SodexoUS was a subsidiary of Sodexo France, a company headed by a billionaire named Pierre Bellon.

SEIU hired Jane and me to write op-eds for French news publications, describing the lawsuit and noting that Sodexo's anti-worker strategy would not be tolerated under French law. I recorded infomercials in French on the same themes. Jane used her piror career experience as video producer to assist the French crew in making me look as presentable as possible. In the video segments, one theme was that the parent Sodexo was allowing its child in the United States to behave in ways that would not be tolerated at home. I challenged M. Bellon to debate.

SEIU used this opportunity to publicize its international labor rights work. They too had noted the increase in wage workers in Third World countries. In Morocco, for example, SEIU worked with labor organizers. In that culture, the married women workers were driven to work by their husbands. If a worker supported the union, she would be transferred to a worksite so far away that it was not possible to make the journey. SEIU asked me to address the issue of global worker rights in a forum in Paris,

A November 2011 *Monthly Review* article, "The Global Reserve Army of Labor and the New Imperialism," provided indispensable research into the changes in the global workforce. I used that and other sources, along with a firm expression of the lawyer's role, and gave two lectures at the University of Paris law school in the Paris suburb of Nanterre, titled "Mondialisation et les droits des ouvriers."

JAPAN

In 2013, Monroe Freedman and Abbe Smith edited a collection of essays by lawyers for those accused of crime. The authors described work with and for clients, and the reasons lawyers choose this work. I contributed a chapter, which was a reprint of what I had written when I accepted the Terry Nichols appointment. The other authors and I appeared at book signings and symposia. I knew, respected, admired, and sometimes disagreed with Monroe from the time I met him in 1966 until his death in 2015. He championed the right of defendants to zealous advocacy and the right of advocates to be zealous.

On October 9, 2013, Monroe hosted a symposium on the book at Hofstra Law School, where he was professor and had been dean. At one of the breaks, a slender Japanese man introduced himself and gave me his card. He was Keiichi Muraoka, from Hitotsubashi Law School in Tokyo. He told me, to my surprise, that my written work was widely read in Japan. He admired Monroe's—and my—commitment to the defense of the accused. Would I be willing to come to Japan and speak?

I agreed. I told him that in 1998 and 1999, Jane and I had represented the CEO of the Honda parent corporation, Yoshihide Munekuni. Jane speaks conversational Japanese. Our first meeting with Mr. Munekuni and his assistants was at a hotel in Vancouver. Jane had taught me a Japanese children's song—the extent of my knowledge beyond menus. She said to our client, "Munekuni-san, Tigar-san knows a children's song in Japanese. But he is shy, He would sing it if you asked." Mr. Munekuni asked, and I sang "Heads and Shoulders, Knees and Toes," appropriate gestures: "Atama, Kata, Hiza, Ashi." Everybody laughed, and we had begun to bridge the distance between lawyer and client.

We did not hear from Keiichi for some time. Monroe died February 15, 2015. In the fall of 2015, Keiichi wrote to us. He had organized a symposium at Hitotsubachi devoted to Monroe and his work. Would Jane and I speak? We went to Japan in February 2016. I spoke at the law school about the duties of advocates. Jane spoke about the influence of Jewish ethics on Monroe's work, the idea of *tikkun olam*, repair of the world, the social responsibility dimension of lawyering. Law teachers and law students gathered around and shared their hope that young lawyers could learn in law school, and put to work in practice, the ideas and skills of which we had spoken.

In Japan, coercive police questioning of criminal suspects is rampant. An arrested person may be held without bail and compelled to confess. The police do not regard the confession as complete until the accused is willing to implicate others and signal willingness to give evidence against them. The scandals of coerced plea bargains had led the Japan Federation of Bar Associations to produce a documentary on the issue. Keiichi arranged for me to speak on this issue at a JFBA meeting attended by hundreds of lawyers,

We met Maiko Tagusari, a law professor who is head of Japan's organization opposed to the death penalty, part of the global network of such groups. Japan maintains the death penalty. Lawyers who represent capital defendants are glad to exchange ideas with those of us from the United States who do that work.

We have visited Maiko and Keiichi each year. Maiko teaches a course on comparative criminal procedure; Keiichi uses excerpts from my books and articles in his classes.

Our work in Japan reinforces the sense that despite language, tradition-based and cultural differences in ways of expressing legal ideas, there is an international consensus about sensing and confronting injustice, and to expose, analyze, and combat the mythologies of state and monopoly power that mask and justify it.

TURKEY, ANOTHER CHILE SEQUEL

On May 16, 2017, Turkey's president Recep Erdogan, visited Washington, D.C. Predictably, people opposed to his regime, including students and Kurdish nationalists, demonstrated against him and his regime's policies. The Turkish ambassador's residence is on Sheridan Circle in northwest Washington, just 50 meters from where a car bomb killed Orlando Letelier and Ronni Karpen Moffitt on September 21, 1976. The demonstrators were acting lawfully and peaceably. District of Columbia police kept the small number of pro-Erdogan demonstrators separated from the anti-Erdogan people. Erdogan arrived in a limousine. Someone, and there is evidence that it was Erdogan himself, gave the order to attack, Turkish security forces from inside the residence, joined by pro-Erdogan civilians, attacked, beat and kicked the anti-Erdogan demonstrators, ignoring police efforts to stop them.

Local prosecutors charged some of the attackers with assault. A team of lawyers, in which I played a small part, filed suit against the Republic of Turkey and individual wrongdoers. The legal team drew on the experience gained in the Letelier-Moffitt litigation.

Turkey moved to dismiss the complaint, alleging—as had Chile in the Letelier case—that its agents were carrying out a discretionary act: combating a terrorist threat by beating up a bunch of young people in the public street. It was not a surprise to see these arguments again in this setting. On February 6, 2020, Judge Kollar-Kotelly denied the motion to dismiss. Turkey's appeal is pending as I write.

I wondered again how learned and civilized people could continue to invoke the mythology of anti-terrorism with a straight face. Turkey's security expert opined that Erdogan was in danger because, among other things, one of the demonstrators was wearing a school backpack and everybody knows that in the past people have carried explosive devices in backpacks. He also noted that the demonstrators were within "handgun range" of Erdogan, even though nobody except the Turkish guards and the D.C. police officers was shown to have a handgun. Turkey's position amounted to this: Within 100 meters of every one of more than a hundred diplomatic premises in Washington, agents of foreign missions have discretion to beat up anybody who wants to protest that government's policies.

JULIAN ASSANGE

Julian Assange registered the Wikileaks domain name on October 4, 2006. Wikileaks published its first story in December 2006. Since that time, Assange and Wikileaks have been at the center of controversy in several countries. In 2019, the U.S. government revealed that it had obtained a grand jury indictment against Assange, in the Eastern District of Virginia, charging him with espionage, computer intrusion, and related crimes. The government began formal proceedings in London to extradite him to the United States.

Gareth Peirce, Assange's solicitor, wrote to ask if Jane and I would act as independent experts in the extradition proceedings, addressing questions about the history and interpretation of the Espionage Act, the recent federal prosecutions of whistleblowers, and the barriers to Assange obtaining a fair trial in the United States. We provided our report, which has been relied on by Assange's barrister Edward Fitzgerald in court proceedings. If you read the discussion in chapter 5, you have some idea of what we wrote about the misuse of espionage law to curtail journalistic freedom. One ought to note that in the past several years, the U.S. government has used the prosecutorial power to deter and punish journalists and leakers who provide information about government misconduct. In 2019, federal prosecutors argued that "leakers"— people who reveal secret documents showing government wrongdoing—are "worse than spies." Federal prosecutors are also interpreting the statutory language in the Espionage Act, that the alleged revelations must be "to the injury of the United States" as allowing prosecution when the "injury" consists of reputational harm to the American "image" because of what is revealed.

Nonsense. In common law history, there is a distinction between "harm" and legally cognizable "injury." In an 1894 *Harvard Law Review* article, Oliver Wendell Holmes posed the hypothetical case of someone who sets up a store near one that is already established. The newcomer may harm the other merchant, but the supervening principle of free competition holds that he has not injured his rival. So, too, if someone reports truthful information about a lawyer's wrongdoing; the supervening value of free expression says no injury has taken place. This principle is firmly established in U.S., UK, and international law.

When the offense element of injury is trivialized to the point of disappearance, the state reveals its true agenda. The government owns "its" information. Hans Magnus Enzensberger has written:

> State secret and espionage as legal concepts are inventions of the late nineteenth century. They were born out of the spirit of imperialism. Their victorious march begins in 1894 with the Dreyfus affair. . . . The mana of the state secret communicates itself to its bearers and immunizes them, each according to the degree of his initiation, against the question; therefore they are free not to answer and, in the real sense of the word, are irresponsible. How many state secrets someone knows becomes the measure of his rank and his privilege in a finely articulated hierarchy. The mass of the governed is without secrets; that is, it has no right to partake of power, to criticize it and watch over it.

MYTHOLOGIES OF STATE AND MONOPOLY POWER

This book grew from a series of blog posts over several years. Without realizing it, I had been building a structure of thought about racism, free expression, worker rights, and social justice.

I have long enjoyed the work of Roland Barthes, the French semioti-cian and literary theorist. He collected some of his essays in a book entitled *Mythologies*—the same word in English and French. Barthes's work, and the title of his book, represented a way of seeing what human rights lawyers do, and what I had been doing in the blog posts I had been writing.. The state demonizes and marginalizes our clients, and portrays their fate, and the injus-tices that beset them as part of a natural, proper, and immutable "way things are." Barthes was writing about a form of alienation. Young Marx had studied this phenomenon. The British psychiatrist R. D. Laing wrote:

> Men have . . . always been weighed down not only by their sense of subordination to fate and chance, to ordained external necessities or con-tingencies, but by a sense that their very own thoughts and feelings, in their most intimate interstices, are the outcome, the resultant of processes which they undergo.

Putting these ideas together, one had another way of seeing and describing what we do for our clients, and the signal importance of client-centered advo-cacy. When the state indicted Angela Davis, it was deploying the mythologies of Black/Woman/Communist/Gun Owner as lenses of refraction through which to view her and her conduct. Angela, speaking for herself, and her law-yers busted the mythology. In Lynne Stewart's case, we succeeded for a time and to some small extent in helping Judge Koeltl see who she really was.

CHAPTER 17

Envoi

Every semester, colleagues at Duke Law School invite me to speak to students who are embarking on clinical legal work. They ask me to address the "busting of mythologies," to remind these students that they are now going to meet people whose lives are very different from theirs. Their first task will be to cast aside the mythologies they have been carrying around. For the first time in a client's life, somebody is going to listen carefully. The sense of injustice is awakened by listening and observing.

There is a new generation of young people rising to continue the work. I hope, by telling the stories in this book, to suggest some paths to explore. As Fran Lebowitz said, "A book is not supposed to be a mirror; it's supposed to be a door." The law, or at least the responsibility for changing it, belongs to this new generation. We remind them not to promise the clients too much. To repeat, we provide outcomes, not solutions. At the same time, we insist that they can and do make a difference now, and often with some prospect of greater change in time to come. Indeed, this is what I have been reminding myself all these years. I am confident of my ability to do my lawyer job, but uncertain about how all of this work will make any lasting difference. We learn to live with this sense of the impermanence and fragility of our accomplishments.

I also ask law students and young lawyers to be open to the changes in them that will be wrought by their experience. Huckleberry Finn's journey to liberation with Jim changed Huck's view of the world.

This "uncertainty principle" need not paralyze us, any more than its existence in the laws of physics prevents physicists from working with electrons. It is just there, a fact of social life.

In early 1989, Justice Brennan asked me to help him write his remarks for the dedication of the Edward Bennett Williams Law Library at Georgetown

Law School. I came to Washington and we sat in Brennan's office poring over transcripts of Ed's Supreme Court arguments and sharing stories about him. As I was leaving, Brennan took hold of my arm and asked, "Did I do any good up here?" I said yes, as meaningfully as I could. So, I thought, all of us who have a sense of purpose are likely to have doubts about the worth of our work.

The doubt is healthy. If you desire social change, and want to assist its arrival, it is always good to keep this sense of doing the next right thing right now, keeping in mind the limits on law's power to foster change and your own fidelity to the larger goal. As I look back on my writing, I see a repeated attention to this duality and contradiction. In my play *The Trial of John Peter Zenger*, the jury has given its verdict:

> Alexander [New York counsel]: You must come with us, sir. To the Black Horse Tavern. They are going to present you the liberty of New York.
> Andrew Hamilton: Alexander, whoever "they" are, they do not have the "liberty of New York." All we did was to free Zenger here. The liberty of New York will have to be won on some other day, and perhaps in some other manner.

My Haymarket play concludes with this exchange between the anarchist leader Lucy Parsons and Clarence Darrow:

> Lucy Parsons: Your lawyer's ego wants you to think you stand at the center of every event by which the world is changed. Your right to stand there is only because some brave soul has risked death or prison in the people's cause and you are called to defend him—or her. When you put law and lawyers at the center of things, you are only getting in the people's way, and doing proxy for the image of the law the state wants us to have. The law is a mask that the state puts on when it wants to commit some indecency upon the oppressed.
> Darrow: (Angry.) If I believed that, I would still be lawyer for the railroad, and not making do with the fees the union can pay. Lucy, the law is a fence built around the people and their rights.
> Lucy Parsons: (Kindly.) What an image! And you, Clarence, are a fierce old dog, set to bark and warn off intruders. Maybe so. I wish it so. We are all on trial in this life we have chosen, Clarence. All we can know is that none of us will live to see the verdict.

And then there is this imperative need that we keep our eye on the injustices we can see and understand and be careful about imposing soaring vision that can cause us to overlook our duties to one another and to our tasks. I had Daniel O'Connell say, in my play *Warrior Bards*, you cannot make a bargain with history, you can only act in it.

In this connection, I am heartened to have at last learned to have some balance in my personal life. So along with nurturing, and increasingly being nurtured by Jane, my children, my grandchildren, and my comrades and friends, I am going to keep sensing injustice: answering an occasional call, writing, speaking, arguing—and perhaps persuading.

Notes and Sources

INTRODUCTION

The Rapoport Center for Human Rights and the Briscoe Center for American History archive is searchable by topic and decade, as well as by subject matter and keyword, https://law. utexas.edu/tigar-event/photos-and-video/. The archive includes almost all of my published work and recorded oral arguments, as well as photos and memorabilia, from the 1940s to 2018. It also includes an oral history, recorded over several days in conversation with University of Texas colleagues, and one can browse the archive for additional background material. Wherever possible, I have included links to source material in that archive. Many of my law review articles can also be found at https://web.law.duke.edu/ fac/tigar/bibliography/.

Many Pacifica Radio broadcasts in which I participated are available from www.pacificaradio-archives.org, a searchable website.

The website and archive were launched on Septmber 20, 2018, with a video introduction by Jeremy Corbyn; a panel with Bernardine Dohrn, Fernando Chávez, Wayne Reaud, Robin Mardemootoo, and Jordan Steiker; an interview with Lois Romano; and a scene from one of my plays.

Many video-recorded advocacy talks and programs, as well as copies of books, jury arguments and other materials are available from Professional Education Group, https://peg.ce21. com/category/michael_e%40%4091_tigar?page=1&displaytype=1.

PROLOGUE

Gutknecht v. United States, 396 U.S. 295 (1970), holding it unlawful for a Selective Service Board to penalize a registrant's delinquency by accelerating their induction to armed services, at https://www.oyez.org/cases/1969/71; and https://law.utexas.edu/tigar/ archive-item/gutknecht-v-united-states-396-u-s-295-1970/; Brief for Petitioner, 1969 WL 119856; also at https://law.utexas.edu/tigar/archive-item/brief-for-petitioner-gutknecht-v-united-states-396-u-s-295-1970/; Brief for the United States, 1969 WL 119855; Reply Brief for Petitioner, 1969 WL 119857.

The other case for which I wrote the brief is *Breen v. Selective Service Local Board No. 16*, 396 U.S. 460 (1970), allowing judicial review of a request for relief against possible future induction, https://www.oyez.org/cases/1969/65. The Brief for Petitioner, 1969 WL 120167, is at https://law.utexas.edu/tigar/archive-item/brief-for-petitioner-breen-v-selective-service-local-board-no-16-396-u-s-460-1970/

The Supreme Court held that *Gutknecht* was to be given retroactive application to free men already convicted. *Davis v. United States*, 417 U.S. 333 (1974), https://www.oyez.org/ cases/1973/72-1454.

The Spock case: *United States v. Spock*, 416 F.2d 165 (1st Cir. 1969). More information on the Selective Service System is in chapter 7 notes below.

David Gutknecht's YouTube oral history: https://www.youtube.com/watch?v=CVwTPPPZusQ&t=5s.

On the legality of the Vietnam War, see Richard A. Falk, ed., *The Vietnam War and International Law*, 3 vols. (Princeton: Princeton University Press, 1968–72). The Supreme Court refused to hear the issue in *Mora v. McNamara*, 389 U.S. 934 (1967), Douglas and Stewart, J.J., dissenting from denial of certiorari, https://supreme.justia.com/cases/federal/us/389/934/.

I recount my draft and military law concerns and experiences more fully in chapter 7.

1. GROWING UP AMONG THE MYTHS

The Heraclitus quote is from Felix S. Cohen, 63 Harv. L. Rev. 1481 (1950), reviewing Edmond Cahn, *The Sense of Injustice*.

Gore Vidal's letter is at https://law.utexas.edu/tigar/archive-item/letter-from-gore-vidal/

Glendale was one of many "sundown towns" that forbade African-Americans from being in the city overnight. See https://en.wikipedia.org/wiki/Sundown_town.

My Father and the Union

Josh Sides, *L.A. City Limits: African American Los Angeles from the Great Depression to the Present* (2004). Anita Seth, "Los Angeles Aircraft Workers and the Consolidation of Cold War Politics," in Peter Westwick, *Blue Sky Metropolis*, 72, at 88–89 (2012), documents IAM Local 727's defiance of the national IAM and its welcoming African-American members. Their opposition continued throughout the war. The article mentioning my father was in *Fortune* magazine, March 1941, 164.

IAM brochure marking fifty years of union recognition at Lockheed, with my father's picture: https://law.utexas.edu/tigar/archive-item/fifty-years-of-cooperation/.

Archival material on the IAM and the aviation industry at http://research.library.gsu.edu/IAMAWCollections. Issues of the IAM monthly newsletter *Get Branded* contain information on Local 727 and my father.

A photograph of my father at the signing of the 1941 Lockheed-IAM contract: https://law.utexas.edu/tigar/archive-item/tigars-father/.

Oral histories of racism in aircraft factories can be found at https://www.loc.gov/folklife/civil-rights/survey/view_collection.php?coll_id=2249.

Schools and Churches

See Patricia L. Bryan and Thomas Wolf, *Midnight Assassin: A Murder in America's Heartland* (2017), a good study of the *Hossack* case, *Trifles*, and the law's treatment of women who kill their abusive partners. I discuss the play, and the issues it raises, in *Nine Principles of Litigation and Life* (2009), https://law.utexas.edu/tigar/archive-item/nine-principles-of-litigation-and-life/.

Working, Learning

History of Kaiser Permanente: https://en.wikipedia.org/wiki/Kaiser_Permanente.

Darrow's 1932 memoir *The Story of My Life* is available at http://gutenberg.net.au/ebooks05/0500951h.html. The Irving Stone biography is *Clarence Darrow for the Defense* (1949). *Attorney for the Damned: Clarence Darrow in the Courtroom* (ed. Weinberg, 1957) contains many of his courtroom arguments. Some biographers have concluded that Darrow was guilty of attempting to bribe a juror in the 1912 McNamara case in Los Angeles. See http://law2.umkc.edu/faculty/projects/ftrials/darrow1912/darrowlinks.html. In 2012, Santa Clara Law School did a reenactment of the case. I portrayed Darrow's lawyer Earl Rogers, Judge Steve Trott prosecuted; information on the mock trial and some video clips can be found at https://law.scu.edu/centennial/trial/. A photo of participants is at https://law.utexas.edu/tigar/archive-item/retrial-of-clarence-darrow/. To prepare, I read the entire 90-volume trial record, and were I a juror I would have voted "not guilty." The case was a frame-up. The state, despite large federal and state resources, was not able to make a convincing presentation.

Arthur Koestler, *Reflections on Hanging* (1957). For an overview on death penalty law, see *Understanding Capital Punishment Law*, ed. Linda E Carter. The book is frequently revised; at this writing the 4th edition is the latest. The 1791 National Assembly debate on the death penalty, including Robespierre's address, is in https://books.google.com/books?id=WFhDAAAAcAAJ&pg=PP1#v=onepage&q&f=false.

2. BERKELEY AND BEYOND
Turned On by the Radio
See https://www.pacifica.org/about_history.php.

Enrolled
Joseph Tussman and Jacobus tenBroek, *The Equal Protection of the Laws*, 37 Calif. L. Rev. 341 (1949).

Jacobus tenBroek, Edward N. Barnhart, and Floyd W. Matson, *Prejudice, War, and the Constitution* (University of California Press, Berkeley, 1975).

Essay on freedom and equality: https://law.utexas.edu/tigar/archive-item/can-we-be-equal-and-free-in-the-unfinished-revolution-c-snow-ed-1976/.

Naval Science
Mahan, *The Influence of Sea Power Upon History, 1660–1783* (12th ed. 1918), http://www.gutenberg.org/files/13529/13529-h/13529-h.htm.

Paul A. Baran, *The Political Economy of Growth* (New York: Monthly Review Press, 1957).

Sophomore Year: 1959–60
The FSM website is at http://www.fsm-a.org/index.html, with abundant material on the free speech issues that led to the events of fall 1964.

Hague v. CIO, 307 U.S. 496, 515 (1939), holds that it is unconstitutional under the First Amendment for the government to completely abridge the right to gather in public spaces, https://supreme.justia.com/cases/federal/us/307/496/. The littering case is *Schneider v. New Jersey*, 308 U.S. 147 (1939), https://www.oyez.org/cases/1900-1940/308us147.

The University as Island
Justice Jackson's statement: *West Virginia State Board of Education v. Barnette*, 319 U.S. 624, 641 (1943), holding that it violates the First and Fourteenth Amendments to compel individuals to salute the American flag, https://www.oyez.org/cases/1940-1955/319us624.

My 1961 essay, "The Brave New University of Clark Kerr," appeared in the November 1961 issue of *the liberal democrat*, https://law.utexas.edu/tigar/archive-item/the-brave-new-university-of-clark-kerr-the-liberal-democrat-november-1961/. For a more extensive account, see https://law.utexas.edu/tigar/archive-item/introduction-to-symposium-student-rights-and-campus-rules-54-calif-l-rev-1-1966/.

Lede: In the days when newspaper copy was set in linotype, line spacing was increased by inserting a strip of metal, called a "lead," like the metal, between lines of linotype. So lede came into being to distinguish it from lead.

Another of my articles was about a right-wing preacher who visited San Francisco, https://law. utexas.edu/tigar/archive-item/a-cable-karl-to-the-top-o-the-marx-frontier-march-1962/.

A history of Berkeley housing discrimination: https://www.berkeleyside.com/2018/09/20/ redlining-the-history-of-berkeleys-segregated-neighborhoods.

I discuss the checkered history of free expression in public places in *Mythologies of State and Monopoly Power* (2018).

No Longer An Island

The Supreme Court case questioning the good faith of investigative committees was *Watkins v. United States*, 354 U.S. 178 (1957), finding that there is "no general authority to expose the private affairs of individuals without justification in terms of the functions of the Congress," https://supreme.justia.com/cases/federal/us/354/178/. The promise that *Watkins* seemed to contain was dashed by the 1961 decisions in *Braden v. United States*, 365 U.S. 431 (1961), holding that a criminal conviction based on an individual's refusal to answer questions during congressional investigation was constitutional, https://supreme.justia.com/cases/federal/us/365/431/; and *Wilkinson v. United States*, 365 U.S. 399 (1961), companion case to *Braden*, affirming the petitioner's conviction on similar grounds, https://supreme.justia.com/cases/federal/us/365/399/.

In 1961, I wrote retrospectively about HCUA's visit: "Black Friday One Year Later," https:// law.utexas.edu/tigar/archive-item/one-year-later-reflections-on-black-friday-the-liberal-democrat-may-1961/. We produced an LP record, *Sounds of Protest*, about the demonstrations, https://law.utexas.edu/tigar/archive-item/sounds-of-protest-audio-documentary/.

David Ossman and I wrote of the imagined appearance of the Bard before a Committee on Un-English Activities, https://law.utexas.edu/tigar/archive-item/the-appearance-of-william-shaksper-before-the-house-committee-on-un-english-activities-1960/.

Into the Summer with Navy and Marines

On lunch counter integration in San Antonio, see https://www.mysanantonio.com/150years/ major-stories/article/Fifty-eight-years-ago-San-Antonio-was-the-first-6145959.php.

Junior Year: 1960-61—Leaving the Navy, Learning Journalism

The case on nontheistic religion to which tenBroek introduced us was *Fellowship of Humanity v. County of Alameda*, discussed in https://en.wikipedia.org/wiki/Fellowship_of_ Humanity_v._County_of_Alameda.

Broadcast Journalist?

The Spanish Civil War documentary is available at https://www.pacificaradioarchives.org/ recording/bb0750?nns=Viznar.

Historian?

My Oppenheimer paper is at https://law.utexas.edu/tigar/archive-item/atomic-science-social-responsibility/. See also Philip M. Stern, *The Oppenheimer Case: Security on Trial* (1970); Kai Bird and Martin J. Sherwin, *American Prometheus: The Triumph and Tragedy of J. Robert Oppenheimer* (2005).

About Clinton Jencks, see Raymond Caballero, *McCarthyism v. Clinton Jencks* (2019); *Jencks v. United States*, 353 U.S. 657 (1957), overturning petitioner's criminal conviction and holding that the defendant has the right to inspect reports that form the basis of

testimony by opposing government witnesses, https://supreme.justia.com/cases/federal/
us/353/657/; Harvey Matusow, *False Witness* (1955).

Lawyer?

A recording of Higgins's hilarious account is available at https://www.pacificaradioarchives.
org/recording/bb1539?nns=Higgins.

The "Fuck the Draft" case is *Cohen v. California*, 403 U.S. 15 (1971), holding that it is unconstitutional under the First Amendment for a state to criminalize the public display of
an expletive, https://supreme.justia.com/cases/federal/us/403/15/. *Smith v. California*,
361 U.S. 147 (1959), holding that a bookseller cannot be liable for the content of books
offered for sale without proof that he knew the contents, https://supreme.justia.com/
cases/federal/us/361/147/.

Communist Party v. Subversive Activities Control Board, 367 U.S. 1 (1961), upholding the
registration requirement of the Subversive Activities Control Act as constitutional
under the First and Fifth Amendments, https://www.law.cornell.edu/supremecourt/
text/367/1. The earlier decision is at 351 U.S. 115 (1956), https://supreme.justia.
com/cases/federal/us/351/115/. The "membership" cases are *Scales v. United States*,
367 U.S. 203 (1961), affirming conviction of an individual based purely on membership in the Communist Party, https://supreme.justia.com/cases/federal/us/367/203/;
and *Noto v. United States*, 367 U.S. 290 (1961), reversing conviction of a member
of the Communist Party based on insufficient evidence that the Party advocated for
a violent overthrow of the government, https://supreme.justia.com/cases/federal/
us/367/290/. In the same volume of Supreme Court reports is a 5 to 4 decision
upholding the firing of a Navy Yard cafeteria worker on "loyalty-security" grounds,
without notice or hearing. *Cafeteria & Restaurant Workers v. McElroy*, 367 U.S. 886
(1961), https://supreme.justia.com/cases/federal/us/367/886/. Justice Brennan wrote
the dissenting opinion.

On Justice Whittaker, see https://en.wikipedia.org/wiki/Charles_Evans_Whittaker.

The passport case is *Aptheker v. Secretary of State*, 378 U.S. 500 (1964), holding that it is
unconstitutional to deny an individual the ability to obtain a passport based on membership in a Communist organization, https://supreme.justia.com/cases/federal/
us/378/500/. In *United States v. Brown*, 381 U.S. 437 (1965), https://supreme.justia.
com/cases/federal/us/381/437/, the Court held that prohibition on a Communist Party
member serving as labor union officer is void as being bill of attainder. The dockyard
worker case is *United States v. Robel*, 389 U.S. 258 (1967), overturning a section of the
Subversive Activities Control Act that made it unlawful for any member of a Communist
organization to seek employment in a defense facility, https://supreme.justia.com/cases/
federal/us/389/258/. *Aptheker* is the first case in U.S. history in which the Supreme
Court invalidated a federal statute on First Amendment grounds.

Personal and Political Decisions

I wrote home to my mother about meeting Pam, a letter that seems jejune now: https://law.
utexas.edu/tigar/archive-item/a-letter-to-my-mother/.

Senior Year: 1961–62

Concerning Harry Bridges, see http://theharrybridgesproject.org/biography.html.

To Finland and to the Radio Station

Material on the Youth Festival, including a photo of Yevtushenko, is at https://law.utexas.edu/
tigar/archive-item/1962-youth-festival-in-helsinki/.

A biography of Konni Zilliacus is Archie Potts, *Zilliacus: A Life for Peace and Socialism* (2002); see also https://en.wikipedia.org/wiki/Konni_Zilliacus; I wrote to the *New York Times* about his obituary, July 15, 1967, https://law.utexas.edu/tigar/archive-item/response-to-the-nyt-obituary-for-konni-zilliacus/.

William Ash and Brendan Foley, *Under the Wire* (2005); Wikipedia lists Bill's novels at https://en.wikipedia.org/wiki/Bill_Ash.

My BBC contract and the script of my presentation are at https://law.utexas.edu/tigar/archive-item/the-americans-have-a-word-for-it-bbc-october-8-1962/.

For Anila Graham, see https://www.theguardian.com/news/2004/nov/18/guardianobituaries.

My report on the Trafalgar Square "riot" can be found at https://www.pacificaradioarchives.org/recording/bb1608?nns=Tigar.

Labour and the Common Market by Tigar and Zilliacus is at https://www.pacificaradioarchives.org/recording/bb0579?nns=Tigar; for Britain and the Cuba Crisis, https://www.pacificaradioarchives.org/recording/bb0581?nns=Tigar.

Lord Russell, Cuba, and the Remnants of Empire

Interview with Bertrand Russell, https://www.pacificaradioarchives.org/recording/bb0597?nns=Tigar; Bertrand Russell, *Autobiography* (2009)

Bombs in Paris

For an overview, see https://en.wikipedia.org/wiki/Organisation_armée_secrète; interview with Claude Bourdet, https://www.pacificaradioarchives.org/recording/bb0335?nns=Tigar.

Music and Politics

See http://www.ewanmaccoll.co.uk/ewan-maccoll-biography/, http://www.peggyseeger.com.For the KPFK RenaissancePleasure Faire. see https://www.youtube.com/watch?v=qmAs_DjQNP0.

3. WHAT WAS TAUGHT, AND WHAT WAS LEARNED, IN LAW SCHOOL
First-Year Courses and Issues

Judge Frank: *United States v. Antonelli Fireworks Co.*, 155 F.2d 631, 662 (2d Cir. 1946); *Lombard v. Louisiana*, 373 U.S. 267, 274 (1963), https://supreme.justia.com/cases/federal/us/373/267/; *Crawley v. Rex*, T.S. (1909) 1105.

The Quebec case was *Johnson v. Sparrow*, [1899] S.C.R. 104, discussed in Constance Backhouse, *Colour-Coded: A Legal History of Racism in Canada, 1900–1950* (1999), 419.

The Oath

Konigsberg v. State Bar of California, 366 U.S. 36 (1961), https://supreme.justia.com/cases/federal/us/366/36/; *In re Anastaplo*, 366 U.S. 82 (1961), https://supreme.justia.com/cases/federal/us/366/82/;

Cramp v. Board of Public Instruction, 368 U.S. 278 (1961), https://supreme.justia.com/cases/federal/us/368/278/.

Law Review and the Free Speech Movement

My law review comment is at 53 Calif. L. Rev. 2242 (1965), https://law.utexas.edu/tigar/archive-item/automatic-extinction-of-cross-demands-compensatio-from-rome-to-california/.

FSM issue: Symposium: Student Rights and Campus Rules, 54 Calif. L. Rev. 1 (1966); my introduction is at https://law.utexas.edu/tigar/archive-item/introduction-to-symposium-student-rights-and-campus-rules-54-calif-l-rev-1-1966/.

Reich, "The New Property," 73 Yale L. J. 733 (1964), arguing that welfare rights and other public entitlements are a form of property.

The resulting book is Jacobus tenBroek and Editors of *California Law Review, The Law of the Poor* (1966).

Stein, Aptheker, Jacobs: Rationing Speech

A summary of the case appears in *Civil Liberties Docket* 11/2 (May 1966).

Justice Brennan

The most complete account is Nat Hentoff's interview with Brennan: https://www.newyorker.com/magazine/1990/03/12/the-constitutionalist.

The University of Texas website has the correspondence and media reports about the Brennan episode: https://law.utexas.edu/tigar/category/the-shadow-of-mccarthyism/.

Julian Bond case, 251 F.Supp. 333 (N.D. Ga. 1966), three-judge federal court, rev. 385 U.S. 116 (1966), https://supreme.justia.com/cases/federal/us/385/116/.

A document from my Freedom of Information Act request, with results of snooping into my political views: https://law.utexas.edu/tigar/archive-item/a-part-of-a-freedom-of-information-act-production/.

Congressman Tuck's comments on the clerkship: https://law.utexas.edu/tigar/archive-item/representative-tuck-on-brennan-clerkship/.

4. WASHINGTON—UNEMPLOYMENT COMPENSATION
Finding a Job, and a Mentor

Williams, *One Man's Freedom* (1962). See also Robert Pack, *Edward Bennett Williams for the Defense* (1983). My book *Persuasion: The Litigator's Art* (1999) is dedicated to Williams and includes some of his courtroom work.

Barbara Babcock's memoir, *Fish Raincoats: A Woman Lawyer's Life* (2016), recounts experiences of women lawyers at the firm, and traces Barbara's pathbreaking career as trial lawyer, law teacher, and mentor.

Bobby Baker

United States v. Baker, 401 F.2d 958 (D.C. Cir. 1968); on remand, 301 F.Supp. 973 (D.D.C. 1969); on appeal from remand, 430 F.2d 499 (D.C. Cir. 1970), argued by Michael Tigar; see Baker and King, *Wheeling and Dealing: Confessions of a Capitol Hill Operator* (1988), a good biography.

Departure

Potomac magazine article about Washington work and departure for UCLA: https://law.utexas.edu/tigar/archive-item/washington-post-article-from-their-weekly-magazine-potomac/.

5. LIKE A BIRD ON A WIRE
Edward Bennett Williams and Eavesdropping

The Las Vegas FBI story appears in 112 Cong. Rec. 13843 (1966). See *Elson v. Bowen*, 83 Nev. 515, 436 P.2d 12 (1967), FBI agents must submit to deposition.

Katz v. United States, 389 U.S. 347 (1967), https://www.oyez.org/cases/1967/35.

Silverman v. United States, 365 U.S. 505 (1961); https://www.oyez.org/cases/1960/66; *United States v. Coplon*, 185 F.2d 629 (2d Cir. 1950), https://law.justia.com/cases/federal/appellate-courts/F2/185/629/50057/.

Alderman and Ivanov

Kolod v. United States 390 U.S. 136 (1968), https://supreme.justia.com/cases/federal/ us/390/136/; *Alderman v. United States*, 394 U.S. 165 (1969), https://www.oyez.org/ cases/1967/133. The *Ivanov* brief, of which I was principal author, is at 1968 WL 112582 (1968).

Warrantless "National Security" Wiretapping

The brief in *United States v. Smith*: https://law.utexas.edu/tigar/archive-item/1971-pleading- from-smith-case/; *321* F.Supp. 424 (C.D. Calif. 1971).

1968: Special Grand Juries, More Wiretaps

The National Association of Criminal Defense Lawyers (NACDL) published a report on grand jury abuse, https://www.nacdl.org/getattachment/0aebc59b-b21b-49ea-b7f9- 7d3b1ea60255/federal-grand-jury-reform-report-and-bill-of-rights.pdf.   See also https://law.utexas.edu/tigar/archive-item/tigar-levy-the-grand-jury-as-the-new-inquisi- tion-50-mich-st-b-j-693-700-1971/.

On use immunity: *Kastigar v. United States*, 406 U.S. 441 (1972), https://www.oyez.org/ cases/1971/70-117, upholding constitutionality of use immunity:

United States v. Calandra, 414 U.S. 338 (1974), https://www.oyez.org/cases/1973/72-734.

Gelbard v. United States, 408 U.S. 41 (1972); brief for petitioner is at 1972 WL 135662; oral argu- ment: https://law.utexas.edu/tigar/archive-item/gelbard-v-united-states-408-u-s-41-1972/.

David Truong: National Security Writ Large

United States v. Truong Dinh Hung, 629 F.2d 908 (4th Cir. 1980), appeal after remand, 667 F.2d 1105 (4th Cir. 1981), cert. denied 454 U.S. 1144 (1982). The brief on appeal by John Mage, John Privitera, Marvin Miller, and me is at 1979 WL 212413. Justice Bren- nan's bail ruling is *Truong Dinh Hung v. United States*, 439 U.S. 1326 (1978), https:// supreme.justia.com/cases/federal/us/439/1326/.

David's obituary: https://www.nytimes.com/2014/07/07/us/david-truong-figure-in-us-wire- tap-case-dies-at-68.html.

The Pentagon Papers case is *New York Times Co. v. United States*, 403 U.S. 713 (1971), https:// www.oyez.org/cases/1970/1873 .

Erwin Griswold article at   https://www.washingtonpost.com/archive/opinions/1989/02/15/ secrets-not-worth-keeping/a115a154-4c6f-41fd-816a-112dd9908115/,

6. CIVIL WRONGS

Law School Days

On federal court injunctive power, see *Dombrowski v. Pfister*, 380 U.S. 479 (1965), the later erosion of which is chronicled in, for example, Owen M. Fiss, Dombrowski, 86 Yale L.J. 1103 (1977).

Attorney General Brownell's opinion is included in President's Power to Use Federal Troops to Suppress Resistance to Enforcement of Federal Court Orders—Little Rock, Ark., 41 U.S. Op. Atty. Gen. 313 (1957). My Mississippi Report scripts can be found at: https:// law.utexas.edu/tigar/media-archive/?decade=1960 .

Federal prosecutorial discretion not to pursue civil rights violations was upheld in *Moses v. Kennedy*, 219 F. Supp. 762 (D.D.C. 1963), aff 'd sub nom. *Moses v. Katzenbach*, 342 F.2d 931 (D.C. Cir. 1965).

The District of Columbia

Jacobus tenBroek, *The Anti-Slavery Origins of the Fourteenth Amendment* (1951), revised and republished as *Equal Under Law* (1965); tenBroek and Tussman, "The Equal Protection of the Laws," 37 Calif. L. Rev (1949). For a discussion of Supreme Court classification lore, see *United States v. Virginia*, 518 U.S. 515 (1996), https://supreme.justia.com/cases/federal/us/518/515/.

Cherokee Nation v. Georgia, 30 U.S. 1 (1831), discussed in https://law.utexas.edu/tigar/archive-item/the-national-security-state-the-end-of-separation-of-powers-monthly-review-july-august-2014/.

Hobson v. Hansen, 269 F.Supp. 401 (D.D.C. 1969), https://law.justia.com/cases/federal/district-courts/FSupp/269/401/1800940/. My Bickel response: https://law.utexas.edu/tigar/archive-item/in-defense-of-skelly-wright/.

7. DRAFT BOARD DAYS AND NIGHTS

My law school valedictory address is at https://law.utexas.edu/tigar/archive-item/may-1966-valedictory-graduation-speech-boalt-hall/.

On the themes in this chapter, see generally Symposium, Selective Service 1970, 17 UCLA L. Rev. 893 (1970); Tigar, "The Rights of the Selective Service Registrant," in *The Rights of Americans* (1970); Tigar and Zweben, "Selective Service: Some Certain Problems and Some Tentative Answers," 37 Geo. Wash. L. Rev. 433 (1969); https://law.utexas.edu/tigar/archive-item/selective-service-some-certain-problems-and-some-tentative-answers/.

Selective Service Law Reporter

The SSLR Practice Manual is at https://law.utexas.edu/tigar/archive-item/selective-service-practice-manual/. Judge Wright's review of SSLR is at https://law.utexas.edu/tigar/archive-item/review-of-the-selective-service-law-reporter/.

Larry

United States v. Wingerter, 423 F.2d 1015 (5th Cir. 1970). See also *United States v. Seeger*, 380 U.S. 163 (1965), https://www.oyez.org/cases/1964/50, holding that a registrant qualifies for conscientious objector status even if he does not believe in an anthropomorphic Supreme Being.

Rosalio

Lefton v. City of Hattiesburg, 333 F.2d 280 (5th Cir. 1964); *Munoz v. Hauk*, 439 F.2d 1176 (9th Cir. 1971), rehearing denied; 446 F.2d 434 (9th Cir.), cert. denied sub nom. *Curtis v. Hauk*, 404 U.S. 1059 (1972). Rosalio's acquittal was reported in the *Los Angeles Times*: https://law.utexas.edu/tigar/archive-item/rosalio-muñoz-draft-case/.

Fernando

Fernando's discussion of the case is on the UT website: https://law.lectures-presentation.la.utexas.edu/paella/ui/watch.html?id=1d5f5340-0981-482b-becb-2eb8910e518e.

Gone Away

See *United States v. Lockwood*, 382 F.Supp. 1111 (E.D.N.Y. 1974), in which court has power to appoint counsel, consider validity of induction orders.

8. MILITARY JUSTICE IS TO JUSTICE . . .

Articles about acquittal: https://law.utexas.edu/tigar/archive-item/texas-lawyer-coverage-of-the-trial-of-major-debra-meeks/; https://law.utexas.edu/tigar/archive-item/cnn-coverage-of-the-trial-of-major-debra-meeks/ .

9. CHICAGO BLUES, SEATTLE TIMES, FREE ANGELA
Chicago

United States v. Spock, 416 F.2d 165 (1st Cir. 1969), https://casetext.com/case/united-states-v-spock. Jessica Mitford's book, *The Trial of Dr. Spock* (1969), is the best account.

On the Chicago case, see Epstein, *The Great Conspiracy Trial* (1970); *United States v. Dellinger*, 472 F.2d 340 (7th Cir. 1972).

The Dellinger trial transcript can be found at https://library.truman.edu/microforms/chicago-seven.asp.

A history and discussion of the inchoate crime of conspiracy: Tigar, "Crime Talk, Rights Talk, and Double-Talk: Thoughts on Reading Encyclopedia of Crime and Justice," 65 Tex. L. Rev. 101, 127–29 (1986), https://law.utexas.edu/tigar/archive-item/essay-crime-talk-rights-talk-and-doubletalk-65-tex-l-rev-101-1986/.

Brandenburg v. Ohio, 395 U.S. 444 (1969); https://supreme.justia.com/cases/federal/us/395/444/#tab-opinion-1948083, on reversing conviction, and applying "clear and present danger" standard to prosecution for criminal syndicalism in which defendant urged crowd to kill cops. On the doctrinal history, see Linde, " 'Clear and Present Danger' Reexamined: Dissonance in the Brandenburg Concerto," 22 Stanf. L. Rev. 1163 (1970).

Seattle

Kim Bakke has written a superb book on the case, *Protest On Trial: The Seattle 7 Conspiracy* (2018).

The exchanges with Judge Boldt are quoted in Dorsen and Friedman, *Disorder in the Court: Report of the Association of the Bar of the City of New York, Special Committee on Courtroom Conduct*, pages 147, 48, 245–48 (1973).

Newspaper coverage of the mistrial: https://www.seattletimes.com/pacific-nw-magazine/protest-on-trial-chronicles-the-chaos-and-the-surprising-conclusion-of-the-1970-trial-of-the-seattle-7/.

The appeal brief is at https://law.utexas.edu/tigar/archive-item/51-f-2d-372-9th-cir-1971-brief-on-appeal. The opinion reversing the contempt citations is *United States v. Marshall*, 451 F.2d 372 (9th Cir. 1971).

Angela

Motion hearing reported here: ; https://law.utexas.edu/tigar/archive-item/angela-daviss-first-court-hearing/.

Bancroft Library, University of California, Berkeley, has the complete Angela Davis record: http://oac2-prd.cdlib.org/findaid/ark:/13030/kt700005j7/.

Motion to dismiss and oral argument: https://law.utexas.edu/tigar/archive-item/case-materials-from-people-v-angela-davis/.

10. CONNECTING LIFE, LAW, AND SOCIAL CHANGE

Leaders of the SDS Weatherman faction authored a reflective book on the movement and its origins, actions, successes, and errors: https://www.sds-1960s.org/PrairieFire-reprint.pdf. Among the errors: believing if you were not with us all the way, you were not with us; mistaking friends for enemies; and too much identification with youth culture.

Goldstucker's life and work is discussed in https://read.dukeupress.edu/new-german-critique/article-abstract/42/1%20(124)/129/33177/Reading-Kafka-Writing-Vita-The-Trials-of-the-Kafka?redirectedFrom=PDF.

The bibliography to my book *Law and the Rise of Capitalism* contains references to many sources.

On the National Lawyers Guild, see https://www.nlg.org. On the Haymarket case, see my play: https://law.utexas.edu/tigar/archive-item/haymarket-whose-name-the-few-still-say-with-tears/.

11. BY ANY MEANS NECESSARY

The Brandeis quote is from *Olmstead v. United States*, 277 U.S. 438, 485 (1928), dissenting opinion.

Cameron Bishop

Justice Jackson's opinion on bail for the Communist Party leaders is *Williamson v. United States*, 184 F.2d 280 (2d Cir. 1950), https://casetext.com/case/williamson-v-united-states-6.

United States v. Bishop, 555 F.2d 771 (10th Cir. 1977), reversed Cam's conviction.

Francisco Martinez

See *United States v. Martinez*, 667 F.2d 886 (10th Cir. 1981). The reversal of Kiko's final conviction is at 855 F.2d 621 (9th Cir. 1988).

John Demjanjuk

A candid assessment of official complicity in bringing Nazis to our shores may be found at www.fas.org/sgp/news/1999/11/naraiwg.html.

The Demjanjuk case is chronicled in *Demjanjuk v. Petrovsky*, 10 F.3d 338 (6th Cir. 1993), cert. denied sub nom; *Rison v. Demjanjuk*, 513 U.S. 914 (1994). The Sixth Circuit's grant of habeas corpus is not reported, but is available at 1993 WL 394773 (6th Cir. 1993). Chief Justice Marshall on the various forms of habeas corpus: *Ex parte Bollman*, 8 U.S. 75 (1807), https://supreme.justia.com/cases/federal/us/8/75/.

Cross-examination of government expert: https://law.utexas.edu/tigar/archive-item/examining-witnesses-2d-ed/ , chap. 1.

My legal opinion on the prosecution's case theory: https://law.utexas.edu/tigar/archive-item/demjanjuk-declaration/.

12. SPEECH PLUS

Robert F. Williams

Williams v. Blount, 314 F.Supp. 1356 (D.D.C. 1970), https://law.justia.com/cases/federal/district-courts/FSupp/314/1356/1472368/.

Rebozo

Biography of Rebozo: https://en.wikipedia.org/wiki/Bebe Rebozo.

Patrick Cunningham

Lefkowitz v. Cunningham, 431 U.S. 801 (1977); the brief is at 1977 WL 189341; oral argument is at https://www.oyez.org/cases/1976/76-260 and https://law.utexas.edu/tigar/archive-item/lefkowitz-v-cunningham-431-u-s-801-1977/.

The state court case is *People v. Cunningham*, 88 Misc.2d 1065 (N.Y. Sup. 1976). Pat was later tried and convicted in federal court for income tax offenses. *United States v. Cunningham*, 723 F.2d 217 (2d Cir. 1983).

Dominic Gentile: Lawyering in the Media Spotlight

Gentile v. State Bar of Nevada, 501 U.S. 1030 (1991); briefs, with extensive history of lawyer speech on public issues, are at 1991 WL 521171 and 1991 WL 521173; oral argument at https://law.utexas.edu/tigar/archive-item/gentile-v-state-bar-of-nevada-501-u-s-1030-1991/.

Charleston Five

Erem & Durrenberger, *On the Global Waterfront: The Fight to Free the Charleston 5* (Monthly Review Press, New York), https://monthlyreview.org/product/on_the_global_waterfront/.

13. DEATH—AND THAT'S FINAL
Buckley and Risotto

Correspondence with Buckley about death penalty and TV program: https://law.utexas.edu/tigar/archive-item/press-release-firing-line-january-1990-and-related-correspondence-2/. See https://en.wikipedia.org/wiki/Gary_McGivern, which cites source material on the case.

Texas Resource Center

Furman v. Georgia, 408 U.S. 238 (1972), https://www.oyez.org/cases/1971/69-5030, holding that death penalty, as applied, constitutes cruel and unusual punishment. As a result of Furman, states quickly moved to revise death penalty statutes, leading to years of litigation. See https://en.wikipedia.org/wiki/Furman_v._Georgia. The website, https://deathpenaltyinfo.org, contains current and historical information on the death penalty.

For more material on the death penalty, see https://law.utexas.edu/tigar/media-archive/?topic=death-penalty; https://law.utexas.edu/tigar/archive-item/essay-lawyers-jails-and-the-laws-fake-bargains-monthly-review-julyaugust-2001/.

Murray v. Giarratano, 492 U.S. 1 (1989), https://www.oyez.org/cases/1988/88-411; https://deathpenaltyinfo.org/news/ex-virginia-death-row-prisoner-with-strong-claim-of-innocence-get-parole-after-38-years.

Witherspoon v. Illinois, 391 U.S. 510 (1968), https://en.wikipedia.org/wiki/Death-qualified_jury.

The case concerning the shackled defendant is *Marquez v. Collins*, 11 F.3d 1241 (5th Cir., 1994).

Graham v. Collins, 506 U.S. 461 (1993), https://www.oyez.org/cases/1992/91-7580. Petitioner's brief is at 1992 WL 526194, reply brief is 1992 WL 526197. Oral argument: https://law.utexas.edu/tigar/archive-item/graham-v-collins-506-u-s-461-1993/.

Johnson v. Texas, 509 U.S. 350 (1993), https://www.oyez.org/cases/1992/92-5653. Petitioner's brief is at 1993 WL 476436, reply brief is 1993 WL 476429. Oral argument: https://law.utexas.edu/tigar/archive-item/johnson-v-texas-509-u-s-350-1993-2/.

Justice Kennedy's apparent change of heart is *Montgomery v. Louisiana*, 577 U.S. (2016), https://www.oyez.org/cases/2015/14-280. See Tigar, "What Are We Doing to the Children?: An Essay on Juvenile (In)justice," 22 Ohio St. Crim. L. J. 849 (2007), https://law.utexas.edu/tigar/archive-item/what-are-we-doing-to-the-children-an-essay-on-juvenile-injustice-22-ohiostatejcriml849-2010/.

For an overview of over-incarceration, see https://en.wikipedia.org/wiki/Incarceration_in_the_United_States. On prison overcrowding in California and the Supreme Court decision, see https://en.wikipedia.org/wiki/Brown_v._Plata. California prisons remain under the supervision of a three-judge federal court.

Oklahoma City

The Nichols transcript is on the UT site: https://law.utexas.edu/tigar/category/transcripts-from-united-states-v-terry-nichols/. My opening statement and closing argument in the trial phase are at https://law.utexas.edu/tigar/archive-item/opening-statement-and-closing-arguments-terry-nichols/.

My essay on defending Terry Nichols is "Defending," 74 Tex. L. Rev. 101 (1995), https://law.utexas.edu/tigar/archive-item/defending-an-essay-74-tex-l-rev-101-1995/. It is also a chapter in Freedman and Smith, *How Can You Represent Those People?* (2013), which has been translated into Japanese.

The decision disqualifying Judge Alley is *Nichols v. Alley*, 71 F.3d 347 (10th Cir. 1995), granting mandamus, ordering recusal, and directing chief judge of the circuit to appoint a trial judge.

Judge Matsch's decision changing venue to Denver is *United States v. McVeigh*, 918 F.Supp. 1467 (W.D. Okla. 1996).

Michael Fortier's cross-examination is chapter 10 of my book *Examining Witnesses* (2d ed., 2013), https://law.utexas.edu/tigar/archive-item/examining-witnesses-2d-ed/.

A long interview with the jury foreperson is at https://law.utexas.edu/tigar/archive-item/the-jewish-journal-the-juror/.

Prof. Jody Madeira has written a book focused on victims' attitudes toward the case, *Killing McVeigh: The Death Penalty and the Myth of Closure* (2012). I reviewed it in "Missing McVeigh," 112 Mich. L. Rev. 1091 (2014), https://law.utexas.edu/tigar/archive-item/missing-mcveigh/; the article also discusses victim impact evidence.

Victims' reaction to verdict: https://www.nytimes.com/1998/01/08/us/oklahoma-city-verdict-the-reaction-families-anger-at-outcome-is-scalding.html.

I like this cartoon about my lawyering style: https://law.utexas.edu/tigar/archive-item/denver-square-terry-nichols-case-cartoon/.

The best book on the Oklahoma City trials is Gumbel and Charles, *Oklahoma City: What the Investigation Missed—And Why It Still Matters* (2012).

Relationship and Forensic Evidence
Jane Tigar: https://law.utexas.edu/tigar/tag/jane-tigar/.

South Africa, Mitigation and the Kenya Embassy Bombing
South African constitutional court judgment: *Mohamed v. President of South Africa*, CCT 17/01 (May 28, 2001).

Orlando Hall
IACHR, Report No. 90/19, Case 12.719: Merits (Final), Orlando Cordia Hall, United States of America, June 10, 2019. The decision will be published at http://www.oas.org/en/iachr/decisions/merits.asp. My expert testimony is at https://law.utexas.edu/tigar/media-type/cases/.

14. POLITICS NOT AS USUAL
Leery of Leary
Greenfield, *Timothy Leary, A Biography* (2006). Leary's decision to testify against erstwhile friends and helpers is well documented in https://en.wikipedia.org/wiki/Timothy_Leary.

John Connally
Bronston v. United States, 409 U.S. 352 (1973), https://www.oyez.org/cases/1972/71-1011.
Letter from Nellie Connally after John's acquittal: https://law.utexas.edu/tigar/archive-item/1368/

I did a mock cross-examination of the informer-witness in the Connally case some years later. On cross-examination, https://law.utexas.edu/tigar/archive-item/examining-witnesses-2d-ed/, chap. 8.

Joan Irvine Smith

Articles about her: https://news.uci.edu/2019/12/20/joan-irvine-smith-passes-away/; https://www.ocregister.com/2019/12/20/joan-irvine-smith-member-of-pioneer-family-who-was-instrumental-in-creation-of-uc-irvine-campus-dies-at-86/.

Robert Mann

See Tigar, "The Right of Property and the Law of Theft," 62 Tex. L. Rev. 1443, 1472–75 (1984), https://law.utexas.edu/tigar/archive-item/the-right-of-property-and-the-law-of-theft-62-tex-l-rev-1443-1984/.

Goldberg v. United States, 425 U.S. 94 (1976), https://www.oyez.org/cases/1975/74-6293.

ABA

New Yorker re Zenger performance: https://law.utexas.edu/tigar/archive-item/review-of-zenger-the-new-yorker-august-25-1986/.

RICO and the Laptop

United States v. Maldonado-Rivera, 922 F.2d 934 (2d Cir. 1990).

United States v. Salerno, 505 U.S. 317 (1992), https://www.oyez.org/cases/1991/91-872; brief is at 1991 WL 530844; oral argument: https://law.utexas.edu/tigar/archive-item/united-states-v-salerno-505-u-s-317-1992/.

Political Commentary

Profile about Murphy case: https://law.utexas.edu/tigar/archive-item/national-law-journal-profile-1980-re-murphy-case/.

Article about Hutchison case: https://law.utexas.edu/tigar/archive-item/houston-post-article-representing-senator-kay-bailey-hutchison/.

15. HUMAN AND GLOBAL RIGHTS
1976

Article on Letelier-Moffitt case: https://law.utexas.edu/tigar/archive-item/the-foreign-sover-eign-immunities-act-and-the-pursued-refugee-lessons-from-letelier-v-chile-1982-mich-igan-yearbook-of-international-legal-studies-421/.

South Africa

Images relating to advocacy teaching in South Africa: https://law.utexas.edu/tigar/archive-item/south-africa-advocacy-training/; https://law.utexas.edu/tigar/archive-item/south-africa-advocacy-training-in-johannesburg-ken-brown-jim-ferguson-and-justice-mloto/.

My lectures at University of the Western Cape on law, state power, and judicial review: https://law.utexas.edu/tigar/archive-item/three-lectures-from-1991-at-the-university-of-the-western-cape-2/; https://law.utexas.edu/tigar/archive-item/south-africa-recordings-1991uwcta-pea1/; https://law.utexas.edu/tigar/archive-item/south-africa-recordings-1991uwcta-peb1/; https://law.utexas.edu/tigar/archive-item/south-africa-recordings-uwctapec1-2/.

Letter from Dullah Omar, Minister of Justice: https://law.utexas.edu/tigar/archive-item/a-let-ter-from-dullah-omar-minister-of-justice/.

Article in *Tejas* (Mexican-American student publication) about South Africa: https://law.utexas.edu/tigar/archive-item/article-about-met-in-south-africa/.

Perspectives from Aix-en-Provence

Tigar, Casey, Giordani and Mardemootoo, "Paul Touvier and the Crime Against Humanity," 30 Tex. Int'l L. J. 286 (1995), https://law.utexas.edu/tigar/archive-item/paul-touvier-and-the-crime-against-humanity-30-tex-intl-l-j-286-1995with-casey-giordani-mardemootoo/.

Chile, the First Sequel

On universal jurisdiction, see my lecture at https://law.utexas.edu/tigar/archive-item/universal-rights-wrongs-roper-v-simmons-torture-and-judge-posner/, and this essay, https://law.utexas.edu/tigar/archive-item/an-essay-on-universal-jurisdiction-drawing-together-thoughts-and-writings/.

Summary of London Proceedings: https://en.wikipedia.org/wiki/Indictment_and_arrest_of_Augusto_Pinochet.

UNROW

Settlement: https://www.nytimes.com/1998/01/16/us/tobacco-concerns-settle-texas-case-for-a-record-sum.html.

Texas Attorney General criminal proceedings: *United States v. Morales*, 807 F.3d 717 (5th Cir. 2015).

Chile, the Second Sequel

Schneider v. Kissinger, 412 F.3d 190 (D.C. Cir. 2005), cert. denied, 547 U.S. 1069 (2006).

Chile, the Third Sequel

Chile Supreme Court ruling: https://ips-dc.org/terrorists-struck-washington-1976-face-murder-charges/; https://cadenaser.com/ser/2015/08/20/tribunales/1440072283_041798.html.

Chagos

I contributed a Foreword to David Vine, *Island of Shame* (2009): https://law.utexas.edu/tigar/archive-item/foreword-island-of-shame/.

The U.S. litigation: *Bancoult v. McNamara*, 445 F.3d 447 (D.C. Cir.), cert denied, 549 U.S. 1166 (2006).

The UK litigation is summarized in https://en.wikipedia.org/wiki/R_v_Secretary_of_State_for_Foreign_and_Commonwealth_Affairs,_ex_parte_Bancoult_(No_2).

International Court of Justice ruling: "Legal Consequences of the Separation of the Chagos Islands Archipelago from Mauritius in 1965," https://www.icj-cij.org/files/case-related/169/169-20190225-01-00-EN.pdf .

UN General Assembly vote: https://www.theguardian.com/world/2019/may/22/uk-suffers-crushing-defeat-un-vote-chagos-islands.

Lynne Stewart

Opinion affirming Rahman conviction: *United States v. Rahman*, 189 F.3d 88 (2d Cir. 1999), cert denied, 528 U.S. 1094 (2000).

Center for Constitutional Rights report on SAMs: https://ccrjustice.org/sites/default/files/attach/2017/09/SAMs%20Report.Final_.pdf.

National Lawyers Guild report on Stewart case: https://www.nlg.org/wp-content/uploads/2017/03/The-Case-of-Lynne-Stewart-2005.pdf.

Koeltl's opinion dismissing some charges, rejecting other defense contentions: *United States v. Sattar*, 272 F.Supp. 2d 348 (S.D.N.Y. 2003).

Justice Department announces new indictment: https://www.justice.gov/archive/opa/pr/2003/November/03_crm_631.htm.

Sentencing: https://www.nytimes.com/2006/10/17/nyregion/17stewart.html.

Opinion affirming Lynne's conviction: *United States v. Stewart*, 590 F.3d 93 (2d Cir. 2009).

Resentencing: https://www.nytimes.com/2010/07/16/nyregion/16stewart.html.

Lynne's obituary: https://www.nytimes.com/2017/03/07/nyregion/lynne-stewart-dead-radical-leftist-lawyer.html.

16. WHAT TO DO WHILE ENJOYING MEDICARE
Writing and Thinking about Terrorism

The Reichstag fire article: https://law.utexas.edu/tigar/archive-item/the-reichstag-fire-trial-1933-2008-the-production-of-law-and-history-with-john-mage-monthly-review-march-2009-p-24/.

Turkey, Another Chile Sequel

Motion to dismiss denied: *Kurd v. Republic of Turkey*, 438 F.Supp. 3d 69 (D.D.C. 2020), appeal pending.

Julian Assange

Our expert report is referred to in counsel's opening brief: https://dontextraditeassange.com/JA_Defence_Opening.pdf. Media reports include https://consortiumnews.com/2020/10/01/live-updates-assange-extradition-day-eighteen-ellsberg-parallel-raised-on-last-day-of-testimony-judgement-day-set-for-jan-4-2021/.

Mythologies

Mythologies of State and Monopoly Power: https://monthlyreview.org/product/mythologies-of-state-and-monopoly-power/.

Reading from the Haymarket play: https://law.lectures-presentation.la.utexas.edu/paella/ui/watch.html?id=1365e372-db62-434b-ad3f-03f29b0aa318. The plays: https://law.utexas.edu/tigar/media-type/plays/.

Index